STUDIES ON THE CIVILIZATION
AND CULTURE OF
NUZI AND THE HURRIANS

Volume 10

Nuzi at Seventy-Five

Edited by
David I. Owen
and
Gernot Wilhelm

CDL Press
Bethesda, Maryland

Published by CDL Press, P.O. Box 34454, Bethesda, MD 20827;
E-Mail: cdlpress@erols.com; website: www.cdlpress.com.

Library of Congress Cataloging-in-Publication Data

Nuzi at seventy-five / edited by David I. Owen and Gernot Wilhelm.
p. cm. — (a Studies on the civilization and culture of Nuzi and the Hurrians ; 10)
Includes bibliographical references and index.
ISBN 1-883053-50-1
1. Nuzi (Extinct city). 2. Hurrians. 3. Akkadian language–Texts. I. Title: Nuzi at 75.
II. Owen, David I. III. Wilhelm, Gernot. IV. Series.
DS70.5.N9 N89 1999
935–dc21 99-052665

The publication of Volume 10 of

Studies on the Civilization and Culture of Nuzi and the Hurrians

Was made possible by a generous subvention by

Charles ("Chuck") Mund, '51 and Carol Winter Mund, '52
Devoted Cornell University alumni
and
The Occasional Publication Fund of the
Department of Near Eastern Studies
Cornell University, Ithaca, New York

Preface

The year 2000 marks not only the turn of the millennium, but also the 75th anniversary of the start of the Nuzi excavations in the winter of 1925/26. It is apparent from the diversity and richness of the material presented below that the study of the Nuzi archives, the associated archaeological remains, and the parallel growth of the corpus of Hurrian texts and archaeological remains from Anatolia and Syria, continue to be productive avenues for research. After three quarters of a century, the finds from Nuzi not only maintain wide scholarly interest but also continue to provide new insights into the languages and civilization of Mesopotamia in the fifteenth and fourteenth centuries B.C.E.

Two special sessions on Nuzi and the Hurrians were organized by Gernot Wilhelm for the XLVe Rencontre assyriologique internationale at Harvard University in July of 1998. They marked the significant role that Nuzi and the Hurrians have played in study of the languages, history, and culture of the ancient Near East. The simultaneous, special exhibition of the archaeological finds from Nuzi at the Harvard Semitic Museum also highlighted the important role the publication of the Nuzi excavations by Richard F. S. Starr had on the field of Near Eastern archaeology. Thanks to the organizers of the XLVe RAI, we are able to include in this volume the (revised) papers submitted for the special sessions. Some of these papers present general overviews on various aspects of Nuzi and Hurrian archives, society, and culture, while others offer more-detailed studies of texts, language, history, and geography. The RAI papers are collected in Part I of this volume. Additional studies on Nuzi and Hurrian texts and society constitute Parts II–III. Unfortunately, due to constraints of time and space, EN 10/3 by Jeanette Fincke could not be included in this volume but will appear in *SCCNH* 13. Dr. Fincke, who has been Prof. Wilhelm's assistant for a number of years, has joined the Assur Project under the direction of Prof. Stefan Maul at the University of Heidelberg. We wish her well in her new position.

The publication of this volume was made possible thanks to the generous subvention provided by two devoted Cornell University alumni, Charles ("Chuck") Mund, '51, and his wife Carol Winter Mund, '52, and the Occasional Publication Fund of the Department of Near Eastern Studies, Cornell University. We are profoundly grateful for the support of the Munds, whose interest in the ancient Near East grew out of their participation in Cornell Adult University study tours to the Middle East with David I. Owen.

Studies on the Civilization and Culture of Nuzi and the Hurrians (*SCCNH*) began in 1981 with the publication of the *Ernest R. Lacheman Anniversary Volume*. Over the past two decades its volumes have honored also Edith Porada, Richard F.S. Starr, and Cyrus H. Gordon—each of whom contributed so much to the understanding of Nuzi and Hurrian civilization. However, it is appropriate, as we look back over the past 75 years, to recall and acknowledge others who have also contributed significantly to this understanding: Moshé Berkooz, Elena Cassin, Edward Chiera, Georges Contenau, Dorothy Cross, Karlheinz Deller, Cyril J. Gadd, Ignace J. Gelb, Ninel Jankowska, Paul Koschaker, Emanuel Laroche, Hildegard Lewy, Herbert Liebesny, Allan A. MacRae, Robert H. Pfeiffer, Pierre M. Purves, Aapili Saarisalo, Ephraim A. Speiser, Francis R. Steele, and Erich Neu, who passed away just as this volume went to press. This volume is dedicated to them for their seminal contributions to the study and interpretation of the Nuzi archives and Hurrian language and civilization.

* * *

The Social Stratification of Alalaḫ, by Eva von Dassow, will be published in *SCCNH* 11. *L'Archive de Paššitilla, fils de Pulaḫali,* by Brigitte Lion, will appear in *SCCNH* 12. We are now accepting papers for *SCCNH* 13. It is scheduled to appear in the winter of 2001/02. The editors will be pleased to consider articles for volume 13 on historical, philological, archaeological, and art historical subjects relating to the general topics of Nuzi, Hurrians, Hurrian and Hurro-Akkadian, Hurro-Hittite, and Urartian in their widest chronological and geographical contexts. In addition, book-length manuscripts will be considered for publication. Accompanying photos must be printed on gloss paper and clearly labeled. Charts and line drawings should be made so that they can be accommodated in the format size of this volume. Manuscripts from Europe and Asia should be sent directly to Professor Gernot Wilhelm, Institut für Orientalische Philologie der Julius-Maximilians-Universität Würzburg, Ludwigstraße 6, D-97070 Würzburg, Germany. Those from North America should be sent to Professor David I. Owen, Near Eastern Studies, Rockefeller Hall 360, Cornell University, Ithaca, NY 14853-2502 USA. Inquiries may also be made by electronic mail to dio1@cornell.edu; by facsimile to (USA) 607-255-1345 or gernot.wilhelm@mail.uni-wuerzburg.de; facsimile (Germany) 049-931-31-2674. Preferably, manuscripts should be submitted in electronic form (IBM or MAC format) with the name and version of the word processor accompanied by a printed copy made on a laser or equivalent printer. Closing date for manuscripts for volume 13 (volumes 11 and 12 will appear in 2000) is June 15, 2001. Contributors will be provided with 25 free reprints of their articles. The printing of additional reprints will not be possible.

Studies on the Civilization and Culture of Nuzi and the Hurrians (*SCCNH*), volumes 1–5 (and following), may be obtained from Eisenbrauns, POB 275, Winona Lake, IN 46590 USA, e-mail orders@eisenbrauns.com; website www.eisenbrauns.com. Volumes 6 and following may be obtained from CDL Press, P. O. Box 34454, Bethesda, MD 20827 USA, e-mail cdlpress@erols.com; website www.cdlpress.com.

David I. Owen &
Gernot Wilhelm
Ithaca and Würzburg
December 1999

TABLE OF CONTENTS

Part I: XLVe Rencontre assyriologique internationale:
The "Nuzi and the Hurrians" Sessions

Introduction

NUZI

Collections

Archives and Scribes

Geography

Society and Law

Archaeology

HURRIANS

Part II: General Studies

Part III: Nuzi Notes, 54-62

Part IV

Part I

XLVe Rencontre assyriologique internationale:

The "Nuzi and the Hurrians" Sessions

Introduction: Recent Trends in Nuzi and Hurrian Studies

GERNOT WILHELM
Julius-Maximilians-Universität, Würzburg

Seventy-five years ago, in the winter of 1927/28, the Harvard Semitic Museum and the Harvard Fogg Art Museum started to finance the excavations at Nuzi that, two years before, had been begun by Edward Chiera on behalf of the American School of Oriental Research at Baghdad. At that time finds were still divided between Iraq and the excavator's institution that resulted in the flow of several thousand cuneiform tablets and fragments into the Harvard Semitic Museum. Therefore it seemed only appropriate that the organizers of the XLVe Rencontre Assyriologique Internationale at Harvard University suggested the allocation of a special session of the congress to be devoted to Nuzi and the Hurrians.

Although the Nuzi texts are written in Akkadian, not every Assyriologist has the time and impetus to follow Nuzi research and even less so Hurrian studies. Both Nuzi and Hurrian studies, however, have seen substantial progress during the last two decades and we felt that the present state of research and the main results should be presented to the wider community of scholars instead of remaining the realm of a small group of the initiated. Consequently, our idea was to focus on a balanced presentation of recent research that need not necessarily lay stress upon the unpublished results of our own research.

Concerning the Nuzi tablets, the most obvious progress made in recent years was the publication of approximately one thousand tablets and fragments. The majority were copied by the late Professor Ernest R. Lacheman, who had published his last volume of copies as early as 1962 but left more than 700 unpublished copies of Nuzi texts at his death in 1982. More than 500 of these copies were of tablets at the Harvard Semitic Museum, with an additional 200 of these at the Chicago Oriental Institute. David I. Owen had inherited Professor Lacheman's scholarly legacy and, with the help of several colleagues, organized the publication of all the copies in the series *SCCNH*, which had begun as a *Festschrift* for Ernest R. Lacheman.[1] Two scholars who are most

1 E.R. Lacheman†, D.I. Owen, and M.A. Morrison, "Excavations at Nuzi 9/1," *SCCNH* 2

Studies on the Civilization and Culture of Nuzi and the Hurrians - 10

intimate with the collections at Chicago and at Harvard, respectively M.P. Maidman (York University) and Jeanette Fincke (Julius-Maximilians-Universität Würzburg) present reports on the properties and organization of the Nuzi tablets of the Oriental Institute in Chicago (pp. 25–34) and the Harvard Semitic Museum (pp. 13–24).

Nevertheless, there still remain significant numbers of unpublished texts. The Harvard Semitic Museum houses a collection of several thousand Nuzi tablet fragments, which is a valuable source for joins. An edition of this collection was started by Jeanette Fincke, who until now has copied approximately 300 fragments.[2] Nearly 300 unpublished Nuzi texts in the British Museum were catalogued in 1987 by M.P. Maidman.[3] A number of them recently were copied and edited by Gerfrid Müller.[4]

Unfortunately most of the several hundred Nuzi-type tablets and fragments unearthed in the late 1960s by Yasin Mahmūd al-Ḫaleṣī in Kurruḫanni, present-day Tall al-Faḫḫār, are available only through unpublished M.A. and Ph.D. theses,[5] or not at all. There are plans, however, to improve the situation.

The Nuzi texts form a unique corpus of sources for the social conditions and economic activities of people of all social strata in a limited space and a short period of time. The potential of these texts for a comprehensive case study of an ancient Near Eastern society has not been exhausted. The best-known contract-type, e.g., the so-called "sale adoption" (*ṭuppi mārūti*), has been referred to again and again more or less casually since the first treatment of the topic,[6] but we are still waiting for the comprehensive monograph that carefully collects and analyzes all the available data. Nevertheless, considerable progress in this field has been made. Carlo Zaccagnini presents a paper on an important aspect of the economy and society of the Nuzi area (pp. 93–102), a field to which he has contributed a number of articles and reviews.

(1987) 355–702; *idem*, "Excavations at Nuzi 9/2," *SCCNH* 4 (1993) 131–398; E.R. Lacheman† and D.I. Owen, "Excavations at Nuzi 9/3," *SCCNH* 5 (1995) 85–357; E.R. Lacheman† and M.P. Maidman, *Joint Expedition with the Iraq Museum at Nuzi VII: Miscellaneous Texts* (SCCNH 3), 1989.

2 J. Fincke, "Excavations at Nuzi 10/1, 1–65," *SCCNH* 8 (1996) 379–468; *eadem*, "Excavations at Nuzi 10/2, 66–174," *SCCNH* 9 (1998) 219–373. "Excavations at Nuzi 10/3" is in preparation.

3 M.P. Maidman, "The Nuzi Texts of the British Museum," *ZA* 76 (1986) 254–88.

4 G.G.W. Müller, *Londoner Nuzi-Texte* (SANTAG 4), Wiesbaden: Harrassowitz Verlag, 1998; see also *idem* (n. 10) with 41 texts in transliteration.

5 A. Fadhil, *Rechtsurkunden und administrative Texte aus Kurruḫanni*, M.A.-Arbeit Heidelberg 1972; F.N.H. Al-Rawi, "Studies in the Commercial Life of an Administrative Area of Eastern Assyria in the Fifteenth Century B.C., Based on Published and Unpublished Cuneiform Texts," Ph.D. thesis, Cardiff 1977; Mundir ʿAlī ʿAbdalmalik al-Mundirī, *nuṣūṣ ʾidārīya wa qaḍāʾīya min Tall al-Faḫḫār (madīna Kurruḫanni)*, Baghdad 1999 (courtesy author and Abdulilah Fadhil).

6 E. Cassin, *L'adoption à Nuzi*, Paris 1938.

One of the major concerns of Nuzi research, apart from the publication of unpublished sources, has been and still is the reconstruction of its archives. Brigitte Lion, who is studying the archive of a family of merchants and landowners (the Pulaḫali archive [*SCCNH* 12, forthcoming]), reports on the various archives and ongoing projects (pp. 35–62).

Much research has been devoted to historical topography, to the analysis of the agricultural landscape, to features of the various kinds of settlements, to local institutions, cults, and prosopography. A monograph by Carlo Zaccagnini on the rural landscape of the land of Arrapḫe[7] should be mentioned here as well as the now published dissertation of Abdulilah Fadhil supervised by Karlheinz Deller.[8] More recently, Jeanette Fincke collected the toponyms from Nuzi texts, published and unpublished, in a volume of the *Répertoire géographique*, indicating as completely as possible the topographical, economic, and administrative features of the individual towns and villages.[9] The last monograph devoted to this topic is Gerfrid Müller's published dissertation, which tries to locate as many towns as possible by systematically using data on roads and communication.[10] Müller presents a paper on this aspect of Nuzi research (pp. 81–91).

The numerous sealings on Nuzi tablets formed the basis for the chapter on ancient Near Eastern art history labelled "Mittanian glyptic" when Edith Porada published and discussed 1011 seal impressions from the Nuzi tablets housed in the Oriental Institute in her 1947 ASOR monograph, *Seal Impressions of Nuzi*. Most of the thousands of seal impressions on tablets from the Harvard Semitic Museum, however, remained unpublished. A major step forward was Diana Stein's dissertation on the seal impressions on the more than 700 tablets from the archive of prince Šilwa-teššup.[11] She not only dealt with the art historical aspects in the narrower sense of style and iconography, but also made full use of all the prosopographical and chronological data supplied by the texts. It may be noted that several thousand seal impressions on tablets from other archives still remain unpublished. Stein's contribution to the XLVe RAI will be published in the framework of a collection of papers on ancient Near Eastern glyptics.

Public and domestic architecture is a topic that demands close cooperation between archaeology and philology. The 200m x 200m mound of Nuzi used to be considered the town of Nuzi, whereas the remains of closely connected houses further to the north, including the houses of Teḫip-tilla and Šilwa-

---

7 C. Zaccagnini, *The Rural Landscape of the Land of Arrapḫe* (Quaderni di Geografia storica), Rome: Università di Roma, Istituto di Studi del Vicino Oriente, 1979.

8 A. Fadhil, *Studien zur Topographie und Prosopographie der Provinzstädte des Königreichs Arrapḫe* (Baghdader Forschungen 6), Mainz: Verlag Philipp von Zabern, 1983.

9 J. Fincke, *Die Orts- und Gewässernamen der Nuzi-Texte* (RGTC 10), Wiesbaden: Dr. Ludwig Reichert Verlag, 1993.

10 G.G.W. Müller, *Studien zur Siedlungsgeographie und Bevölkerung des mittleren Osttigrisgebiets* (HSAO 7), Heidelberg: Heidelberger Orientverlag, 1994.

11 D. Stein, *The Seal Impressions. Text; Catalogue* (Das Archiv des Šilwa-teššup 8–9), Wiesbaden: Harrassowitz Verlag, 1993.

teššup, have been labelled "suburban dwellings." The texts, however, repeatedly refer to private houses in the *kerḫu* of Nuzi. Thus it is clear that Nuzi had a *kerḫu*, an upper city, which has to be identified with the main mound, whereas the so-called "suburban dwellings" are the remains of a lower town, which mostly fell victim to erosion and plowing. The buying and selling of houses, parts of houses, and building plots are frequently attested in the texts. The excavation of Nuzi yielded a large part of the city plan. The paper of Judy Bjorkman provides a surprising, fresh interpretation of the history of the Ishtar temple at Nuzi (pp. 103–22). The private houses were recently analyzed by Mirko Novák,[12] whose paper deals with this aspect of Nuzi research (pp. 123–40).

The language of the Nuzi tablets has not been extensively dealt with since 1970.[13] Fortunately, the dictionaries have carefully included lexical material from Nuzi, especially as far as rare words are concerned. The enormous increase of published texts, however, has added considerably to the lexicon. The study of words of Hurrian origin would be stimulated if there were more scholars of Hurrian who, at the same time, work with the Nuzi texts and vice versa. Combining the two fields yields many insights, especially after the recent increase of intelligible Hurrian vocabulary. To give two examples: (1) the dictionaries mention a word *kapparnu* attested at Nuzi; according to *AHw* it is a "Kupferkanne," according to *CAD* "a pitcher." *AHw* asks whether the word is Hurrian; *CAD* calls it "foreign." An analysis based on new lexical data reveals that the word contains the Hurrian root *kapp-* "to fill," and the iterative suffix *-ar-*.[14] (2) *AHw* mentions a word *paḫussu* of "u.H." ("unknown origin") attested at Nuzi and Alalaḫ. *AHw* calls it "ein Frauengewand," *CAD* K 544b, "a headgear." Actually *CAD* is correct; the word is a substantivized adjective of appropriateness in *-ussi* based on *paġe* "head."[15]

---

12 M. Novák, "Eine Typologie der Wohnhäuser von Nuzi," *Baghdader Mitteilungen* 25 (1994) 341–446.

13 G. Wilhelm, *Untersuchungen zum Ḫurro-Akkadischen von Nuzi* (AOAT 9), Kevelaer/ Neukirchen-Vluyn: Neukirchener Verlag, 1970.

14 G. Wilhelm, "Hurritische Lexikographie und Grammatik: Die hurritisch-hethitische Bilingue aus Boğazköy," *Or*NS 61 (1992) 131.

15 G. Wilhelm, "Hurritische Berufsbezeichnungen auf *–li*," *SMEA* 29 (1992) 241 n. 6. – More examples are: (1) *teḫampašḫu*, *AHw* 1344 ("churr. Fw.", "eine Art von Silber?"): *teġ-* "grow" (tr. and intr.); *-am-* factitive, *-b-* "?"; *-aš(še)* abstract suffix; *-ḫe* adjective of appurtenance: *teġ=am(=)b=aš=ḫe*, "pertaining to the raising" (payment for nursing a child), see J. Fincke, "Beiträge zum Lexikon des Hurritischen von Nuzi," *SCCNH* 7 (1995) 6–11. (2) *ampannu*, *AHw* 44 ("churr. Fw.", "eine Holzart"), *CAD* A/2, 77 ("a wooden implement," "Hurr. word"): *amb-*, "burn" (intr., s. *am-*, "burn" tr.); *-a-* intrans.; *-nni* nominal suffix: *amb=a=nni* "s.th. burning" (fire wood), see G. Wilhelm, *Das Archiv des Šilwa-teššup, Heft 4: Darlehensurkunden und verwandte Texte*, Wiesbaden 1992, 59f. (s. noch J. Fincke, l.c., 19). (3) *ḫašartennu*, *AHw* 333 ("churr. Fw.", "?"), *CAD* Ḫ 138 ("mng. uncert.," "Hurr. word"): *ḫāž-* "anoint"; *-ar-*, iterative suffix; *-denni* (*-de=nni*?), suffix of profession: *ḫāž=ar=denni*, "s.o. who anoints again and again" (female perfume maker, = *muraqqītu*?), see G. Wilhelm, *SMEA* 29 (1992) 245–47.

In the field of grammar a careful analysis of scribal practices and traditions, of their competence and incompetence, is prerequisite. Paola Negri Scafa presents a paper on this important aspect (pp. 63–79). A new grammar is, in fact, desirable, but it cannot follow established paths of Akkadian dialect grammars because the Nuzi corpus of Akkadian texts cannot be treated as a uniform linguistic corpus originating from people using Akkadian as their mother tongue. There are varying degrees of scribal competence and varying degrees of Hurrian influence; there is the early Middle Babylonian formular of deeds and there also are Assyrian influences.

As far as Hurrian studies are concerned, the most important discovery of the last decades has been the Hurro-Hittite bilingual series of tablets called "*kirenzi*" in Hurrian, that means "manumission," "release from slavery." For Hurrian studies the series *kirenzi* has already attained the same prominence the Mittani letter has held for more than a century. The tablets were found in 1983. Eight years later, Heinrich Otten and Christel Rüster published the cuneiform copies[16] and in 1996 Erich Neu published a transliteration and translation with a copious commentary.[17] A bibliography of research on the bilingual would now contain close to a hundred entries.

Apart from the gains for Hurrian lexicography and grammar, the series *kirenzi* is a most remarkable addition to our corpus of ancient Near Eastern literature. There are three components whose interrelations are still in dispute: (1) a myth narrating Teššob's visit to the palace of Allani, the Hurrian queen of the netherworld; (2) a collection of similes, most of which focus on the punishment of misbehaving sons or state functionaries; and (3) a tale of a disputed manumission in the city of Ebla.

Even agreement on the structure of the Ebla tale has not yet been reached. As this author sees it,[18] the preserved part of the Ebla story begins with an overview of several previous kings of Ebla whose names are Arib-Ebla, Paib-Ebla, and Ešeb-abu (KBo 32, 20). They belong to a line of six kings of Ebla who had all been served by a certain Purra. This Purra was a citizen of the city of Igingalliš, where he had served under the reigns of three kings until he, together with the population of his city, was enslaved by the Eblaites, presumably as a consequence of a war. The next tablet, according to my reconstruction (KBo 32, 19), also refers to Purra. After he had served nine kings—three in Igingalliš and

---

16 H. Otten / Ch. Rüster: *Die hurritisch-hethitische Bilingue und weitere Texte aus der Oberstadt* (KBo 32), Berlin: Gebr. Mann Verlag, 1990 [appeared 1991].

17 E. Neu, *Das hurritische Epos der Freilassung. Untersuchungen zu einem hurritisch-hethitischen Textensemble aus Ḫattuša* (StBoT 32), Wiesbaden: Harrassowitz Verlag, 1996.

18 G. Wilhelm, "Die Könige von Ebla nach der hurritisch-hethitischen Serie 'Freilassung'," *AoF* 24 (1997) 277–93. It should be taken into consideration, however, that the tablet KBo 32, 12, which contains similes just as KBo 32, 14, a tablet without a colophon, might not belong to the series *kirenzi*; according to the colophon it is the second tablet of a series whose title is broken. This would leave the question open, whether the myth of Teššob's descent to the Netherworld (KBo 32, 13) precedes or follows the Ebla tale. See now also the comments of S. Martino, *JAOS* 119 (1999) 339–41.

six in Ebla—his tenth lord, Megi, the last king of Ebla, received an order from the main god of his city, the weather-god Teššob, to release Purra and the inhabitants of Igingalliš. Teššob threatens the city with destruction if it does not give its consent to the manumission, and Megi repeats the words of the god to the elders of Ebla. The next tablet in this reconstruction, the fifth of the whole series (KBo 32, 15), relates that the elders of Ebla resisted Megi's demand of a manumission. They even ridiculed the god's demand through irony. The preserved part of the tale ends with Megi's second visit to the temple of Teššob, where he informed the god about the negative reaction of the elders. He then cleansed himself and cast impurity on the city of Ebla. We do not know whether this led to the destruction of the city because the Ebla tale breaks off at this point. In addition there is much dispute on other questions raised by the bilingual texts. E. Neu presents his view on some points below (pp. 293–304).

The series *kirenzi* has enriched the Hurrian dictionary by more than 200 words and it has led to a much better understanding of many grammatical features. Mauro Giorgieri (pp. 223–56) and Margaret Khačikyan (pp. 257–65) deal with nominal inflection and the verbal system.

The verbal system of the series *kirenzi* helps to understand a pattern that appears in Hurrian personal names as well as in the Hurrian texts from Urkeš, Mari, Babylonia, and Ḫattuša. It has become evident that Hurrian names like Unap-teššup, Ḫašip-teššup, and Arum-atal contain a finite verbal form (*un=a=b*, "he came," *ḫaž=i=b*, "he heard [yielded to the plea]," *ar=o=m*, "he gave"; the vowels /a/, /i/, /o/ mark intransitivity, transitivity/non-ergativity, and ergativity).[19] This new insight not only opens a path to a better understanding of the Hurrian texts, especially those from Boğazköy, but it also raises a fundamental problem. The type of Hurrian personal names just mentioned consists of two elements, namely a finite verbal form in initial position and a theophoric element, e.g., Arip-Ugur, "(The god) Ugur has given," exactly like the Akkadian Iddin-Dagan, "Dagan has given," or the Amorite Yasmaᶜ-Addu, "Addu has heard." It is interesting that the position of the verb in these names is not the normal position in Hurrian; usually the verbal form occupies the final position of a sentence. One may ask whether the Hurrian phrase names were formed according to the Akkadian and Northwest-Semitic model. If this is true, one would have to assume a rather long period of Hurro-Akkadian symbiosis as early as the third millennium, because this type of phrase name is already well attested among the earliest Hurrian personal names. It may be important in this context to note that Urartian, a language closely related to Hurrian, which, however, was never in a *Sprachbund* with Semitic languages, does not utilize phrase names at all.

---

19 G. Wilhelm, "Zum hurritischen Verbalsystem," in: S.R. Anschütz (ed.), *Texte, Sätze, Wörter und Moneme. Festschrift für Klaus Heger zum 65. Geburtstag*, Heidelberg: Heidelberger Orientverlag, 1992, 659–71; *idem*, "Name, Namengebung. Bei den Hurritern," *RlA* 9/1–2 (1998) 121–27.

Though the series *kirenzi* yielded the most spectacular results in Hurrian studies during the last decades, there was also progress in other areas. As far as new texts are concerned, the cuneiform edition of all the Hurrian texts from Boğazköy, as far as they were still unpublished, has to be mentioned. The *Corpus der hurritischen Sprachdenkmäler* provides transliterations and indices for most of the Boğazköy Hurrian corpus and thus facilitates research considerably.[20] Since 1990, Hurrian texts were reported to have been found at Ortaköy northeast of Boğazköy[21]; they are still unpublished.[22] At Tuttul (Tell Bīᶜa) at the mouth of the Baliḫ river, an incantation has been found that, according to the epigraphist of the expedition, Manfred Krebernik, duplicates a tablet from Mari. A Hurrian fragment from the late Old Babylonian period that comes from clandestine diggings in the still unidentified city of Tigunanu has been published recently by Mirjo Salvini.[23] Most important is a tablet with a trilingual word list found at Ugarit in 1994.[24] Béatrice André-Salvini and Mirjo Salvini present a résumé and additional reflections on this important find (pp. 267–75, 434–35).

Astonishingly enough, even the best-studied Hurrian document, the so-called Mittani letter of king Tušratta found at el-Amarna more than a century ago, has stimulated a number of recent studies that help to understand considerably more of its grammar, lexicon, and content.[25] The increase of the

---

20 The following volumes have appeared so far (1999): V. Haas, *Die Serien* itkaḫi *und* itkalzi *des* AZU-*Priesters, Rituale für Tašmišarri und Tatuḫepa sowie weitere Texte mit Bezug auf Tašmišarri* (ChS I/1), Rome: Multigrafica Editrice, 1984; M. Salvini / I. Wegner, *Die hethitisch-hurritischen Rituale des* AZU-*Priesters*. Teil 1 (Die Texte), Teil 2 (Das Glossar) (ChS I/2), Rome: Multigrafica Editrice, 1986; I. Wegner, *Hurritiscbe Opferlisten aus hethitischen Festbeschreibungen*, Teil 1 (Texte für Ištar-Ša(w)uška) (ChS I/3,1), Rome: Bonsignori Editore, 1995; I. Wegner / M. Salvini, *Die hethitisch-hurritischen Ritualtafeln des* (ḫ)išuwa-*Festes* (ChS I/4), Rome: Multigrafica Editrice, 1991; V. Haas und I. Wegner, *Die Rituale der Beschwörerinnen* SALŠU.GI, Teil 1 (Die Texte), Teil 2 (Das Glossar) (ChS I/5), Rome: Multigrafica Editrice, 1988; St. de Martino, *Die mantischen Texte* (ChS I/7), Rome: Bonsignori Editore, 1992; V. Haas, *Die hurritischen Ritualtermini in hethitischem Kontext* (ChS I/9), Rome: CNR – Istituto per gli studi micenei ed egeo-anatolici, 1998; G. Wilhelm, *Ein Ritual des* AZU-*Priesters* (mit einer Autographie von Hans Gustav Güterbock) (ChS I, Ergänzungsheft 1), Rome: Bonsignori Editore, 1995.

21 A. Süel, "Eine hethitische Stadt mit hethitischen und hurritischen Tontafelentdeckungen," in *Hittite and Other Anatolian and Near Eastern Studies in Honour of Sedat Alp*, Ankara 1992, 487–92; *eadem*, "Ortaköy'ün Hitit çağındaki adı," *Belleten* 59 (1995) 271–83; *eadem*, "Ortaköy-Şapinuwa: Bir Hitit merkezi", *TÜBA-AR* 1 (1998) 43.

22 See, however, the publication of three Hurrian fragments from the museum of Çorum, that, though having been purchased, presumably come from Ortaköy: A. Ünal, *Hittite and Hurrian Cuneiform Tablets from Ortaköy (Çorum), Central Turkey*, Istanbul: Simurg, 1998, 57–65.

23 M. Salvini, *The Ḫabiru Prism of King Tunip-teššup of Tikunani* (Documenta Asiana 3), Rome: Istituti Editoriali Poligrafici Internazionali, 1996, 123–28.

24 B. André-Salvini / M. Salvini, "Un nouveau vocabulaire trilingue sumérien-akkadien-hourrite de Ras Shamra," *SCCNH* 9 (1998) 3–40.

25 For the latest contributions, see "Notes on the Mittani Letter" in *SCCNH* 7–9.

Hurrian dictionary and the discovery of new grammatical forms have again stimulated the comparative approach to Hurrian and Urartian that was successfully advanced by Igor M. Diakonoff in the 1950s and 60s.

As far as history is concerned, new data on the Hurrians in the third millennium have appeared. The most important discovery certainly is the identification of Tell Mozan in the northern Ḫabur area.[26] Giorgio and Marilyn Buccellati found sufficient evidence for their hypothesis that Tell Mozan is ancient Urkeš. The sealings found in an Akkad-period building refer to a ruler, Tupkiš of Urkeš, who bears the same title as the ruler Tišatal, known from his foundation inscription, which still is the oldest-known Hurrian text.[27] Southern Mesopotamia came into close contact with the Hurrian-speaking zone in the northeastern part of the Fertile Crescent through the military expansion of the Third Dynasty of Ur. This early phase of Hurrian history is treated in a paper by Douglas Frayne (pp. 141–201).

The history of the Mittani empire in the second millennium rests very much on the well-known sources, the Amarna letters and the Šuppiluliuma-Šattiwazza treaty. However, additional information was provided recently by textual finds at Tell Brak, Terqa, and Emar. The contribution of Cord Kühne (pp. 203–21) provides an updated survey of the history of Mittani.

Last but not least, Hurrian religion has to be mentioned. During the last twenty years it has become even more evident that the gods worshipped in Hurrian-speaking parts of the Near East were of mixed origin. There were gods that the Hurrians brought from their early homeland on the northeastern fringes of the Ancient Near Eastern world. But when the Hurrians moved westward, they met old cults of indigenous gods, which they adopted or renamed or identified with their own gods. Marie-Claude Trémouille, who recently published a book on the goddess Ḫebat,[28] contributes a paper that deals with aspects of Hurrian religion (pp. 277–91).

The special sessions on Nuzi and Hurrian studies at the XLVe RAI were to provide an overview of recent research and also to raise questions and contribute to the changing of attitudes, where necessary. It should be emphasized that Hurrian and the Hurrians were part and parcel of ancient Near Eastern civilization. A traditional assyriological concept that views them as barbarians who

---

26 G. Buccellati / M. Kelly–Buccellati, "The Royal Storehouse of Urkesh: The Glyptic Evidence from the Southwestern Wing," *AfO* 42/43 (1995/96) 1–32; M. Kelly-Buccellati, "Nuzi Viewed from Urkesh, Urkesh Viewed from Nuzi," *SCCNH* 8 (1996) 247–68; G. Buccellati / M. Kelly-Buccellati, "Urkesh. The First Hurrian Capital," *Biblical Archaeologist* 60/2 (1997); *idem*, "The Courtiers of the Queen of Urkesh," *Subartu* 4/2 (1998) 195–216; all with additional literature.

27 For a new edition with ample commentary, see G. Wilhelm, "Die Inschrift des Tišatal von Urkeš," in: G. Buccellati / M. Kelly-Buccellati (eds.): *Urkesh and the Hurrians. Studies in Honor of Lloyd Cotsen* (Urkesh/Mozan Studies 3; BibMes 26), 117–43, Pl. XIII–XV.

28 M.-C. Trémouille, *^{d}Ḫebat. Une divinité syro-anatolienne* (Eothen 7), Florence: LoGisma editore, 1997.

bastardized the Akkadian language ("barbarisiertes Akkadisch" instead of "languages in contact") is ideology, not history. What made the Hurrians different from many other peoples who migrated into the Fertile Crescent is that they not only maintained their language, but that their rulers, priests, and scribes used it as a means of learning and written communication. This was not an act of barbarism but of full-scale participation in cross-cultural intellectual developments and exchanges within a multilingual world.

The Nuzi Collection of the Harvard Semitic Museum*

JEANETTE FINCKE
Julius-Maximilians-Universität, Würzburg

The four seasons of excavations at the site of Yorġān Tepe / Nuzi produced nearly 5000 texts and fragments. Almost 3000 have been published, but many, mostly fragmentary, texts remain in the collections of the Oriental Institute in Chicago and the Harvard Semitic Museum in Cambridge. This paper surveys the history of the organization and publication of these texts, particularly those in the collection of the Harvard Semitic Museum.

In order to understand the character and the structure of the Nuzi tablet collection of the Harvard Semitic Museum [HSM], Cambridge, Mass., we have to go back in time, to the year 1925.[1] It was in the winter of that year[2] when Gertrude Bell, the Honorary Director of Antiquities of the newly established Iraq, asked Edward Chiera, then Annual Professor of the American School of Oriental Research in Baghdad, to begin an excavation at Kirkūk, east of the Tigris and south of the lower Zāb. She had hoped they might find more of the so-called Kirkūk tablets that were known to Assyriologists since 1896.[3] Because a modern town existed on the ancient city mound, it was impossible to dig in Kirkūk itself.[4] When Dr. William Corner, a resident of Kirkūk, told Chiera about a small

* Tracing the history of the Harvard Semitic Museum as well as the history the HSM Nuzi Collection could not have been accomplished without the help of various people: I thank my teacher, Professor G. Wilhelm, Würzburg, as well as Professor D.I. Owen, Ithaca, N.Y., Dr. Diana L. Stein, London, Dr. Joseph Green, Assistant Director of the Harvard Semitic Museum, and especially Dr. James Armstrong, Assistant Curator at the Harvard Semitic Museum, who read the version of this paper that was given at the XLVe RAI, corrected my English, and also eliminated some errors.

1 The following description of the excavation at Nuzi (Yorġān Tepe) is based on the excavation report by R.F.S. Starr, *Nuzi* Vol. I: Text, Cambridge, Mass., 1939.

2 R.F.S. Starr, *Nuzi*, Vol. I, XXIX; *idem*, *BASOR* 17 (February, 1925) 19. E. Chiera, *BASOR* 20 (December, 1925) 21.

3 The first Nuzi tablet was bought by the British Museum in 1891 and published by T.G. Pinches, CT 2 (1896), No. 21 (BU 91-5-9,296).

4 See E. Chiera, *BASOR* 20 (December, 1925) 22–23.

mound where a native found inscribed tablets some years before,[5] it was decided to go there. Good surface indications encouraged Chiera to select the small mound near the foot of the larger mound of Yorġān Tepe, situated 3 kms southwest of the village of Tarkhalan and 13 kms southwest of Kirkūk. During two months of excavation in March/April 1925, supported by the Iraq Museum and the American Schools of Oriental Research at Baghdad [ASOR], Chiera exposed one house and uncovered an archive of more than one thousand tablets.[6] According to those tablets, Yorġān Tepe covered ancient Nuzi, a major city in the kingdom of Arrapḫe, a vassal state of the Hurrian kingdom of Ḫanigalbat.

Two years later, in 1927, the Semitic Museum and the Fogg Art Museum of Harvard University joined with the American Schools of Oriental Research at Baghdad in a joint expedition to continue the excavation at Nuzi. Four seasons were conducted under the leadership of these institutions with the additional collaboration of the University of Pennsylvania Museum during the last two seasons (1929/30 and 1930/31).

Figure 1 is a plan showing the excavated areas of the different seasons. This is Plan No. 4 of the excavation report by Richard F.S. Starr, to which is added the grid of the main mound and the letters of each excavated area.

Edward Chiera was Field Director during the first season of this joint expedition (1927/28). At first, the houses of Šurki tilla and of Teḫip-tilla—see figure 1: the house in the northwest of the plan marked with the letter "T"—were excavated and cleared. Although Chiera had unearthed *ca.* 2800 tablets and fragments[7] in the house of Šurki-tilla two years earlier, more tablets and fragments continued to be found.

East of this house, the houses of Šilwa-teššup and Zike—designated by the letter A on the plan—were excavated and almost completely cleared. A cablegram of December 9, 1927, reported,[8] "Library of eight hundred tablets discovered. Everything well," and referred to the house of Šilwa-teššup. Some days later 200 more tablets were found in a room belonging to the adjoining house of Zike.

---

5 See E. Chiera, *BASOR* 20 (December, 1925) 23; R.F.S. Starr, *Nuzi*, Vol. I, XXIX.

6 See E. Chiera, *BASOR* 20 (December, 1925), 24. According to the terms of the excavation, Chiera was to publish all the tablets of this campaign. Because he was Professor of Assyriology at the University of Pennsylvania at that time, the tablets first went to Philadelphia (see E. Chiera, *BASOR* 20 [December, 1925] 25, and JEN I, 1927). But after he had accepted a position at the University of Chicago during the season 1927/28, the tablets were moved to the Oriental Institute.

7 This total has been given by M.P. Maidman in a paper presented at the XLV[e] RAI [see this volume]. But the excavation report noted only about 1000 tablets unearthed in this house. These tablets are those of the Oriental Institute, Chicago, and are published in the series, Joint Expedition with the Iraq Museum at Nuzi (JEN).

8 See David G. Lyon, *BASOR* 30 (April, 1928) 3.

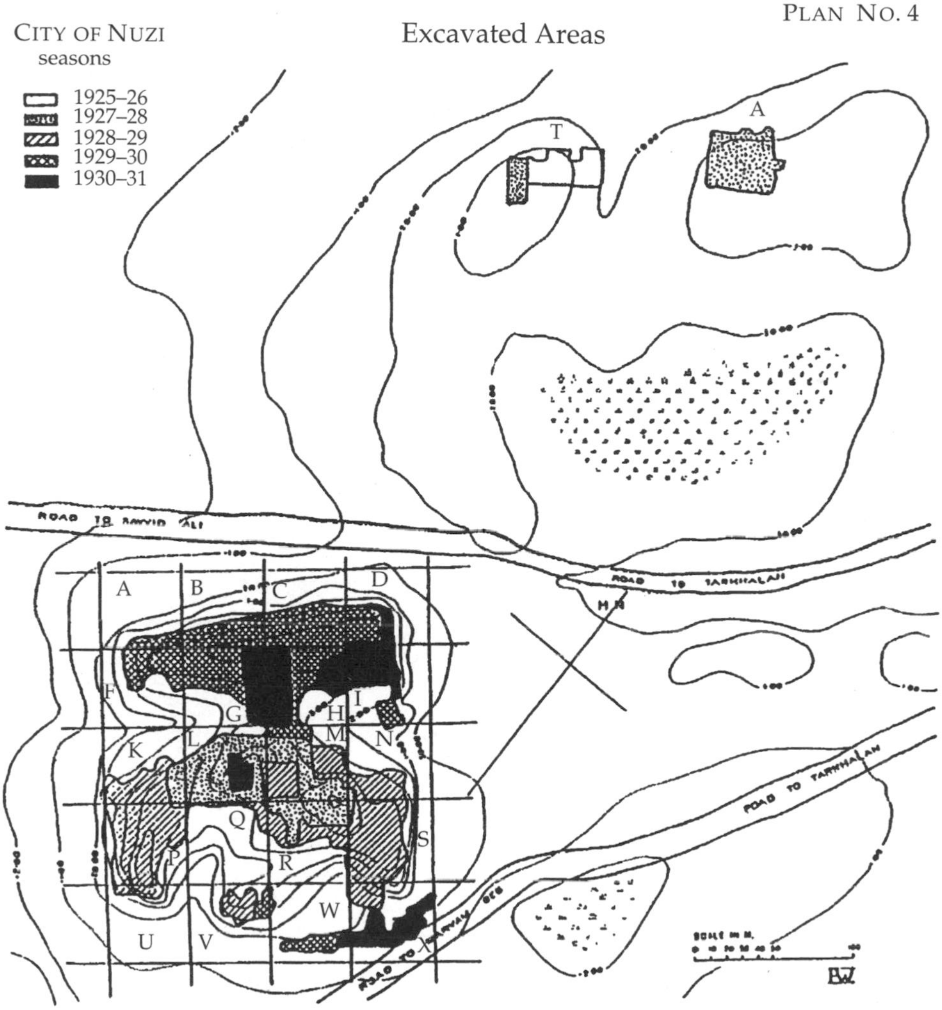

FIGURE 1

The excavated areas of the different seasons at Yorġān Tepe (Nuzi) (R.F.S. Starr, Nuzi plan no. 4), to which the grid to the main mound and the letter to each excavated area have been added.

At the same time, the archaeologists began excavating the main mound, opening up a large part of the palace containing *ca.* 90 rooms. During the excavation, Edward Chiera used the letter "C" for the entire palace area but, because of the considerable dimensions of the excavated city of Nuzi, the mound was subsequently subdivided into squares. These later subdivisions were utilized throughout the excavation report and they are added to the plan in figure 1. However, the early publications and references used the letter "C" assigned by Chiera. This means that, with respect to the tablets, "C" has to be changed into "K", "L", "M", "N", "R", "S", and some into "P", for each tablet with an SMN number below 2500.[9]

During the second season (1928/29), Professor Robert H. Pfeiffer was Field Director. The palace was cleared almost completely as were two large areas to the southwest (squares K/P) and northeast of the palace (squares M, N, R, and S). In the reception room of the governor (room L 4, located somewhere in the black spot in square L of the plan), digging below the pavement, a Cappadocian letter was unearthed. Digging deeper, down to the fourth pavement, two archaic contract tablets were found. In total, more than 700 tablets were said to have been unearthed during this season.

Richard F.S. Starr, from the Fogg Art Museum, was Field Director of the third and fourth campaigns. He had been the General Assistant during the first two seasons. In the third season (1929/30), mainly, the northern and northwestern sections of the mound were excavated and the temple was cleared completely—the temple is represented by the black mark in squares B/C and G/H of the plan. A small number of tablets were found during this campaign. By the end of 1929 (Dec. 1929) an archive of about 80 tablets, in more or less good condition, and the so-called bronze tablet, were unearthed in room F 24 (published as HSS 14, 1). Recently, this "bronze" tablet has been shown to be of nearly pure copper.[10]

During the final season (1930/31), the city-wall area of Nuzi at the southeastern foot of the mound (square X) was excavated, but the main object of this campaign was to expose the earlier levels of the mound. About 227 Sumerian, Old Akkadian, and Old Assyrian tablets, as well as the well-known geographical map (room L 4),[11] were found in these levels. Dr. T.J. Meek, the epigraphist

---

9 Tablets with an SMN number above 3000 come from the northwest and northeast ridges of the mound, squares A to H, where "A" and "C" are different from the letters used in HSS 5, 9, 13, 14, and AASOR 16 for tablets below 2000.

In HSS 14, 1950, XIX–XX, E.R. Lacheman provided a list of rooms, formerly designated as "C", with the letters used in Starr's plans: "L 1 (A 1?), L 2 (M 2 ?), L 6, L 8, L 13, 17(?), L 20, L 24, L 27, L 29, L 31, K 32, K 35 (certainly not P 35 for the tablets with this room designation came to the Museum before this section of the mound was excavated), R 48, R 49, R 50, R 56, R 57, M 61, M 74, R 75, R 76, M 77, M 78, M 79, R 81, R 84, M 89, M 91, R 96." Add to this list: L 14, L 44, M 70, S 110, S 112, S 113, N 120, S 132, S 133, S 151, P 382, P 465, P 470.

10 Courtesy Dr. J. Armstrong, Assistant Curator of the Harvard Semitic Museum.

11 First publication of the map by T.J. Meek in *BASOR* 42 (April, 1931) 7–10, with photo and drawing on p. 8.

of this season, who published all the tablets from the earlier levels in HSS 10,[12] proved that the earlier name of the city had been Gasur.

According to the terms of the excavations, all tablets unearthed during the years 1927–1931 were brought to the Harvard Semitic Museum for publication. In general, this was done in the Harvard Semitic Series (HSS), with a new sub-series, Excavations at Nuzi (EN). In the bibliography appended to this paper, Part IIa contains a list of the main publications of these Nuzi texts. It also serves as a kind of concordance between the two series HSS and EN. To date, more than 2800 Nuzi tablets and fragments unearthed during the years 1927–1931 have been published.

It was also agreed that half of the published material was the property of the Iraq Museum, Baghdad, and was to be returned to Iraq after publication. In general, the division was carried out for the texts published in AASOR 16 and in the Harvard Semitic Series. The last eight boxes were sent back to the Iraq Museum in 1982 and contained selected texts from HSS 14, 15, 16, and 19. The preparations concerning the division of the EN 9 texts were interrupted in 1990 because of the Gulf War.

In the late 1970s, a project was initiated at the Harvard Semitic Museum to produce casts of the tablets that were to be returned to Iraq. This project was begun but could not be completed because of the lack of funds. As to the tablets that already had been sent back, only a few reproductions exist at the HSM. As a result, anyone who wishes to collate a Nuzi text published in the Harvard Semitic Series first should determine whether the tablet in question is at the HSM or at the Iraq Museum.

The list of major publications of the HSM Nuzi texts shows that, beginning in 1937, it was E.R. Lacheman who published the texts. Lacheman had studied with both Pfeiffer and Chiera and, in 1935, completed a doctoral dissertation on the Nuzi tablets at Harvard.[13] As a result, when the Harvard Semitic Museum was closed during World War II, Pfeiffer, who at the time was curator of the Museum, assigned the unpublished Nuzi tablets to Lacheman for publication. The Museum remained without support even after the war and was finally closed to the public in 1958. Lacheman, who taught at Wellesley College and later at Brandeis University, kept the tablets at his home and continued to publish them. When the Harvard Semitic Museum was reorganized in the 1970s, Lacheman began returning the tablets to the Museum. During the following years several small collections of tablets and fragments were brought back. Professor David I. Owen returned the last group of tablets to the HSM in the years following Lacheman's death in 1982.

Originally, the plan was to provide every single tablet and fragment unearthed during the four seasons of excavation its own "Semitic Museum:

---

12 HSS 10 = EN 3, published in 1935.

13 E.R. Lacheman, "Selected Cuneiform Texts from Nuzi in the Harvard Semitic Museum," Ph. D. dissertation, Cambridge 1935.

Nuzi" (= SMN) number. Thereafter, the assignment of SMN numbers was to reflect the order of the tablets found during each subsequent campaign.[14] But each season so many tablets were being found, that the HSM staff could not finish cataloguing them before boxes[15] from the next season began arriving. This created complications when it was decided that the tablets from the earlier levels unearthed during the last campaign (1930/31) should also be assigned SMN numbers—something which, in fact, was misleading because these tablets came from the earlier Gasur period, and not from the Nuzi period. It is now obvious that when T.J. Meek was ready to publish the Gasur texts, four years after they had been unearthed, not all of the boxes had been unpacked. So, the approximate number of tablets and fragments in each box was estimated. Based on information the excavators themselves provided during their campaigns, it was decided to start with the number 4001 for texts from the earlier levels.

The Harvard Semitic Museum Nuzi tablets can be divided into two major groups according to their publication status. The first group is the collection of published texts. It is the largest Nuzi collection at the Museum and is organized by publication number. The second group consists of the unpublished Nuzi texts and is divided into five minor sub-collections. They are:

(1) collection of the texts with SMN numbers.[16] In this collection groups of fragments are often collected under single SMN numbers.

(2) collection of the unnumbered tablets and fragments.

The tablets in these two collections vary according to size and condition of preservation. There are whole tablets as well as very small fragments.[17]

(3) NTF collection (= Nuzi Tablet Fragments) of unpublished fragments.

---

14 Nos. 1–2000 should have been found during the 1927/28 campaign, 2001–3000 in 1928/29, 3001–4000 in 1929/30 (see E.R. Lacheman, HSS XIV, Introduction); or Nos. 1–2148 in 1927/28 and 2149–3760 during the years 1928 to 1931 (see E.R. Lacheman, "Selected Cuneiform Texts from Nuzi in the Harvard Semitic Museum," Ph. D. dissertation, Cambridge 1935, p. IV, Introduction).

15 See, e.g., the description by Carney E.S. Gavin, *SCCNH* 1 (1981) 137, "When Professor Ernest Lacheman first came to the Harvard Semitic Museum in 1930, he was taken by the second Curator of the *HSM*, the late Professor Robert Pfeiffer, to an immense wooden box ('four feet by four feet by four feet') full of Nuzi cuneiform tablets."

16 Many texts were used for research prior to publication and therefore were quoted often by their SMN numbers. Since most of these texts were eventually published, a concordance between the SMN and publication numbers is essential. The only available concordance, including publications until 1972, was published by M. Dietrich - O. Loretz - W. Mayer, *Nuzi-Bibliographie* (AOAT-S 11), Kevelaer/Neukirchen-Vluyn 1972, pp. 209–40. A revised and completed SMN-concordance including joins to previously published tablets is in preparation. It will appear in a future *SCCNH* volume.

17 As for the whole or nearly whole tablets, the surface very often is abraded and the cuneiform signs are difficult to see or read.

Unfortunately, it is not known who organized this collection or why the numbering system was created. It uses the letters "M", "MM", "N", "P", and "Q" followed by numbers to which sometimes letters are appended to indicate further subdivisions. Usually, there are several fragments in these NTF boxes but their numbers vary. Some of these fragment groups carry a SMN number and occasionally a slip of paper with the date of excavation and the room number. Very seldom do the fragments in one box come from the same tablet—usually they belong to different tablets—and, beyond that, sometimes to tablets unearthed in different rooms and/or squares. It is obvious that the system does not correspond to the excavation records. According to a rough calculation, the NTF collection contains *ca.* 3000 fragments—most of them are very small.

(4) the so-called "clay-bullae" collection.[18]

In fact, the name "clay-bullae" collection is not accurate since this collection contains 750 sealed clay objects, including tablet fragments, bullae, fragments of envelopes, and so on, all organized in numerical order. Additionally, within the NTF collection, most of the sealed fragments are also numbered and grouped together in plastic bags, but still kept within the NTF boxes—the numbers of these sealed fragments within the NTF collection are higher than 750; the highest number is 1498. Recent investigation[19] has revealed that the clay-bullae and these numbered NTF fragments belong to the same numbering system, and that these numbers refer to the "seal impression" or "glyptic" project of the Museum in the 1970s,[20] which produced 1498 photos of unpublished sealed fragments. There is further evidence that the so-called clay-bullae were selected from the NTF collection, but separated from the boxes to create a kind of separate "glyptic" collection, a project that was never completed.

(5) the ERL (= Ernest Rene Lacheman) collection.[21]

The tablet fragments in this collection are those unnumbered fragments that D.I. Owen, M.A. Morrison, and others catalogued in the Lacheman home while Owen was organizing the return of the Nuzi texts to the HSM. Some of the ERL fragments have since been assigned SMN numbers, while others are not numbered according to the SMN system. A few have been

---

18 See J. Fincke, *SCCNH* 8 (1996) 379ff., n. 3.

19 I thank James Armstrong for his efforts to inquire into the problem of this collection. Without his investigation at the Museum, the results could never have been achieved from abroad.

20 See Carney E.S. Gavin, *SCCNH* 1 (1981) 140–47.

21 See D.I. Owen and M.A. Morrison, *SCCNH* 2 (1987) 341–42.

joined to other tablets.[22] The highest ERL number in the Nuzi collection is 145.

Within these sub-collections at the Harvard Semitic Museum there are still thousands of unpublished fragments of Nuzi tablets. The potential value of these collections for joins has already been demonstrated in the *SCCNH* series and elsewhere. Some of these joins have been made with texts published in EN 9. Fortunately, these texts have not yet been sent back to the Iraq Museum. As for joins with texts that have already been returned to Baghdad, for the time being they can no longer be checked. Unfortunately, the fragments in the NTF collection are usually too small to provide sufficient evidence for a potential join based solely upon its content. The original tablets are needed to verify joins. Nevertheless, even these small fragments can be very important to understand the contents of a tablet.

Although most of the complete Nuzi tablets of the HSM collection are published, there is still enough unpublished material left for much additional research. Furthermore, the Nuzi collection is far from being edited completely. Much remains to be done.

BIBLIOGRAPHY OF THE PUBLICATION OF THE HARVARD SEMITIC MUSEUM (HSM) NUZI TEXTS[23]

I. Excavation Report:

Starr, Reginald F.S.
Nuzi. Report on the Excavations at Yorgan Tepa near Kirkuk, Iraq. Conducted by Harvard University in Conjunction with the American Schools of Oriental Research and the University Museum of Philadelphia 1927–1931. Vol. I. Texts (1939); Vol. II. Plates and Plans (1937). Harvard University Press, Cambridge, Mass.

II. Publication of the HSM Nuzi Texts:

II.a. The series *Excavations at Nuzi* (EN) and additional main publications (AASOR [1936] 16, *RA* [1937] 24, *RA* [1939] 36).

1929	EN 1	HSS 5	E. Chiera	*Texts of Varied Contents* [107 texts]
1932	EN 2	HSS 9	R.H. Pfeiffer	*The Archives of Shilwateshub Son of the King* [158 texts]
(1935	EN 3	HSS 10	T.J. Meek	*Old Akkadian, Sumerian and Cappadocian Texts from Nuzi* [223 texts])
1936		AASOR 16	R.H. Pfeiffer / E.A. Speiser	*One Hundred New Selected Nuzi Texts* [100 texts in transliteration]

---

22 See, e.g., G. Wilhelm, *SCCNH* 7 (1995) 151ff. Nuzi Notes 16 "Identifikationen von ERL-Nummern."

23 With additional remarks of the author in square brackets.

1937		*RA* 34	E.R. Lacheman	
				(pp. 1–8) "An Omen Text from Nuzi" [1 text]
1939		*RA* 36	E.R. Lacheman	
				"Nuziana", Part I [7 school-tablets] and Part II [almost every text of Part II is reedited in HSS 14, HSS 15 and some in HSS 13]
1942	EN 4	HSS 13	R.H. Pfeiffer / E.R. Lacheman	
				Miscellaneous Texts from Nuzi, Part I [389 texts, almost all in transliteration]
1950	EN 5	HSS 14	E.R. Lacheman	
				Miscellaneous Texts from Nuzi, Part II: The Palace and Temple Archives [265 texts + 108 in transliteration]
1955	EN 6	HSS 15	E.R. Lacheman	
				The Administrative Archives [335 texts + about 86 fragments]
1958	EN 7	HSS 16	E.R. Lacheman	
				Economic and Social Documents [467 texts]
1962	EN 8	HSS 19	E.R. Lacheman	
				Family Law Documents [147 texts]
1987	EN 9/1	*SCCNH* 2	E.R. Lacheman / D.I. Owen, M. Morrison	
1993	EN 9/2	*SCCNH* 4	E.R. Lacheman / D.I. Owen, M. Morrison	
1995	EN 9/3	*SCCNH* 5	E.R. Lacheman / D.I. Owen	[EN 9 = 529 text numbers]
1996	EN 10/1	*SCCNH* 8	J. Fincke	[65 texts and fragments]
1998	EN 10/2	*SCCNH* 9	J. Fincke	[109 texts and fragments]
2001	EN 10/3	*SCCNH* 13	J. Fincke	in preparation

II.b. Monographs including transliterations of previously unpublished HSM Nuzi texts (most of the texts transliterated in one of these dissertations were published in the EN 9-series).

Chow, Wilson Wing-Kin

"Kings and Queens of Nuzi" (Brandeis University, Ph. D., 1973; History, ancient. UMI 73-32,371).

Eichler, Barry L.

Indenture at Nuzi: The Personal Tidennūtu Contract and Its Mesopotamian Analogues (Yale Near Eastern Researches 5; Yale University Press, 1973).

Hayden, Roy E.

"Court Procedure at Nuzu" [CPN] (Brandeis University, Ph. D., 1962; History, ancient. UMI 63-5842).

Frymer-Kensky, Tikva S.

"The Judicial Ordeal in the Ancient Near East" (Yale University Ph. D., 1977; UMI 80-2726).

Lacheman, Ernest R.

"Selected Cuneiform Texts from Nuzi in the Harvard Semitic Museum" (Harvard University, Ph. D., 1935).

Lieberman, Alvin I.

"Studies in the Trial-By-River Ordeal in the Ancient Near East during the Second Millennium BCE" (Brandeis University, Ph. D., 1969; History, ancient. UMI 69-20,729).

Morrison, Martha

"Šilwa-tešup: Portrait of a Hurrian Prince" (Brandeis University, Ph. D., 1974; History, ancient. UMI 74-28,003).

Owen, David I.

"The Loan Documents from Nuzi" [LDN] (Brandeis University, Ph. D., 1969; Economics, history. UMI 70-12,031).

Wilhelm, Gernot

Das Archiv des Šilwa-teššup. Heft 2: Rationenlisten I. (Wiesbaden, 1980).
Das Archiv des Šilwa-teššup. Heft 3: Rationenlisten II. (Wiesbaden, 1985).
Das Archiv des Šilwa-teššup. Heft 4: Darlehensurkunden und verwandte Texte. (Wiesbaden, 1992).

II.c. Publication of HSM Nuzi texts in articles:

Fincke, Jeanette

"Nuzi Note 31. SMN 2799 and One Unnumbered Fragment Joined to EN 9/2 455," *SCCNH* 8 (1996) 365–66 [SMN 2799+; SMN 2371].

"Nuzi Note 37. NTF P 230(1) Joined to EN 9/1, 30," *SCCNH* 9 (1998) 190–91.

"Nuzi Note 38. 'Clay Bulla' no. 161 and SMN 2463 Joined to EN 9/2, 106," *SCCNH* 9 (1998) 191–93.

"Nuzi Note 39. NTF P 2(1) and 'Clay Bulla' no. 748 Joined to EN 9/2, 157," *SCCNH* 9 (1998) 193–94.

"Nuzi Note 40. Unnumbered Fragment Joined to EN 9/2, 163," *SCCNH* 9 (1998) 194–96.

"Nuzi Note 41. SMN 3718 Joined to EN 9/1, 170," *SCCNH* 9 (1998) 196–97.

"Nuzi Note 42. SMN 2975 Joined to EN 9/2, 175," *SCCNH* 9 (1998) 197–98.

"Nuzi Note 43. NTF P 233(1) and NTF P 173(1) Joined to EN 9/1, 500," *SCCNH* 9 (1998) 199–200.

"Nuzi Note 44. 'Clay Bulla' no. 125 Joined to HSS 13, 273," *SCCNH* 9 (1998) 200–1.

"Nuzi Note 45. Unnumbered Fragment Joined to HSS 15, 140," *SCCNH* 9 (1998) 201–2.

"Nuzi Note 46. 'Clay Bulla' no. 13 Joined to EN 9/3, 328," *SCCNH* 9 (1998) 202–3.

"Nuzi Note 47. HSS 19, 26 + HSS 19, 34 + EN 9/1, 241 + 'Clay Bullae' nos. 623+624+561," *SCCNH* 9 (1998) 203–4.

"Nuzi Note 48. ERL 6 Joined to HSS 9, 158 (= IM 50841)," *SCCNH* 9 (1998) 205.

"Nuzi Note 54. A New Writing of the Arrapḫa Place Name, URU.Turanzi / Dūranzi," *SCCNH* 10 (1999) 425.

"Nuzi Note 55. EN 10/1, 38 Joined to HSS 13, 300," *SCCNH* 10 (1999) 425–26.

"Nuzi Note 56. One Fragment from NTF P 181 Joined to HSS 15, 26," *SCCNH* 10 (1999) 426–28.

"Nuzi Note 57. HSS 19, 108 Joined to EN 9/1, 139," *SCCNH* 10 (1999) 428–29.

"Nuzi Note 58. Two Fragments from NTF P 2 and 'Clay Bullae' nos. 770 and 772 Joined to EN 9/2, 16," *SCCNH* 10 (1999) 429–30.

"Nuzi Note 59. SMN 2797 Joined to HSS 19, 30," *SCCNH* 10 (1999) 430–32.

"Nuzi Note 60. 'Clay Bulla' no. 573 Joined to EN 9/2, 362," *SCCNH* 10 (1999) 432.

Grosz, Katarzyna

"Nuzi Note 8. A New Fragment from the Archive of the Family of Akkuja," *SCCNH* 2 (1987) 352–54 [SMN 1655; SMN 1655 + 1 unnumb. frg. + 6 frgs. from NTF M 28 A = EN 10/2, 77].

Klein, Michael

"Nuzi Notes 14. HSS 15, 50 Joined to HSS 15, 111," *SCCNH* 7 (1995) 150.

"Nuzi Notes 15. One Fragment from NTF M 16 A joined to HSS 16, 370," *SCCNH* 7 (1995) 151.

"Nuzi Notes 20. HSS 14, 60 Incorrectly Joined," *SCCNH* 8 (1996) 349–51 [SMN 3392a; SMN 3392b].

"Nuzi Note 32. HSS 15, 317," *SCCNH* 8 (1996) 366–67 [HSS 15, 317 F+G+L; HSS 15, 317 wrongly joined].

Maidman, M.P.

"Nuzi Notes 2. A Tale of Two Cities," *SCCNH* 2 (1987) 345–49 [JEN 13 + SMN 1584].

"Nuzi Notes 3. A Second Teḫip-Tilla Fragment at Harvard," *SCCNH* 2 (1987) 349 [SMN 1721; SMN 1721 = EN 10/2, 110].

Owen, David I.

"Nuzi Notes 4. A *tidennūtu* Fragment," *SCCNH* 2 (1987) 349–50 [SMN 1594; SMN 1534 = EN 10/1, 32].

"Nuzi Notes 5. A New Reference to *irana*," *SCCNH* 2 (1987) 350–51 [SMN 1631].

"Nuzi Notes 6. A Typical Loan Fragment," *SCCNH* 2 (1987) 351 [SMN 2790].

"Nuzi Notes 7. A *ṭuppi zitti* Fragment," *SCCNH* 2 (1987) 351–52 [SMN 2797].

"An Old Assyrian Letter from Nuzi," *SCCNH* 7 (1995) 65–67 [SMN 1002; this text is not identical with SMN 1002 = HSS 16, 407].

Wilhelm, Gernot

"Zusammenschlüsse von Nuzi-Texten," *SCCNH* 1 = *Fs.* Lacheman, 1981, 341–47 [HSS 19, 42 + 1 frg. from NTF M 25 A; HSS 19, 19 + 1 frg. from NTF N 18; HSS 16, 279 + HSS 16, 299; HSS 15, 138 + 1 unnumbered frg.; HSS 9, 156 +? 1 frg. from NTF M 8 B].

"Marginalien zu Herodot Klio 199," in: T. Abush *et.al.*, eds., *Lingering over Words: Studies in Ancient Near Eastern Literature in Honor of William L. Moran* (Harvard Semitic Studies 37; Cambridge, Mass., 1990), pp. 505–24 [SMN 1670].

"Ein neuer Text zum Ordal in Nuzi (JEN 659 + SMN 1651)," *SCCNH* 5 (1995) 71–74 [SMN 1651+ = EN 10/2, 73].

"*Bīt papāḫi* in Nuzi," *SCCNH* 7 (1995) 121–28 [ERL 82 + SMN 2963].

"Nuzi Notes 9. SMN 1636 Joined to HSS 13, 340," *SCCNH* 7 (1995) 143–44.

"Nuzi Notes 10. SMN 1687 Joined to HSS 19, 22," *SCCNH* 7 (1995) 144–46.

"Nuzi Notes 11. SMN 1696 Joined to EN 9/1, 122," *SCCNH* 7 (1995) 146.

"Nuzi Notes 12. SMN 1780 Joined to EN 9/2, 18," *SCCNH* 7 (1995) 147–48.

"Nuzi Notes 13. SMN 2957 Joined to EN 9/2, 19," *SCCNH* 7 (1995) 148–49.

"Nuzi Notes 16. Identifikationen von ERL-Nummern," *SCCNH* 7 (1995) 151–55 [ERL 2 = SMN 1173; ERL 29 = SMN 2356; ERL 104 = SMN 2786; ERL 105 = SMN 1638; SMN 1173 + AASOR 16, 3 = EN 10/1, 10; SMN 1638 + 1 Frg. from NTF P 63 = EN 10/1, 56].

"Nuzi Notes 22. SMN 1621 Joined to HSS 13, 218," *SCCNH* 8 (1996) 351–52.

"Nuzi Note 30. SMN 1669 Joined to HSS 13, 100," *SCCNH* 8 (1996) 364–65.

III. Studies on the Seal Impressions of the HSM Nuzi Texts.

Stein, Diana L.

"A Reappraisal of the 'Sauštatar Letter' from Nuzi," *ZA* 79 (1989) 36–60.

Das Archiv des Šilwa-teššup. Heft 9: The Seal Impressions (Wiesbaden, 1993).

The University of Chicago Nuzi Texts: History and Prospects

M. P. MAIDMAN
York University

The winter of 1925/26 marked the first of five seasons of excavation at Nuzi. The tablets from that season were eventually housed at the Oriental Institute of the University of Chicago. These artifacts are prominent both for their large number and for their having been part of extensive private archives from Nuzi's suburbs.

This article reviews the modern history of the Chicago texts and the plans for their continuing publication. A description of the number, contents, and provenience of these texts is followed by a more detailed outline of the nature of the texts yet to be published. Elements to be noted are: new and unusual text genres, new types of data, and expanded attestations of personal and geographical names. Finally, preliminary thoughts are presented regarding the implications of this fresh material for further research and for the history of Nuzi.

It is now just over a century since Theophilus G. Pinches published the first Nuzi text. The document was a labor contract and appeared in CT II.[1] This initiated a flurry of publications, which continues to this day, of similar tablets obtained in the antiquities market. Hundreds of these texts from Nuzi and nearby Kirkuk found their way to the British Museum, the Louvre, the Hermitage, and other museums and libraries in Europe and the United States. The crowning example of the publication and edition of these texts remains Cyril J. Gadd's masterful "Tablets from Kirkuk," published in 1926.[2] Through his copies, transliterations, and translations of over eighty British Museum tablets, but even more so through his brilliant commentary to those then novel texts, Gadd established Nuzi studies as a distinct and viable branch of Assyriology.

Shortly before the time of Gadd's crucial publication, in the winter of 1925/26, another event, this one epochal for Nuzi studies, had taken place. Under the

---

[1] CT II, 21, published in 1896. Abbreviations follow Erica Reiner, ed., *The Assyrian Dictionary of the Oriental Institute of the University of Chicago,* Š/3 (Chicago: The Oriental Institute, 1992), pp. v–xxii.

[2] C.J. Gadd, "Tablets from Kirkuk," *RA* 23 (1926) 49–161.

Studies on the Civilization and Culture of Nuzi and the Hurrians - 10

auspices of the American Schools of Oriental Research, Edward Chiera of the University of Pennsylvania undertook excavation in what turned out to be a suburb of Nuzi. Many hundreds of tablets and tablet fragments were unearthed during that winter, the first of five seasons undertaken in the suburbs and main mound of Nuzi. Scholars soon recognized that Nuzi was a source of the texts published by Pinches, Gadd, and others. Chiera's industry was such that the first volume of tablets, containing one hundred Nuzi texts from that dig, of a total of five volumes he was to produce in rapid succession, appeared in the very same year, 1926, at about the same time as Gadd's article.[3]

The documents excavated by Chiera were shipped to Philadelphia where Chiera could study them. The next year, 1927, Chiera was called to the University of Chicago, and with Chiera went all the tablets from that first season of excavation. Thus did Chicago's Oriental Institute end up with the second largest Nuzi tablet collection after Harvard's, adding new meaning to the observation, *ex oriente lux*, "light comes from the east," in this case, from Philadelphia.

It is this Chicago collection, the tablets and fragments that went to the American midwest with Chiera, that has been the core of my own research and upon which this paper focuses.

The collection is amenable to brief definition. It consists of just over 2,800 tablets, fragments, and other archival artifacts excavated from the first season at Yorghan Tepe. It comes from the so-called "western suburban area"[4] and comprises part of the private archives of four discrete families.[5] The largest of the archives is that of the family of Teḫip-tilla son of Puḫi-šenni, a family documented for five generations. The archives describe the private business and other economic affairs of the four families that collected and preserved these texts. In general, the state of preservation of the tablets varies by archive. The surviving tablets from one family's archive, that of Ḫutiya son of Kuššiya, are often in wretched shape, of only partially washed clay, unbaked in antiquity except perhaps by destructive fire, frequently brick red, badly cracked, and often impossible to decipher. Moreover, the family's scribes often seemed also to have exhibited poor penmanship. The largest archive, Teḫip-tilla's, happily contains mostly tablets of clean clay, well baked, usually well written, and sometimes appearing as if they had been written only a few days ago.

Of the 2,800 items in the Chicago collection, just under 900 have been published, these by Chiera, Ernest R. Lacheman, and myself.[6] This number

---

[3] JEN I. The others appeared within eight years: JEN II (1930), III (1931), IV (1934), V (1934).

[4] For this designation, see, for example, Ernest R. Lacheman, HSS XVI, p. v.

[5] For details, see Lacheman, HSS XVI, pp. v–vi.

[6] Major publications include Chiera: JEN I–V; Lacheman: JEN VI; Lacheman and Maidman: JEN VII (=*SCCNH* 3). Minor publications include E.R. Lacheman, "New Nuzi Texts and a New Method of Copying Cuneiform Tablets," *JAOS* 55 (1935) 429–31 + pll. I–III;

includes most of the relatively complete tablets and some major fragments. The remaining 1,900 pieces include about 110 tablets and 460 sizable fragments whose context is relatively clear and significant. The remainder, about 1,300 pieces, consists of minor fragments ranging from parts of a few lines, often with identifiable content and recoverable data, to mere chips preserving a sign or two.

Although the assignment of one piece or another to the category of minor fragment versus significant fragment versus tablet is to some extent subjective, the general breakdown of these items is sound and the numbers comprising the collection secure. This latter assertion regarding the number of Chicago artifacts is based on my catalogue of the Nuzi collection of the Oriental Institute in which 2,866 items are assigned numbers, which represent 2,806 artifacts after joins. The number of artifacts will, of course, decrease further as more joins are made.

As for future publication, I plan, in addition to completing text editions for the Chicago texts in JEN VII, to publish an additional 120 tablets and major fragments. This will bring the published corpus to over 1,000 items, including almost all the remaining tablets. At that point, I shall complete an annotated catalogue of the entire Chicago collection, including descriptions of the remaining unpublished 1,800 items, mostly small fragments, some significant fragments, and a few—mostly badly damaged—tablets.

Having defined the corpus of Chicago Nuzi texts, and having outlined the course of past and future publication, I should now like to sketch the contents of the decipherable unpublished tablets and fragments insofar as they exhibit significant or novel data or patterns. In short, the remainder of this paper consists of "coming attractions."

The number of texts to be noted in the various categories are, of course, approximate. These numbers represent unambiguous texts. The number of examples of one category of text or another would be augmented by other tablets from the collection as yet not clearly identifiable as belonging to the category. On the other hand, the numbers noted will be diminished by as yet unrecognized joins among the fragments that I count as individual items. On balance, I judge that my numbers are probably minimal, when not below minimal.

The first salient feature of the unpublished 1,900 items is that, as a whole, they mirror the texts already published. With one possible exception—to be discussed below—they will not force a fundamental re-evaluation of the current pictures of Nuzi society. Thus, as in the published corpus, unpublished texts of the Teḫip-tilla Family easily outnumber those of the other western

---

M.P. Maidman, "A Revised Publication of a Unique Nuzi Text," in *DUMU-E$_2$-DUB-BA-A: Studies in Honor of Åke W. Sjöberg*, ed. H. Behrens, *et al.* (Philadelphia, 1989), pp. 371–81; "Joins to Five Published Nuzi Texts," *JCS* 42 (1990) 71–85; and assorted contributions in *SCCNH* 2, 3, 6, and 9.

suburban archives; and texts involving Teḫip-tilla himself outnumber those of other members of his family. These texts and fragments include 44 additional Teḫip-tilla real estate adoptions,[7] 5 additional exchanges,[8] as well as 7 personnel contracts of various sorts,[9] and 6 trial texts involving both real estate and mobilia.[10] In short, the profile of Teḫip-tilla's own economic activity is not altered by the unpublished texts; it is made more precise, more nuanced.

The picture of the rest of the family remains substantially unaltered as well. Transactions of nine other family members over four generations may be identified, including 12 texts for Teḫip-tilla's firstborn son, Enna-mati,[11] and an unexpected 14 from the subsidiary archive of Tarmi-tilla, grandson of Teḫip-tilla by his second-born son.[12] Puḫi-šenni, Teḫip-tilla's poorly attested father, appears in one or two or three texts.[13] This last gain and the fact that some half dozen of these texts involve intra-family transactions will allow for a significantly richer elucidation of the family history than is presently possible.

As the overall character of the several family archives appears to be unaffected by the still unpublished texts, so does the picture of Nuzi's toponymy. Among the hundreds of items examined, I could identify but a single new toponym, a town called Nupašḫina.[14] The lexicon is similarly unaffected. I believe I have isolated possibly one heretofore unattested lexeme[15] and a second rare word.[16] But even the commonplace is useful for refining our knowledge. Twelve additional antichretic loans,[17] both personal and real estate,

---

7 JEN*u* 22a, 36a, 41b (with a real estate exchange), 62a, 323, 333a, 371, 390a+390b+538a+538b, 438a, 562?, 568b, 667b?, 716a(+)716d, 731a, 943?, 967a?, 968a, 973a+1077f(+)973b, 983a, 996, 1026, 1027+1049f+1123e, 1035b, 1035d, 1037g, 1038c?, 1049b, 1055g (a declaration of real estate adoption), 1089o, 1101m, 1103a, 1113e, 1118h?, 1120i, 1126a, 1126g?, 1127a (a declaration of real estate adoption), 1141z, 1147a, 1152l, 1163, 1165a (a declaration of real estate adoption), 1183, 1185.

8 JEN*u* 41b, 64a, 255, 602a, 1076f (involving buildings rather than land).

9 JEN*u* 58, 88a, 393 (an antichretic loan), 638?, 667a, 956, 1109c.

10 JEN*u* 332a (involving paternal authority), 471a (stolen pigs), 1044b (sheep and cereals?), 1054+1061a (real estate), 1101b, 1104x.

11 JEN*u* 87b?, 131, 350b?, 687, 1003, 1035g, 1040a, 1068a, 1070, 1104h, 1118c, 1149a.

12 JEN*u* 9c, 21a, 94a, 112a, 116, 120b, 120c, 123, 130, 199, 911, 1036a, 1112a, 1123b?. Note the marked clustering of Tarmi-tilla texts (from room 13) among the lower JEN*u* numbers.

13 JEN*u* 1082a, 1095b?, 1133a?.

14 JEN*u* 1169:12; cf. l. 6.

15 $^{\text{LÚ.MEŠ}}$ *ḫi-ta-nu* (JEN*u* 1188:4), occurring in a witness list.

16 *pa-*⌜*š*⌝*u-nu* (JEN*u* 255:34, identifying a witness. Cf. *AHw*, p. 846b s.v. *pašunu* for the two other known examples, both from Nuzi.

17 JEN*u* 94a, 149, 393, 703, 729a (a trial dealing with a personal antichretic loan), 927, 1002, 1069a, 1071a, 1116b, 1148a, 1164a. Of the texts where the relevant data are preserved, all such contracts appear to be traceable to the later Nuzi generations.

will help clarify the role of this transaction in the economic development of Nuzi, and the same may be said of 14 more personnel and labor contracts.[18]

And there are the novelties to be considered. In addition to a new toponym and new words, the unpublished Chicago texts yield unusual or unique data about Nuzi. A real estate adoption is described as rewritten according to a damaged original.[19] A contract identifies a slave by his personal name and patronymic.[20] An Assyrian slave seems to be identified,[21] and on and on.

Unusual, even unique, text types are also attested in the unpublished material. There is a list of 15 witnesses,[22] pure and simple, and another list of individuals who, it appears, paid the *ilku*-tax.[23] There is a declaration that title to a field has been cleared[24] and a possible list of tablets pertaining to holdings in different towns.[25] Other lists include one detailing peculiar implements[26] and a list of unidentifiable items, written in two columns,[27] a most unusual format among the Nuzi texts.

Four pieces of a single envelope[28] contain an inscription more appropriate to a docket than an envelope. And envelopes themselves are well represented. About 30 pieces have been isolated,[29] adding significantly to the envelope corpus already published. Other unusual artifacts include door sealings[30] and dockets,[31] the latter a category to which I shall return presently. On some of these latter items cylinder seals have been impressed *into* the clay as if they were stamp seals, leaving trough-like impressions in the clay.[32] Unusually well preserved and impressively beautiful seal impressions occasionally appear[33]

---

18 JEN*u* 58, 88a, 112a, 393, 638?, 667a, 895, 956, 987a, 1062, 1073a, 1106b?, 1109a, 1109c.

19 JEN*u* 983a.

20 JEN*u* 1024a.

21 JEN*u* 1109c.

22 JEN*u* 557.

23 JEN*u* 674.

24 JEN*u* 725a.

25 JEN*u* 1162ad.

26 JEN*u* 1068c.

27 JEN*u* 1071e.

28 JEN*u* 1083a–1083d.

29 JEN*u* 21b–21h, 21j–21l, 1083a–1083d, 1087b?, 1087h?, 1088 (many), 1089e, 1089bd?, 1109a?, 1150d?, 1162n, 1182. As for JEN*u* 1088 "many": 1088a–1088z, 1088aa–1088ad are uninscribed pieces. Many, if not all, seem to be pieces of envelope.

30 For example, JEN*u* 1091b, 1091c, 1102d?, 1202?.

31 See below, note 36.

32 For example, JEN*u* 1034c, 1034j, 1139e, 1139g. The function(s) of items such as these is not known for certain.

33 For example, JEN*u* 1101ab (fish, scorpion, mammals), 1101ad (splendidly clear), 1139f (tree with sphinx; on a docket).

and one carefully prepared lump of clay contains the rolling out of a single seal and nothing more,[34] as if to identify it for future reference.[35]

Now this catalogue of "goodies" may make one's mouth water—if one has sufficiently unusual culinary tastes—and may even contribute substantial gains toward an appreciation of Nuzi society and history. However, they are presently merely "goodies." Two categories of unpublished items, however, promise immediate dividends for our understanding of Nuzi's archives and of Nuzi society at large. These categories are dockets, present in relatively large numbers, and tablets from the earliest attested stage of late Bronze Age Nuzi. It is to these categories and their significance that we now turn.

In one way, the most impressive category of unpublished Chicago texts are the dockets or labels. In terms of sheer numbers relative to already published examples, there are about 80 possible dockets and docket fragments catalogued versus 3, possibly more, published, those stemming from the Harvard collection.[36] Of the 80, about half are certainly dockets and somewhat over half of *those* are inscribed. Twenty-one of the inscribed examples yield some sense.

By docket or label, I mean a lump of clay originally impressed upon string or rope that was used to secure a basket or box containing cuneiform tablets. Furthermore, the docket was frequently inscribed with a brief note indicating the type of tablet stored in the container.[37]

The presence of dockets in significant number within the Chicago corpus demonstrates that which can already be deduced from both the number of tablets recovered and from other artifacts recovered from archival chambers,

---

34 JEN*u* 1156. The impression consists of two registers separated by a guilloche. In each, two sphinxes face each other. The feet of all four approach the guilloche, with the heads near the upper and lower borders, the pattern resembling that of jacks, queens, and kings in a deck of playing cards.

35 A similar object, dubbed a "tag," appears as figure 2 in Michelle I. Marcus, "'In His Lips He Held a Spell'," *Source: Notes in the History of Art*, 13/4 (Summer 1994) [=Porada Festschrift], 11. Possible functions and further examples of such tags are noted by Marcus, pp. 11–12, with notes. See also Prudence O. Harper, *et al.*, *Discoveries at Ashur on the Tigris: Antiquities in the Vorderasiatisches Museum, Berlin* (New York: The Metropolitan Museum of Art, 1995), pp. 99–103, describing items ##63–65. There, Joan Aruz discusses three Middle Assyrian tags. Note p. 100, n. 2, referring to Dominique Collon, *First Impressions: Cylinder Seals of the Ancient Near East* (London: British Museum Publications, 1987), p. 119.

36 The mere listing and subdivision of fourscore catalogue numbers is of doubtful utility at present. Full data for each of these items is forthcoming in my annotated catalogue of the University of Chicago Nuzi texts and in the publication of twenty-two dockets as JEN 882–903. Particular dockets are identified below.

Published Harvard dockets include HSS XVI, 327B; EN 9, 370, 453. For the edition of EN 9, 370, see Gernot Wilhelm, *Das Archiv des Šilwa-teššup, vol. 4: Darlehensurkunden und verwandte Texte* (Wiesbaden: Harrassowitz Verlag, 1992), #186 (p. 31).

37 For a recent brief discussion of Neo-Assyrian dockets and their functions, see F.M. Fales and J.N. Postgate, *Imperial Administrative Records, Part II: Provincial and Military Administration* (SAA 11; Helsinki: Helsinki University Press, 1995), pp. XX–XXIII (written by Fales). Neo-Assyrian practice, it appears, largely parallels Nuzi practice.

namely, some private households held large numbers of real estate documents whose utility hinged upon the ability to get the right tablet at the right time. The dockets, by identifying classes of documents, helped ensure that utility. Furthermore, the suburban archival texts comprising the Chicago corpus neatly confirm the document profile derived from the docket inscriptions. Thus, for example, from the Teḫip-tilla Family archives come at least three dockets describing the contents of containers as "tablets pertaining to the town of Nuzi,"[38] whereas no other toponym is mentioned more than once. And, in fact, the number of real estate documents pertaining to land in Nuzi and recovered from the rooms where the dockets were found far exceeds texts mentioning other towns. This suggests that, where dockets yield data not mirrored in the surviving documents, we may nevertheless depend on those dockets to help fill out the picture of the once extant archive.

Two examples may here be adduced. First, a docket from the Teḫip-tilla house identifies a container as holding tablets pertaining to one district—*dimtu*—of a nearby town.[39] This shores up a supposition derived from some tablets that this district was an object of intense economic interest on the part of Teḫip-tilla.[40]

A second example involves archives other than Teḫip-tilla's. Five inscribed dockets derive from other, minor, suburban archives,[41] archives whose tablets are not at all well preserved, many, as noted earlier, not having been baked in antiquity. The fortuitous preservation and survival of dockets from these rooms provide information otherwise unavailable or unrecognizable from those badly broken tablets.

The unpublished Chicago dockets contribute to our appreciation of archival taxonomy in yet another way. All the inscribed and decipherable dockets we have from the Teḫip-tilla archives classify the tablets by place name, either a town name, such as Unap-še or Nuzi,[42] or a district name, such as the *dimtu* of *piršanni*.[43] Dockets deriving from the suburban archives of at least two other families classify the tablets as deriving from, or pertaining to, particular individuals.[44] If indeed these latter dockets are also meant to indicate real estate activity, then the principle of organization is the identity of the ceder of land rather than the location of land. This difference in taxonomy, if correctly per-

---

38 JEN*u* 1075, 1147b, 1154f.

39 JEN*u* 1104a. The location is the *dimtu ša piršanni* in the jurisdiction of the town of Zizza.

40 See, for example, JEN 641, an important list of Teḫip-tilla's holdings in this *dimtu*. This text is edited in M.P. Maidman, "A Socio-economic Analysis of a Nuzi Family Archive" (diss. Pennsylvania, 1976), 174–83.

41 JEN*u* 1089d, 1145c from room "6" (*sic*); JEN*u* 1128a, 1128b, 1135j from room 12.

42 Unap-še: JEN*u* 1111a (here the contents are described as tablets of PN of Unap-še); Nuzi: JEN*u* 1075, 1147b, 1154f.

43 JEN*u* 1104a.

44 For these five texts, see above, note 41.

ceived, appears logical. For the Teḫip-tilla Family archive, where hundreds of documents involving land in over two dozen towns were stored, classification by place is a reasonable first cut to finding the right tablet at the right time. For the far smaller collections of these minor archives, classification by the names of the other contracting parties—presumably where the co-contractor is involved in more than one contract—such classification by personal name would be more efficient.[45] From a larger perspective, this difference of classification is important because it warns us against assuming homogeneity in the way the ancients organized archives, even within one town, at one moment, and pertaining to a single type of activity undertaken by a single segment of society. On the positive side, we may exploit such differences in taxonomy by deducing, on the basis of the docket inscriptions alone, the size of the underlying archive and, ultimately, the economic standing of the proprietor of such an archive. The more general the rubric of the docket, the larger the archive.

If the unpublished dockets afford us insight into the archival dynamics of private landowners, another segment of the unpublished corpus illuminates broader aspects of Nuzi's economic life.

Possibly the most intriguing class of unpublished Chicago Nuzi tablets are the "old texts," texts dating mostly to generation 2 (=Puḫi-šenni) or, in a very few cases, to generation 3 (=Teḫip-tilla). (Generation 1 = Tur-šenni is represented solely by the patronyms of individuals attested later.) These early texts are identifiable using a combination of criteria. The orthography of the texts is idiosyncratic, employing spellings unattested in documents from later generations. The palaeography is distinctive, frequently archaic in form. Often lines of text are separated from each other by rulings, sometimes between every line, sometimes not. Such rulings are absent from later documents. Standard contract formulas are more flexibly couched in the older texts than in others. Finally, where the state of preservation permits, prosopographical analysis confirms the relative antiquity of the early texts. One might note, in passing, that, conversely, all texts in which members of generation 2 are parties possess formal features of these "old" texts as just described.

In the published corpus of the Chicago texts, there are perhaps a dozen early texts.[46] Among the unpublished artifacts, I have identified a minimum of 20 and a maximum of 25 early texts and text fragments.[47] Taking into account

---

45 No analyses of the documentary contents of rooms "6" or 12, or any of the other minor archives from Nuzi's western suburban area, have yet been undertaken. Definition of the precise relationship of dockets from those rooms to the tablets of those archives depends on such analyses.

46 See, for example, JEN 82, 552, 560–62. Cf. also EN 9, 1–3.

47 Certainly or very probably "old" are: JEN*u* 731b, 1015a, 1015b, 1016e, 1035l, 1041a, 1055e+1193, 1057, 1072c, 1082a, 1082b, 1082c, 1090a, 1093i, 1095a, 1095b, 1118r, 1120a, 1133a, 1133d.

Possibly "old" are: JEN*u* 782b, 1013b, 1016b, 1102c, 1151b.

Where an archaeological context is recorded, all texts come from rooms 13, 15, and 16; i.e.,

possible joins and incorrectly identified items, on the one hand, and, on the other, unrecognized examples of this class of text, it seems reasonable to assert that there exist twice as many unpublished "old" texts as published ones. Parenthetically, there appear to be very few such early texts in the Harvard collection or elsewhere. This would make sense since the Chicago corpus alone consists exclusively of private archival records, precisely that category of archive where old texts—especially those describing real estate acquisition—retain value and utility over the generations.

The significance of this small group of artifacts is manifold. First, the fact of their existence in such numbers compels us to weigh more seriously the level of private economic activity of generation 2. Second, the vigor of this activity focuses especially on the acquisition of real estate, as just intimated. Of the 25 unpublished documents considered, 11 lack sufficient context to identify the activity being described—although some, perhaps even most, of these may well pertain to real estate transfer. Of the remaining 14, 11 definitely pertain to real estate purchase and 8 of those are real estate adoptions,[48] that is, *ṭuppi mārūti* texts, transactions that are a hallmark of later Nuzi private economic activity.

Thus these early texts demonstrate an impressive level of acquisitive real estate activity at the outset of the Nuzi period at Nuzi, activity characterized by a legal device, fictive adoption, which was ubiquitous down to the latest-attested generation. One may conclude with greater certainty than ever that fictive real estate adoption was not a late device to circumvent some hypothetical ban on alienation of land. It was in place for as far back as there are records, although—as suggested immediately below—it may not go back farther than that. Explanation for the origin of the form must be sought elsewhere. Hence, a fundamental economic and legal continuity characterizes this community throughout the history of the Nuzi period.

But these early texts, the published and unpublished alike, point to *dis*continuity as well. Especially noteworthy is the elasticity of legal formulas in texts of generation 2. These formulas become rigidly standardized in generation 3 and on to the end of the Nuzi period. One might surmise, then, that the continuity of economic activity and contract type from generation 2 to the end of the Nuzi texts, which has just been asserted, has its origin only in generation 2 itself, since the forms and economic tactics would appear to have been novel in generation 2 and the start of 3, then to become fixed, standardized, truly formulaic. It is tempting to link this discontinuity with that represented by the marked shift of palaeography and, to a lesser degree, orthography. The forms of the early texts are distinctive. Those of all the subsequent generations are indistinguishable from each other. What catalyzed this shift eludes me at

---

all "old" Chicago texts seem to have belonged to the several Teḫip-tilla Family archives.

48 The eight real estate adoptions are: JEN*u* 1013b, 1016e, 1041a, 1055e+1193, 1093i, 1095a, 1120a, 1151b?.

The remaining three real estate texts are: JEN*u* 731b, 1090a, 1118r.

present. It does not suffice to assert that writing at Nuzi was new, a foreign import, later localized and homogenized. For, despite traces and hints of Babylonian and Assyrian influence,[49] such an assertion is more a description of what happened than an explanation of why it happened. And even the force of the description is hobbled by the lack of direct evidence for such a process.

And so these early texts in their newly augmented numbers bear witness to economic continuity from the start to the end of the Nuzi period. But they also bear witness to discontinuity and so sharpen the intriguing questions surrounding Nuzi's early history. Whence and under what circumstances came the script and the cultural package of which it was part? What, in other words, occurred perhaps at the time of the poorly attested generation 1? And what stimulated the sharp—not gradual—change between generations 2 and 3? And why did these changes affect certain aspects of Nuzi life and not others? The answer to this last question may lie in the nature of the phenomena marked by continuity and discontinuity. The underlying economic and legal forms of Nuzi remained stable, while the superimposed operational device, writing, was introduced to enable those underlying forms to work on a larger scale and more efficiently. As such, the formal elements of the bureaucracy underwent change and subsequent homogenization while the basic structural features of Nuzi's economic dynamic continued relatively unchanged.

The implications of this survey of the unpublished Chicago corpus are threefold. First, these texts and fragments will enrich and deepen our current understanding of the Nuzi phenomenon by the resulting accretions to features already recognized and analyzed. Ultimately, this may well be the major contribution of this unpublished corpus. Second, this material will contribute a host of new data and other features, many relatively minor, to be sure, to Nuzi and to late Bronze Age Mesopotamian society. Some of these may result in changes, presently unexpected, in the general picture we currently work with. Third, and finally, regarding the dockets and especially the "old" texts, the new documents will bring into sharper focus early late Bronze Age Nuzi and so, in important ways, the entire Nuzi period, its modes of operation and its economic development in the private sector.

Thus, the continued publication of the riches from Chicago's Oriental Institute will bring about change, change to which students of Nuzi and late Bronze Age Mesopotamian society in general should eagerly look forward. *Ex occidente flux.*

---

49 See, for example, Gernot Wilhelm, *Untersuchungen zum Ḫurro-Akkadischen von Nuzi* (AOAT 9; Kevelaer/Neukirchen-Vluyn: Butzon & Bercker/Neukirchener Verlag, 1970), pp. 35–47, especially p. 35 with reference.

Les archives privées d'Arrapḫa et de Nuzi *

BRIGITTE LION
Université Paris I-Panthéon-Sorbonne

The recent accelerated publication of Nuzi texts and fragments, especially in the *SCCNH* series, has provided us with many new documents, mostly concerned with private archives. The present article reports on the history of the archival studies of the Nuzi tablets. Several recent studies have clarified the makeup and organization of the more significant family archives while other archival groups have not yet received the same attention. The availability of new sources, coupled with a more accurate reconstruction of the findspots and the family archives to which they belong, open up new prospects for the study of the society and economy at Nuzi.

Les premières données concernant les textes exhumés sur le site de Yorgan Tepe, l'antique Nuzi, figurent dans les rapports de fouilles partiels parus dans *BASOR*[1] et surtout dans le rapport archéologique final de R.F.S. Starr[2]. Les directeurs

---

* Juste après avoir présenté à Harvard une conférence intitulée «Nuzi Archives: Studies and Results», j'ai découvert le livre d'O. Pedersén, *Archives and Libraries in the Ancient Near East, 1500–300 BC*, Bethesda, 1998, dont les pages 15 à 32, consacrées aux tablettes de Nuzi, Kurruḫanni et Arrapḫa, recoupent en grande partie la description que j'avais pu donner des différents lots d'archives. O. Pedersén m'a néanmoins encouragée à publier ce travail et je l'en remercie. Le livre d'O. Pedersén offre une excellente présentation des lots de textes de Nuzi, en les plaçant dans la perspective d'une reflexion plus générale sur les archives. Si je ne fais pas, dans l'article qui suit, référence à cet ouvrage, c'est parce que j'ai travaillé, en très grande partie, antérieurement à sa parution et de façon indépendante.

1 Ces données sur les fouilles figurent sans *BASOR* 18 (1925) 1–5; 19 (1925) 21; 20 (1925) 19–25; 27 (1927) 14; 28 (1927) 14 et 18; 30 (1928) 1–6; 32 (1928) 15–17; 33 (1929) 11; 34 (1929) 2–7; 35 (1929) 27–29; 38 (1930) 3–8; 41 (1931) 24–27; 42 (1931) 1–10; 48 (1932) 2–5; il s'agit de lettres envoyées par les directeurs des fouilles de Nuzi, E. Chiera, E.A. Speiser, puis R.F.S. Starr. Cf. aussi E. Chiera et E.A. Speiser, «A New Factor in in the History of the Ancient East», AASOR 6 (1926) 75–92.

2 *Nuzi, volume I, Text*, et *Nuzi, volume II, Plates and Plans*, Cambridge (Mass.), 1939 et 1937 (cités ci-après *Nuzi* I et *Nuzi* II). Il faut ajouter à ce rapport les lettres de R.F.S. Starr, écrites durant ses missions en Iraq: «Letters from the Field, 1927–1930», *SCCNH* 8 (1996) 13–125; elles contiennent parfois des détails notés sur le vif, mais ne donnent que peu d'informations sur la localisation des tablettes.

Studies on the Civilization and Culture of Nuzi and the Hurrians - 10

successifs de la mission signalent la présence de tablettes dans certaines pièces et précisent parfois leur nombre, leur contenu ou les noms propres qui y apparaissent le plus souvent. Les documents écrits, mis à part ceux découverts lors du sondage dans la pièce L 4 du palais[3], proviennent tous du «*stratum* II» et datent du XIVe s. av. J.-C.[4]

En 1958, E.R. Lacheman a fait le point sur la répartition des textes par quartiers et lots d'archives[5]: il distinguait dix principaux lieux de découverte, correspondant à dix ensembles de tablettes dont il indiquait brièvement le contenu. Par la suite, il a encore affiné cette description et précisé la teneur de certains lots[6].

Aujourd'hui, un nouveau bilan s'impose. La publication des tablettes de Nuzi n'a pas toujours tenu compte de leur lieu de provenance. Or les recherches menées depuis quelques années ont montré l'intérêt qu'il y avait à regrouper ces textes par lots d'archives. C'est pourquoi, après un bref historique des éditions de textes de Nuzi, cet article tentera de faire le bilan des travaux archivistiques récents et d'indiquer quelques directions de recherches à explorer[7].

Mon propos se limite ici aux archives privées familiales, excluant la documentation administrative[8] pourtant abondante. Néanmoins, de nombreux textes de cette nature, par exemple ceux provenant du palais, du temple, ou des quartiers au nord et au sud-ouest du temple, attendent encore une exploitation systématique. En outre, des archives administratives ont parfois été trouvées dans les mêmes pièces que des archives privées, sans que l'existence de liens éventuels entre ces deux types de textes apparaisse clairement.

---

3 R.F.S. Starr, *Nuzi* I, pp. 18–30. Les tablettes du IIIe et du début du IIe millénaire ont été publiées par T.H. Meek, HSS 10 = EN 3, 1935.

4 Pour cette datation, cf. D.L. Stein, «A Reappraisal of the "Sauštatar Letter" from Nuzi», *ZA* 79 (1989) 36–60.

5 HSS 16, Preface, pp. v–viii.

6 «Le palais et la royauté de la ville de Nuzi: les rapports entre les données archéologiques et les données épigraphiques», dans P. Garelli (éd.), *Le palais et la royauté, CRRAI 19 (Paris, 1971)*, Paris 1974, 359–72 (cet article est cité ci-après *CRRAI* 19).

7 Je laisse ici de côté la documentation trouvée à Tell al-Faḫḫar, l'antique Kurruḫanni: deux campagnes de fouilles irakiennes, de 1967 à 1969, y ont mis à jour un bâtiment administratif, dit «Green Palace», qui a livré plusieurs centaines de tablettes. Elles sont semblables à celles de Nuzi et d'Arrapḫa, et des liens prosopographiques entre les documents issus des sites de Tell al-Faḫḫar et de Yorgan Tepe ont pu être mis en évidence. Les textes qui ont été édités semblent, en grande partie, relever d'archives privées, mais n'ont que peu été étudiés dans cette perspective. Cf. G. Wilhelm, «Kurruḫanni», *RlA* 6 (1980–83) 371–72, qui donne la bibliographie antérieure.

8 Je renvoie à la définition donnée par M. Morrison, *SCCNH* 4 (1993) 7: «Administrative archives are composed of the texts that document the inflow and outflow of goods, services, personnel, and equipment from a central agency such as the palace or a large estate».

Planche n° 1

Le site de Nuzi, plan général

(R.F.S. Starr, *Nuzi*, II, plan n° 2)

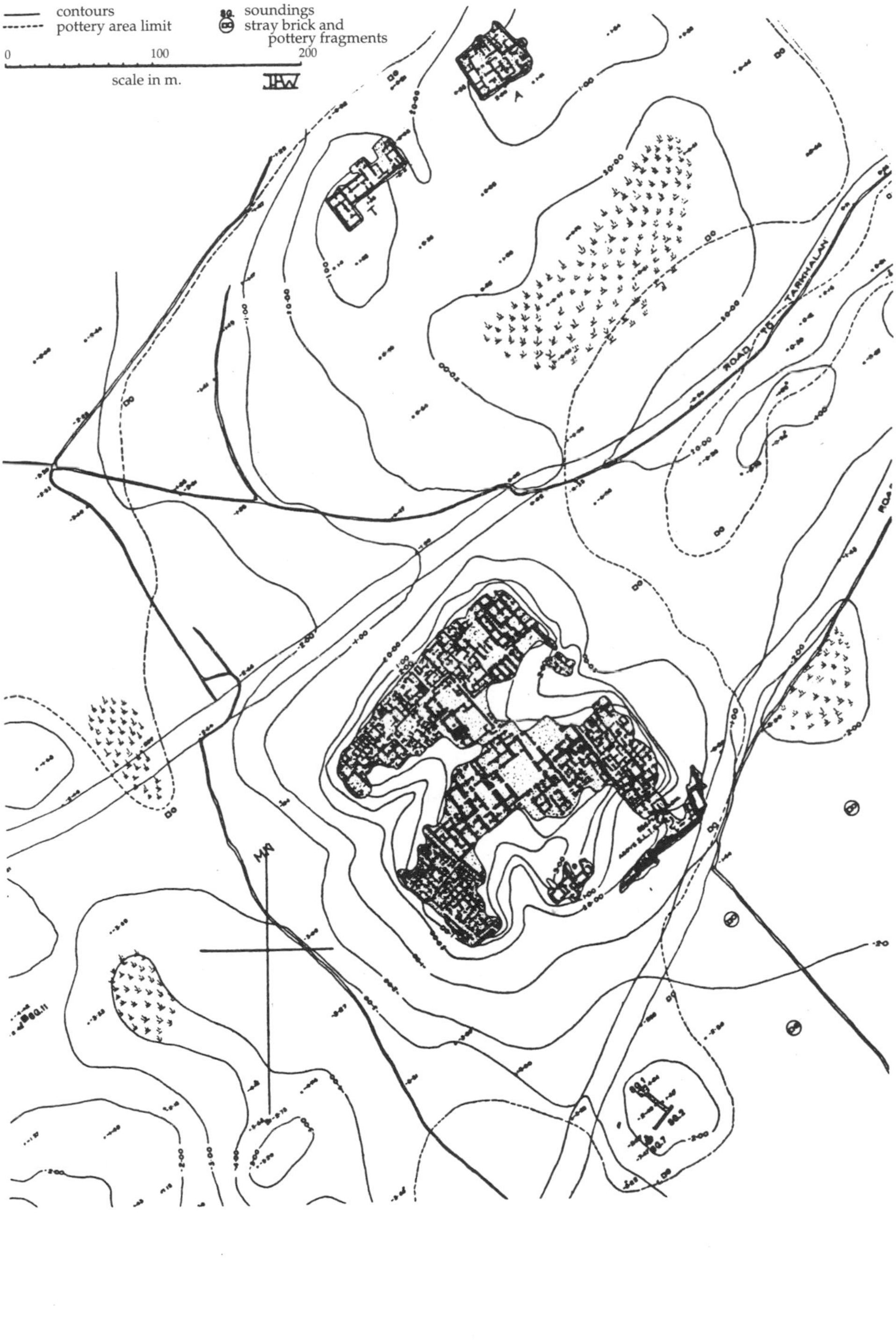

1. Publication et Étude des Textes

1.1. Les publications

Dans un premier temps, la publication des tablettes ne s'est guère souciée de la répartition par archives; elle correspond aux différentes phases de la fouille (planche n° 1). On peut en distinguer trois:

1.1.1. Textes issus des fouilles clandestines

Les premières tablettes publiées sont issues de fouilles clandestines qui ont eu lieu à la fin du XIXe siècle et au début du XXe, sur les sites de Yorgan Tepe (Nuzi) et Kirkouk (Arrapḫa). Elles ont circulé sur le marché des antiquités et ont abouti dans divers musées. Les collections les plus importantes se trouvent au British Museum, au Louvre, dans les musées russes, à l'Iraq Museum, à Yale... Quelques tablettes appartiennent à des collections privées. Les lieux de provenance exacts des textes sont inconnus; seul un examen interne a permis de séparer les documents d'Arrapḫa de ceux de Nuzi et de les regrouper par archives.

1.1.2. Première campagne de fouilles régulières à Yorgan Tepe, 1925/26

Les tablettes exhumées pendant la première saison de fouilles régulières, dirigée par E. Chiera en 1925/26, ont été ramenées à Chicago et sont publiées dans la série des JEN[9]. Leur nombre dépasse le millier. Elles sont issues de trois maisons voisines, situées sur une butte (T) au nord-ouest du tell central. Le lieu de provenance des textes est précisément connu. Le groupement en archives, malgré l'abondance des documents, est relativement simple, puisque les lots de ce petit tell n'ont pas été mélangés à d'autres après leur découverte.

1.1.3. Les campagnes de fouilles régulières à Yorgan Tepe de 1927 à 1931

Les quatre campagnes suivantes ont été menées par la Harvard-Baghdad School expedition. Elles ont porté sur les deux petites buttes (T et A) et sur le tell principal. Les tablettes, envoyées à Harvard, y ont reçu des numéros de musée SMN (Semitic Museum, Nuzi). Elles ont été publiées dans les volumes des HSS, dans une série ayant pour sigle EN[10]; cette série EN continue dans les volumes

---

[9] JEN = Joint Expedition with the Irak Museum at Nuzi (les tablettes inédites portent le sigle JEN*u*). Copies cunéiformes publiées par E. Chiera, JEN 1 (1929); JEN 2 (1930); JEN 3 (1931); JEN 4 et 5 (1934); E.R. Lacheman, JEN 6 (1939); E.R. Lacheman et M.P. Maidman, JEN 7 = *SCCNH* 3 (1989). M.P. Maidman a transcrit, traduit et commenté 107 textes de JEN 7 = *SCCNH* 3 (ou, plus précisément, 99 textes, certains ayant reçu deux, voire trois numéros d'inventaire différents) dans *SCCNH* 6, 1994 (JEN 674 à 774) et dans *SCCNH* 9, 1998, pp. 95–123 (JEN 675 à 780).

[10] EN = Excavations at Nuzi. E. Chiera, HSS 5 = EN 1 (1929); R.H. Pfeiffer, HSS 9 = EN 2 (1932); R.H. Pfeiffer et E.R. Lacheman, HSS 13 = EN 4 (1942); E.R. Lacheman, HSS 14 = EN 5 (1950); HSS 15 = EN 6 (1955); HSS 16 = EN 7 (1958); HSS 19 = EN 8 (1962). HSS 5, 15 et 19 sont des recueils de planches cunéiformes; HSS 13 et 16 en revanche donnent surtout des translittérations et très peu de copies; HSS 9 et 14 contiennent à la fois des translittérations et des copies cunéiformes.

SCCNH[11]. Par ailleurs, une centaine de documents ont été transcrits par R.H. Pfeiffer et traduits par E.A. Speiser dans AASOR 16 (1936).

Ces publications n'ont pas retenu un seul critère pour le regroupement des textes, mais plusieurs critères successifs:

— les deux premiers volumes tiennent compte du lieu de découverte: tous les textes sont issus d'une petite butte (A) au nord-est du tell principal. HSS 5 présente les textes trouvés dans une même pièce, A 34. HSS 9, «The Archives of Shilwateshub son of the King», publie surtout les archives de la maison voisine.

— Les cinq volumes suivants de la série HSS contiennent à la fois les tablettes issues de la butte nord-est (A) et celles du tell central. HSS 13 et 14 ne retiennent pas de critères précis, comme l'indique leur titre, «Miscellaneous Texts». Les trois derniers recueils choisissent une approche typologique: HSS 15, «The Administrative Archives» (inventaires); HSS 16, «Economic and Social Documents» (comptes et listes) et HSS 19, «Family Law Documents» (contrats).

— AASOR 16 regroupe des textes de types et provenances divers: l'archive de Tulpunnaya, les plaintes contre le *ḫazannu* Kuššši-ḫarbe et les rations d'huile pour les divinités forment trois lots bien individualisés, issus de trois pièces différentes du palais. Les autres documents ont été trouvés en divers endroits du palais et des deux buttes septentrionales.

Quant à EN 9 et 10, ils contiennent les textes qui demeuraient inédits après la parution des volumes HSS et correspondent à plusieurs ensembles différents.

Ainsi, les publications n'ont pas été faites systématiquement par lots d'archives. Conséquence de ce phénomène, beaucoup de petites ou moyennes archives privées sont dispersées dans ces différents volumes.

1.2. Le début des études archivistiques

Les études consacrées aux textes de Nuzi, dans un premier temps, n'ont pas privilégié l'aspect archivistique[12]. Elles se sont davantage attachées aux aspects thématiques et typologiques de la documentation: les adoptions (E. Cassin), la propriété du sol (H. Lewy), les procès (R. Hayden), les contrats de prêts (D.I. Owen), pour ne citer que quelques exemples. Ces études ont permis d'avoir une bonne vue d'ensemble sur les types de documents qui se trouvaient à Nuzi, ou sur les mécanismes économiques et sociaux. Elles continuent avec, entre autres, les travaux de K. van der Toorn sur la religion, ou de C. Zaccagnini sur

---

11 E.R. Lacheman, D.I. Owen et M.A. Morrison, *SCCNH* 2 (1987) 355–702 = EN 9/1 et *SCCNH* 4 (1993) 131–398 = EN 9/2; E.R. Lacheman et D.I. Owen, *SCCNH* 5 (1995) 85–357 = EN 9/3; J. Fincke, *SCCNH* 8 (1996) 379–468 = EN 10/1 et *SCCNH* 9 (1998) 217–384 = EN 10/2.

12 Il faut néanmoins mentionner les remarques d'E. Chiera et E.A. Speiser, «A New Factor in the History of the Ancient Near East», AASOR 6 (1926) 75–92, les pp. 85–90 de cet article sont consacrées à l'archive de Teḫip-Tilla.

l'économie. Il faut mentionner également les avancées rapides de la philologie hourrite.

En 1971, E.R. Lacheman pouvait encore écrire: «Jusqu'à présent les cunéiformistes qui ont étudié les tablettes de Nuzi n'ont pas tenu compte des données archéologiques»[13]. L'idée de rassembler les textes provenant du même endroit n'est en effet apparue que dans un second temps[14]. Le premier travail de grande ampleur a été la thèse de M.P. Maidman en 1976 sur la famille de Teḫip-Tilla, puis les autres articles du même auteur, qui ont posé les questions fondamentales: qu'est-ce qu'une archive familiale? Quelle est la fonction des documents conservés? Comment une famille gère-t-elle ses biens, et comment évoluent les stratégies économiques sur plusieurs générations, dans les différentes branches d'une même famille? Les comportements économiques sont-ils différents selon les groupes familiaux?[15]

Pour tenter de répondre à ces questions, il est nécessaire de commencer par regrouper les textes trouvés ensemble, dans une même maison, ou dans une même pièce. Deux critères sont utilisables à cette fin:

— le lieu de découverte a en général été noté par les fouilleurs, pièce par pièce, et ces indications figurent dans les publications. Ces précieux renseignements demeurent toutefois incomplets. L'information n'existe évidemment pas pour les documents issus des fouilles clandestines. Quant aux tablettes exhumées lors des fouilles légales, plusieurs sont réputées de provenance inconnue; quelques erreurs d'enregistrement sont également repérables. Enfin, le site de Nuzi ayant été détruit et pillé, des tablettes ont pu être déplacées au moment de la chute de la ville.

— les critères internes doivent également être considérés: il s'agit des données contenues dans les textes eux-mêmes, en premier lieu la prosopographie. Les indications géographiques aussi peuvent être précieuses: le travail d'A. Fadhil lui a permis, en considérant les contrats rédigés dans une même localité ou ayant trait à des transactions dans une localité particulière, de remembrer les dossiers relevant de certaines familles, et de noter que «Stadtgeschichte ist immer zugleich Familiengeschichte»[16].

---

13 *CRRAI* 19, p. 359.

14 Ces étapes successives: édition des documents, réflexion thématique, puis regroupement par archives, ne sont pas caractéristiques des études consacrées à Nuzi: la même évolution est perceptible dans le traitement des documents paléo-assyriens de Kültepe, ou dans celui des archives royales de Mari, publiées désormais par grands «dossiers».

15 La réflexion sur la notion même d'archives familiales a été menée par M.P. Maidman, *A Socio-Economic Analysis of a Nuzi Family Archive*, 1976, Ann Arbor 1982, et également dans «A Nuzi Private Archive: Morphological Considerations», *Assur* 1/9 (1979) pp. 179–86. Cf. aussi sur ce point M. Morrison, *SCCNH* 4, p. 7.

16 *Studien zur Topographie und Prosopographie der Provinzstädte des Königreichs Arrapḫe*, Baghdader Forschungen 6, Mainz, 1983 (citation p. 4). Cet ouvrage sera cité ci-après *STPPKA*.

L'intérêt pour les archives s'est beaucoup développé durant les dernières décennies. Néanmoins, il reste encore de nombreuses études à mener. En 1993, D. Stein notait que six lots d'archives avaient été rassemblés, dont trois seulement avaient fait l'objet d'une étude systématique[17]. Ces chiffres doivent être aujourd'hui révisés à la hausse.

2. Les Groupes d'Archives

2.1. Les tablettes d'Arrapḫa

Les textes issus des fouilles clandestines, provenant de plusieurs endroits différents, ont été mélangés, apparemment avant même leur entrée dans les musées ou collections. Dans ce cas, la seule possibilité pour retrouver leur origine consiste en leur examen interne.

Un premier ensemble ne vient pas de Nuzi, mais d'Arrapḫa. Les tablettes ont été découvertes accidentellement au début du siècle, suite à deux glissements de terrain. Le site, recouvert par la ville actuelle de Kirkouk, n'a pas pu être fouillé. J. Fincke a récemment regroupé les informations disponibles concernant l'origine de ces tablettes.

K. Grosz a rassemblé une grande partie des documents d'Arrapḫa, 142 en tout. L'archive la plus importante, celle de Wullu et de ses descendants, compte 71 textes. Mais l'auteur a aussi identifié sept autres groupes, de dimensions plus modestes. Par ailleurs, il est possible que la petite archive de Ziliya fils d'Ipša-ḫalu, étudiée par A.R. Millard, se rattache à la documentation d'Arrapḫa.

Bibliographie[18]

FINCKE J., «More Joins Among the Texts from Arrapḫa (Kirkūk)», *SCCNH* 9 (1998) 49–62.

GROSZ K., *The Archive of the Wullu Family*, Copenhagen 1988.

MILLARD A.R., «Strays From a 'Nuzi' Archive, with an appendix: Two 'Nuzi' Texts in the Wellcome Institute for the History of Medicine», *SCCNH* 1 (1981) 433–41.

MÜLLER G.G.W., «Anmerkungen zu neupublizierten Texten aus Kirkuk im British Museum», *NABU* 1991/74.

NEGRI SCAFA P., Compte rendu de K. Grosz, The Archive of the Wullu Family, *Or* NS 65 (1996) 43–46.

OWEN D.I., «Texts Fragments from Arrapḫa in the Kelsey Museum of Art and Archaeology, The University of Michigan», *SCCNH* 1 (1981) 455–68.

STEIN D., «Seal Impressions on Texts from Arrapḫa and Nuzi in the Yale Babylonian Collection», *SCCNH* 2 (1987) 225–320.

17 *Das Archiv des Šilwa-Teššup, Heft 8*, Wiesbaden 1993, 17.

18 Les indications bibliographiques données dans cet article ne se veulent pas exhaustives. Elles se limitent aux études archivistiques, ainsi qu'aux publications récentes permettant, le cas échéant, de compléter les données relatives à certaines archives. Elles sont classées par ordre chronologique de publication.

WILHELM G., «Collations of the Wullu Archive in the Louvre», *SCCNH* 7 (1995) 129–33.

2.2. Les fouilles clandestines de Nuzi: l'archive de Zike fils de Šurki-Tilla

D'autres documents issus de fouilles clandestines ont été exhumés à Nuzi. Parmi eux, nombreux sont ceux qui appartenaient à Šurki-Tilla fils de Teḫip-Tilla et à son fils Zike: leur maison a donc fait l'objet de fouilles illicites, mais, lors des campagnes régulières, elle ne semble pas avoir été localisée. La plupart de ces textes étaient encore inédits lorsque M.P. Maidman a étudié à la famille de Teḫip-Tilla, et de ce fait cet auteur n'a pu en prendre qu'un très petit nombre en considération[19]. Des lots d'archives plus modestes, comme ceux de Zilip-Tilla fils de Kelip-šarri, ou d'Urḫi-Teššup fils de Tarmiya, ne semblent pas directement liés à ce dossier.

La plupart des tablettes sont conservées au British Museum et ont été publiées par G.G.W. Müller.

Bibliographie

MAIDMAN M.P., «Some Late Bronze Age Legal Tablets from the British Museum: Problems of Context and Meaning», dans B. Halpern and D.W. Hobson (éds.), *Law, Politics and Society in the Ancient Mediterranean World*, Sheffield 1993, 42–89 (sur l'archive d'Urḫi-Teššup fils de Tarmiya).

MÜLLER G.G.W., *Studien zur Siedlungsgeographie und Bevölkerung des mittleren Osttigrisgebietes*, Heidelberg 1994, 236–71 (transcription de 41 textes du British Museum).

MÜLLER G.G.W., *Londoner Nuzi-Texte*, Wiesbaden 1998 (édition de 163 textes du British Museum, la plupart relevant de l'archive de Zike).

2.3. Les fouilles régulières de Nuzi: «Western Suburban Area»

Pour les textes issus des fouilles régulières, on peut reprendre avec quelques variantes l'itinéraire suivi par E.R. Lacheman voici plus de 25 ans, pour situer dans leur contexte d'origine les lots retrouvés. Sur certains points, notamment pour les archives des petits tells du nord ou du palais, il n'y a que peu de modifications à apporter à cette excellente synthèse, sinon pour en compléter la bibliographie.

La petite butte au nord-ouest du tell central (Western Suburban Area) a d'abord été appelée T par les archéologues, parce que de nombreux textes retrouvés dans ce secteur relevaient de l'archive de Teḫip-Tilla: le sigle T+n° correspond donc à cette zone (il n'y a pas de carré T sur le tell central). Trois maisons y ont été fouillées (planche n° 2):

19 M.P. Maidman, *A Socio-Economic Analysis of a Nuzi Family Archive*, 1976, Ann Arbor 1982, 56–59 et 287–89.

Planche n° 2

Tell nord-ouest (= Western Suburban Area = T)

(R.F.S. Starr, *Nuzi*, II, plan n° 30)

Les numéros des pièces ayant livré des tablettes sont indiqués entre parenthèses

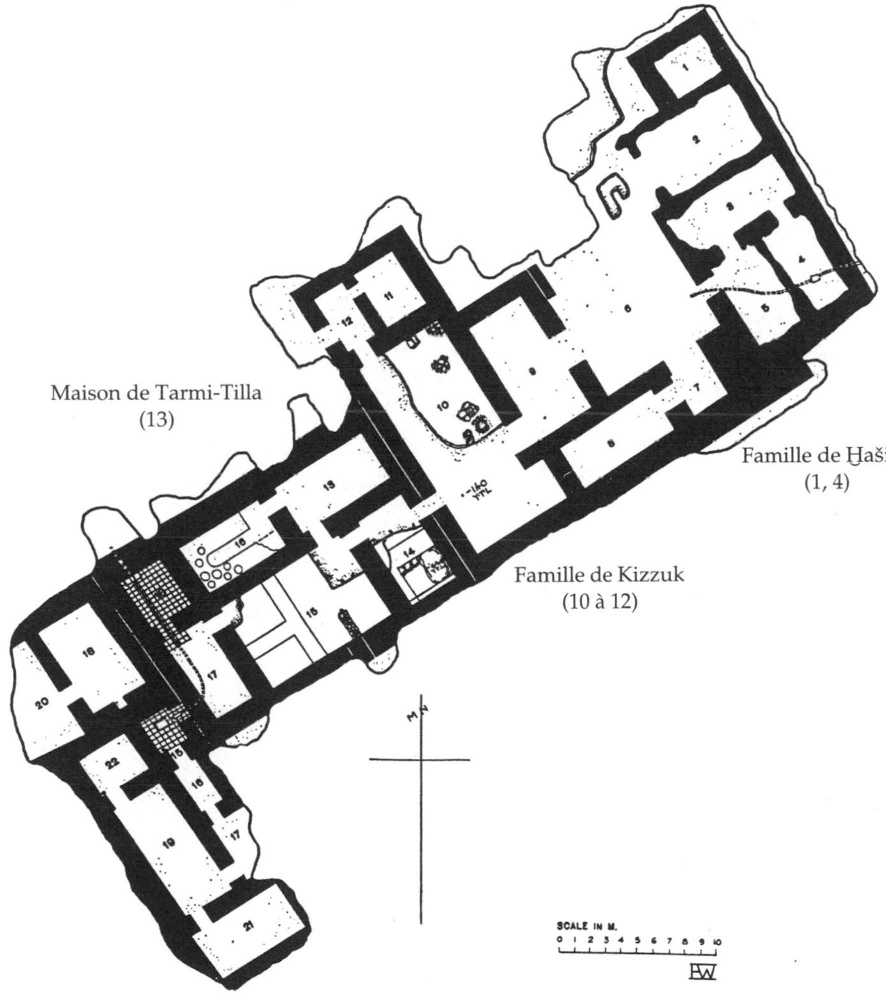

2.3.1. Les maisons de Teḫip-Tilla et de Tarmi-Tilla

La maison située au sud-ouest, correspondant aux pièces 15 à 22, contenait l'une des plus grosses archives privées du Proche-Orient ancien, celle de Teḫip-Tilla, réunissant plusieurs centaines de tablettes. Elle a été occupée par Teḫip-Tilla, puis par son fils aîné Enna-mati et ses descendants.

Dans la maison centrale (pièces 13 à 18)[20], seule la pièce 13 abritait quelques dizaines de tablettes; leur nombre exact pose problème[21]. Cette maison appartenait à Tarmi-Tilla, fils de Šurki-Tilla et petit-fils de Teḫip-Tilla, qui y conservait ses archives.

L'ensemble de cette énorme archive (Teḫip-Tilla + Tarmi-Tilla), qui dépasse le millier de documents[22], a été étudié de façon approfondie par M.P. Maidman et il convient de se reporter surtout à sa bibliographie.

Pour une étude générale de cette famille, il faut désormais prendre en compte les textes du British Museum récemment publiés par G.G.W. Müller, qui apportent de nombreuses informations sur Zike, un autre fils de Šurki-Tilla, frère de Tarmi-Tilla. Une nouvelle branche de cette famille se trouve ainsi documentée, mais le lieu où ses archives ont été découvertes demeure inconnu (cf. ci-dessus, § 2.2.).

Bibliographie

MAIDMAN M.P., *A Socio-Economic Analysis of a Nuzi Family Archive*, Ann Arbor 1982.

MAIDMAN M.P., «The Teḫip-tilla Family of Nuzi: A Genealogical Reconstruction», *JCS* 28 (1976) 127–55.

MAIDMAN M.P., «The Teḫip-tilla Family Tree», *JCS* 29 (1977) 64.

MAIDMAN M.P., «A Nuzi Private Archive: Morphological Considerations», *Assur* 1/9 (1979) 179–86.

MAIDMAN M.P., «*JEN* VII 812: an Unusual Personnel Text from Nuzi», *SCCNH* 2 (1987) 157–66.

---

20 Les pièces 15 à 18 de cette maison centrale portent donc des numéros identiques à ceux de certaines pièces de la maison sud-ouest; mais elles ne contenaient pas de tablettes, ce qui évite les confusions.

21 «Environ 70», d'après E.R. Lacheman, *CRRAI* 19, pp. 360–61. N. Jankowska, *SCCNH* 1 (1981) 196 n. 2, compte 26 tablettes publiées dans la pièce 13, ou 30 en postulant des erreurs d'enregistrement ou un déplacement des tablettes. M.P. Maidman, *A Socio-Economic Analysis of a Nuzi Family Archive*, 1976, Ann Arbor 1982, 272–74, compte 29 documents se rapportant à Tarmi-Tilla (dont 19 publiés et 10 inédits à cette date); la liste qu'il en donne est en partie différente de celle de N. Jankowska; dans JEN 7 = *SCCNH* 3, il publie 13 inédits provenant de cette même pièce (dont 10 n'étaient pas mentionnés dans sa thèse).

22 Cette archive a longtemps été tenue pour la plus vaste archive privée retrouvée dans le Proche-Orient ancien. Les fouilles belges de Tell ed-Dēr (Sippar Amnânum ou d'Annunîtum) ont mis au jour une archive encore plus considérable, dans la maison du gala-maḫ Ur-Utu, qui comptait plus de 2500 tablettes et fragments. C. Michel me signale que plusieurs archives privées de marchands assyriens exhumées à Kültepe dépassent également le millier de tablettes.

MAIDMAN M.P., «A Tale of Two Cities», *SCCNH* 2 (1987) 345–49.

MAIDMAN M.P., «A Second Teḫip-Tilla Fragment at Harvard», *SCCNH* 2 (1987) 349.

MAIDMAN M.P., «A Unique Teḫip-tilla Family Document from the British Museum», *SCCNH* 7 (1995) 57–63.

MAIDMAN M.P., «A New Teḫip-tilla Text Fragment», dans G.D. Young, M.W. Chavalas, R.E. Averbeck (éds), *Crossing Boundaries and Linking Horizons = Mél. M. C. Astour*, Bethesda 1997, 335–38.

MÜLLER G.G.W., *Londoner Nuzi-Texte*, Wiesbaden 1998, donne à la dernière page de son ouvrage une nouvelle version de l'arbre généalogique de cette famille.

WILHELM G., «Ein neuer Text zum Ordal in Nuzi» (JEN 659 + SMN 1651), *SCCNH* 5 (1995) 71–74.

2.3.2. La maison nord-est

Cette troisième maison comprend trois ailes:

— l'aile orientale (pièces 1 à 5). Dans les pièces 1 et 4 se trouvait l'archive de Ḫašiya fils de Waḫr-api, ses fils Mušeya et Itḫ-apu, et Ḫuite fils de Mušeya, comprenant quelques dizaines de tablettes. A. Fadhil a noté que cette petite archive, fermée sur elle-même, concernait la localité de Ḫurazina ṣeḫru[23].

— dans l'aile centrale, ni le rapport de fouilles ni les publications ne font état de tablettes pour les pièces 6 à 9.

— dans l'aile occidentale, les pièces 10, 11 et 12 ont livré de nombreuses tablettes, mais l'estimation de leur nombre varie selon les différents auteurs. Les documents de la pièce 10 concernent Ḫilpiš-šuḫ fils de Šuḫun-zirira et son fils Kurpa-saḫ; ils ont été rédigés dans la ville de Temtena[24]. Les archives des pièces 11 et 12 sont celles de Ḫutiya fils de Kuššiya et de son fils Kel-Teššup; les textes de la pièce 11 auraient été écrits en majorité dans la ville de Šuriniwe, ceux de la pièce 12 dans les villes de Šuriniwe et Kizzukwe, et quelques-uns à Puruliwe et Temtena[25].

---

[23] Sur cette archive, cf. G. Dosch et K. Deller, *SCCNH* 1 (1981) 93, et A. Fadhil, *STPPKA*, p. 8.N. Jankowska, *SCCNH* 1 (1981) 197, n. 5, compte 31 tablettes dont 7 inédites, pour ces pièces 1 et 4. A. Fadhil compte 25 inédits. M.P. Maidman, dans JEN 7 = *SCCNH* 3, a publié 10 documents de la pièce 1 et 6 de la pièce 4.

[24] G. Dosch et K. Deller, *SCCNH* 1 (1981) 93. Il y aurait une douzaine de tablettes selon E.R. Lacheman, *CRRAI* 19, p. 361 et G. Dosch et K. Deller, *SCCNH* 1 (1981) 92, n. 2, qui donnent la liste des textes. N. Jankowska, *SCCNH* 1 (1981) 195, n. 1, fournit une liste légèrement différente, avec 11 tablettes publiées et 3 inédites (mais publiées depuis, par M.P. Maidman, dans JEN 7 = *SCCNH* 3, comme provenant de la pièce 11); elle propose d'y ajouter 3 autres tablettes considérées comme provenant des pièces voisines.

[25] Selon G. Dosch et K. Deller, *SCCNH* 1 (1981) 92, n. 2, il y avait 26 textes dans la pièce 11 et 21 textes dans la pièce 12; les auteurs en donnent la liste. Mais pour ces deux mêmes pièces, E.R. Lacheman, *CRRAI* 19, p. 361, compte environ 80 tablettes, et N. Jankowska, *SCCNH* 1 (1981) 197 n. 6, 30 ou 32, avec une liste moins complète que celle de G. Dosch et K.

G. Dosch et K. Deller ont montré que ces archives de l'aile ouest relevaient toutes d'une même famille d'origine kassite, Šuḫun-zirira et Ḫutiya étant des cousins éloignés (leurs pères sont cousins germains), ayant pour ancêtre commun Kizzuk. Néanmoins, les deux lots relèvent de branches différentes et de générations différentes.

Bibliographie

DOSCH G. et DELLER K., «Die Familie Kizzuk. Sieben Kassitengenerationen in Temtena und Šuriniwe», *SCCNH* 1 (1981) 91–113.

JANKOWSKA N., «Life of the Military Elite in Arrapḫe», *SCCNH* 1 (1981) 195–200.

MAIDMAN M.P., «Kassites among the Hurrians: A Case Study from Nuzi», *BSMS* 8 (1984) 15–21.

Les archives de ce secteur «T» ont été trouvées en grand nombre dès la première campagne de fouilles et sont donc publiées dans la série des JEN. Les six premiers volumes donnent les copies cunéiformes des tablettes, il en existe parfois des transcriptions et traductions dispersées, mais il n'y a pas eu d'édition scientifique systématique de l'ensemble de ces archives. Les tablettes de JEN 7 = *SCCNH* 3 ont été, pour plus de la moitié d'entre elles, transcrites, traduites et commentées par M.P. Maidman[26], avec des index, ainsi qu'un «catalogue of interrelated texts», ce qui inaugure une nouvelle façon d'aborder ces documents.

Il reste de nombreux inédits (numéros JEN*u*), estimés par M.P. Maidman à 110 tablettes complètes, 458 fragments assez conséquents et 1300 petits fragments[27], dont cet auteur est en train de préparer l'édition, ainsi qu'un catalogue complet des textes de Chicago. De tels travaux devraient donner une vision complète des archives et permettre d'évaluer exactement ce qui a été trouvé dans chaque lot. Pour l'instant, par exemple, l'estimation de ce qui a été exhumé dans chaque pièce demeure imprécise et varie beaucoup selon que les auteurs ont eu ou non accès aux inédits. Ce problème est d'ailleurs général pour l'ensemble des textes trouvés à Nuzi, et ne se pose pas seulement pour ceux de la butte nord-ouest.

Lors de la seconde campagne, les fouilles de la maison de Teḫip-Tilla se sont poursuivies[28]. Cela explique probablement la présence, dans la collection de Harvard, de quelques documents trouvés dans cette maison. Ils ont été publiés dans HSS 13, 14, 15 et EN 9[29].

Deller. Aux tablettes comptées par G. Dosch, K. Deller et N. Jankowska, il faut ajouter 11 textes provenant de la pièce 11 et 2 de la pièce 12 publiés depuis par M.P. Maidman, dans JEN 7 = *SCCNH* 3. Cf. aussi A. Fadhil, *STPPKA*, p. 8.

26 *Two Hundred Nuzi Texts from the Oriental Institute of the University of Chicago, Part I, SCCNH* 6 (JEN 674 à JEN 774), «JEN 775–780: The Text Editions», *SCCNH* 9 (1998) 95–123 et «JEN 781–789: The Text Editions», *SCCNH* 10 (1999) 329–74.

27 *SCCNH* 6 (1994) xiii.

28 R.F.S. Starr, *Nuzi* I, p. xxxiv et *Nuzi* II, plan n° 4.

29 M.P. Maidman, *SCCNH* 2, pp. 345–49, a publié des fragments de l'archive de Teḫip-Tilla conservés à Harvard, en particulier un joint entre un fragment de Chicago (JEN 13) et

2.4. Les fouilles régulières de Nuzi: «Eastern Suburban Area»

Une seconde petite butte, au nord-est du tell central, a été fouillée lors de la seconde campagne (planche n° 3). Les archéologues ont dans un premier temps appelé ce site A. Le sigle A+n° correspond donc à cette zone, non au carré A du tell central qui n'a pas livré de tablettes. Deux maisons y ont été fouillées:

Planche n° 3

Tell nord-est (= Eastern Suburban Area = A)

(R.F.S. Starr, *Nuzi*, II, plan n° 34)

---

un autre du Semitic Museum (SMN 1584); il signale: «We are left with the disquieting conclusion that JEN*u* materiel from Chicago has infiltrated the SMN collection in Cambridge...» (p. 348). La poursuite des fouilles dans ce même secteur lors de la seconde campagne pourrait éclairer cette «infiltration». Même phénomène pour JEN 659 + EN 10/2 73, cf. G. Wilhelm, *SCCNH* 5 (1995) 71–74

2.4.1. La maison de la famille d'Akkuya

La maison dite de Zike occupait la partie nord-est de la butte. Selon E.R. Lacheman, «trois salles nous ont produit des tablettes: 30 (21 tablettes), 34 (168 tablettes) et 35 (5 tablettes)»[30]. 107 des tablettes de la pièce 34 ont été publiées dans HSS 5. Près d'une centaine d'autres réputées provenir du même endroit, ainsi qu'une vingtaine de la pièce A 30 ont paru dans HSS 9, 13 à 16 et 19, EN 9 et 10[31]. Néanmoins, de nombreuses erreurs d'enregistrement sont repérables, et il semble qu'une partie des tablettes se rapporte en fait à la maison voisine, celle de Šilwa-Teššup.

Les principaux lots de la pièce A 34 sont:

- les archives d'Akkuya fils de Katiri et des trois générations suivantes, dont Zike fils d'Akkuya (74 textes); les fouilleurs ont retenu le nom de Zike pour désigner la maison.
- les archives d'Ilanu fils de Tauki et de ses descendants (60 textes).
- des listes de *rākib narkabti*, dont certaines comptent parmi les plus anciennes retrouvées à Nuzi. Leur présence serait à mettre en rapport avec les activités d'Akap-šenni fils de Zike (29 textes).

Dans le petit lot trouvé en A 30, plusieurs textes font partie des archives des fils d'Ennaya.

Bibliographie

DOSCH G., *Die Texte aus Room A 34 des Archivs von Nuzi*, Heidelberg 1976, Magister-Arbeit inédit, qui doit bientôt être publié[32].

GROSZ K., «A New Fragment from the Archive of the Family of Akkuya», *SCCNH* 2 (1987) 352–54.

2.4.2. La maison de Šilwa-Teššup, fils du roi

L'autre maison de la butte «A» a livré l'archive de Šilwa-Teššup, fils du roi, la plus grosse archive de Nuzi après celle de Teḫip-Tilla, comptant plus de 730 tablettes, trouvées surtout dans les pièces A 23 et A 26. Celles-ci ont été publiées dans HSS 9, puis dans HSS 13 à 16, HSS 19, EN 9 et 10.

Les premières synthèses ont été faites par M. Morrison. G. Wilhelm fournit actuellement une nouvelle édition de ces textes, comprenant transcriptions après collations systématiques, traductions et commentaires; les volumes parus concernent les archives administratives de la maison du prince et les contrats

---

30 *CRRAI* 19, p. 362. La même remarque, mais sans indication du nombre de tablettes, figure dans HSS 16, p. vi.

31 Je n'ai pas trouvé trace de publication de tablettes de A 35. EN 9/1 317, réputée provenir de A 33 (*SCCNH* 2 [1987] 370, indication reprise dans *SCCNH* 5 [1995] 118 et 145), dans la même maison, doit plus vraisemblablement être attribuée à A 23 (*SCCNH* 2 [1987] 381)

32 Madame G. Dosch a bien voulu m'envoyer son manuscrit; qu'elle en soit ici vivement remerciée.

de prêts. D. Stein a étudié les sceaux apposés sur ces tablettes. Trois volumes de textes et un volume d'introduction sont encore en préparation. Cette série devrait servir de modèle aux travaux archivistiques ultérieurs; ceux-ci, à l'exception des études concernant la famille de Teḫip-Tilla, porteront de toute façon sur des corpus de taille beaucoup plus modeste.

Bibliographie

MORRISON M., *Šilwa-Tešup: Portrait of a Hurrian Prince*, Ann Arbor 1976.

MORRISON M., «The Family of Šilwa-Tešub, mâr šarri», *JCS* 31 (1976) 3–29.

STEIN D., *Das Archiv des Šilwa-teššup Heft 8. The Seals Impressions (Text)*, Wiesbaden 1993.

STEIN D., *Das Archiv des Šilwa-teššup Heft 9. The Seals Impressions (Catalogue)*, Wiesbaden 1993.

WILHELM G., *Das Archiv des Šilwa-teššup Heft 2. Rationenlisten I*, Wiesbaden 1980.

WILHELM G., *Das Archiv des Šilwa-teššup Heft 3, Rationenlisten II*, Wiesbaden 1985.

WILHELM G., *Das Archiv des Šilwa-teššup Heft 4, Darlehensurkunden und verwandte Texte*, Wiesbaden 1992.

2.5. Les fouilles régulières de Nuzi: Tell principal

Les archives trouvées sur le tell principal (planche n° 4) ont été étudiées de façon très inégale. L'un des principaux problèmes tient une fois de plus aux incertitudes quant à la provenance exacte des tablettes[33]. Il existe des divergences entre le nombre de tablettes indiqué par R.F.S. Starr pour telle ou telle pièce dans son rapport de fouilles et les textes qui ont effectivement été enregistrés comme provenant de cette pièce. De plus, l'étude interne montre qu'il y a eu parfois des erreurs d'enregistrement.

2.5.1. Le palais

Les textes du palais sont publiés dans AASOR 16, HSS 13 à 16 et 19 et EN 9.

W.M. Mayer a fourni un inventaire précis de 600 textes trouvés dans le palais, classés par lieu de découverte, avec un résumé de chaque document. Il s'agit en général de textes économiques. Néanmoins, dans la pièce N 120, l'archive d'une femme, Tulpunnaya, fille de ᶠŠeltunnaya, a été retrouvée. Elle comprend plus d'une trentaine de contrats, du même type que ceux figurant dans les autres archives privées de Nuzi: adoptions qui lui permettent d'acquérir des vergers dans les régions de Temtena et de Zizza, *titennūtu* de personnes, adoptions de jeunes filles à marier, achats d'esclaves… La plupart de ces textes n'ont pas été copiés, mais ont été transcrits et traduits par R.H. Pfeiffer et E.A. Speiser.

---

33 Cf. M. Morrison, *SCCNH* 2 (1987) 168–69.

Planche n° 4

Tell Central

(R.F.S. Starr, *Nuzi*, II, plan n° 13)

Bibliographie sur l'archive de Tulpunnaya

MAYER W.M., *Nuzi-Studien I. Die Archive des Palastes und die Prosopographie der Berufe*, AOAT 205/1, Neukirchen-Vluyn 1978, 40–49.

PFEIFFER R.H. et SPEISER E.A., *One Hundred New Selected Nuzi Texts*, AASOR 16 (1935–36) 20–35 et 75–97 (n° 15 à 45).

2.5.2. Le temple

Le temple de Nuzi, correspondant au «groupe 29» de R.F.S. Starr, s'étend sur les carrés G et H (planche n° 5). Des tablettes ont été retrouvées dans ses deux *cellae*, G 53 et G 29–G 73 et plus d'une soixantaine d'entre elles sont

Planche n° 5

Temple

(R.F.S. Starr, *Nuzi*, II, plan n° 13)

Archive de Kerip-šeri
(G 29, G 53)

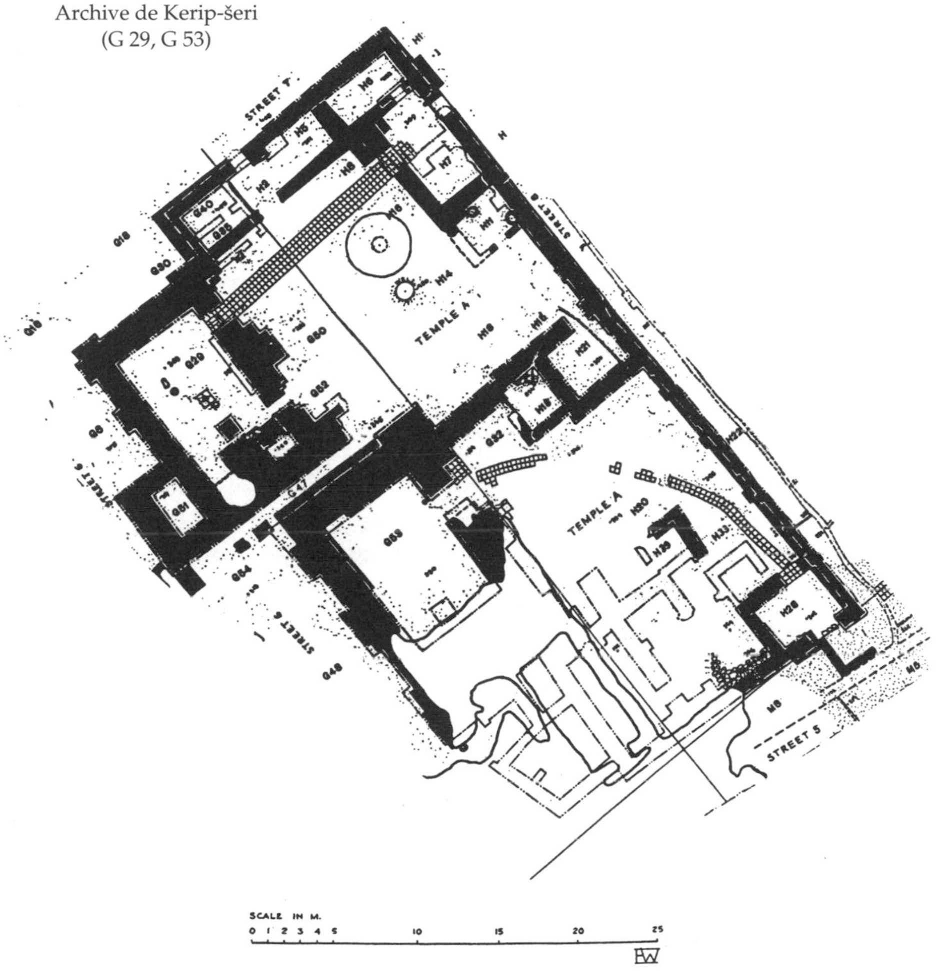

publiées[34]. A côté de listes et d'inventaires, les groupes les plus importants sont surtout des contrats d'adoptions et de *titennūtu*, et des procès. Une quinzaine

34 La pièce G 73, non indiquée dans *Nuzi* II, plan n° 13, qui correspond au «stratum II», figure en revanche sur les plans n° 8 et 9, qui montrent des états antérieurs du temple; elle se situe dans l'angle est de la *cella* G 29; cf. aussi E.R. Lacheman, *CRRAI* 19, p. 367. Les tablettes publiées proviennent pour l'essentiel de G 29 et G 73, et quelques-unes de G 53. E.R. Lacheman mentionne aussi des tablettes en G 55 et H 15 (HSS 16, p. vii); EN 9/3 447 vient de la cour H 15, mais je n'ai trouvé aucune publication de tablette de G 55. EN 9/3 259 est réputée provenir de G 23, mais… cette pièce n'existe pas: elle ne figure dans *Nuzi* II ni dans l'«index of rooms» de la p. 22, ni sur le plan n° 13, ni sur les divers plans du temple antérieur au «stratum II».

de textes concerne Kerip-šeri fils de Ḫut-Teššup; ils étaient répartis entre les deux *cellae*. Les autres archives appartiennent à des personnages très variés. Dans le temple, comme dans le palais, on trouve donc des archives privées. E.R. Lacheman en avait déjà fait la remarque: «on se demande ce que faisaient ces archives dans le temple»[35]. La plupart d'entre elles ont été publiées dans EN 9/3 et elles n'ont pas encore été étudiées.

2.5.3. Les maisons

Les autres bâtiments du tell central de Nuzi sont des maisons privées, les «groupes» de R.F.S. Starr, dont l'étude a été reprise récemment par M. Novak[36]. Elles contiennent quelquefois des documents administratifs, mais surtout des archives familiales, moins abondantes que les très gros lots décrits ci-dessus: elles représentent quelques tablettes, parfois quelques dizaines. Leur publication se trouve dans HSS 14 à 16, HSS 19, ainsi que dans la série EN 9. Des études récentes ont permis de mieux connaître les habitants de certains quartiers.

2.5.3.1. Les bâtiments au nord du temple

Les carrés de fouille C, D, H, I correspondent aux groupes 30 à 36 (planche n° 6). Seuls trois d'entre eux auraient livré des tablettes:

— Dans le groupe 31, en C 19 et C 28, environ 160 tablettes[37] formaient les archives de la famille de Zike fils d'Artimi, son fils Utḫap-Tae et son petit-fils Šar-Teššup. Celles de C 19 concernent surtout des reçus de grain, alors que C 28 renfermait surtout des contrats et quelques textes administratifs[38].

— Dans le groupe 33, la pièce C 30 aurait livré quelques tablettes[39].

— Dans le groupe 36, en D 3 et D 6, se trouvaient environ 280 documents[40]: reçus de grains pour les chevaux du roi, les fonctionnaires, la reine et les dieux, ainsi que des listes. D 6 a fourni aussi un extrait du recueil de présages *Enuma Anu Enlil*. Selon R.F.S. Starr, quelques tablettes se trouvaient également dans les pièces I 27–30, une dans I 24, une dans I 23–26[41].

---

35 *CRRAI* 19, p. 367.

36 «Eine Typologie der Wohnhäuser von Nuzi», *Bag. Mitt.* 25 (1994) 341–446.

37 Chiffre donné par E.R. Lacheman, HSS 16, p. vii. Sur ces 160 tablettes, 110 sont publiées.

38 Selon R.F.S. Starr, *Nuzi* I, p. 234, C 19 contenait environ 75 tablettes et C 28 environ 80. 57 textes issus de C 19 sont publiés, ainsi que 54 de C 28.

39 Selon R.F.S. Starr, *Nuzi* I, p. 238. Cette information n'a pas été reprise par E.R. Lacheman. Seules deux tablettes réputées venir de cette pièce ont été publiées.

40 E.R. Lacheman, HSS 16, p. viii. 111 textes de D 3 et 73 de D 6 sont publiés.

41 R.F.S. Starr, *Nuzi* I, pp. 249–50. Seules les deux tablettes de I 24 et I 23–26 sont publiées, mais pas celles de I 27–30.

Planche n° 6

Quartier au nord du temple

(R.F.S. Starr, *Nuzi*, II, plan n° 13)

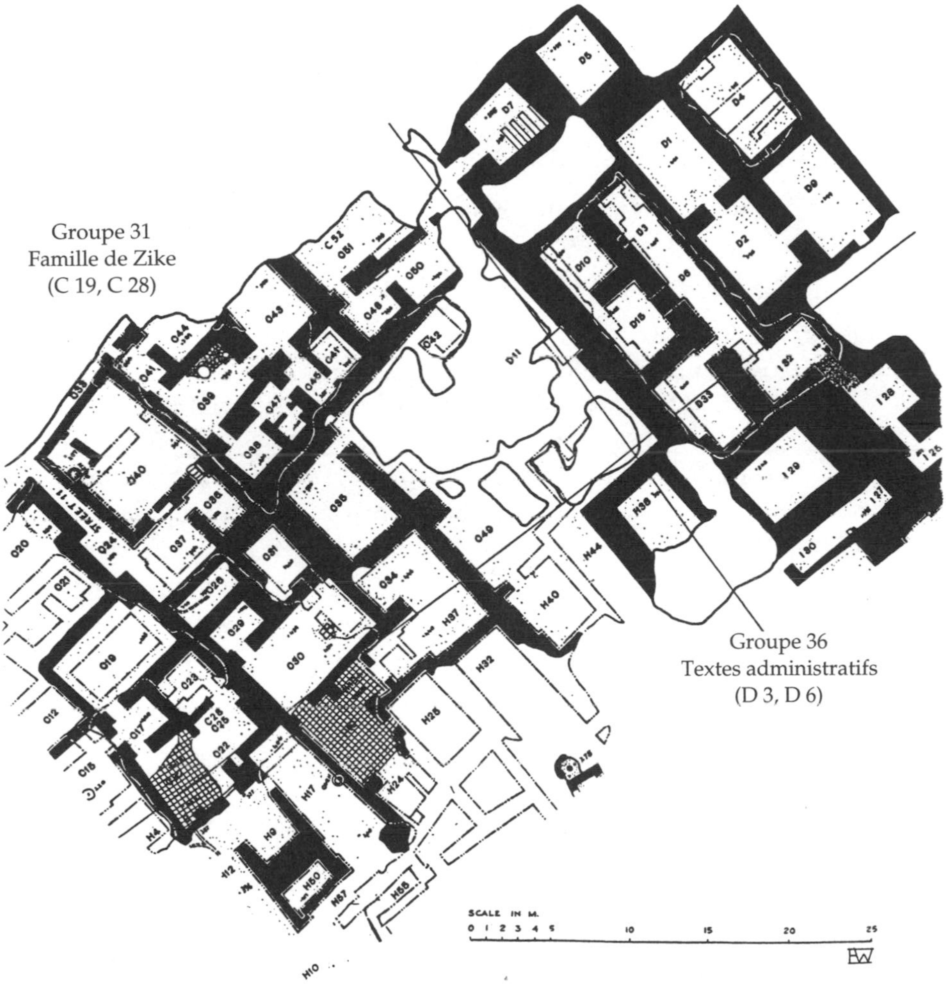

Ces textes ressemblent beaucoup à ceux du palais et E.R. Lacheman, comme W. Mayer[42], ont supposé que les gens vivant dans ce secteur étaient liés au palais. Néanmoins, aucune étude précise n'a permis d'approfondir cette question.

2.5.3.2. Les bâtiments au sud-ouest du temple.

Les maisons au sud-ouest du temple se situent dans le carré F (planche n° 7). Il s'agit des groupes 22 à 28 où, selon E.R. Lacheman, «quelques tablettes en petit nombre furent trouvées»[43]. Parmi les textes publiés, environ 70 sont issus de ce secteur. Ils n'ont pas fait l'objet d'études particulières. Ils proviennent de quatre groupes:

— Dans le groupe 22, les pièces F 26 et F 32 ont livré des textes administratifs; 8 d'entre eux sont publiés.

— Dans le groupe 23, seuls 3 textes administratifs des pièces F 4 et F 6 sont publiés.

— Le groupe 24 a fourni les documents les plus nombreux, en provenance des pièces F 24 (35 textes publiés, parmi lesquels la tablette de cuivre HSS 14 1)[44], F 25 (12 textes publiés) et F 38 (1 texte publié). Cette maison contenait, outre quelques documents administratifs, de nombreux contrats, dans lesquels prédominent les noms des membres de la famille de Ṣill-apuḫe et de celle de Niḫriya.

— Dans le groupe 25, les 8 tablettes publiées de la pièce F 16 font apparaître plusieurs fois le nom de Ḫutanni, peut-être fils de Turar-Teššup. De la pièce F 19 n'a été publiée qu'une liste de bétail.

Seules ces deux dernières maisons abritaient donc des archives familiales.

2.5.3.3. Les bâtiments au sud-ouest du palais

Dans les carrés K et P, les groupes 1 à 13 ont été dégagés (planche n° 8); les groupes 2 et 8 ont livré les archives les plus abondantes. Elles sont en partie publiées dans HSS 14, 15, 16 et 19; EN 9/1 complète ce corpus.

M. Morrison a pu répertorier 130 textes trouvés dans ce quartier, dont une trentaine, surtout des fragments, seraient encore inédits. Ils correspondent à plusieurs petites archives privées. Chacune contient quelques textes, rarement plus d'une dizaine. L'auteur distingue onze lots de textes, qui devaient appartenir à quatre ou cinq familles principales. Les familles ainsi représentées sont celles de Taya, Ṣupr-Adad, Taya fils d'Arim-matka, Šerta-ma-ilu, Šellapai,

---

42 *Nuzi-Studien I. Die Archive des Palastes und die Prosopographie der Berufe* (AOAT 205/1), Neukirchen-Vluyn 1978, 11.

43 *CRRAI* 19, p. 368. Dans HSS 16, p. viii, E.R. Lacheman ne donne aucun chiffre pour ce secteur.

44 Selon R.F.S. Starr, Nuzi I, p. 218, il y aurait eu 75 tablettes dans F 24. Si l'on considère les textes publiés, soit il reste de nombreux inédits provenant de F 24, ce qui est peu

Planche n° 7

Quartier au sud-ouest du temple

(R.F.S. Starr, *Nuzi*, II, plan n° 13)

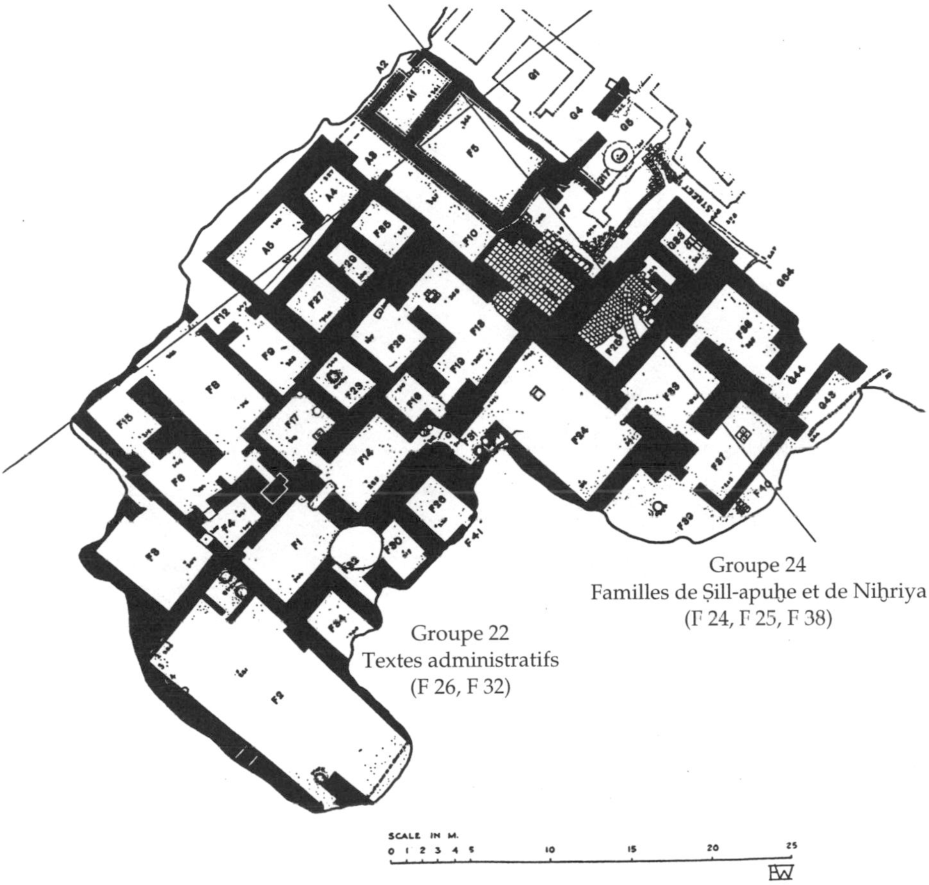

Tamar-Tae, Paikku, Puḫiya et Artaya; M. Morrison a pu reconstruire plusieurs arbres généalogiques. Du même secteur proviennent les rares textes scolaires trouvés à Nuzi[45].

L'enregistrement des textes, une fois encore, semble avoir posé des problèmes: ceux qui relèvent d'une même archive sont parfois réputés provenir de

vraisemblable, soit ce chiffre de 75 représente l'ensemble des tablettes trouvées dans ce carré F et non dans la seule pièce F 24.

45 E.R. Lacheman, «Nuziana», *RA* 36 (1939) 81–95. Selon cet article, cinq d'entre eux proviennent de P 313 et un de K 465. Le dernier aurait été trouvé en S 151, donc dans le secteur à l'est du palais (groupe 18A). En revanche, dans HSS 16, p. viii, E.R. Lacheman attribue les sept textes à la pièce P 313.

Planche n° 8

Quartier au sud-ouest du palais

(R.F.S. Starr, *Nuzi*, II, plan n° 13)

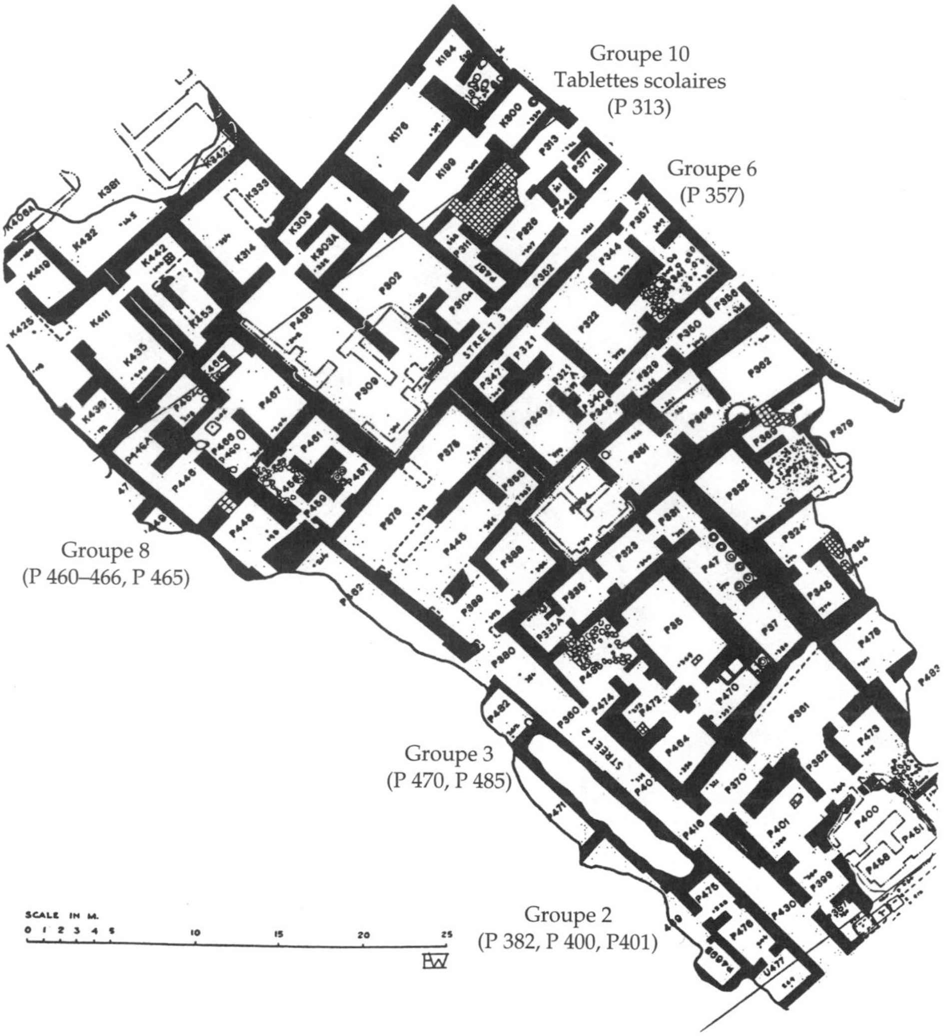

pièces différentes, voire de groupes différents, au point qu'il devient difficile d'assigner une maison à une famille précise.

L'intérêt de l'étude de M. Morrison est d'avoir mis en lumière ces archives modestes, appartenant à des familles certainement moins riches que celles de grands propriétaires fonciers comme Teḫip-Tilla, et de montrer les relations économiques et sociales que pouvaient entretenir les gens d'un même quartier.

Planche n° 9

Quartier à l'est du palais

(R.F.S. Starr, *Nuzi*, II, plan n° 13)

Bibliographie

MORRISON M., «The Southwest Archives at Nuzi», *SCCNH* 2 (1987) 167–201.

2.5.3.4. Les bâtiments à l'est du palais

Les groupes 15 à 20A se trouvent dans les carrés de fouilles N et S (planche n° 9). La plus grande partie des textes trouvés dans ce secteur a été publiée sous forme de copies sous le sigle EN 9/2. Une bonne présentation en a été donnée là encore par M. Morrison. A peu près 340 textes sont répertoriés; parmi eux, plus de 100 fragments demeurent inédits. Comme pour le quartier précédemment cité, M. Morrison fournit une liste très utile des textes retrouvés pour chaque pièce et pour chaque groupe.

Le groupe 15 n'a livré qu'une seule tablette issue de S 150; le groupe 18, trois tablettes trouvées en S 131. En revanche, trois autres groupes ont fourni des archives plus abondantes, comprenant fréquemment quelques dizaines de textes:

- Dans le groupe 17, il y avait deux lots d'archives, trouvés en S 110 et S 113: ceux de la famille d'Ar-tura fils de Kuššiya, et de ses fils, en particulier Utḫap-Tae; et ceux de Šeḫal-Teššup fils de Teḫup-šenni, *gugallu*.
- Dans le groupe 18A, les tablettes proviennent toutes de la petite pièce S 151, un corridor; R.F.S. Starr a proposé qu'elles aient été jetées là depuis la pièce voisine (S 307). Elles constituent l'archive des descendants de Ḫuya fils de Šimika-atal, et principalement de Tarmiya, le fils cadet de Ḫuya. Leurs biens fonciers sont localisés dans le *dimtu* de Ḫuya, d'après le nom de l'ancêtre de cette famille; ils font également des transactions immobilières dans la ville de Nuzi.
- Plusieurs lots d'archives étaient conservés dans le groupe 19: ceux d'Urḫi-Kušuḫ «dumu lugal», des descendants de Muš-apu et de ceux de Pula-ḫali; dans S 112 a aussi été retrouvée la bulle d'argile creuse qui contenait 48 jetons, correspondant au nombre de têtes de petit bétail confiées à un berger[46]. La famille de Muš-apu est basée à Unapšewe, où elle investit dans les terres et possède du bétail. La famille de Pula-ḫali offre un cas intéressant, car il s'agit d'une famille de marchands, dont les investissements diffèrent des stratégies foncières habituelles: les documents les plus fréquents sont des contrats de prêts. Cette archive concerne presqu'exclusivement la ville de Ṭupšarriniwe.

Ce dernier quartier révèle donc l'existence de familles aisées, mais dont toute l'activité n'était pas centrée sur Nuzi, bien au contraire. Elles étaient aussi implantées dans d'autres villes du royaume d'Arrapḫa.

Bibliographie

CASSIN E., «Une querelle de famille», *SCCNH* 1 (1981) 37–46 (famille de Ḫuya).

DELLER K., «Die Hausgötter der Familie Šukrija S. Huja», *SCCNH* 1 (1981) 47–76 (famille de Ḫuya).

MORRISON M., «The Eastern Archives of Nuzi», *SCCNH* 4 (1993) 3–130.

NEGRI SCAFA P., «Alcune Osservazioni sui Testi HSS XIX 113 e HSS XIX 114», *SCCNH* 1 (1981) 325–31 (archive d'Utḫap-tae fils d'Ar-tura).

46 HSS 16 449, cf. A.L. Oppenheim, «On an Operational Device in Mesopotamian Bureaucracy», *JNES* 18 (1959) 121–28: trouvée dans la pièce S 129 de la même maison, la tablette HSS 16 311 se rapporte à la même opération. Cf. T. Abusch, «Notes on a Pair of Matching Texts: A Shepherd's Bulla and an Owner's Receipt», *SCCNH* 1 (1981) 1–9.

3. Familles Connues et Méconnues

3.1. L'établissement des archives

3.1.1. Les tablettes issues des fouilles clandestines

K. Grosz a opéré un gros travail de rassemblement des textes d'Arrapḫa, en particulier ceux de la famille de Wullu; elle a aussi remembré plusieurs autres petites archives provenant d'Arrapḫa. Les textes trouvés sur ce site ont donc pu être isolés et ont fait l'objet d'une étude par lots d'archives.

Pour les tablettes provenant des fouilles clandestines de Nuzi, le travail reste en partie à faire. La plupart sont désormais publiées et, dans les volumes de *SCCNH*, plusieurs joints ont été opérés entre des textes appartenant soit à une même collection, soit à des collections différentes, ce qui clarifie la situation. Néanmoins, si des lots d'archives se dessinent nettement, en particulier la grosse archive de Zike, fils de Šurki-Tilla et petit-fils de Teḫip-Tilla[47], ainsi que plusieurs petits groupes indépendants[48], les études des familles et de leurs activités n'a pas été systématiquement menée. Le lieu de provenance de ces textes demeurant inconnu, il n'est pas possible de savoir s'ils sont issus d'une ou de plusieurs maisons.

3.1.2. Les archives des tells nord-est et nord-ouest

Les textes provenant de ces deux secteurs sont en général bien identifiés et de nombreux travaux ont déjà été faits sur ces archives; on a déjà mentionné les ouvrages de M.P. Maidman, D. Stein et G. Wilhelm, ainsi que le Magister-Arbeit de G. Dosch, dont la publication est prochaine. Mais étant donnée l'abondance du matériel, beaucoup reste à faire. Sur le tell T, les archives de la maison orientale, souvent citées, n'ont pas reçu l'édition critique qu'elles méritent. Sur le tell A, le petit lot de textes trouvé dans la pièce A 30 de la maison ouest n'a pas été étudié.

3.1.3. Les archives du tell central

Les archives privées du tell principal, comme l'a fait remarquer M. Morrison[49], ont été moins bien étudiées que celles des zones du nord-est et du nord-ouest, en partie parce qu'elles sont restées longtemps inédites. La publication de EN 9 et 10 vient désormais quasiment clore le corpus. Or tous ces textes, parus ces dix dernières années, ont encore été très peu exploités, voire pas du tout. De nombreuses archives, moyennes ou petites, devraient encore pouvoir être rassemblées et les perspectives d'études sont multiples.

Le tri et la description du matériel demeurent incomplets. W. Mayer a fait l'inventaire des documents du palais. M. Morrison, dans *SCCNH* 2 et 4, a fourni la liste complète des textes réputés provenir des quartiers situés de part et

---

47 G.G.W. Müller, *Londoner Nuzi-Texte*, Wiesbaden 1998, 19–23.

48 Cf. M.P. Maidman, «The Nuzi Texts in the British Museum», *ZA* 76 (1986) 255–58.

49 *SCCNH* 2 (1987) 167.

d'autre du palais. Dans *SCCNH* 5, D.I. Owen a publié un «Cumulative Catalogue» qui indique, pour toutes les tablettes publiées dans EN 9, le lieu exact de provenance lorsque celui-ci est connu. Ces travaux très utiles permettent de voir d'un seul coup d'œil quelles tablettes ont été trouvées dans une même pièce ou un même bâtiment. Pour les textes publiés antérieurement à *SCCNH* 5, dans HSS 13 à 16 et 19, le lieu de découverte des tablettes est indiqué dans chaque publication séparément. Mais il manque un catalogue général, incluant toutes ces données, qui serait intéressant surtout pour les quartiers n'ayant pas encore été l'objet d'études spécifiques.

Certains lots ont en effet été jusqu'à présent complètement négligés: les textes trouvés dans le temple et dans les quartiers proches du temple n'ont reçu aucune attention particulière. Les quartiers situés de part et d'autre du palais ont été mieux étudiés, grâce aux travaux par secteurs de M. Morrison; néanmoins ces textes gagneraient à être réédités très précisément, archive par archive[50].

Pour de nombreuses tablettes se pose le problème du lieu d'origine. La comparaison entre les relevés de fouille de R.F.S. Starr et le catalogue des textes publiés montre de grandes divergences. Les études archivistiques mettent en évidence certaines erreurs d'enregistrement: des tablettes relevant de l'archive de Šilwa-Teššup ont ainsi été attribuées à différents endroits situés hors de sa demeure, ce qui est fort peu vraisemblable[51]. Par ailleurs, le nombre des tablettes sans indication de provenance est élevé. Sur plus de 500 tablettes publiées dans EN 9, 145 n'ont pas de lieu de provenance connu, soit plus du quart; quant aux fragments parus depuis dans EN 10, la grande majorité d'entre eux s'inscrit dans la rubrique «Room number: none». Le remembrement des archives devrait permettre de rattacher à un lieu de découverte ces textes dont l'origine est aujourd'hui incertaine. Par exemple, parmi les 55 tablettes correspondant à l'archive des descendants de Pula-ḫali, 11, soit 20 %, sont réputées de provenance inconnue; leur étude interne permet de supposer qu'elles sont certainement issues du groupe 19, comme les autres.

3.2. Des archives familiales à découvrir

L'établissement correct des archives permet de compléter les études prosopographiques, en premier lieu celle de la famille la mieux documentée, celle de Teḫip-Tilla, dont une autre branche est désormais révélée; même si les textes de Zike n'apportent pas de bouleversement complet aux conclusions de M.P. Maidman, qui a déjà largement étudié cette famille, il devient possible d'affiner encore l'évolution du patrimoine et des stratégies économiques sur plusieurs générations.

---

50 Je dois éditer bientôt les transcriptions et traductions d'une cinquantaine de textes, relevant des archives de Pašši-Tilla, fils du marchand Pula-ḫali, trouvées dans le groupe 19 [*SCCNH* 12 (2000) sous presse]. D. Stein prépare l'étude des sceaux de cette même archive.

51 Les lieux de découverte supposés de plusieurs de ces tablettes s'avèrent, après reconstitution de l'archive, «falsche»: G. Wilhelm, *Das Archiv des Šilwa-Teššup, Heft* 2, 12; *Heft* 3, 17; *Heft* 4, 5. La même expérience peut être faite sur des lots plus petits.

A côté des énormes archives de puissants personnages, comme Teḫip-Tilla ou Šilwa-Teššup, apparaissent désormais de nombreux lots petits ou moyens, documentant des familles aisées. Des comparaisons entre ces lots de tailles très différentes devraient mieux mettre en lumière la stratification sociale.

S'il est évident qu'une grande fortune comme celle de Teḫip-Tilla et une fortune moyenne ou modeste ne peuvent être gérées de la même façon, il semble toutefois que les mêmes opérations aient été pratiquées à tous les niveaux de la société. Les adoptions avec cession de biens immobiliers, très abondantes dans les textes de Teḫip-Tilla, sont pratiquées dans à peu près toutes les familles. Néanmoins, des situations diverses peuvent exister. M.P. Maidman a remarqué que, si Teḫip-Tilla investissait prioritairement dans la terre, ses descendants étaient moins portés sur des acquisitions massives, préférant gérer leur patrimoine ou acheter des esclaves pour l'exploiter. Ainsi, des variations sont observables d'une génération à l'autre. D'autres ensembles fournissent des renseignements d'un ordre différent: les textes de Šilwa-Teššup, incluant de nombreuses tablettes administratives, donnent beaucoup d'informations sur la gestion du personnel d'une grande maisonnée. Un lot d'archives de taille moyenne, comme celui de Pašši-Tilla, fils de Pula-ḫali, montre un marchand qui accroît sa fortune par des prêts de métaux, ses fonctions lui permettant certainement de se procurer étain, cuivre ou bronze; en revanche, les investissements fonciers sont assez peu représentés, la fortune mobilière est privilégiée. Ainsi, il existe plusieurs façons d'être riche à Nuzi, et les études archivistiques devraient permettre d'affiner nos connaissances des comportements économiques.

L'étude des maisons et des quartiers d'habitation qu'a menée M. Novák[52] confirme l'idée de quartiers résidentiels différenciés, caractérisés par une richesse plus ou moins grande de l'habitat domestique. Reste à voir si cette géographie sociale se reflète dans les archives des gens de ces quartiers. Cela n'est pas certain; dans les quatres principaux secteurs se trouvaient à la fois des maisons abritant des tablettes et d'autres vides d'écrits: une moitié environ des «groupes» ne contenait pas de textes, or ces bâtiments se répartissent sur l'ensemble du site et ne semblent pas se distinguer des autres maisons. Cela pose le problème de l'usage et de la conservation de l'écrit chez les habitants de ces lieux.

Les données archéologiques, là encore, sont insuffisantes pour venir à notre aide, dans la mesure où elles ne fournissent pas d'indications sur la manière dont étaient rangés les documents—si toutefois ils étaient rangés. Comment comprendre que, dans certaines pièces, on ne trouve par exemple qu'une unique tablette? Faut-il supposer dans certains cas que des documents étaient conservés dans un contexte secondaire, en remploi? Le problème se complique du fait que le site a connu une fin violente: R.F.S. Starr a supposé à plusieurs reprises que des tablettes avaient pu être déplacées, et donc retrouvées ailleurs que dans leur lieu de conservation habituel. D. Stein a fait la même hypothèse

52 Cf. ci-dessus, n. 36.

pour les textes de l'archive de Šilwa-Teššup réputés provenir de la maison voisine de la sienne (pièces A 30, A 33 et A 34), où ils auraient pu tomber depuis la pièce A 26[53].

Même si la destruction finale de la ville a pu provoquer le déplacement de certaines tablettes, elles n'ont probablement pas été entraînées très loin de leur lieu de stockage. Or l'attention portée au lieu de provenance des textes soulève plusieurs questions, à ce jour sans réponse:

— que faisaient des archives privées dans une pièce du palais, dans le cas de Tulpunnaya, et dans les deux *cellae* du temple?

— inversement, dans les maisons, en particulier dans le secteur situé au nord du temple, que faisaient les multiples listes d'hommes ou d'armes retrouvées dans les mêmes pièces que les transactions privées? Faut-il y voir des documents officiels conservés chez des fonctionnaires[54]?

— pourquoi, dans certaines maisons, plusieurs archives de familles différentes, apparemment sans aucun lien de parenté entre elles, ont-elles été retrouvées?

— les propriétaires des archives résidaient-ils à Nuzi, ou ailleurs, ou avaient-ils deux résidences? Dans certains cas, une partie de l'archive, et parfois presque l'ensemble, concerne des transactions effectuées dans d'autres villes. Faut-il également supposer que ces familles conservaient, ailleurs dans le royaume d'Arrapḫa, d'autres lots de textes? Les nombreux liens prosopographiques qui ont pu être montrés entre les archives de Nuzi et celles de Kurruḫanni peuvent le laisser penser.

Enfin, l'étude complète du matériel devrait permettre de mieux estimer, dans un dernier stade, l'importance de ce qui a été perdu. M.P. Maidman a bien noté que, malgré l'abondance des documents relatifs à la famille de Teḫip-Tilla, son archive restait incomplète[55]: Ḫaiš-Teššup, frère de Teḫip-Tilla, devait ainsi avoir une archive à Nuzi, mais sa maison n'a apparemment pas été retrouvée. En outre, il est vraisemblable qu'il existait des lots d'archives conservés ailleurs qu'à Nuzi: pour cette même famille, Enna-mati et Akip-Tašenni, les fils de Teḫip-Tilla, devaient avoir des archives à Turša. De même, pour les autres familles, à partir de ce qui reste, on devrait pouvoir dresser un inventaire de ce qui n'a pas été retrouvé: documents détruits, ou transmis à d'autres descendants dont les maisons n'ont pas été fouillées, ou entreposés ailleurs qu'à Nuzi… Les archives perdues de Nuzi mériteraient à leur tour une étude.

---

53 D. Stein, *Das Archiv des Šilwa-Teššup, Heft 8*, 25.

54 D'autres sites peuvent présenter des phénomènes tout aussi complexes. A Ugarit, les maisons dites de Rap'anu et d'Urtenu abritaient des types de textes variés: exercices scolaires, documents de la pratique et correspondance internationale; certains de ces documents étaient rédigés en akkadien, d'autres en ugaritique. Il est difficile de trouver une logique à ces groupements de tablettes. Sur ce point, cf. S. Lackenbacher, «La correspondance internationale dans les archives d'Ugarit», *RA* 89 (1995) 67–76.

55 M.P. Maidman, *A Socio-Economic Analysis of a Nuzi Family Archive*, Ann Arbor 1976, 488.

The Scribes of Nuzi*

PAOLA NEGRI SCAFA
Rome

Since the first texts from the Kingdom of Arrapḫa were published, interest in the Hurro-Akkadian dialect of Nuzi and the scribes who wrote in that dialect has been a major focus of research. This article reviews the scholarship associated with the study of the scribes and scribal practice at Nuzi and presents some new avenues of research as well as suggestions for future work on the subject.

INTRODUCTION

The excavation of the city of Nuzi during the decade of the twenties inaugurated a new line of research that was immediately very promising. The exposure of the town, of its buildings, the architectural remains of its palace and temple, each provided significant new comparative material for Near Eastern archaeology. Wall paintings, ceramics, glyptic, and, to a lesser extent, small finds and glass attracted the attention of many scholars and almost became a separate field of study.

The thousands of tablets found in the ruins of Yorghan Tepe and in the nearby mounds certainly have been among the most important finds at Nuzi. Texts from earlier clandestine digs in the area were recognized quickly as relating to the tablets coming from the excavations. As a consequence, a corpus of about 5,000 texts has been collected to which the texts found in Kurruḫanni/Tell al-Faḫḫār some decades later were added.[1] From these texts it has been possible to recreate a general picture of the small kingdom of Arrapḫa, which was subject to the Mittani Empire and was inhabited primarily by a Hurrian-speaking population.

Nuzi studies began with the clandestine recovery of texts, even before the the town itself had been discovered. The work on Nuzi developed over the decades in different phases and according to different themes, thereby becoming a specialized area within Assyriology. In the earliest stages of Nuzi studies, scholars concentrated on defining the dialect and script of the Nuzi texts, which had been identified as a kind of "peripheral Akkadian" heavily influenced by

---

* I thank Prof. D.I. Owen for his help in correcting the English text of my article.

1 See Appendix.

the Hurrian language. In addition, great emphasis was placed on the study of the social structure and economy; family law,[2] including a particular kind of adoption introduced by the formula *ṭuppi mārūti*;[3] practices connected to slavery,[4] loans,[5] and credit; and legal and court records.[6] Each has been studied in depth and compared with data coming from other areas of Mesopotamia and often with the Hebrew Bible. Less attention was paid in these earliest endeavors to administrative archives from the palace and from the private sector.

The more recent attention to social and economic aspects of the life in the kingdom of Arrapḫa resulted from careful and close examination of texts, such as lists of personnel, lists of witnesses, receipts, as well as various other types of archival documents. Thanks to the investigation of palace lists and rolls,[7] of the larger archive of Teḫip-Tilla[8] and Šilwa-Teššup,[9] and of smaller private archives found in the different areas of Nuzi, family histories and activities have been reconstructed. Thus our knowledge of Nuzi society and its economy has increased greatly. The analysis of the numerous geographical names occurring in the texts, often referring to unexcavated centers and towns in and around the kingdom of Arrapḫa, has resulted in a clearer understanding of the geography of the area.[10]

---

2 Cf. e.g., J. Paradise, "Nuzi Inheritance Practices," unpublished Ph. D. dissertation, University of Pennsylvania, 1972.

3 Because of their importance, *ṭuppi mārūti* have been the subject of frequent studies; in particular, cf. E. Cassin, *L'Adoption à Nuzi*, Paris, 1938.

4 E.g., E. Cassin in J. Bottéro, *Le Problème des ḫabiru* (4e Rencontre Internationale d'Assyriologie), Paris 1954; A. Saarisalo, *New Kirkuk Documents Relating to Slaves* (StOr 5/3), Helsinki, 1934; G. Dosch, *Zur Struktur der Gesellschaft des Königreichs Arrapḫe*, (HSAO 5), Heidelberg, 1993, 155–62.

5 Cf. D.I. Owen, "The Loan Documents from Nuzu," unpublished Ph. D. dissertation, Brandeis University, 1969. B.L. Eichler, *Indenture at Nuzi*, New Haven: Yale University Press, 1973.

6 Cf. R.E. Hayden, "Court Procedure at Nuzu," unpublished Ph. D. dissertation, Brandeis University, 1962.

7 W. Mayer, *Nuzi-Studien I*, Kevelaer/Neukirchen-Vluyn, 1978.

8 M.P. Maidman, "A Socio-Economic Analysis of a Nuzi Family Archive," unpublished Ph. D. dissertation, University Pennsylvania, 1976.

9 G. Wilhelm, *Das Archiv des Šilwa-teššup: Heft 2 – Rationenlisten I*, Wiesbaden: Harrassowitz, 1980; *Heft 3 – Rationenlisten II*, Wiesbaden 1985; *Heft 4 – Darlehensurkunden und verwandte Texte*, Wiesbaden: Harrassowitz, 1992.

10 L.R. Fisher, "Nuzi Geographical Names," unpublished Ph. D. dissertation, Brandeis University, 1959; C. Zaccagnini, *The Rural Landscape of the Land Arrapḫe* (QGS 1), Rome: Università di Roma, Istituto di Studi del Vicino Oriente, 1979; A. Fadhil, *Studien zur Topographie und Prosopographie des Königsreichs Arrapḫe* (BaF 6), Mainz: Philipp von Zabern, 1983; J. Fincke, *Die Orts- und Gewässernamen der Nuzi Texte* (RGTC 10), Wiesbaden: Dr. Ludwig Reichert, 1993; G.G.W. Müller, *Studien zur Siedlungsgeogaphie und Bevölkerung des mittleren Osttigrisgebietes*, (HSAO 7), Heidelberg: Orient-Verlag, 1994.

During the last decades new avenues of inquiry into Assyriology and Near Eastern society, particularly in "peripheral areas," have been developed. Discoveries of more Hurrian texts have increased our understanding of the Hurrian language and culture, thereby providing a better understanding of Nuzi language and society. Accordingly, the most recent trends in Assyriology, Hurrian studies, historiography—coupled with disciplines such as anthropology, ethnology, and linguistics—have each contributed to the development of the most recent phases of Nuzi studies.

All the elements indicated above also affect our study of the scribes of the kingdom of Arrapḫa. The study of scribal activity is very important. It can enlighten topics such as (1) archives and archive organization; (2) paleography and analysis of the evolution and diffusion of cuneiform writing; (3) the beginning of literature and the diffusion of the literary tradition; (4) linguistic elements, in particular when referring to those phases and periods when political differences within Mesopotamia and the periphery created problems concerning the use of a *lingua franca* in a multi-ethnic environment.

With respect to Nuzi scribes, the lack of literary texts makes it impossible to say anything about literature at Nuzi. In any case, the ability to write in cuneiform required intense training that included the study of traditional literary texts. Therefore it is possible to infer that Nuzi scribes, to some extent, belonged to the "mainstream" of Mesopotamian scribal tradition, as did scribes in other peripheral areas, e.g., Ugarit, Emar, and Ḫattuša. The Nuzi scribes exhibit local peculiarities that have drawn the attention of many scholars. For these reasons there have been many studies and analyses of Nuzi scribal practices since the discovery of the archives. It is possible to organize them according to the following major themes.

Number of Scribes

In the corpus of Nuzi texts more than 250 scribal names occur, but the number of scribes was certainly larger. In particular, there are different scribes who bear the same name. Fortunately it is often possible to distinguish between them thanks to the use of patronymics. This allows us to reconstruct certain scribal families (see below). The scribal family of Apil-Sîn, in particular, is very important for the study of the Nuzi archives because it covers the entire span of time during which the texts were composed and can therefore be used for prosopographical comparisons and chronological reconstruction.

Chronology of the Texts

One of the most vexing problems in the study of the Nuzi corpus is the internal and absolute chronology of the texts. In the corpus of Nuzi texts practically no historical events that can connect the history of the kingdom of Arrapḫa to the history of neighboring countries and kingdoms are recorded. Until now the absolute date of the Nuzi texts has been tied to the presence of the seal of Sauštatar, king of Mittani, on a Nuzi tablet.[11] But when it was recognized that the seal was, in fact, a dynastic seal, in use for a long time, the synchronism between the kingdom of Arrapḫa and the reign of Sauštatar was no longer tenable. In addition, the internal chronology of the texts was equally problematic. Unlike the texts of other corpora from the ancient Near East, only a few Nuzi texts bear any date formulae, none of which is useful for dating the texts. Moreover, the data relating to the kings and queens of Arrapḫa, who are mentioned several times in the texts, do not allow for a reconstruction of the internal chronology at Nuzi nor of a royal genealogy. Therefore the documents have been arranged according to archival groups. An internal chronology was established according to the genealogical lines preserved in each archival group with the aid of prosopographical comparisons. The most relevant archive for this purpose is the family archive of Teḫip-Tilla, which covers the entire span of time the texts were written. The same situation applies to the well-attested scribal family of Apil-Sîn,[12] which, through prosopographical analysis, is the primary control to establish ties between lists and documents. Other well-attested families used for chronological purposes and prosopographical comparisons are those of Akkuya and Katiri.[13]

A reconstruction of the relative chronology of Nuzi has been proposed recently by Friedmann.[14] Perhaps the first to utilize a computer for the analysis of the Nuzi texts, he extracted the data concerning members of all these families (chronology PNs) from a database "that incorporates data from some 3,600 Nuzi tablets" and synchronized them with the attestations of scribes of the Apil-Sîn family. The five charts he created depict co-attestations of chronological PNs and scribes. On the basis of the Teḫip-Tilla and Apil-Sîn families, which served as a chronological check, "bands of contemporaneity" were constructed. The charts also offer the possibility of studying the duration and overlapping of generations. According to Friedmann's calculations, the time

---

11 Discovered in 1927, the text (now known as HSS 9, 1) was promptly reported by Chiera in *BASOR* 32 (1928) and studied by E.A. Speiser, "A Letter of Shaushtatar and the Date of the Kirkuk Tablets," *JAOS* 49 (1929) 269–75. Cf also B.L. Eichler, *Indenture at Nuzi* (YNER 5), New Haven: Yale University Press, 1973, 2 n. 7; G. Wilhelm, "Parrattarna, Sauštatar und die absolute Datierung der Nuzi-Tafeln," *Acta Antiqua Academiae Scientiarum Hungaricae* 24 (1976) 154–55; *idem*, "Die Siegel des Königs Itḫi-tessup von Arrapḫa," *WO* 12 (1981) 5–7. The traditional chronological interpretation has been criticized by D. Stein; cf. D. Stein, "A Reappraisal of the 'Saustatar Letter' from Nuzi," *ZA* 79 (1989) 36–60.

12 As described by G. Wilhelm, *Untersuchungen zum Hurro-Akkadischen von Nuzi* (AOAT 9), Kevelaer/Neukirchen-Vluyn: Butzon und Bercker/Neukirchener Verlag, 1970.

13 The texts of these families have been published mainly in HSS 5 and HSS 9; their genealogies were reconstructed for the first time by E. Chiera in the preface to his HSS 5. All the texts of these archives were collected and analyzed by G. Dosch, *Die Texte aus Room A 34 des Archivs von Nuzi*, Magister-Arbeit, Heidelberg 1976.

14 A.H. Friedmann, "Toward a Relative Chronology at Nuzi," *SCCNH* 2 (1987) 109–29.

span of the Nuzi corpus was 85 ± 15 years. His conclusion agrees with the most recent chronological assessments.[15]

Another method of calculating the chronology of the texts was used by Wilhelm in his study of the Archive of Šilwa-Teššup. He analyzed the rations given to different individuals during the various phases of their lives. Through the comparison of ration lists it is possible to follow the life of certain individuals from young slave to adult slave or from young slave girl to adult woman. Prosopographical comparisons among lists make the reconstruction of the internal chronology of the archive of Šilwa-Teššup easier.

Place of Writing

Nuzi scribes carried out their activity not only in Nuzi, Arrapḫa, and Kurruḫanni, where the texts were excavated, but also in other until now unexcavated towns all over the kingdom. The picture is to some extent fragmentary because it is based only on scribes for whom more than one text has been identified. According to the available evidence, some scribes worked only in one city: for example Ir-muša, Adad-bāni, and Adad-nūḫir worked in Ḫurazina-ṣeḫru; *warad ekalli* scribes like Aḫa-ai-amši, Arip-šarri, Tarmi-Teššup, and Unap-Teššup seem to have been connected to the town of Nuzi where the palace was located. But in the majority of the cases, the scribes wrote their tablets in many different towns. It seems possible to draw the conclusion that the scribes were associated more with various archives than with specific towns and moved according to the exigencies of the owners of the archives. There is evidence that the scribes belonging to the earlier generations travelled from town to town within the kingdom, whereas scribes of the later generations seemed to travel within only a few, neighboring locations. Also, connections with archives appear to vary. From the earlier generations, documents belonging to a few important family archives are attested, whereas texts belonging to small family archives are attested mostly in the later generations—this may be due to the fact that documents from the later periods are more numerous, but it may indicate also that the later scribes carried out their activities in a different and more widespread manner.[16]

Scribes often wrote their tablets by the city or palace gates; studies on city gates as a place for writing texts have been undertaken recently.[17] Some scribes also spent their time in activities other than writing texts, as references to scribes as messengers (*mār šipri*) demonstrate[18] (see below).

---

15 G. Wilhelm suggested this possibility in 1983 and M.A. Morrison also agreed with this time span. Cf. Friedmann, *cit.*, 113 n. 15.

16 P. Negri Scafa, "Scribes locaux et scribes itinérantes," in D. Charpin / F. Joannès (eds.) *La circulation des biens, des personnes et des idées dans le Proche Orient ancien* [CRRA 38], Paris: Edition Recherche sur les civilisation, 1992, 235–40.

17 P. Negri Scafa, "Gates in the Texts of the City of Nuzi," *SCCNH* 9 (1998) 139–62.

18 Cf. P. Negri Scafa, "Gli scribi di Nuzi in funzioni diverse da redattori di testi," *Mesopotamia* 21 (1986) 249–59; *idem*, "The Scribes of Nuzi and Their Activities Relative to Arms

Scribal Names

Another area of interest in the study of the scribes of the kingdom of Arrapḫa is their name types. Special attention was paid to this by the authors of *Nuzi Personal Names*[19] in an attempt to determine the ethnic composition of the Nuzi scribes. In particular, they focused on the possibility that scribes bearing Akkadian names were actually Akkadian, an assumption that was proved to be erroneous. A study of the early scribes at Nuzi was also undertaken by Purves, who analyzed the writing styles of four scribes: Apil-Sîn, Amurru-šar-ilāni, Ḫūb-milk-abi, and the unknown scribe of JEN 570. He determined that their correct usage of Akkadian syntax indicated that these four scribes were probably not Hurrians but rather Akkadians who worked in a Hurrian milieu and who had set themselves apart from other scribes.[20]

PALEOGRAPHY AND SYLLABARY

In a general survey of scribal studies, obviously there would be emphasis on writing and language. During the first years after the discovery of the Nuzi texts, scholars studied the peculiarities of the writing and language. In particular, the earliest studies focused on: (1) the problem of the origin of the Nuzi writing; and (2) the definition of the features of Nuzi paleography.

Pinches,[21] Contenau,[22] and Gadd,[23] who were among the first to study the texts stemming from clandestine finds, pointed out Early Assyrian features in the writing. In particular, Gadd suggested that it was via Old Assyrian that the scribes of the Kirkūk tablets received their knowledge. Koschaker,[24] on the other hand, identified features in the Nuzi script as having Babylonian peculiarities, and, therefore, classified the writing as Babylonian.

After careful analysis of Contenau's comparative list of signs, Berkooz[25] suggested that the Nuzi script was "... to be classified... as a group by itself" closely related to the Akkado-Hittite syllabary, in which a large number of characters is similar to those of the Babylonian script, but on which some Assyrian influence is recognizable. In his analysis Berkooz collected and evaluated material related to orthography and phonology. Inconsistencies in use of determinatives, problems concerning vowels and consonants, and usage

according to Palace Texts," *SCCNH* 5 (1995) 53–69.

19 P.M. Purves, I.G. Gelb, A.A. MacRae, *Nuzi Personal Names* (=*NPN*), Chicago: University of Chicago Press, 1943, and in particular the section by MacRae on Akkadian and Sumerian names.

20 P.M. Purves, "The Early Scribes of Nuzi," *AJSL* 57 (1940) 171.

22 G. Contenau, "Les tablettes de Kerkouk et les origines de la civilisation assyrienne," *Babyloniaca* 9 (1926) 69–151; 157–212.

23 C.J. Gadd, "Tablets from Kirkuk," *RA* 23 (1926) 49–151 (p. 53).

24 P. Koschaker, *Neue Keilschriftliche Rechtsurkunden aus der El-Amarna Zeit*, (= *NKRUA*), Leipzig 1928, 9–20.

25 M. Berkooz, *The Nuzi Dialect of Akkadian. Orthography and Phonology*, Philadelphia 1937.

of rare signs, were collected and studied. Peculiarities of writing were considered to be the result of a phonology strongly influenced by Hurrian (e.g., metatheses that actually reflected dialectal differences between the eastern Hurrian of Nuzi and that of western Hurrian).

Von Soden summarized all these elements in the introduction to his *Syllabar*:[26] In particular, he underlined the internal consistency of the Nuzi syllabary, while acknowledging that Middle Assyrian and Middle Babylonian peculiarities are recognizable as well. According to von Soden, some values, such as *šúk*, *šina*, and $\check{s}ir_9$ were the result of an internal development in the Nuzi syllabary that, in any case, can be connected directly to the Hurrian syllabary. In his study of the Akkadian of Nuzi, Wilhelm[27] determined that certain elements of the syllabary belong to the beginning stage of Middle Babylonian, where the signs for emphatic consonants and the use of intervocalic /*w*/ or /*m*/, in particular, can be used to establish the date of the Nuzi syllabary.

These studies on paleography and the syllabary present only some of the elements that have attracted the attention of scholars. Detailed studies were also carried out on other relevant phenomena, such as (1) variations in the use of ideogrammatic or syllabic writing; (2) variations in the use of phonetic complements; (3) inconsistent writing of stops; (4) variation in the use of CV-VC or CVC signs—the use of the latter increasing during the latest scribal generations.

A significant aspect of the Nuzi texts are the variations in writing within the same text or context. Some scribes wrote the same word in different ways either in the same or different texts, but always in the same context. For example, (1) Aḫa-ai-amši writes *abullu* as KÁ.GAL and *a-bu-ul-li*; (2) the ratio in the use/lack of phonetic complements in Ḫutiya son of Arip-šarri is 2:7; and (3) Taya son of Apil-Sîn in the heading of the *ṭuppi mārūti* can alternatively use either *ēpuš* or *ētepuš*. These are only a few examples drawn from a systematic analysis of graphemic, grammatical, and syntactical features of the scribes.

For this reason an analytical description of graphemic features of every scribe can be useful. There are many graphemic features that must be taken into consideration for an exhaustive analysis of the data. Some examples, in addition to what has been mentioned above, are the alternation in the writing of personal name elements, the graphemes used in verbal forms, the insertion of new vowels, and modifying consonants. Through a complex analysis of the data it is possible to reconstruct distinctive features of each scribe and compare them with other scribes in order to identify groups, schools, and trends in the scribal system at Nuzi. In any case, all these variations in writing appear to demonstrate that Nuzi scribes, their school, and scribal system, were dynamic and active in every phase of their history.

---

26 W. von Soden, *Das Akkadische Syllabar*, Rome 1967^2, p. xxxvii.

27 G. Wilhelm, AOAT 9, 15–16.

LINGUISTIC FEATURES

Scholars, including Gordon,[28] Speiser,[29] and Lacheman,[30] oriented their pioneering analyses to shed light on various peculiarities present in the Nuzi texts. Because of the differences with Standard Babylonian and the presence of elements similar to the language known from the Mittani Letter, the language of the Nuzi texts was identified early on as a kind of peripheral Akkadian heavily influenced by Hurrian.

Gordon described the language of the Nuzi texts for those who intended to study Akkadian dialects. He focused his attention on peculiarities that made the interpretation of the texts more difficult, such as the confusion of person, number, and gender; the use of the masculine forms of verbal suffixes instead of feminine forms; and the interchange of subject and object.

Tablets from Alalaḫ offered interesting parallels for the study of Nuzi texts.[31] Some linguistic features were occasionally noted in von Soden's, GAG,[32] which remains the standard reference work for the study of Akkadian and its dialects. But the major work on the Hurro-Akkadian dialect of Nuzi was carried out by Wilhelm.[33] Wilhelm provided a descriptive grammar in which features of the Nuzi language were studied analytically. The presence of both Old and Middle Babylonian features indicates that the Nuzi dialect may have been an intermediate stage between both these Babylonian dialects (agreeing with Gordon's earlier conclusions). The presence of some Middle Assyrian features (in the writings of about 25% of the scribes) indicates the influence of that dialect. Hurrian elements analyzed in depth in Wilhelm's study consist of syntactical peculiarities of the verb that, hitherto, usually had not been taken into consideration. Wilhelm also noted the differences among scribal generations, as indicated in his analysis of the Hurrian *anīna*-sentence in use in texts of the third and fourth generations.

---

28 C.H. Gordon; "Numerals in the Nuzi Tablets," *RA* 31 (1934) 53–60; *idem*, "The Pronoun in the Nuzi Tablets," *AJSL* 51 (1934/35) 1–21; *idem*, "Nouns in the Nuzi Tablets," *Babyloniaca* 16 (1936) 1–153; *idem*, "The Dialect of the Nuzu Tablets," *Or*NS 7 (1938) 32–63; 215–32.

29 Cf., e.g., E.A. Speiser, "New Kirkuk Documents Relating to Family Laws," *AASOR* 10 (1932) 1–73; *idem*, "New Kirkuk Documents Relating to Security Transaction," *JAOS* 52 (1932), 350–67, *JAOS* 53 (1933) 24–46; *idem*, "Nuzi Marginalia," *Or*NS 25 (1956) 1–23; *idem*, "A Significant New Will from Nuzi," *JCS* 17 (1963) 65–71.

30 Cf. e.g., E.R. Lacheman, "New Nuzi Texts and a New Method of Copying Cuneiform Tablets," *JAOS* 55 (1935) 429–31; *idem*, "An Omen Text from Nuzi," *RA* 34 (1937) 1–8; *idem* "Epigraphic Evidence of the Material Culture of the Nuzians," in R.F. Starr, *Nuzi* I, Cambridge, Mass. 1939, Appendix D, 528–44; *idem*, "Nuziana I: Tablettes Scolaires," *RA* 36 (1939) 81–95; *idem*, "Nuziana II" *RA* 36 (1940) 113–219.

31 E.A. Speiser, *Introduction to Hurrian* (AASOR 20), New Haven 1941.

32 W. von Soden, *Grundriß der Akkadischen Grammatik*, (=GAG; AnOr 33), Rome: Pontificium Institutum Biblicum, 1952.

33 G. Wilhelm, AOAT 9, *cit*. For the definition of the language of the Nuzi texts as "Hurro-Akkadisch," see p. 12, n. 6.

Probably only a few scribes were native-speakers of Akkadian (see above); it is likely that for most scribes, Akkadian was a foreign language to be mastered in school. However, Nuzi scribes rapidly developed their own style. It was a complex development that can be partially reconstructed from the existing texts. This process is discernible in their attempt to standardize contract clauses. In late *ṭuppi mārūti* texts, scribes could employ at least seven clauses:[34] *ṭuppi mārūti, ana mārūti epēšu, kīma zitti, kīma qīsti, birqu/bāqirānu rasû, ilku*-clause, *nabalkutu*-clause, to which the *mušelwû*-clause in the witness lists could be added. Some of these clauses were present among the texts of the earliest scribes (e.g., *ṭuppi mārūti* occurs in the texts of Apil-Sîn). It is also possible to follow the evolution of different clauses through the generations of scribes. However, some scribes never used these clauses, whereas others used them sporadically. Therefore an analysis of the internal structure of the texts, and, in particular, the presence or absence of clauses and formulaic sentences, along with parallels from other areas and a comparison with lexical lists,[35] offers the possibility to better understand certain aspects of the Nuzi dialect.

Another important line of research relates to the presence of Hurrian elements. It is interesting to observe that practically no complete Hurrian sentence has been found in the Nuzi tablets even though Hurrian words and clauses are incorporated frequently into the texts. A significant amount of recent research focuses on the Hurrian lexicon and grammatical forms in the Nuzi texts, providing new data for interpreting obscure passages in the tablets.

Scribal Status

Distribution in Different Social Classes

According to recent studies on Nuzi society, the kingdom of Arrapḫa reflects the same complexity as other surrounding regions. The population was comprised of distinct classes and groups to which different duties and obligations were attached and people could be free, enslaved, or of varying degrees of freedom.[36] Scribes were found in almost all social classes. Many members of the scribal family of Apil-Sîn belonged to the upper class of the charioteers (*rākib narkabti*); their names appear in lists and rolls together with princes (*mār šarri*).

Scribes such as Kase, the scribe of the *bīt ḫurizati*, belonged to the *nakkuššu* class.[37] Four scribes are known to have been palace servants (*warad ekalli*)—

---

34 A. Fadhil, "Ein frühes *ṭuppi mārūti* aus Tell al-Faḫḫār/Kurruḫanni," *SCCNH* 1 (1981) 363–76.

35 G. Dosch, "Ein neues Nuzi-Graphem für den Ausdruck *abbutta muššuru* und neue Gedanken zu den Strafklauseln," *SCCNH* 2 (1987) 77–87.

36 Cf. G. Dosch, *Zur Struktur der Gesellschaft des Königreichs Arrapḫe* (HSAO 5), Heidelberg: Heidelberger Orientverlag, 1993.

37 IM 49137.

Aḫa-ai-amši, Arip-šarri, Tarmi-Teššup, and Unap-Teššup. They were clearly high-ranking officials and had a close, working relationship with the palace. Yet, one of them, Arip-šarri, seems to have enjoyed some degree of professional freedom, as he also practiced as a scribe in private matters (e.g., he seals the documents he writes). The scribe Attilammu entered the house of Teḫip-Tilla as an Assyrian *ḫabiru*, yet his writings do not reveal any distinctive Assyrian features. The scribe Ir-muša seems to have been a slave (he is identified as ÌR Keliya), but he may be the official mentioned in a private archive, which would indicate some degree of autonomy.

Non-Scribal Activities

Scribal activity were not limited to writing. Some certainly occupied administrative posts, and that sphere of activity was quite broad. An analysis of certain administrative texts provides evidence of how scribes were responsible to specific sections in the administration. In particular, they were concerned with the control of goods circulating inside or outside the palace. They could also seal texts as witnesses. Their appearance in military rolls and lists is proof of their involvement in military activities. Furthermore, professions such as priests and diviners usually required some scribal training. Scribes were divided or organized into several groups or categories. Designations such as *ṭupšar šarri* or *ṭupšar bīt ḫurizati* (as with Kase, see above) reflect categories of scribes, a practice known from other Mesopotamian sources.

Data from the Nuzi texts are, in general, very scarce and do not permit the full reconstruction of the scribal system. However, there is sufficient evidence that the organization of this important profession was quite complex. The existence of *warad ekalli* scribes, palace scribes, recalls the situation in the Hittite bureaucracy. It is also possible to suppose the existence of an internal hierarchy indicated only by the fact that *warad ekalli* scribes could work for private households. An analysis of the scribal connections to these families might reveal the background to their activities.

THE SCHOOL

Among the texts found in private houses, a small group of texts that have been categorized as "school texts" was excavated in the southwest area of the town of Nuzi.[38] Starr suggested that there was a "scribal quarter in that area."[39] Other data do not support this suggestion,[40] even if the southwest area of Nuzi was a place where many texts were written[41] and where scribes were very active. This recalls the situation in the House of Ku-Ningal on no. 7 Quiet Street at Ur,

38 E.R. Lacheman, "Nuziana I: Tablettes Scolaires," *RA* 36 (1939) 81–95.

39 R. Starr, *Nuzi I*, 285.

40 M. Morrison, "The Southwest Archives at Nuzi," *SCCNH* 2 (1987) 167–201, esp. p. 187.

41 P. Negri Scafa, "Gates in the Texts of the City of Nuzi," *SCCNH* 9 (1998) 139–62 (161),

where school tablets were found, but which does not seem to have been an é-dub-ba even if some school activity was carried out there.[42]

Our difficulties in understanding the transmission of the scribal arts in Nuzi involve the interpretation of the phrase, "NP_1 scribe son of NP_2." It is possible that, as in other areas of the ancient Near East, a scribe would train his own children to be scribes, passing the craft on within the family. Another possibility is that "son of..." is to be interpreted as "pupil of...." This interpretation has been suggested for Apil-Sîn and his scribal family, taking into consideration the high number of "sons" of Apil-Sîn. Wilhelm, in his reconstructed family tree of the scribe Apil-Sîn concluded that these scribes were pupils of Apil-Sîn ("die Schule des Apil-Sîn").[43] In some cases, however, it is possible to demonstrate from lists of personnel and military rolls that "son of..." indicates the true patronymics of the scribes. Therefore, the interpretation of the phrase "son of" remains an open question. One possible resolution may come from a comparison between the graphemic, grammatical, and syntactical features and characteristics of the "scribe father" and "scribe son," in order to determine if they belong to the same school tradition. If features of the scribal "father's" written language differ from those of the "son," it may be an indication that the "scribe's father" is the natural father of "the son," but not his teacher.

Concluding Remarks

It is evident that Nuzi scribes developed a coherent system to express their dialect. A comparison with other writing systems in use in the second millennium may be very useful to better define the Nuzi system and appreciate its relationships with other peripheral systems. Some elements suggest that this method is particularly fruitful. For example, the writing of the personal name *Pa-an-ti-ya* in a text of Apil-Sîn, which is written by later scribes as *Wa-an-ti-ya,* may be related to the personal name *Pa-ti-ib-šarri* in Tell Brak 7035, a parallel of which is Wanti-šarri. The fact that Apil-Sîn is an early Nuzi scribe may be important for understanding developmental relationships. Other elements that are similar in Nuzi writing to those in surrounding areas are perhaps to be connected to earlier traditions. Among these are the writing ^{d}*Ne/Ni-ri-ig-la* in JEN 29 for the name of Nergal, to be compared (according to Wilhelm) with ^{d}*Ni-ri-ig-lá* at Tell Leilan; or a list in a school text of Emar (Emar VI/2 540) to be partially compared with SMN 2559. Furthermore, cases of the confusion in the writing of voiced and voiceless stops in a Mari letter (A. 2995 + M 14337) written in Dêr by a local scribe—who writes *Ter* instead of *Der, tabābum* instead of

where *abullu ša šupūli* is identified with *abullu ša Tiššae;* the southwestern area of the city was a very important place for the redaction of contracts and many texts were written there.

42 D. Charpin, *Le clergé d'Ur au siècle d'Hammurabi (XIXe–XVIIIe siècles av. J.-C.)*, Genève-Paris: Librairie Droz, 1986.

43 G. Wilhelm, AOAT 9, l.c.

dabābum, *târum* instead of *dârum*—seem to be determined by phonological factors.

These comparisons derive from the regions of Upper Mesopotamia and Syria, where the Mittani Kingdom originated. Therefore, it might be useful to widen the analyses of internal data to include materials from other areas to try to reconstruct the origin and development of the Nuzi writing system and dialect. Studies like these should not only improve our knowledge of the Nuzi linguistic system, but also reveal the extent to which this system was innovative. Other valuable studies and analyses remain to be undertaken, such as a study of the organization of groups or families of scribes, or an analysis of unsigned texts in order to identify different scribal hands as a preliminary stage in the reconstruction of the internal organization of administrative bureaus. Much remains to be done.

Appendix

Nuzi Text Editions

During the last few years many new Nuzi texts and fragments have been published and many previously published texts and fragments have been collated or joined. The following is an up-to-date list of all editions of Nuzi texts from the earliest to the most recent (not including those in the current volume).

Series and Monographs

AASOR 16	R.H. Pfeiffer and E.A. Speiser, *One Hundred New Selected Nuzi Texts* (AASOR 16), New Haven 1936 [AASOR 16 51 = E.R. Lacheman, *Sumer* 32, 9; AASOR 16 76 = HSS XIV 20].
AdŠ	G. Wilhelm, *Das Archiv des Šilwa-teššup, Heft 2: Rationenlisten I*, Wiesbaden 1980.
	G. Wilhelm, *Das Archiv des Šilwa-teššup, Heft 3: Rationenlisten II*, Wiesbaden 1985.
	G. Wilhelm, *Das Archiv des Šilwa-teššup, Heft 4: Darlehensurkunden und verwandte Texte*, Wiesbaden 1992.
Al-Rawi	F.N.H. Al-Rawi, *Studies in the Commercial Life of an Administrative Area of Eastern Assyria in the Fifteenth Century B.C.*, Based on Published and Unpublished Cuneiform Texts, Ph.D. Thesis, University of Wales, 1977.
CNI 5	K. Grosz, *The Archive of the Wullu Family* (The Carsten Niebuhr Institute of Ancient Near Eastern Studies Publications 5), Copenhagen 1988.
CT 2	T.G. Pinches, *Cuneiform Texts from Babylonian Tablets in the British Museum* 2, London 1896.
CT 51	B.F. Walker, *Miscellaneous Texts, Cuneiform Texts from Babylonian Tablets in the British Museum* 51, London 1972.

EN 9/1 — E.R. Lacheman, D.I. Owen, and M.A.Morrison, "Excavations at Nuzi 9/1," *SCCNH* 2 (1987) 355–702.

EN 9/2 — E.R. Lacheman, D.I. Owen, and M.A. Morrison, "Excavations at Nuzi 9/2," *SCCNH* 4 (1993) 131–398.

EN 9/3 — E.R. Lacheman, D.I. Owen, and M.A. Morrison, "Excavations at Nuzi 9/3," *SCCNH* 5 (1995) 85–357.

EN 10/1 — J. Fincke, "Excavations at Nuzi" 10/1: nos. 1–65, *SCCNH* 8 (1996) 379–468.

EN 10/2 — J. Fincke, "Excavations at Nuzi" 10/2: nos. 66–174, *SCCNH* 9 (1997) 219–384.

HSS V — E. Chiera, *Texts of Varied Contents* (Excavations at Nuzi 1 - HSS V), Cambridge, Mass.: Harvard University Press, 1929.

HSS IX — R.H. Pfeiffer, *The Archives of Shilwateshub Son of the King* (Excavations at Nuzi 2 - HSS IX), *ibid.* 1932.

HSS X — T.J. Meek, *Old Akkadian, Sumerian, and Cappadocian Texts from Nuzi* (Excavations at Nuzi 3 - HSS X), *ibid.* 1935 [Nr. 231].

HSS XIII — R.H. Pfeiffer and E.R. Lacheman, *Miscellaneous Texts from Nuzi, Part* (Excavations at Nuzi 4 - HSS XIII), *ibid.* 1942.

HSS XIV — E.R. Lacheman, *Miscellaneous Texts from Nuzi, Part II: The Palace and Temple Archives* (Excavations at Nuzi 5 - HSS XIV), *ibid.* 1950.

HSS XV — E.R. Lacheman, *The Administrative Archives* (Excavations at Nuzi 6 - HSS XV), *ibid.* 1955.

HSS XVI — E.R. Lacheman, *Economic and Social Documents* (Excavations at Nuzi 7 - HSS XVI), *ibid.* 1958.

HSS XIX — E.R. Lacheman, *Family Law Documents* (Excavations at Nuzi 8 - HSS XIX), *ibid.* 1962.

JEN I — E. Chiera, *Inheritance Texts* (ASOR, Publications of the Baghdad School, Texts I: Joint Expedition with the Iraq Museum at Nuzi), Paris: Geuthner, 1927.

JEN II — E. Chiera, *Declarations in Court* (ASOR, Publications of the Baghdad School, Texts II: Joint Expedition with the Iraq Museum at Nuzi), Paris: Geuthner, 1930.

JEN III — E. Chiera, *Exchange and Security Documents*, (ASOR, Publications of the Baghdad School, Texts III: Joint Expedition with the Iraq Museum at Nuzi), Paris: Geuthner, 1931.

JEN IV — E. Chiera, *Proceedings in Court* (ASOR, Publications of the Baghdad School, Texts IV: Joint Expedition with the Iraq Museum at Nuzi), Philadelphia: University of Pennsylvania Press, 1934.

JEN V — E. Chiera, *Mixed Texts* (ASOR, Publications of the Baghdad School, Texts V: Joint Expedition with the Iraq Museum at Nuzi), Philadelphia: University of Pennsylvania Press, 1934.

JEN VI — E.R. Lacheman, *Miscellaneous Texts*, (ASOR, Publications of the Baghdad School, Texts VI: Joint Expedition with the Iraq Museum at Nuzi), New Haven: American Schools of Oriental Research, 1939.

JEN VII — E.R. Lacheman and M.P. Maidman, "Joint Expedition with the Iraq Museum at Nuzi VII. Miscellaneous Texts," *SCCNH* 3 (1989).

LNT — G.G.W. Müller, *Londoner Nuzi-Texte* (SANTAG 4), Wiesbaden: Harrassowitz, 1998.

Lutz, UCP 9,11 H.F. Lutz, "A Legal Document from Nuzi," *University of California Publications in Semitic Philologie* Vol. 9, No. 11, Berkeley: University of California Press, 1931, 405–12, pl. 12.

MCB L. Speleers, *Recueil des Inscriptions de l'Asie Anterieure des Musees Royaux du Cinquantenaire à Bruxelles, Textes sumeriens, babyloniens et assyriens*, Brussels 1995, Nr. 309 and Nr. 310.

MLS 11 F.M.Th. de Liagre Bohl, *Mededeelingen uit de Leidsche verzameling van spijkerschrift-inscripties 2: Oorkonden uit de periode van 2000 – 1200 v.Chr.* (Mededeelingen der Koninglijke Akademie van Wetenschappen, Afdeeling Letterkunde), Amsterdam 1934, p. 44.

RATK A. Fadhil, *Rechtsurkunden und administrative Texte aus Kurruḫanni*, Magister-Arbeit, Universität Heidelberg, 1972.

TCL 9 G. Contenau, *Contrats et Lettres d'Assyrie et de Babylonie* (Textes Cuneiformes du Louvre 9), Paris 1926, Nr. 1–46.

VS 1 *Vorderasiatische Schriftdenkmaler der königlichen Museen zu Berlin* 1, Leipzig: J.C. Hinrichs, 1907, Nr. 106–11 (copied by A. Ungnad).

Articles

'Atiqot S. Levy and P. Artzi, "Sumerian and Akkadian Documents from Public and Private Collections in Israel," *'Atiqot* 4 (1964), pl. 45–47, no. 93 (= JEN 20).

Al-Rawi, *Sumer* 36 F.N.H. Al-Rawi, "Two Tidennutu Documents From Tell Al-Fahar," *Sumer* 36 (1980) 133–8 [IM 70882 = Fadhil, RATK No. 18].

Arnaud, *RA* 68 D. Arnaud: [Review with] "Annexe I: Quatre fragments de Nuzi" [AO 2161, AO 8151, AO 8152, AO 8153], *RA* 68 (1974) 174–79.

Brinkman/Donbaz, *OrAnt* 16
A. Brinkman and V. Donbaz, "A Nuzi-Type *Ṭidennūtu* Tablet Involving Real Estate," *OrAnt* 16 (1977) 99–104, Tav. V–VII.

Cassin, *RA* 56 E. Cassin, "Tablettes inédites de Nuzi," *RA* 56 (1962) 57–80.

Contenau, *RA* 28 G. Contenau, "Textes et Monuments, I: Tablettes de Kerkouk du Musee du Louvre," *RA* 28 (1931) 27–39.

Deller, *WO* 9 K. Deller, [Rezension zu.] B.L. Eichler, Indenture at Nuzi, *WO* 9 (1977–78) 297–305.

Donbaz, *SCCNH* 2 Donbaz, "Two Documents from the Diverse Collections in Istanbul," *SCCNH* 2 (1987) 69–75.

Donbaz/Kalaç, *ZA* 71 V. Donbaz and M. Kalaç, "Two Tablets from Nuzi Housed in Istanbul," *ZA* 71 (1981) 205–14 (Nu. 2, Nu. 3).

Ebeling, *OrNS* 22 E. Ebeling, "Ein Brief aus Nuzi im Besitz des Athener Archäologischen Museums," *Or*NS 22 (1953) 355–58.

Fadhil, *SCCNH* 1 A. Fadhil, "Ein frühes *ṭuppi mārūti* aus Tell al-Faḫḫār / Kurruḫanni," *SCCNH* 1 (= Fs. Lacheman, 1981) 363–76.

Fincke, *AoF* 21 J. Fincke, "Noch einmal zum mittelassyrischen *šiluḫli*," *AoF* 21 (1994) 339–51.

Fincke, *SCCNH* 7a J. Fincke, "Beiträge zum Lexikon des Hurritischen von Nuzi," *SCCNH* 7 (1995) 5–22.

Fincke, *SCCNH* 7b J. Fincke, "Einige Joins von Nuzi-Texten des British Museum," *SCCNH* 7 (1995) 23–36.

Fincke, *SCCNH* 8 — J. Fincke, "Weitere Joins von Nuzi-Texten," *SCCNH* 8 (1996) 273–81.

Fincke, *SCCNH* 9a — J. Fincke, "Beiträge zum Lexikon des Hurritischen von Nuzi, Teil 2," *SCCNH* 9 (1998) 41–48.

Fincke, *SCCNH* 9b — J. Fincke, "More Joins Among the Texts from Arrapḫa (Kirkuk)," *SCCNH* 9 (1998) 49–62.

Fincke, *SCCNH* 9c — J. Fincke, "Nuzi Fragments from the Estate of R.F.S. Starr," *SCCNH* 9 (1998) 63–70.

Gadd *RA* 23 — C.J. Gadd, "Tablets from Kirkuk," *RA* 23 (1926) 19–161.

Ismail/Müller, *WO* 9 — B. Khalil Ismail and M. Müller, "Einige bemerkenswerte Urkunden aus Tell al-Faḫḫār zur altmesopotamischen Rechts-, Sozial- und Wirtschaftsgeschichte," *WO* 9 (1977) 14–34.

Deller/Fadhil, *Mesopotamia* 7 — K. Deller and A. Fadhil, "nin.dingir.ra / *entu* in den Texten aus Nuzi und Kurruḫanni," *Mesopotamia* 7 (1972) 193–213.

Jank. — N.B. Jankowskaja, "Juridičeskie dokumenty iz Arrapachi v sobranijach SSSR," *Peredneaziatskij Sbornik: Voprosy Chettologii i Churritologii*, Moskva 1961, 424–580, 603–4.

Koschaker, *ZA* 48 — P. Koschaker, "Drei Rechtsurkunden aus Arrapḫa," *ZA* 48 (1944) 161–221.

Krebernik, *SCCNH* 8 — M. Krebemik, "Eine 'Memorandum'-Tafel (*ṭuppi taḫsilti*)," *SCCNH* 8 (1996) 305–8.

Lacheman, *Genava* — E.R. Lacheman, "Les tablettes de Kerkouk au Musee d' art et d'histoire de Geneve," *Genava N.S.* 15 (1967) 5–23.

Lacheman, *JAOS* 55 — E.R. Lacheman, "New Nuzi Texts and a New Method of Copying Cuneiform Tablets," *JAOS* 55 (1935) 429–31, Plates I–VI.

Lacheman, *RA* 34 — E.R. Lacheman, "An Omen Text from Nuzi," *RA* 34 (1937) 1–8.

Lacheman, *RA* 36 — E.R. Lacheman, "Nuziana," *RA* 36 (1939) 81–95, 113–219.

Lacheman, *Sumer* 32 — E.R. Lacheman, "Tablets from Arraphe and Nuzi in the Iraq Museum," *Sumer* 32 (1976) 113–48.

Maidman — M.P. Maidman, "Some Late Bronze Age Legal Tablets from the British Museum: Problems of Context and Meaning," in B. Halpern and D.W. Hobson, eds., *Law, Politics and Society in the Ancient Mediterranean World*, Sheffield, 1993, pp. 42–89.

Maidman, *SCCNH* 7 — M.P. Maidman, "A Unique Teḫip-Tilla Family Document from the British Museum" *SCCNH* 7 (1995) 57–64.

Maidman, *SCCNH* 9 — M.P. Maidman, "JEN 775–780: The Text Editions," *SCCNH* 9 (1998) 95–124.

Maidman, *SCCNH* 10 — M.P. Maidman, "JEN 781–789: The Text Editions," *SCCNH* 10 (1999) 329–73.

Meissner, *OLZ* 5 — B. Meissner, "Thontafeln aus Vyran sehir," *OLZ* 5 (1902) 245–46 [= V. Scheil, Nouvelles notes d'epigraphie et d'archeologie assyriennes, II. Lettre assyrienne de Kerkouk, *RT* 31 (1909) 56–58].

Millard, *SCCNH* 1 — A.R. Millard, "Strays from a 'Nuzi' Archive, with an appendix: Two Nuzi Texts in the Wellcome Institute for the History of Medicine," *SCCNH* 1 (= Fs. Lacheman, 1981) 433–41.

Müller, *SCCNH* 5	M. Müller, "Ein Prozess um einen Kreditkauf in Nuzi," *SCCNH* 1 (= Fs. Lacheman, 1981) 443–54.
Müller, HSAO 7	G.G.W. Müller, "Studien zur Siedlungsgeographie und Bevölkerung des mittleren Osttigrisgebietes," *Heidelberger Studien zum alten Orient* 7, Heidelberg 1994, pp. 235–71.
Müller, *SCCNH* 8	G.G.W. Müller, "Bemerkungen zu Nuzi-Texten aus dem P.A. Hearst Museum/Berkeley," *SCCNH* 8 (1996) 309–19.
Nougayrol, *RA* 47	J. Nougayrol, "Une nouvelle 'mise a mort de Humbaba'," *RA* 47 (1953) 34.
Owen, *SCCNH* 1	D.I. Owen, "Text Fragments from Arrapḫa in the Kelsey Museum of Art and Archaeology, The University of Michigan," *SCCNH* 1 (= Fs. Lacheman, 1981) 455–68.
Owen, *SCCNH* 7	D.I. Owen, "An Old Assyrian Letter from Nuzi," *SCCNH* 7 (1995) 65–68.
Scheil, *RA* 15	V. Scheil, "Tablettes de Kerkouk," *RA* 15 (1918) 65–73.
Scheil, *RT* 31	V. Scheil, "Nouvelles notes d'épigraphie et d'archéologie assyriennes, 11. Lettre assyrienne de Kerkouk," *RT* 31 (1909) 56–58 [= B. Meissner, Thontafeln aus Vyran sehir, *OLZ* 5 (1902) 245–46].
Shaffer, *Fs. Oppenheim*	A. Shaffer, "*kitru/kiterru:* New Documentation for a Nuzi Legal Term," *Studies Presented to Leo A. Oppenheim*, Chicago 1964, 181–94.
Wilhelm, *SCCNH* 1	G. Wilhelm, "Zusammenschlüsse von Nuzi-Texten," *SCCNH* 1 (= Fs. Lacheman, 1981) 341–47.
Wilhelm, Xenia 21	G. Wilhelm, "Gedanken zur Frühgeschichte der Hurriter und zum hurritisch-urartäischen Sprachvergleich," in: V. Haas (ed.), *Hurriter und Hurritisch* (Xenia 21), Konstanz 1988, 58 [copy of HSS XVI 415].
Wilhelm, *SCCNH* 7	G. Wilhelm, "*Bīt papāḫi* in Nuzi," *SCCNH* 7 (1995) 121–28.
Wilhelm, *SCCNH* 7	G. Wilhelm, "Collations of the Wullu Archive in the Louvre," *SCCNH* 7 (1995) 129–34.
Yale	E.R. Lacheman - D.I. Owen, "Texts from Arrapḫa and from Nuzi in the Yale Babylonian Collection," *SCCNH* 1 (= Fs. Lacheman, 1981) 377–432.
Young, AOAT 22	G.D. Young, "Nuzu Texts in the Free Library of Philadelphia," (Fs. Gordon, AOAT 22), Kevelaer/Neukirchen-Vluyn 1973, 223–33.
Zaccagnini, *RA* 77	C. Zaccagnini, "A Nuzi-Type Loan-Contract," *RA* 77 (1983) 72–74.

"Nuzi Notes" Containing Texts

Nuzi Note 2	M.P. Maidman, "A Tale of Two Cities," *SCCNH* 2 (1987) 345–49.
Nuzi Note 3	M.P. Maidman, "A Second Teḫip-Tilla Fragment at Harvard," *SCCNH* 2 (1987) 349.
Nuzi Note 4	D.I. Owen, "A *tidennūtu* Fragment," *SCCNH* 2 (1987) 349–50.
Nuzi Note 5	D.I. Owen, "A New Reference to *irana*," *SCCNH* 2 (1987) 350–51.
Nuzi Note 6	D.I. Owen, "A Typical Loan Fragment," *SCCNH* 2 (1987) 350–51.
Nuzi Note 7	D.I. Owen, "A *ṭuppi zitti* Fragment," *SCCNH* 2 (1987) 351–52.

Nuzi Note 8	K. Grosz, "A New Fragment from the Archive of the Family of Akkuja," *SCCNH* 2 (1987) 352–54.
Nuzi Note 9	G. Wilhelm, "SMN 1636 Joined to HSS 13, 340," *SCCNH* 7 (1995) 143.
Nuzi Note 10	G. Wilhelm, "SMN 1687 Joined to HSS 19, 22," *SCCNH* 7 (1995) 144.
Nuzi Note 11	G. Wilhelm, "SMN 1696 Joined to EN 9/1, 122," *SCCNH* 7 (1995) 146.
Nuzi Note 12	G. Wilhelm, "SMN 1780 Joined to EN 9/1, 18," *SCCNH* 7 (1995) 147.
Nuzi Note 13	G. Wilhelm, "SMN 2957 Joined to EN 9/1, 19," *SCCNH* 7 (1995) 148.
Nuzi Note 14	M. Klein, "HSS 15, 50 Joined to HSS 15, 111," *SCCNH* 7 (1995) 150.
Nuzi Note 15	M. Klein, "One Fragment from NTF M 16 A Joined to HSS 16, 370," *SCCNH* 7 (1995) 151.
Nuzi Note 16	G. Wilhelm, "Identifikationen von ERL-Nummern," *SCCNH* 7 (1995) 151.
Nuzi Note 20	M. Klein, "HSS 14, 60 incorrectly joined," *SCCNH* 8 (1996) 349.
Nuzi Note 22	G. Wilhelm, "SMN 1621 joined to HSS 13, 218," *SCCNH* 8 (1996) 351.
Nuzi Note 27	J. Fincke, "*pizipsumma epēšu*," *SCCNH* 8 (1996) 357.
Nuzi Note 28	G. Wilhelm, "*aladumma epēšu* 'begleichen; kaufen'," *SCCNH* 8 (1996) 361.
Nuzi Note 29	G. Wilhelm, "SMN 1669 joined to HSS 13, 100," *SCCNH* 8 (1996) 364.
Nuzi Note 31	J. Fincke, "SMN 2799 and one unnumbered fragment joined to EN 9/2 455," *SCCNH* 8 (1996) 365.
Nuzi Note 32	M. Klein, "HSS 15, 317," *SCCNH* 8 (1996) 366.
Nuzi Note 36	J.W. Carnahan and A.D. Kilmer, "Nuzi Texts in the Hearst Museum, Additions and Corrections," *SCCNH* 9 (1998) 189.
Nuzi Note 37	J. Fincke, "NTF P 230(1) Joined to EN 9/1, 30," *SCCNH* 9 (1998) 190.
Nuzi Note 38	J. Fincke, "'Clay Bulla' no. 161 and SMN 2463 Joined to EN 9/2, 106," *SCCNH* 9 (1998) 191.
Nuzi Note 39	J. Fincke, "NTF P 2(1) and 'Clay Bulla' no. 748 Joined to EN 9/2, 157," *SCCNH* 9 (1998) 193.
Nuzi Note 40	J. Fincke, "Unnumbered Fragment Joined to EN 9/2, 163," *SCCNH* 9 (1998) 194.
Nuzi Note 41	J. Fincke, "SMN 3718 Joined to EN 9/1, 170," *SCCNH* 9 (1998) 196.
Nuzi Note 42	J. Fincke, "SMN 2975 Joined to EN 9/2, 175," *SCCNH* 9 (1998) 197.
Nuzi Note 43	J. Fincke, "NTF P 233(1) and NTF P 173(1) Joined to EN 9/1, 500," *SCCNH* 9 (1998) 199.
Nuzi Note 44	J. Fincke, "'Clay Bulla' no. 125 Joined to HSS 13, 273," *SCCNH* 9 (1998) 200.
Nuzi Note 45	J. Fincke, "Unnumbered Fragment Joined to HSS 15, 140," *SCCNH* 9 (1998) 201.
Nuzi Note 46	J. Fincke, "'Clay Bulla' no. 13 Joined to EN 9/3, 328," *SCCNH* 9 (1998) 202.
Nuzi Note 47	J. Fincke, "HSS 19, 26 + HSS 19, 34 + EN 9/1, 241+ 'Clay Bulla' nos. 623+624+561," *SCCNH* 9 (1998) 203.
Nuzi Note 48	J. Fincke, "ERL 6 Joined to HSS 9, 158 (= IM 50841)," *SCCNH* 9 (1998) 205.
Nuzi Note 49	H. Schneider-Ludorff, "**tuḫbal* ," *SCCNH* 9 (1998) 206.
Nuzi Note 50	H. Schneider-Ludorff, "Zu UCLMA 9-3027," *SCCNH* 9 (1998) 208.

Nuzi Note 52 G. Wilhelm, "Fragment No. 1091 from NTF-P 51 Joined to EN 9/2, 345," *SCCNH* 9 (1996) 213.

Nuzi Note 53 G. Wilhelm, "Miscellaneous Collations," *SCCNH* 9 (1998) 214.

The Geography of the Nuzi Area

GERFRID G. W. MÜLLER
Wilhelms-Universität Münster

The study of the topography of the kingdom of Arrapḫa has been a focus of scholarly investigation almost since the publication of the first Nuzi texts. This paper outlines the progress made in the location of various towns and settlements mentioned in the texts from Arrapḫa and Nuzi and the roads that connected them.

A map of the kingdom of Arrapḫa can be drawn today on the basis of our knowledge of the toponomy and topography of the area. However, it is far from being a map in the modern sense that leads us from tell to tell over ancient tracks. It is rather a tool of our imagination that provides us with an idea of what we will have to look for once we will be able again to do field work in this area.

The following is a brief outline of how I reconstructed the basic grid of towns connected by roads mentioned in the Nuzi texts. At its core, the reconstruction is, in my opinion, quite reliable. But as long as we do not have more fixed points, all the localizations around the central roads and towns will remain quite speculative. Circles are used on the maps below to indicate tentative locations of towns and settlements.

The starting point and the destination of as many roads as possible had to be determined in order to begin my reconstruction. In 1938, when A. Leo Oppenheim made the first attempt to reconstruct the topography of the Nuzi area,[1] he could use only those roads whose starting points and destinations were mentioned in the texts. However, in many instances, only the destination of a road was given. The starting point had to be determined by an evaluation of the prosopographical data, a tedious task subsequently partly undertaken by Deller, Fadhil,[2] and Zaccagnini.[3] In the course of this study, a number of ghost towns, originating from misreadings, were eliminated. Work on recently

---

1 A.L. Oppenheim, "Étude sur la topographie de Nuzi," *RA* 35 (1938) 136–55.

2 A. Fadhil, *Studien zur Topographie und Prosopographie der Provinzstädte des Königreichs Arrapḫe* (Baghdader Forschungen 6), Mainz, 1983.

3 C. Zaccagnini, *The Rural Landscape of the Land of Arrapḫe*, Rome, 1979.

Studies on the Civilization and Culture of Nuzi and the Hurrians - 10

published texts, especially those from Arrapḫa in the British Museum[4] and from Nuzi in *Excavations at Nuzi* 9,[5] filled in some important gaps.

When the first reconstruction of the topography of the Nuzi area was attempted, there were only two fixed points—Arrapḫa (Kirkuk) and Nuzi (Yorghan Tepe). But when I began my study, two more had been determined —Kurruḫanni (Tell al-Faḫār) and Natmani (Tell ᶜAli), the Atmani of the Middle Assyrian tablets found at this site. Natmani is the most distant city from Nuzi and therefore the best place to begin to trace the routes to Nuzi from town to town on roads mentioned in the texts (see Map 1[6]). We know of two roads going

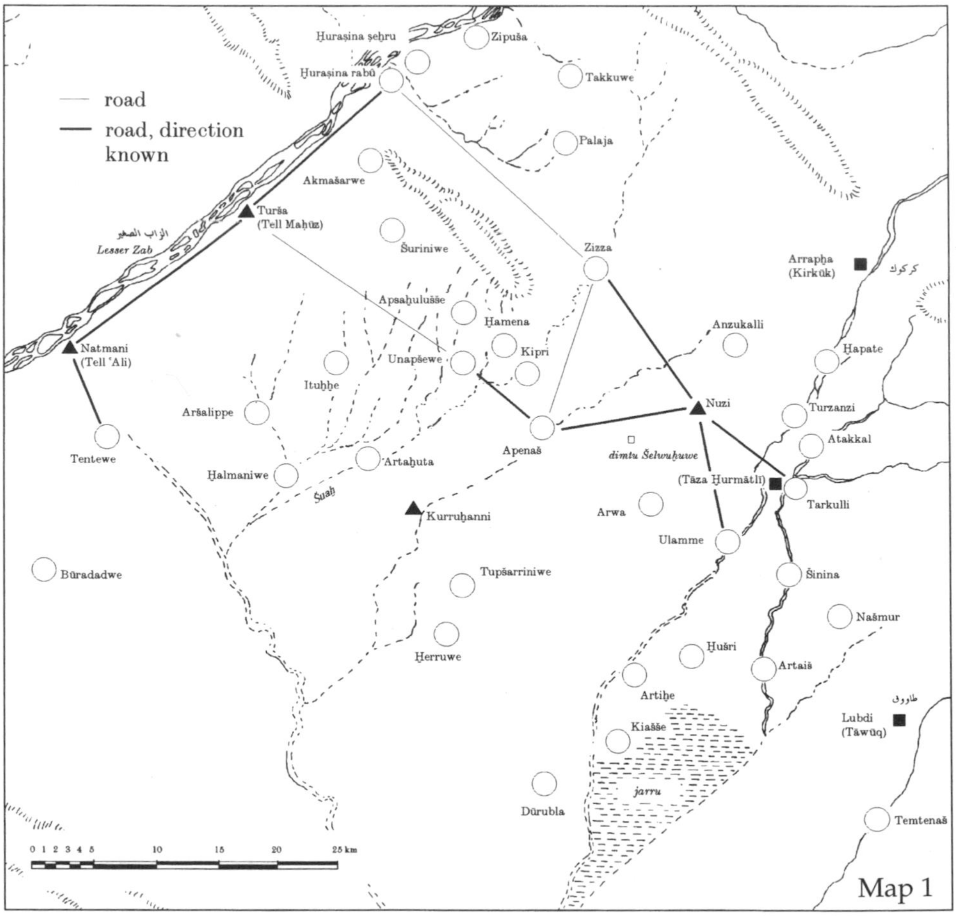

Map 1

4 See G.G.W. Müller, *Londoner Nuzi-Texte* (SANTAG 4), Wiesbaden: Harrassowitz, 1998, with further references, p. 16.

5 E.R. Lacheman†, M.A. Morrison, and D.I. Owen: "Excavations at Nuzi 9," published in three parts: EN 9/1 in *SCCNH* 2 (1987), EN 9/2 in *SCCNH* 4 (1993), EN 9/3 in *SCCNH* 5 (1995).

6 Only roads mentioned in this paper will be found on the map. For more details on the reconstruction, see G.G.W. Müller, *Studien zur Siedlungsgeographie und Bevölkerung des mittleren Osttigrisgebietes, Heidelberger Studien zum Alten Orient* (HSAO 7), Heidelberg, 1994.

from or to Natmani—one to Tentewe, the other to Turša. On the basis of the topographical data, Fadhil came to the conclusion that Turša was located on the bank of the Lower Zab and suggested this important settlement is probably buried under the huge Tell Maḫūz.[7] A Spanish expedition planned to investigate this tell but, because of the Gulf war, was, unfortunately, never able to begin work at the site.

From Turša two more roads go respectively to Ḫuraṣina rabû[8] and to Unapšewe. The latter is another important town surrounded by many *dimātu*, "hamlets." One of several roads connecting Unapšewe with other settlements in the area leads us to Apenaš, which is directly linked to Nuzi. The distance between Nuzi and Tell Maḫūz is approximately 40 km and between Tell Maḫūz and Tell ᶜAli about 18 km. Now there is not much doubt about the approximate location of the towns on the way from Natmani to Nuzi.

Ḫuraṣina rabû could also be reached from Turša. Ḫuraṣina rabû was close to Ḫuraṣina ṣeḫru, which was located to the east at a river, presumably the Lower Zab. Ḫuraṣina rabû was connected by another road with Zizza, which itself was linked by roads to Apenaš and Nuzi. Thus a second route from Natmani to Nuzi can be determined.

The descriptions of field locations, from which we get most of our information about roads, offers us clues to the direction of these roads. They describe fields in relation to roads, from which we can conclude that roads run basically (or at least when they pass fields) in east–west or north–south directions. The directions of roads determined from an analysis of the descriptions of field locations turn out to be quite reliable, especially if we take the north–south axis as parallel to the Zagros range.[9] As a result, I used these locations for the approximate positioning of other settlements that were not situated between firmly established locations.

A study of the general pattern of the watercourses provided additional clues. We know, e.g., that Unapšewe and Zizza were both at or close to a watercourse called Šuaḫ. We also know that Artiḫe was near a geographic feature called *jarru*, something like a lake, but most likely the swamp found on old (modern) maps of the area. However, the most complicated area to reconstruct was the region of Nuzi itself. This is no place to go into further detail, but the once proposed identification of Tarkulliwe with modern Tarkhalan is no longer tenable—the roads to Ulamme and Tarkulliwe run in a north–south direction. North of Nuzi there is no space at all for these settlements and also they are connected with other towns that have to be located in the south.

This topographical reconstruction provides us with an opportunity to raise further questions. One interesting point is the ethnic distribution in the region around Arrapḫa and Nuzi (Map 2). We find in the texts quite a few individuals

---

7 Fadhil, *Studien zur Topographie*, 194ff.

8 The text, Jank. 30, is restored, but not beyond any doubt.

9 The four points of the Babylonian compass follow the main directions of the winds.

from Ḫanigalbat, mainly charioteers, who were stationed in the vassal kingdom of Arrapḫa.[10] There were also many slaves from Lullubu (Nulluāju), who came as prisoners of war or were imported by merchants from the Zagros northeast of Nuzi. But what is of more interest to us here is the distribution of the settled population, the Hurrian Arrapḫeans, the Assyrians, the Babylonians, and the Kassites.

Basically the inhabitants of the land of Arrapḫa were Hurrians, as reflected in their personal names and toponyms. If we look at the map of settlements that can be tentatively located, we find only a few towns with non-Hurrian names. The most western is Būr-Adadwe, definitely an Akkadian name ("calf of Adad") with a Hurrian genitive suffix ("town of B.").[11] Ibašši-il-we may be located in the same area; but this cannot be determined with certainty.

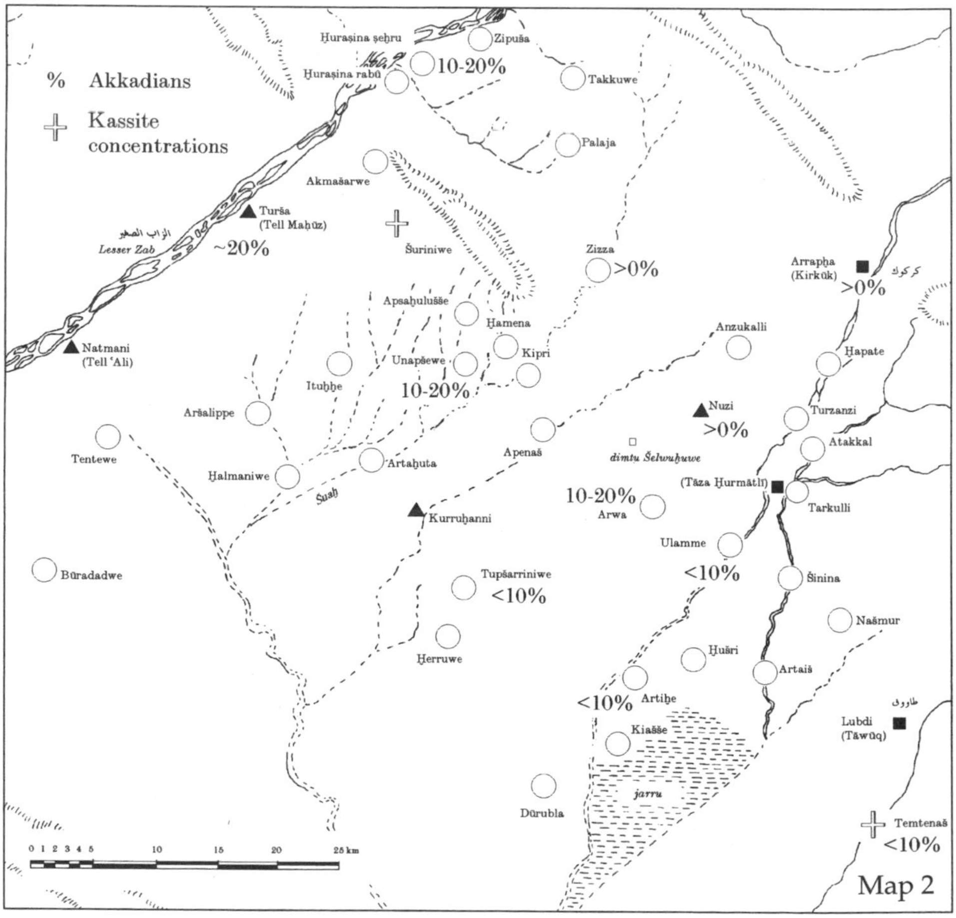

Map 2

---

[10] Cf. C. Zaccagnini, "Les rapports entre Nuzi et Hanigalbat," *Assur* 2/1 (1979) 1–27. See also K. Deller, "Ḫanigalbatäische Personennamen," *NABU* 1987/53.

[11] Since designations of settlements by personal names (of the founder or the like) are very common, a derivation from *būru*, "well," is most unlikely.

In the north we see Ḫuraṣina ṣeḫru and rabû, derived from Akkadian *ḫurāṣu*, "gold."[12] The *dimtu* of Bēlānu was adjacent to the area of Ḫuraṣina ṣeḫru. Further south, close to Unapšewe, there was, though not on the map, the *dimtu ša išparāti*, "hamlet of the weavers," in the area of Apsaḫulušše by the "big road" to Karāna. The location of Karāna, derived from Akkadian *karānu*, "wine," is a crux to the reconstruction. Unfortunately, the location of Karāna has not been determined, but we assume it was situated somewhere close to the Lower Zab, probably on its right bank, i.e., north of the river.

In the region of Apsaḫulušše we find also the *dimtu ša* Nulluenašwe, the "hamlet of the Lullubeans." Apart from this case, the Lullubeans never appear as a group but only as slaves and usually without personal names. In the same area we have to look for (*dimtu* or URU) Adad-šemiwe.

Another settlement called Irēm-Adad-we ("Adad showed mercy"), adjoined the *dimtu* Kizzuk, the latter named after the ancestor of the well-known Kassite family. There are some hints that the *dimtu* Kizzuk was close to Šuriniwe, between Unapšewe and the Lower Zab, although the reconstruction of this area is problematic. Even more uncertain is the location of Maškani(we), possibly west of Unapšewe, towards the Lower Zab. In the same region we have to look for Bēl-aḫḫē-šu-we.

The closer one comes to Aššur or the Lower Zab, the more Assyrian influence becomes evident. On the other hand, we find *dimātu*, like Bēlu-qarrād and Bēl-abi, in the vicinity of Nuzi, in the very heartland of Arrapḫa.

In the south there are two more places with names that may be Akkadian—Tupšarriniwe and Dūr-ubla. The latter is already attested in the Old Akkadian period, while the former may be derived from a Hurrian form *tupšarri* from Akkadian *ṭupšarru*, "scribe."

If we examine the names of people who are known to have been from the better-documented towns, we find only a few Akkadian names. In the center of the country, in Arrapḫa, Zizza, and Nuzi, the number of individuals with Akkadian names owning fields or houses is very small. The same holds true for the debtors we know from Tašenniwe, which must be sought not far from Arrapḫa. Only Arwa seems to have had a higher percentage of people with Akkadian names (between 10–20%); but the sample is rather small. Towards the south in Ulamme, Artiḫe, and Temtenaš, their share is under 10%.

In the west, Tupšarriniwe and Kurruḫanni, and even Šuriniwe in the north near the Lower Zab, each shows less than 10% Akkadian names. The important Unapšewe and Ḫuraṣina ṣeḫru on the Lower Zab have 10–20% among the owners of fields and houses and witnesses. In contrast, the individuals mentioned in the Puḫišenni S. Mušapu archive, which Fadhil ascribed to Unapšewe, reveal a very low frequency of Akkadian names, suggesting that not all these texts belong there. Finally, the case of Turša on the Lower Zab is not very clear. The landowners in the time of Teḫiptilla bearing Akkadian names make up 20% of the total; whereas, in later times, their share is less than 10%. On the other

12 Possibly an indication for gold that was washed out there from the river.

hand, we have clear evidence for some foreign migration into the region south of the Lower Zab. There exist a number of contracts in which Assyrian refugees (*ḫapiru*) voluntarily make themselves slaves of Teḫiptilla.[13] The reduction of the percentage of Akkadian names may be a result of assimilation.

As for the Kassites, the matter is more complicated. First of all, who is a Kassite? There are a number of personal names identified as Kassite since the publication of *Nuzi Personal Names*[14] and K. Balkan's *Kassitenstudien.*[15] A few of them are hybrid names, Kassite and Hurrian (e.g., Bula-nikir), but most are rarely attested or very short. The name Ḫašuar, for instance, seems to be a variant of Kassite *ḫašmar*, "falcon." Unfortunately, this name is quite common in contrast to most other alleged Kassite names—thereby introducing some Kassite presence into many households. Even a prince is called Ḫašuar; maybe his mother was a Kassite. But in most cases, Ḫašuar is the only Kassite name in the family.

Another example that illustrates the difficulties in recognizing Kassite names is the suffix *-uk*. Balkan[16] lists the names Sambi-ḫaruk (a horse name, besides Sambi-ḫari), Ula-gisuk, Kissuk (from Nuzi, besides Kissi-Ḫarbe and Kissi), and Galduk (also from Nuzi). Now we can add the name Nizzuk from recently published Nuzi texts in the British Museum where an individual bearing this name is explicitly called *kaššû* (without the determinative LÚ).[17] But does this mean that all the names with *-uk* are Kassite? In the "Ḫapiru Prism" of King Tunip-Teššup of Tikunani, published by M. Salvini in 1996, we find among perfectly good Hurrian names such names as *A-mu-ul-tu-uk* (VI 34, VIII 26), *A-wa-ar-tu-uk* (VI 41), *Ep-šu-un-tu-uk* (an overseer, VI 43), *E-zu-uk* (I 34), *Ḫe-er-ru-uk* (VII 35; cf. Ḫerri), and finally, under an overseer named *Gi-iz-zi* (cf. Kizzuk), *Ki-ir-tu-uk* (VIII 32) and *Ḫé-lu-uk* (VIII 36) (together with others with perfectly good Hurrian names like Kušuḫ-atal and Ari-n). Furthermore, *Pu-la-ḫa-li* (IV 54, VII 51) and *Ša-ka-ar-ak-ti* (V 9) appear in this prism—both claimed to be Kassite and both were present at Nuzi. The latter is known also as an element in Šagarakti-šuriaš, Šagarakti-Saḫ, and Šagarakti-Enlil, but the former is claimed only as being Kassite on the basis of the element *Ḫala*, the Kassite equivalent for ^{d}Gula.[18] Which name is really Kassite[19] and which person is Kassite?

---

13 E.g., JEN 456, 611, 613.

14 I.J. Gelb, P.M. Purves, A.A. McRae, *Nuzi Personal Names* (OIP 57), Chicago, 1949.

15 K. Balkan, *Kassitenstudien: 1. Die Sprache der Kassiten* (AOS 37), New Haven, 1954.

16 K. Balkan, *Kassitenstudien,* 223, Par. 74 b.

17 G.G.W. Müller, *Londoner Nuzi-Texte* (SANTAG 4), Wiesbaden, 1998, nos. 20 and 23.

18 Although Salvini recognized only one Kassite name (Šakarakti), Th. Richter recently pointed out that there might be more ("Anmerkungen zu den hurritischen Personennamen des *ḫapiru*-Prismas aus Tigunānu," *SCCNH* 9 [1998] 125–34).

19 To avoid further confusion: the mentioned names with *tuk* are definitely Hurrian (cf. *tukke* at Nuzi as well as the verbal elements in front of *-tuk*). I tend also to interpret at least Ḫerruk and Ḫeluk as Hurrian (cf. the honorific *-k-* that also appears in several names of deities; cf. I. Wegner, "Grammatikalische und lexikalische Untersuchungen hurritischer

The seals and seal impressions do not help either. The Kassite style seals—maybe we should better say seals with designs of Kassite inspiration—were used by individuals with Akkadian and Hurrian names as well as by persons with Kassite background (e.g., Ariḫḫamanna S. Turi-kintar) and appear to have been popular among scribes. On the other hand, the seals of the Kizzuk family mostly show Mittani designs.

If we accept the results of Balkan, Gelb, and Purves, as well as the rather optimistic ones of Deller and Dosch in their study on the Kizzuk family,[20] we come to the conclusion that Kassites lived everywhere in the land of Arrapḫa and even held high offices, such as held by the mayor of Nuzi, Kušši-Ḫarbe. Two of the three towns that are connected with the estates of the Kizzuk family are on our map: Temtenaš in the south and Šuriniwe in the north somewhere between Unapšewe and the Lower Zab. These two towns obviously were not situated side by side, as suggested by Deller and Dosch. The concentration of people of Kassite origin in the area around Šuriniwe is emphasized by the names of two nearby *dimātu*, Kizzuk and Ukin-Zaḫ.

Let us now turn to the economic geography. The domains of the royal household were concentrated, as far as we know, around Nuzi and down to Atakkal and Šinina. Other fields of the palace were in Tilpašte, probably situated somewhere in the vicinity of Atakkal and Šinina, as well as in Ḫulumeniwe (possibly near Zizza). Finally, there were fields in Turša. All these areas had a good water supply. Fields of queens were also situated in Nuzi, Atakkal, and Ulamme, as well as to the west of Unapšewe. The estates of Prince Šilwateššup were probably somewhere in the triangle Palaja - Arrapḫa - Nuzi resp. Arwa. Tašenniwe was probably near Arrapḫa but cannot be located with certainty. Other estates were also at Ṣillijawe near Nuzi and at Zizza.

The most important data for the reconstruction of the topography of the Nuzi area comes from the well-known Teḫiptilla archive. The fields of Teḫiptilla and his family, acquired by adoption, were mainly situated in or around Turša, Unapšewe, Zizza, Apenaš, Nuzi, Ulamme, Šinina, Ḫušri, and Artiḫe. The wide range of the estates (Map 3) now provides us with an idea of the mobility of the upper strata of Arrapḫean society. According to the witness lists, Teḫiptilla used to travel together with some confidants.

J. Fincke systematically collected all references to goods in connection with place names[21] in her volume of the *Repertoire géographique*. Whereas barley can be found virtually everywhere, wheat shows a specific distribution. Wheat came from Turša on the Lower Zab and from the best-watered area down from

---

Beschwörungsformeln aus Boğazköy," in V. Haas [Hrsg.], *Hurriter und Hurritisch* [Xenia 21], Konstanz, 1988, 149–50).

20 K. Deller and G. Dosch, "Die Familie Kizzuk – Sieben Kassitengenerationen in Temtena und Šuriniwe," *SCCNH* 1 [= Fs. Lacheman] (1981) 47–76. On the Kassite ethnicity, cf. M.P. Maidman, "Kassites among the Hurrians: A Case Study from Nuzi," *Bulletin of the Society for Mesopotamian Studies* [=*BSMS*] 8 (1984) 15–21.

21 RGTC 10, 428ff.

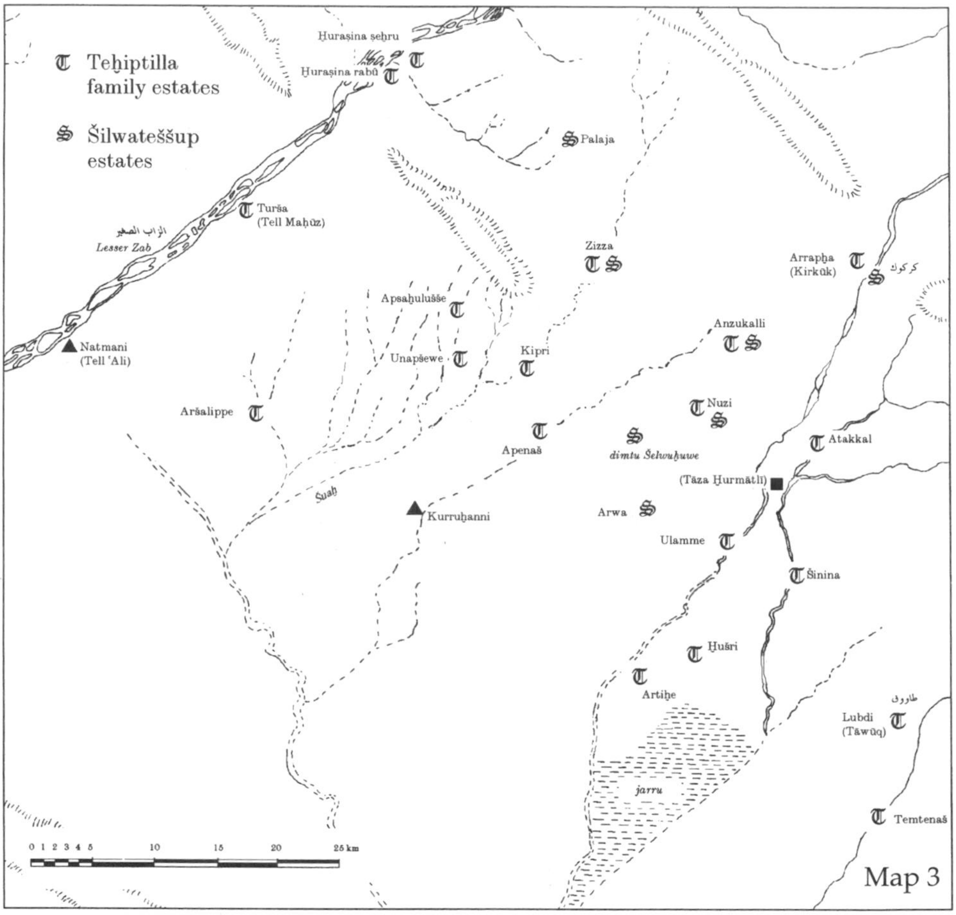

Palaja via Arrapḫa, Anzukalli, Nuzi, Tarkulli, Šinina, and Našmur, insofar as we can approximately fix the places of origin (Map 4). We find wheat also at Unapšewe close to the river Šuaḫ.

The percentage of irrigated fields cannot be determined with certainty because of the uneven distribution of the sources. In the better-documented towns of Turša, Unapšewe, Zizza, Nuzi, and Artiḫe, the percentage of fields that are explicitly said to be irrigated lies roughly between 10 and 20% with the lowest rate at Unapšewe with 12% according to Zaccagnini's calculation.[22] But in Apenaš, where the sources do not mention any canal, eight out of ten mentioned fields are irrigated. At the beginning of our century there was no agriculture at all in this area. However, the area of the fields in this region is much smaller than in the aforementioned cases. If we limit our sample to the *ṭuppi mārūti* texts, the percentage of irrigated field area looks somewhat different: Apenaš 88%, Zizza 64%, Turša 38%, Artiḫe 24%, Nuzi 22%, and

---

22 Zaccagnini, *Rural Landscape*, 111f. Cf. also *idem*, "Again on the Yield of Fields at Nuzi," *BSA* 5/2 (1990) 201–17.

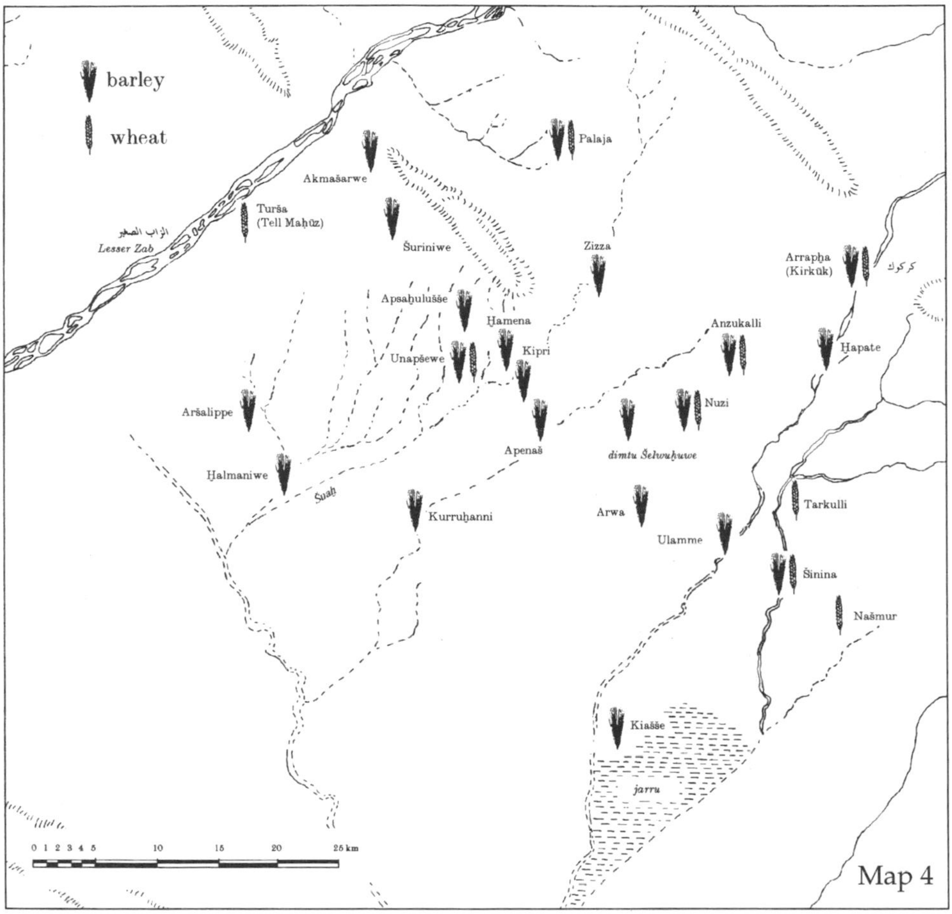

Map 4

Unapšewe 21%. Among other cities and unlocated fields, Zaccagnini counted only an 11% irrigated area. This is in contrast to the amount of irrigated fields in Unapšewe and again points to the importance of the river Šuaḫ in this area.

The yields, as far as we can calculate, reveal the most favorable conditions to be around Ulamme, Šinina, and Artiḫe, possibly also Apenaš with a ratio of roughly 1:8, followed by Nuzi, Zizza, Unapšewe, and Ḫuraṣina ṣeḫru at around 1:6. Turša and Tentewe, as well as Arrapḫa, possibly had lower yields, but the documentation is rather scarce in these cases.[23]

A good impression of the hydrological situation is provided by the distribution of settlements with gardens (Map 5). The fact that we find gardens also in Šuriniwe and Tentewe raises some doubt as to the exact location of these settlements. Interesting to note is the provenience of sesame seed from Ulamme, which was issued to people from Apenaš, Temtenaš, and Lubdi,[24] all places that

---

23 C. Zaccagnini, "The Yields of the Fields at Nuzi," *OrAnt* 14 (1975) 181–225; G.G.W. Müller, HSAO 7, 228–34.

24 HSS 14, 72.

were presumably rich in water, especially those at the foot of the mountains. *Uḫinnu,* "fresh, green dates," were delivered to Anzukalli and Lubdi.[25] The land of Arrapḫa is quite far north for the cultivation of dates since winter frost might make the palm trees burst. Thus the dates might not have originated from the Nuzi area.

Several spices, such as *kamūnu* (cumin) and *kusibarratu/ kussibirru* (coriander), and vegetables, such as *šimeru* (fennel), are mentioned as coming from Zizza, Ziziwe, and Durzanzi, but they grow everywhere.

Several items were imported—horses from the Lullubu in the northwest mountains, from Ḫanigalbat, and from the countries of Murkunaš/Murkušanni and Kuššuḫḫe, the land of the Kassites (perhaps beyond the Hamrin ridge). Also tin, as well as copper, came from Lullubu and was also imported from Akkad.

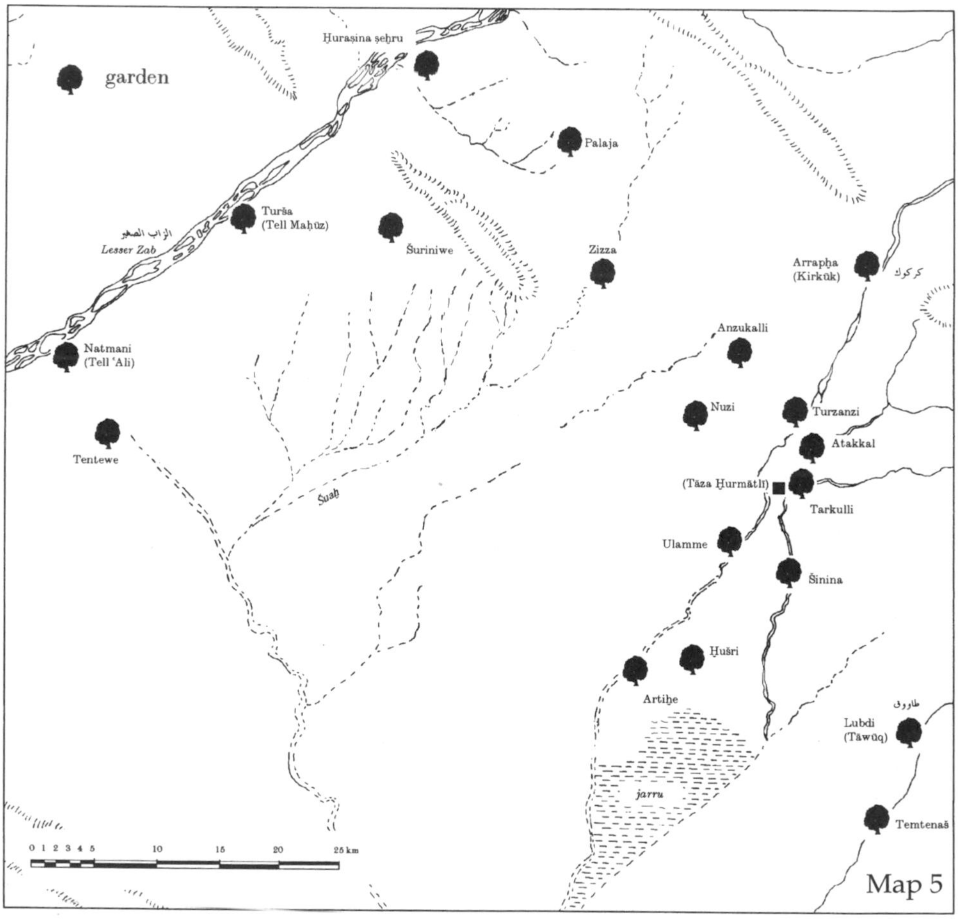

Map 5

25 HSS 14, 215.

Textiles were not only produced in the country, but also were imported from the surrounding countries of Akkad, Murkunaš/Murkušanni, Inzalzi, and Ḫanigalbat. Lower-quality textiles came from Nullu, the country of the Lullubeans.

We can look forward with great expectations to a future survey of the Arrapḫa area to improve and refine our reconstruction and to perhaps provide us with a picture of the actual settlement pattern. In addition, such a survey might give us more insight into the agricultural structure and climatic variations in the area. The finds from Nuzi and Kurruḫanni allow us the opportunity to obtain a clearer and more accurate image of the inner workings of the social and political structure of this little kingdom on the periphery of the cuneiform world.

Features of the Economy and Society of Nuzi: An Assessment in the Light of Recent Research

CARLO ZACCAGNINI

Istituto Universitario Orientale (Napoli)

During the past two decades research in Nuzi civilization has made great strides. This overview provides a summary of the recent research. It concludes with comments on two issues that have evoked much attention—that of the yield of grain in Nuzi agriculture and on the *ilku*-duties—along with observations on current trends in scholarship in Near Eastern society and economy.

During the past two decades, progress in the research field of Nuzi civilization has attained significant achievements. After a long lethargy, that was in part broken only by Jankovska's efforts to propose a new historiographic model for the interpretation of the Nuzi features of land ownership and transfer (see, e.g., Jankovska 1969; Jankovska 1969a), on the one hand, and on the other by certain University of Pennsylvania dissertations devoted to the investigation of a selection of relevant topics pertinent to the juridical and socio-economic aspects of the Nuzi public and private institutions (Eichler 1967, cf. Eichler 1973; Paradise 1972; Maidman 1976), fresh impetus was provided by the preliminary study of the *ca.* 850 Nuzi-type tablets retrieved some 30 years ago at Tell el-Faḫḫār—Kurruḫanni, most of which however are still unavailable, aside from those published in Fadhil and al-Rawi's dissertations and the few selected documents published by Ismail - Müller 1977; the meritorious publication of *ca.* 530 Harvard cuneiform copies drawn by Lacheman (Excavations at Nuzi, 9/1-2-3, in *SCCNH* 2 [1987], 4 [1993], 5 [1995]); the ongoing publication by J. Fincke of the remaining fragmentary tablets housed in the Harvard Semitic Museum (EN 10, in *SCCNH* 8 [1996], 9 [1998]); the *ca.* 200 Chicago copies by Lacheman (JEN 7: *SCCNH* 3 [1989], with Maidman's philological elaborations in *SCCNH* 6 [1994], *SCCNH* 9 [1998] 95–123, *SCCNH* 10 [1999], below, and elsewhere); the progressive availability of the *ca.* 360 [cf. below, J. Fincke, p. 307] texts presently housed in the British Museum (catalogue: Maidman 1986; *ca.* 41 texts have been treated by Müller 1994, 235–71, 39 texts by Grosz 1988, 159–82, and 163 texts by Müller 1998). The long-term project undertaken by G. Wilhelm continues to offer a comprehensive and philologically reliable new edition of the huge archive of Šilwa-teššup, the "king's son" (see as of now AdŠ 2 [1980]; AdŠ 3

Studies on the Civilization and Culture of Nuzi and the Hurrians - 10

[1985]; AdŠ 4 [1992]; cf. Stein, D., AdŠ 8–9 [1993]). As far as I know, the philological elaboration of this massive wealth of "new" textual material is still in a preliminary stage, although a number of scholars have benefited from access to it for some time.

Be that as it may, I have the impression that the basic documentary evidence relevant to the main features of the Nuzi civilization has not undergone substantial change. On the other hand, new and at times decidedly challenging research trends have come to the fore. It is to be asked whether they will eventually provide fresh and fruitful insights for an updated historical appreciation of this extraordinary and still largely unexplored corpus of ancient Near Eastern documentation.

In the early seventies, independently of one another, Maidman and Deller had perceived the importance of putting some order to the *mare magnum* of the Nuzi evidence by singling out the identity, consistency, chronological sequences, and geographical relevance of the various private family archives (as a parallel to the palace archives, for which see the preliminary and unsatisfactory sketch of Mayer 1978, commented on, among others, by Zaccagnini 1982), and by creating dossiers of texts with reference to the geographical (and administrative) subdivisions of the Arrapḫean territory. A combination of both criteria, primarily based on a comprehensive filing of the witnesses and scribes recorded in the tablets, yielded fundamental progress in reconstructing the spacial and chronological location of the evidence. Identification and detailed study of other major archives, such as those of Šilwa-teššup (cf. above), of the Wullu family (see the provisional attempt of Grosz 1988, with the philological improvements of Wilhelm in *SCCNH* 7 [1995] 129–33), and of those retrieved in the southwestern and eastern areas of Yorghan Tepe (see Morrison 1987; Morrison 1993) have laid the foundations of a long-awaited new approach that, I hope, will allow the attainment of an adequate historical evaluation of the single blocks of textual material. In this regard, it might incidentally be noted that a closely similar trend is exhibited, at least in part, by contemporary research devoted to the study of the Old Assyrian texts (cf., e.g., Ichisar 1981; Michel 1991; Dercksen 1996). At the same time, comparative investigations on general matters or on issues of detail have marked an increasing scholarly commitment to the multi-faceted and highly debated controversial field of Nuzi socio-economic institutions and juridical practices. This resulted from the attentive scrutiny of the inner documentary evidence and by comparative historical analyses of other related and/or comparable archival corpuses (mainly those of Emar, Ugarit, and Alalaḫ).

This is certainly not the place to single out and comment on a selection of more or less relevant contributions that have appeared in recent times. Rather, I prefer to focus briefly on some issues that significantly reflect the current and notably divergent methodological approaches to the study of Nuzi socio-economic structures, juridical institutions, and legal practices. My aim is to suggest certain basic guidelines for an updated agenda for future research and methodological options.

There is hardly any need to underscore that no substantial gains have been achieved in the study of the vast, yet still largely elusive, "public" sector of the Arrapḫe state organization. Of course, this should not be surprising, were it not that the evidence stemming from the palace archives provides only sectorial and marginal bits of information that faintly mirror the evidence originating in private archives. Even more meagre is the documentation concerning the temples' organization and economic activities, as well as institutional relations with the palace bureaucracy. We know close to nothing about all this.

Leaving aside the issue of the relationships between the Mittanian overlord and the "vassal" king of Arrapḫe—for which, again, we possess very poor and marginal pieces of information, mainly referring to the final period of the Nuzi archives (cf. Zaccagnini 1979; Lion 1995)—interactions between the central palace authority and the private sectors of Nuzi socio-economic milieu are far from being elucidated. A relatively minor topic, such as that of international trade, that was controlled by the palace organization but was also open to private participation (see most recently Zaccagnini in press, with selected bibliography), certainly does not suffice to encourage a much wider and intricate investigation.

As is well known, a major and highly relevant issue for discussion is the nature, extent, and legal implications of the (royal) "proclamations" (*šūdûtu*) that are often mentioned in the final clauses of real estate transactions concluded among private parties. The question of whether these "proclamations" should be compared with earlier Mesopotamian edicts of remission of debts is still open to debate (see most recently Maidman 1996 and Zaccagnini in press). Clearly enough, the ascertainment of what the Nuzi *šūdûtu* in fact were and, more precisely, what their functional aims and juridical effects constituted, is a matter of decisive importance in any attempt to reconstruct the basic features of Nuzi private land ownership and transfer, as well as—on a more general level—the impact of state intervention into the sector of family household economies.

Particular attention has been devoted to singling out and defining the Nuzi "social classes," as attested in the documents stemming from private and palace archives (cf., among others, Zaccagnini 1984a; Maidman 1993; Dosch 1993). Notwithstanding the fact that the concept of "class" has been understood in substantially different ways and that the close parallels with the more or less contemporary evidence from the Alalaḫ and Ugarit archives (cf. Dietrich - Loretz 1969–70; Dietrich - Loretz 1970; Serangeli 1978; Liverani 1979; Heltzer 1982; Heltzer 1987; etc.) have been only partially explored, while the data of the Emar archives still need appropriate investigation (see however the preliminary studies of Bellotto 1995 and Yamada 1995), by now it seems likely that the basic structure of the Nuzi social stratification included: (1) the palace dependents (*arad ekalli*), (2) the military élite (charioteers: *rākib narkabti*), (3) the various members of the "free" sector of the population that were comprised of private landowners, tenants, and lower groups deprived of any title to real estate property, (4) the slaves (*ardu*).

The institutional and functional relationships between the "free" sector and the palace administration, as well the relationships that intervened between the various "sub-classes" of the "free" sector (I refer to the well-known groups of *ālik ilki, aššābu,* and *nakkuššu,* for which cf. Zaccagnini 1984; Zaccagnini 1984a; Maidman 1993; Dosch 1993), certainly need further inquiry. *Pace* Maidman, other "social classes" like the "king's sons" (*mār šarri*) and the *ḫapiru* only refer to (noble) rich and enterprising landlords and businessmen, on the one hand, and on the other, to indigent people—frequently foreigners—who entered the households of wealthy Arrapḫean lords for a lifetime of servitude.

A few words are needed concerning the "slaves" (*ardu*). The Nuzi evidence mirrors the situation revealed in the more or less contemporary late Bronze Age Syrian archives. Both palace officials and dependents (regardless of their professional capacities and bureaucratic ranks) and family household chattel are qualified as *ardu*. Yet this label does not necessarily imply—and in fact did not—an identical personal situation both from a juridical and a social viewpoint. It is not possible here to dwell on the intricate and highly controversial matter of slavery and serfdom in ancient Near Eastern economies and specifically in those of the late second millennium (cf., among others, the various contributions edited by Powell 1987). However, as far as Nuzi is concerned and in accordance with comparable evidence, we can reasonably argue that the economic organization and management of the palace sector were not based primarily on a slave labor force, in the spheres of primary production (i.e., crop-raising and stock-breeding), of non-specialized work performance and—if I correctly understand—of qualified craftsmanship. However, it would seem that consistent seasonal and/or occasional implementation of work services, forcibly imposed on vast sectors of the "free" members of the Arrapḫe community (the *ilku*-duty in the first place), played an important part in the entire budget of the public sector of the economy.

As concerns the private sector, the situation is much more differentiated and complex. The management of small or medium-size estates belonging to free peasant family units (be they of a nuclear or extended/patriarchal kind—I leave aside the vexed question of the existence and functions of village communities, for which cf. Jankovska 1969; Jankovska 1969a; Recueils 1983; Liverani 1978; etc.), as well as stock-raising activities, were ensured by recourse to an internal labor force. Agricultural activities on latifundia, owned by a restricted number of absentee landlords, were carried out by resident peasantry that in most cases had forfeited their own title to their family land and had transferred it to rich entrepreneurs in order to overcome economic difficulties. Large-scale stock raising was entrusted to free herdsmen whose yearly obligations in kind were the object of *ad hoc* stipulations (cf. Morrison 1981). To all appearances, specialized handicraft (textile industry in the first place) was carried out by slaves (cf. especially the data from Šilwa-teššup's archive).

Clearly enough, any reliable reconstruction of the real dimensions and economic significance of the slave labor force within the general framework of

Nuzi palace and private economies presupposes a careful and detailed scrutiny of the data referring to the *ardu*, the sources and procedures of their recruitment, their current purchase prices, their professional qualifications, and their means of maintenance (i.e., basically, food rations). In addition to this, it would be essential to attempt a demographic evaluation of the records that attest to their presence in palace or private economic set-ups, bearing in mind, by way of comparison, the average figures that characterize the standard composition of ancient Near Eastern family units not affected by partial or total disintegration. Once all this has been done, we would find ourselves in a much more confident situation for evaluating and discussing the juridical and the socio-economic features of Nuzi slavery and/or serfdom—a subject that obviously includes a full appraisal of the other forms of non-free personal status and labor obligations attested at Nuzi, such as, e.g., those of the *ḫapiru* and the (life-long) *tidennu*. As a final and, perhaps, obvious remark, I would like to stress the extreme complexity and sectoral diversification of the many components of the Nuzi economic world in their institutional and functional interactions. By resorting to an old, and nowadays almost totally ignored historiographic model, I would say that what ought to be ascertained and defined is the Nuzi "mode of production," as a whole and as a result of its structural components, which may well include different "relationships of production" variously interacting and/or conflicting (cf. Zaccagnini 1989, esp. 1–56 with extensive bibliography).

At any rate, any tentative assessment of the Nuzi economic and social structures presupposes the elucidation of certain basic issues. In what follows, I will limit myself to pointing out and briefly discussing two of them. The first one concerns the expected and/or actual average corn yields and the possible crop-sharing between, (a) title holders of farmland (i.e., the absentee landlords) and resident farmers (i.e., the former owners who had sold portions or the entirety of their real estates, thus becoming simple tenants), in the private sector of land ownership and exploitation, (b) the palace landed properties and dependent farmers, in the public sector. Without entering into unnecessary detail, may I be permitted to recall that my preliminary calculation of the Nuzi cereal yields (Zaccagnini 1975), later integrated with comments based on the additional textual material stemming from Šilwa-teššup's archive (Zaccagnini 1990; Zaccagnini 1990a, esp. 42–43) have been widely accepted but also challenged (Dosch 1993, 139–44 and Müller 1995). Both scholars argued for substantially higher yield rates and further suggested different budgetary patterns with respect to the institutional and standard relations between title holders of real estate and rural workers. Regardless of my disagreement with Dosch and Müller's conclusions, I believe that this crucial matter deserves further and unbiased investigation that, in any case, should take into account the valuable pieces of comparative evidence offered by late third, early and late second millennium, northern Mesopotamian and Syrian archives, both as concerns cereal yield rates and—what is perhaps even more important—the general evolutionary pattern of private peasant land ownership (the pertinent bibliography is too vast to be quoted here).

The second issue concerns the *ilku*-duties. Given that these compulsory services, at least in principle, were incumbent on privately owned real estate (primarily fields), with the possible exception of *ad hoc* royal exemptions, it is still a matter of debate whether or not the obligations due to the central Arrapḫe administration were not only *de facto* but also juridically imposed on the former peasant landowners who had ceded portions of their properties to rich investors and continued to reside and work on the land (in contrast with the few deeds of transfer in which the sellers "raised their foot," *scil.* moved out of the conveyed real estates). This crucial and highly debated issue has been discussed at length but has not yet been definitely settled. Among many discussions, I single out Maidman 1976, p. VI (s.v. *ilku*); Zaccagnini 1984a, 714–22; Zaccagnini 1991/92, 177; Maidman, *SCCNH* 6 (1994), esp. p. 102.

I would like to conclude this short and somewhat rhapsodic discourse with a general, but not irrelevant, comment. The present and ongoing radical dismissal of allegedly obsolete and inadequate theoretical models and analytical tools that previously had been applied to the study of ancient economies and societies, including those of the pre-classical Near East (cf. Zaccagnini 1989 and the bibliography quoted therein; see most recently Giardina 1999, esp. pp. 177–80) is a pervasive feature nowadays displayed by the great majority of scholars. Marxian "orthodox" or "heterodox" concepts, formalizations and research guidelines are at a very low ebb, to say the least. In parallel, the Polanyian model, and its nuanced elaborations followed by a number of anthropologists and economists, have been the object of severe criticism. The most recent methodological alternatives unambiguously reflect scientific options that issue from the drastically changed—and still changing—world-wide political, economic, and cultural scenarios.

It is certainly not a mere chance that, starting from the early 1990s, the concepts of market economy and market exchange, characterized by the logic and dynamics of supply and demand, of profit and investment, of private capital gain and accumulation, occasionally matched and counterbalanced by the "redistributive" effects of "social" state interventions and support, have rapidly gained a privileged space in the discussion of ancient Near Eastern economies. They have been taken over as a whole and with specific reference to some of their segments (suffice it to cite the well-known case of the Old Assyrian corpus and, in most recent times, that of the Neo- and Late Babylonian evidence). On the other hand, it is also not by chance that alternative models often have been developed by invoking questionable parallels with the private juridical institutions of the Roman world in a superficial and sterile revival of the old Pandectistic paradigms. In both cases, the current literature is too abundant (and incessant) to be selected and quoted here.

I refrain from taking personal issue on this state of scholarship that concerns much wider and multi-faceted issues than that of the Nuzi archives. However, at the risk of appearing too brief and simplistic, it is my impression that, once again, we observe a further case of problematic and inconclusive confrontation (perhaps better, pseudo-dialogue) between "modernist" and "primitivist" approaches to the study of ancient economies, a confrontation that reminds us of the famous Bücher – Meyer controversy. Be that as it may, the stimulating intricacies of the rich Nuzi evidence offer an optimal ground for renewed methodological and historiographic challenges in the study of the ancient Near East.

BIBLIOGRAPHY

Al-Rawi, F.N.H.

1977 "Studies in the Commercial Life of an Administrative Area of Eastern Assyria in the Fifteenth Century B.C., Based on Published and Unpublished Cuneiform Texts," unpublished Ph.D. dissertation, University of Wales.

Bellotto, N.

1995 "I LÚ.MEŠ.*aḫ-ḫi-a* a Emar," *AoF* 22, 210–28.

Dercksen, J.G.

1996 *The Old Assyrian copper trade in Anatolia,* Istanbul.

Dietrich, M. - Loretz, O.

1969–70 "Die soziale Struktur von Alalaḫ und Ugarit (II)," *WO* 5, 57–93.

1970 "Die soziale Struktur von Alalaḫ und Ugarit (IV)," *ZA* 60, 88–123.

Dosch, G.

1986 "Gesellschaftsformen, die in Nuzi-Texten nachgewiesen werden können," *Mesopotamia* 21, 191–207.

1987 "Non-Slave Labor in Nuzi," in: Powell 1987, 223–35.

1993 *Zur Struktur der Gesellschaft des Königsreichs Arrapḫe,* Heidelberg.

Eichler, B.L.

1967 "Nuzi Personal *ditennūtu* Transactions and Their Mesopotamian Analogues, unpublished Ph.D. dissertation, University of Pennsylvania.

1973 *Indenture at Nuzi. The Personal* tidennūtu *Contract and Its Mesopotamian Analogues,* New Haven - London.

Fadhil, A.

1972 "Rechtsurkunden und administrative Texte aus Kurruḫanni," unpublished MA thesis, University of Heidelberg.

1983 *Studien zur Topographie und Prosopographie der Provinzstädte des Königreichs Arrapḫe,* Mainz am Rhein.

Giardina, A.

1999 "Esplosione di Tardoantico," *Studi storici* 40, 157–80.

Grosz, K.

1988 *The Archive of the Wullu Family,* Copenhagen.

Heltzer, M.

1982 *The Internal Organization of the Kingdom of Ugarit*, Wiesbaden.

1987 "Labour in Ugarit," in: Powell 1987, 237–50.

Ichisar, M.

1981 *Les archives cappadociennes du marchand Imdilum*, Paris.

Ismail, B.Kh. - Müller, M.

1977 "Einige bemerkenswerte Urkunden aus Tell al-Faḫḫār zur altmesopotamischen Rechts-, Sozial- und Wirtschaftsgeschichte," *WO* 9, 14–34.

Jankovska, N.B.

1969 "Communal Self-Government and the King of the State of Arrapḫa," *JESHO* 12, 233–82.

1969a "Extended Family Commune and Civil Self-Government in Arrapḫa in the Fifteenth Century B.C.," in: D'jakonov, I.M. (ed.), *Ancient Mesopotamia. Socio-economic History*, Moscow.

Lion, B.

1995 "La fin du site de Nuzi et la distribution chronologique des archives," *RA* 89, 77–88.

Liverani, M.

1978 "Sulle tracce delle comunità rurali. In margine ai lavori della Société J. Bodin," *OA* 17, 63–72.

1979 "Ras Shamra," in: *Supplément au Dictionnaire de la Bible*, 9, Paris, 1295–1348.

Maidman, M.P.

1976 "A Socio-Economic Analysis of a Nuzi Family Archive," unpublished Ph.D. dissertation, University of Pennsylvania.

1986 "The Nuzi Texts of the British Museum," *ZA* 76, 254–88.

1993 "Le classi sociali di Nuzi," in: *CNR - Istituto per gli Studi Micenei ed Egeo-Anatolici. Seminari - anno 1992*, Rome, 29–49 (original English text translated by P. Negri-Scafa).

1996 "'Privatization' and Private Property at Nuzi: The Limits of Evidence," in: Hudson, M. and B.A. Levine, (eds.), *Privatization in the Ancient Near East and Classical World*, Cambridge. Mass., 153–76 (with discussion on pp. 164–70).

Mayer, W.

1978 *Nuzi-Studien* I. *Die Archive des Palastes und die Prosopographie der Berufe*, Kevelaer - Neukirchen-Vluyn.

Michel, C.

1991 *Innāya dans les tablettes paléo-assyriennes*, I–II, Paris.

Morrison, M.

1981 "Evidence for Herdsmen and Animal Husbandry in the Nuzi Documents," *SCCNH* 1, 257–96.

1987 "The Southwest Archives at Nuzi," *SCCNH* 2, 167–201.
1993 "The Eastern Archives of Nuzi," *SCCNH* 4, 3–130.

Müller, G.G.W.
1994 *Studien zur Siedlungsgeographie und Bevölkerung des Mittleren Osttigrisgebietes*, Heidelberg.
1998 *Londoner Nuzi Texte*, SANTAG 4, Wiesbaden.

Müller, M.
1995 "Getreideertragsabgaben an den 'Palast' im hurritischen Staat Arrapḫe," *SCCNH* 5, 29–43.

Paradise, J.
1972 "Nuzi Inheritance Practices," unpublished Ph.D. dissertation, University of Pennsylvania.

Powell, M.A. (ed.)
1987 *Labor in the Ancient Near East*, New Haven.

Recueils
1983 *Les communautés rurales*, II: *Antiquité*, in: *Recueils de la Société Jean Bodin pour l'Histoire Comparative des Institutions*, XLI (Warsaw 1976), Paris.

Serangeli, F.
1978 "Le liste di censo di Alalaḫ IV," *VO* 1, 99–131.

Yamada, M.
1995 "The Hittite Social Concept of 'Free' in the Light of the Emar Texts," *AoF* 22, 297–316.

Zaccagnini, C.
1975 "The Yield of the Fields at Nuzi," *OA* 14, 181–225.
1976 "Osservazioni sui contratti di 'anticresi' a Nuzi," *OA* 15, 191–207.
1979 "Les rapports entre Nuzi et Ḫanigalbat," *Assur* 2/1, 1–27.
1982 Review of Mayer 1978, *Or*NS 51, 276–81.
1984 "Land Tenure and Transfer of Land at Nuzi (XV–XIV Century B.C.)," in: Khalidi, T. (ed.), *Land Tenure and Social Transformation in the Middle East*, Beirut, 79–94.
1984a "Proprietà fondiaria e dipendenza rurale nella Mesopotamia settentrionale (XV–XIV secolo a.C.)," *Studi storici* 25, 697–723.
1989 "Asiatic Mode of Production and Ancient Near East. Notes Towards a Discussion," in: Zaccagnini, C. (ed.), *Production and Consumption in the Ancient Near East*, Budapest, 1–126. [Original Italian version published in *Dialoghi di archeologia* NS 3/3 (1981), 3–65.]
1990 "Again on the Yield of the Fields at Nuzi," *BSA* 5, 201–17.
1990a Review of Wilhelm, G., *Das Archiv des Šilwa-teššup*, 3 (Wiesbaden 1985), *OLZ* 85, 40–43.
1991/92 Review of Maidman, M.P., *SCCNH* 3 (1989), *AfO* 38/39, 174–79.

1998 Review of Dosch 1993, *BO* 55, 187–89.

in press "Debt and Debt Cancellation at Nuzi," in: Van De Mieroop, M. and M. Hudson, (eds.), *Clean Slates and Economic Renewal*, New York.

How to Bury a Temple: The Case of Nuzi's Ishtar Temple A

JUDY BJORKMAN
Syracuse, New York

R.F.S. Starr, the excavator of Nuzi, used the familiar model of wanton, looting soldiers to explain the presence of the large quantity of fragmentary cultic remains found in the last manifestation of Nuzi's "Ishtar" temple. Fortunately, Starr's published reports are sufficiently detailed to allow for a different scenario, viz., that any "destruction" was more likely to have been a deliberate activity accompanying the religious "de-commissioning" and burial of the building. Specific aspects of the archaeological data are analyzed in support of this hypothesis. General parallels with the burial of other Mesopotamian temples are cited, along with suggestive fragments of literary material, to indicate that such artifactual evidence belongs, not to any history of looting activities, but to the history of Mesopotamian religion.

In the sixty years since R.F.S. Starr wrote his lucid account of the excavations at Nuzi, nearly all scholarly attention has focussed on the fascinating texts found there. Seldom have Starr's interpretations of the non-textual archaeological remains been analyzed. Fortunately, his work is sufficiently detailed that alternative interpretations of those remains can be offered, as in the following case of Nuzi's "Ishtar" Temple A.

Ishtar Temple A (see Plan 1), also known as the "northwestern temple," is the last of several manifestations of this temple at Nuzi, going back to at least the Akkadian period (Heinrich 1982: 152, 221). Temple A is a double temple; the northwestern cella is traditionally assigned to the worship of Ishtar (on the basis of the type of artifacts found there [Heinrich 1982: 221; Starr 1939: 90]). The southeastern cella has therefore been assigned to Teshub, considered to be Ishtar's spouse at Nuzi (Starr 1939: 113; Heinrich 1982: 221). Ishtar Temple A is completely preserved, whereas the Teshub segment is about half gone, due to later erosion (Starr 1939:111).

Temple A was traditionally dated to the mid-15th century B.C. (e.g., Heinrich 1982: 221). More recently, the evidence has been re-evaluated and the Temple's date lowered by about a century (see Stein 1989 and Moorey 1994: 196). The date of Nuzi's destruction is now given as 1330/1325 B.C. (Stein 1989).

Studies on the Civilization and Culture of Nuzi and the Hurrians - 10

PLAN 1

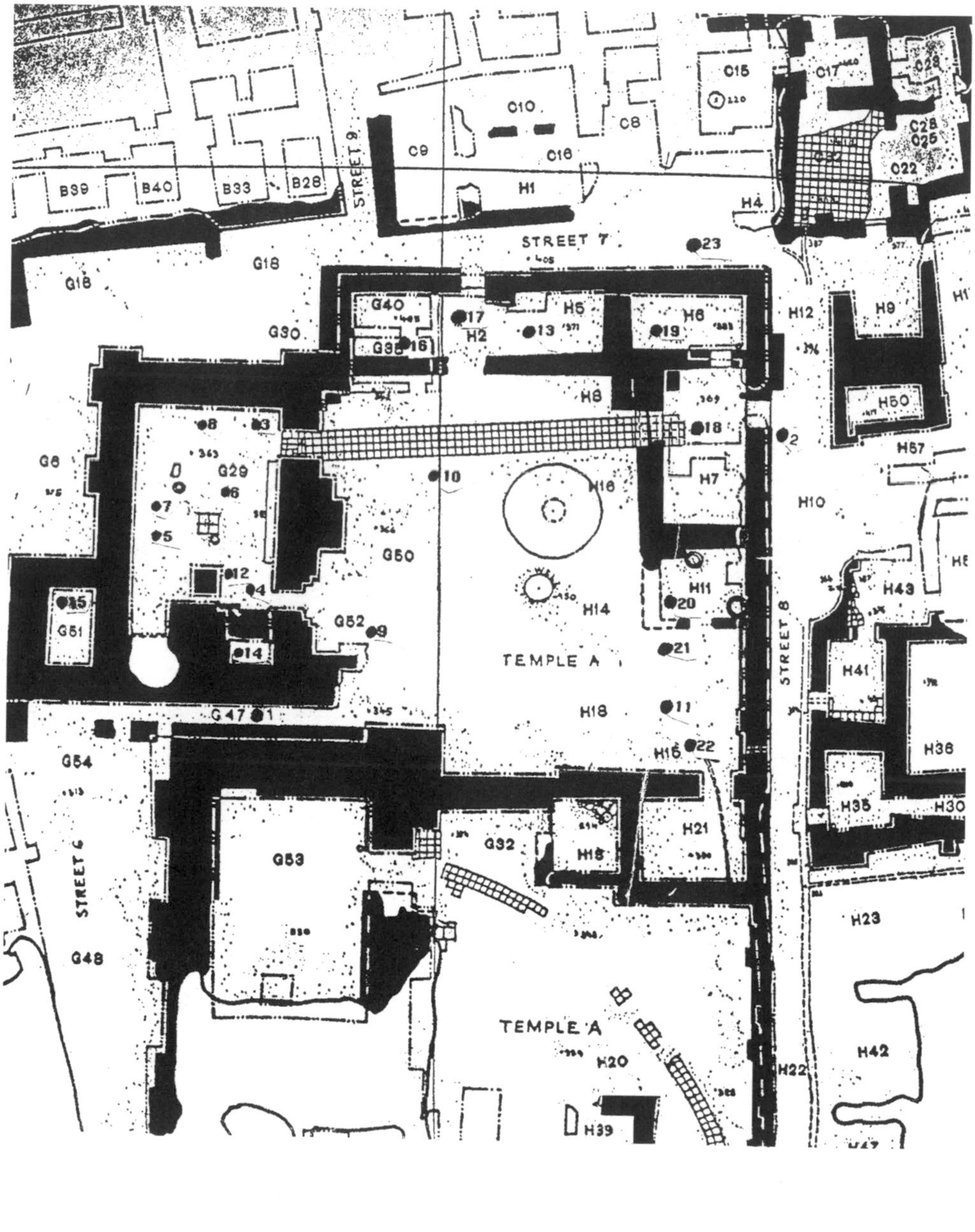
STREET 9
STREET 7
STREET 8
STREET 6
TEMPLE A
TEMPLE A
B39
B40
B33
B28
C9
C10
C8
C15
C16
C17
C22
H1
H2
H4
H5
H6
H7
H8
H9
H10
H11
H12
H14
H15
H16
H18
H20
H21
H22
H23
H35
H36
H39
H41
H42
H43
H50
H57
G6
G18
G29
G30
G32
G38
G40
G47
G48
G50
G51
G52
G53
G54
WELL

Numerous fragments of beautiful glass and glazed terracotta artifacts were found scattered over several areas of Temple A. The preponderance of beads, maceheads, wall nails, plaques, and statues led the excavators to propose that these were the remains of the cultic paraphernalia of the goddess and that they had once been arranged inside the cella (Starr 1939: 87ff.). The fact that so many of such artifacts were made of glass seems to reinforce their role as high-status artifacts. Sometime in the 16th century B.C. a great flowering of glass technology had begun, which for the first time exploited glass's unique properties (Moorey 1994: 193ff.). At Nuzi, the finds of more elaborate glass artifacts tended to be concentrated in Temple A and in the Palace, as one would expect of luxury items (*ibid.*: 196–97). Over 16,000 beads, mostly of glass but some also of frit and stone, were found in Temple A. One of Starr's letters, published in the recent *Richard F. S. Starr Memorial Volume*, complained about the time needed to clean all those beads, half of which were too deteriorated to be saved in any case. Starr concluded, "I never want to see another bead as long as I live" (Owen and Wilhelm 1996: 114).

Not only were artifacts scattered about the cella and courtyard of Temple A, but a few also were found in the fill above the building and many more in a grain storage pit and in a deep shaft, both located within the courtyard. See Table 1 for the type, location, and references of all artifacts related to Ishtar Temple A.

Starr's suggested reconstruction of what led to this situation is approximately as follows. Temple A was attacked, pillaged at this time, and never rebuilt (Starr 1939: 87). The looters (perhaps Assyrians [*ibid.*: 89]), looking for the most valuable items among the temple's contents, went into the cella,[1] which probably received light only through the two doorways leading onto the courtyard. Because of the poor lighting (*ibid.*: 102), the looters dragged most of the cultic artifacts out into the courtyard, where they sorted out what they wanted (*ibid.*: 92), and threw the remains around them with great abandon, mostly into the northern and northwestern parts of the courtyard (*ibid.*: 103), but also into the far eastern corner (*ibid.*: 109). In addition, they stuffed full the deep shaft in the center of the courtyard, which, Starr suggests, may originally have been used for libations to the underworld (*ibid.*: 104). The cultic statue, perhaps built of the terracotta with which the Nuzians knew how to work so well, was stripped of its valuable accoutrements, leaving only one large and beautifully-made eye, found in the grain storage pit. Then the statue was utterly smashed so that nothing remained of it except the eye and possibly the glazed terracotta female breast found in the cella (*ibid.*: 88–90). The degree of wantonness that the looters exhibited can be seen in their apparently having pulled down the walls around the courtyard, so that a few smashed remains from the cella were found in the fill above the courtyard pavement (*ibid.*: 103–4). The invaders also set a fire, as is shown by the burned condition of some pottery

---

1 Starr has a very interesting reconstruction of the possible appearance of the cella (*ibid.*: 102–3).

outside G 29's eastern door. This fire may have led to the collapse of the aforementioned walls onto the courtyard (*ibid.*: 104).

As Starr notes (1939: 115ff.), "...the devastation of Stratum II was one from which the Nuzians never fully recovered," and, there was

> no attempt at a rebuilding of the temple, but, instead of that, a new pavement violating the temple enclosure, running indiscriminately over its walls and rooms. It seems certain that this could not have been built by the same people who formerly had venerated this spot (*ibid.*: 116).

On this later pavement were found some fragments of the grotesque lion-bodied terracotta statues of Temple A. But since they were isolated fragments, Starr believed they were probably the result of intrusive digging in this area (*ibid.*), not evidence of continuation of the same culture.

Starr's careful proposals may be accurate. But I suggest that the same data can be interpreted rather differently, leading to an improved hypothesis for what actually happened to this Nuzi temple. I propose instead that the "destruction" was a deliberate activity of officials of this temple, performed in order to de-commission or de-sacralize the temple. In so doing, they left behind certain remnants, mostly broken, of cult artifacts, spread about as a type of deposit that I have suggested be given the name "fill deposit" (Bjorkman 1994: 300ff.).

I propose that Temple A was abandoned (for reasons presently not clear to us) but not pillaged. It was "de-commissioned," by cult personnel, as were many other Mesopotamian temples, in other times and places (see below). Assuming that there was a cult statue, some of it would have been re-cycled. Since it is probable that most anthropomorphic cult statues were made of wood and plated with sheet metal, probably the metal plating over the wooden core was removed (mostly for re-cycling). The remains of this process may be seen in the small copper nails, scraps of sheet copper, and tiny fragments of thin sheet gold that Starr found in the cella (Starr 1939: 95). One could even imagine (and here I am being very speculative) that the evidence of a fire set in the courtyard outside the eastern door of the cella (*ibid.*) was due to the wooden core of the cult statue having been moved from the cella, straight out the nearest (eastern) doorway, onto the court, where, after special rituals, it was burned completely. Then the bricks in the vicinity of this fire, which, as Starr says, had been partially "baked to a friable and crumbling condition" (*ibid.*: 109), were turned over, in order to restore the appearance of the temple courtyard (*ibid.*). This may have been the formal end of the cult statue. The large eye and the glazed terracotta female breast might have been, as Starr claimed, parts of the cult statue, but they could also be pieces of some other artifacts.

It seems likely to me that, as Starr proposed, the cult paraphernalia were removed or displaced from their settings within the cella. However, this activity, according to my hypothesis, was carried out by temple personnel. They were the ones who broke up the larger artifacts—storage jars, terracotta lion figures, etc. Many fragments were then deliberately separated from others of the same artifact. Such fragments, plus thousands of beads and single examples of particular artifacts, were spread out over the area of the temple complex and buried in the shaft and in the pit, in ways that may exhibit general patterns for the cultically appropriate burial of a temple at this time and place.

In addition, I suggest that the new, later pavement mentioned above, which Starr said ran indiscriminately above the walls and rooms of the temple complex, was not done, as he suggests, by a different people who had no veneration for this spot.[2] I propose that it, too, was done by the cultic personnel, who laid out the fill deposit, filled everything in, and then created a "cap" over the area, probably including the new pavement, as the final step in the de-commissioning of the old temple.[3]

Two very different "scenarios" for the end-time of Temple A are given above. I will present several points of evidence which, although they cannot furnish absolute proof of my "fill deposit" hypothesis, should show why I find Starr's "wanton looters" hypothesis to be inadequate.

(1) *The Shaft in the Middle of the Temple Courtyard*

Starr notes that this shaft, which is nearly nine meters deep, cannot have been a well (despite the label on Plan 1), since its bottom is still eleven meters above the water level of Nuzi times, and it is very large for a well—a little over a meter and a half in diameter. Starr (1939: 104) both describes and offers an explanation of the situation, as follows:

> It could not have been anything other than wanton and mischievous destruction that led the invaders to throw so much of their loot down the shaft in the center of the courtyard. From bottom to top it was filled with objects from the cella.... That these [artifacts] were evenly interspersed in

2 Stein (1989: 54) notes, "What little remains of stratum I, above the destruction level, is identical with that of stratum II underneath; even the tablets from room D 3/6 of stratum I are indistinguishable prosopographically." This indicates that stratum I probably was mixed and thus not a reliable indicator of a "different people" who might have built the new pavement.

3 Presumably, the remains of the "Teshub" temple were included under this "cap," as well. Even though this temple had suffered more from later erosion, it was clear that, like the Ishtar Temple, it had not been rebuilt after the end of Stratum II. However, the remaining contents of its cella (G53) and its courtyard were meager indeed, compared to those of the Ishtar Temple—less than 300 beads (compared to 16,000) and perhaps two dozen fragments of miscellaneous artifacts and tablets (Starr 1939: 112—"a considerable quantity" of tablets; Pedersén 1998: 20—"a few" tablets), compared to the hundreds of artifact fragments found in the Ishtar segment. There was a complete absence of glazed ware in the Teshub Temple, which seems to indicate, as Starr (1939: 113) observed, that it was a special feature of the cult of Ishtar. The scarcity of objects was attributed by Starr to differences in the cult requirements of the two deities. Starr is probably correct in seeing a more "austere" cult in the Teshub Temple, but the arrangement of the few artifacts still present does not seem to suggest that Starr's proposed "looters" had proceeded here with the same wild abandon he had proposed for the Ishtar Temple.

> the fill from top to bottom is strong evidence that there was a structure around the mouth of the shaft, which was demolished and thrown down simultaneously with the temple objects. Unfortunately, this destruction was so complete that not even the foundations of such a structure could be found.

It is to Starr's credit that he reported this even interspersing of artifacts and fill in the shaft. His solution for the presence and even distribution of this fill (viz., that there had been some structure, now completely demolished, around the mouth of the shaft) is rather ingenious, but perhaps Starr also recognized what I suggest, that there is a certain incongruity between the evenly-spaced fill-plus-artifacts and the wanton looters.

I propose instead that the arrangement of fill and artifacts in this shaft was deliberate and was done by cult adherents, not by looters who supposedly threw things all over the temple complex, yet also spent time nicely sandwiching fill and artifacts in this shaft. Perhaps the shaft was constructed specifically for the purpose of disposal of the cult artifacts found within it. It represents a great amount of work. For its construction, two sets of steps had been cut into opposing sides of the shaft. It was not lined with brick except in its constricted mouth, which was mostly destroyed (Starr 1939: 104–5). Starr suggested (*ibid.*: 104) that the shaft may have been used for libations to the gods of the underworld. Perhaps this is so, but the rest of Starr's discussion on this shaft seems to leave open the matter of its original function.

In Appendix A of Starr (1939: 521), H.W. Eliot describes the shaft as "peculiar," as well as "needlessly great" in diameter for purposes of libation. Adding to the mystery of this shaft is the fact that when the excavators, continuing it as a test pit (G50) to reach virgin soil, dug down 85 cm below the shaft's bottom, "through undisturbed soil" (*ibid.*: 40; cf. Mrs. Starr's description in Owen and Wilhelm 1996: 226–27), they came to a solid clay pavement on which "lay a cache of twenty-five stamp and four cylinder seals..." (Starr 1939: 521). Along with them lay 23 stone beads, 23 pierced shells and a quartz fragment (*ibid.*: 40). The pavement and the deposit were "covered by a layer of sand 2 or 3 cm thick, which in turn was overlaid with a thin deposit of sherds of coarse reddish and greenish ware, fragmentary and undistinguished" (*ibid.*). The pavement on which they lay was slightly blackened (*ibid.*). Eliot adds, "That the 85 cm of matter immediately above the pavement could not have come from above, or have been the result of a cave-in of the sides, seems to have been carefully established by the excavators at the time "(*ibid.*: 521). He suggests that the stamp and cylinder seals are Uruk in date but probably were deposited as antiquarian treasures in a later level, since a bowl of some later date was found below the clay pavement (*ibid.*: 522). In any case, the cache of seals has the appearance of a deliberate deposit, but without wider exposure of this test pit (G50) it is impossible to confirm whether or not the cache might have been connected with the shaft and its contents. The possibility of a connection seems hinted at by Mrs. Dorothy Starr in her diary reference to this "well" that ended "in a pavement which never could have produced water, and to make it even more fantastic, the shaft happens to lead to the one spot on the *tepa* where a cache of archaic seals lay buried...." (Owen and Wilhelm 1996: 227).

(2) *The Grain Storage Pit*

Near the shaft was a beehive-shaped pit typical of those used for storage of grain. It is described as follows:

> The pit is chopped out of the underlying soil and is entirely without brick or *libin* support. The bottom is slightly concave with a diameter of 420 cm and a depth of 304 cm below the courtyard pavement. Again it is impossible to tell with any accuracy the diameter of the opening or whether there was any construction to protect its mouth (Starr 1939: 105).

The pit "was bare of signs of any stored material" (*ibid.*); the materials that were found in this pit are detailed in Table 1. Starr observes that it must have been empty "at the time of the invasion" (*ibid.*), since in the haste of looting it would have been unlikely to have been cleaned out so completely. I propose instead that the pit may have been cleaned out by cultic personnel, for use as another place to bury and to spread out fragmentary artifacts from the cella. In any case, given the large volume of the pit, a relatively small volume of artifacts was found buried in it.

(3) *The Wide Separation of Pieces of the Same Artifacts*

The best examples of this activity are the remains of two pairs of glazed terracotta lions, which Starr suggested had flanked and fronted the cult statue (*ibid.*: 97). One pair was green-glazed and standing, the other pair couchant and yellow-glazed over red-painted bodies.[4] I will arbitrarily label them Green (1 and 2) and Yellow (1 and 2). Their fragments were found as follows: Green-1 (Starr 1939: 97) was found relatively unbroken but out of context at the northwest end of the cella. The head of Yellow-1 was found in pieces near the pedestal in the cella (*ibid.*). Much of Yellow-2 was found outside the temple compound in H 10 in Street 8 (Starr 1937: 28 [description of Plate 111]). In the courtyard, near the northern cella door, fragments of three of the four lions were found (Starr 1939: 103). Near the doorway to H 11 were the front legs of Green-2 (*ibid.*: 108). Down inside the shaft in G 50 were the broken bases and stands of Green-1 and-2 (*ibid.*: 104). Thus, parts of the pair, Green-1 and -2, were found in four completely different places, and parts of Yellow-1 and -2 in three different places. Some of the fragments of one lion were separated by as much as 19 meters. While this is not absolute proof that wanton looters did not do this, the combination of a wide separation of pieces and the burial in the shaft of other parts of these same artifacts raises the likelihood that another scenario could better explain the situation.[5]

---

4 These two pairs of glazed lions were reunited for the first time in almost 3,330 years in the display of Nuzi artifacts in Harvard's Semitic Museum, on the occasion of the 45th annual meeting there of the Rencontre Assyriologique Internationale, July 5–8, 1998.

5 Another Nuzi example of this seemingly deliberate separation of fragments of cult

My hypothesis is that the de-commissioning of Ishtar Temple A is, in fact, another example of similar ritual activity that occurs throughout Mesopotamia and its environs, during most of its history, comprising, in fact, the most frequently occurring form of Mesopotamian ritual deposit.[6] As noted above, I have proposed (Bjorkman 1994: 300ff.) the name, "fill deposit," for this type of activity.

Occasionally, others have suggested that the concept of "wanton looters" does not explain the nature of excavated remains. For example, at Tell Brak, on the courtyard of the Akkadian monumental complex in Area SS was found a heap of interesting artifacts, some broken, several of great intrinsic value (e.g., gold, silver, lapis, copper). Since the monumental complex had been deliberately filled in, the excavators suggested that the heap was a "ritual offering" (D. and J. Oates 1991: 135) and that the filling-in of the complex also represented "some ritual gesture" (D. and J. Oates 1989: 204), in fact, its "formal entombment" (*ibid.*: 206). Other characteristics of the complex's burial that seem to emphasize its deliberate, ritual nature are that joins were made of "potsherds found at different levels in the fill" (*ibid.*: 202), and that deposits comprised of "small groups of complete pottery cups and bowls, usually inverted" (D. and J. Oates 1991: 135) were found at the top of the fill, as well.

Other examples of fill deposits, involving the re-evaluation of data from older excavations, come from Mari, Tello, and Uruk. Börker-Klähn (1979) denied that looters were involved in the final destruction of the Ishtarat and Ninnizaza temples at Mari (cf. Bjorkman 1994: 353ff.), proposing instead that the two temples were formally buried, and that the uppermost of their last two floors was never used for normal traffic but only for the "funeral" (*Beisetzung*) of the buildings before they were filled in (Börker-Klähn 1979: 229–30). She (*ibid.*: 229, n. 56) also proposed that the "Construction Inférieure" at Tello and the Riemchengebäude and Steingebäude at Uruk were additional examples of "buried" buildings. Crawford (1987) suggested that the "Construction Inférieure" at Tello (see Bjorkman 1994: 428ff.) had a religious function, despite the lack of an altar, and that its second stage of construction may have been quite short-lived (Crawford 1987: 73–74), before the building was carefully sealed in and overbuilt by the "Construction d'Urnanshe" (sometimes also termed the "Maison des Fruits"). The Riemchengebäude at Uruk (see Bjorkman 1994:

---

artifacts occurs in Ishtar Temple F, dating to the Akkadian period (Heinrich 1982: 152–53). Pieces of a house model offering-stand of terracotta were found as follows: the largest group of fragments was on the floor next to the left-hand (NE) side of the altar; one piece was on top of the altar; other fragments were scattered around the cella (G29) and in the entry-room (G78) (see Starr 1939: 66–67; 1937: Plan 7, and Plates 5A and 61A,B). Some fragments were separated by as much as nine meters (horizontal, straight-line distance).

6 Acts of votive deposition can be observed at widely dispersed sites in the ancient Near East, at least as early as the ninth millennium BC (Bjorkman 1994: 116–19). An excellent account of such activity in the Neolithic and Chalcolithic periods in the Near East is by Yosef Garfinkel, "Ritual Burial of Cultic Objects: The Earliest Evidence," *Cambridge Archaeological Journal* 4/2 (1994) 159–88.

445ff.) is a signal example of a structure clearly laid out for ritual purposes, in which valuable cult artifacts were buried in a ritual involving limited use of fire. It has been suggested that the purpose of the Riemchengebäude was as a ritual burial of artifacts from the Steinstifttempel that had been devoted to the gods (Lenzen 1974: 127; Crawford 1987: 75). However, I much prefer Heinrich's (1982: 73, 135) suggestion that the burial of valuables devoted to the gods was not the sole purpose, perhaps not even a major purpose, of the Riemchengebäude and certainly not of the Steingebäude (since it essentially contained no artifacts), and that perhaps they were both cenotaphs, i.e., buried buildings, serving as monuments to "dead" temples (Bjorkman 1994: 451–52).

Yet another example of the burial of a "dead" temple may be that of the Kleiner Anten-Tempel at Tell Chuera (Bjorkman 1994: 415ff.). When Moortgat originally excavated the area, the nature of the deposits found in Level 2 seemed to him to indicate a kind of burial of the temple itself (Moortgat 1965: 17), even though he subsequently broadened his interpretation to include other possibilities (Moortgat 1967: 14).

In addition, in all of the above examples from Tell Brak, Mari, Tello, Uruk, and Tell Chuera there are examples of pieces of the same artifacts that are found in widely separated locations, as was noted earlier for the Nuzi glazed lion statues. It is not possible here to discuss the details of this issue further,[7] but I will note that the majority of the over 70 examples that I have collected of this practice of separating pieces of the same artifact come from fill deposits.

A few objects were found in the fill above the Ishtar Temple A courtyard at Nuzi.[8] This, too, is a common characteristic of fill deposits. For example, in the so-called "Sammelfund" at Uruk, Heinrich (1936: 4) observed how artifacts were on the floor and in the fill, and the fill itself was permeated with an enormous number of beads and inlay pieces (Bjorkman 1994: 455ff.).

At Nuzi, some artifacts (including much of one of the four glazed lion statues) were found just outside the main door into the temple complex, in the street. This practice finds a parallel in a fill deposit at Assur, with artifacts from Archaic Ishtar Temple G (see Andrae 1922, pls. 3 and 6; Bjorkman 1994: 312ff.).

In general, the broken and sometimes scattered nature of the Nuzi temple artifacts parallels nearly all other fill deposits. For example, the huge and fascinating fill deposit found near the base of the platform of the Ninhursag temple at Al-Ubaid (Bjorkman 1994: 304ff.) contains artifacts that have been reconstructed, but almost none of them were found intact. Hall and Woolley

---

7 For more discussion, see Bjorkman 1994: 300ff., especially in regard to the following fill deposits: Mari #10 and #11, Tell Brak #10, Tell Chuera #9, Tello #1, and Uruk #1.

8 Starr (1939: 103–4) explains their presence as follows:

> That one of the large couchant unglazed lions was 35 cm above the pavement ...suggests that a willful destruction of the walls accompanied the general looting. This and a single macehead must have been thrown there after the upper portion of the wall had been thrown down.

(1927: 77) observed that most things had been broken before being put at the platform's base.

The *types* of artifacts present may prove to be of significance—for example, like all other fill deposits, no cult statue was found at Nuzi. Several other fill deposits have, like Nuzi, yielded one large statue eye, and several single examples of some unusual artifacts. Like Nuzi, most fill deposits have a very limited number of artifacts of intrinsic value, especially gold, silver, and lapis, and slightly larger numbers of copper artifacts. But one could propose, as I do, that precious metals and stones are present only in *symbolic* amounts (Bjorkman 1994: 474–75).

As noted above, Starr (1939: 104; cf. 110) had proposed that the "looters" set a fire in the courtyard just outside the cella's eastern door. Yet there is no evidence for wider use of fire.[9] None of the artifacts in Table 1 are said to be fire-damaged, except for the plain pots from that burnt area at the cella's eastern door. I have suggested that the use of fire there may have been ritual in nature, perhaps to consume the cult statue's wooden core (and other flammable cult furnishings?) as part of the de-commissioning of Temple A. The lack of evidence for fire damage on artifacts was one of the reasons why Börker-Klähn (1979: 224–25) suggested that Parrot's description of fire and violence as causes for the destruction of Mari's Ishtarat and Ninnizaza temples needed to be

---

[9] Starr (1939: 107) reports evidence for fire at one other place in the Temple area, viz., the H 7 face of the northwestern, double-width jamb of the door leading from H 7 into the courtyard (G 50). Both the *libin* and the plaster of this jamb are said to bear evidence of intense fire.

Even in the palace and in the housing areas of Stratum II there does not seem to be consistent evidence for a fiery destruction of the city. In all the rooms of the palace, only the following are described as having some evidence of fire:

- M 100 (remnants of wooden beam-ends found close to walls);
- N 120 ("charcoal far in excess of the amount one would expect from the burned rafters alone");
- M 79 (charcoal and inlay remnants, possibly from a couch);
- M 90 (signs of intense fire from flammable materials kept in this storeroom);
- L 20 and L 11 (charcoal remnants of rafters and of a large door between these two rooms);
- L 27 (mixed with the charcoal that "filled the interior" of the room were a few artifacts and a large number of cuneiform tablets [NB: for locations of archives of Nuzi tablets, see Pedersén 1998: 15–28]);
- L 6 (in the debris "was a quantity of charcoal in excess of what might be expected from the ruined rafters," and, among other things, "a number of inscribed clay tablets were on the pavement...");
- L 41 ("much charcoal and ashes of straw were found on the floor");
- M 74 (the walls showed signs of intense burning; charcoal from two burned doors that did not belong to this room);
- R 50 (carbonized barley in a terracotta basin);
- R 179 (one end of room showed signs of continued hot fire).

Apparently, in only 12 out of over 80 palace rooms described by Starr are there varying types of evidence for fire. How convincing is this as an indicator of enemy destruction?

reconsidered. The importance of better determining the nature of a building's end-time can be seen in the ways that such data are used. There is a tendency to assume that a temple's "destruction" marks the violent end of that period in a city's history. In the next conceptual step, a link is proposed with what little may be known from textual evidence regarding such an event. (If textual mention of warfare is not known, a battle may be conjectured.) Then, this "fixed point" will be used as a basis for further speculations on chronology, foreign relations, economics, history, religion, etc. The case of those two Mari temples also furnishes an example of this. Although, as noted above, I found Börker-Klähn's interpretation of the end of those adjoining temples as a deliberate burial to be convincing, I consider her additional, speculative attempts to flesh out historical events (viz., that ED Mari was destroyed by an Eblaite general, Enna-Dagan, who also buried the two temples [*ibid.*: 232–33]) to be unconvincing (Bjorkman 1994: 357). The nature of the relations between Mari and Ebla is still in the process of being assessed. It is unlikely that the battle proposed by Börker-Klähn ever took place.

I have suggested that an earthen "cap" was put over the Nuzi temple to mark the end of its time of veneration, essentially to signify a funeral for and burial of the building and a fraction of its contents. This is a feature that I suggest can be observed in deposits at several other sites—the red brick cover of the artifacts of the Ninhursag Temple at Al-Ubaid, the two meters of fill on the floor of the last manifestation of the Eye Temple at Tell Brak, the whole Riemchengebäude at Uruk, the temples of Ishtarat and Ninnizaza at Mari, the Level 2 Kleiner Anten-Tempel at Tell Chuera, the ED IIIa Nintu Temple at Khafajah, and others.

In summary, I have proposed that the remains of Nuzi's Ishtar Temple A portray the deliberate burial of the building, not its looting by enemy soldiers. This proposal is no more than an hypothesis that needs further testing. It leaves many questions unanswered, most notably that of the factors that led to the Temple's burial. What happened to extinguish the institutional life of a building that apparently had been rebuilt over a period of a thousand years?[10] The entire town of Nuzi seems to have come to an end around the same time as the Temple. Was that due to an enemy attack on the city (for which there is not good archaeological evidence, in my opinion)? Or was it due to other causes, such as tactical surrender and eventual deportation or eviction or even voluntary evacuation? Were there internal power struggles that resulted in the destruction of Nuzi's economic organization and finally its life?[11] The textual evidence

---

10 Whether or not it was always Ishtar who was worshipped here cannot be stated with certainty, even though Starr says this (Starr 1939: 113). There was a period of "long abandonment between Temple F and the end of Temple E" (*ibid.*: 76; see also 72ff.). Starr implies that an "intrusive culture" then rebuilt the northwestern temple at the end of E (*ibid.*: 62, 77).

11 Diana Stein is preparing an analysis of Nuzi iconography, pointing to factors that may well have led to strains on the local economy.

from Nuzi does not shed a great deal of light on the matter, although Stein notes,

> The Nuzi records of the last generation do reflect a period of upheaval. Palace rations were reduced to a wartime minimum while large military detachments of chariots were assembled on the northern and southern borders of Arrapha (Stein 1989: 51–52).

Aspects of the remains of Temple A, as well as those of the Nuzi Palace, and even of the private houses, seem to show that a kind of deliberation, rather than haste, marked the "destruction" of Nuzi.

I conclude by summarizing some thoughts on why fill deposits were made at all. Obviously, I believe that the purposes behind fill deposits were religious in nature and that fill deposits were not made for "practical" reasons such as getting rid of old temple inventory or just filling space when old buildings were levelled up (Bjorkman 1994: 483ff.). In fact, I think that fill deposits are a type of theological "statement," which I have not yet found expressed systematically in any Mesopotamian literature. Nonetheless, what strikes me as a beginning point is the Mesopotamian belief that both the temple and its furnishings, as the property of the god or goddess, were in some sense alive (Jacobsen 1987a: 387; Bjorkman 1994: 486ff.). This feature is consistent in Mesopotamian literature—in some of the earliest understandable cuneiform texts, those from the Fara period, offerings are made to various temple artifacts and to the temple itself. Items such as drums, harps, and spears could have their own personal names and even be objects of independent cults (Selz 1997: 167ff.). Later textual materials describe the ritual activities needed to cause the cult statue of a god or goddess to come alive (see Jacobsen 1987b: 23ff. and Walker and Dick 1999) for the "mouth-washing" [*mīs pî*] ritual), and similar rituals existed for enlivening such things as the Standard and the Footstool of the god Shamash (*CAD* Š/3 346a: *ARM* 18 69:15), the temple kettledrum and a cultic torch (Pritchard 1955: 337–38: RAcc. 12, 8ff. and 119, 29). The function of worshipper statues in praying on behalf of their donors (e.g., Frankfort 1939: 11) clearly implies that these statues were in some sense "alive." When any temple cult came to an end, presumably these "living" artifacts had to be properly disposed of.[12] I suggest that the life-filled aspect of these artifacts led to the necessity for their breakage. Such life-force needed to be dissipated and thus controlled.[13] It may have been

---

12 Given the dearth of archaeological examples of the remains of a cult statue, I propose that they were dealt with differently from other temple artifacts. This is a topic to which I hope to return at another time.

13 Although much later and from a different context, a biblical passage may illustrate potential problems with spiritual powers that are not appropriately dealt with.

> When an unclean spirit goes out of someone it wanders through waterless country looking for a place to rest, and not finding one it says, "I will go back to the home I came from." But on arrival, finding it swept and tidied, it then goes off and brings seven other spirits more wicked than itself, and they go in and set up house there, and so that person ends up worse off than before (Luke 11:24–26 [NJB]).

understood as impossible to destroy it and perhaps disrespectful to attempt to do so. The "taming of the spirits," represented by the breakage of artifacts and the dispersal of their fragments, resembles a type of defensive magic that Faraone (1992) describes from later Greek contexts in his book, *Talismans and Trojan Horses*.

Assuming that fill deposits do represent a theological statement, it is about how things were appropriately *ended* in Mesopotamia, just as foundation deposits speak (more intelligibly) about how and why things were begun. In order to accurately infer past ways of thought from material remains, very careful and detailed excavation and recording are needed, of course. But what sense is made of that data also depends on the models used to interpret it. In the case of Nuzi's Ishtar Temple A, I have proposed that the "wanton looting soldiers" be put on the shelf and that the "fill deposit" hypothesis be tested instead. I believe that the latter produces a better "fit," both for Nuzi and for a very large body of other Mesopotamian archaeological data, as well.

The point here is that spirits did not just go out of existence when leaving a person but might reappear and wreak havoc. Efforts to evict spirits and to make them stay away are detailed in Neo-Assyrian magical texts designed for that purpose. See, e.g., J. Scurlock, "Magical Means of Dealing with Ghosts in Ancient Mesopotamia," (Ph. D. dissertation, Department of Near Eastern Languages and Civilizations, University of Chicago; 1988), texts 58–60, 62–64 (=BAM 323:79–88; 89–107; LKA 85:1–25; KAR 267:31–r.25; LKA 84:1–r.12; KAR 56:12–r.10).

Table 1*

LOCATION OF ARTIFACTS FROM NUZI'S ISHTAR TEMPLE A

LOCATION		PAGE	PLATE	
•1	G47	88	97,L	several *glazed wall nails*
		—	75,Y	glazed terracotta [t.c.] *bottle*
•2	H10	88, 108	98,G	(a) 3 *glazed wall-nails* (one combination of nail + wall plate)
		99	—	(b) fragments of *large crude t.c.animal* figures
		108	102,C	(c) *bronze statuette* of standing female figure
		108	111,A	(d) 2 small *standing t.c. lions*, green-glazed and very disintegrated
		108	—	(e) many glass and frit *beads*
		108	—	(f) fragments of *inlaid glass vessels*
		97	111,B	(g) *couchant t.c. lion statue*, yellow-glazed, red-painted
•3	G29	90	102,E	(a) green-glazed *t.c. woman's breast* (<life-size) + fragments
		91	—	(b) large straight-sided *storage jar* smashed into fragments
•4	G29	91	10,A, 94,K	(a) 2 plain *pot-stands* found near SE door; crenelated base
		101–2		(b) over 15 shattered *tablets* "near the eastern doorway"
•5	G29	91	—	(a) simple *blue frit cup* of delicate proportions
		91,101	—	(b) at least 3 small *glazed pots or bottles*
		91	cf.92,Z	(c) 2 glazed *tripod bowls*
		91	cf.56,I,L	(d) fragment of *frit vessel* w/lip pierced vertically for string handle
		101	—	(e) glazed t.c. *pot lid*
		—	117,H	(f) *burnisher* made from a sherd
•6	G29	91	10,A	(a) massive *whetstone* on pavement between brick altar and N. corner
		91	10,A, 133,A,B	(b) near whetstone, a bottle-shaped *basket*, woven of twigs and covered on outside with bitumen [uses suggested]
•7	G29	92	119,K,L, S; 120, M,II,KK, VV,ZZ	(a) thousands of *beads* scattered over floor of cella, some with remnants of copper wire; mostly glass, a few blue frit, fewer in various stones; some multi-colored (see p. 92)
		93	—	(b) tiny *gold sun disk*
		94	98,A	(c) 2 *glazed wall nails*
		95	—	(d) small *copper nails* scattered in considerable quantity over the floor + occasional flat *scraps of copper* with nail holes
		95	—	(e) several frags. of thin *sheet gold* (scraps from larger sheets)
		96	121,P	(f) *glass macehead*, broken anciently and mended with bitumen

* Bulleted numbers (e.g., "•1") refer to approximate locations of groups of artifacts, as indicated here on Plan 1.
Location indicators (e.g., "G47") refer to Starr 1937, Plan 13, reproduced here as Plan 1.
Page numbers refer to Starr 1939.
Plate numbers refer to Starr 1937.

LOCATION		PAGE	PLATE	
		96	cf.121,U	(g) fragments of larger *glass macehead*
		96	121,S	(h) circular *macehead of limestone*
		96	121,A, 130,B	(i) two delicate *glass staff-heads*, flower-shaped, in 2–3 colors
		96	—	(j) white *glass macehead*, 78x28mm, shaped like spindle whorl
		98	112,B	(k) green-glazed *boar's head*, found in fragments in cella, + 2 tusk-like objects of blue frit
		98	110,C	(l) part of green-glazed *sheep's head*
		—	110,B	(m) glazed t.c. *brick*
		98	99,A	(n) white glazed *hollow t.c. socket* found in fragments on pavement
		101	125,Y, Z,BB;L	(o) 3 small *copper arrowheads* and a *pike* (for ritual use)
		96	101,H	(p) glazed t.c. free-standing *figurine* [p. 90: said to be from the court]
		97	110,B	(q) fragment of crude glazed t.c. *bird*
•8	G29	92	119,K	(a) found at NW end of G29—*unbaked brick* set w/a row of elliptical and circular eye-beads
		96	101,I	(b) small *bone statuette*, "Hittite" type, with pegs (pc. of furniture?)
		97	110,A	(c) (relatively) unbroken *green-glazed standing lion statue* found resting partly on brick with inset eye beads & a few cm from the bone statuette (b)
		101	—	(d) part of *wooden platter*, ca. 5 cm high, red interior, bitumen exterior
•9	G52	93	131,A	(a) limestone *plaque* overlaid with tree-of-life design in colored glass
		103–4	—	(b) "a few objects outside the cella's eastern door ... many...were *small vessels* of the usual household type." "...much-burned..."
•10	G50	93	131,B	(a) t.c. *plaque* overlaid with tree-of-life design in colored glass
		93, 94, 103	30,C,D; 119,N, M,Q,R, U;120,B, D,E,G, I,J,N–T, W,Y,Z, AA,CC, FF,OO, RR–UU, XX,YY, AAA–DDD	(b) many *eye and other beads and amulets*, intermixed with large nos. of small pierced *seashells*
		93	121,B	(c) small circular *plaque* of red frit, pierced and inlaid
		93	126,S	(d) small lunate *gold earring* wrapped around a copper core
		94, 103	98,F	(e) 25 glazed *wall-nails* found in the court
		96	121,N, U,Y	(f) 3 *maceheads* of magnetite, marble, and haematite; [pp. 103–4: one of these was found ca. 35 cm above the pavement; NB: 121,N is also said to be from the storage pit (p. 105)]

	LOCATION	PAGE	PLATE	
		99	107,D, 108,109	(g) frags. of several *large crude t.c. animal* figures; 3 main types [see p. 99 and p. 103—one large couchant unglazed lion figure was found 35 cm above the pavement]
		101	102,S	(h) 5 small unglazed *animal figurines* of the usual household type
		103	111,B	(i) fragments of 3 of the 4 *green- and yellow-glazed lions*
		101	133,C	(j) *wooden cup* covered with bitumen inside and out
		—	127,Q	(k) bone *peg*
		—	130,H,O	(l) vari-colored *glass beads*
		—	131,H,I	(m) stone *pendant and bead*
		—	133,C	(n) wood *cup* with bitumen coating
		—	116,O	(o) pierced t.c. *lug*
		—	102,AA	(p) t.c. *animal figurine*, pierced chest
		—	104,A,B	(q) zoomorphic t.c. *jars*
		—	105,A–D	(r) zoomorphic t.c. *jars* and fragments
		—	106,A, B,E,G	(s) zoomorphic t.c. *jars* and fragments
		—	107,A,B	(t) zoomorphic t.c. *jar* fragments
		—	110,B	(u) glazed t.c. *sheep's head*
		—	121,C	(v) marble *plaque*
		—	121,F	(w) disc shaped shell *bead*
		—	126,Q	(x) copper *pendant*
		—	127,D	(y) copper *bosses*
		—	79,T	(z) t.c. high *cup* fragment, incised lip
[*Note: some of the above may have come from inside the shaft in G50—see below for its contents.*]				
•11	H18	96	121,Z	(a) 1/2 *ceremonial axe*, green rhyolite lava (Hittite double-axe)
		103, 108	—	(b) *beads* were scattered all across the court "as far as the eastern corner"
		108	—	(c) several *wall nails*
		108	—	(d) a *cylinder seal*
		108	—	(e) a *lamp* fragment
		108	—	(f) many fragments of *inlaid glass*
		108	—	(g) lots of *amulets* of glass, frit, and stone
•12	G29	97	111,B	fragments of *yellow-glazed couchant lion's head* found "close to and northeast of the pedestal in G29"
•13	H5	99, 106	103,L	(a) fragments of large, *crude t.c. animal figures*
		106	—	(b) many *glass beads*
		106	—	(c) fragments of *blue glass vessel*(?), crushed
		106	—	(d) a plain *Ishtar figurine*
		106	—	(e) a *wall-nail*
		106	103,L	(f) a small t.c. *lion-shaped jar*
•14	G73	101	—	[doorless alcove] "Within it was a considerable store of [unbaked & shattered—p. 102] *tablets* of the ordinary contract type, two *glazed pots...*, a glazed *wall-nuil* and many *beads*." Tablets had "no inscriptional connection with the temple" (p. 102).

LOCATION		PAGE	PLATE	
●15	G51	102	—	(a) [doorless room] "abundantly supplied with temple *beads*"
		—	102,Y	(b) t.c. *animal figurine*
●16	G35	106	114,B	unbaked *clay offering stand* (see p. 106 for description)
●17	H2	106	126,U	several *beads*, a *cylinder seal*, and a *copper spoon* (illustrated)
●18	H7	108	98,C	(a) six glazed *wall-nails*
		108	—	(b) many *beads* of glass, frit, and stone
		108	—	(c) a *copper pin*
		108	—	(d) a *copper spoon*, similar to that of H2
		108	98,I	(e) a *chariot wheel*
		108	—	(f) fragment of a pottery *lamp*
●19	H6	108	—	(a) a *shouldered cup*
		108	—	(b) a few glass *beads*
		108	97,M 98,B,D	(c) 5 glazed *wall nails*
		108	99,B	(d) fragment of a square glazed *wall-nail plate* of unusual design
●20	H11	108	97,N	(a) a glazed *wall-nail*
		109	98,H	(b) part of a glazed *wall-nail plate* found on the pavement under the oven in the east corner of H11 [pp. 109–10]
		108	—	(c) a *cylinder seal*
		108	—	(d) several *beads*
		108	—	(e) 2 very large copper arrowheads
●21	H11	108		Near doorway to H11 are front legs of the green-glazed lion of G29
●22	H15	—	120,NN	Glass sun disc pendant
●23		115		On the earliest level (p. 122: "Assyrian") of the scrap-brick pavement of Stratum I were several frags. of the fantastic lion-bodied figures of Temple A (Pl. 109). This pavement was built over the walls of H6, H7, H9, H10, and H12. A later pavement here is Parthian (p. 122), traceable only by storage pits sunk from above into the temple building.

TEMPLE A

ARTIFACTS FOUND IN GRAIN STORAGE PIT IN G50 (= ca. H16)

[no signs of any stored grain]

PAGE	PLATE	
89,105	102,F	(a) one complete eye ("part of cult statue") + fragment of another
105	102,G	(b) near the above "was a triangular, flat piece of dolomite, hollowed in the center—the eye of another and far from lifelike figure"
105	121,N	(c) magnetite macehead [p. 96: also said to be from courtyard]
105	—	(d) a glazed wall-nail
105	—	(e) many glass and frit beads

ARTIFACTS FOUND IN SHAFT IN G50 (labelled "well")

[p. 104: "filled from bottom to top"]

PAGE	PLATE	
104	—	(a) "most of the zoomorphic jars"
104	—	(b) "broken bases and stands of the two green-glazed lions"
104	—	(c) "the sheep's head"
104	92,Z	(d) "two glazed tripod bowls"
104	—	(e) "many wall nails"
104	—	(f) "lesser objects and fragments" [no great quantity of *libin*]
(521)	40,A–Y	(g) 25 marble stamp seals [=deposit found below bottom of shaft]
(521)	41,C–F	(h) 3 marble and 1 limestone cylinder seals: [" " " "]
(522)	49,E	(i) crude t.c. bowl [=found below pavement on which stamp and cylinder seals were found]

BIBLIOGRAPHY

Andrae, Walter

1922 *Die Archaischen Ischtar-Tempel in Assur* (*WVDOG* 39; Leipzig).

Bjorkman, Judith

1994 "Hoards and Deposits in Bronze Age Mesopotamia" (Ph. D. dissertation, University of Pennsylvania, Philadelphia).

Börker-Klähn, Jutta

1979 "Eine folgenreiche Fundbeobachtung in Mari," *ZA* 69: 221–33.

Crawford, Harriet

1987 "The *Construction Inférieure* at Tello. A Reassessment," *Iraq* 49: 71–76.

Faraone, Christopher

1992 *Talismans and Trojan Horses—Guardian Statues in Ancient Greek Myth and Ritual* (Oxford).

Frankfort, Henri

1939 *Sculpture of the Third Millennium from Tell Asmar and Khafajah* (OIP 44; University of Chicago Press).

Hall, H.R., and C. Leonard Woolley

1927 *Al-'Ubaid.* Ur Excavations I. (Oxford: Oxford University Press).

Heinrich, Ernst

1936 *Kleinfunde aus den Archaischen Tempelschichten in Uruk.* (Ausgrabungen der Deutschen Forschungsgemeinschaft in Uruk-Warka. Band 1; Berlin).

1982 *Die Tempel und Heiligtümer im alten Mesopotamien: Typologie, Morphologie, und Geschichte.* 2 vols. (Berlin: deGruyter).

Jacobsen, Thorkild

1987a *The Harps that Once...* (New Haven: Yale University Press).

1987b "The Graven Image," in P.D. Miller, Jr., P.D. Hanson, and S.D. McBride (eds.), *Ancient Israelite Religion—Essays in Honor of Frank Moore Cross* (Philadelphia:Fortress Press) pp. 15–32.

Lenzen, H.J.

1974 "Die Architektur in Eanna in der Uruk IV Periode," *Iraq* 36: 111ff.

Moorey, P.R.S.

1994 *Ancient Mesopotamian Materials and Industries—The Archaeological Evidence* (Oxford: Clarendon Press).

Moortgat, Anton

1965 *Tell Chuera in Nordost-Syrien. Vorläufiger Bericht über die vierte Grabungskampagne 1963.* (Wissenschaftliche Abhandlungen der Arbeitsgemeinschaft für Forschung des Landes Nordrhein-Westfalen, 31; Köln and Opladen).

1967 *Tell Chuera in Nordost-Syrien. Vorläufiger Bericht über die fünfte Grabungskampagne 1964.* (Wiesbaden: Schriften der Max Freiherr von Oppenheim-Stiftung, 6).

Oates, David, and Joan Oates

1989 "Akkadian Buildings at Tell Brak," *Iraq* 51: 193–211.

1991 "Excavations at Tell Brak," *Iraq* 53: 127–49.

Owen, David I., and Gernot Wilhelm (eds.)

1996 *Richard F. S. Starr Memorial Volume (Studies in the Civilization and Culture of Nuzi and the Hurrians*, 8; Bethesda, Md.: CDL Press).

Pedersén, Olof

1998 *Archives and Libraries in the Ancient Near East, 1500–300 B.C.* (Bethesda, Md.: CDL Press)

Pritchard, James B. (ed.)

1955 *Ancient Near Eastern Texts Relating to the Old Testament* (2nd edition: Princeton).

Starr, R.F.S.

1937 *Nuzi: Report on the Excavations at Yorghan Tepa near Kirkuk, Iraq...1927–1931.* Vol. II – Plates and Plans. (Cambridge, Mass.).

1939 *Nuzi: Report on the Excavations at Yorghan Tepa near Kirkuk, Iraq...1927–1931.* Vol. I. – Text. (Cambridge, Mass.).

Selz, Gebhard

1997 "The Holy Drum, the Spear, and the Harp—Towards an Understanding of the Problems of Deification in Third Millennium Mesopotamia," in I. Finkel and M. Geller (eds.), *Sumerian Gods and Their Representations* (Styx) pp. 167–209.

Stein, Diana

1989 "A Reappraisal of the 'Saushtatar Letter' from Nuzi," *ZA* 79: 36–60.

Walker, Christopher and M.B. Dick

1999 "The Induction of the Cult Image in Ancient Mesopotamia: The Mesopotamian *mīs pî* Ritual," in Michael B. Dick (ed.), *Born in Heaven, Made on Earth: The Making of the Cult Image in the Ancient Near East* (Eisenbrauns), pp. 55–121.

The Architecture of Nuzi and Its Significance in the Architectural History of Mesopotamia*

MIRKO NOVÁK
Eberhard-Karls Universität, Tübingen

The numerous excavations conducted in the Near East since the Nuzi excavations were completed have added a great deal of new information on the architectural history of Mesopotamia, particularly with respect to the public architecture of temples and palaces. However, only recently have private dwellings been subjected to the kind of excavation and analysis that public structures have had. This survey discusses both public and private architecture at Nuzi in the light of recent finds throughout Mesopotamia.

In 1939 R.F.S. Starr published the results of the excavations conducted by the Harvard University expedition at Yorğan Tepe.[1] Since then there have been only a few studies concerning the architecture of this important site.[2] The focus of nearly all these studies has been public architecture, represented by a temple of long use and a well-decorated and large-scale palace. The private dwellings, on the other hand, have just recently begun to be subject of further analysis.

A large number of excavations in the Near East and the publication of their major results in the last fifty years have shed new light on the architectural history of ancient Mesopotamia, for which Nuzi has remained an important source. In turn, the architecture of Nuzi can now be understood much better than at the time of publication.

Since the interests of most scholars in several aspects of archaeology and history have changed in recent decades, new questions have arisen with respect to the material. The socio-economic aspects of archaeology and, especially, architecture have become very important issues. In this context it has become clear that the well-investigated town of Nuzi, with its large corpus of written sources, may offer new and important information. Therefore, it seems to be opportune

* I thank Dr. Anthony Green for helping me compose this paper in acceptable English.

1 On the excavations at Nuzi and its history, stratigraphy, architecture, and art, see Starr 1939 and Stein 1997.

2 See references below.

Studies on the Civilization and Culture of Nuzi and the Hurrians - 10

to take a look at the architecture of Nuzi with regard both to pure architectural history as well as socio-economics. No final answers, of course, can be offered in a short paper. It is impossible to reflect on all aspects of the architecture of Nuzi. Here, just a brief overview and a consideration of context can be presented, in the hope that further research on the material might be undertaken.

First the outer shape and inner structure of the whole town will be briefly discussed; then the development and organization of the public and private buildings. Thereupon follow some concluding remarks on the significance of Nuzi in the architectural history of Mesopotamia.

1. The Town

The general plan of the ruins shows a nearly square main mound measuring about 200 m in length and width (Fig. 1). A rectangular town wall formed the outer shape of the town.[3]

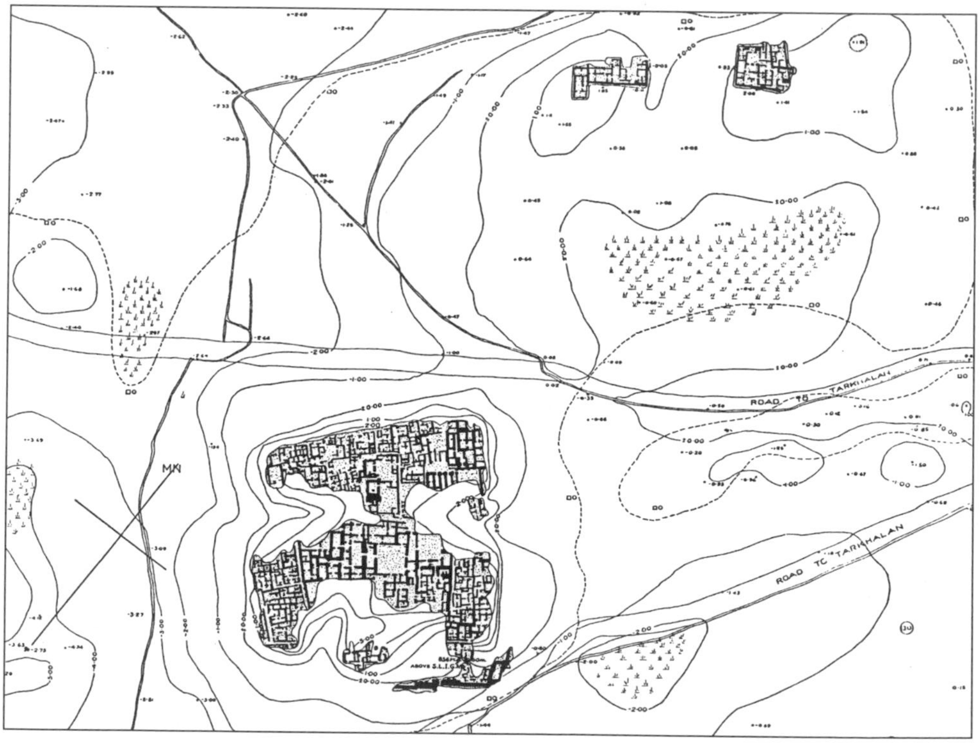

Fig. 1: General plan of Nuzi (from Starr 1939, Plan 2)

---

3 McAdam 1981.

Some 300 m north of the fortified town, a group of wealthy private houses, the residences of rich landowners, was investigated. The excavators thought that they were *extra muros*. Several modern excavations in the Near East now have made clear that many ancient cities were characterized by a separation between an "inner" and an "outer" town, a separation that was created sometimes by an inner fortification wall. On the other hand, large parts of flat outer towns often have been totally destroyed by modern agricultural activities.

This leads to the suggestion that the *villae* indeed were part of a—possibly also fortified—outer or lower town, which is no longer preserved. G. Wilhelm has drawn attention to another piece of evidence that supports this theory; in the Nuzi texts there is reference to a *kerḫu* of Nuzi, a Hurrian word meaning "inner town."[4] Thus the area surrounding the temple and the palace may therefore be identified as the *kerḫu,* i.e., the inner town of a larger scale Nuzi. However, only a small portion of the city wall—which probably was the separation wall between the inner and outer town—has been investigated. Though the fortification as a whole was nearly rectangular, the construction of the wall itself was irregular.

None of the gates was excavated; therefore their number and structure remain unknown. The alignment of the streets and the existence of three deep *wādīs* suggest that the city had at least three accesses, one in the northeast (Square "N"), a second in the southwest (Square "F" or "K"), and a third one in the southeast (Square "P", "Q", or "V").

The street system of Nuzi is characterized by a three-step hierarchy with one straight main axis, several regular quarter access streets, and some dead-end alleys in the dwelling quarters (Fig. 2).[5] It seems that several streets ran along the inner sides of the city wall. Although only the existence of one of them—Street 10—has been proved, the spatial organization of certain houses makes it clear that more streets of that kind must have existed.

The main thoroughfare, Street 5, connected two gates—the one in the northeast and that in the southwest—and separated the temple and the palace. This, and the fact that the well-built main drainage channel ran under its pavement, shows the importance of this intra-urban axis. Street 4 connected the third gate with Street 5 and was therefore the second prominent axis of the town. Some other streets (e.g., 11, 12, 14, and 15) were dead-end streets.

The inner town was divided into four parts: the official space with palace and temple in the center and three quarters with private dwellings. The "Northwestern Ridge" (NWR) stretched north of Street 5, the "Southwestern Section" (SWS) west of the palace, and the "Northeastern Section" (NES) east of it.

Analysis of the houses and their inventories revealed that different social classes of inhabitants used different quarters—a distinct case of social segre-

---

4 Haas – Wegner 1995: 193ff.

5 Wirth 1975: 66ff.

gation.[6] The most prominent quarter was the Northwestern Ridge, where the richest people lived. The most standardized houses existed in the southwestern section. The houses in the northeastern section show a large variation in the social status of the inhabitants.[7]

In general, the town gives the impression of a planned organization. The main features were the rectangular outer shape, straight-running, and almost regular streets and the centralized position of palace and temple. The differences in the forms of the houses and alignments of the streets between Stratum III and the later Stratum II may indicate that the earlier phase of the town was more regular. Through time, a kind of urban dynamic took place: due to social differences among the inhabitants, some houses occupied former open spaces or parts of other houses. This, perhaps, is good evidence of the social inequality in ancient Nuzi.

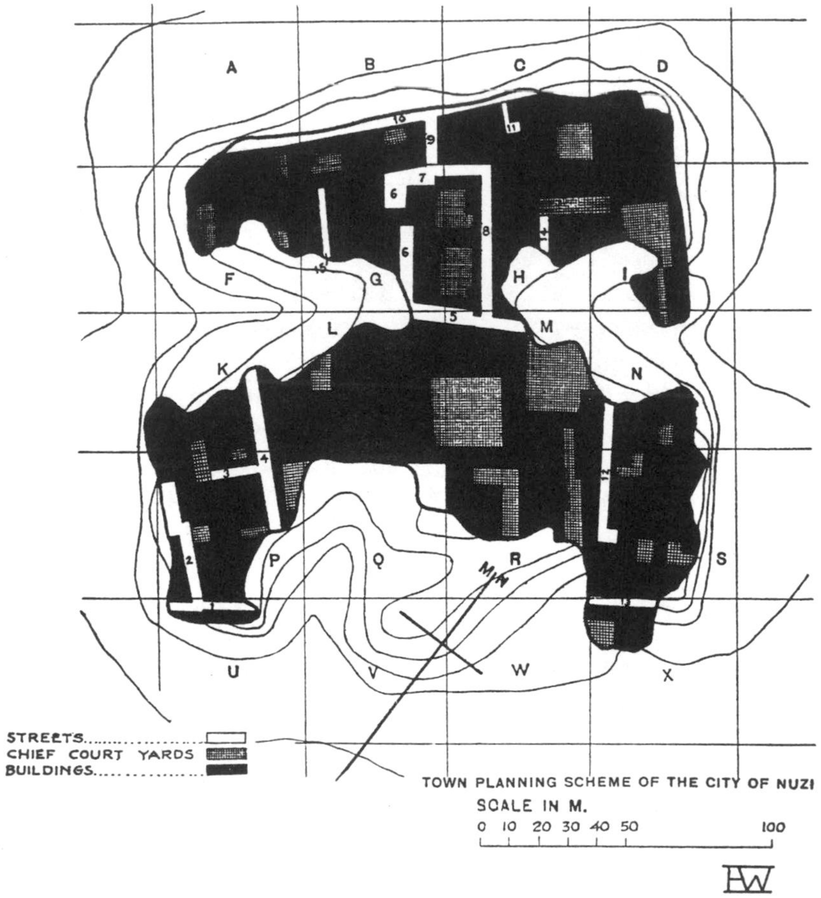

Fig. 2: Street system of the town (from Starr 1939, Plan 16)

6 Novák 1994.

7 For the textual evidence, see Morrison 1987 and Morrison 1993.

2. The Palace

The royal palace was situated in the center of the town, south of the temple (Fig. 3).[8] The main entrance is not preserved but was probably situated in the northern or northwestern part of the building and led from Street 5 via a vestibule into court M 94. The street itself, as the main axis through the town, connected the palace with the temple area.[9] The palace was divided into three parts. The first, surrounding the paved courtyard M 94 with its benches on the southwestern and southeastern walls, was obviously an "official" quarter. To the east lay the administrative and supply area, with kitchens and baths, as well as production and storage rooms.

The first audience hall (M 89) separated this part of the building from the central one with its main court (M 100)—the largest in the whole palace. To the southeast a sequence of large rooms with Q 103 was accessible. Its structure is reminiscent of the later Neo-Assyrian scheme, well known in palaces and residential houses.[10] Additional living rooms, with baths and storage chambers lay northwest of court M 100.

The most important room arrangement stretched to the southwest of M 100—the two large halls L 20 and L 11. L 20, the smaller one, had a broad entrance from the court. Two brick pillars in front of the entrance may have supported a wooden roof. The construction of such an anteroom is reminiscent of the medieval Islamic *Tarima*. A similar architectural element is known from Syrian palaces, for example at Ebla and Alalaḫ, and became part of the later *ḫilāni*.[11] The largest room of the palace, L 11, was situated behind L 20. The arrangement, as a whole, can be identified as a typical Old Babylonian audience hall suite found, for example, in the palace of Zimri-Lim at Mari.

The third part of the palace, of a more private character, lay behind the audience rooms in the southwest. It is characterized by several sequences of rooms serving different functions.

The entire palace was richly decorated with wall paintings and furnished with brick and marble paving, and had a well-organized drainage system.

The two main features of the palace were inner courtyards in the center of different suites and sequences of rooms—in German *Raumketten*—which created so-called *Agglutinate*. Elements of Old Babylonian palace architecture, such as

---

8 A description and typological classification of the building in relation to the palace architecture of Mesopotamia has been presented by E. Heinrich (Orthmann 1975: 267f.; Heinrich 1984: 82ff.); its spatial system and inner structure have been analyzed by J. Margueron (Margueron 1982: 425ff.).

9 Heinrich 1984: 82f.

10 Heinrich 1984: 83.

11 Novák 1996: 338f.

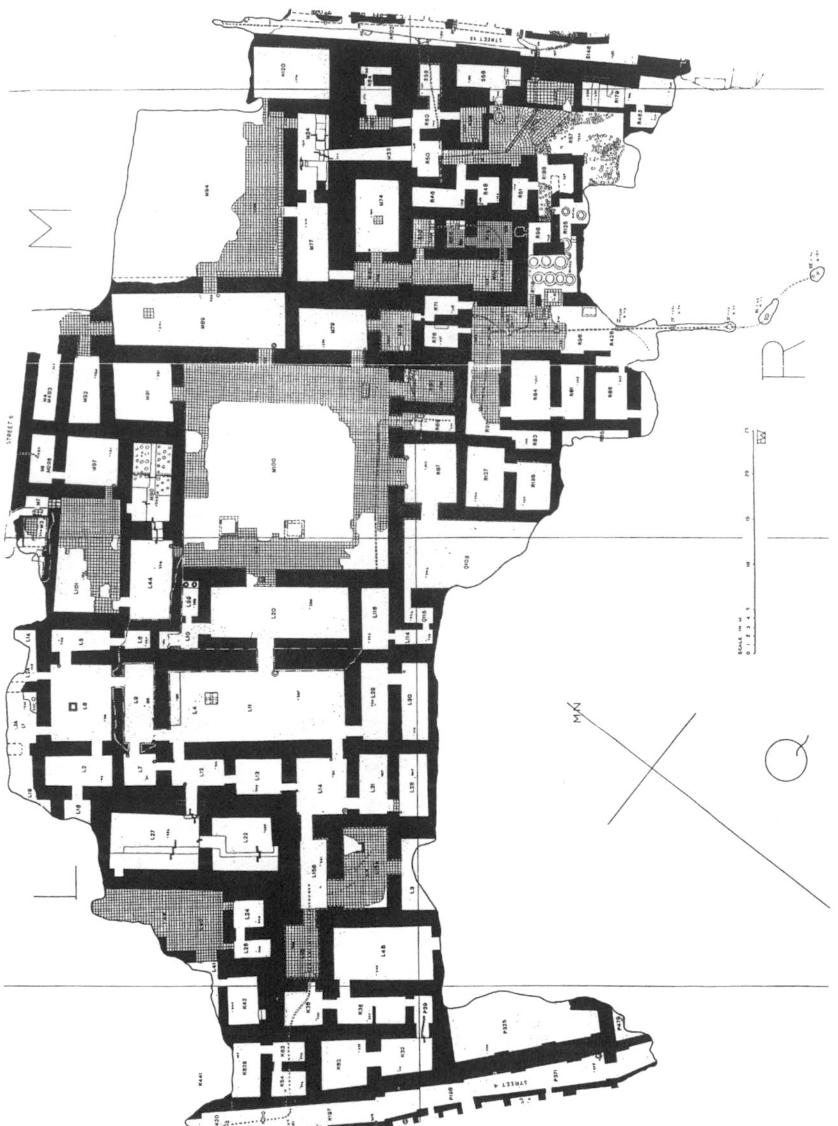

Fig. 3: The royal palace (from Heinrich 1984, Abb. 43, after Starr 1939, Plan 13)

the audience hall group, were mixed with new ones characteristic of the later Middle and Neo-Assyrian palaces—for example the structure with a series of several courtyards maintaining different degrees of "privacy." This shows that the building was erected at a time of changing architectural movements; it marks a time when new forms began to evolve and old ones started to lose importance.

3. The Temple

The only identified sacral building in Nuzi was situated north of Street 5, neighboring the palace (Fig. 4). As excavations have shown, the temple was built in the third millennium and was in use until the end of the occupation of the town. In the earliest phase, G, dating to the late third millennium, only the northwestern shrine existed. But in phase F, that is during the Old Babylonian Period, it was transformed into a double shrine and remained so up until the latest phase, A. One of the shrines was probably dedicated to Ištar-Šawuška, the principal goddess of Nuzi.[12] The other may have served as the temple of Teššub, although there are no direct references for this identification.

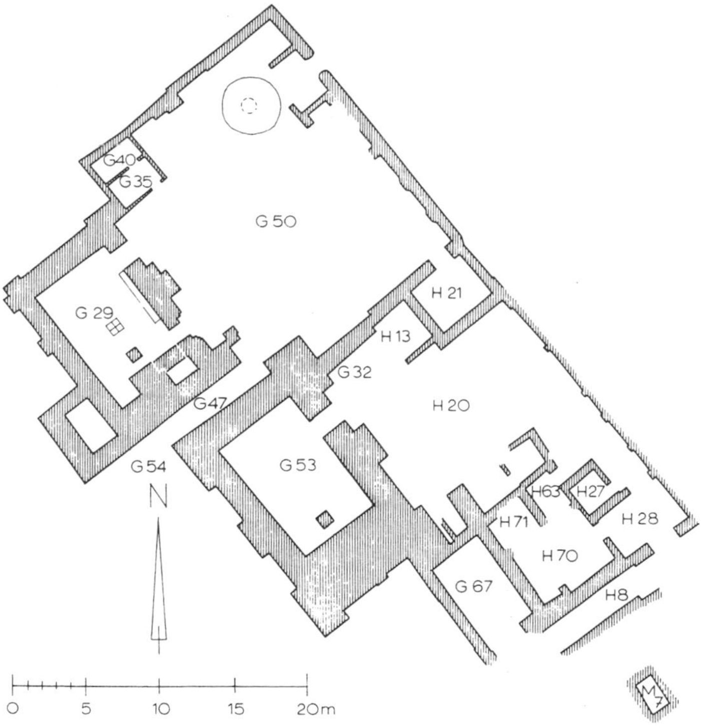

Fig. 4: Temple with double shrine of Šawuška and Teššub (?). Phase B (from Heinrich 1982, Abb. 294, after Starr 1939, Plan 12)

12 Stein 1997: 173.

The form of the double temple—with its two shrines—has been analyzed by Ernst Heinrich,[13] who classified it as a so-called *Herdhaus*.[14] It was formed by an enclosed court and the two *cellae*. The main feature of both was the *Knickachs-schema*, the "bent axis-scheme"; this means that the visitor to the shrine had to turn at a right angle after entering the room.[15]

Barthel Hrouda has stressed in several papers that the *Knickachsschema* was associated with early Hurrian civilization, and thereafter mainly developed in Assur and the area east of the Tigris for the cult of Ištar-Šawuška.[16] But the earliest phases F and G, which date to the pre-Hurrian "Gasur"-period, and the later phases A–D, all show the "bent axis-scheme." Due to the lack of a hiatus, it seems that the temple kept in general its original plan following an old principle.

The "*Knickachsschema*" was known in northern Babylonia already in the third millennium, and probably derived from the Uruk-period *Mittelsaalhaus*, as it is seen in the temple of Sîn in Ḫafāǧī.[17] In the Ur III period it disappeared in Babylonia itself but was—on a small scale—still in use in Assyria and some other parts of northern Mesopotamia. Worthy of note are the temples of Ištar and Aššur in the town of Assur—but also some smaller shrines, for example in Dūr-Šarrukēn, which followed this principle until Late Neo-Assyrian times.

That such an outdated scheme was used in Nuzi makes it clear that there was no real break in the worship of the main deity of Gasur/Nuzi in spite of the new ethnic components and even the change of the city's name. Indeed, the cult architecture in this town was very conservative and traditional. New influences like the Babylonian temple type with its *Breitraum*, or the Assyrian one with the *Langraum*, were never copied. The decoration shows Assyrian influences, such as the glazed *sikkātu*.

4. Private Dwellings

In addition to the palace and temple of Nuzi, many private dwellings were excavated.[18] Much attention was paid to the residences of rich landowners in the northern "suburb"—or rather "outer town." The most prominent of these was the house of Šilwa-Teššub, whose architecture shows typologically a close connection to the palace (Fig. 5).[19]

---

13 Orthmann 1975: 267f.; Heinrich 1982: 152f., 221.

14 For this term, see Heinrich 1982: 1ff.

15 For the development of the "Knickachstempel," see Novák, forthcoming.

16 See, e.g., the paper published in 1995, "Zur Frühgeschichte der Hurriter" in *Eski Yakın Doğu Kültürleri Üzerine Incelemeler* (In Memoriam I. Metin Akyurt, Bahattin Devam, Anı Kitabı), 17375. Istanbul.

17 Novák forthcoming.

18 Starr 1939; Novák 1994; Bardeschi 1998a; Bardeschi 1998b; Miglus 1999.

19 Orthmann 1975: 265f.; Heinrich 1984: 86f.; Bardeschi 1998a: 225ff.

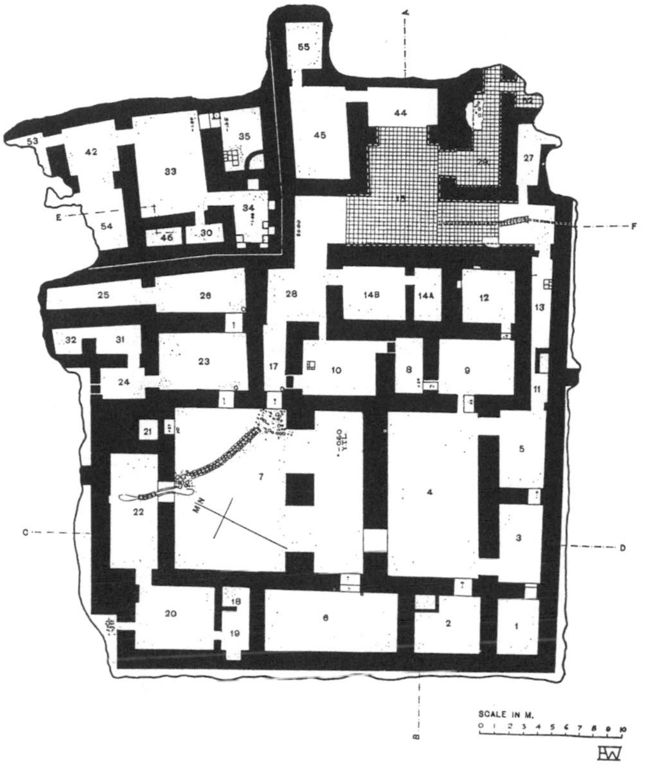

Fig. 5: House of Šilwa-Teššub as example of the so-called "suburban dwellings" (from Starr 1939, Plan 34)

The houses of the inner town can be classified in two ways: formal and functional.[20] Four different forms of houses were used at Nuzi:[21] The most important was the *reguliertes Agglutinat*, a house with several rooms of almost equal size (Fig. 6) that were arranged to form a more or less regular block. The second prominent form was the *Mittelsaalhaus*, an often tripartite house that was dominated by a central hall connected with several smaller rooms (Fig. 7). In contrast, Babylonian-like *Hofhäuser*, with a central and dominating court, were rarely used (Fig. 8).

The *Agglutinat* was a regular and simple, but also very outdated, concept for building a house. It became rare in elaborate Mesopotamian architecture during the second and first millennia.[22] Also the *Mittelsaalhaus*-scheme was an early design—most popular throughout Mesopotamia during the Uruk period. Only in Assyria was it still in use until the first millennium, as evidenced by the private houses seen at Assur.

---

20 Novák 1994.

21 For the terminology of the classification of house forms, see E. Heinrich 1975, 177ff.

22 Miglus 1999.

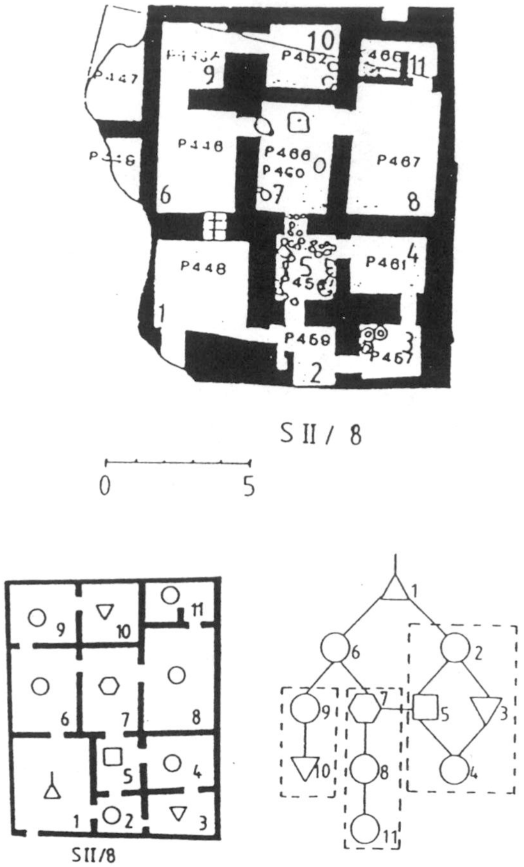

Fig. 6: Group SII/8 as an example of the "reguliertes Agglutinat" (from Novák 1994, Abb. 10, partly after Starr 1939, Plan 13)

The house-forms at Nuzi give the impression of a conservative architecture, on the one hand, and of close relations to Assyria on the other. Babylonian influences were not present on a large scale. A dominating feature was, as in parts of the palace, the sequence of rooms, the so-called *Raumkette*. A good example is Group 17 in Stratum II, where at least 11 rooms were constructed in a single row.[23]

There is no marked difference between the houses in Stratum III and II, except that the latter became more irregular in shape and the sizes of the units differed more markedly.

The functional classification of the houses is based on the analysis of their inventories and installations. Both provide distinct archaeological evidence for

23 Novák 1994: 424, Abb. 17.

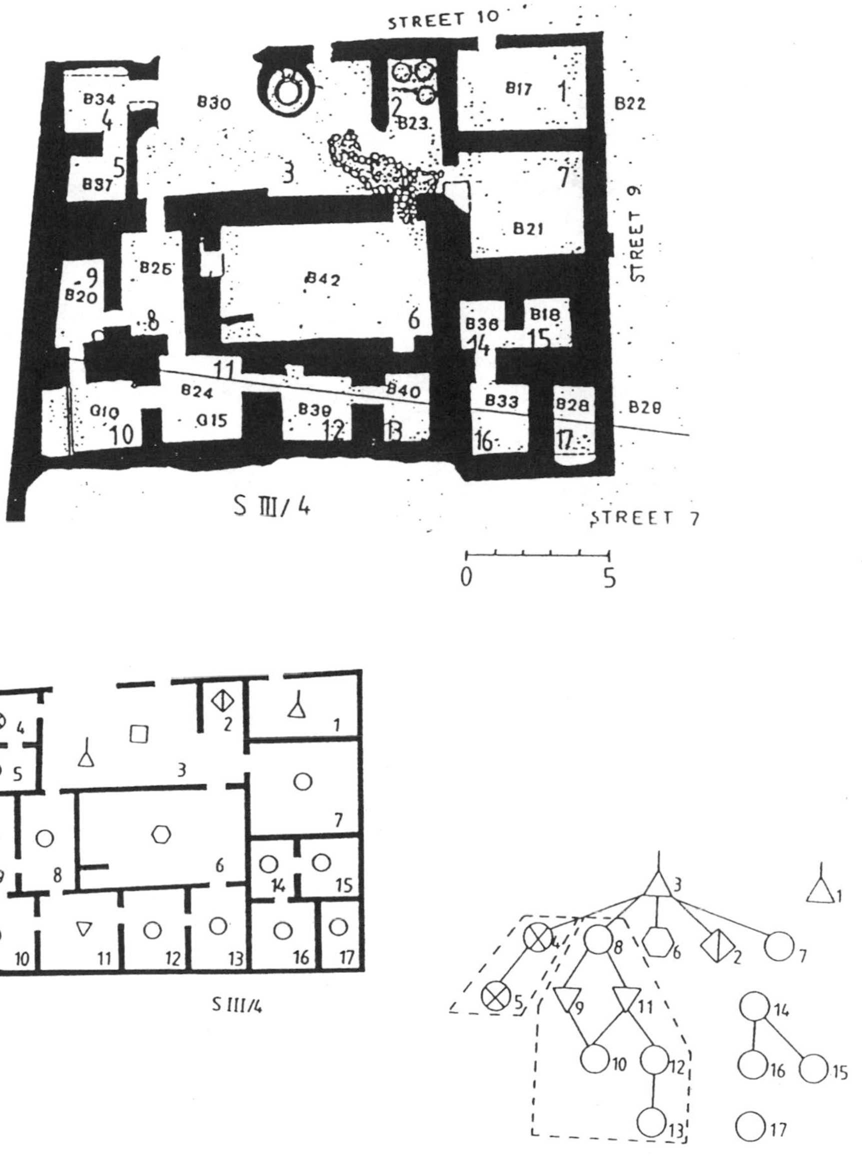

Fig. 7: Group SIII/4 as an example of the "Mittelsaalhaus"
(from Novák 1994, Abb. 31, partly after Starr 1939, Plan 11)

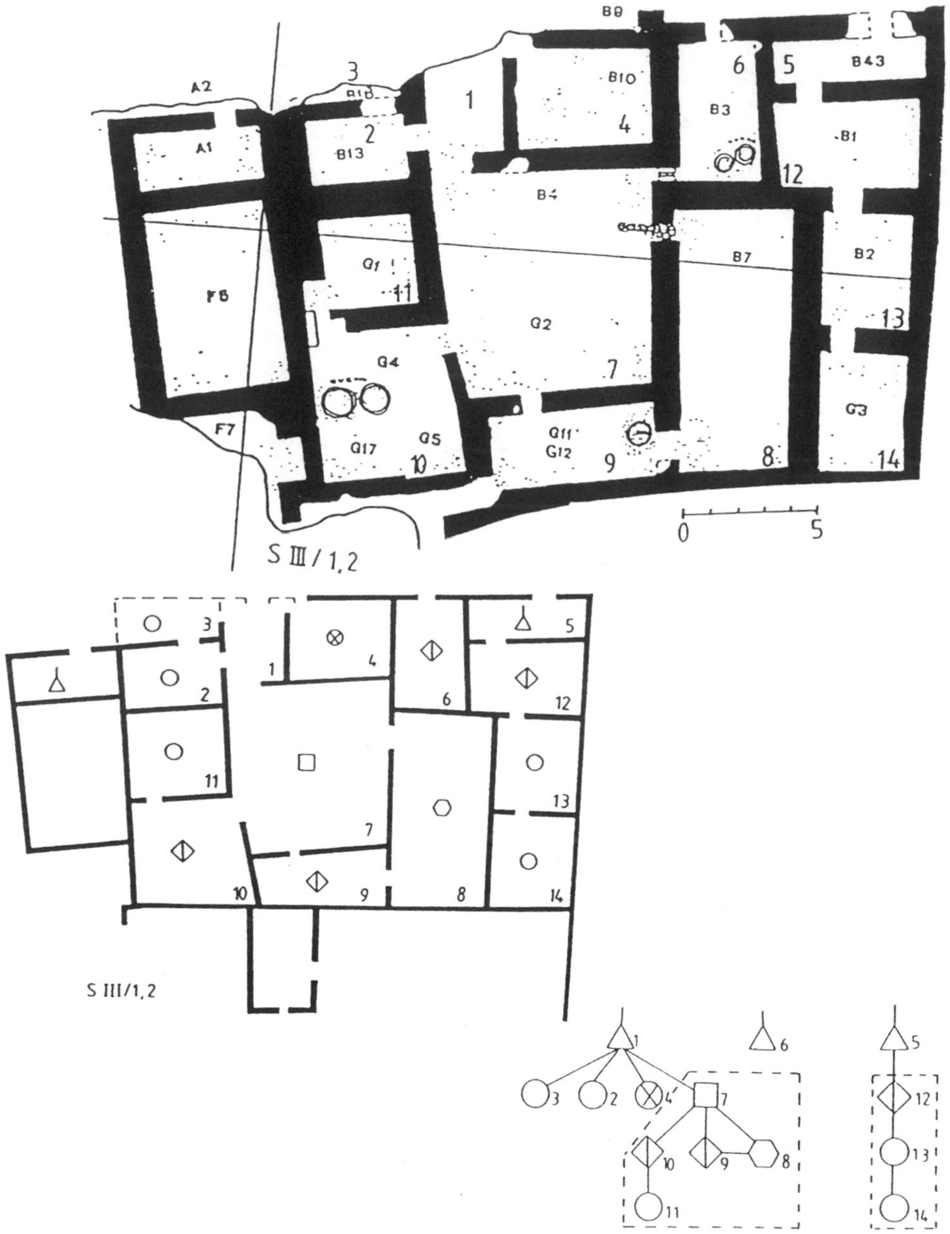

Fig. 8: Group SIII/2 as an example of the "Hofhaus"
(from Novák 1994, Abb. 30, partly after Starr 1939, Plan 11)

the activities that took place in the different chambers and courts. Although every room in a Mesopotamian house was multifunctional, each one did have a primary use, such as for washing or cooking. Therefore, each could be classified as a "bath," "kitchen," or "reception room," etc.[24] This corresponds to Akkadian expressions for different types of rooms, such as *bīt rimki, bīt ḫuršī, kisallu, ekallu* or *pāpāḫu*.[25]

The so-defined main functions of the different rooms provide, in connection with the formal structure and organization of the units and apartments, an opportunity to determine the functional structure of the houses.[26] This can be presented distinctly by a schema (Fig. 9): each room is marked by a special symbol indicating its function (Fig. 10).

On the basis of functional structure, four types of houses can be distinguished. *Type 1* is characterized by a single suite, used by only one household. *Type 2*, also used by only one household, shows a separation between an official and a private part of the house. *Type 3* has only one official but two private suites. Houses of *Type 4* were used by two households and have at least two separate official and private units. This type appears only twice at Nuzi. This functional analysis gives some information about the customs of housing. As a rule, every nucleus family possessed its own house; dwellings used by extended families were rather rare.[27] In many cases, a separation was created between a private and a reception suite (Fig. 11), suggesting that privacy was very important to the people of ancient Nuzi.

As stressed above, the social structure of the inhabitants of the several quarters differed markedly. Spacious rooms, especially reception rooms, richly decorated walls and floors, proper installations, and a large quantity of luxury goods indicated wealth. Cuneiform tablets with administrative texts and letters provide additional information about the mercantile position of the families and their social status. It is interesting that both textual and archaeological evidence leads to a similar interpretation of social structure and status at Nuzi.[28]

---

24 Novák 1994: 364.

25 Kalla 1996: 247ff.; Miglus 1996: 218, fig. 9.

26 Novák 1994: 380ff.

27 For the family structure in Nuzi, see G. Dosch 1996, 301ff. Contrary to her view (that extended families lived together), the domestic architecture at Nuzi clearly shows that only nucleus families used the houses. This corresponds to the results of a study undertaken by Kalla 1996, 252.

28 Morrison 1987; Morrison 1993.

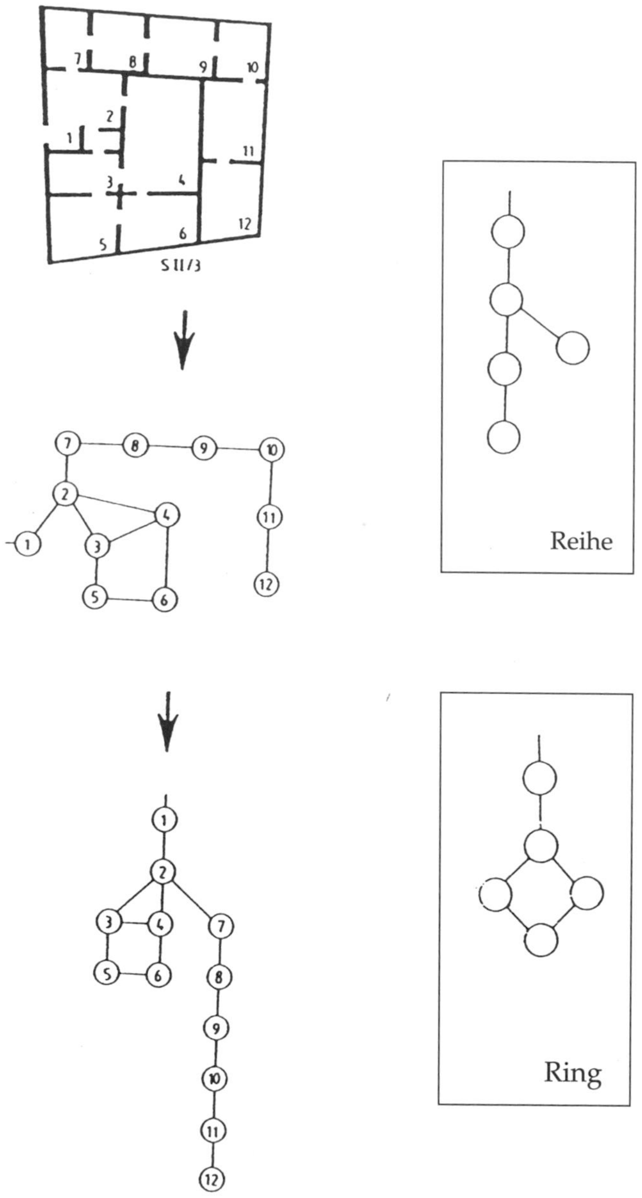

Fig. 9: Systematical scheme for analysing house forms by marking formal units (from Novák 1994, Abb. 4).

TYPES OF ROOMS AND THEIR SYMBOLS

Vestibule		⊗	*biwāba* (Doorkeeper's Room)
Reception Room		□	Court
Bath		▽	Storage Room
Kitchen		○	Living Room

Fig. 10: Scheme to mark functional room categories (after Novák 1994, 410).

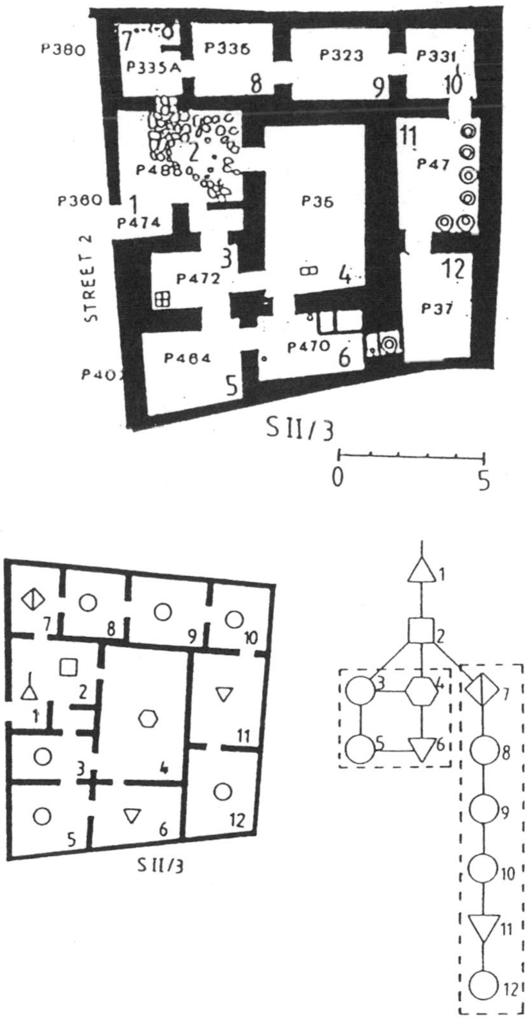

Fig. 11:
Group SII/3 with significant separation of private and reception suite
(from Novák 1994, Abb. 6, partly after Starr 1939, Plan 13).

5. Conclusion

In general, Nuzi with its rectangular outer shape, straight-running and almost regular streets and the centralized position of palace and temple gives the impression of a planned and thoroughly organized town. In the time between Stratum III and II, an urban dynamic led to a successive loss of regularity of the houses as well as of the street alignments. But the process of degeneration of urban structure, which is characteristic of Near Eastern cities,[29] was not very marked by the time the town had been destroyed and abandoned.[30] This suggests that the town was founded or refounded with a regular shape and structure only a short time before the period of Stratum III.

In contrast, the traditional and archaic form of the temple with its "bent axis scheme" proves the long continuity in worship and architecture from the third millennium onwards. The stratigraphy demonstrates the long use of this building. This leads to the question of how the immigration of the Hurrians and the change between "Gasur" and "Nuzi" took place. Was there a sudden break, as the layout of the town seems to indicate, or a slow and insidious change with definite continuity, as the form of the temple suggests? At the present time, it is not possible to give a satisfactory answer.

The palace shows a mixture of traditional and innovative elements, thereby indicating a link between Old Babylonian and Middle Assyrian architecture. It was obviously erected at a time of changing architectural movements. Unfortunately, nothing is known about its earlier phases or preceding buildings.

The houses at Nuzi represent a conservative domestic architecture with some outdated forms and arrangements, and a moderate affinity to Assyrian buildings. The separation created in most houses between an official and a private suite suggests that privacy was of utmost importance.

Since the excavation reports give very detailed information about the architecture of Nuzi, only a few further studies have been undertaken during recent decades. Unfortunately neither the temple, with its archaic plan, nor the palace have been the subject of detailed analysis in regard to questions of programmatic messages in architecture and decoration or of functional categories and their relationship to social structures. In contrast to its importance as an archaeological site, the significance of Nuzi in the architectural history of the Ancient Near East has, to date, not been satisfactorily investigated.

---

29 Wirth 1975; Wirth 1997.

30 Novák 1994: 401ff.

References

Bardeschi, Ch. D.

1998a *Architettura domestica nella Mesopotamia settentrionale nel II Millenio A.C.* Florence.

1998b Quelques Considerations à propos de'lArchitecture de l'Agglomeration Hourrite de Nuzi. In: S. de Martino – F. Imparati (eds.), *Studi e Testi I.* Florence.

Dosch, G.

1996 Houses and Households in Nuzi: The Inhabitants, the Family, and those dependent on it. In: K.R. Veenhof (ed.), *Houses and Households in Ancient Mesopotamia* (Papers read at the 40e Rencontre Assyriologique Internationale), 301–8. Leiden.

Haas, V. – Wegner, I.

1995 Stadtverfluchungen in den Texten aus Boğazköy sowie die hurritischen Termini für „Oberstadt", „Unterstadt" und „Herd". U. Finkbeiner – R. Dittmann – H. Hauptmann, *Beiträge zur Kulturgeschichte Vorderasiens, Festschrift für R. M. Boehmer,* 187–94. Mainz.

Heinrich, E.

1975 Stichwort „Haus", B. Archäologisch. *Reallexikon der Assyriologie und Vorderasiatischen Archäologie* 4, 176–220.

1982 *Tempel und Heiligtümer im Alten Mesopotamien.* Berlin.

1984 *Paläste im Alten Mesopotamien.* Berlin.

Kalla, G.

1996 Das altbabylonische Wohnhaus und seine Struktur. In: K.R. Veenhof (ed.) *Houses and Households in Ancient Mesopotamia* (Papers read at the 40e Rencontre Assyriologique Internationale), 247–56. Leiden.

Margueron, J.

1982 *Recherches sur les Palais Mésopotamiens de l'Age du Bronze.* Paris.

McAdam, E.

1981 "Town Planning and domestic Architecture in Ancient Mesopotamia from earliest Times until the middle of the Second Millenium B.C.," Ph. D. dissertation, Somerville College.

Miglus, P.A.

1996 Die räumliche Organisation des altbabylonischen Hofhauses. In: K.R. Veenhof (ed.) *Houses and Households in Ancient Mesopotamia* (Papers read at the 40e Rencontre Assyriologique Internationale), 211–20. Leiden.

1999 *Städtische Wohnhausarchitektur in Babylonien und Assyrien.* Baghdader Forschungen. Mainz.

Morrison, M.

1987 The Southwest Archives at Nuzi. *Studies on the Civilization and Culture of Nuzi and the Hurrians* 2, 167–201.

1993 The Eastern Archives of Nuzi. *Studies on the Civilization and Culture of Nuzi and the Hurrians* 4, 3–130.

Novák, M.

1994 Eine Typologie der Wohnhäuser von Nuzi. *Baghdader Mitteilungen* 25, 341–446.

1996 Der Landschaftsbezug in der orientalischen Palastarchitektur. *Altorientalische Forschungen* 23/2, 335–78.

forth. Hofhaus und Antentempel—Zur Entwicklung des assyrischen Tempelbaus. In: Meyer, J.-W. – Novák, M. – Pruß, A. (eds.), *Festschrift Winfried Orthmann.*

Orthmann, W.

(Hrsg.) 1975 *Der Alte Orient.* Propyläen Kunstgeschichte 14. Berlin.

Starr, R.F.S.

1939 *Nuzi. Report on the Excavations at Yorgan Tepe near Kirkuk.* Cambridge Mass.

Stein, D.L.

1997 "Nuzi." *The Oxford Encyclopedia of Archaeology in the Near East,* 171–75. New York and Oxford.

Wirth, E.

1975 Die orientalische Stadt. *Saeculum* 26, 45–94.

1997 Kontinuität und Wandel der orientalischen Stadt—Zur Prägung von städtischen Institutionen durch jahrtausendealte kulturspezifische Handlungsgrammatiken. In: G. Wilhelm (ed.), *Die orientalische Stadt: Kontinuität, Wandel, Bruch.* CDOG 1, 1–44. Saarbrücken.

The Zagros Campaigns of Šulgi and Amar-Suena

DOUGLAS FRAYNE

RIM Project, Toronto

A study of the toponyms mentioned in the year names, royal inscriptions, and economic tablets dating to the last half of the reigns of Šulgi and Amar-Suena, coupled with a detailed study of modern topographical maps of the area around the Zagros foothills road, have enabled the identification of tentative locations for many of the cities attacked by the Ur III kings during their Zagros campaigns. The evidence of the Ur III sources is supplemented by evidence from the royal inscriptions of Narām-Sîn of Akkad, Kutik-Inšušinak and Šilḫak-Inšušinak of Elam, in addition to the evidence of the Early Dynastic List of Geographical Names (=LGN), the Gudea cylinders, Nuzi archival texts, and modern place names.

Studies on the Civilization and Culture of Nuzi and the Hurrians - 10

4.12 Temtena(š)
4.13 Lami
4.14 Šelwuḫu(we)
4.15 Tašenni(we)
4.16 Ḫuḫnuri
4.17 Ayyinu
4.18 Ašuḫiš
4.19 Terqa
4.20 Lassi
4.21 Ḫumpurše
4.22 Mumam
4.23 Arwa
4.24 Ḫapate
4.25 Šenkur
5. Summary

1. INTRODUCTION[1]

In a recent publication, B. Lafont called attention to a small yet intriguing Ur III archival text from Girsu that mentions "mountain-mining-smiths" (simug-ḫur-sag-ba-al-me) going to the Elamite city of Adamšaḫ.[2] In his discussion of the text Lafont raises doubts about the commonly (but not universally) accepted location of ancient Kimaš (attested as a source of copper in the Gudea inscriptions) in the area of the Jabal Ḥamrīn or Zagros Mountains not far from modern Kirkūk. A northeasterly location for Kimaš was proposed already in 1930 by Poebel,[3] and reiterated by several scholars, including Goetze, Falkenstein, Edzard, Muhly, Jacobsen, Carter, and Stolper.[4] Steinkeller and Vallat, on the other hand, have held a dissenting view, suggesting a more easterly location for Kimaš. Steinkeller argues for a location for Kimaš in the western part of the modern province of Kermānšāh.[5] Vallat, on the other hand, proposes, as a working hypothesis, a location of Kimaš in the region of Anarak, near the Caspian Sea, where copper deposits were apparently exploited in ancient times.[6] Lafont concludes his article with the suggestion that a location for Kimaš in Elam better fits the (admittedly limited) evidence we have for Kimaš.

1 The toponyms cited in this study use the form found in the map A I 4 "Mesopotamia: Relief, Gewässer und Seidlungen," in the *Tübinger Atlas des Vorderen Orients*, 1985.

2 Lafont (1996), 87. For the rendering of the GN Adamšaḫ instead of the previous reading Adamdun, see Civil (1998), 11–14. I am thankful to Professor Civil for allowing me to see this article before its publication.

3 Poebel (1930), 137.

4 For the relevant bibliography, see Lafont (1996), 92 nn. 18–22.

5 Steinkeller (1988), 201 n. 31.

6 Vallat (1993), 140.

Now, Lafont is likely correct that a city named Kimaš was located somewhere in Elam. The evidence for this assertion comes from an Old Babylonian copy of a literary text or royal inscription that mentions Kimaš in connection with a whole roster of well-attested Elamite cities, namely: Ḫuḫnuri, Sabum, Kašdadun, and Anšan.[7] The same Kimaš, in all likelihood, is also named in an Ur III archival tablet described by Delaporte; it mentions the cities of Susa, Adamšaḫ, Urua, Sabum, and Anšan.[8] However, since it is not uncommon to find pairs or even triplets of geographical names in the ancient Near East, we cannot conclude, *prima facie*, that this "Elamite" Kimaš refers to the Kimaš mentioned in the Ur III year names. Clearly, a more detailed study of the question is needed.

In connection with our preparation of the edition of the Ur III royal inscriptions for the Royal Inscriptions of Mesopotamia Project, we made a study of the Zagros toponyms mentioned in the year names and archival texts of the Ur III period. As part of this research, detailed topographical maps of the eastern region of Iraq prepared by the British Army (1942 edition) were consulted with profit. Since the results of this investigation bear directly on the question of the location of the Kimaš mentioned in the Ur III sources, we decided to publish them here as a response to Lafont's provocative article.

2. Methodological Considerations

In the research for this study, we have, in several cases, compared modern GNs to ancient toponyms. Of course, there are potential pitfalls with this investigative approach. Reade notes:

> The actual names of modern places provide another line of approach, since linguists can suggest their likely ancient forms. There is a methodological problem here, since it is only too easy to pick and choose one's evidence, taking a handful of ancient names and hunting for modern derivatives. A proper procedure would be more thorough: take the known modern or medieval names of all important towns, regions, rivers and mountains, deduce how they may have evolved, and then look for a consistent pattern of relationships with ancient toponyms.
>
> ... It is difficult to avoid admiration, for instance, that Boehmer, looking for ancient Musasir in a small part of Iraqi Kurdistan, came on an appropriate site which turned out to be named Mujeisir; that the modern village of Ziwiye in what was once Mannean territory adjoins the ruins of an important town, and that an important Mannean town was named Izibia; or that the excavators of the mound of Shemshara encountered the archives of a previously unknown Old Babylonian town with the name of Shusharra. There is manifestly much more to be done on these lines. For instance, at the 1994 Berlin rencontre assyriologique, Medvedskaya argued that Assyrian Sagbat might have become modern Hamadan.[9]

7 Çığ and Kızılyay (1969), 179 (pl. 121 Ni 9717).

8 Delaporte (1912), 84 no. 7980.

9 Reade (1995), 40.

Although Reade's comments are perfectly reasonable, a detailed work in progress by the author in which numerous ancient GNs are correlated with modern GNs has revealed that in most cases the modern Arabic, Turkish, or Kurdish "etymologies" of the modern name are irrelevant to the question of the origin of the name. They simply represent a relatively modern attempt to explain proper names that had apparently been handed down over a very long time and whose original meaning had long been lost. In a very large number of cases ancient toponyms survive, but in forms somewhat mangled from their original form, thanks to processes such as metathesis.

In this study we have limited the comparative study of ancient and modern GNs to toponyms lying on land or water routes in relatively small and well-defined areas, such as, for example, the valley of the Sarkapkān River north of Rāniyah. As a general rule, chances for success for the comparative method increases in reverse proportion to the size of the area being considered. A simple correlation between a modern GN and an ancient toponym is unlikely to be convincing unless the two GNs can be shown, on the basis of other data—especially itineraries—to have lain in the same area.

In a many cases we have suggested that the particular form of a modern GN may have resulted from its interpretation through *Volksetymologie* (Folk etymology). The process involved can perhaps best be illustrated by an example.

The fact that the Walters Art Gallery Sennacherib inscription describes the ancient town of Surmarrāti (with a likely Akkadian etymology *sur marrāte* "bitter [water] ditch") as being situated on the Tigris,[10] and that this town is listed in the fragment K. 4384 immediately after Ekallāte,[11] strongly suggest that ancient Surmarrāti should be connected with modern Sāmarrāʾ. Sachs notes the possible connection, but is noncommittal as to endorsing it.[12] He is, however, unequivocal on seeing the modern GN Sāmarrāʾ as resulting from an Arabic popular etymology. He writes:

> It was pointed out many years ago that the Arabic spelling surra-man-raʾā "Delighted-Is-He-Who-Beholds" for Sāmarrā rests upon an Arabic popular etymology. One Arabic tradition, in a valiant effort to square the orthography with the pronunciation, maintains that the city was called surrā-man-rāʾa when it flourished, and, after it was abandoned, saʾā-man-rāʾa "Displeased-Is-He-Who-Beholds." Other curious etymologies, included some with a Persian basis, are listed in the second part of M. Streck's *Die alte Landschaft Babylonien nach dem arabischen Geographien* (Leiden, 1901), pp. 183–84.[13]

In this study, we will suggest that a large number of ancient toponyms take a modern form that has been influenced by the process of *Volksetymologie*.

---

10 Grayson (1963), 94–95 line 115.

11 Forrer (1920), 104.

12 Sachs (1937), 419–20.

13 *Ibid.*, 420.

3. THE ZAGROS WARS OF ŠULGI AND AMAR-SUENA.

3.1 *General Overview*

According to W.W. Hallo's reconstruction of historical events, Šulgi waged three distinct "Hurrian" wars in the lands situated on the northeastern periphery of the Ur III state.[14] Here we briefly reiterate the data noted by Hallo. In view of the uncertainty as to the precise ethnic and linguistic makeup of this region in Ur III times—it almost certainly was a multi-ethnic region[15]—we have preferred to label these campaigns as the "Zagros Wars of Šulgi."

The First Zagros War began with an offensive against the city of Karaḫar that is commemorated in the year name for Š(ulgi) 24. A second stage of the conflict included the first and second campaigns against Simurrum; they provided the names for the years Š 25 and 26 respectively. Finally, the third stage of the First Zagros War saw an attack on Ḫarši; it provided the name for year Š 27.

After a hiatus of four years, Šulgi's Second Zagros War began; it involved campaigns directed, once again, against Karaḫar (year name for Š 31) and Simurrum (year name for Š 32).

Then, after a gap of seven years, a final major offensive, Šulgi's Third Zagros War, commenced. It began with the defeat of Šašrum, commemorated in the name of Š 42. The year name for Š 45, in turn, records the defeat of several cities: Urbillum, Simurrum, Lullubu, and Karaḫar, and the year name for Š 46 records the defeat of Kimaš and Ḫuwurtum. Finally, the year name for Š 48 commemorates the conquest of Ḫarši, Kimaš, and Ḫuwurtum.

In our discussion of the Zagros campaigns we will attempt to show that Šulgi and Amar-Suena proceeded in a northwesterly direction in their efforts to expand the territories under Ur's control. Many of the cities they conquered lay along the ancient road that led from the area where the Diyālā River cuts through the Jabal Ḥamrīn, to the city of Arrapḫa. The particular route of the main road running along the Zagros foothills has been described (most recently) by Postgate;[16] he has provided scholars with a most useful map showing the general course of the road.[17] In this study we shall refer to this important land route as the "Arrapḫa Road." The designation is apt in view of the fact that it apparently corresponds to the ancient name of this route. The evidence for this assertion comes from a Mari letter published by Lafont; it refers (in a restored text) to the "Arrapḫa Road" (*girri Arrapḫa*) as a route taken

---

14 Hallo (1978), 74–79.

15 While it is clear that Hurrian personal names and Hurrian toponyms appear in Ur archival texts connected with this region, the ethnic and linguistic makeup of the area remains to be sorted out. On this question one may refer, for the present, to a very useful discussion in Eidem (1992), 46–54 and Zadok (1993), 224–26.

16 Postgate (1979), 593–95; *ibid*. (1983), 150–51.

17 Postgate (1983), 150.

by messengers who were traveling from Ekallātum to Ešnunna.[18] The strategic importance of Arrapḫa is evident from its location; it lies at the hub of a network of radiating roads.

3.2 *Cities along the Diyālā River and Its Tributaries*

3.2.1 General Overview

The Diyālā River is the largest of all the eastern tributaries of the Tigris. Since it flows through the southern section of territory that was attacked by the Ur III kings during their Zagros wars, a brief discussion of this river name is relevant to the present discussion.

Although the exact details are not entirely clear, scholars have generally agreed that the modern river name Diyālā is ultimately derived from an ancient river name.[19] The hydronym occurs in three forms in cuneiform texts: Turul (the earliest-attested form),[20] Turrān, and Turnat.[21] Of interest, in this connection, is Hannoon's observation[22] that one of the river names given by Yaqut to refer to the Diyālā, the "Tamarra" River, is likely a distortion of the Assyrian river name Turrān.[23]

The confluence of two important tributaries of the Diyālā: (a) the Ḥulwān (or Alwānd) River, and (b) the Sirwān River, is found just east of the point where the Diyālā River cuts through the Jabal Ḥamrīn; the names of these tributaries are discussed immediately below.

3.2.2 Cities along the Ḥulwān (or Alwānd) River

3.2.2.1 General Overview

The Ḥulwān River (also designated as the Alwānd River on modern maps) is the most easterly of the tributaries of the Diyālā discussed in this study. Of importance for determining the ancient name of this river is R. Borger's publication of a *kudurru* that was found, likely *in situ*, at modern Sar-e Pol-e Ẕahāb; the town lies at a point on the modern Ḥulwān River where it is joined by the Kazara River, a tributary of the Ḥulwān.[24] The fact that fields described in the *kudurru* mention the Turrān River as a border[25] led Borger to conclude that the course marked by the modern Ḥulwān River was denoted in ancient

---

18 Lafont (1988), 498 no. 523 ll. 39–40: *gi-ir-ri ar-ra-ap-ḫ*[*i-im*.KI *le-qé-e-ma*] *a-na èš-nun-na*.KI [*ku-uš-da-nim*] "Take the Arrapḫa road to arrive at Ešnunna."

19 For the most detailed study, see Streck, *Enzyklopaedie des Islam* 1, 1022ff., and cf. Borger (1970), 1.

20 See Edzard and Farber (1974), 259; Leemans (1966), 36 n. 4.

21 See Borger (1970), 1 for the references.

22 Hannoon (1986), 356.

23 *Ibid.*, 356.

24 Borger (1970), 1–11.

25 *Ibid.*, 2 col. i line 2.

times as the Turrān.[26] The proper name Ḥulwān, in turn, is generally connected by scholars with the ancient GN Armān (var. Ḫalmān) mentioned in inscriptions of Shalmaneser III; this is the mountain town where the rebel leader Marduk-bēl-usāte took refuge.[27] The evidence of the *kudurru* published by Borger led him to conclude that ancient Ḫalmān (or Armān) can be linked with modern GN Ḥulwān; it is very likely to be located at modern Sar-e Pol-e Ẕahāb.[28]

Strangely enough, apart from Karaḫar, we find no references in Ur III archival texts to cities that, according to the evidence presented in our monograph on the Early Dynastic list of geographical names from Abū Ṣalābīḫ and Ebla[29] (the list is hereafter cited in this study as the LGN), and in our article on the location of Simurrum,[30] lay along the Ḥulwān River, namely: Mê-Turrān,[31] Batir, Nīqum,[32] Namar, Madar, and Padān.

3.2.2.2 Karaḫar

The first major city in the Zagros region defeated by Šulgi was Karaḫar; as noted, the conquest of this city is commemorated in the year name for Š 24.

Now, according to our interpretation of the LGN, the city Karaḫar was located along the course of the Ḥulwān River not far west of modern Sar-e Pol-e Ẕahāb, likely at a point where the Great Ḫurāsān Road meets the river.[33] More specifically, in our article on the location of Simurrum, we posited a location for ancient Karaḫar at or near modern Qaṣr-e Šīrīn.[34] This Karaḫar is clearly different from the Ḫarḫar appearing in Assyrian sources and provisionally located by Levine in the vicinity of the Great Ḫurāsān Road in central or eastern Māhidāšt.[35]

---

26 This datum might be seen to conflict with the fact that the land or mountain of Zabbān was said to lie on the Turrān River (see Freydank [1974], 82) and our identification of Zabbān/Simurrum with modern Qalᶜah Širwānah. It seems not improbable that both the Sirwān as well as the Ḥulwān rivers may have been designated in a general sense as the Turrān by the ancient Mesopotamians.

27 For a discussion of this Arman/Ḫalman, see J.A. Brinkman (1968), 195 n. 1195. For the textual references, see Grayson (1996), 30 (A.0.102.5 col. v line 2); 37 (A.0.102.6 col. ii line 46); and 46 (A.0.102.8 line 25').

28 Borger (1970), 1.

29 Frayne (1992), 63–65.

30 Frayne (1997a), 253–59.

31 For a possible connection with ancient Rašap, see section 3.3.2 below.

32 One possible reference to Nīqum in an Ur III royal inscription is discussed in section 3.2.2.3 below.

33 Frayne (1992), 65.

34 Frayne (1997a), 257–58.

35 Levine (1974), 116–17.

The equation of LGN 242: *kak-kà-ra* with *kà-kà-ra-an* of the Tell as-Sulaimah tablets,[36] and with Ur III Karaḫar, later Ḫarḫar, leads us to postulate an original form *kar(a)kar for this toponym. The alternation between the velar stop (k) and the velar fricative (ḫ) found in the spellings of this toponym is attested for other GNs located in the northeast region, namely: Ṭaqṭaq/Tikitiḫum (see section 3.7.2) and Šuknir/Šuḫnir (see section 3.4.3).

The data concerning the various cities along this stretch of the Ḥulwān (based on our earlier investigation) are displayed in Chart 1.

Unfortunately, there are no known archival texts that can be connected with Šulgi's campaigns against the city and region of Karaḫar. A text dated to ix AS 5, refers to Ea-rabi, governor of Karaḫar,[37] and might conceivably be related in some way to Amar-Suena's second campaign against Šašrum, but this is uncertain. Ea-rabi, governor of Karaḫar, also appears in an undated tablet published by Jones and Snyder[38] and Karaḫar appears in a tablet dated to ŠS 9.[39] Karaḫar's neighboring city Armān (that is the Armān/Ḫalmān of later sources noted above) is mentioned in a tablet dated to the same year.[40]

3.2.2.3 Nīqum = ? Nīḫi

One city along the Ḥulwān River may possibly have been unrecognized in the corpus of Ur III royal inscriptions. In lines 22–24 of the doorsocket inscription of Ir-Nanna, the sukkal-maḫ and governor of Lagaš under Šū-Sîn, Ir-Nanna gives the following titles: énsi-ḫa-àm-zi.KI ù kára (Text: GÁNA)-ḫar.KI GÌR.NÍTA NI.ḪI.KI "governor of Ḫam(a)zi and Karaḫar, and general of NI.ḪI."[41] Ni-ḫi is also attested in two Ur III archival texts.[42] In view of the alternations between velar stop (k) and spirant (ḫ) noted in section 3.2.2.2 above, we are inclined to posit Nīḫi as a conceivable variant of the city name Nīqum. Admittedly, the expected form would be *Nīḫum, not Nīḫi. Nīqum is well attested from both Sargonic[43] and Old Babylonian sources.[44] Further, bearing in mind that -ḫe is attested as a "gentilic suffix of adjectival character" in Hurrian,[45] we suggest a connection between the GN Nīqum and the GN Nīgimḫi found in Middle Assyrian sources.[46] Its mention together with Turukkûm in those

36 Rashid (1981), tablet 5 col. i line 6: GA-GA-*ra-an*.KI.

37 A 4316, as yet unpublished see Hallo (1953), 23.

38 Jones and Snyder (1961), 72 no. 114 line 29.

39 Owen (1975), pl. LXXXV no. 299 line 4.

40 de Genouillac (1911b), pl. X no. 50 line 3.

41 Steible (1991), 265–68 Šusuen 13 ll. ii 6–8; Frayne (1997b), 323–24 E3/1.1.4.13 ll. 22–24.

42 Edzard and Farber (1974), 148.

43 Edzard, Farber and Sollberger (1977), 133.

44 It occurs in an early Old Babylonian letter, see Whiting, (1987), 37–38.

45 Gelb, Purves and MacRae (1943), 215.

46 Nashef (1982b), 205.

Chart 1: Cities along the Ḥulwān (Alwānd) River

Source	*Mê-Turrān*	*Batir*	*Nīqum*	*Namar*	*Madar*	*Karaḫar*	*Padān*	*Ḫalmān*
LGN[a]	—	258: ba-tá-ar	—	237: na-mar	241: ma-dar	242: kak-kà-ra		244: ʾà-ir-rìm
Old Akkadian Texts: Tell as-Sulaimah[b]	—	ba-tá-rí no. 29 l. 10 no. 42 l. 12		na-ma-rí no. 5 col. ii 9		kà-kà-ra-an no. 5 col. i 6	pá-da-ni no. 34 line 8	
Early OB letter from Ešnunna[c]	—	—	ni-qi$_4$-[im] Letter 2 line 2	—	—	—	—	ḫa-al-⌜ma-ni⌝ Letter 2 line 5
Tall Ḥarmal Geographical List[d]	me-tu-ra-an line 78	—	ni-qum line 77	—	—	kára-ur line 76	—	—
Tamītu text of Ḫammu-rāpi[e]	—	—	—	—	—	—	URU.pad-ni ll. 5 and 10	KUR.ḫal-man line 24
Mustafa, Mê-Turan no. 916[f]	—	—	—	na-mar	—	kára-ḫar	—	—
Ibidem, no. 114	me-tu-ra-an	ba-ti-ir	—	—	—	—	—	—
Samsuilūna Gen.[g]	—	—	—	—	ma-da-ra	ḫa-ar-ḫa-ar	—	—
MB kudurru[h]	—	—	—	na-mar	—	—	—	ḫal-man
MB kudurru[i]	—	—	—	na-mar	—	—	—	ḫal-man
Agum-Kakrime[j]	—	—	—	—	—	—	pa-da-an	al-ma-an
ḪAR-gud[k]	—	—	—	—	—	—	pa-din	ár-man

a. Pettinato (1978), 54–73; *ibid.* (1981), 217–41. LGN entry nos. are in the chart.
b. Rasheed (1981). Tablet and lines nos. are in the chart.
c. Whiting (1987), 37–38 letter 2.
d. Reiner, and Civil (1974) 87 col. iii 74–86. Line nos. are in the chart.
e. K 3703+5966+9957+16238; transliteration courtesy W.G. Lambert.
f. Mustafa (1983). Tablet nos. are in the chart.
g. Schroeder (1917), no. 156 3'.
h. Borger (1970), 2 col. i 14.
i. King (1912), 35 col. ii 22–23.
j. Pinches (1880), 33 col. i 37–38.
k. Reiner, and Civil (1974), 36 Rec. B Tab. V 6.

sources points to a location somewhere in the east Transtigris. Elsewhere, we have suggested a location for Nīqum at a point on the great Ḫurāsān Road between ancient Mê-Turrān and Armān/Ḫalmān, probably at modern Ḫānaqīn.[47] The modern GN could conceivably be a compound of Persian *ḫān* "caravansary" + *naqīn*.

3.2.3 Cities along the Sirwān River

Having seen that the modern names for both the Diyālā and one of its major tributaries can be linked to ancient river names, the question arises whether the same might hold true for the river name Sirwān; it was a second major tributary of the Diyālā.

An affirmative answer to the question would be indicated if the hypothesis put forward in our article "On the Location of Simurrum," turns out to be true. In that article we suggested that the ancient city of Simurrum should be located at the mound Qalᶜat Šīrwānah; it is situated at a point where the modern mountain road running in a southeasterly direction down the valley of the Pungla River from modern Kifrī meets the Sirwān River.[48] Support for this hypothesis comes from the fact that the name equated with Simurrum in lexical texts, Zabbān, is likely to be connected with the modern mountain name Kušk-e Zang; the mountain runs parallel to and southwest of the Pungla River. These conclusions are in accord with Müller's recent assessment of the data concerning Zabbān:

> Da das Land Zaban bis an den Diyala reichte, ist es im Gebiet südöstlich von Kifri zu lokalisieren ...[49]

Now, bearing in mind the not infrequent alternation between "w" and "m" in Akkadian vocables,[50] we have suggested in our article on the location of Simurrum that the modern river name Sirwān might be a reflex (through metathesis) of the ancient GN Simurrum, that is */simur+ān/ (or) */siwur+ān/ > /sirwān/.[51] We note, in passing, that scholars have identified another major tributary of the Diyālā, the Šaṭṭ al-ᶜAẓaim with the ancient Radānu River.[52] Of interest in this connection is Hannoon's remark:

> In more modern times a dry branch of the al-ᶜUdaim, closely paralleled by the Baghdad-Kirkuk road, was known as the "Nahr Rathan" and is at present known as the Wadi Shṭaiṭ.[53]

---

47 Frayne (1992), 70; *ibid.*, (1977), 257–58.

48 Frayne (1997a), 266–67. The road is clearly indicated on pl. 104 in the *Atlas of Archaeological Sites of Iraq* published by the Republic of Iraq, Ministry of Information, Directorate General of Antiquities (Baghdad 1975–76).

49 Müller (1994), 219.

50 von Soden (1952), 21 § 21b.

51 Frayne (1997a), 266.

52 For literature on this subject, see Nashef (1982), 314, sub Radānu.

53 Hannoon (1986), 355.

Turning once again to historical sources, we note that a second stage of Šulgi's First Zagros War included an attack on the city of Simurrum. If our hypothesis that ancient Simurrum was located at Qalᶜat Šīrwānah is true, then we could see the campaign against Simurrum as an attempt to gain control over cities that lay along the course of the Sirwān River. The Iraq Directorate General of Antiquities' *Atlas of the Archeological Sites in Iraq* shows a number of mounds on the road that runs beside the Sirwān River.[54] However, since we are completely ignorant as to the names of these settlements in ancient times, no correlations with GNs occurring in the Ur III archival texts are possible at present.

3.3 *Cities Along The Road from Rašap to Matka*

3.3.1 General Overview

Having gained a foothold over the settlements in the valleys of the Ḥulwān and Sirwān Rivers, Šulgi apparently directed his attention to points that (according to our understanding) lay further north and west. As noted, the data for this discussion comes from year names.

While we cannot, as yet, actually document the process from archival sources, it is likely that a necessary first step in Šulgi's wars against the region of Ḫarši, Kimaš, and Ḫuwurtum was to gain control over the route that led from the town of Rašap[55] to the town of Matka.[56] Based on our study of the LGN we have posited that three ancient settlements: Abal (LGN 34: ù-wa-al.KI/ù-al); Bazude (LGN 35: ba-zú-⸢dì⸣.KI, ba-zu-dè.KI) and Gidānu (LGN 36: gi-da-nu, gi-da:nu) lay on the route that connected ancient Rašap with Matka.

3.3.2 Rašap

Of interest in the context of this study are references in booty lists dated to AS 5 of a GN written variously URU.MES.LAM.TA.È.A[57] or URU.ᵈNERGAL,[58] which, following Steinkeller,[59] we have suggested refers to the city Rašap;[60] Rašap occurs as entry 33 in the LGN: *ᵈra-sa-ap*. This conclusion was accepted by Kessler,[61] who suggested, in view of the evidence pointing to an important cult of the god Nergal at Tell Ḥaddād,[62] that Rašap may well have been the name of Tell Ḥaddād/Tulūl as-Sīb in pre-Old Babylonian times. Rašap, then, is

---

54 *Atlas of Archaeological Sites of Iraq*.

55 See the discussion in § 3.3.2 below.

56 See the discussion in § 3.4.1 below.

57 Salonen, Çiğ, and Kızılyay (1954), 41 no. 120 line 3.

58 Keiser and Kang (1971), pl. LXX no. 532 line 3.

59 Steinkeller (1986), 37 n. 51.

60 Frayne (1992), 56.

61 Kessler (1995), 282.

62 *Ibid.*, 281–83. Cf. Rasheed (1981b).

attested in Early Dynastic and Ur III sources; its non-appearance in the Sargonic texts from Tell as-Sulaimah is a puzzling omission. The city name Mê-Turrān, on the other hand, is first attested in Old Babylonian times in the building inscription of Arīm-Līm,[63] and in the tablets from Tulūl Ḥaddād.[64] Accepting Kessler's hypothesis concerning Rašap and Tell Ḥaddād/Tulūl as-Sīb, we now interpret LGN entries 31–42 as referring to a route that went up the Diyālā River, through the Jabal Ḥamrīn, to Rašap (= ? Tell Ḥaddād / Tulūl as-Sīb), and thence northwest to Terqa.

3.3.3 Abal

Ancient Abal seems to have been a very important town; it is mentioned in Sargonic,[65] Ur III[66] and Old Babylonian[67] sources.

In Ur III archival texts the city name appears in variety of spellings. One form is a-ba-al found in NMW 303276 (AS 5);[68] another writing, e-ba-al occurs in Walker Art Center 10 (AS 5).[69] In the tablet ASM (Arizona State Museum) 12059 (Š 46) the GN is written a-ba-al.[70] Further, a writing a-ʾwa-alʾ occurs in the seal inscription of Babati, Šū-Sîn's uncle.[71] In Old Babylonian times the city was defeated by Samsu-ilūna, who commemorated his victory in the name of his thirty-fifth year (there Abal is written a-ma-al).[72]

Now, due to the frequent mention of Abal in the tablets excavated at Tell as-Sulaimah, F. Rashid suggested that Tell as-Sulaimah might mark the site of ancient Abal.[73] However, as noted by the author, the evidence of a brick and seal inscription from Tell as-Sulaimah points to an identification of Tell as-Sulaimah with ancient Batir.[74] In our study of the LGN we have proposed a location of Abal in the general vicinity of modern Qara Tappe, that is, in the area that lay not far northwest of Tell Ḥaddād.[75]

---

[63] Frayne (1990), 700 text E4.16.1.

[64] See Mustafa (1983); Muhamed (1985) and (1992).

[65] Edzard, Farber, and Sollberger (1977), 20.

[66] Edzard and Farber, (1974), 20 sub Awal.

[67] Groneberg (1980), 27 sub Awal.

[68] Whiting (1976), 180; Owen (1981a), 247 and *ibid.*, (1981b), 65.

[69] Jones and Snyder (1961), 6 no. 10 line 5. See also Whiting (1976), 180.

[70] Whiting (1976), 180.

[71] *Ibid.*, 178.

[72] See Groneberg (1980), 27.

[73] Rasheed (1983), 55–56.

[74] Frayne (1992), 67.

[75] *Ibid.*, 56–57.

3.3.4 Bazude

The toponym Bazude, as far as can be determined, does not appear in any Ur III (or other) archival source. Our interpretation of the LGN suggests that it lay in the region between modern Tall Ḥaddād and Kifrī.[76]

3.3.5 Zidānum

While a city Gidānum named in the LGN is not actually attested in Ur III texts, a city Zidānum is known, and, bearing in mind the not infrequent variation between GI and ZI in cuneiform texts, we have suggested that the two names might be linked.[77] Zidānum appears in a tablet (dated to AS 3) following a mention of Ḫarši,[78] and in another tablet (dated to AS 9) after a mention of Ḫuwurtum.[79] These facts accord well with our tentative placement of Zidānu (as shown in Map 1) in the area southeast of ancient Ḫarši and Ḫuwurtum.

3.4 *Cities along the Road from Matka to Arrapḫa*

As noted, Šulgi and Amar-Suena waged a prolonged war against the cities on the Mê-Turrān-Matka-Arrapḫa Road. Seven cities may tentatively be located on this road, namely: Matka, Ḫarši, *Šuḫnir, Terrabān/Terqa, Kimaš, Ḫuwurtum, and Arrapḫa.

Unfortunately, the precise order of the cities along this road is not certain. We have used as a working hypothesis the assumption that the order given in the year name for Š 48: Ḫarši, Kimaš, and Ḫuwurtum, is geographical, and that the sequence is from southeast to northwest. We have also assumed that the settlements: Ḫarši, *Šuḫnir/Šuknir, Terrabān/Terqa, Kimaš, and Ḫuwurtum were located at strategic points where the ancient road from Matka to Arrapḫa crossed tributaries of the Saṭṭ al-ᶜAẓaim (the river that waters the whole of this area), namely: (a) the ᶜĀq Ṣū (at Ḫarši); (b) the Kura Çai (at *Šuḫnir/Šuknir); (c) the Ṭāwūq Çai (at Terqa and Kimaš), and (d) the Kaur Darre (at Ḫuwurtum).[80]

3.4.1 Ḫarši

Little is known about the location of Ḫarši; all we can say is that it seems to have lain in the same general area as Ḫuwurtum and Kimaš.

As noted, Šulgi's defeat of Ḫarši is commemorated in his year names for years 27 and 48. In the latter case we have a small group of Ur III archival texts alluding to the defeat of Ḫarši. The city is named in various booty lists: (a) AO 5485 (de Genouillac 1911a: pl. VIII line 1) dated to vii Š 48; (b) PTS 473 (Sigrist, 1990: no. 60 ll. 11–12) dated to vii Š 48; (c) YBC 1531 (see Owen [1991]: no. 252)

---

76 *Ibid.*, 57.

77 *Ibid.*, 57.

78 Delaporte (1911), 188–89 no. 7.

79 Dhorme (1912), 61 (SA 200 ll. 5–6).

80 For a map showing these rivers, see Fincke (1993), map after p. 440.

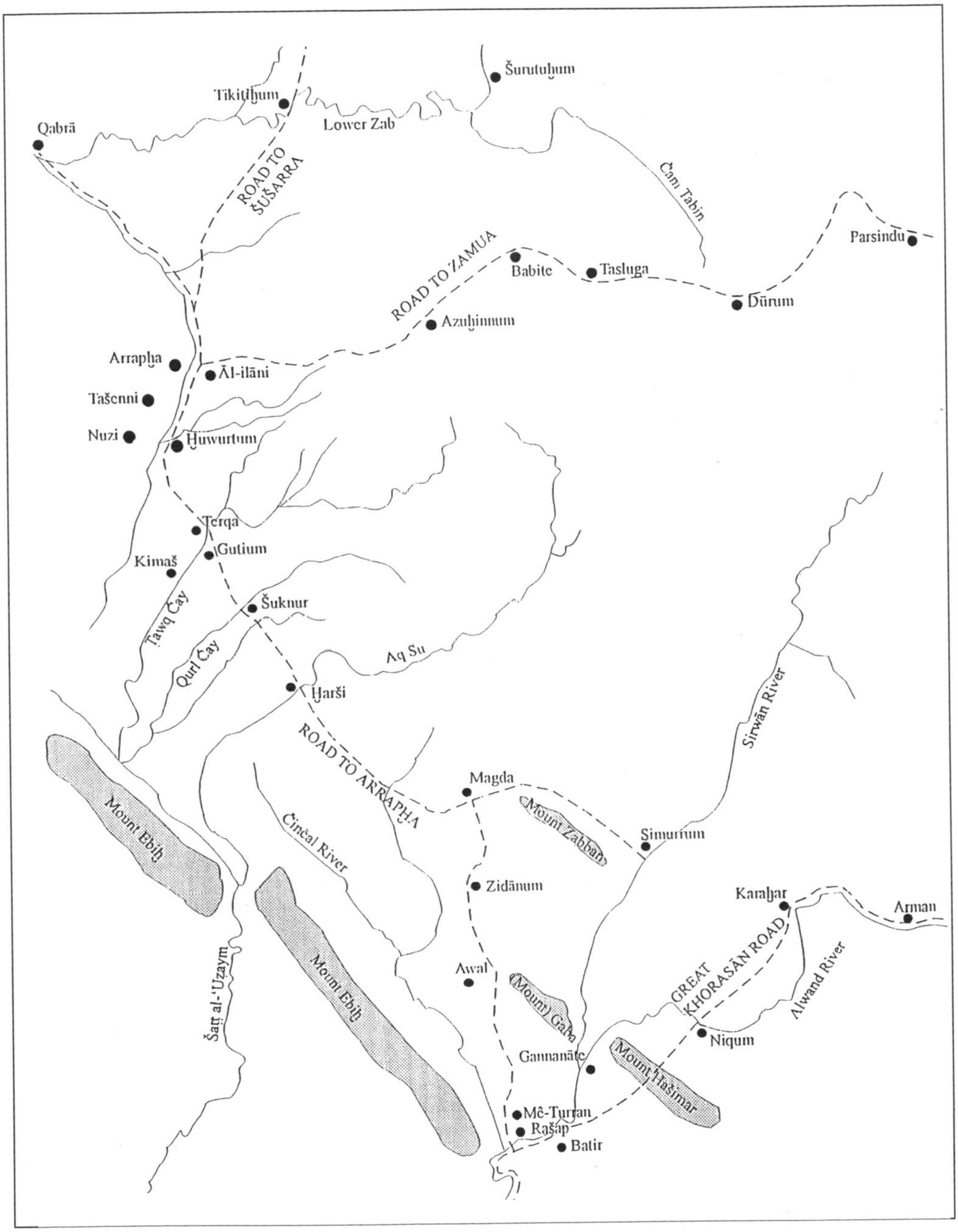
Šurutuḫum
Tikitiḫum
Qabrā
Lower Zab
ROAD TO ŠUŠARRA
Čani Tabin
Parsindu
ROAD TO ZAMUA
Babite
Tasluga
Dūrum
Azuḫinnum
Arrapḫa
Āl-ilāni
Tašenni
Nuzi
Ḫuwurtum
Terqa
Gutium
Kimaš
Šuknur
Tawq Čay
Quri Čay
Aq Su
Ḫarši
Sirwān River
ROAD TO ARRAPḪA
Magda
Mount Zabban
Simurrum
Mount Ebiḫ
Čirčal River
Zidānum
Karaḫar
Arman
Šaṭṭ al-ʿUzaym
Mount Ebiḫ
Awal
(Mount) Gaba
GREAT KHORASĀN ROAD
Alwand River
Niqum
Gannanāte
Mount Hašimar
Mê-Turran
Rašap
Batir

MAP 1

dated to vii Š 48; and (d) AUAM 73.0568: Sigrist (1988: no. 364 rev. 8) (undated). Also to be noted is a Drehem tablet, PD 538 (Salonen, Çığ, and Kızılyay: 1954 no. 538) dated to viii Š 48; it records (ll. 1–2) the receipt of "forty able-bodied young men from Ḫarši" (40 guruš-sig$_7$-a lú-ḫa-ar-ši.KI). They likely were prisoners of war from that city. Another tablet (private collection, Goetze [1957]: 77) dated to the viii Š 48, refers (lines 1–3) to cattle that are described as being: "part of the revenue brought from the campaign" (šà máš-da-ri-a kaskal-ta ir-ra).

A possible clue as to the location of Ḫarši is provided by an Old Babylonian brick inscription of a ruler named Puḫīia, who adopted the title "King of the Land of Ḫuršītum" (LUGAL *ma-a-at ḫu-ur-ši-ti-im*).[81] Scheil indicated that bricks with this inscription were found on a mound beside the ᶜĀq Ṣū, near modern Ṭūz Ḫūrmātū.[82] Also of note is the occurrence of the GN *ma-at ḫu-ur-ši-tim* in an Old Babylonian letter apparently sent by a ruler of Ešnunna.[83] If we were to take the expression *māt ḫuršītim* of the brick published by Scheil to be related to the Ur III GN Ḫarši, then a case could be made for a location for Ḫarši at or near modern Ṭūz Ḫūrmātū. Admittedly, the evidence is far from conclusive.

3.4.2 *Šuḫnir/Šuknir

While the toponym *Šuḫnir/Šuknir is not actually attested in the extant cuneiform record, the element Šuḫnir in the divine name Bēlat-Šuḫnir "Lady of Šuḫnir" has been taken by scholars to point to the existence of a GN *Šuḫnir/Šuknir.[84] A wide variety of spellings of the DN Šuḫnir/Šuknir is attested; Sallaberger notes: ᵈ*be-la-at-*ᵈ*šuḫ-nir*, ᵈ*be-la-at-*ᵈ*šuḫ-nir*ⁱʳ, ᵈ*be-la-at-šuḫ-ne-er*, ᵈ*be-la-at-*ᵈ*šu-nir*, ᵈ*be-la-at-šu-ku$_8$-nir*, ᵈ*be-la-at-*ᵈ*šuk-nir*;[85] in an Old Babylonian text the writing [d]NIN-*šuk-nir* appears.[86] In Ur III texts Bēlat-Šuḫnir is named with the goddess Bēlat-Terrabān[87]; the two deities occur, for example, in the titulary of the personal seal of Babati, the uncle of Šū-Sîn.[88] As noted by various commentators, the fact that the cults of these two goddesses appear in Ur III texts from Ur about the same time that references to Šulgi-simtī, Šulgi's (second?) wife are first found, is hardly a coincidence.[89] Sallaberger, in fact, has argued that these two goddesses were the personal deities of Šulgi-simtī; he notes that no other

---

81 Scheil (1894), 186, *ibid.*, (1897), 64. For the latest edition, see Frayne (1990), 718.

82 Scheil (1894), 186.

83 Van Dijk (1973), 65.

84 Sallaberger (1993), 19 notes: "Die Namen der beiden Göttinnen [Bēlat-Šuḫnir and Bēlat-Terrabān] sind sicher jeweils as 'Herrin von ON' zu verstehen."

85 Sallaberger (1993), 19 n. 64.

86 Frayne (1990), 810.

87 Sallaberger (1993), 19.

88 Whiting (1976), 178–79. Walker (1983), 91–96; Kärki (1986), 105–6; Frayne (1997b), 340–41 (E3/2.1.4.32).

89 Jacobsen (1940), 143 n. *. Sallaberger (1993), 18 n. 59.

deities are mentioned for years Š 29–30 in the Šulgi-Simtī archive![90] Jacobsen has suggested that the sudden appearance of these two "new" deities in the Ur III archival record resulted from Šulgi's campaigns in the Zagros region.[91] Of note is that fact that Šulgi-simtī probably appears for the first time in the archival record in a text dated to ii Š 28;[92] this comes just after the year named for the defeat of Ḫarši. According to our interpretation of the data, the home territory of Šulgi-simtī likely lay in the territory around ancient *Šuḫnir/Šuknir and Terqa/Terrabān. Ancient Šuknir is likely to be equated (through metathesis) to the GN Šenkuru named in an inscription of the Elamite king Šilḫak-Inšušinak that records his campaigns in the Zagros region.[93] Šenkuru, in turn, is likely to be connected with the modern village of Sunkur located on the modern road between modern Kifrī and Ṭuz Ḫurmātū (see discussion in § 4.25).

3.4.3 Matka

LGN entry 37: ma-DA-GA is clearly to be connected with the ma-AD-GA named in Sargonic tablets from Tell as-Sulaimah[94] and Girsu,[95] as ma-AD-GA in Gudea Cylinder B (there named as a source of bitumen),[96] as ma-AD-GA (var.) ma-AD-DA-GA in Ur III texts[97] (again as a source of bitumen),[98] and as ma-at-ka in Nuzi texts.[99] That Matka was situated on an important road is made clear by a Nuzi text that refers to a "road to Matka."[100] A scholarly consensus favoring a location of ancient Matka somewhere in the region between modern Kifrī and Tūz Ḫūrmātū has emerged.[101] Gadd received a report that bitumen is obtained from the Jabal Qumar southeast of Kifrī[102] and Forbes has provided us with a useful map showing a number of surface deposits of asphaltic bitumen in the region between Kirkūk and Kifrī.[103] Most recently, N. Hannoon has noted that a bitumen source is located at the village of Nau Saliḫ, only 3.2 km southeast of

---

90 Sallaberger (1993), 19.

91 Jacobsen (1940), 143: "It is reasonable to assume that the introduction of these new goddesses to the official pantheon reflects a political event, a recent inclusion of their cult-cities in the empire."

92 Sallaberger (1993), 18 n. 58: "Das erste Mal vielleicht UET 3 289 (ii Š 28)."

93 König (1977), 127–28 § 29.

94 Rasheed (1981a), 202 text 35 col. iii line 10.

95 Thureau-Dangin (1903), 92 no. 235 (AO 3401) line 2.

96 Edzard (1997), 35 (E3/1.1.7 StB ll. 51–56).

97 Edzard and Farber (1974), 113.

98 See Frayne (1997b), 294.

99 Fincke (1993), 176.

100 Lewy (1968), 159 and n. 75.

101 For the extensive literature on this question, see M. Walker (1985), 34–36 and Fincke (1993), 176.

102 Gadd (1926), 65.

103 Forbes (1964), map after p. 2.

Kifrī.[104] G. Müller has indicated a location of the Matka of the Nuzi sources not too far south of the modern town of Ṭāwūq. This would accord extremely well with H. Lewy's suggestion that Nuzi Matka is to be identified with the modern settlement of Matika, which is 2.5 miles south-southwest of Ṭāwūq.[105] Müller's skepticism about the connection is, to my mind, unjustified. The modern name Matika suggests a normalization of the ancient name as Matka. An Akkadian etymology from *matāku* "to be sweet" is conceivable; perhaps it referred to a particularly sweet type of crude oil or bitumen from the spring at Matka.

3.4.4 Terqa/Terqān/Terrabān

As noted in § 3.4.2, the divine name Bēlat-Šuḫnir generally occurs in Ur III archival sources together with the goddess Bēlat-Terrabān; in the latter DN the element Terrabān, like *Šuḫnir/Šuknir, is thought to be derived from a GN. Jacobsen[106] connected it with the city Terrabān that is mentioned in Sargonic texts from Gasur.[107]

Bearing in mind the alternation q/b found in contrasting pairs of site names such as (ancient) Burullum = ? (modern) Qurulla,[108] the GN Terrabān could conceivably be linked with the toponym found in LGN 42: ter$_5$-GA. Its location, according to our understanding of the LGN, should be in the area somewhere northwest of ancient Matka. A tentative location of this Terqa at or near Ṭāwūq on the Ṭāwūq Çai is conceivable, since Ṭāwūq a very short distance northeast of Matka/Matika. If this be true, then the modern GN Ṭāwūq could conceivably be a reflex of the ancient GN Terqa.

This Terqa is clearly to be connected with the "Terqān opposite Gutium" named in a lexical source[109] in which it is equated with the city LU-ti, interpreted by Hallo to be a reference to the ancient Lubdi that is thought to have lain between Arrapḫa and the Ṭāwūq Çai.[110] This fits well with our suggestion that ancient Terqa lay at or near modern Ṭāwūq. The fact that a "road to Lubdi" is attested in the Nuzi archives[111] suggests that Terqa/Lubdi lay on an important land route. Further, the aforementioned lexical text seems to indicate that Gutium—conceivably a reference to the eponymous city that served as the stronghold (and even capital?) of the Gutians in Late Sargonic and Post-Sargonic times—lay in this region. Indeed, a place name *gu-tum* is attested in a list of toponyms in the general region of Ḫuḫunri/Nuri and *a-in-un-ak* in the inscription published by Scheil in MDP 14.

---

104 Hannoon (1986), 397.

105 Lewy (1968), 160.

106 Jacobsen (1940), 143.

107 The Gasur references are Meek (1935), no. 146 line 16 and no. 154 col. iv line 17.

108 For a tentative association of the two names, see Eidem (1992), 56.

109 Reiner and Civil (1974), 35 line 14.

110 Hallo (1971), 719.

111 Lewy (1968), 159.

Curiously, we have only one reference to the northeastern Terqa in Ur III archival sources; this tablet mentions also the eastern settlements of Tašil and Urguḫalam.[112] Also of note is a tablet from the reign of Sîn-iddinam of Larsa that mentions, in succeeding entries, men of the (likely neighboring) cities of Kimaš and Terqa.[113] That Terqa was an important center in Late Old Babylonian times is clearly indicated by its occurrence in the tablets from Tell Ḥaddād studied in an unpublished dissertation by Mustafa.[114] In these Tell Ḥaddād texts Terqa is named eight times. This compares with a mention of Zabbān (apparently the Late Old Babylonian name for Simurrum) thirteen times, Mê-Turran itself eight times, and Karaḫar six times. Of particular interest is a tablet (no. 2 in Mustafa's dissertation) that mentions a trip made from Arrapḫa via Terqa (to Mê-Turran).[115] Other Tell Ḥaddād tablets speak of trips made from Zabbān to Terqa.[116]

This northeastern Terqa is clearly different from both the well-known Terqa located on the middle Euphrates at Tell al-ᶜAšārah,[117] and the ancient GN Tiriqān; the latter, according to the one source mentioning it, a Middle Babylonian *kudurru* from Susa, was situated on the Ṭābān River.[118]

3.4.5 Kimaš

Relatively little is known about the location of Kimaš of Ur III sources. The fact that it occurs with Ḫuwurtum in the year name of Š 46 (the year name is also to be linked with a temporal clause in a Šulgi royal inscription[119]) and with Ḫuwurtum and Ḫarši in the name of Š 48, suggests that the three cities of Kimaš, Ḫuwurtum, and Ḫarši lay in the same general area.

Of importance for the question of the location of Kimaš is its appearance in Gudea Statue B (VI: 21–23) as a source of copper: KÁ.GAL-*at*.KI ḫur-sag ki-maš-ka urudu mi-ni-ba-al "In Abullāt, on the mountain range of Kimaš, he mined copper."[120] The Abullāt of this text could conceivably be linked to the GN Abul-Adad (taking the latter to be a corruption[121]) that appears as an eastern toponym

---

112 de Genouillac (1911b), no. 54 col. i line 3.

113 Goetze, (1950), 110 (UIOM 2040 ll. 4–6).

114 Mustafa (1983). The references are: tablets 1:17; 2:19–20, 3:13, 17:3, 44:3, 53:7, 75: 10–12; 11:12.

115 Mustafa (1983), tablet 2 ll. 19–20: 1 BÁN ZÌ.ŠE *a-na* KASKAL ᵈŠEŠ.KI.MA.AN.SUM *ša iš-tu* URU *ar-ra-ap-ḫi-im*.KI *i-tu-ta-an-ma a-na* URU *tir-ga*.KI "1 seah barley for the journey of Nanna-iddinam, who returned from Arrapḫa and passed to Tirqa."

116 Mustafa (1983), tablets nos. 3, 44, and 53.

117 For a report on the most recent excavations there and a bibliography of articles dealing with the site, see Rouault (1997).

118 Nashef (1982a), 122.

119 See von Schuler (1967), 293–95 and Frayne (1997b), 140–41 (E3/2.1.2.33).

120 Edzard (1997), 34 (Gudea E3/1.1.7. StB).

121 The possible connection was suggested to me by G. McEwan in an oral communication.

in the so-called "Sargon Geography"; line 14 of the geography reads: TA *ḫi-iz-za-at* DIŠ KÁ.GAL-^{d}10 KUR *ak-ka-di-i*.KI "From Ḫizzat to Abul-Adad: the land of Akkad."[122] Now, we have suggested, following McEwan[123] that the *ḫi-iz-za-at* of the Sargon geography is to be connected with the GN Ḫiza named in the Sumerian Temple hymns.[124] It may possibly be linked as well with the ḪA.A.KI. named in a doorsocket found at Tell Ḫarāʾib Ghḍairīfah/Tell Duhūbah, which records the construction of the temple of Ninḫursag of ḪA.A.KI.[125] If so, we expect Abul-Adad of the Sargon Geography, if related to Abullāt, to be situated somewhere in the Zagros foothills.

In Gudea Cylinder A (XVI 15–17) Kimaš is mentioned once again in connection with copper: ḫur-sag urudu-ke$_4$ ki-maš-ta ní-bi mu-na-ab-pà uruda-bi gi-si-a-ba mu-ni-ba-al "From Kimaš, the copper mountain range made itself known to him, and he dug its copper into baskets."[126]

But, as is noted in the introduction to this study, it is not clear whether the Kimaš named in the Gudea inscriptions refers to the city that is noted in the Ur III year names or to the Kimaš that was apparently located further east in Elam. If the connection with Abul-Adad of the Sargon Geography holds true, it suggests the location of Kimaš of the Gudea inscriptions to be in the north-eastern Zagros region. It is in this same general area that we have located ancient Matka, a source of bitumen for Gudea. Further, the mountain Barme, noted as a source of building stone for Gudea's reconstruction of the Eninnu temple, might conceivably be connected with the modern GN Marīvān near Lake Zeribor.[127] It appears, then, that Gudea obtained much of his building material for the construction of the Eninnu temple from the eastern Zagros region.

Unequivocal evidence that a city named Kimaš was located in the greater vicinity of the middle Tigris is found in one (or more) year names on tablets of Old Babylonian date from Iščālī that mention the two cities of Kimaš and Ekallātum being attacked by an apparent king of Ešnunna.[128] Now, Ekallātum was certainly located on the Tigris River, and is likely to be identified with modern Tell Haikal about 16 km north of Aššur.[129] This fact, if nothing more, clearly refutes Lafont's hypothesis that there was no city named Kimaš in the east Transtigridian area.

---

122 For the relevant lines of the Sargon Geography, see Grayson (1974–77), 59 ll. 14–15.

123 McEwan (1982), 11–12.

124 Sjöberg and Bergmann (1969), 46–47.

125 See Al-Rawi and Black (1993), 147–48; Frayne (1992) 105, n. 80; *ibid*., (1993), 80 (E2.1.3.6) and finally Steinkeller (1995), 275–81. I cannot concur with the conclusions reached by Steinkeller in his article.

126 Edzard (1997), 79 (E3.1.1.7 Cyl A ll. 15–17).

127 See Frayne (1992), 80 for a discussion of ancient *ba-ra-mu*.KI, *bar-ra-an*.KI, and *bar-me-um*.KI.

128 Greengus (1979), 28 (year date 25) and 31 (year date 33).

129 As measured on the British topographical map. The figure 25 km given in Hallo (1964) 72 would appear to be incorrect.

A small group of Ur III archival texts are to be connected with the defeat of Kimaš that is recorded in the year name for Š 46. They are listed here in chronological order; the citations have been collected by P. Michalowski,[130] T. Maeda,[131] and M. Cooper (personal communication). Tablet (a) (Legrain [1912]: 63 no. 144) dated to 27 iv Š 45, refers to troops (érin) of Kimaš (see Maeda [1992]: 157) where érin should be read for u_4; tablet (b) NCBT 1624 (unpublished, information courtesy W.W. Hallo) dates to v Š 45 and contains the remark "when Kimaš was destroyed" (u_4 ki-maš.KI ba-ḫul); tablet (c) dated to ii Š 46 (YBC 504, Keiser [1919] no. 74) contains the note (ll. 2–3) "banquet when Kimaš was destroyed" (kaš-dé-a u_4 ki-maš.KI ba-ḫul); tablet (d) dated to ii Š 46 (HSM 911.10.231: Michalowski [1976]: 82) contains the expression "offering during the (course of) the campaign when [Kimaš?] was smitten with weapons (siskur šà-kaskal-la u_4 GIŠ.tukul ba-sìg); tablet (e) dated to iii Š 46 (Hirose no. 50: Gomi, Hirose, and Hirose [1990]: no. 50) records (ll. 1–2) various cattle of the troops of Kimaš (érin ki-maš.KI); and finally, tablet (i) dated to v Š 46 (A 5080 [Chicago], reference courtesy W.W. Hallo) indicates that the governor of Kimaš himself was captured during the campaign (u_4 énsi-ki-maš.KI im-ma-dab_5-ba). Further, as was pointed out by Hallo, an echo of Šulgi's defeat of Kimaš is likely found in the later omen and chronicle tradition.[132]

If we are correct in our supposition that the year name for Š 48 lists its three cities — Ḫarši, Kimaš and Ḫuwurtum — in geographical order, and that ancient Ḫarši was located somewhere on or near the ᶜĀq Ṣū, then Kimaš should be located in the region northwest of the ᶜĀq Ṣū. We offer a tentative location of Kimaš at modern Qūš Tepe, a very large mound (as would be expected for the important city of Kimaš) located beside the Ṭāwūq Çai at a point about 1.8 kms south of Ṭāwūq. If we bear in mind the alternation noted earlier between "w" and "m" in Akkadian vocables, the modern GN Qūš Tepe could conceivably contain a reflex of the ancient GN Kimaš: /kimaš (or) kiwaš/ > /qūš/.

3.4.6 Ḫuwurtum

As with Kimaš, little is known about the location of ancient Ḫuwurtum; all we can say is that it seems to have been situated in the same general area as Ḫarši and Kimaš. The GN occurs in various spellings: ḫu-MUR-ti, ḫu-MUR-tum, ḫu-ur-ti and ḪUR-ti. A normalization of the GN as Ḫuwurtum is used in this study.

A small group of Ur III archival texts can be connected with the defeat of Ḫuwurtum that is commemorated in name of Š 46. The relevant dossier of tablets is numbered here in chronological order as tablets (a) to (c). Tablet (a) dated to 14 iv Š 46 (AUAM 73.1571: Sigrist [1984]: no. 683) contains the remark (ll. 3–4) "banquet when Ḫuwurtum was destroyed" (kaš-dé-a ḫu-MUR-ti.KI ba-

---

130 Michalowski (1976), 82.

131 Maeda (1992), 157.

132 Hallo (1978), 76.

ḫul); tablet (b) dated to 14 iv Š 46 (Kelsey 89217: Owen [1991]: no. 201) records (line 17) various cattle as being "part of the booty of Ḫuwurtum" (šà nam-ra-ak ḫu-MUR-ti.KI); tablet (c), dating to 24 iv Š 46 (ROM 295 925.62.283a: Sigrist [1995]: no. 44) registers (ll. 4–5) disbursements for "the banquet in the temple of the god Enlil, when Ḫuwurtum was destroyed for the second time" (gizbun$_x$ [KI.KAŠ] šà-é-^{d}en-líl mu ḫu-MUR-ti.KI a-rá-2-kam-aš ba-ḫul).

The fact that these texts date to the time period just after those dealing with the defeat of Kimaš suggests that the conquest of Ḫuwurtum occurred shortly after the defeat of Kimaš.

As for the location of Ḫuwurtum, we note that the next stream crossed by the modern Kifrī–Kirkūk road after it crosses the Ṭāwūq Çai is the Kaur Derre[133]; at the junction of the modern road and stream lies the town named Tāze Ḫurmātū. The element Ḫurmāt in these modern GNs could be connected with Persian *ḫurma* "date" by *Volksetymologie*, but it is more likely that Ḫurmātu is a reflex of the ancient GN Ḫuwurtum. One would postulate a development /*ḫuwurtu/ (or) */ḫumurtu/ (through metathesis) to /ḫurmāt/. Metathesis is very commonly found in transformations of ancient toponyms to their modern equivalents.

3.4.7 Arrapḫa

The end point of the road discussed in this section was ancient Arrapḫa. Although traditionally located by scholars at modern Qal^{c}ah Kirkūk,[134] N. Hannoon has asserted that Arrapḫa is more likely to be located at the modern tell named ^{c}Arafah: He writes:[135]

> In summary, Arrapha was a city and provincial centre, which in the middle of the second millennium B.C. had a religious and administrative complex known as Āl-ilāni with a part of it called Āl-Taššeniwe. Apparently, the views about the location of these three places expounded above were established on the identification of Qal^{c}at Kirkuk itself with Arrapḫa. This has to be taken cautiously, for the identification of Arrapḫa with modern Kirkuk means that one has to deal with Qal^{c}at Kirkuk and its surroundings, which are covered by the city at present. The city of Kirkuk was confined to the citadel mound until the first half of the eighteenth century when it started to extend around the citadel This extension inc1uded some archeo1ogica1 sites which might be important for the relationship between the Qal^{c}ah and the surrounding area. The most important site in that area survived until the Summer of 1948 when it was removed by the Iraq Oil Company. That site had been known as ^{c}Arafah, which became the name of the modern living quarter established at the same spot.

---

133 See the map in Fincke (1993) after p. 440.

134 For the literature on this identification, see Fincke (1993), 38.

135 Hannoon (1986), 369.

ᶜArafah is located within the modern city of Kirkūk, about 3 km west of Qalᶜah Kirkūk.[136] Some scholars have suggested that the GN Āl-ilāni (URU DINGIR.MEŠ) named in tablets found at Qalᶜah Kirkūk[137] was a religious and administrative complex within Arrapḫa,[138] or that Āl-ilāni was simply a graphemic equivalent for Arrapḫa.[139] According to H. Lewy, Āl-ilāni was a twin city with Tašenniwe.[140] As for the location of the latter city, Müller writes:

> Tašenniwe steht in enger Verbindung mit Arrapḫa. Das wird zum einen aus dem Archiv des Šilwateššup deutlich, worin die Haushalte von Arrapḫa und Tašenniwe nicht deutlich geschieden werden ...[141]

Finally, Tašenniwe has been plausibly identified by Gelb with the modern tell named Tasᶜīn;[142] it lies about 4.8 km south of Qalᶜah Kirkūk.

Although we have no archival texts or year names referring specifically to the event, it is highly likely that by Š 44 (if not already by Š 42) Šulgi had taken control of the city and district of Arrapḫa. The name of year Š 45 commemorates the defeat of Urbillum and, as is noted below, the road that led from the area of Kimaš and Ḫuwurtum (where Šulgi had been campaigning earlier) to Urbillum passed by Arrapḫa.

As far as can be determined, there are only four attestations of Arrapḫa in Ur III archival texts.[143] Of interest is a tablet dated to v AS 5 that mentions the general Ḫašip-atal in connection with "soldiers of Arrapḫa" (érin ar-ra-ap-ḫu-um.KI).[144]

3.5 *Cities in the Vicinity of Arrapḫa and in the Eastern Marches*

Ancient Arrapḫa was situated not far from the point where three important Transtigridian roads converged, namely: (a) an eastern road that led from Arrapḫa, probably by ancient Azuḫinnum, through the Bazian Pass and through the mountains, to the area of Lake Zeribor ("The Road to Zamua"); (b) a road that ran in a northwesterly direction via modern Altūn Kūprū on the Lower Zab to modern Erbil ("The Road to Urbillum"); and (c) the road that ran northeast via the river crossing on the Lower Zab at modern Ṭaqṭaq to the area of the modern Rāniyah Plain ("The Road to Šušārra").

An important source dealing with cities in the vicinity of Arrapḫa and points further east is an intriguing and informative tablet published by

---

136 Hannoon (1986), 370. Hannoon also points out that the small mound of Tell Mulla ᶜAbdullah may also have formed part of greater Arrapḫa.

137 For references in the Nuzi texts to Āl-ilāni, see Fincke (1993), 9–16.

138 So Lewy (1968), 156.

139 So Müller (1994), 17.

140 So Lewy (1968), 156.

141 Müller (1994), 111.

142 Gelb, Purves, and MacRae (1943), 263a.

143 See Edzard and Farber (1974), 16 and Owen (1981a), 247 [=Owen 1991, no. 66:6].

144 Salonen, Çığ, and Kızılyay (1954), no. 166 line 11. Read érin for Salonen's u_4.

Sigrist[145]; it dates to 8-v-AS 8. The text mentions érin "soldiers" of ten GNs, namely: (a) Arrapḫa, (b) Durmaš, (c) Agaz, (d) Lullubu, (e) Ḫamazi, (f) Šuʾirḫum, (g) Šuʾaḫ, (h) Gablaš, (i) Zaqtum and (j) Dūr-Ibla.

(a) Arrapḫa as noted, can be located at ᶜArafah within the modern city of Kirkūk.

(b) Durmaš is, as far as can be determined, otherwise unattested.

(c) Agaz was apparently a large eastern city; it is attested in sources dating from Pre-Sargonic to Old Babylonian times.[146] The city (with a variant spelling Agsi'a) was of sufficient importance to have the destruction of its city wall commemorated in an Old Babylonian year name found on a tablet from Tulūl as-Sīb: MU BÀD URU *ag-si-a*.KI BA.GUL.[147]

(d) Lullubu is extremely well attested; in a recent survey, H. Klengel lists references to Lullubu in Sargonic, Ur III, Old Babylonian, Middle Babylonian, Middle Assyrian, and Neo-Assyrian sources.[148] The fact that ancient toponyms often find a reflex in the modern name of their site leads to posit a location of Lullubu at Ḥalubja.

(e) Ḫamazi is thought to have been a very important eastern land, but relatively few references to it (in Sargonic and Ur III archival texts) are known.[149] The Ḫamazi attested in a letter of Late Early Dynastic date from Ebla, which is addressed to the "chief steward" (agrig) of Ḫamazi,[150] almost certainly does not refer to this eastern Ḫamazi, but rather to another Ḫamazi that is likely to be located at Qalᶜat Ḥomṣ, the "citadel hill" of modern Ḥomṣ. According to M. Moussli, the site exhibits ceramics dating from the Early Bronze period.[151]

(f) Šuʾirḫum. As far as can be determined, this GN is otherwise unattested.

(g) Šuʾaḫ. In view of the fact that Arrapḫa is mentioned in line 1 of the Sigrist tablet, the GN Šuʾaḫ, which appears in line 12 could conceivably be linked (following G. Müller[152]) to the river name Šuʾaḫ attested in the Nuzi tablets; it is identified by Müller with the modern wadi Ḫirr Abū Naft.

(h) Gablaš. As far as can be determined, the GN is otherwise unattested.

(i) Zaqtum. Again, the GN is not otherwise known. If the GN is related to Akkadian *zaqtu*(*m*) "pointed," a connection with a mountain peak is conceivable.

---

145 Sigrist (1979).

146 See Frayne (1992), 84–85.

147 Mustafa (1983), 39 year name (v).

148 Klengel (1988), 164.

149 Edzard (1972), 70–71.

150 See Pettinato (1981), 96–99; Shea (1984); Chiera (1986).

151 Moussli (1984), 11.

152 Müller (1994), 204.

(j) Dūr-Ibla. In view of the Nuzi connections noted above for entries (a) and (c), Dūr-Ibla of line 18 of the Sigrist tablet may be linked to the GN Dūr-ubla found in the Nuzi archives.[153] The various Pre-Sargonic (or Sargonic) and Ur III references to the city have been listed by Fadhil.[154] According to Müller, it lay at or near the southern border of the province of Arrapḫa.[155] Another possibility is that it is connected with the *maškan* BÀD *ebla* of the Gasur map, which we have suggested was located on or near the southern shore of Lake Zeribor.[156]

3.6 *Cities along the Road from Arrapḫa to Urbillum*

3.6.1 General Overview

The year name for Š 45 gives the first mention of an attack of Šulgi against the city of Urbillum (modern Arbīl). In order to reach this city, Šulgi would have travelled along the road that ran from Arrapḫa in a northwesterly direction[157] to the area of modern Altūn Kūprū on the Lower Zab, and thence west to Arbīl.

3.6.2 Arrapḫa

See section 3.3.7.

3.6.3 Qabrā/Qabarā

Since the land of Urbillum was attacked not only by Šulgi in Ur III times, but also by the combined forces of Šamšī-Adad of Ekallātum and Dāduša of Ešnunna in Old Babylonian times, a study of the Old Babylonian data may be helpful for a better understanding of the Ur III campaign.

We are fortunate in possessing several sources for the campaign directed against Qabrā by Šamši-Adad and Dāduša.[158] These include two steles (one of Šamšī-Adad in the Louvre[159] and one of Dāduša in the Iraq Museum[160]) and several letters, both from Mari[161] and Šimšārah.[162] Further, the defeat of Qabrā/ Qabārā was commemorated by Dāduša in the name of his last year.[163]

---

153 *Ibid.*, 131–32.

154 Fadhil (1983), 253.

155 Müller (1994), n. *.

156 Frayne (1992), 81–82.

157 East of the range known today as the Kani Dolman Dagh; for the geography of this area, see Levine (1989), 84.

158 A study of this campaign is given in Charpin and Durand (1985), 312–15, Eidem (1985), 83–88, and Wu Yuhong (1994), 181–90. I am informed by Charpin that a study of Mari documents relevant to the Šamšī-Adad campaign will be forthcoming in ARM 29; an article on this subject is also to appear in *Amurru* 2.

159 For the latest edition, see Grayson (1987), 63–65 (RIMA 1 1001).

160 See Ismail Khalil (1986) for a summary of the contents of this important monument.

161 See Charpin and Durand (1985), 312–15 and Wu Yuhong (1994), 181–90.

162 See Eidem (1985), 83–88.

163 See Baqir (1949), 45.

The Old Babylonian data has led various scholars to posit a location for ancient Qabrā/Qabarā. H. Lewy writes:

> Since, according to all the evidence available, the Lesser Zab is easily crossed only at the site of present-day Altin Köprü, "The Gold Bridge," it appears that the town of Al-Qanṭarah, "The Bridge," it appears that Turša and Qabra faced each other across the river, Turša standing on the southern and Qabra on the northern side of the river crossing of Altin Köprü.[164]

J. Eidem, editor of the Šimšārah economic texts, notes:

> The town of Qabra, although probably close to the town of Altin Köprü, cannot be located precisely, but the land of Qabrā must have incorporated a major part of the large and fertile plain between the Zābs, including the town of Urbēl (Erbil) in the north.[165]

Most recently, Deller has discussed the situation of ancient Qabrā/Qabarā, indicating a location:

> etwa 15–20 km. nordwestlich von Altın Köprü zwischen den Strassen nach Erbil und nach Dibaga-Guwair.[166]

The fact that important cities in ancient Mesopotamia often lay at the points where roads crossed major rivers leads us to posit the location of ancient Qabrā/Qabārā at Altūn Kūprū itself (the latter is the Arabic name found on the Répertoire map; the Turkish form is Altın Köprü). In this case the meaning of the apparent name Altın Köprü "Golden Bridge" makes excellent sense, but again I see this as likely being an example of *Volksetymologie*. Altın Köprü lies on an island in the middle of the Lower Zāb, and thus would have had a very defensible position in ancient times. If our connection of Qabārā = Altın Köprü hold true, then this might account for its being the last major city to fall during the campaign led by Šamši-Adad and Dāduša.

3.6.4 Māḫāzum

It is clear that the Old Babylonian kings of Ešnunna, like their Ur III predecessors, strove to control the territory northwest of Ešnunna as far as the Lower Zāb river. The first evidence of Ešnunna's expansion into the region is found in a chronicle text from Mari that records the conquest of Arrapḫa by Ipiq-Adad II of Ešnunna.[167] Further, as noted, king Dāduša named his last year for the defeat of Qabārā/Qabrā, a city probably located not far north of Arrapḫa. Also of interest is the name of year four of Ibāl-pî-El, Dāduša's successor; it commemorates the taking of the land of Māḫāzum (*māt maḫāzim*).[168] The GN Māḫāzum in this case may be compared with the GN Māḫāzu found as the

---

164 Lewy (1968), 151.

165 Eidem (1985), 84.

166 Deller (1990b), 62–63.

167 Birot (1985), 229 line 12: *i-na da-da-a-ia* MÌN *i-pí-iq*-^{d}IŠKUR *ar-ra-ap-ḫa-am*.KI *iṣ-ba-*[*at*].

168 Baqir (1949), 64. See also Greengus (1979), 33 year name 48.

name of a *dimtu* in the Nuzi archives.[169] In his discussion of the Nuzi GN, Fadhil notes the appearance of the term in the Hurrian column of a quadrilingual lexical text from Ugarit. The line in question, col. ii line 21' in Nougayrol's edition,[170] is as follows: (logogram) KAR, (Akkadian) *ka-a-ru*, (Hurrian) *ma-ḫa-[z]i*, (Ugaritic) *ma-aḫ-ḫa-[zu]*. Fadhil argues that in the Nuzi context the word refers to a landing place for boats,[171] suggesting then that Māḫāzu was a harbor settlement.[172] If we bear this in mind, the GN Māḫāzum of the Ibāl-pî-el year name could plausibly be linked with modern Tell Maḥūz,[173] a high tell[174] located on the left bank of the Lower Zāb River about 38 km downstream from Altūn Kūprū.

It is uncertain whether this Māḫāzu is the same city that is mentioned (in the spelling *ma-ḫa-zum*.KI) in an Ur III archival text, whose date, unfortunately, is broken away.[175] Māḫāzum appears there immediately after an entry mentioning the GN Kismar; the latter is thought to be an east Transtigridian city. Kismar, in turn, is mentioned in two Ur III tablets along with the GN Maškan-šarrum.[176] Maškan-šarrum, in turn, is thought to have lain on the Tigris River along the southern border of the land of Assyria. Steinkeller notes:

> The earliest references to Maškan-šarrum come from Ur III texts. The crucial evidence of the location of Maškan-šarrum is provided by the so-called Sargon Geography. Line 8 of the document reads: [*ultu* ...]-⌜*x*⌝ ⌜*adi*⌝ *maš-kán-*LUGAL *māt aš-šur*^{ki}, "[from ...]-⌜x⌝ to Maškan-šarru/šarri (is) the country of Assyria." Based on this passage, W. F. Albright located Maškan-šarrum on the Tigris a little south of Assur, near the mouth of the Lower Zab ... [177]

A location of Ur III Māḫāzum at modern Tell Maḥūz on the Lower Zāb would put the city at a point only 50 km northeast of the junction of the Lower Zāb and Tigris, and not far from the point where Albright suggested ancient Maškan-šarrum was situated.

Māḫāzum also occurs as a city conquered by an unnamed king in an Old Babylonian copy of a royal inscription belonging to either Šū-Sîn of Ur or Narām-Sîn of Akkad.[178] Finally, the city name appears in a Nestorian chronicle. Astour writes:

---

169 Fincke (1993), 169.

170 Nougayrol (1968), 242.

171 Fadhil (1983), 44.

172 *Ibid.*, 44.

173 For the location, see the map after p. 144 in Fincke (1993).

174 Fadhil (1983), 208 refers to Tell Maḥūs as "ein relativ hoch anstehender Ruinenhügel." He suggests an identification with ancient Turša.

175 Nies (1920), no. 91 line 341.

176 For the references, see Edzard and Farber (1974), 104 sub Kismar.

177 Steinkeller (1982), 289.

178 See Frayne (1997), 300–1 E3/2.1.4.2.

After a long gap the city maḥōzê de-Ariwān appears in a chronicle of Thomas of Margâ (ninth century A.D.). It belonged to the district of Bēt-Garmai (between the Lesser Zab, the Tigris, the Ḥamrīn Range, reaching east of Kirkuk), and as apparently situated on the Lesser Zab.[179]

Of interest in the context of this study is the possible mention of the district of Maškan-šarrum in the Nuzi archives. Müller has noted the occurrence of the GNs Maškani(we)[180] and Šarri (LUGAL.KI)[181] in the Nuzi tablets. One of the cited texts[182] indicates that Maškaniwe lay in "Kuššuḫḫe land," a designation possibly meaning "Kassite land."[183] Of note is the occurrence of the GNs Maškan and Šarri together in one tablet.[184] While Müller indicates that the close geographical connection between the two GNs remains an open question, a connection of Nuzi Maškani(we) and Šarri with Ur III Maškan-šarrum would make excellent sense if we understood Maškan-šarrum to be a twin city (comparable to Uruk-Kullaba). If so, the towns of Maškani(we) and Šarri apparently lay at the most westerly point of the principality of Arrapḫa.

3.6.5 Urbillum

The year name for Š 45 commemorates Šulgi's victory over a number of Transtigridian cities, including Urbillum:

> mu ^{d}šul-gi nita-kala-ga lugal-uri$_5$.KI-ma lugal-an-ub-da-límmu-ba-ke$_4$ ur-bí-lum.KI si-mu-ru-um.KI lu-lu-bu.KI ù kára-ḫar.KI-ra AŠ-eš šu du$_{11}$-ga šu-tibir-ra im-mi-ra
>
> The year Šulgi, mighty man, king of Ur, king of the four quarters, having overtaken Urbillum, Simurrum, Lullubu, and Karaḫar as a single group, struck them down.[185]

In this case we do not have to speculate as to the location of Urbillum, since it is known to lie at modern Arbīl; the city appears in imperial Aramaic as *ʾrbl* and in classical sources as Arbela.[186]

The defeat of Urbillum by Šulgi is alluded to in three Ur III economic tablets. Tablet (a), a Drehem tablet dated to 17 vii Š 44 (Musées Royaux d'Art et d'Histoire O.70: de Genouillac 1911b: no. 86 = Limet 1976: no. 39), describes (rev. line 6) various metal objects that are designated as "booty of Urbillum" (nam-ra-ak ur-bìl-lum.KI-ma); tablet (b), a Drehem tablet dated to xi Š 45 (FLP

---

179 I am thankful to M. Astour for permission to quote this passage in advance of his publication of the full article.

180 Müller (1994), 74.

181 *Ibid.*, 98.

182 Lacheman (1955), no. 283.

183 Müller (1994), 221 n. 59 notes that Kuššuḫḫe may be a variant of Kaššiḫe, the Hurrian adjectival form of Akkadian *kaššû(m)* "Cassite."

184 Lacheman (1955), no. 283.

185 King (1898), pl. 18 col x ll. 15ff.

186 Astour (1987), 39.

1248: Sigrist, Owen and Young 1984: 423), records (line 27) a disbursement said to be "part of the booty of Urbillum" (šà-nam-ra-ak ur-bíl-lum.KI); tablet (c), dated to xii Š 45 (AUAM 73.1377+73.0717: Sigrist 1988: no. 326+336, see also Sallaberger 1993: Vol. 1: 16 n. 50), also records booty of Urbillum. Already by i Š 47 an economic tablet (NBC 2150 [Keiser and Kang 1971: no. 18]) mentions (ll. 6–7) revenue of the territory of Urbillum (maš-da-ri-a ma-da ur-bí-lum.KI-ka).

3.7 *Cities Along the Road from Arrapḫa to Šašrum*

3.7.1 General Overview

The year name for Š 42, which commemorates Šulgi's taking of the city of Šašrum, marks the beginning of Šulgi's Third Hurrian War and signals a major expansion of the Ur III empire towards the north. Now, the obvious route for Šulgi to travel from the area of Arrapḫa, where he was apparently campaigning shortly after his conquest of Ḫarši, would be by the modern road that runs in a northeasterly direction from (modern) Kirkūk to the ford on the Lower Zāb at Ṭaqṭaq, and thence via the town of Kūysanjaq (Arabic form found in the Répertoire map; the Turkish form is Koi Sancaq) to Rāniyah. In this section we discuss three settlements that likely lay on the Arrapḫa to Šašrum Road: Tikitiḫum, Kakmium, and Šašrum.

3.7.2 Tikitiḫum

The GN Tikitiḫum occurs with two spellings in Ur III texts: ti-ki-ti-ḫu-um and ti-gi-ti-in-ḫi.[187] That the spellings refer to the same place is virtually certain in view of the fact that the tablets both mention the same man, a certain ga-da-bi, as coming from Tikitiḫum. In one tablet (de Genouillac 1911a no. 5500) Tikitiḫum occurs with the GN ša-aš-ru (as noted below, modern Šimšārah). A plausible location for Tikitiḫum, assuming a derivation of the modern town name from an ancient toponym, is modern Ṭaqṭaq, which is situated at an important ford on the Lower Zāb, where the route from Kirkūk to Kūysanjaq crosses the river. If the equation of ancient and modern GNs hold true, then the ancient name would provide a further example of the name type C_1VC_2-C_1VC_2 (here *tik-tik), in which the velar of the second syllable is found in a spirantized form (cf. ancient Karaḫar from *kar-kar discussed above). The modern form suggests that the ancient name was Ṭikiṭiḫum.

3.7.3 Kakmi

Although Kakmi seems to have been a very important regional center, as far as can be determined, there is only one clear reference to the GN in Ur III sources (Langdon 1911: no. 67); Kakmi is mentioned there with the GNs Gumaraši and Šerši. The city is attested more frequently in Old Babylonian texts[188]; of note is the name of year 37 of Ḫammu-rāpi, which mentions Kakmûm together with

187 Edzard and Farber (1974), 192–93; M. Walker (1985), 39–40; Astour (1987), 38.

188 Groneberg (1980), 129–30.

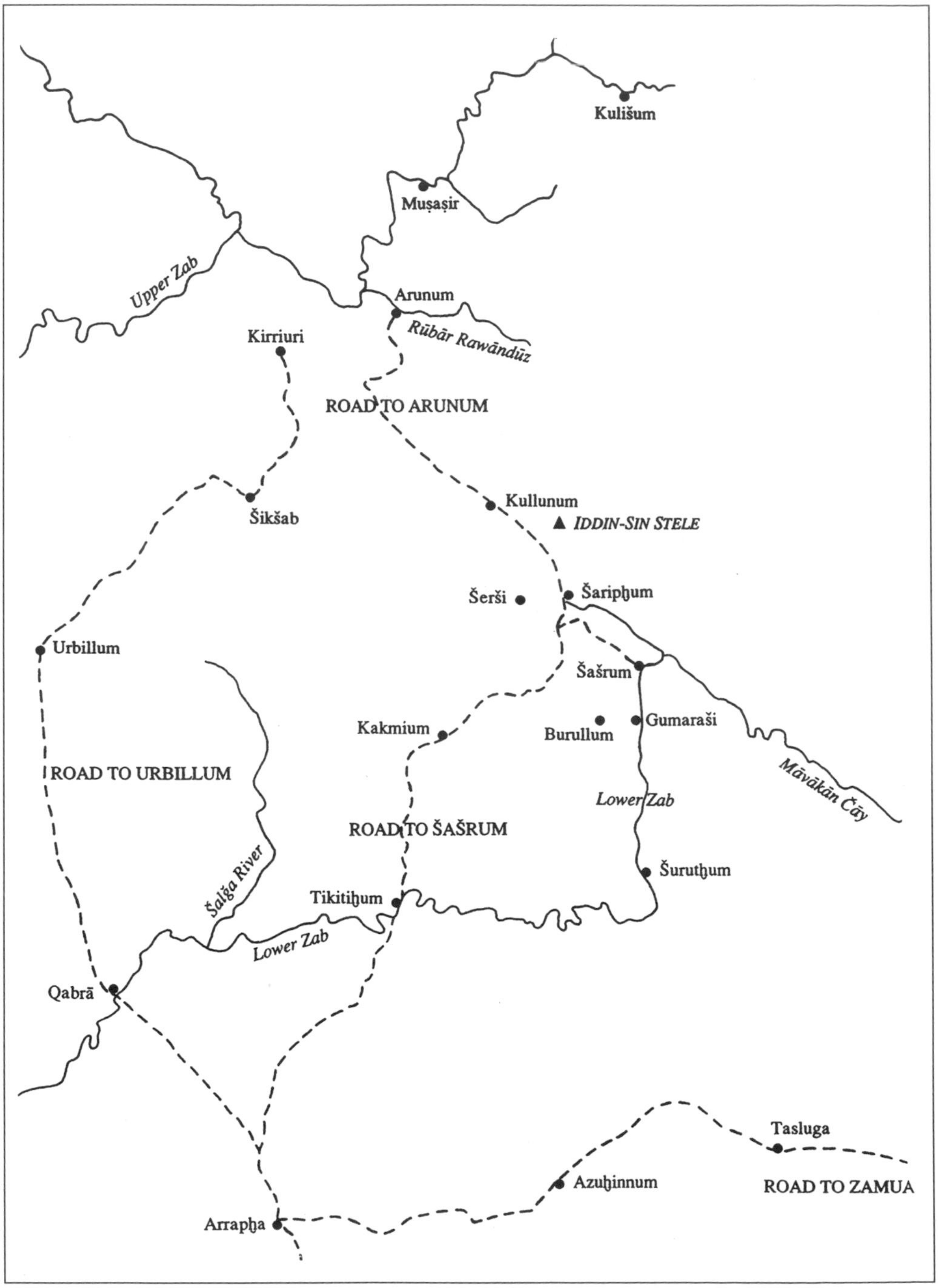
Kulišum
Muṣaṣir
Upper Zab
Arunum
Rūbār Rawāndūz
Kirriuri
ROAD TO ARUNUM
Šikšab
Kullunum
IDDIN-SIN STELE
Šerši
Šariphum
Urbillum
Šašrum
Kakmium
Burullum
Gumaraši
ROAD TO URBILLUM
Lower Zab
Māvākān Čāy
ROAD TO ŠAŠRUM
Šalga River
Šuruthum
Tikitihum
Lower Zab
Qabrā
Tasluga
Azuhinnum
ROAD TO ZAMUA
Arrapha

MAP 2

Turrukûm.[189] Laessøe has suggested a location for Old Babylonian Kakmûm in the Rāniyah district,[190] and this would accord well with the evidence of the tablet published by Langdon as TAD no. 67.[191] This east-Transtigridian Kakmi/Kakmûm is to be kept distinct from the Kakmium found in the Ebla archive.[192] As Astour has pointed out to me (personal communication), *kak-me* occurs as the name of a gate of in the eastern wall of the Tigris, pointing to a location of the city east of Aššur. I would suggest that the ancient GN Kakmiʾum survives in the modern GN Kūysanjaq (Turkish Koi Sancaq). Although Astour also pointed out to me that the Turkish name sancak means "flag; standard, formerly a division of a vilayet," once again I would suggest that this name results from the process of *Volksetymologie*.

3.7.4 Šašrum

A likely terminus on the road from Arrapḫa to the area of the Rāniyah Plain was the Ur III city named Šašrum. We are fortunate in knowing the precise location of this GN. The evidence comes from the excavations of the Danish Dōḫān expedition at Tell Šimšārah.[193] The Old Babylonian tablets found at the site clearly identify it as ancient Šušarrā; the GN is also known from roughly contemporaneous texts from Mari and Tell ar-Rimā.[194] In turn, there can be little doubt that Old Babylonian Šušarrā corresponds to the GN Šašrum (variant spellings: Šašrum, Šaššuru, Šassurum, Aššuru) of Ur III sources (including the year name for Š 42). Tell Šimšārah lies in the fertile Rāniyah plain about 6.5 km southeast of the modern town of Rāniyah. If this location for Šašrum is correct (as seems virtually certain), then it would be an important starting point for determining the location of the toponyms of the lands of Šašrum and Šurutḫum mentioned in Ur III archival texts.

Now, the (second) defeat of the city Šašrum is well known from the year name for AS 6. Curiously, while we have no archival texts that can be unequivocally linked (by the appearance of the GN Šašrum) to this (second) campaign against Šašrum and Šurutḫum, three texts, all dating to AS 4, are clearly connected with an earlier (first) attack on Šašrum. They provide evidence that the first attack against Šašrum dated to AS 4. The relevant texts are listed here in chronological order and noted as tablets (a) to (c). Tablet (a), dated to vii AS 4, notes (rev. 25–26): "when Amar-Suena destroyed Šašrum and Šurutḫum" (u_4 ^{d}amar-^{d}EN.ZU-ke_4 ša-aš-ru-um.KI ù šu-ru-ut-ḫu-um.KI ḫul-a)[195]; tablet (b),

---

189 Stol (1976), 38.

190 Laessøe (1963), 148.

191 Langdon (1911), no. 67.

192 Bonechi (1996), no. 92.

193 See Laessøe (1957) and (1959); Ingholt (1957); Weidner (1958); Falkner (1959–60); Eidem (1985) and (1992).

194 Groneberg (1980), 229–30.

195 Riedel (1913), 209.

dated to 29 viii AS 4), notes (obv. 4) "part of the delivery of the booty of Šašru and Šuruthum" (šà mu-DU nam-ra-ak ša-aš-ru.KI ù šu-ru-ut-ḫu-um.KI)[196]; and tablet (c), (de Genouillac, 1911b no. 2) dated to viii AS 4, contains the remark (rev. 6): "when Amar-Suena destroyed Šašrum and Šuruthum" (u_4 ^{d}amar-^{d}EN.ZU-ke_4 ša-aš-ru-um.KI ù šu-ru-ut-ḫu-um.KI mu-ḫul-a).[197] Three other tablets dated to AS 4[198] record booty from a campaign of Amar-Suena, but unfortunately do not specify its provenance. We would have expected that the attack on Šašrum that occurred in AS 4 would have supplied the name for AS 5. Instead, the installation of the new *en* of Inanna was used to name that year.

3.8 *Cities Along the Road from Šašrum to Arunum*

3.8.1 General Overview

We are fortunate in possessing a small number of Ur III archival texts that mention towns that were taken by Amar-Suena during his thrust from the area of Šašrum, north through the valley of the Sarkapkān River, to the ancient city of Arunum. Four tablets are particularly informative for this campaign: de Genouillac (TCL 2 5500), Langdon (TAD 67), B(ryn) M(awr) C(ollege) 2 (Ellis [1979]: 35–36) and Keiser YOS 4, 67; their data is displayed in Chart 2 below. For this research we have utilized the evidence of a detailed British topographical map of the region of the Rāniyah Plain (1942 edition) and the map provided by J. Eidem in his edition of the Old Babylonian Šimšārah tablets.[199] We have also taken into account the evidence of the rock inscriptions of the Early Old Babylonian king, Iddi(n)-Sîn of Simurrum, found in the Bītwātah district,[200] since, as will be clear from the following discussion, Iddi(n)-Sîn campaigned in this very same area. Further, the evidence of the Sargonic period archival texts from Tell as-Sulaimah[201] and the Old Babylonian tablets from Tulūl Ḥaddād studied by Mustafa[202] will be taken into account. Also relevant to the discussion is a chronicle, or "chronicle-like," text dealing with campaigns of the Middle Assyrian king Arik-dēn-ili (c. 1317–1306 B.C.).[203]

---

196 de Genouillac (1911a), pl. 35.

197 de Genouillac (1911b), no. 2.

198 Maeda (1992), 158.

199 Eidem (1992), 55.

200 Al-Fouadi (1978).

201 Rasheed (1981a).

202 Mustafa (1983).

203 Grayson (1987), 120–21 (A.0.75.1). Scholars have placed the eastern boundary of the land of Assyria in the 14th to 12th centuries B.C. somewhere in the region of Arrapḫa (see, for example, the map in Roaf [1990], 140); a campaign of Arik-dēn-ili in the area around Šušarrā would seem to fit the historical data.

Chart 2: Ancient Settlements on the Road from Šašrum to Arunum.

Ur III Sources					*OB Sources*			*MA Sources*	*Modern*
Year names	TCL 2 5500[a]	TAD 67[b]	BMC 2[c]	YOS 4 67[d]	Iddi(n)-Sîn of Simurrum[e]	Šimšārah Tablets[f]	Tell Ḥaddād Tablets[g]		
šu-ru-ut-ḫu-um	ša-ri-it-ḫu-um								Duḫān(?)
						bu-ru-ul-li-we			Quralla
	gu-ma-ra-ši	gu-ma-ra-ši	gu-ma-ra-ši						Qorašina
ša-aš-ru-um	ša-aš-ru					šu-ša-ra-(a)			Šimšārah
				ša-rí-ip-ḫu-um					Sarkupkān
		še-er-ši							Seručawa
					ku-lu-un-nu-um		ku-la-an		Gulān
			ḫa-bu-ra			ḫa-ba-ru		ḫa-ba-ru-ḫa	
			a-ru$_9$-⌜nu⌝-um			a-ru-ni-im e-ri-na		ar-nu-na ar-nu-ni	Rāwandūz
						na-ga-pi-ni-we		na-gab-bil-ḫi	
			ki-ri-[ú-ri]					kir-ri-ú-ri	Ḥarīr

a. de Genouillac 1911a.
b. Langdon 1911.
c Ellis 1979.
d. Keiser 1919.
e. Al-Fouadi 1978.
f. Eidem 1992.
g. Mustafa 1983.

3.8.2 Šaruthum

The fact that the GN Šaruthum (variant spelling Šarithum) occurs with Šašrum in the year name for AS 6 suggests that it was a town of first-rank importance in the Rāniyah region. Unfortunately, we are not sure of its location. A comparison of the GN Šaruthum with the PN Šuruhtuh found in an Old Babylonian letter from Šimšārah as the name of the king of Elam[204] suggests that the GN Šaruthum is of Elamite origin, a not entirely unexpected fact in view of its eastern location. Of interest in this connection is an apparent reference to this GN in an inscription of the Elamite king Šilhak-Inšušinak; it mentions: *ni-ri-bu-ni šu-ru-tu$_4$-ha*,[205] a phrase interpreted by Hinz and Koch to mean the "mountain pass of *šu-ru-tu$_4$-ha*" (*Gebirgspaß von Šurutuha*).[206] Perhaps the reference is to the gorge at Dōhān.

3.8.3 Burullum

Although we have as yet no Ur III references to the city named Burullum, mention should be made of this city in the context of this study.

The GN Burullum is attested in a most informative Old Babylonian letter from Mari that has been discussed by Laessøe. He writes:

> The "country of *Utûm" (*māt Utîm*) is mentioned in one instance in the Mari correspondence, in the letter ARM 1, 5 (24 ff.), where it is reported that Lidaja, a commander of an army of Turukkaeans, frightened by the din created by the Assyrian army under Išmē-Dagan, has abandoned Burullum, his city, whereupon Išmē-Dagan has conquered Burullum and the entire country of *Utûm. This would certainly suggest that Burullum was a town located in the country of *Utûm, and A. Finet suggested, reasonably, that Burullum was the capital of that country (ARM 15, 123).
>
> Evidence with regard to the whereabouts of the country of *Utûm, of a somewhat clearer description, has been recovered from the Shemshāra archives. In the letter SH. 812 (= IM. 62091), published in Sh. T., pp. 78ff., when writing to Kuwari, the governor of Šušarrā, a certain Šepratu encourages him to leave his army in garrison if there is a danger that Šamši-Adad may turn against the city, "so that it may protect the country of *Utûm and the city of Šušarrā" (line 60: *ma-at Uś-te-em ù* URU.KI *Šu-šar-ra-e*^{ki} *li-ṣur*). In another letter, SH. 827 (= IM 62100), published in *AS* 16 (1965), 191 ff., the same correspondent advises Kuwari to establish friendly relations with the kings of Lullum (Lullubum; Lullumu) so that they may be counted upon to act favourably towards the country of *Utûm and the city of Šušarrā and the *harrānum* (ll. 25–27: *sa-li-im-šu-nu le-qé ki-ma a-na ma-at Ú-te-em ù* URU.KI *Š[u-š]ar-ra-e*.KI *ù a-na* KASKAL *i-ṭà-bu*).[207]

---

204 Laessøe (1965), 194 line 50.

205 König (1977), 132 no. 54a § 3.

206 Hinz and Koch (1987), 1003.

207 Laessøe (1968), 121–22.

We expect, then, that ancient Burullum lay in the general vicinity of Tell Šimšārah. This evidence is completely concordant with Eidem's suggestion of a possible connection of ancient Burullum with the modern mound named Qurulla[208]; the latter is situated about 12 km almost due south of modern Rāniyah. Further, a GN referring to the same place is plausibly found in the toponym *bu-ru-ul-li-we* attested in four Old Babylonian tablets from Tell Šimšārah.[209]

3.8.4 Gumaraši

Four Ur III attestations are known for the GN Gumaraši.[210] Its association with Šašrum in one text[211] suggests a possible location in the Rāniyah district. If we bear in mind the not uncommon variation between "w" and "m" in Akkadian vocables, a posited alternation /gumaraši/ (or) /guwaraši/ would point to a connection with the important mound named Qorašinah.[212] The site was excavated in 1956 and 1958 by the Iraqi Directorate General of Antiquities, but unfortunately, no details on the excavations have been published.[213]

3.8.5 Šariphum

An archival text dated to viii (Umma month name) AS 4 and known, curiously enough, from four tablet copies: (a) YBC 1472 (Keiser 1919: no. 67); (b) unknown collection (Scheil 1918: 61–62 = Scheil 1927: 44–45); (c) University of Hiroshima no. 14 (Yoshikawa 1985: 191–93); and (d) Ligabue Collection (Fales 1988: no. 33), which records various personnel who are named (ll. 5–7) as "booty dedicated to the god Šara, (from) the city Šariphum" (nam-ra-ak a-ru-a ^{d}šára URU.ša-rí-ip-ḫu-um-ma.KI). While some scholars (see Edzard and Farber 1974:177 and Yoshikawa 1985: 192) have indicated that Šariphum is likely a variant spelling of the GN Šarithum, modern evidence argues against this connection. An examination of the British topographical map of the region of the Rāniyah Plain reveals the existence of a village named Sarkapkān, located 10.4 km northwest of Rāniyah. Also of note is the appearance of the Sarkapkān River in Levine's map of the northern and central Zagros.[214] This village and river name, in all likelihood, contain a reflex of the ancient GN Šariphum.

---

208 Eidem (1992), 56.

209 *Ibid.*, 56 and 88. The GN Burullum is clearly derived from the Hurrian *purli* "house" and, not surprisingly, a number of ancient toponyms bore this name. Thus the GN Purulli(we) of the Nuzi tablets is likely distinct from the Burullum of the Šimšārah and Mari archives and the Burallum situated on the road from Aššur to Kaniš. On this question, see Müller (1994), 95.

210 See Edzard and Farber (1974), 70; Owen (1981a), 252; and Sigrist (1988), no. 344 line 4.

211 de Genouillac (1911a), no. 5500 co. ii line 5.

212 Eidem (1992), 54.

213 *Ibid.*, 54.

214 Levine (1973), 6.

3.8.6 Šerši

Only one certain reference to Šerši is found in Ur III sources.[215] The mention of the GNs Gumaraši and Kakmium in this same tablet suggests that ancient Šerši lay in the Rāniyah region. If so, the GN Šerši can plausibly be connected with the modern village named Saručawah, located about 20 km northwest of Rāniyah.[216]

3.8.7 Barbanazu

The GN Barbanazu is named in one Ur III tablet.[217] Its listing there with the GN Gumaraši (line 12) is suggestive of a possible connection with the area of the Rāniyah Plain. If so, Barbanazu can likely be connected with the modern village named Bardi Sanjian, cited by Al-Fouadi as the findspot of the famous Iddin-Sîn rock inscriptions.[218] Bardi Sanjian is located 20 km northwest of Rāniyah on the modern road that proceeds through the valley of the Sarkapkān River.

3.8.8 Kullunum/Kullānum

Ancient Kullunu, an apparently important settlement in the Rāniyah region, is named in the Iddi(n)-Sîn rock inscriptions published by Al-Fouadi; the town is singled out as the instigator of a revolt against the king of Simurrum:

> ^{d}*i-dì*-^{d}EN.ZU LUGAL *da-núm* LUGAL *si-mu-ri-im*.KI ^{d}*za-ba-zu-na* DUMU.NI *ku-lu-un-nu-um*.KI *ik-ki-ir-ma a-na* ^{d}*za-ba-zu-na gi-ra-am i-ta-ba-al*
>
> Iddi(n)-Sîn, the mighty, king of Simurrum: Zabazuna is his son. Kullunum became hostile and waged war against Zabazuna.[219]

The fact that the Iddi(n)-Sîn inscription was found near the village named Bardi Sanjian indicates that ancient Kullunum should be located in this same district.

Kullunum is attested in textual sources dating from Sargonic to Late Old Babylonian times. In the Sargonic tablets from Tell as-Sulaimah mention is made in one tablet of the GN: *be-al*-GUL-*ni*;[220] a second tablet gives a variant writing: [*be*]-*al*-GUL-*la-ni*.[221] The proper name "Lord of G/Kullāni" would

---

215 Langdon (1911), no. 67 line 9.

216 A similarly named but clearly different GN is the Šereše appearing in the annals of Tiglath-pileser I, according to which "it was located on the eastern bank of the Tigris, across from the land of Kadmuḫi, on a steep mountain, in or near the land of Papḫi" (Astour [1987], 33). This Šereše is located too far west to be considered (as Astour suggests) as a conquest by Amar-Suena; the maximum northern extent of the Ur III domains in Amar-Suena's time, we would argue, was the area of Ḥarīr. Astour points out that this western Šereše corresponds to classical Sareisa.

217 Ellis (1979), 35 BMC 2 line 14.

218 Al-Fouadi (1978), 122.

219 *Ibid.*, 125 ll. 1–11.

220 Rashid (1981a), 179 no. 1 col. iv line 3.

221 *Ibid.*, 203 no. 38 line 5'.

appear to be a DN that was also used as a GN, comparable, for example, to the divine and geographical name Aššur. The second element of the GN Beʾāl-Kullāni, then, can likely be linked to the GN Kullunum of the Iddi(n)-Sîn inscription. That we are indeed dealing with the general area of the Rāniyah in these Tell as-Sulaimah tablets is strongly suggested by the occurrence of the GN *ú-ta*.KI as the previous entry to Beʾal-G/Kullāni in the first tablet cited above.[222] *Uś-tá*.KI is likely to be connected with the GN Utûm found as the name of a land (and possibly a city) in the Old Babylonian texts from Šimšārah.[223] Further, Kullānum appears in the form *kul-la-an* in the Late Old Babylonian archive from Tulūl Ḥaddād that has been studied by Mustafa. One tablet of the archive mentions a certain Sîn-abum, a citizen of Kullān.[224] Finally, the GN Kullunum/Kullān can very plausibly be linked with the modern village named Gulān, located only 4.4 km west of Bardi Sanjian!

3.8.9 Ḫabura

In the tablet BMC 2, published by M. Ellis,[225] a GN ḫa-bu-ra.KI occurs two entries after the GN bar-ba-na-zu.KI (in line 16). In light of the associations of the GNs in the Bryn Mawr tablet with the modern toponyms of the Rāniyah region and the ancient toponyms named in the Old Babylonian Šimšārah archives, we suggest that this Ḫabura is to be connected with the GN Ḫabaru named in one Old Babylonian administrative tablet from Šimšārah.[226] It might conceivably be connected as well with the GN Ḫabaruḫa named in a chronicle, or "chronicle-like," text of Arik-dēn-ili.[227]

3.8.10 Arunum

We have seen that a number of toponyms in the Ur III texts can be plausibly located along a route that runs from the town of Rāniyah in a northwesterly direction past the modern villages of Sarkupkān, Bardi Sanjian, and Gulān. How far north did the Ur III kings campaign along this road? An answer is suggested by Levine who notes:

> Another final route to Ruwandiz follows the Serkapkan river up out of the Rania plain, and then over the Garu Manjal pass to the valley leading to Ruwandiz.[228]

So, an apparent *terminus* on this road north from Gulān is marked by the modern town of Rāwandūz; the city is today an important regional center. Can

---

222 *Ibid.*, 179 no. 1 col. iii line 12.

223 Eidem (1992), 41 suggests that an Akkadian (popular?) etymology of *utûm* as "gate-keeper" is likely, bearing in mind the particular geography of the region.

224 Mustafa (1983), no. 112 line 1.

225 Ellis (1979), 35 BMC 2 line 16.

226 Eidem (1992), text no. 24 ll. 2 and 10.

227 Grayson (1987), 126 line 19'.

228 Levine (1973), 7.

an ancient GN be linked to the modern GN Rāwandūz? A tentative "yes" is provided by J. Savoury (in an oral communication to the author)[229]; he indicates that Rāwandūz is almost certainly a compound of two elements, the first Rāwān-, and the second -dūz. The etymology of the second element -dūz is clear; it stands for older Persian *dizh* with the meaning "castle, fortress" (cf. modern Dizful). The first element Rāwān is almost certainly to be connected with the GN Arunum (a-ruḫ-⌜nu⌝-um.KI) found in BMC 2.[230] While we have only this one Ur III reference to Arunum, the GN does reappear in the Old Babylonian archive from Šimšārah; the siege of this apparently important center is mentioned in the letter SH 812 discussed by Laessøe[231] and Eidem.[232] The city may appear (following Eidem's suggestion[233]) in the spelling e-ri-na.KI in the Old Babylonian administrative tablets from Šimšārah.[234] Further, a gentilic possibly formed from this GN appears in personal names in Middle Babylonian tablets noted by Nashef.[235] In addition, a connection with the GN Arnuna/Arnuni named in the aforementioned Middle Assyrian text of Arik-dēn-ili is possible, albeit less certain. Finally, the GN may occur in the form *a-ri-in-ni* in a list of 34 countries conquered by Tukulti-Ninurta I of Assyria,[236] especially since it appears there only two entries before a mention of Arrapḫa. On the other hand, the GN URU *a-ri-na/a-ri-ni/a-ri-nu* (of the land of Muṣri) appearing in an inscription of Tiglath-pileser III[237] is clearly too far west to be considered as a conceivable conquest of Amar-Suena.

3.8.11 Ki-r[i-ú-ri]

Since we have accepted the equation of Ur III Arunum with modern Rāwandūz, the entry immediately preceding Arunum in BMC 2 assumes special interest. The GN in question is broken; it was restored as ki-z[i-ri] by Owen (Owen 1981a: 254), but the text as copied reads ki-r[i-x]. When we recall Levine's location of the ancient land of Kirriuri/Kirrûri (well known from Neo-Assyrian texts) in the area between Arbīl and Rāwandūz (and probably including the Šaqlāwah Valley and the Dāsht-e Ḥarīr),[238] a suggested restoration of the GN as ki-r[i-ú-ri] is inescapable. The GN is normally connected by

---

229 Professor Savoury is Professor Emeritus, Department of Near and Middle Eastern Civilizations, University of Toronto.

230 Ellis (1979), 35 BMC 2 line 17.

231 Laessøe (1959), 77–87.

232 Eidem (1985), 89–90.

233 *Ibid.*, 56.

234 *Ibid.*, 56 and 88.

235 Nashef (1982b), 39, sub Arunāju.

236 Weidner (1959), 27 col. iii line 78.

237 See Astour (1987), 22 no. 1.

238 Levine (1980), 606–7. For further studies of the location of the land of Kirrûri, see Reade (1978) 141, and Saggs (1980), 79–83.

scholars with modern GN Ḥarīr. The association was not noted by Levine, perhaps because he was considering the (erroneous) possibility that this GN was to be read as Habr(i)uri. If our restoration of the line in the Ur III text as ki-r[i-ú-ri] is correct and the connection with Kirriuri/Kirrûri is valid, then the reading *Habr(i)uri should be abandoned.

3.8.12 Nakkabniwe

Of interest in the context of this study is an Ur III toponym that is written NE-*gi*-NE-*ḫu-um*, so far, attested in only two texts.[239] The name has been normalized by some scholars as *dè-gi-dè-ḫu-um*, and seen as an alternate spelling of the GN Tikitiḫum, which we have discussed above.[240] This hypothesis seems to be supported by the fact that both texts referring to NE-*gi*-NE-*ḫu-um* and *ti-ki-ti-ḫu-um* mention a certain ga-da-bi as coming from this place.[241] However, in light of the fact that the value DÈ is, according to von Soden's *Syllabar*, much rarer than either NE or BIL (the primary attested values of the sign NE),[242] we suggest an alternate reading for the GN: *ne-gi-bil-ḫu-um*. This GN, then, could be linked to the GN *na-ga-bil-ḫi* that is found in the aforementioned Arik-dēn-ili chronicle, or "chronicle-like," inscription.[243] In turn, if we bear in mind the not uncommon alternation of l/n in Hurrian names, [244] it may correspond to the GN Nakabbiniwe found in Old Babylonian archival texts from Šimšārah.[245]

3.9 *Cities along the Road from Urbillum to Arunum*

We have seen that Amar-Suena was able to extend the area under Ur's influence to include settlements along a road that led north of the Rāniyah district, all the way to the ancient city of Arunum, probably modern Rāwandūz. Further, we have noted that Šulgi was able, certainly by year Š 45, to exercise control over the city of Urbillum. An important road leads from modern Arbīl to Rāwandūz, and we expect that the Ur III kings, in attempting to consolidate their hold over the region, would have sought to control towns along this road. The major town on the modern road from Arbīl to Rāwandūz is Šaqlāwah. Can this GN be linked to a ancient toponym?

A possible candidate does come to mind, namely ancient Šikšabbum. The city is first mentioned in an Ur III text dated to Š 47 where a reference to a lú-ši-ik-ša-bi.KI ("man" of Šišabbi) is found.[246] A second Ur III reference may

---

239 See Edzard and Farber (1974), 193 and Owen (1981a), 263.

240 Edzard and Farber (1974), 193.

241 See M. Walker (1985), 39–40.

242 von Soden (1976), 22 no. 122.

243 Grayson (1987), 127 line 26'.

244 Berkooz (1937), 54; Gelb, Purves, and MacRae (1943), 285.

245 See Eidem (1992), 89 for a list of the references.

246 Fish (1932), 32 no. 191.

possibly be seen in the tablet TAD no. 67 line 11.[247] According to Langdon's copy it reads: lú-še-ša-bi.KI; the toponym, if copied correctly, is otherwise unattested. An emendation of the copy to read lú-šik!-ša-bi.KI is conceivable, albeit not supported by the fact that Gelb does not list a syllabic value ŠIK for Ur III period texts.[248] Collation of the line would appear to be impossible; according to Grégoire,[249] the tablet TAD no. 67 has been lost. Šikšabbum reappears in the Old Babylonian tablets from Šimšārah in a variety of spellings: ši-ik-ša-ab-bu-um, ši-ik-ša-ab-bu, and ši-ik-ša-am-bi.[250] If we bear in mind the phonetic development: OB -št- > MA -lt- > NA -ss found, for example, in the variations of the spelling of the GN: OB Kaštappum, MA Kaltappu and NA Kassappa/i (likely modern Tell Kašāf/Kešāf/Kušāf two km upstream from the confluence of the Upper Zab with the Tigris),[251] we suggest a development OB Sikšabbum > MA *Šiklabbu > modern Šaqlāwah.

Does a location of Šikšabbum at Šaqlāwah fit the available data for the location of Old Babylonian Šikšabbum? Unfortunately, the Old Babylonian evidence is hardly conclusive. In his earliest discussion of the city, Laessøe notes:

> Šikšambum ... would appear to be a city between Assyrian and Qutean spheres of influence.[252]

In a later article restricted to ancient Šikšabbum Laessøe indicates:

> ... it could well be that its [Šikšabbum's] remains are irretrievably lost, now, in the waters behind the High Dam at Dokān. Or is Šikšabbum to be looked for in the next valley, to the east of the Rānia Plain, the Dasht-i-Bitwain? The large mound of Qal^{c}a Dizeh for instance? ... Or should one search in the foothills of the Zagros Range?[253]

In a still later discussion, Laessøe and Jacobsen write:

> Shikshabbum was a neighbouring city [to Shushāra] that kept up a running feud with Shusharrâ. It may be identical with the large mound of Qal^{c}a Dizeh in the valley east of the Dasht-i-Bitwain ...[254]

Eidem, on the other hand, suggests a more westerly location. He writes in discussion of the letters from Šimšārah:

> There are basically three different, but related themes which dominate the Assyrian correspondence. The first is relations to a certain Jašub-Addu, ruler of a land called Aḫāzum with is capital Šikšabbum, located somewhere on the Lower Zab downstream from Šušarrā.[255]

---

247 Langdon (1911), no. 67.

248 Gelb (1961), 117 no. 320.

249 Grégoire (1996), pl. 17.

250 Groneberg (1980), 221.

251 See Deller (1990a), 61–62 no. 83.

252 Laessøe (1959), 35.

253 Laessøe (1985), 182.

254 Laessøe and Jacobsen (1990), 132.

255 Eidem (1985), 95.

Finally, according to Wu Yuhong, the land of Aḫāzum, which Eidem indicates had its capital at Šikšabbum, was located somewhere between the Upper and Lower Zābs.[256] This area would provide an excellent fit for modern Šaqlāwah, since it is located between the two Zāb Rivers. Clearly, more data is needed to elucidate this question.

4. Other Comparative Matter

The Ur III kings were not the only rulers to have campaigned in the foothills of the Zagros mountains. Indeed, a number of sources complement the picture provided by the Ur III texts. The relevant material comes from eight sources:

(a) the LGN,[257]

(b) an Old Babylonian tablet copy of a royal inscription of Narām-Sîn of Akkad,[258]

(c) an Old Babylonian tablet copy of royal inscriptions of the Gutian king Erridu-pizir,[259]

(d) references to toponyms in the cylinders of Gudea,

(e–f) a list of Zagros GNs in two inscriptions of the Elamite king Kutik-Inšušinak,[260]

(g) a royal inscription of the Elamite king Šilḫak-Inšušinak,[261]

(h) the Middle Babylonian period Nuzi archives,[262] and

(i) modern toponyms.

Here we have listed the toponyms, for the most part, in the order found in the most detailed list, source (f), the Kutik-Inšušinak inscription published by Scheil in MDP 14. The GNs are normalized following Fincke in *Répertoire géographique*, vol. 10.

4.1 Zuya(we)/Suʾawe

According to Müller, the GN Zuyawe is derived from the Hurrian PN Zuya and is likely to be connected with the GN Suʾawe.[263] The likely same city appears as *su-a*-PI.KI along with the GN Azuḫinnum in an Old Akkadian inscription of king Narām-Sîn of Akkad,[264] our source (b) here. The location of Suʾawe/Zuya(we) is uncertain.

---

256 Yuhong (1994), 208.

257 Frayne (1992).

258 Michalowski (1986).

259 Kutscher (1989).

260 Scheil (1905) and (1913).

261 König (1965), 118–132 no. 54.

262 Fincke(1993); Müller (1994).

263 Müller (1994), 161–642 § 2.228.

264 Müller (1994), 214.

4.2 Azuḫinnum

According to Charpin, there were (at least) two ancient cities named Azuḫinnum.[265] He notes:

> Azuhinni, d'après les textes de Nuzi, est situé dans le royaume d'Arrapḫa (p. 77–78). Dans les textes de Mari, Azuhinnum est située au nord du Sinjar, mais à l'ouest du Tigre, non loin de Razamâ (cf. *Fragmenta Historiae Elamicae, Mélanges Steve*, p. 136, n. 51, voir aussi *ARM* 26/1, no. 127, n. b); noter OBTR 145, qui mentionne un transport de grain à dos d'âne depuis Azuhinnum jusqu'à Tell Rimah, ce qui est difficilement concevable si Azuhinnum est dans la région de Zab inférieur (cf. d'ailleurs p. 81 *a*)! L'on est donc conduit à se demander s'il ne faut pas admettre qu'on a affaire à des villes différentes, situées de part et d'autre du Tigre.[266]

The city of Azuḫinni is first attested in a year name of Narām-Sîn of Akkad that also names the city's defeated ruler, a certain Daḫisatili[267]; his name is clearly Hurrian. Unfortunately, we do not know to which of the two Azuḫinnis this year name refers. Azuḫinni also occurs in the Narām-Sîn royal inscription cited as source (b) in our study.[268] In this case, however, evidence clearly points to its location east of the Tigris. Of importance for the question is the concluding rubric of the inscription: URU.KI.URU.KI [*a*]-*bar-ti* [I]DIGNA.IṬ "cities [ac]ross the [T]igris River." But what does "across the Tigris" mean in this context?

Relevant to this question is a section of the much later Cyrus Cylinder, discussed by Beaulieu, which lists cities said to lie "across the Tigris":

> From [Ninev]eh, Aššur, and Susa, Agade, Ešnunna, Zambān, Mêturnu (and) Dēr, until the border of Gutium, the cult cent[ers acr]oss the Tigris, whose (divine) dwellings had lain in ruins for a long time, I returned to their places the gods who dwelt in them and established (for them) an everlasting dwelling.[269]

All the cities mentioned in this passage whose locations are known lay either on the Tigris or at points to the east of it. But, the decisive piece of data indicating that the Narām-Sîn inscription (source b) refers to an eastern Azuḫinnum is the already noted appearance of Azuḫinnum together with Suʾawe in that text.[270]

Also of note is the appearance in Middle and Neo-Assyrian sources of (N)arzuhina/Urzuhina as the name of the eastern gate of Arrapḫa[271]—the road that led from this gate headed in an easterly direction to the Lullubu land, indicating that (N)arzuhina/Urzuhina lay east of Arrapḫa. According to the

265 Charpin (1990), 94.

266 Charpin (1990), 94–95.

267 Foster (1982).

268 Michalowski (1986).

269 Beaulieu (1989).

270 Michalowski (1986), 7 rev. col. iv' 6–8.

271 Müller (1994), 36 § 2.43.2.

Zamua itinerary[272] Arzuhina lay one day's journey from Sare. Sare, in turn, is to be identified with the Sarrima in the land of Qabrā, defeated by the Old Babylonian king Šamši-Addu.[273] Fadhil has followed Speiser in suggesting a location of the eastern Azuḫinnum with Gök Tepe.[274] Levine suggests a location of the province of Arzuḫinnum further east in the direction of modern Chemchemal.[275]

4.3 Matka

Most of the data concerning Matka has been given above in § 3.4.3. Müller points out that the territory of the province of Arrapḫa in general terms lay in the area between the Lower Zāb and Ṭauq Çai, and, as noted in § 3.4.3, he has indicated a location of the Matka of the Nuzi sources not too far south of the modern town of Ṭāwūq. As noted, this would accord extremely well with H. Lewy's suggestion that the Nuzi Matka is to be identified with the modern settlement of Matika that lies two and one half miles SSW of Ṭāwūq.[276]

4.4 Ulamme

Bearing in mind that the element ḫun- apparently occurs in Elamite as an afformative element,[277] we suggest a connection of the GN u-lam(?)-ḫu-un of source (f) (Kutik-Inšušinak)[278] with source (g), Nuzi GN ú-la-me.[279] Müller notes that Ulamme is associated with the GNs Tilturi und Tarkulli in the Nuzi sources.[280] In this connection we may question Müller's rejection of Lacheman's proposed connection of Nuzi Tarkulli with modern GN Tār kulān.[281] Müller denies the identification due to his belief that no toponyms in the Nuzi area can be connected with modern GNs. The evidence assembled in this study would suggest otherwise.

4.7 Tun(ni)

The GN tu-un of source (f) (Kutik-Inšušinak)[282] is almost certainly to be connected with the GN tu_4-un-ni of source (g) (Šilḫak-Inšušinak).[283] No other correlations are known at present from the other comparative material.

272 Levine (1989) and earlier literature cited there; Frayne (1992), 72–81.

273 Charpin and Durand (1985), 314 n. 92.

274 Fadhil (1983), 91.

275 Levine (1989), 84.

276 Lewy (1968), 160.

277 Hinz and Koch (1987), 717–21.

278 Scheil (1913), 11 col. i line 32.

279 Fincke (1993), 319–22 sub Ullame; Müller (1994), 134–37 § 2.1.9.3.

280 Müller (1994), 135.

281 Lacheman (1941), 12.

282 Scheil (1913), 11 col. i line 34.

283 König (1965), 127 § 35 line 72.

4.6 Ḫuḫu

The GN ḫu-uḫ that appears in our source (f)[284] as a toponym, possibly of Elamite origin,[285] may be connected with the restored GN [ḫu]-⌜ùḫ(?)⌝-ḫu of our source (b) (Narām-Sîn).[286] The correlation is uncertain in view of the broken nature of source (b).

4.7 Ḫašiyawe

The ⌜ḫa⌝-ši-ia-we of the Nuzi archives[287] may be connected to the GN ḫa-zi-BI of source (f) (Kutik-Inšušinak).[288] The GN also likely appears in source (b) in the broken GN Michalowski read as: ḫa(?)-su/ba-an-šè.[289] A comparison of the name, but certainly not the place, may be made with Eblaite ḫa-zu-wa-an[290] and Hittite ḫa-aš-šu-wa-an, ḫa-aš-šu.[291] The equation of the GN of source (b) (Narām-Sîn) with source (f)(Kutik-Inšušinak) is strongly supported by the evidence given in § 4.8.

4.8 Ḫuranna

While the reading of this GN at Nuzi is uncertain—it is attested only twice, once as ḫu-⌜ra-x⌝-na, and a second time as ḫu-ra-⌜x⌝-na[292] —the reading ḫu-ra-⌜an(?)⌝-na is strongly supported by comparative evidence. The name can be connected with the ⌜ḫur⌝-a-núm of source (b) (Narām-Sîn)[293] and the ḫur-nam of source (c) (Erridu-pizir).[294] The sequences ḫa-su-an-šè, ⌜ḫur⌝-a-núm, ḫa-ḫu-un of source (b)[295] (Narām-Sîn); ḫa-zi-BI, ḫu-ḫu-un of source (f) (Kutik-Inšušinak)[296]; and ḫa-ši-ia, ḫu-ra-⌜an(?)⌝-na of source (h) (Nuzi texts) are noteworthy. Also of interest is the fact that ḫu-ra-⌜an(?)⌝-na is mentioned with ḫa-ši-ia in HSS XV 74,[297] which strongly supports the geographical proximity of the two cities.

---

284 Scheil (1913), 11 col. i line 33.

285 Hinz and Koch (1987), 714.

286 Michalowski (1986), 6 Ex. B col ii' line 23.

287 Fincke (1993), 96 sub Ḫašia(we).

288 Scheil (1913), p. 11 col. i line 35.

289 Michalowski (1986), 6 Ex. B col ii' line 29.

290 Bonechi (1993), 178–79 sub Ḫazuwan(nu), Ḫašuwan.

291 Del Monte and Tischler (1978), 97–99 sub Ḫašuwa.

292 Fincke (1993), 104–5 sub Ḫu-ra-x-na.

293 Michalowski (1986), 6 Ex. B col ii' line 24.

294 Kutscher (1989), 59 col. x line 12'.

295 Michalowski (1986), 6 Ex. B col ii' ll. 29, 24, and 4.

296 Scheil (1913), p. 11 col. i ll. 35–36.

297 See Fincke (1993), 105.

4.9 Ḫaḫun/Ḫaḫum/Ḫuḫun

Ha-ḫu-un of source (b) (Narām-Sîn)[298] almost certainly is connected with ḫa-ḫu-um of source (d) (Gudea)[299] and ḫu-ḫu-un of source (f) (Kutik-Inšušinak).[300] The word appears to be Elamite, but the meaning of the name is unclear.

4.10 Zarizar[a]

Za-ar-za-[x] of source (e) (Kutik-Inšušinak)[301] is connected with za-ar-zal(?) of source (f) (Kutik-Inšušinak)[302] and za-ri-za-r[a-we] of source (h) (Nuzi).[303] It is mentioned in one Nuzi tablet together with the city Šannaš(we),[304] and Šannaš(we), in turn, is mentioned together with the cities of Ki'aššе, Ḫušri, and Dūr-ubla, located by Müller in the southern part of the province of Arrapḫa.[305]

4.11 Ḫalu

The GN ḫa-lu of source (v)[306] and ḫa-a-la of source (g)[307] can conceivably be linked to the GN Ḫal(u)-šenni of the Nuzi documents, since the Nuzi GN is apparently derived from the compound PN Ḫalu-šenni.[308] It was probably located near Hašiya(we),[309] as noted in § 4.7 of this study.

4.12 Temtena(š)

The GN ti-in-tin of source (f)[310] is likely to be connected with the GN te-em-te-na-(aš) of the Nuzi tablets.[311] Müller notes that Temten(aš) is mentioned in two sources in connection with a road to Lubdi, and in another with a road to Matka. He thus locates Temten(aš) not far southwest of Ṭauq (= ancient Lubdi[?]).[312]

---

298 Michalowski (1986), 6 Ex. B col ii' line 4.

299 Edzard (1997), 34 col. vi line 34.

300 Scheil (1913), p. 11 col. i line 4.

301 Scheil (1905), col. iii line 1.

302 Scheil (1913), p. 11 col. 2 line 6.

303 Fincke (1993), 347, sub Zarizawa(we).

304 Müller (1994), 98 § 2.136.

305 Müller (1994), 331–32 § 2.185.1

306 Scheil (1913), p. 11 col. 2 line 9.

307 König (1965), 127–28 § 37 line 33.

308 Fincke (1993), 86 sub Ḫalu-šenni.

309 Fincke (1993), 86.

310 Scheil (1913), p. 11 col. 2 line 10.

311 Fincke (1993), 290–92 sub Temtena(š); Müller (1994), 113–20, § 2.170.

312 Müller (1994), 113.

4.13 Lami

The GN la-ni of source (f)[313] is likely to be connected with the GN ⌜la⌝-a-mi of the Nuzi tablets.[314] The correlation fits the Nuzi data perfectly, since Zaccagnini indicates that Nuzi Lami lay in the vicinity of Temtemna(š),[315] the city appearing immediately before Lami/Lani in source (f).

4.14 Šelwuḫu(we)

The GN *še-el*-WI-*an* of source (f)[316] possibly is linked to the še-el-wu-ḫu-(we) of the Nuzi sources.[317] Müller places the city a little northwest of modern Taza Ḫurmatli.[318]

4.15 Tašenni(we)

The GN *tá-še-un* of source (f)[319] likely correlates to the ta-še-en-ni-(we) of Nuzi documents.[320] The GN may possibly be located at modern Tisᶜin.[321]

4.16 Ḫuḫnuri

Bearing in mind that the element ḫuḫ- is apparently a nominal stem in Elamite,[322] we can posit a possible connection between the ḫu-ḫu-un-rí of source (f)[323] and the nu-ri of LGN 39[324]; the former would be a compound of ḫuḫun- plus -nuri. This correlation is very strongly supported by the fact that the GN that follows nu-ri, LGN 40: ʾà-i-nu, can be connected with the GN a-in-un-ak that follows Ḫuḫunri in source (f).[325] Moreover, this correlation indicates that the Ḫuḫnuri appearing in the name of year 7 of Amar-Suena does not refer to the Ḫuḫnuri that lay far off to the east in Elam, but rather the Ḫuḫnuri that was situated in the Zagros, probably not far from Lubdi. Indeed, if we were to assume that the Ḫuḫnuri of AS 7 lay in Elam, a very strange pattern would emerge from the historical data. We would find Šulgi and Amar-Suena campaigning year after year in the Zagros foothills, only to shift

---

313 Scheil (1913), p. 11 col. 2 line 11.

314 Fincke (1993), 165, sub Lami.

315 Zaccagnini (1959), 192.

316 Scheil (1913), 11 col. 2 ll. 17–18.

317 Fincke (1993), 249–50; Müller (1994), 98–99 § 2.140.

318 Müller (1984), map.

319 Scheil (1913), 11 col. 2 line 119. The line was read *it-tu-un*-(ki) by Scheil, but the reading *tá-še-un*.KI is supported by the copy.

320 Fincke (1993), 281–84; Müller (1994), 111–12 § 2.166.

321 For the literature on this equation, see Fincke (1993), 283–84.

322 Hinz and Koch (1987), 714 sub Ḫu-úḫ.

323 Scheil (1913), 13 col. iii line 1.

324 Pettinato (1978), 64–65 LGN 39a.

325 Scheil (1913), 13 col. iii line 3.

suddenly the locus of the conflict several hundred miles to the east for one solitary year, and then a return to further battles in the Zagros region. It may be noted that the defeat of Ḫuḫnuri apparently marked the end of the Zagros campaigns of the Ur III kings.

4.17 Ayyinu

As noted in § 4.16 the ʾà-i-nu of LGN 17 corresponds to a-in-un-ak of source (f). If probably lay near ancient Terqa/Lubdi.

4.18 Ašuḫiš

The GN Ašuḫiš found in the Nuzi archives[326] may be linked to the GN a-šu-ḫa-áš appearing in source g (Šilḫak-Inšušinak),[327] where it occurs along with pi-it la-as-si-i(?) and ma-at-ka_4. It may conceivably be connected with the a-$šu_{12}$/a-ša of LGN 41, but this is most uncertain. It probably lay not far from Terqa/Lubdi.

4.19 Terqa

The data concerning ancient Terqa is given in § 3.4.4 above, where a connection with modern Ṭauq is suggested.

4.20 Lassi

The GN la-sá of LGN 43 may be compared with the la-as-si-i appearing in source (h) (Šilḫak-Inšušinak).[328] It likely lay not far from ancient Terqa/Lubdi.

4.21 Ḫumpurše

The GN ḫu-un-pur-še-⸢x⸣ of source (g)[329] (Kutik-Inšušinak) may be connected with the GN Ḫumpurše occurring in the Nuzi archives.[330] Its particular location in the Kutik-Inšušinak inscription suggests it lay close to Ayyinu and Ḫuḫunri.

4.22 Mumam

The mountain name Mumam, occurring in the inscription of Erridu-pizir as the pass leading to the city of Urbillum,[331] may conceivably be connected with the GN mu-i-um-an of source (f) (Kutik-Inšušinak).[332]

326 Fincke (1993), 57–58; Müller (1994), 32–33 § 2.35.

327 König (1965), 127 § 37 line 81.

328 König (1965), 127 § 37 line 81.

329 Scheil (1913), 13 col. iii line 4.

330 Fincke (1993), 103; Müller (1994), 47–48 § 2.68.

331 Kutscher (1989), 59 col. xi BT 3 line 4.

332 Scheil (1913), 13 col. iii line 8.

Chart 3: Other Comparative Matter

LGN	*Narām-Sîn*	*Erridu-pizir*	*Gudea*	*MDP 6: Kutik-Inšušinak*	*MDP 14: Kutik-Inšušinak*	*Šilḫak-Inšušinak*	*Nuzi*	*Modern*
—	su-a-we	—	—	—	—	—	zu-ia-we	—
—	a-zu-ḫi-núm	—	—	—	—	—	a-zu-ḫi-in-ni	—
ma-tá-kà	—	[ma]-a[t-kà]	ma-at-kà	—	—	ma-at-ka_4	⸢ma⸣-at-qa_4	Matika
—	—	—	—	—	u-lam-ḫu-un		ú-la-me	—
—	[ḫu(?)]-ùḫ(?)-ḫu	—	—	—	ḫu-uḫ	—	—	—
—	—	—	—	—	tu-un	tu_4-un-ni	—	—
—	ḫa-su-an-šè	—	—	—	ḫa-zi-BI	—	⸢ḫa⸣-ši-ia-we	—
—	⸢ḫur⸣-a-núm	ḫur-nam	—		—	—	ḫu-⸢ra-an⸣-na	—
—	ḫa-ḫu-un	—	ḫa-ḫu-um	—	ḫu-ḫu-un	—	—	—
—		—	—	za-ar-za-[x]	za-ar-zal(?)	—	za-ri-za-r[a-we]	—
—	—	—	—	—	ḫa-lu	ḫa-a-la	—	—
—	—	—	—	—	ti-in-tin	—	te-em-te-en	—
—	—	—	—	—	la-ni	—	⸢la⸣-a-mi	—
—	šè-wi-in	—	—	—	še-il-wi-an	—	še-el-wu-ḫu	—
—	—	—	—	—	tá-še-un	—	ta-še-en	Tisᶜin

Chart 3: Other Comparative Matter

LGN	*Narām-Sîn*	*Erridu-pizir*	*Gudea*	*MDP 6 Kutik-Inšušinak*	*MDP 14: Kutik-Inšušinak*	*Šilḫak-Inšušinak*	*Nuzi*	*Modern*
nu-ri	—	—	—	—	ḫu-ḫu-un-ri	—	—	—
ʾà-i-nu	—	—	—	—	a-in-un-ak	—	—	—
ter-qa	—	—	—	—		—		Ṭauq
la-sá	—	—	—	—	—	la-as-si-i	—	—
—	—	—	—	—	ḫu-un-bur-še	—	ḫu(!)-um(?)-pu-ur-še	—
—	—	mu-ma-am	—		mu-i-um-ma	—	—	—
—	àm-mi-ra	—	—		x-àm-ra	—	ar-wa	—
—	—	—	—	—	ḫa-an-ba-te	ḫa-pa-te	—	—
—	—	—	—	—	—	nu-ú-za	nu-zi	—
—	—	—	—	—	—	ar-ra-ap-ḫa	a-ra-ap-ḫe	ᶜArafah
—	—	—	—	—	—	še-en-ku-ru		Sungur

4.23 Arwa

The GN àm-mi-ra of source (b) (Narām-Sîn)[333] may likely be connected with the GN x-àm-ra of source (f) and the GN ar-wa occurring in the Nuzi archives.[334] Müller places Arwa a little distance southwest of Nuzi.[335]

4.24. Ḫapate

As noted by Müller,[336] the GN Ḫapate of the Nuzi archives is connected with the GN ḫa-an-ba-te, which appears in source (g) (Šilḫak-Inšušinak)[337]—in the same section of source (g) Arrapḫa and Nuza are mentioned.

4.25 Šenkur

A noted in § 3.4.2, a GN še-en-ku-ru is named as a settlement in a section of source (g) (Šilḫak-Inšušinak).[338] Other toponyms found in this section include [pi-it-na-a]p-pa-ḫi-e and ša im-mi-ri-e; they correspond to the GNs Nappāḫî[339] and Imēri[340] of the Nuzi archives. This ancient GN is possibly connected with the modern GN Sungur, as noted in § 3.4.2 above.

5. SUMMARY

A study of the toponyms mentioned in the year names, royal inscriptions, and economic tablets dating to the last half of the reign of Šulgi and the reign of Amar-Suena, coupled with a detailed study of modern topographical maps of the area around the Zagros foothills road, has enabled us to posit tentative locations for many of the cities attacked by the Ur III kings during their Zagros wars. The evidence of the Ur III sources can be supplemented by evidence from the royal inscriptions of Narām-Sîn of Akkad, Kutik-Inšušinak, and Šilḫak-Inšušinak of Elam, in addition to the evidence of the LGN, the Gudea cylinders, the Nuzi archival texts, and modern place names.

In general, the Ur III kings expanded the territory of Ur along a corridor that stretched in the southeast from the area where the Diyālā River cuts through the Jebel Ḥamrīn to the modern city of Rāwandūz in the northwest.

---

333 Michalowski (1986), 7 Ex. B col iv' line 27.

334 Fincke (1993), 55–56; Müller (1994), 31–32 § 2.31.

335 Müller (1994), map at end of book.

336 Müller (1994), 43–44 § 2.56.

337 König (1965), 128 § 40 line 96.

338 König (1965), 126–27 § 29 line 44.

339 Fincke (1994), 182.

340 Fincke (1993), 117.

BIBLIOGRAPHY

Astour, Michael

1987 "Semites and Hurrians in Northern Tigris," *Studies on the Civilization and Culture of Nuzi and the Hurrians* 2. Edited by D. I. Owen and M. Morrison. (General Studies and Excavations at Nuzi 9/1). Winona Lake, Ind.

Baqir, Taha

1949 "Date-Formulae and Date-Lists from Harmal," *Sumer* 5, 34–86.

Beaulieu, Paul-Alain

1989 "Agade in the Late Babylonian Period," *NABU* 1989/3 no. 66.

Berkooz, Moshé

1937 *The Nuzi Dialect of Akkadian: Orthography and Phonology.* (Language Dissertations Published by the Linguistic Society of America no. 23). Philadelphia.

Birot, Maurice

1985 "Les chroniques assyriennes," *M.A.R.I.* 4. Edited by Beyer and Charpin. Paris, 219–42.

Birot, Maurice, Jean-Robert Kupper, and Olivier Rouault

1979 *Répertoire analytique. Tomes* I–XIV, XVIII *et textes divers hors-collection. Première partie: Noms propres.* (ARMT 16/1). Paris.

Börker-Klähn, Jutta

1982 *Altvorderasiatische Bildstelen und vergleichbare Felsreliefs.* Mainz am Rhein.

Bonechi, Marco

1996 "Remarks on the 'Road to Zamua'," NABU 1996 no. 92.

Borger, Rykle

1970 "Vier Grenzsteinurkunden Merodachbaladans I. von Babylonien," *AfO* 23, 1–26.

Brinkman, John

1968 *A Political History of Post-Kassite Babylonia.* (Analecta Orientalia 43). Rome.

Charpin, Dominique

1990 Review of Abdullah Fadhil, Studien zur Topographie und Prosopographie der Provinzstädte des Königsreichs Arrapḫe, *RA* 74, 94–96.

Charpin, Dominique and Jean-Marie Durand

1985 "La prise du pouvoir par Zimri-Lim," *M.A.R.I.* 4, 293–343.

Chiera, Giovanna

1986 "Il Messaggero di Ibubu," *OrAnt* 25, 81–86.

Çığ, Muazzez and Hatice Kızılyay

1969 *Sumer Edebî Tablet ve Parçaları.* (Vol. I). Ankara.

Civil, Miguel

1998 "Adamdun, the Hippopotamus, and the Crocodile," *JCS* 50, 11–14.

Delaporte, Louis

1911 "Tablettes de Drehem," *RA* 8 ,183–98.

1912 *Textes de l'époque d'Ur.* (Inventaire des Tablettes de Tello IV). Paris.

Deller, Karlheinz

1990a "aB Kaštappum, mA Kaltappu, nA Kassappa/i," *NABU* no. 83.

1990b "Eine Erwägung zur Lokalisierung des aB ON Qabrā/Qabarā," *NABU* no. 84.

Del Monte, Giuseppe F. and Johannes Tischler

1978 *Die Orts- und Gewässernamen der hethitischen Texte* (Répertoire Géographique des Textes Cunéiformes VI). Wiesbaden.

Dhorme, Paul

1912 "Tablettes de Dréhem à Jerusalem," *RA* 9, 39–63.

Edzard, Dietz O.

1972 "Ḫamazi," *RLA* 4/,1 70–71.

1997 *Gudea and His Dynasty.* (The Royal Inscriptions of Mesopotamia. Early Periods Volume 3/1). Toronto.

Edzard, Dietz O. and Gertrud Farber,

1974 *Die Orts- und Gewässernamen der Zeit der 3. Dynastie von Ur.* (Répertoire Géographique des Textes Cunéiformes II). Wiesbaden.

Edzard, Dietz O., Gertrud Farber, and Edmond Sollberger

1977 *Die Orts und Gewässernamen der präsargonischen und sargonischen Zeit.* (Répertoire Géographique des Textes Cunéiformes I). Wiesbaden.

Eidem, Jesper

1985 "News from the Eastern Front: The Evidence from Tell Shemshara," *Iraq* 47, 83–107.

1992 *The Shemshāra Archives 2: The Administrative Texts.* Copenhagen.

Ellis, Maria de Jong

1979 "Cuneiform Tablets at Bryn Mawr College," *JCS* 31, 30–55.

Fadhil, Abduillah

1983 *Studien zur Topographie und Prosopographie der Provinzstädte des Königreichs Arrapḫa.* (Baghdader Forschungen 6). Main am Rhein.

Fales, Mario

1988 *Prima dell'alfabeto: La storia della scrittura attraverso testi cuneiformi inediti.* Venice.

Falkner, Margarete

1959–60 "Tell Shemshara," *AfO* 19, 201–2.

Fincke, Jeanette

1993 *Die Orts- und Gewässernamen der Nuzi-Texte.* (Répertoire Géographique des Textes Cunéiformes X). Wiesbaden.

Fish, Thomas

1931 *Catalogue of Sumerian Tablets in the John Rylands Library.* Manchester.

Forbes, R.

1964 *Studies in Ancient Technology* (Vol. 1). Leiden.

Forrer, Emil

1920 *Die Provinzeinteilung des assyrischen Reiches.* Leipzig.

Foster, Benjamin

1982 "An Agricultural Archive from Sargonic Akkad," *ASJ* 4, 7–51.

Al-Fouadi, Abdul-Hadi

1978 "Inscriptions and Reliefs from Bitwāta," *Sumer* 34, 122–29.

Frayne, Douglas

1990 *Old Babylonian Period (2003–1595 BC).* (The Royal Inscriptions of Mesopotamia, Early Periods Volume 4). Toronto.

1992 *The Early Dynastic List of Geographical Names.* (American Oriental Series 74). New Haven.

1993 *Sargonic and Gutian Periods* (*2334–2113 BC*). (The Royal Inscriptions of Mesopotamia, Early Periods Volume 2). Toronto.

1997a "On the Location of Simurrum," *Crossing Boundaries and Linking Horizons: Studies in Honor of Michael C. Astour on His 80th Birthday.* Ed. by G. Young, M. Chavalas, and R. Averbeck, Bethesda, Md.

1997b *Ur III Period* (*2112–2004 BC*). (The Royal Inscriptions of Mesopotamia, Early Periods Volume 3/2). Toronto.

Freydank, Helmut

1974 "Zwei Verpflegungstexte aus Kār-Tukultī-Ninurta," *AoF* 1, 55–89.

Gadd, Cyril

1926 "Tablets from Kirkuk," *RA* 23, 49–161.

Gelb, Ignace

1961 *Old Akkadian Writing and Grammar.* (MAD 2^2). Chicago.

Gelb, Ignace, Pierre Purves, and Allan MacRae

1943 *Nuzi Personal Names.* (OIP 57). Chicago.

de Genouillac, Henri

1911a *Tablettes de Drehem publiées avec inventaire et tables.* (TCL 2). Paris.

1911b *La trouvaille de Drehem: Étude avec une choix de textes de Constantinople et Bruxelles.* Paris.

1921 *Époque présargonique, époque d'Agade, époque d'Ur.* (ITT 5). Paris.

Goetze, Albrecht

1950 "Sin-iddinam of Larsa. New Tablets from his Reign," *JCS* 4, 83–118.

1957 "Texts and Fragments," *JCS* 11, 77–78.

Gomi, Tohru, Yoko Hirose, and Kazutaka Hirose

1990 *Neo-Sumerian Administrative Texts of the Hirose Collection*. Potomac, Md.

Grayson, A. Kirk

1963 "The Walters Art Gallery Sennacherib Inscription," *AfO* 20, 83–96.

1974–77 "The Empire of Sargon of Akkad," *AfO* 25, 56–64.

1987 *Assyrian Rulers of the Third and Second Millennia BC (To 1115 BC)*. (The Royal Inscriptions of Mesopotamia, Assyrian Periods Volume 1). Toronto.

1996 *Assyrian Rulers of the Early First Millennium BC II (858–745 BC)*. (The Royal Inscriptions of Mesopotamia, Assyrian Periods Volume 3). Toronto.

Greengus, Samuel

1979 *Old Babylonian Tablets from Ishchali and Vicinity*. (PIHANS 44). Leiden.

Grégoire, Jean-Pierre

1996 *Archives administratives et inscriptions cunéiformes: Ashmolean Museum, Bodleian Collection, Oxford*. (Contribution à l'histoire sociale, économique, politique et culturelle du proche-orient ancien 1/1). Paris.

Groneberg, Brigitte

1980 *Die Orts- und Gewässernamen der altbabylonischen Zeit*. (Répertoire Géographique des Textes Cunéiformes 2). Wiesbaden.

Hallo, William W.

1953 *The Ensi's of the Ur III Dynasty*. (M.A. thesis).

1964 "The Road to Emar," *JCS* 18, 57–88.

1971 "Gutium (Qutium)," *RLA* 3/9, 708–20.

1978 "Simurrum and the Hurrian Frontier," *RHA* 36, 71–83.

1996 *Origins: The Ancient Near Eastern Background of Some Modern Institutions*. Leiden.

Hannoon, Nail

1986 "Studies in the Historical Geography of Northern Iraq During the Middle and Neo-Assyrian Periods" (Ph. D. Dissertation, University of Toronto).

Hinz, Walther and Heidemarie Koch

1987 *Elamisches Wörterbuch*. (Deutsches Archäologisches Institut Abteilung Teheran. Archäologische Mitteilungen aus Iran Ergänzungsband 17). Berlin.

Ingholt, Harald

1957 "The Danish Dokan Expedition," *Sumer* 13, 214–15.

Iraq, Directorate General of Antiquities

1975–76 *Atlas of the Archeaological Sites in Iraq*. Baghdad.

Khalil Ismail, Bahijah

1986 "Eine Siegesstele des Königs Daduša von Ešnunna," *Im Bannkreis des Alten Orients. Studien zur Sprach- und Kulturgeschichte des Alten Orients und seines Ausstrahlungsraumes, Karl Oberhuber zum 70. Geburtstag gewidmet*. Ed. by W. Meid and H. in Meid. Innsbruck, 105–8.

Jones, Tom and John Snyder

1961 *Sumerian Economic Texts from the Third Ur Dynasty*. Minneapolis, Minn.

Kärki

1986 *Die Königsinschriften der dritten Dynastie von Ur* (Studia Orientalia 58). Helsinki.

Keiser, Clarence

1919 *Selected Documents of the Ur Dynasty*. (YOS 4). New Haven.

Keiser, Clarence and Shin Teke Kang

1971 *Neo-Sumerian Account Texts from Drehem*. (BIN 3). New Haven.

Kessler, Karlheinz

1995 "Drei Keilschrifttexte aus Tell Baradān," *Beiträge zur Kulturgeschichte Vorderasiens: Festschrift für Rainer Michael Boehmer*. Ed. by U. Finkbeiner, R. Dittmann, und H. Hauptmann. Mainz, 281–88.

King, Leonard

1898 *Cuneiform Tablets from Babylonian Tablets, &c., in the British Museum* (Part V). London.

1912 *Babylonian Boundary Stones and Memorial Tablets in the British Museum*. London.

Klengel, Horst

1988 "Lullu(bum)," *RLA* 7 3/4, 164–68.

König, Friedrich

1965 *Die elamischen Königsinschriften*. Graz.

1977 *Die elamischen Königsinschriften*. (*AfO* Beihefte 16). Osnabrück.

Kutscher, Raphael

1989 *The Brockmon Tablets at the University of Haifa: Royal Inscriptions*. Haifa.

Lacheman, Ernest

1941 "Nuzi Geographical Names II," *BASOR* 81, 10–15.

1955 *The Administrative Archives*. (Excavations at Nuzi 6. HSS 6). Cambridge, Mass.

Laessøe, Jørgen

1957 "An Old Babylonian Archive Discovered at Tell Shemshara," *Sumer* 13, 216–18.

1959 *The Shemshāra Tablets: A Preliminary Report*. København.

1963 *People of Ancient Assyria*. London.

1965 "IM 62100: A Letter from Tell Shemshara," *Studies in Honor of Benno Landsberger on his Seventy-fifth Birthday, April* 21, 1965. Ed. by H. Güterbock and Th. Jacobsen. (AS 16). Chicago.

1968 "The Quest for the Country of *Utûm," *JAOS* 88, 120–22.

1985 "Šikšabbum: An Elusive City," *OrNS* 54, 182–88.

Laessøe, Jørgen and Thorkild Jacobsen

1990 "Šikšabbum Again," *JCS* 42, 127–78.

Lafont, Bertrand

1988 "La Correspondance d'Iddiyatum," *Archives épistolaires de Mari* 1/2. Joint authors, D. Charpin, F. Joannès, S. Lackenbacher et B. Lafont. Paris, 461–508.

1996 "L'extraction du minerai du cuivre en Iran à la fin du IIIe milléniare," *Tablettes et Images aux Pays de Sumer et d'Akkad, Mélanges offerts à Monsier H. Limet*, (A.P.H.A. mémoire no. 1). Edited by Ö. Tunca and D. Deheselle. Liège.

Landsberger, Benno

1933 "Lexikalisches Archiv," *ZA* 41, 216–36.

Langdon, Stephen

1911 *Tablets from the Archives of Drehem*. Paris.

Leemans , Wilhelmus

1966 "Cuneiform Texts in the Collection of Dr. Ugo Sissa," *JCS* 20, 34–47.

Legrain, Léon

1912 *Le temps des rois d'Ur, recherche sur la société antique, d'après des textes noveau*. Paris.

Levine, Louis

1973 "Geographical Studies in the Neo-Assyrian Zagros-I," *Iran* 11, 1- 27.

1974 "Geographical Studies in the Neo-Assyrian Zagros-II," *Iran* 12, 99–124.

1980 "Kirruri, Kirriuri," *RlA* 5, 606–7.

1989 "K. 4675+ - The Zamua Itinerary," *SAAB* 3, 75–92.

Lewy, Hildegard

1968 "A Contribution to the Historical Geography of the Nuzi Texts," *JAOS* 88, 150–62.

Limet, Henri

1976 *Textes sumériens de la IIIe Dynastie d'Ur*. (Documents du Proche Orient Ancient, Épigraphie1). Brussels.

Maeda, Tohru

1992 "The Defense Zone during the Rule of the Ur III Dynasty," *ASJ* 14, 135–72.

McEwan, Gilbert

1982 "Agade after the Gutian Destruction: the Afterlife of a Mesopotamian City," *AfO* Beiheft 19, 8–15.

Meek, Theophile

1935 *Old Akkadian, Sumerian and Cappadocian Tablets from Nuzi.* (HSS 10). Cambridge, Mass.

Michalowski,

1976 "The Royal Correspondence of Ur" (Ph. D. dissertation Yale University, University Microfilms 76-30, 236). Ann Arbor, Mich.

1986 "The Earliest Hurrian Toponymy," *ZA* 76, 4–11.

Moussli, Majid

1984 "Tell Ḥomṣ (Qal^{c}at Ḥomṣ)," *Zeitschrift des Deutschen Palästina-Vereins* 100, 9–11.

Müller, Gerfrid

1994 *Studien zur Siedlungsgeographie und Bevölkerung des Mittleren Osttigrisgebiets.* (Heidelberger Studien zum Alten Orient, Vol. 7). Heidelberg.

Muhamed, Ahmad

1985 "Studies on Unpublished Cuneiform Texts from the Diyālā Region — Basin of Himrin — Tell Haddad" (M.A. thesis, Baghdad University).

1992 *Old Babylonian Cuneiform Texts from the Hamrin Basin: Tell Haddad.* (Nabu Publications: Edubba 1). London.

Mustafa, Ahmad

1983 "The Old Babylonian Tablets from Me-Turan (Tell al-Sib and Tell Haddad" (Ph. D. dissertation, University of Glasgow).

Nashef, Khalid

1982a "Der Ṭaban-Fluss," *Bagh. Mitt.* 13, 117–41.

1982b *Die Orts- und Gewässernamen der mittelbabylonischen und mittelassyrischen Zeit.* (Répertoire Géographique des Textes Cunéiformes V). Wiesbaden.

Nies, James

1920 *Ur Dynasty Tablets Chiefly from Tello and Drehem.* (Assyriologische Bibliothek 25). Leipzig.

Owen, David I.

1975 *The John Frederick Collection.* (MVN 3). Rome.

1981a Review of Edzard and Farber, *Die Orts- und Gewässernamen der Zeit der 3. Dynastie von Ur.* (Répertoire Géographique des Textes Cunéiformes 2). In *JCS* 33, 244–70.

1981b "Tax Payments from Some City Elders in the Northeast," *ASJ* 3, 63–68.

1991 *Neo-Sumerian Texts from American Collections.* (MVN 15). Rome.

Pettinato, Giovanni

1978 "L'atlante Geografico del Vicino Oriente Antico attestato ad Ebla e ad Abū Ṣalābīkh (I). *Or* 47, 50–73.

1981a Testi lessicali monolingui della biblioteca L. 2769. (Materiali Epigrafici di Ebla 3). Naples.

1981b *The Archives of Ebla: An Empire Inscribed in Clay*. Garden City, N.Y.

Pinches, Theophilus

1909 *The Cuneiform Inscriptions of Western Asia*. Vol. 5. London.

Poebel, Arno

1930 "Sumerische Untersuchungen IV," *ZA* 39, 129–64.

Postgate, Nicholas

1979 "The Historical Geography of the Hamrin Basin," *Sumer* 35, 586–94.

1983 "The Historical Geography of the Hamrin Basin," *Sumer* 40, 149–59.

Rasheed, Fawzi

1981a *The Ancient Inscriptions in Himrin Area*. (Himrin 4: Results of the Salvage Excavations at Himrin Reservoir). Baghdad.

1981b "A Royal Inscription from Tell Ḥaddād," *Sumer* 37, 72–80 (Arabic section).

1983 "Akkadian Texts from Tell Sleimah," *Sumer* 40, 55–56.

Al-Rawi, Farouk and Jeremy Black

1995 "A Rediscovered Akkadian City?" *Iraq* 55, 147–48.

Reade, Julian

1978 "Kassites and Assyrians in Iran," *Iran* 16, 141.

1995 "Iran in the Neo-Assyrian Period," *Neo-Assyrian Geography*. (Quaderni di Geografia Storica 5). Ed. by Mario Liverani, Rome, 31–42.

Reiner, Erica and Miguel Civil

1974 *The Series ḪAR-ra = ḫubullu Tablets* XX–XXIV. (MSL 11). Rome.

Riedel, Wilhelm

1913 "Weitere Tafeln aus Drehem," *RA* 10, 207–10.

Roaf, Michael

1990 *Cultural Atlas of Mesopotamia and the Ancient Near East*. Oxford.

Rouault, Olivier

1977 "Terqa: Rapport préliminaire (1987–89), Introduction," *M.A.R.I.* 8. Edited by D. Beyer, D. Charpin, B. Muller, and M. Sauvage. Paris, 73–82.

Sachs, Abraham

1937 "Another Occurrence of the Alleged Ancient Name of Sāmarrā," *JAOS* 57, 419–20.

Saggs, Harry

1958 "The Nimrud Letters, 1952 — Part IV," *Iraq* 22, 182–212.

1980 "The Land of Kirruri," *Iraq* 42, 79–83.

Sallaberger, Walther
1993 *Der kultische Kalender der Ur III-Zeit*. Vols. 1 and 2. Berlin.

Salonen, Armas, Muazzez Çığ, and Hatice Kızılyay
1954 Istanbul Arkeoloji Müzelerinde Bulunan Puzriš-Dagan Metinleri. Vol. I. Helsinki.

Scheil, Père Vincent
1894 "Notes d'épigraphie et d'archéologie assyriennes," *RT* 16, 186–90.
1897 "Notes d'épigraphie et d'archéologie assyriennes," *RT* 19, 44–64.
1905 *Textes Élamites-Sémitiques.* (MDP 6). Paris, 14–15 and pl. 4.
1913 *Textes Élamites-Sémitiques.* (MDP 14). Paris, 7–16.
1918 L'admission d'un esclave au service liturgique," *RA* 15, 61–62.
1927 "Butin du guerre voué à Šara," *RA* 24, 44–45.

Schroeder, Otto
1917 *Altbabylonische Briefe.* (VS 16). Leipzig.

von Schuler, Einar
1967 "Eine neue Inschrift Šulgis," *BJVF* 7, 293–95.

Shea, William
1984 "The Form and the Significance of the Eblaite Letter to Ḫamazi," *OrAnt* 23, 143–58.

Sigrist, René Marcel
1979 "Nouveaux noms géographiques de l'empire d'Ur III," *JCS* 31, 166–70.
1984 *Neo-Sumerian Account Texts in the Horn Archaeological Museum* 1. (AUCT 1). Berrien Springs, Mich.
1988 *Neo-Sumerian Account Texts in the Horn Archaeological Museum* 2. (AUCT 2). Berrien Springs, Mich.
1990 *Tablettes du Princeton Theological Seminary, époque d'Ur III.* (OPKF 10). Philadelphia.
1995 *Neo-Sumerian Texts from the Royal Ontario Museum* I: *The Administration at Drehem*. Bethesda, Md.

Sigrist, René Marcel, David I. Owen, and Gordon D. Young
1984 *The John Frederick Lewis Collection Part II.* (MVN 13). Rome.

Sjöberg, Åke W. and Eugene Bergmann S.J.
1969 *The Collection of the Sumerian Temple Hymns.* (TCS 3). Locust Valley, N.Y.

von Soden, Wolfram
1952 *Grundriß der akkadischen Grammatik* (Analecta Orientalia 22). Rome.

Steible, Horst
1991 *Die neusumerischen Bau- und Weihinschriften.* (Freiburger altorientalische Studien 9). Stuttgart.

Steinkeller, Piotr

1982 "The Mesopotamian God Kakka," *JNES* 41, 289–94.

1986 "Seal of Išma-Ilum, Son of the Governor of Matar," *Vicino Oriente* 6, 27– 40.

1988 "On the Identity of the Toponym LÚ.SU(.A)," *JAOS* 108, 197–202.

1995 "A Rediscovered Akkadian City?" *ASJ* 17, 275–81.

Stol, Marten

1976 *Studies in Old Babylonian History*. (PIHANS 40). Leiden.

Thureau-Dangin, François

1903 *Recueil de Tablettes Chaldéennes*. Paris.

Vallat, François

1993 *Les noms géographiques des sources suso-élamites*. (Répertoire Géographique des Textes Cunéiformes XI). Wiesbaden.

Walker, Christopher B.F.

1983 "Another Babati Inscription," *JCS* 35, 91–96.

Walker, Marcie Finkel

1985 "The Tigris Frontier from Sargon to Hammurabi: A Philologic and Historical Synthesis." (Ph. D. dissertation, Yale University, University Microfilms 8613633). Ann Arbor, Mich.

Weidner, Ernst

1958 "Dokan," *AfO* 18, 178–80; 458–59.

1959 *Die Inschriften Tukulti-Ninurtas I. und seiner Nachfolger*. (*AfO* Beiheft 12). Graz.

Westenholz, Aage

1987 *Old Sumerian and Old Akkadian Texts in Philadelphia. Part Two: The 'Akkadian' Texts, the Enlilmaba Texts, and the Onion Archive*. (CNI Publications 3). Copenhagen.

Whiting, Robert

1976 "Tiš-atal of Nineveh and Babati, Uncle of Šu-Sin," *JCS* 28, 173–82.

1987 *Old Babylonian Letters from Tell Asmar*. (AS 22). Chicago.

Wu Yuhong

1994 *A Political History of Eshnunna, Mari and Assyria During the Early Old Babylonian Period (From the End of the Ur III Period to the Death of Šamši-Adad)*. (Institute of History of Ancient Civilizations, Periodical Publications on Ancient Civilizations 2). Chanchun, China.

Yoshikawa, Mamoru

1985 "A New Duplicate of YOS IV, No. 67 // V. Scheil, *RA* 24/1 No. 8c," *ASJ* 7, 191–92.

Zaccagnini, Carlo

1979 *The Rural Landscape of the Land of Arrapḫe*. (Quaderni di geographica storica 1). Rome.

Zadok, Ran
1993 "Hurrians as well as Individuals Bearing Hurrian and Strange Names in Sumerian Sources," *Kinattūtu ša dārâti: Raphael Kutscher Memorial Volume.* Ed., A. Rainey. (Tel Aviv Occasional Publications 1). Tel Aviv.

Imperial Mittani: An Attempt at Historical Reconstruction

CORD KÜHNE
Universität des Saarlandes, Saarbrücken

A reconstruction of the history of Mittani must be based entirely on external sources since neither the capital of Mittani nor any of its state archives has been discovered. This sketch of Mittani history is based on sources from Ḫatti, Syro-Canaan, Mesopotamia, and Egypt and attempts to provide a coherent overview of that history.

A reconstruction of the history of the Mittani state has to cope with well-known problems impeding, at least from the late second millennium B.C. onward, any synthetic historical research in the ancient Near East. There is a lack of an exact overall chronology,[1] as well as a scarcity of reliable synchronisms (partly due to the narrow propagandistic scope of the few original historiographical records) that, in general, willfully ignore the names of respective adversaries on the interstate level. In addition, the haphazard and often ambiguous state of the historic documentation available allows only for an incomplete picture, resulting in many gaps that can be bridged only by hypotheses.

---

1 I dispense with the long-cherished idea of obtaining reliable results from the evaluation of the relevant Babylonian astronomical dates. In this synthesis, I rely strictly on historical considerations and propose the decade between 1550 and 1540 as a transitional decade for the end of the Old Babylonian Dynasty instead of its so-called short chronology approximation of 1539 resp. 1531 (earlier supported by me in my "Politische Szenerie und internationale Beziehungen Vorderasiens um die Mitte des 2. Jahrtausends vor Chr. [zugleich ein Konzept der Kurzchronologie]," in H.-J. Nissen/ J. Renger [eds.], *Mesopotamien und seine Nachbarn*, Berliner Beiträge zum Vorderen Orient [henceforth BBVO] 1, Berlin 1982, 203–67, pl. xxxiv). Even less can I endorse the still recent reduction of the date to 1499 as proposed by H. Gasche, *et al.*, *Dating the Fall of Babylon* (Mesopotamian History and Environment, Series II, Memoirs IV), Ghent-Chicago 1998 (with corrections in *Akkadica* 108 [1998] 1–4) that does not provide enough space for the development of Hittite history, something completely disregarded by the authors. Instead, recent dendrochronological research "supports either a Low or lower Middle chronology" (P.I. Kuniholm, *et al.*, *Nature* 381 [1996] 780–82, and cf. P.I. Kuniholm in M. Mellink, *et al.* [eds.], *Aspects of Art and Iconography, Anatolia and Its Neighbors, Studies in Honor of Nimet Özgüç*, Ankara 1993, 371–73, connecting trees cut for timber in 1791 ± 37 [*ibid.*, p. 372, to be corrected to 1752 ± 37, author's personal communication, Nov. 1996] more or less closely with bullae dated to the 10th year of Šamšī-Adad I, favoring a date *ca.* 1541 ± 37 for the end of the Old Babylonian dynasty).

Studies on the Civilization and Culture of Nuzi and the Hurrians - 10

A synthesis of the historical data about Mittani presents a special problem. Except for the late Mittani period, these data are furnished nearly exclusively by external sources,[2] i.e., by passing and mostly tendentious statements mainly made by enemies along Mittani's periphery. This situation, in no way corresponding to Mittani's importance as a major power on the international scene of her day, is due, so to speak, to modern circumstances. Despite intensive efforts, Mittani's administrative centers, to be sought in the Syro-Turkish northern Ğazira, and their archives have so far not been discovered.

A feature of the external documentation relating to Mittani is the circumscribed and thereby ambiguous way she is mentioned, especially with respect to her earliest historical phase. This fact adds to our incomplete knowledge of Mittani's entry into history and may be explained by the sheer enmity of the sources. It may also be conditioned by a hesitation to use an unaccustomed name that did not evoke (rightly or not) any historic or traditional associations, especially, as we shall see, if the name was derived from an eponym. The other options were either to allude to Mittani's geographical situation in the northern Ğezira or to call her the Hurrian Land.[3] This would have referred to her predominant ethnic makeup, namely the Hurrians, originally eastern invaders and settlers of the Ğezira who had spread beyond the Euphrates. Alternatively, Egyptian sources often use the ethno-geographical term Naharena, "(the Land of) Two[4] Rivers."[5] In the same way, Syro-Canaanite sources may speak of *māt Nahrêma*,[6] while other neighbors now and then refer

---

2 For a most convenient compilation of the pertinent documentary evidence available up to the late seventies, see H. Klengel, "Mitanni: Probleme seiner Expansion und politischen Struktur," *RHA* 38 (1978[1980]) 91ff. In this collection of meanwhile only slightly expanded material, only two short clearly Mittanian documents dating before 1400 are to be found: *AlT*, nos. 13–14 (see also below, n. 11); but *AlT* nos. 108 and 112 may perhaps be added (Klengel, *ibid.*, 93f. with n. 16). For the Nuzi letter HSS IX 1, see D. Stein, *ZA* 79 (1989) 36ff. The scant, newly published material (KBo XXVII 110; *Iraq* 47 [1985] 181ff. [see *infra*, n. 106]; *Iraq* 49 [1987] 188, and, e.g., allusions from Emar [*infra*, n. 35]) do not contain early Mittanian sources.

3 See below and nn. 17–20.

4 If reconstructed as **Nahrêna* <**Nahraina* (I.M. Diakonoff, *Or*NS 41 [1972] 117 n. 97).

5 A. Gardiner, *Ancient Egyptian Onomastica* I (Oxford 1947), 171*ff.; R.T. O'Callaghan, *Aram Naharaim* (AnOr 26, 1948), 132ff. (add the Hieratic docket of Amarna letter 27 [J. Knudtzon, VAB II, 241] describing the Mittani king's letter as Naharinian). Often used for the sphere of political influence of Mittani including western Syria, the name refers to the physical situation of northern Mesopotamia with its Euphrates and (most probably as later on) Tigris rivers. See e.g., below, n. 12. A different location (between the Jordan and Litani or Litani and Orontes rivers) recently proposed by C. Vandersleyen, *L'Egypte et la vallée du Nil* II, Paris 1995, 260, cannot be accepted. The crossing of the river, "Water of Naharina," mentioned in connection with the region (opposite) Carchemish (Urk. IV 891= ARE II, § 583) definitely refers to the Euphrates (see also *infra*, n. 59). The location of Mittani proper is also indicated in the evidence from Boğazköy (KBo I 1.3 etc.) and, implicitly, in Assyrian sources.

6 Less probably *Nahrīma* "(land of) rivers."

to Mittani by using the old geographical designation, Subartu,[7] in a cosmological sense meaning "North (Country)," which had already been applied for centuries to Hurrian-settled territory.[8] Another synonym, Ḫanigalbat, reminiscent of the Ḫanaean tribe and the territory of their wanderings and earlier political activity,[9] is etymologically unclear. It is much better attested and seems to have designated the central area of upper Mesopotamia where the core of Mittani is to be sought. Its use, both externally[10] and internally,[11] for describing that core, as well as the somewhat larger political entity (without its satellites),[12] can be traced to the 15th century. Eventually Ḫanigalbat became the official name of Mittani's truncated successor state.[13] After its annexation by the Middle Assyrian Empire, the Habur triangle and probably the bulk of Assyria's

---

7 Cf. Ebeling *ap.* J.A. Knudtzon, VAB II, 1579; W. Helck, *Die Beziehungen Ägyptens zu Vorderasien im 3. und 2. Jahrtausend v. Chr.* (Ägyptologische Abhandlungen, 5) Wiesbaden 1962, 290; I. Singer, StBoT 27, 58 n. 11; G.F. del Monte, RGTC 6/1, 367; 6/2, 131; G. Wilhelm, *Grundzüge der Geschichte und Kultur der Hurriter*, Darmstadt 1982, 9.

8 Cf. D.O. Edzard - G. Farber, RGTC 2, 174f. *s.v.* Subir.

9 Cf. B. Groneberg, RGTC 3, 89, and B. Landsberger, *JCS* 8 (1954) 62ff., for the Old (and late Old) Babylonian period. But compare also *infra*, n. 68, and the continuation of Ḫana into the late second millennium B.C. as a regional, respectively political, entity mentioned as Ḫanu in a Middle Assyrian letter found at Dūr-Katlimmu (E. Cancik-Kirschbaum, *Die mittelassyrischen Briefe aus Tall Šēḫ Ḥamad* [Berichte der Ausgrabung Tall Šēḫ Ḥamad/Dūr-Katlimmu, Band 4, Texte 1] Berlin 1996, 108, 5. 14; 30[122]) as well as the (petty) kingdom of Ḫana (e.g., J.-R. Kupper, *RlA* IV, 76; H.M. Kümmel, *ZA* 79 [1989] 193[7]).

10 For the Nuzi evidence, see J. Fincke, RGTC 10, 89–91; cf. also EA 255, 10.20 (from southern Canaan); Amenophis III, EA 1, 38 (gentilic), and Aššur-uballiṭ I, EA 16, 22 (gentilic).

11 Besides attestations of the name in King Tušratta's letters EA 20, 17; 29, 49, the derived formation *ḫanigalbatūtu* "ḫanigalbatship" is used as a term of (inter)national law (*pace* E. von Weiher, *RlA* IV, 105) in a legal decision by King Saušsatatar, *AlT* 13, 4 (second half of the 15th century).

12 The territory between the bend of the Euphrates and the upper reaches of the Tigris, probably up to the Ṭūr-ᶜAbdīn and possibly even including the plain around Diyarbakir: G. Wilhelm, *l.c.*, 34f.

13 See e.g., the royal letter *IBoT* I 34, 2(!): H. Klengel, *Or*NS 32 (1963) 280ff. (also E. von Weiher, *l.c.*, 106). But compare Suppiluliuma's and Šattiwaza's treaties, KBo I 1 and 3, namely the former, which, in reviewing the past and by specifying international contractual terms, differs decisively from the latter (cf. G. Beckman in M.E. Cohen, *et al.*, *The Tablet and the Scroll, Near Eastern Studies in Honor of William W. Hallo*, Bethesda, Md. 1993, 55ff.). Keeping the name and assuming the more or less fictive restoration of the former "great" Mittani (KBo I 1 obv. 57 [instead of Mittani, used frequently, the text only once offers synonymous *māt Ḫurri*: rev. 37]), on the one hand, KBo I 1 concedes parity to Šattiwaza (obv. 66) though never calling him "great king," restricting this title, formerly born by Šattiwaza's father, to the Hittite ruler, and curtailing the alleged equality on the other hand, as was so aptly proven by V. Korošec, *Hethitische Staatsverträge* (Leipziger Rechtswissenschaftliche Studien, 60) Leipzig 1931, 7f., 13, 27, 32f., 48, 64, 81, 86, 91, 101f. Nevertheless, Muwattalli II (first quarter of the 13th century) still officially regards the king of Ḫanigalbat as his equal (KUB XXI 5 [*CTH* 76] iii 25f.: J. Friedrich, *Staatsverträge des Ḫatti-Reiches* II [MVAeG 34/1], Leipzig 1930, 68f.; G. Beckman, *Hittite Diplomatic Texts* [ed. H. Hoffner], Atlanta 1996, 85 '11). See also below, n. 29.

western provinces still would be called Ḫanigalbat.[14] On the other hand, early Hittite records, mainly preserved in later copies or redactions, often seem to mean Mittani when they speak of "the Hurrian(s),"[15] or the "Hurrian enemy,"[16] or, as the later redactions also might put it, the "Hurrian Country."[17] Mittanians, too, could and did use the descriptive term "Hurrian Country" more or less officially for their territory[18] (others following their example[19]), while texts of the Hittite Empire apply the plural, "Hurrian countries" (alongside of "lands of Mittani-land"[20]) to the Mittani confederation, especially Mittani's satellites.[21] Closing this list of Mittani's synonyms, I note that the presently used spelling of Mittani deviates slightly from the widely used form, Mitanni. The reading adopted here follows orthographies viewed today as the most developed and correct. The Indian etymologies proposed earlier, based on the idea that a part of Mittani's upper class bore Indian names, have been seriously criticized and superseded by a cautious *non liquet*, tentatively suggesting a derivation from the Nuzi-attested, linguistically obscure, personal name Maitta.[22]

Among the scraps of evidence of mostly external origin, information about Mittani's economic role is lacking except for a list of gifts and some notes about

---

14 See E. von Weiher, *l.c.* 106f. and, e.g., G.F. del Monte, RGTC 6 (1978), 77f.

15 Evidence discussed by O. Soysal, *Hethitica* 7 (1987) 246ff.[236] (writings with determinative, lú$^{\text{(MEŠ)}}$*ḫurla-*, judged as later). See also G.F. del Monte, *l.c.*, 119ff.

16 KBo X 2 (*CTH* 4) i 24; the Akkadian version has ^{lú}kúr uru *Ḫa-ni-kal-bat* (KBo X 1 obv. 11).

17 KUB XXVI 72 (*CTH* 11), 10′: (lú^{MEŠ}) kur ^{URU}*Ḫur-la-aš-*. Later texts usually write (kur) ^{URU}*Ḫur-ri* (e.g., MH/NS KUB XXIII 11 [*CTH* 142] iii 28 vs. NH KBo III 3 [*CTH* 63] i 4), *Ḫur-ri* being the usual form (genitive in the construction *māt Ḫurri*) applied in Akkadian texts, in Hittite context thus really to be taken as an Akkadiogram. The vast later Egyptian evidence for *ḫù-rú* as a term for the Egyptian zone of influence in Syro-Canaan and its inhabitants refers to the Hurrian infiltration (and dominance) before and during the rise of the XVIIIth dynasty (see e.g., W. Helck, *Beziehungen*,[1] 275). Relics of Hurrian presence in southern Canaan are to be found also with the Horites of the Old Testament (*pace* R. De Vaux, *Revue Biblique*, 74 [1967] 481ff.).

18 Mostly so in the last Mittani king Tušratta's Hurrian letter EA 24 (VS XII 200) i 11; ii 67.72; iii 6.113; iv 127 vs. iii 104.

19 For use in Syria, see e.g., EA 56, 44 (alongside *māt Mi-it-ta-an-ni, ibid.*, l. 39); M. Sigrist, in: A.F. Rainey, *kinattūtu ša dārâti* (R. Kutscher Memorial Volume, Tell Aviv [Journal], Occasional Publications, 1, 1993), 176, 11, 13 (*šar māt Ḫur-ri*).

20 KBo I 1 (*CTH* 51) rev. 14 (E. Weidner, *Politische Dokumente aus Kleinasien* [*BoSt* 8/9], Leipzig 1923, 22 = G. Beckman, *Hittite Diplomatic Texts*, 41).

21 See the evidence for kur.kur$^{\text{MEŠ/ḪI.A (URU)}}$*Ḫur-ri* in F.G. del Monte, RGTC 6/1, 120, and kur.kur^{MEŠ} *ŠA* kur ^{URU}*Mi-it-ta-an-ni* "the lands (dependent) on Mittani-Land," KBo I 1 rev. 14ff., regarding the northern and southwestern segments of the chain of Mittani's protectorates, cf. obv. 25–47; compare EA 60 (VS XI 27), 13f.: *gab-bi* lugal$^{\text{ḪI.A}}$ *ša* lugal érin^{MEŠ} *Ḫurri* "all the kings (in the following) of the 'King of the Hurrian Troops'," and below, n. 34f. for this title.

22 Cf. *NPN*, 94; G. Wilhelm, *RlA* 8 (1995–97) 290 with lit.

various presents King Tušratta sent to Amenophis III and Akhenaten. The archives of Mittani's satellites, Arrapḫa and Alalaḫ IV, indicate the area as being under their control. Utilizing them in order to understand Mittani's economic system remains hypothetical. Our reconstruction of Mittani's history, especially regarding her origins, will tend to restrict itself to an outline of her political development with a minimum use of hypotheses.

During the second third of the 16th century, the Old Hittite Kingdom began to expand towards and beyond the Taurus Range. In the second year of his annals, Hattusili I mentions his apparent first foray into northern Syria, which led him from Alalaḫ through territories of the eastern slope of the Taurus to Uršu on the western bank of the Euphrates.[23] For the following year the annals record an invasion into Anatolia by the "Hurrian foe," who, through swift action, struck Hattusili's realm with a nearly fatal blow.[24] At first glance, one might understand the term "Hurrian foe" as a collective term for the small and medium-sized political entities of the upper Euphrates region, such as Uršum, Ḫaḫḫum, and Ḫaššum, seen by their Hittite opponent from an ethno-linguistic point of view.[25] However, from the Old Hittite story of the siege of Uršu, a contemporary literary source, we learn that among Uršu's allies, to which belonged such famous kingdoms as Ḫalab and Carchemish, was included a group called the "Hurrian troops." They were paid in money and goods and were regarded as especially important for Uršu's relief. The collector and distributor of such payments was the agent of a (probably deceased) king who is mentioned as the "Son of the Weather-God"[26] and whose sons are reported to have been contending for the kingship.[27] We do not know if these royal contenders are the same individuals mentioned in another literary-historical text, the so-called cannibal story (*Menschenfressergeschichte*), in which four "kings of the Hurrian troops" are mentioned as having been paid to rescue a member of an anti-Hittite coalition, two parties of which (the king of Ḫalab and a prince[?] named Zuppa) also were allies of Uršu in this story of a roughly contemporary Uršu siege.[28] Nor can it be proved that the epithet "Son of the

---

23 KBo X 1 obv. 6–10; 2 i 15–21 (*CTH* 4: F. Imparati - C. Saporetti, *Studi Classici e Orientali* 14 (1965) 77, 80.44f.; H.M. Kümmel in: *Texte aus der Umwelt des Alten Testaments* [ed. O. Kaiser] I/5, Gütersloh 1985, 456, 460 and G.F. del Monte, RGTC 6/1, 476; B. Groneberg, RGTC 3, 250).

24 KBo X 1 obv. 10–12; 2 i 22–26.

25 For such Hurrian presence, see e.g., G. Wilhelm, *Grundzüge*, 17f., and recently M. Salvini in: G. Buccellati - M. Kelly-Buccellati (eds.), *Urkesh and the Hurrians. Studies in Honor of Lloyd Cotsen* (Biblioteca Mesopotamica 26) Malibu 1998, esp. pp. 111–15. Implicitly also V. Donbaz, *AoF* 25 (1998) 178–81.

26 KBo I 11 (*CTH* 7) rev. 27–32 (H.G. Güterbock, *ZA* 44 [1938] 124f.).

27 *Ibid.*, rev. 7 (H.G. Güterbock, *l.c.*, 120f.).

28 Compare KBo III 60 (*CTH* 17,1) col. iii (Güterbock, *l.c.*, 106–9) with KBo I 11 rev. 25, 28ff. and Güterbock, *l.c.*, 135; C. Kühne, BBVO 1, 237 n. 33; S. de Martino, *Seminari 1990* (Istituto per gli Studi Micenei ed Egeo-anatolici) 78; *id.*, *Hethitica* 11 (1992) 28.

Weather-God" belonged to the titulary of the kings of Hurri-Mittani.[29] However, both texts convey vivid impressions of an anti-Hittite resistance of north Syrian principalities, who were forced together by Hittite pressure. They show clearly that opposition against Ḫatti depended preponderantly on the military power of the "Hurrian troops" (érin[MEŠ] *ḫurri*), "troops"—seemingly opposed to just Hurrian "men" or "people," which the same text renders as lú[MEŠ] *Ḫurri*.[30] These Hurrian troops formed a distinct entity that also will have played the leading and coordinating role in striking the blow credited to the Hurrian foe by the Annalist in Hattusili's third recorded year.[31]

It is possible that these events belong to the early, if not the formative, stage of Mittani's statehood.[32] This also would explain the origin of the remarkable epithet or title, "King of the Hurrian troops," by which another annalistic text of Hattusili or his successor Mursili I mentions as a, or rather *the*, leading figure of the anti-Hittite coalition.[33] The title "King of the Hurrian troops" (lugal érin[MEŠ] *Ḫurri*) is attested at different times and places for later kings of Mittani,[34]

---

29 The possibility remains, however, that (if not for the reading in KBo I 1 obv. 49, which is not followed by the duplicate) the so far only other occurrence of this epithet, KUB XXI 38 obv. 15′ (from a letter of Queen Puduhepa, see E. Edel, *Die ägyptisch-hethitische Korrespondenz aus Boghazköi* [Abhandlungen der Rheinisch-Westfälischen Akademie der Wissenschaften, 77] Opladen 1994, I, 216f.; II, 330f.), refers to Šattuara II, the infelicitous last king of Ḫanigalbat, as guessed by E. Forrer (*RLA*, I, 55), F. Sommer agreeing (*Die Aḫḫijavā-Urkunden*, München 1932, 259). Puduḫepa's letter should then antedate the annexation of Ḫanigalbat by Shalmaneser I, occurring some time after Šattuara's defection from the inherited Assyrian bonds to the earlier Ḫanigalbatean dependence on Ḫatti. The royal Ḫanigalbatean letter IBoT I 34, addressed to the Hittite king (Hattusili III) seems to belong to this phase and to Šattuara's authorship; cf. H. Klengel, *Or*NS 32 (1963) 280ff.

For the central position of the storm-god (Teššup) in the Hurrian pantheon, see the literature cited by de Martino, *Seminari* 1990, 83[81].

30 At least regarding the Hittite use (cf. also e.g., KBo XXII 2 [CTH 3] rev. 7′ vs. 12′ or § 54 of the Hittite Laws), but see also, roughly contemporary, *CAD* Ṣ, *s.v. ṣābu* d, f2′, 4′, g, i), I am now less reluctant than earlier (BBVO I, 238 n. 34 *ad ib.* 206f.: "Hurrimannen") to render érin[MEŠ] here as "troop(s)." See also e.g., M. Astour in *Emar* (ed. M. Chavalas), Bethesda, Md. 1996, 31ff. (though not regarding the implications of the early Hittite evidence, p. 33 n. 31). The problematic non-Hurrian (Akkadianizing) construction, *ḫurad ḫurri* in KUB XXVII 38 iv 19f. (S. de Martino, *SMEA* 31, 1993, 129 n. 63), occurring in a clearly anachronistic epithet, *e-we$_e$-er-ne šar-ra uš-ta-e* [*ḫu-r*]*a-ad ḫur-ri*, referring to a third-millennium king (calling to mind Idrimi's lugal *dan-nu* lugal érin[MEŠ] *ḫurri*, for which see below, n. 34), may well be the written syllabic realization of what Hurro-Akkadian scribes pronounced when their text offered the writing érin[MEŠ] *ḫurri*. The name Hurri may itself be derived from the stem *ḫur-* "warrior" (e.g., I. Wegner in *Hurriter und Hurritisch* [ed. V. Haas; Xenia 21], Konstanz 1988, 149 with lit.).

31 For the problem of the counting of years in these annals, see O. Soysal, *Hethitica* 7 (1987) 203f.

32 M. Astour, *JNES* 31 (1972) 102ff. (partly outdated); H.G. Güterbock, *JCS* 25 (1973) 101; D.B. Redford, *JAOS* 99 (1979) 278f.; C. Kühne, BBVO I, 206f.; G. Wilhelm, *Grundzüge*, 28f.

33 KBo III 54, 8′, C. Kühne, *ZA* 67 (1977) 246 n. 11.

34 Idrimi, l. 71, 73; *AlT* 2, 73f. (both 15th century); EA 60, 14 (14th century). For an eventual application to a king of the third millennium (KUB XXVII 38: V. Haas - I. Wegner, *Die Rituale und Beschwörungen der* [SAL]ŠU.GI (ChS I/5, Rome 1988, no. 87 iv 19f.), see *supra*, n. 30.

and it seems that, even after the downfall of the Mittanian empire, it was applied, at least by foreigners, to the rulers of epigonic Ḫanigalbat in the first half of the 13th century.[35] The title seems to fit perfectly the influential role of the Hurrian troops as depicted in our early texts and reveals the exceptionally *ethnic and military* source and legitimacy of their early bearer's royalty. To explain this remarkable feature, we may hint at the linguistic fact that the Hurrian dialect used by the Mittani chancellery in the 14th century was markedly different from *pre-Mittani* Hurrian that was transmitted as a more or less "literary" language (or dialect) in Syria and Anatolia.[36] It seems probable that the "Hurrian troops" meant by our annalistic texts were drawn from a recent wave of Hurrian invaders who had descended from the mountainous flanks of northwestern Iran and superseded the older Hurrian ethnic layers,[37] eventually expanding the territory of settlement. It seems natural for these newly arrived founders of a political entity to have clung to their dialect when handling their internal affairs, while, on the interstate level, yielding to the conventional use of Babylonian, as indeed they did. In support of a fairly recent arrival of a substantial part of these Hurrians is the convincing theory that their military and political success, and perhaps even their emigration, was due to the leading role of a group of Indo-Arians. They may have settled temporarily in the mountainous Hurrian homelands, become Hurrianized, and left the early second-millennium migration of their India-bound kinsmen. Perhaps they searched, together with their new partners, for better homesteads in the lush plains of Mesopotamia and provided successful leadership, crowned by royal claims, for the eventual establishment of the kingdom of Mittani. Their dominance and influence may be traced by a few occurrences of their ancestors' Indo-Arian mother tongue. To these traces,[38] attested for the 15th and 14th

---

35 See A. Skaist, *ZA* 88 (1998) 65ff. (differently M.C. Astour in *Emar* [n. 30], 31ff. [35]), regarding evidence from Emar and its environs, dating to the earlier half of the 13th century, published by D. Arnaud, *Recherches au pays d'Aštata* VI, Paris 1986, 42, 9; G. Beckman, *Texts from the Vicinity of Emar in the Collection of Jonathan Rosen* (History of the Ancient Near East/ Monographs, II) Padova 1996, nos. 70, 28; 77, 35; M. Sigrist, in A.F. Rainey, *kinattūtu ša dārâti* (R. Kutscher Memorial Volume, Tell Aviv [Journal], Occasional Publications, 1, 1993), 176, 11,13.

36 See e.g., G. Wilhelm, *Or*NS 61 (1992) 137 and *idem* in: J. Sasson (ed.), *Civilizations of the Ancient Near East* II, New York 1995, 1245f.

37 For these, cf. M. Salvini, *l.c.* (n. 25), 99ff.

38 For their quantification and verifiability, cf. M. Mayrhofer, *Die Indo-Arier im Alten Vorderasien*, Wiesbaden 1966, and A. Kammenhuber's monographic (often hypercritical) response, *Die Arier im Vorderen Orient*, Heidelberg 1968, as well as the affirmative review of the latter by I.M. Diakonoff, *Or*NS 41 (1972) 91ff., and the response to both by Mayrhofer, *Die Arier im Vorderen Orient—ein Mythos?* (Österreichische Akademie der Wissenschaften, philosoph.-hist. Kl., Sitzungsberichte 294/3), Vienna 1974, as well as his contribution "Welches Material aus dem Indo-Arischen von Mitanni verbleibt für eine selektive Darstellung?," in: *Investigationes Philologicae et Comparativae. Gedenkschrift für Heinz Kronasser* (ed. E. Neu), Wiesbaden 1982, 72ff. For later detailed studies I confine myself to P. Raulwing - R. Schmitt, "Zur etymologischen Beurteilung der Berufsbezeichnung *aššuššanni*

centuries and, in at least three cases, for the 13th century,[39] belong technical terms concerning the training of horse teams necessary for pulling the tactically decisive, two-wheeled chariots. In addition, the names of a few Indian gods occur. Further, and above all, a corpus of male personal names, kept mainly in the dynastic tradition, were utilized when a Mittanian ruler, in case he bore a non-Indian (i.e., Hurrian) name by birth, needed to choose a throne name.[40] Also, of Indian etymology is the (Hurrianized) word *mariyanni*, a social term introduced for a new, elite class of chariot warriors. They were of paramount importance in demanding military circumstances and, in the course of time (at least in certain regions), they achieved the status of hereditary nobility.[41]

Based on early Hittite sources, we interpret the existence of a Mittani state, beginning about the mid-16th century, as resulting from the clash of two young and powerful forces trying to establish their respective roles, as did their predecessors, by expanding through military or diplomatic action and reaction. Ḫatti, at first, preferred to turn conquered territories into new provinces.[42] Mittani, early on, may have come to the aid of attacked or threatened neighboring states, thereafter binding them by treaties of loyalty that stipulated Mittani's position of superior strength, which automatically led to suzerainty.[43] Ḫatti, and then Mittani, thus threatened the long-established international order. When, for example, Hattusili attacked Alalaḫ, he automatically and knowingly went to war with Alalaḫ's traditional overlord, Ḫalab-Yamḫad, as well as Ḫalab's other satellites (among them Emar and probably Ebla, which are both mentioned in the Hittite annals[44]). Thus, through the same act, he found

---

des Pferdetrainers Kikkuli von Mittani" in *Man and the Animal World. Studies in Archaeozoology, Archaeology, Anthropology and Palaeolinguistics in memoriam Sándor Bökönyi* (Archaeolingua 8; eds. P. Anreiter, *et al.*), Budapest 1996, 675ff.

39 The Ḫanigalbatean names Šattuara and Wazašatta and the (Hurrianized) social term *mariyanni* (see n. 41), which had become a loanword in Akkadian, Ugaritic, and Egyptian (here still attested for the 12th century: W. Helck, *Beziehungen*[1], 524).

40 Evidence for such dichotomy between birth and throne names in the royal line of Mittani is so far given only in the late case of King Tušratta's son, Šattiwaza, whose birth name Kili-Tešub is clearly Hurrian (cf. H.G. Güterbock, *JCS* 10 [1956] 121).

41 H. Reviv, *IEJ* 22 [1972] 218ff.; G. Wilhelm, *Grundzüge*, 27, 60.

42 Cf. e.g., KBo III 1 (*CTH* 19) i 6′–11′, 16′–19′ (E.H. Sturtevant - G. Bechtel, *A Hittite Chrestomathy*, Philadelphia 1935, 182f.; lately H.M. Kümmel in: *Texte aus der Umwelt des Alten Testaments* (ed. O. Kaiser) I/5, Gütersloh 1985, 464f.).

43 Idrimi, ll. 45–58 (M. Dietrich - O. Loretz, *UF* 13 [1981] 205 and my comments in BBVO I, 246 tending to show an early dependence of Ḫalab on Mittani). Further *AIT* 2, 73–75 (cf. O. Loretz in: *Crossing Boundaries and Linking Horizons. Studies in Honor of Michael C. Astour* [eds. G.D. Young, *et al.*, Bethesda, Md. 1997, 211ff.); 3, 40–43, and cf. also KBo I 5 i 30–39 (G. Beckman, *Hittite Diplomatic Texts* [ed. H. Hoffner], Atlanta 1996, 15); 2 obv. 30–47 (Beckman, *l.c.*, 39f.), and *supra*, n. 21. See especially H. Klengel, *RHA* 36 (1978) 111ff. Ḫatti, with a few exceptions, had adopted and developed this method since the decline of her Old Kingdom (C. Kühne, *l.c.*, 212).

44 See C. Kühne, *ZA* 62 (1973) 244f. with n. 32.

himself at war with Ḫalab's allies. Mittani, for policy considerations just stated, was also drawn into the conflict. Hattusili reports to have crossed the Euphrates,[45] thereby threatening Mittani's heartland, albeit from a distance. When, after a series of Hittite setbacks, Mursili I managed to conquer Ḫalab,[46] the opposing network of existing alliances seems to have continued and, perhaps, spread. We may surmise that even faraway Babylon was bound to Ḫalab by a pact of mutual assistance.[47] We do not know if Babylon demonstrated signs of solidarity or not, but Mursili gained more glory and booty by attacking Babylon,[48] dumbfounding and winning over to his side, or intimidating, the petty kingdoms stationed along the Euphrates.[49] Upon returning home after the victory that caused the downfall of Hammurabi's Amorite dynasty, Mursili had to fend off "the Hurrians,"[50] Mittani's somewhat belated, but not ineffectual, attempt to stop him.

Mursili, perhaps not long after these events, was assassinated at home and Ḫatti subsequently became engaged in a bloody dynastic feud.[51] Mittani soon found herself filling the vacuum left by the shattered old system of powers after Ḫatti's retreat. Weakened Ḫalab was no longer able to live up to her former glories and from then on, as long as circumstances allowed, followed in Mittani's wake. Idrimi, who ruled by Mittani's grace as king of Alalaḫ in the mid-15th century, recalled that his fathers toiled[52] to keep the bonds of Parattarna's, his overlord's forbears. Nothing seems to have hindered Mittani's ability to spread her influence quickly in all directions, especially southward along the Orontes river and deep into southern Canaan, where (as at Syrian Qadeš), still in the 14th century, we find Indo-Iranian-named princelings[53] and where the (Hurrianized) term *mariyanni* seems well established before the middle of the 15th century.[54] By pushing her influence so far, Mittani could use her Syrian satellites, probably among them the prince of Qadeš, who, at least in

---

45 KBo X 2 (*CTH* 4) ii 17f, iii 29; 1 obv. 34f. (F. Imparati - C. Saporetti, *Studi Classici e Orientali* 14 [1965] 48ff., 81, 83; Kümmel, *l.c.*, 461, 463, 457).

46 KBo III 1 i 27′f. (Sturtevant-Bechtel, *l.c.*, 184f., Kümmel, *l.c.*, 465).

47 Cf. H. Klengel, *Geschichte Syriens* I, Berlin 1965, 160f.; H. Otten in: E. Cassin, *et al.* (eds.), *Fischer Weltgeschichte* III, Frankfurt/M. 1966, 119f.

48 KBo III 1 i 28′–30′ (cf. *supra*, n. 46); BM 96152 rev. 10′: A.K. Grayson, *Assyrian and Babylonian Chronicles* (Texts from Cuneiform Sources, V), 156.

49 B. Landsberger, *JCS* 8 (1954) 62ff. (p. 65 suggesting common Hittite-Hanaean interests).

50 KBo III 1 i 29a.

51 *Ibid.*, I 30ff. See now also O. Soysal, *AoF* 25 (1998) 6ff. [30f.] for a re-evaluation (and dating) of *CTH* 10.12.

52 E.g., C. Kühne, BBVO I, 246.

53 *Id.*, 238 n. 37.

54 *Id.*, 236 n. 25 (ad Urk. IV 665, 7 [*ARE* II, § 436]), arguing for Hurrian and Mittani-Hurrian presence and influence south of Qatna, as against A. Kammenhuber's categorical denial, *Or*NS 46 (1977) 132 (who, *i.a.* refers to R. de Vaux, *Revue Biblique* 74 [1967] 481ff.). See also the evidence referred to *infra*, n. 63.

the middle of that century, was their leader.[55] Of course, Mittani could be successful only during a period of weakness or inactivity by Egypt, the international power with traditional claims to a sort of overlordship of Palestine and Phoenicia. Indeed, two or three such periods may be considered. The first period ended in the 1520s, when Ahmose, second Pharaoh of the XVIIIth Dynasty, liberated Egypt from the yoke of the century-long and insignificant rule of the Hyksos. He pursued the vanquished Hyksos into their southern Canaanite refuge,[56] thus renewing Egypt's historic claim to the Levant and occasionally establishing a military presence.[57] This *terminus ad quem*, though leaving open a choice of options, would also provide for the much discussed possibility that the appearance of the Hyksos in Egypt was linked to a more or less massive arrival of Hurrians in Canaan,[58] even before there is evidence for Mittani's existence. Since reliable information about Egyptian military activity in Asia is lacking for the era of Ahmose's successor, Amenophis I, i.e., from *ca.* 1514 to 1493 B.C.,[59] a second, less likely opportunity for that initial Hurrian penetration may be suggested for those years. The third and latest (if not too

---

55 See below, n. 73. W. Helck, *Beziehungen*, 117ff.

56 Urk. IV 4 (*ARE* II, § 13). The end of the three-year siege of the last Hyksos stronghold, Sharuhen, is dated by Helck, *Jahresbericht des Instituts für Vorgeschichte der Universität Frankfurt* 1977, 9, to Ahmose's 22nd regnal year, *ca.* 1520.

57 Urk. IV 18.35 (*ARE* II, § 20).

58 One theory presuming the Hyksos ("rulers of foreign lands") were Syro-Canaanites pressed southward by the Hurrians (e.g., G. Wilhelm, *Grundzüge*, 27f.), the other surmising that the Hyksos were of Hurrian stock (see e.g., W. Helck, *Beziehungen*, 92ff., as against views that regard them as descendants of Semitic nomads who more or less peacefully infiltrated the Delta at least since the end of the Middle Kingdom [mid-18th century]).

59 The statement about (Egypt's) northern border as being formed by the "inverse water" flowing southward (in contrast to the northward flow of the Nile) made on Thutmose I's Tumbos stela of his regnal year 2 (Urk. IV 85, 13f. = ARE II, § 73) was taken for a long time as evidence for a very early appearance of this pharaoh on the banks of the Euphrates (e.g., T.G.S. James in *The Cambridge Ancient History*^{3} II/1 [1973], 309, supposing lasting and comparable basic achievements by the king's predecessor, Amenophis I). However, E. Hornung has argued that, for practical reasons, the presumed campaign is precluded and credit for the claimed boundary line should be given solely to the Asia-directed activities of a predecessor of Thutmose, probably to Amenophis I (*Untersuchungen zur Geschichte und Chronologie des Neuen Reiches*, Wiesbaden 1964, 32, 70; cf. also D.B. Redford, *JAOS* 99 [1979] 276f.). Relevant sources lacking, C. Vandersleyen now categorically denies the probability of Asiatic campaigns of Amenophis I (*L'Egypte et la vallée du Nil* II, 241 n. 2, against D.B. Redford's tentative attribution of lastly indecisive evidence, *l.c.*, 270ff.), promoting a new interpretation that relates the abovementioned northern border to Egypt's Nubian territory in identifying the said river with an inverse bend of the upper Nile (*ibid.*, 225 n. 3, 257f., referring to a Ramesside attestation). Since references dating from the 15th century clearly localize the "inverse water" in northern Syria, especially as the border between Naharena and the Syrian territory claimed by Egypt (e.g., Urk. IV 1232, 1245 [*ANET*, 240b.a], 587 [ARE II, § 631]. See also n. 60 and, for the cosmological reputation of the Euphrates as a border line, C. Kühne, BBVO 1, 242 n. 63), this theory probably will find little support. It shows, however indirectly, that the question about Amenophis I's Asian policy cannot be settled as yet.

late) time for this occurrence is during the inactive era of Hatshepsut, between 1480 and 1460 B.C. A plausible argument *against* this late date is the fact that, about 1490, Amenophis I's successor, Thutmose I, was definitely at war with Mittani, even making a foray as far north as Carchemish and beyond, to the eastern bank of the Euphrates.[60] His operation is to be seen as a reaction to Mittani's Syro-Canaanite policy and presence, which opposed Egyptian claims to the area. This is made clear by a statement in the tomb inscription of Amenemhet, the Egyptian inventor of the clepsydra,[61] who, either starting his career or (rather!) being just born in Ahmose's 15th regnal year, had earned his first decoration under Amenophis I.[62] Reviewing his life and times, which may well have lasted into the era of Thutmose I and even longer, he refers to Mittani and her "evil" (activity) that, in his and, implicitly, in the pharaoh's eyes, deserved Egypt's "revenge."[63] This inscription provides us with the very first mention of Mittani's name. To date, the only other early (possibly contemporaneous) reference is on a seal inscription reading "Sutarna, son of Kirta, King of Maitani." This inscription, however, is known only from impressions owed to later dynastic use of a seal that belonged to one of the early Mittani rulers, who, we assume, was Sutarna I.[64]

In spite of Thutmose I's remarkable campaign, Egypt's northern opponent was not easily vanquished. About thirty years later, Thutmose III, seizing power *ca.* 1457, found Canaan up to Egypt's border (and, of course, all of Syria), if indirectly, under Mittani's control. It is possible that Parattarna, "King of the Hurrian warriors," may, at this time, have been his distant opponent. Parattarna is attested as overlord of a still young Idrimi of Alalaḫ, as well as of

---

60 Urk. IV 697 (ARE II, 478f.): Thutmose III's reference to his grandfather's memorial stela opposite Carchemish, cf. Urk. IV 891 [*ARE* II, 583]. Cf. also *ib.*, 1232 [*ANET*, 240b] and W. Helck, *Chronique d'Egypte* 56, 1981, 242ff.]); for the chronology, cf. D.B. Redford, *l.c.*, 277.

61 The damaged, now lost, text published in 1920 by L. Borchardt *ap.* E. von Bassermann-Jordan, *Die Geschichte der Zeitmessung und der Uhren*, I, 60–63, pl. 18 has, for the relevant part, been re-edited and commented on by H. Brunner, *MIO* 4 (1956) 323–27.

62 Brunner's argument (*ib.*, 325f.) that in l. 4'f.: "I spent 10 years under king *Nb-pḥtj-R*ᶜ (Ahmose)" and "I [spent] 21 years under king ... *Ḏśr-k3-R*ᶜ (Amenophis I) [...]" are to be understood as giving the duration of offices held by the author, who, comparing evidence of a contemporary's biography (Urk IV 2 = *ARE* II, § 7), could not have taken over his first office before he was at least ten years old (which would lead to a birth date not later than year 5 of Ahmose [*ca.*1534]), was founded on the conception, now generally dismissed, that Amenophis I's reign lasted longer than 21 years (*ibid.*, 325). So L. Borchardt's interpretation of "spending x years" as "living x years," dating the author's birth to Ahmose's 15th year, remains acceptable.

63 Though interrupted by a lacuna, the mention of Mittani and enemies in l. 1', and pharaoh's accomplishment of revenge for evil, l. 2, the interpretation is obvious in the light of the evidence cited in n. 60. See also D.B. Redford, *l.c.*, 284 n. 93, for literature.

64 D. Stein, *RlA* 8 (1995–97) 296f. This assumes that if filiations in royal inscriptions as a rule are stated in a legitimizing sense, Šutarna's father Kirta will have to be taken as a royal predecessor. He probably still belongs in the 16th century.

Idrimi's probably elder colleague and neighbor, Pilliya,[65] who may well have been a king of Kizzuwatna in southeastern Anatolia. He may also be identified with a king Pilliya of Kizzuwatna who once had been allied to a king Zidanta of Ḫatti[66] (with respect to the chronology adopted here, these latter kings could, though not without reservations, be identified with the first royal bearers of their names, Pilliya I and Zidanta I[67]). There is little doubt that Parattarna also exacted suzerainty over the petty kingdom of Ḫana on the middle Euphrates,[68] over trans-Tigridian Arrapḫa,[69] as well as over a host of dominions surrounding Mittani proper. These are mentioned, if only for a small southwestern section (together with their towns), in Thutmose's toponym lists.[70]

When young Thutmose acted to relieve Egypt from the threat of a second foreign takeover, he encountered an army consisting of contingents furnished by 330 princelings (all bearing royal titles), mostly representing territories traditionally claimed by Egypt.[71] Among them were also rulers and detachments from northern Syria up to Naharena, very probably including the aforementioned kingdom of Kizzuwatna.[72] They were led by the prince of Qadeš, whom we may regard as Mittani's mightiest representative in the South acting on behalf of his overlord.[73] After the pharaoh's famous victory at Megiddo,

---

65 *AlT* no. 3. Cf. C. Kühne, BBVO I, 248 n. 88; R.H. Beal, *Or*NS 55 (1986) 429 n. 26.

66 KUB XXXVI 108 (CTH 25), for which see H. Otten, *JCS* 5 (1951) 129ff.

67 In spite of its archaic appearance, KUB XXXVI 108 is now mostly dated later by at least half a century and attributed to Zidanta II, whose partner should then be Pilliya II and who could hardly be a senior colleague of Idrimi, as AlT no. 3, 40–43, compared with *Idrimi*, ll. 43–58, would suggest. The argument against Zidanta I is derived from a passage in Telipinu's edict stating (§ 21) that the land of Adaniya, together with Arzawa and other territories, had become hostile to Ḫatti under Zidanta I's successor, Ammuna. If Adaniya (as known from later sources) was part of Kizzuwatna, the latter's earlier existence as an autonomous state *prima facie* seems doubtful if not precluded (cf. A. Goetze, *JCS* 11 [1957] 72f.; O.R. Gurney, *CAH* II/1, 661; H.M. Kümmel, *RlA* 5 [1976–80] 628 and myself, *l.c.*, 211f., 217; R.H. Beal, *l.c.*, 428ff.). On the other hand, can we dismiss altogether the possibility that Telipinu might have encouraged the defection under Ammuna of an already existing buffer state in the (then perhaps slightly arrogant?) way the edict does? Further study seems necessary considering Idrimi's report of his campaign against Ḫatti, *Idrimi*, ll. 64–77, and the possibility that it was a venture undertaken by a group of allies including Pilliya (cf. H. Klengel, *Geschichte Syriens* I, 230).

68 O. Rouault, *SMEA* 30 (1992) 254 (the dominion seems to have lasted until the end of the empire, when Suppiluliuma of Ḫatti made the region part of the kingdom of Carchemish: KBo I 1 obv. 19).

69 Here at least his death is mentioned in an (unofficial) dating: HSS XIII 165, 2f., cf. C. Kühne, BBVO I, 252 n. 122.

70 Urk. IV 788–94 (W. Helck, *Beziehungen*, 142ff.), and see also n. 71.

71 *Ibid.*, 780–86, places and dominions indirectly attached to Mittani by their local overlords residing in Megiddo, Qadeš, and Tunip (cf. Helck, *l.c.*, 127ff.).

72 For hieroglyphic *qdj* (Urk. IV 649, 10 [*ANET*, 235b]) as synonymous with Kizzuwatna, see Helck, *l.c.*, 288f.

73 Urk. IV. 649, 658 (ARE II, §§ 420, 430), 1234 (*ANET*, 238a), 184ff.

Thutmose still required many campaigns and a decade until he could, at least for a short while, reverse the situation. Systematically fighting and weakening the kingdoms of Qadeš and its northwestern neighbor Tunip,[74] Thutmose crossed the Euphrates *ca.* 1447 and, putting the royal defender to rout, appeared for a moment at Mittani's front door.[75] Although he, of course, could not hold a territory so far north, he acted as victor, proudly erecting his stele of triumph at the side of his grandfather's monument.[76] And, as he had done in Canaan,[77] he seems to have received oaths of fealty from his archenemy's north Syrian vassals.[78] He left them to their fate—to be dethroned for disloyalty—as soon as the Mittanian army returned following the Egyptian army's return home.[79] (Such a fate surely befell the king of Alalaḫ, who, after its neighbor, Nuḫašše, had been devastated by the Egyptians *ca.* 1442, sent tribute to the pharaoh.[80] Perhaps that prince was Idrimi's son and successor, Addu-nērārī, the evidence for whose short reign is provided by the inscription on his father's famous statue.)[81] Indeed, Thutmose's efforts did not earn Egypt lasting influence in the affairs of northern Syria. Mittani showed herself tenacious and *ca.* 1445 engaged Thutmose in a battle near Ḫalab or perhaps south of Apamea, stopping another enemy advance.[82] Still, later during this continued struggle, borders, or rather front lines, oscillated roughly within the area of central Syria. Mittani sent troops to strengthen certain dependencies of Qadeš,[83] seeking in vain to bar Egypt's access to the Orontes valley. Incessantly instigating opposition and defection even as far as southern Canaan, Mittani challenged Egypt well into the era of Thutmose's son, Amenophis II.[84]

As could be expected, Thutmose's Asiatic campaigns, starting with his victory at Megiddo, later followed by his crossing of the Euphrates and his (though marginal) inroad into Mittani proper, had international repercussions

---

74 *Ibid.*, 689, 686, 691 (ARE II, §§ 465, 459, 470), 1234f. (*ANET*, 239b).

75 *Ibid.*, 697f. (ARE II, § 478–80), 1246, 1230 (both *ANET*, 240a), 662f. (ARE II, § 434f.).

76 *Ibid.*, 698 (ARE II, § 481), 1232 (*ANET*, 240b).

77 *Ibid.*, 1234f.

78 Cf. EA 51, obv. 4–9 (and rev. 2ff.), regarding, as now mostly done, Manaḫpiya as Mn-ḫpr-R^{c} = Thutmose III. Compare Urk. 1304, 1313 (*ANET*, 246a: Amenophis II). In this context note the tribute sent by the king of Alalakh to Thutmose in 1442 (see *infra*, n. 80).

79 Compare in principle Urk. IV 1308 (*ANET*, 247a); KBo I 1 (*CTH* 51, G. Beckman, *Hittite Diplomatic Texts*, Atlanta 1996, 38ff.) obv. 30ff.; 4 (*CTH* 53, Beckman, *l.c.*, 50ff.) i 2ff. Such was the fate of vassals who had, forcedly or not, become disloyal to their suzerain, keeping attached to their new master.

80 Urk. IV 719f. = ARE II, § 512.

81 Idrimi. l. 91; cf. C. Kühne, BBVO I, 216.

82 Urk. IV 710 (ARE II, § 498f.), Kühne, *l.c.*, 214. Differing from an earlier proposal (e.g., Helck, *Beziehungen*, 152), M. Astour recently localized the battleground as far south as ^{c}Ašarna on the Orontes (in G.D. Young [ed.], *Ugarit in Retrospect*, Winona Lake, Ind. 1981, 11).

83 Urk. IV 730f. (ARE II, § 531f.).

84 *Ibid.*, 1304f. (*ANET*, 246a), 1314.

in general. Mittani and her king, then either Parsatatar or his son Sauš(sa)-tatar,[85] the latter again attested as overlord of Ḫana,[86] had shown weakness. Her Hittite and Kassite rivals, as well as Assyria (whose former ruler, Puzur-Aššur III, had not too much earlier concluded a treaty with Burna-Buriaš I of Babylon, perhaps after having freed himself from Mittanian bonds, thereby risking revenge),[87] all felt some relief and, entering into diplomatic relations with Egypt,[88] dreamt of isolating their menacing neighbor. Though her power was still unbroken, Mittani's subsequent attempts to restore her former influence on the Levant were of but limited consequence. She could not regain lasting control over territories lying south of Mukiš and Nuḫašše.[89] Kizzuwatna vacillated between Mittani and Ḫatti,[90] while in the east Mittani could, (also) under Sauš(sa)tatar, take revenge and ransack Aššur, thereby, for a short time, renewing her hold on Assyria.[91] However, perhaps some years later, Sauš(sa)-tatar's failure to gain the upper hand over Ḫatti in a struggle for Išuwa on the upper Euphrates (while Ḫatti was engaged in a war on several Anatolian fronts)[92] foreshadowed serious trouble for Mittani. Near the close of the 15th century, Tudḫaliya I of Ḫatti (usually identified as the second king of this name) appeared on the Syrian scene and, raising old claims, managed to draw not only

85 See D. Stein, *RlA* 8 (1995–97) 297, and compare *supra*, n. 64.

86 O. Rouault, *SMEA* 30 (1992) 254.

87 "Synchronistic History" i 5–7 (A.K. Grayson, *Chronicles*, 158); Kühne, BBVO I, 210.

88 As reflected in Urk. IV 668, 671, 700f., 727 (*ARE* II, §§ 521, 446, 449, 484f., 525) indicating the accompanying gifts of courtesy as tributes, according to the ideology of Egyptian universal rule.

89 Under the auspices of the "king of the Hurrian warriors," probably Sauš(sa)tatar (cf. *AlT* no. 13f.), Idrimi's son Niqmepa^{c}, concluded the treaty *AlT* no. 2 with Ir-Tešub of Tunip. It seems difficult to say if this happened before, between, or (some time) after Thutmose fought with Tunip (Urk. IV 686, 691 = ARE II, §§ 459, 470), i.e., starting *ca.* 1441, and devastated it (*ibid.*, 729, *ca.* 1438), but for a possibility of a rather late date, see my discussion BBVO I, 220 (after 1442).

90 Compare the treaties *CTH* 21, 26 (for the latter, see G. Beckman, *l.c.* [n. 79], 11ff.), KBo XXVIII 107–9, and *AlT* no. 14, a treaty under Saušsatatar's auspices concluded with Šunaššura, who most likely was king of Kizzuwatna (see e.g., H. Klengel, *Geschichte Syriens* I, 220; Kühne, *l.c.*, 221) and as such should probably be identical with king Šunaššura of Kizzuwatna, who, after his defection from Mittani, became the partner of Tudḫaliya I/II of Ḫatti and whose alliance is stipulated in KBo I 5 (*CTH* 41: for the reading of the Hittite king's name in col. i 1, see now G. Wilhelm, in: *Documentum Asiae Minoris Antiquae. Festschrift für Heinrich Otten zum 75. Geburtstag*, Wiesbaden 1988, 359ff.; for the identification of both kings, see R.H. Beal, *OrNS* 55 [1986] 424ff. [442–45] and H.Ph.J. Houwink ten Cate, *AoF* 25 [1998] 39ff.; for a juridical evaluation, see A. Altman, *Bar-Ilan Studies in Assyriology Dedicated to Pinhas Artzi* [eds. J. Klein - A. Skaist], Ramat Gan 1990, 177ff. A new translation, also for *CTH* 26, is provided by G. Beckman, *l.c.* [n. 79], 13ff.).

91 KBo I 3 (CTH 52, Beckman, *l.c.*, 44ff.) obv. 8f. (cf. Kühne, BBVO I, 217f.).

92 For the fragmentary evidence, KUB XXIII 14 ii 1ff.; 11 *CTH* 142 (iii 28ff.) etc., see O. Carruba, *SMEA* 18 (1977) (137ff.) 172, 158ff.; S. de Martino, *L'Anatolia occidentale nel Medio Regno Ittita* (Eothen 5) Florence 1996, 13ff., and myself, *l.c.*, 223, 262 n. 221.

Kizzuwatna[93] but also Ḫalab to his side.[94] The Mittani king would not accept this reduction of his western flank and, presumably by military action, restored control over both dominions, thereby inviting a furious Hittite reaction. Tudḫaliya annexed Kizzuwatna[95] and, pursuing the Mittanians, destroyed Ḫalab.[96] It must have been about the same time that Assyria rid herself of Mittanian control and Aššur-bēl-nišēšu (*ca.* 1409–1400) renewed the alliance with Babylon, King Karaindaš acting as his partner.[97]

It seems easy to imagine that, at this juncture, the Mittani king—either the aging Sauš(sa)tatar or his successor—weighed the tactical stalemate in central Syria against the renewed threat from the West and uneasy developments in the southeast and resolved to end the century-long, exhausting competition with Egypt. Indeed, Amenophis II (*ca.* 1426–1400), who, still in his 9th regnal year, felt himself compelled to campaign in Canaan,[98] in the usual pretentious official tone, boasts of receiving, along with delegations from the Hittite and Babylonian rulers, an embassy sent by the "prince of Naharen," all of them begging for peace.[99] This latter statement seems unduly exaggerated, since Ḫatti and Babylon had long been on friendly terms with Egypt.[100] Perhaps it reflects the reaction evoked by the appearance of the archenemy's envoy. For Egypt, the Mittani initiative was, of course, most welcome. Thus peace between the two powers eventually was established on the basis of the status quo.[101]

When the short-lived Hittite danger had passed[102] and Mittani's lost satellite states had been restored to her, Egypto-Mittani relations, under a new generation of royal partners, moved to a higher plane. Following a proposal of

---

93 KBo I 5 i 30ff., see *infra*, n. 89.

94 KBo I 6 (– 75, Beckman, *l.c.*, 88f.) obv. 15f., to restore according to the parallel redaction (21/c, 7′f.); see H. Klengel, *ZA* 56 (1964) 213ff.

95 See the evidence discussed by R.H. Beal, *Or*NS 55 (1986) 435ff. H.Ph.J. Houwink ten Cate, *AoF* 25 (1998) 45ff., not reckoning with the assumed defection of Šunaššura, argues for a peaceful unification with Ḫatti by marriages of Kizzuwatnaen princesses to Tudḫaliya and his successor Arnuwanda I.

96 KBo I 6 obv. 15–18 (H. Klengel, *l.c.*, 177, 184, Kühne, *l.c.*, 223 and, regarding Alalaḫ, n. 230). For the extent of the area claimed, see *ib.*, obv. 19ff.

97 Synchronistic History i 1′–4′ (A.K. Grayson, *Chronicles*, 158).

98 Urk. IV 1305ff. (*ANET*, 246, 247).

99 *Ibid.*, 1309 (Memphis stele, cf. *ANET*, 247b), relating this incident (rather: chronologically different incidents) immediately to the pharaoh's victorious campaign, a combination that must be doubted, all the more, as the otherwise parallel Karnak stele (*ibid.*, 1315f.) omits any such information, proving itself to belong to an earlier redaction.

100 See above, n. 88. Urk. IV 1326 (ARE II, § 804) therefore mentions only Mittani "great ones" (referring to the Mittani king by his Syrian vassals. Differently H. Klengel, *RHA* 36 (1978) 97, merging lú.MEŠ *ḫurri* and érin.MEŠ *ḫurri* as asking for "grace."

101 Cf. H. Klengel, *l.c.*, 110.

102 Cf., e.g., KBo I 6 [n. 94] obv. 19–27, accepting a king Hattusili II as successor to Tudḫaliya I/II (e.g., C. Kühne, BBVO I, 261f., 215).

Thutmose IV (*ca.* 1400–1390) and after very extended negotiations, the young pharaoh received a daughter of king Artadama in marriage, an event that took place in the late 1390s.[103] For a generation, Mittani again could bask in glory as the undisputed master of north Syria and the Ǧezira. Her dominion also included trans-Tigridian Arrapḫe[104] and, presumably, Assyria.[105] This was the seemingly blissful era of King Šutarna II, who also gave a daughter in marriage to the pharaoh, Amenophis III, in the latter's tenth regnal year (*ca.* 1381).[106] Šutarna's son, King Artaššumara (whose judicial procedure was found at Tell Braq[107]), appears to have reigned only for a short time before he was murdered.[108] He was replaced by a brother, Tušratta, then still a minor.[109] Thereafter Mittani's situation became precarious. A Hittite attack was launched against her western flank, but was repulsed.[110] In the East, Kassite Babylonia invaded Arrapḫe and forced that kingdom, bound to Mittani for generations, to become a Babylonian vassal.[111] It is also possible that Assyria had to recognize

---

103 EA 29, 16–18 (also 24 iii 37f.); cf. C. Kühne, AOAT 17, 20 n. 85.

104 As documented e.g., by a royal Mittani letter found at Nuzi and dated to the first half of the 14th century, regarding a grant of real property: D. Stein, *ZA* 79 (1989) 36ff.; *RlA* 8 (1995–97) 297.

105 Aššur-uballiṭ's letters EA 15 and 16, written some decades later, show clearly enough that after his seemingly independent ancestor Aššur-nādin-aḫḫē (II, *ca.* 1390–1381), Assyria's contact with Egypt had been interrupted, a situation that, seen in accordance with claims to Assyria's servitude raised by Mittani (and Babylon, but see n. 111), would suggest another change for the worse in the political status of Assyria.

106 EA 17, 26f.; 29,18–20 (also 24 iii 35f.); Urk. IV, 1738 (ARE II, § 867); cf. C. Kühne, AOAT 17, 21.

107 I. Finkel, *Iraq* 47 (1985) 191ff.

108 EA 17, 19; cf. Kühne; *l.c.*, 19 n. 82. Cf. *ibid.*, 39.

109 EA 17, 11f.; cf. Kühne, *l.c.*,18 n. 80.

110 EA 17, 30–35. Cf. perhaps KBo I 1 [n. 79] obv. 10b–13.

111 For a period dating to Nuzi generations IV/V (about the middle of the century, including the forties) we are informed of severe military aggression against Arrapḫe's southern and western central districts, Mittanian forces fighting on the side of Arrapḫe (e.g., HSS 14 no. 249, and cf. G. Dosch, *Zur Struktur der Gesellschaft des Königreichs Arrapḫe* [HSAO 5] Heidelberg 1993, 12[36–39]. For the cited topographic evidence, see the map of G. Müller, *Studien zur Siedlungsgeographie und Bevölkerung des mittleren Osttigrisgebietes* [HSAO 7] Heidelberg 1994). Since the invaded territories lie north of the Babylonian border, the first guess as to the aggressor's identity goes to Arrapḫe's southern neighbor, Babylonia. Assyria, bordering on the northwest, is only the second candidate. Following A. Fadhil, *Studien zur Topographie der Provinzstädte des Königreichs Arrapḫe* (BaF 6), Mainz 1983, 162f., HSS 13 no. 63 indeed shows that both Babylonia and Assyria were at war with Arrapḫe. Probably not long after, the same Arrapḫaean prince, Ḫut-Tešup, who was engaged in the defense (HSS 14 no. 249, 2), is seen returning from a diplomatic mission, traveling with a Babylonian envoy after having delivered in "Akkad," i.e., at the Kassite king's respective residence, a consignment of items (*unūtu*, HSS 14 no. 91, 8), probably as gifts. It cannot be excluded that the 30 golden and silver goblets (one of them in use by the king himself) that at that time had been transferred from different departments of the palace of Nuzi to

Kassite sovereignty for some time.[112] While Tušratta could give a daughter in marriage to the aged Amenophis III,[113] the subsequent intended marriage of another daughter to Amenophis IV never seems to have been realized,[114] either because of the collapse of Tušratta's empire or perhaps as a consequence of deteriorating relations, as can be inferred by Tušratta's campaign in northern and central Syria in violation of her agreement with Egypt as to their spheres of influence.[115] This campaign, however, had been forced on him by renewed hostilities with King Suppiluliuma of Ḫatti, who had concluded a pact with Artadama, a pretender to the Mittani throne, and had launched a foray into the Mittani protectorates on the west bank of the Euphrates as far as central Syria

---

Arrapḫe (HSS 14 no. 136) were used at a banquet honoring the Babylonian envoy. But even if Ḫut-Tešup's mission here had been mentioned only for dating the goblets' release, this would point to the importance of the diplomatic event. To be sure, a mission like this must have run counter to the conduct a loyal vassal of Mittani could afford in time of war. This, however, is not the only evidence for a shift in Arrapḫe's relations. Even more conspicuous is the sojourn in "Akkad" of Ḫut-Tešup's father, the return of whom and of whose entourage, including his queen, his brother, three of his sons (Ḫut-Tešup among them) as well as a number of courtiers of rank, together with attendants, horses and mules, is attested in HSS 14 no. 46. The entourage, especially the queen's presence, does not convey a warlike impression. It seems as if the Arrapḫean king returned, be it after a temporary deportation (instances, though with different outcome, for example referred to by Suppilu-liuma in KBo I 1 [*supra*, n. 79] obv. 31–43. Cf. also details of a royal deportation of the 13th century: E. Cancik-Kirschbaum, *l.c.* [*supra*, n. 9], no. 10), or after a sumptuous visit to demonstrate submission in dignity to the Kassite ruler. In any case, this would mean that the king of Arrapḫe now came as representative of a pax Babyloniaca.

A partly different interpretation of the alluded events is given by N.B. Jankowska in: *Societies and Languages of the Ancient Near East, Studies in Honour of I.M. Diakonoff*, Warminster 1982, 138ff.

112 Taking at face value Babylonian claims mentioned in EA 9, 31ff. (*pace* W. Mayer, *Politik und Kriegskunst der Assyrer* [ALASPM 9], 189), Babylonia, at some perhaps not too distant time, had interfered in Assyria's political circumstances (a procedure that, of course, would not have been acknowledged by Mittani, cf. KBo I 3 [*CTH* 52, cf. *supra*, n. 90] obv. 6f.). Given the evidence of HSS 13 no. 63 as shown by Fadhil, *l.c.*, 162, Assyria had been at war with Arrapḫe at the time of the Babylonian aggression, and it would seem perfectly credible that Assyria, experiencing the above-inferred period of weakness after Aššur-nādin-aḫḫē II (n. 105, assuming a then re-established Mittani overlordship), had already become a victim of Kassite expansion and was bound to cooperate against the Mittani party. Also evidence for the presence of Assyrian fugitives in Arrapḫe (e.g., G. Müller, HSAO 7, 221) dating from the third Nuzi generation onward may point to unregulated relations between both states, a situation not fitting for members of the same commonwealth (for Mittani, cf. *AlT* nos. 2 and 14), thus suggesting years of Assyro-Arrapḫean enmity.

113 EA 24 iii 1f., 11ff.; cf. C. Kühne, AOAT 17, 33, 38f., dating the event to the fifties of the 14th century.

114 Regarding the state of affairs as shown by EA 29, Tušratta's last remaining letter to the pharaoh. For this and the problematic reading of the date on its hieratic docket, see C. Kühne, AOAT 17, 47.

115 EA 58, 4–6; 85, 51ff.; 86, 10–12 as compared with 109, 39f.; 90, 19–21; 95, 27f.; cf. KBo I 1 [*supra*, n. 79] obv. 5–9; 4 [n. 79] i 2–8.

and even beyond into the Lebanon.[116] In the late 1340s, a well-prepared second Hittite onslaught put an end to Mittani's role as a great power. Suppiluliuma crossed the upper reaches of the Euphrates and advanced as far as the Ṭūr-ᶜAbdīn. He rewarded the open defection of Antar-atal of Alše, Tušratta's northern vassal, by extending his realm. Then he moved southward, raiding the Mittani heartland. He plundered the absent Tušratta's capital, Waššukanni, subsequently turning west to annex the states on the west bank of the Euphrates as far south as Qadeš, where he encountered the only serious resistance.[117] In the north, the Alšean king and, in the east, young Aššur-uballiṭ of Assyria seized the opportunity to annex as much as they could of the territories bordering Mittani. The Assyrian king probably also annexed parts or all of Arrapḫe (thereby automatically rejecting the above presumed Kassite claim to his loyalty).

In the Mittani heartland, a protracted period of turmoil had begun. Luckless Tušratta was killed by his own son. Probably a majority of the empire's elite were disenfranchised as the pretender, Artadama (recognized as king by the grace of now distant and otherwise occupied Suppiluliuma), eventually gained firm hold of the Mittani throne by ruthless pragmatism. Artadama (II) accepted the territorial status quo created by both Antar-atal and Aššur-uballiṭ. He shared power with his son, Šutarna, and won the support of the kings of Alše and Assyria by handing over to them the wealth of Tušratta's treasury and turning over to the Assyrians many prominent followers of Tušratta, abandoning these men to the cruel death of impalement.[118] International order, however, could not easily be restored by such gestures and Artadama and his son found themselves overwhelmed by Assyria's ambitious policy of filling the power vacuum created by the absence of a strong Mittanian empire. This development (eventually leading to Aššur-uballiṭ's recognition as ruler over a great sovereign power by Pharaoh Tutankhamen, at the very latest[119]) ran counter to the intentions of the Hittite pact with Artadama. The flight to Ḫatti of Šattiwaza, a younger son of Tušratta who had been persecuted by Šutarna, provided Suppiluliuma with an excuse to interfere. He made the prince his son-in-law and ordered his own son, Piyassili, whom he had installed as king of Carchemish, to launch another campaign against Mittani. This action was intended to rid that country of Šutarna and to secure Artadama's succession in Šattiwaza,[120] whose truncated realm of Mittani (Ḫanigalbat) would become a

116 KBo I 1 obv. 1–4; 4 i 12ff.; EA 75, 35–39.

117 KBo I 1 obv. 14–47; PRU IV, 35f., 40f.

118 For all these details, see KBo I 1 [n. 79] obv. 48–50; 3 [n. 91] obv. 2–14; cf. G. Wilhelm, *Grundzüge*, 50ff.

119 Cf. EA 16, 6ff.; C. Kühne, AOAT 77ff.; for an early dating well into the reign of Amenophis IV and before Tusratta's downfall, see R. Krauss, *Das Ende der Amarnazeit* (Hildesheimer Ägyptologische Beiträge, 7), Hildesheim 1978, 73f.

120 KBo I 1 obv. 52–58; 3 obv. 14–36. The possibility that Akitteššup's flight (KBo I 3 obv. 14f.) as well as Šattiwaza's return from his (presumed) flight to Babylonia (*ibid.*, obv. 16b–

buffer state between Ḫatti and Assyria, although fully integrated into the Hittite empire. This undertaking, probably dating to the late 1330s, some time after the death of Amenophis IV (as now widely believed),[121] led to a clash with Šutarna and his Assyrian ally and ended with the Hittites achieving their goal. They secured for their protégé the territory from the (simultaneously much extended) borders of Carchemish eastward, at least as far as the eastern end of the Habur triangle.[122] Formal treaties were drawn that defined for Mittani her duties, as well as providing her a highly privileged rank in the hierarchy of the Hittite protectorates.[123] Suppiluliuma's achievement, overshadowed from the outset by the Assyrian threat, lasted only a short time and not without serious interruptions.[124] The imperial glories formerly attached to the Mittani name were never again to be restored to what now remained of the Land of Mittani, more properly called Ḫanigalbat.

17, but compare KBo I 1 obv. 54!) were reflected in the documents of the latest-attested Nuzi generation has been (positively) discussed by N.B. Jankowska (*supra*, n. 111), 138ff. (143ff.).

121 P/Nipḫururiya, the name of the pharaoh whose death is mentioned in KBo V 6 iii 5; XIV 12 iv 18, earlier understood as prenomen of Tutankhamen (*Nb-ḫpr.w-R*ᶜ [died *ca.* 1323], e.g., E. Edel, *JNES* 7 [1948] 14f.), has recently been identified with *Nfr-ḫpr.w-R*ᶜ, a prenomen of Amenophis IV (died *ca.* 1335) by G. Fecht and R. Krauss (R. Krauss, [*supra*, n. 119], 9–19). In the year of *P/Nipḫururiya*'s death, Piyassili was installed as king of Carchemish: KBo V 6 (*CTH* 40) iii 1–43 and duplicate XIV 12 iii 15–20 (H.G. Güterbock, *JCS* 10 [1956] 94–96).

122 KBo I 3 (*CTH* 52; n. 91) obv. 35ff.; KUB XIX 13 (*CTH* 40) ii 20'ff. (Güterbock, *l.c.*, 111). Taide, tentatively identified with Tall Braq, belonged to Šattiwaza as his eastern residence; cf. KBo I 1 rev. 28.

123 Cf. *supra*, n. 13.

124 Already Suppiluliuma's son Mursili II complains about Mittani's defection (inevitable and compulsory, regarding aggressive Assyria's proximity and Ḫatti's weakness at the time of Mursili's accession): KUB XXIV 3+ (*CTH* 376) ii 26–28 (A. Goetze, *ANET*, 306). For the further history of Mittani-Ḫanigalbat, see, e.g., A. Harrak, *Assyria and Hanigalbat*, Hildesheim-Zürich-New York 1987.

Die hurritischen Kasusendungen *

MAURO GIORGIERI

CNR, Istituto per gli Studi Micenei ed Egeo-Anatolici, Roma

The article provides a detailed discussion of the research literature on Hurrian case suffixes from the appearance of F.W. Bush's *Grammar of the Hurrian Language* in 1964 until today. It highlights unanswered questions and offers new insights and suggestions from the author.

> Anders als flektierende Sprachen erlauben agglutinierende Sprachen in der Tat Paradigmen auch mit mehr als zehn Kasus, so daß auch einer weiteren Kasus-Suche durchaus noch Erfolg beschieden sein kann.
>
> (Plank 1988: 82)

Das Hurritische, eine agglutinierende, ergativische Sprache, verfügte, wie man heute weiß, über mindestens dreizehn bis vierzehn Morpheme, die als Kasusendungen betrachtet werden können, wenn man diesen Begriff im weiteren Sinn verwendet[1].

Vorliegender Überblick über die hurritischen Kasusendungen will eine zusammenfassende Darstellung des heutigen Forschungsstandes in einem Bereich der hurritischen Grammatik bieten, in dem einerseits neue wichtige Erkentnisse in den letzten Jahren gewonnen wurden, andererseits aber erst jüngst hervorgetretene, vieldiskutierte Probleme noch keine befriedigende, umbestrittene Lösung gefunden haben[2].

Diese Darstellung ist vor allem bibliographisch und philologisch orientiert und hat ein rein deskriptivisches Ziel. Spezifisch sprachwissenschaftliche, theoretische Fragen, die etwa strukturelle Probleme des Kasussystems betreffen bzw. dessen interne Rekonstruktion oder die Bestimmung der Bedingungen,

---

* Der auf der Rencontre vorgetragene Text wurde für die Drucklegung überarbeitet.

1 Dazu s. § 2.1.1.

2 Die jüngste eingehende, zusammenfassende Darstellung der hurr. Kasusendungen, die aber nunmehr überholt ist, befindet sich in Khačikyan 1985: 72 ff.; s. auch den knappen Überblick bei Wilhelm 1995a: 114, 132 Anm. 4–5. Leider unzulänglich Dietrich, Mayer 1993.

Studies on the Civilization and Culture of Nuzi and the Hurrians - 10

die die Verwendung von einigen Kasusendungen in besonderen syntaktischen Konstruktionen regeln, werden absichtlich nicht erörtert, da dem ausführliche Untersuchungen, die auf systematischen Sammlungen von Belegen aus dem ganzen textlichen Material beruhen, besonders über Probleme der Kasussyntax erst noch vorausgehen müssen[3].

1. Zur Geschichte der Forschung (1964–1998)

Als erster Punkt des vorliegenden Beitrags werden die wichtigsten Etappen der Forschungsgeschichte in den letzten dreißig Jahren behandelt, die zum heutigen Kenntnisstand im Bereich der hurritischen Kasusendungen geführt haben.

1.1. 1964, in seiner *Grammar of the Hurrian Language*, die noch heute als die beste zur Verfügung stehende, umfassende Beschreibung der hurritischen Grammatik gilt und daher Ausgangspunkt dieses forschungsgeschichtlichen Abrisses sein wird, betrachtete Frederic William Bush acht Suffixe als Kasusendungen, die er allerdings „relational suffixes" nannte (Bush 1964: 119–147 „The relational or 'case' suffixes"). Das von Bush gebotene Bild des hurritischen Kasusystems orientierte sich bis auf einige Details an dem von Ephraim Speiser (Speiser 1941: 105–14 „The So-called Case-endings"). Diese die Kasus-Beziehungen zum Ausdruck bringenden acht Suffixe waren nach Speiser und Bush die folgenden (Speiser 1941: 114; Bush 1964: 120):

	Sg.	Pl.
Subject-case (od. zero-suffix)	ø	*-až*
Agentive	*-ž*	*-až=už*
Genitive	*-ve*	*-až=e*
Dative	*-va*	*-až=a*
Directive	*-da*	*-aš=ta*
Comitative	*-ra*	*-až=ura*
Locative	*-(j)a*	
Stative	*-a*	

---

[3] An wichtigen, grundlegenden Arbeiten fehlt es im Rahmen der Kasusyntax eigentlich nicht; vgl. etwa einige Beiträge von E. Neu (1988a; 1992; 1996b), I. Wegner (1994) und G. Wilhelm (1983; im Druck), die aber noch auf begrenzter Materialbasis beruhen und eine reine Deskription der Phänomene bieten.

Die Voraussetzungen für wirklich umfassende, systematische Grundarbeiten sind allerdings dadurch erschwert, daß die zahlreichen, einsprachig-hurritischen religiösen Texte aus Ḫattuša trotz mancher Fortschritte der jüngsten Zeiten immer noch weithin unverständlich bleiben, zumal man m.E. bei diesem an sich reichlichen Textmaterial leider nicht selten mit Überlieferungs- und Schreiberfehler rechnen muß.

1.2. Einige in den späteren 60er und in den 70er Jahren erschienene hurritologische Beiträge konnten bezüglich der Kasusendungen durch Präzisierungen und Korrekturen zu einem besseren Verständnis der schon von Speiser und Bush gekannten und im Wesentlichen beschriebenen Phänomene führen.

1.2.1. So erwog z.B. Emmanuel Laroche (1968: 460), das bis dahin als gerundial-adverbiales Morphem gedeutete Suffix *-ae/i* habe manchmal die Funktion eines Instrumentals[4].

1.2.2. Die Zahl der Kasusendungen wurde von Johannes Friedrich in seinem 1969 im *Handbuch der Orientalistik* erschienenen grammatikalischen Abriß des Hurritischen vermehrt, indem er im Unterschied zu Speiser und Bush auch das ablativische Suffix *-dan* ins Paradigma der Kasusendungen mit einbezog (Friedrich 1969: 14)[5]. Die Einbeziehung des Ablativs auf *-dan* ins Paradigma der Kasusuffixe fand 1971 Eingang in *Hurrisch und Urartäisch* von Igor Diakonoff (Diakonoff 1971: 93 f.).

Das Paradigma der hurritischen Kasusendungen am Anfang der 70er Jahren war nach Friedrich bzw. Diakonoff das folgende:

	Sg.	Pl.
Stammkasus bzw.Casus absolutus	ø	*-až, -na*
Agentiv bzw. Ergativ	*-ž*	*-až=už*
Genitiv	*-ve*	*-až=e*
Dativ	*-va*	*-až=a*
Direktiv (Allativ)	*-da*	*-aš=ta*
Ablativ bzw. Ablativ-Instrumentalis	*-dan*	*-aš=tan*
Komitativ	*-ra*	*-až=ura*
Lokalis bzw. Lokativ	*-(j)a*	*-až=a*
Stativ	*-a*	*-až=a*

1.2.3. 1971 erschien in *Orientalia* NS 40 ein wichtiger Beitrag von Walter Farber über einige hurritische Enklitika im Mittani-Brief (fortan abgekürzt Mit.), in dem er unter anderem nachweisen konnte, daß sich das enklitische Pronominalsuffix *-nna* an das vorausgehende Ergativmorphem *-ž* assimiliert, und zwar wird *-ž* + *-nna* zu *-šša* (Farber 1971: 34 ff.).

1.2.4. Zitiert sei noch die 1974, in *Hurritische und luwische Riten aus Kizzuwatna* von Volkert Haas und Gernot Wilhelm gebotene Behandlung der von Speiser und Bush als „Stativ" bezeichneten Endung auf *-a*, für die sie die Bezeichnung

---

4 Einen forschungsgeschichtlichen Überblick über die Endung *-ae* bietet Wilhelm 1998a: 177 f.

5 Es sei aber bemerkt, daß, obwohl erst 1969 erschienen, der Friedrichsche Abriß deutlich vor der Grammatik von Bush geschrieben wurde, da Friedrich dieses Werk nicht erwähnt.

„Essiv" als angemessener betrachteten. Durch eine kombinierte Analyse des Sprachmaterials aus Boğazköy, Nuzi und Mittani konnten die beiden Autoren überzeugend nachweisen, daß die Kasusendung auf *-a* nicht nur eine essivische, sondern auch eine destinativische Funktion hat (Haas, Wilhelm 1974: 130 ff.).

1.3. Eine gänzlich neue Situation ergab sich aber seit Beginn der 80er Jahre: In den letzten fünfzehn Jahren konnten vier neue Kasusendungen identifiziert werden und darüber hinaus gelangte man zu neuen wichtigen Erkentnissen auch im Rahmen der Syntax der Kasus.

Diese hervorragenden Ergebnisse ermöglichten einerseits der Fund der sogenannten hurritisch-hethitischen Bilingue aus Boğazköy (fortan abgekürzt Bo.Bil.), andererseits eine neue intensive Beschäftigung mit dem Mittani-Brief, mit den hurritischen religiösen Texten aus Boğazköy und mit dem Hurro-Akkadischen von Nuzi, die sich schon vor dem Bekanntwerden der Bilingue als besonders ergiebig erwies.

1.3.1. Die Bestimmung eines neuen Kasusgrammems *-ne* in der Funktion eines Ablativs und eines Instrumentals verdankt man einer grundlegenden Untersuchung von Gernot Wilhelm, die 1983 in der *Zeitschrift für Assyriologie* erschien (Wilhelm 1983). Dieses Ergebnis hat 1985 Eingang gefunden in die russische Überarbeitung von I.M. Diakonoffs Werk *Hurrisch und Urartäisch* durch Margarit Khačikyan (Khačikyan 1985: 72, 74)[6]. Im folgenden werde ich versuchsweise diese Endung, die im Kapitel 3 ausführlich besprochen wird, als „Instrumental-Dimensional" bezeichnen (s. auch § 1.3.5.4, 1.3.5.4.1–2).

1.3.2. Ein weiteres Kasusgrammem *-ne/i*, das die Funktion einer adverbialen Bestimmung des Zweckes hat, wurde ebenfalls von G. Wilhelm bei einigen Infinitivformen auf *-ummene/i* im Hurro-Akkadischen von Nuzi isoliert (Wilhelm 1987). Damals (der Aufsatz wurde 1984 abgeschlossen und erst 1987 in *Studies on the Civilisation and Culture of Nuzi and the Hurrians* 2 publiziert) standen dem Verfasser aber die Daten der Bo.Bil. noch nicht zur Verfügung, so daß die für diese Endung bestimmte direktivische Dimension anscheinend in Widerspruch mit der des ablativischen, gleichlautenden Kasus auf *-ne* stand (s. jedoch unten 1.3.5.4)[7].

---

6 Diakonoff 1971: 94 hatte bereits ein ablativisches Element *-n*, das er mit dem urartäischen Ablativ-Instrumental *-ne* verglich, im hurritischen Ablativ *-dan* erkannt. Diese Endung war nach Diakonoff eigentlich als Direktiv *-da* + Ablativ *-n* zu analysieren; dazu s. auch Wilhelm 1980a: 136; 1983: 112 f. Davon ausgehend, nennt Khačikyan 1985: 72 die Endung auf *-dan* „*direktiv-ablativ*". Im Unterschied zu Diakonoff und zur herkömmlichen Auffassung setzt Khačikyan 1985: 72 zwei Direktive an, nämlich einen „*direktiv* I" auf *-da* und einen „*direktiv* II" auf *–də*, der ihrer Meinung nach in den hurritischen Texten aus Mari und Boğazköy begegnet.

Zum Kasus auf *-ne* als Instrumental bei den im *itkaḫi*-Ritual enthaltenen Opfertermini s. jetzt auch Schwemer 1995: 90 mit Anm. 38 und Haas 1998: 4, 13.

7 Dazu s. auch Wilhelm 1993: 102 ff. *contra* Dietrich, Mayer 1991: 125 f. Vgl. auch unten, § 2.3.4.3.2.

1.3.3. Bei seiner Beschäftigung mit dem Text des Mittani-Briefes konnte Christian Girbal in einem 1988 ebenfalls in der *Zeitschrift für Assyriologie* erschienenen, ausgezeichneten Aufsatz auf eine bis dahin nicht erkannte Kasusendung auf *-nn(i)=a* hinweisen, die die Gleichheit ausdrückt und die er deshalb „Äquativ" nannte (Girbal 1988: 130, 131 ff.)[8]. Diese Endung wurde 1995 von Gernot Wilhelm als „Assoziativ" bezeichnet und als Kombination des adjektivischen Suffixes *-nni*[9] mit dem Essiv *-a* analysiert (Wilhelm 1995a: 119 f., 132 Anm. 5; 1995b: 140 Anm. 26). Daß dieser Suffixkomplex *-nn(i)=a* nunmehr tatsächlich als Kasusendung aufgefaßt werden kann, zeigt seine Stellung direkt nach dem sogenannten Relator (oder Artikel) *-ne* (Giorgieri 1998: 76 f. mit Anm. 13).

1.3.4. Girbal glaubte in dem oben zitierten Aufsatz auch, bei einigen Stellen des Mittani-Briefes eine ebenfalls bis dahin nicht bemerkte Satzkonstruktion mit doppeltem Absolutiv ansetzen zu können (Girbal 1988: 127 ff.; auch Girbal 1990: 98; 1994a: 82 f.). Die Entdeckung—allerdings unter falschen Voraussetzungen (s. unten § 1.3.5.3.1)—dieses für eine ergativische Sprache syntaktisch auffallenden Phänomens fand große Resonanz in weiteren, in den letzten Jahren erschienenen Studien besonders von Erich Neu (etwa Neu 1996a: 304; 1996b: 67 ff.), Jean Catsanicos (Catsanicos 1996: 258, 268) und Ilse Wegner (Wegner 1994: 165 ff.; vgl. auch Haas, Wegner 1997: 446 ff.), die auf Grund auch des Befundes der inzwischen bekanntgewordenen hurritisch-hethitischen Bilingue aus Boğazköy auf verschiedenartige Satzkonstruktionen mit doppeltem Absolutiv hingewiesen haben.

1.3.5. Wie es zu erwarten war, so verdanken wir auch im Bereich der Kasussuffixe der in den Jahren 1983–85 entdeckten, sogenannten hurritisch-hethitischen Bilingue aus Boğazköy eine Reihe neue Erkentnisse[10].

1.3.5.1. Zunächst wurden auf Grund der Bo.Bil. zwei neue Kasusendungen identifiziert. Dabei handelt es sich um den sogenannten Äquativ auf *-o=ž*, der 1988 (besonders in der *Festschrift für Heinrich Otten*) von Erich Neu angesetzt (Neu 1988b: 236 ff.) und 1990 von Ilse Wegner in der *Gedenkschrift für Einar von Schuler* weiter behandelt wurde (Wegner 1990: 303 Anm. 13)[11], und um einen

8 Zu diesem Suffix s. aber schon Wilhelm 1985: 494, der von einer „adverbielle[n] Ableitung (*-o=nn=a*, Lokativ)" spricht. Wie auch Girbal 1988: 132 notiert, hat die Endung *-nn(i)=a* neben einer äquativen Funktion auch die Funktion eines „Adverbialis"; darüber s. unten § 2.2.1.

9 Dieses Suffix hat eine ähnliche Bedeutung und Funktion wie *-nn(i)=a*; s. unten § 2.1.1.

10 S. nunmehr Neu 1996a für die Edition sämtlicher Texte und Fragmente in Transkription und Übersetzung mit ausführlichem philologischen und sprachlichen Kommentar. Zu einem Überblick über die Kasusendungen in der Bo.Bil. s. Wilhelm 1992a: 135 f.; Catsanicos 1996: 284 f.

11 Zu den Belegen der Bo.Bil. s. auch Catsanicos 1996: 285.

Kasus auf *-ē*, der 1991 in *Iraq* 53 von Gernot Wilhelm durch die kombinierte Analyse von Belegen aus der Bo.Bil. und dem Mittani-Brief etabliert wurde (Wilhelm 1991a: 163 f. Anm. 20)[12].

1.3.5.2. Die Bo.Bil. erbrachte auch die Bestätigung der bereits von E. Laroche erkannten Funktion der Endung *-ae/i* als Instrumental in den hurritischen Texten aus Boğazköy (Neu 1988c: 16 Anm. 43, 30; 1988d: 512; Wilhelm 1992a: 136; 1998a: 177 f.; Catsanicos 1996: 285). Gleichzeitig hat E. Neu auch eine Verbindung der Verbalnomina auf *-l=ai* und *-m=ai* mit der Instrumentalendung *-ae/i* vorgeschlagen (Neu 1988d; zu diesen Formen s. auch Wilhelm 1992: 140; Catsanicos 1996: 287 und besonders unten § 2.3.4.1–2)[13].

1.3.5.3. Was die Kasussyntax betrifft, so konnte man durch die Bilingue zu neuen Einsichten z.B. bei dem sogenannten Essiv gelangen. Hierüber ist der wichtige Beitrag von Erich Neu in *Hethitica* 9 (1988) zu zitieren, der einen Überblick über die verschiedenen Funktionen des Essivs in der Bilingue bietet (Neu 1988a). Daraus ist es nunmehr klar geworden, daß der Essiv auch eine lokativische Funktion hat, so daß der herkömmliche Unterschied zwischen einem Lokativ auf *-a/-ja* und einem Stativ-Essiv auf *-a* wahrscheinlich aufzugeben ist[14].

1.3.5.3.1. Besonders beachtenswert ist auch die durch das Studium der Bilingue angeregte Entdeckung einer neuen Satzkonstruktion, bei der der Essiv als Objekt eines transitivischen, nicht-ergativischen Verbs (des sog. „Antipassivs") auftritt, dessen Subjekt im Absolutiv steht (Neu 1988a: 161 f.). Obwohl die Existenz dieses Satzmusters (die sog. „Absolutiv-Essiv-Konstruktion") inzwischen unbezweifelbares Gemeingut der Hurritologie geworden ist (Neu 1995a: 198 mit Anm. 19; 1996a: 304; 1996b: 65 ff.; Haas, Wegner 1997: 445 f.), sind aber manchmal einige Beispiele solcher syntaktischen Konstruktion falsch als Sätze mit doppeltem Absolutiv interpretiert worden (Girbal 1990: 98; Neu 1996a: 304; 1996b: 67 ff.). Für eine ausführliche Diskussion dieses syntaktischen Phänomens verweise ich auf einen eingehenden Aufsatz von Gernot Wilhelm in der *Festschrift für R. Schmitt-Brandt* (Wilhelm im Druck)[15], in dem eine Reihe von Beispielen der „Absolutiv-Essiv-Konstruktion" gesammelt ist

---

12 S. auch Wilhelm 1992a: 136; 1995a: 119, 132 Anm. 4; 1997: 284 f Anm. 40. Ein „suffixe de direction" auf *-e*, das dem sumerischen Terminativ -šè sowie dem akkadischen *ana* entspricht, hatte allerdings bereits Thureau-Dangin 1931: 260 f. auf Grund sowohl einiger hurritischer Formen in dem sumerisch-hurritischen Vorläufer zu ḪAR-ra = *ḫubullu* Tafel II aus Ugarit als auch einiger Stellen des Mittani-Briefes erwogen (frdl. Hinweis G. Wilhelm).

13 Zu der von Neu 1988d: 511 ff. angesetzten, angeblichen Form auf **-kạì* s. Wilhelm 1992: 133, 140.

14 Dieser Unterschied befindet sich noch in Khačikyan 1985: 72, 74 („*lokativ-illativ*" *vs.* „*stativ-(destinativ)*"). S. aber Zweifel bereits bei Wilhelm 1987: 331 Anm. 7.

15 Ich danke Herrn Prof. Dr. G. Wilhelm herzlichst dafür, daß er mir das Manuskript seines Aufsatzes schon vor der Veröffentlichung zur Verfügung gestellt hat.

und gleichzeitig alle vermeintlichen Belege einer Satzkonstruktion mit doppeltem Absolutiv kritisch besprochen werden. Daraus ergibt sich, daß ausschlaggebende Argumente fehlen, um eine „Absolutiv-Absolutiv-Konstruktion" nachweisen zu können (vgl. auch oben § 1.3.4)[16].

1.3.5.3.2. Was den Absolutiv wiederum betrifft, so hat G. Wilhelm jüngst auf Grund der Tišatal-Inschrift (Ende 3. Jht.) auf eine Satzkonstruktion mit Anakoluth hingewiesen, bei der eine Art *absolutivus pendens* an die Stelle des syntaktisch zu erwartenden Ergativs tritt (Wilhelm 1998c: 122 f., 125, 138, 141)[17].

1.3.5.4. Die Existenz einer weiteren, mit dem von Wilhelm angesetzten Instrumental- bzw. Ablativmorphem auf *-ne* vergleichbaren Kasusendung auf *-ne/i* als Richtungspartikel wurde 1988 auf Grund einiger Stellen der Bilingue von Erich Neu erwogen (Neu 1988e: 109; 1988b: 247 mit Anm. 46; s. auch Haas, Wegner 1991: 390; Wilhelm 1992a: 136). Der Gelehrte gab bald diese meines Erachtens richtige Feststellung jedoch auf und versuchte, diese auf *-ne/i* endenden Formen, die vornehmlich in direktivischer (auf die Frage „Wohin?"), seltener aber auch in lokativischer Funktion (auf die Frage „Wo?") verwendet werden[18], eher als mit dem Relator (oder Artikel) Singular *-ne* determinierte Absolutive zu erklären (Neu 1988c: 31 f.). Diese vermeintliche Funktion des angeblich mit dem Relator *-ne* versehenen Absolutivs als Ortskasus wurde von Neu 1992 in dem Beitrag für die *Festschrift Sedat Alp* eingehend behandelt (Neu 1992; s. auch Catsanicos 1996: 284). E. Neu unterscheidet daher die ablativischen bzw. instrumentalen Formen mit Endung *-ne*, bei denen er die herkömmliche Deutung des Morphems als Kasusendung (Ablativ-Instrumental) beibehält[19], von den auf *-ne/i* endenden Formen in direktivischer und lokativischer Funktion, die er als Absolutive + Relator *-ne* erklärt[20].

---

16 In diesem Zusammenhang soll aber folgendes Beispiel erwähnt werden, in dem eine Konstruktion mit zwei Absolutiven (enkl. Pronomina 1. Pers. Sg. *-tta* und 2. Pers. Sg. *-mma*) beim Imperativ auf *-i/e* (*ḫāž=i*) vorliegt: *anammi=tta ḫāž=i=mma Tado-ḫeba=tta* „So erhöre mich, Tatu-ḫepa, doch!" (ChS I/1 Nr. 41 III 63; Wilhelm 1991b: 43). Auf andere mögliche Belege solcher Konstruktion in der Bo.Bil. haben soeben Haas, Wegner 1997: 454 hingewiesen; vgl. auch Wilhelm im Druck: Anm. 25.

17 Dieses syntaktische Verhalten des Absolutivs ist m.E. mit seiner Funktion als Vokativ zu verbinden, die am besten aus der folgenden Stelle der Bo.Bil. zu entnehmen ist: *Mēgi fē=va abi=va* „vor dich, Meki" KBo 32.19 I 10 (so mit Neu 1996a: 406; Wilhelm 1997: 288 mit Anm. 48).

18 Zum angeblich als Ortskasus auf die Frage „Wo?" fungierenden Absolutiv ohne *-ne* s. ebenfalls Neu 1988c: 25; 1988e: 109; 1992: 400; 1996a: 36 f. Dagegen s. aber Wilhelm 1992a: 132 f.

19 S. etwa Neu 1996a: 167.

20 Dagegen betrachten Dietrich, Mayer 1991: 110 sowie Catsanicos 1996: 284 auch die Formen auf *-ne* mit ablativischer und instrumentaler Bedeutung als Absolutive + Relator *-ne*.

1.3.5.4.1. Zum Problem dieses Ortskasus auf *-ne/i* sowie seines Verhältnisses einerseits zu dem Ablativ-Instrumental auf *-ne*, andererseits zu dem gleichlautenden Relator Singular hat sich wiederum Gernot Wilhelm 1993 in der *Zeitschrift für Assyriologie* ausführlich geäußert (Wilhelm 1993: 105 ff.). Seiner Meinung nach ist der Sachverhalt dahingehend zu erklären, daß dem Relator *-ne* eine allgemeine relationale Kasusfunktion zukommt. Wir hätten demzufolge mit einem Kasusgrammem auf *-ne* zu tun, das eventuell nur sprachgeschichtlich identisch mit dem Relator Singular ist, auf der Ebene des vorliegenden Sprachmaterials aber als echte Kasusendung in ablativischer bzw. direktivischer oder instrumentaler Funktion zu betrachten ist[21].

1.3.5.4.2. Kürzlich hat aber Gernot Wilhelm in der *Festschrift für Horst Klengel* eine andere mögliche Lösung vorgeschlagen: in den auf *-ne/i* endenden Formen, die eine Richtungskomponente (Direktiv und Ablativ) haben, könnte man vielleicht den von ihm selbst beobachteten *ē*-Kasus in defektiver Schreibung isolieren, der dem Relator *-ne* suffigiert ist (*-n(e)=ē*). Die Endung *-ne/i* (mit ihrer Kurzform *-n*), die mit dem urartäischen Ablativ-Instrumental *-ne* zu vergleichen ist, wäre dagegen nur auf den Instrumental beschränkt.

Zum noch offenen Problem solcher Formen auf *-ne/i* in direktivischer, lokativischer, ablativischer bzw. instrumentaler Funktion und zu ihrem Verhältnis zu der Endung *-ē* und zu dem Relator Sg. s. *ad* Kapitel 3.

1.4. Als letzte wichtige Beiträge zu den Kasusendungen seien die umfassenden Studien Ilse Wegners und Gernot Wilhelms über die sogenannte „Suffixaufnahme" zitiert, die 1995 publiziert wurden und einen reichlich dokumentierten Überblick über diese morphosyntaktische Besonderheit (s. unten, § 2.6) des Hurritischen bieten (Wegner 1995b; Wilhelm 1995a).

2. Morphologie der hurritischen Kasusendungen

Im vorliegenden Abschnitt werden die morphologischen Aspekte der hurritischen Kasusendungen kurz behandelt. Es sei vorerst betont, daß die Bezeichnung einiger Kasus als rein etikettenartig gilt. Weitere Beschäftigungen mit Problemen der Kasussyntax werden sicher zu einer besseren Definition der exakten Funktionen solcher Morpheme führen.

2.1. Das Paradigma der hurritischen Kasusgrammeme, wie es nach heutigem Kenntnisstand rekonstruiert werden kann, besteht aus den folgenden Morphemen:

21 Vgl. auch Wegner 1995a: 119.

Absolutiv	ø
Ergativ	*-ž*
Genitiv	*-ve/i*
Dativ	*-va*
Komitativ	*-ra*
Essiv	*-a*
Assoziativ/Äquativ	*-nni; -nn(i)=a* (< *-nni* + *-a*)
Direktiv	*-da*
Ablativ	*-dan(i)* (< *-da* + *ne/i*)
Instrumental-Dimensional	*-ne/i*
Lokativ(-Dimensional)	*-ē*
Instrumental-Adverbial	*-ae/i*
Äquativ	*-o=ž* (< *-o=ži*)

Für eine ausführlichere Darstellung des Paradigmas der Kasusendungen verweise ich auf Tab. 1 (S. 252), die die verschiedenen Allomorphe[22] der einzelnen Kasus im Singular und im Plural sowie ihre syntaktischen Funktionen verzeichnet.

2.1.1. Als Kasusendungen habe ich auch Morpheme betrachtet, deren Ursprung eigentlich eher im Bereich der adjektivischen Suffixe zu suchen ist, denen aber ein kasusähnlicher Status konventionell zugeschrieben wird. Dabei handelt es sich um die zwei assoziativ-äquativartigen Suffixe auf *-nni*[23] bzw. *-o=ž*[24], die adverbialen Charakter haben. Das Kasusgrammem *-nni* entspricht nämlich morphologisch völlig dem adjektivischen Derivationssuffix *-ni*/*-nni*[25], während die Endung *-o=ž* eigentlich wohl einen kristallisierten Suffixkomplex

---

22 Hier sei nur das Problem des Auslautvokals *e* oder *i* bei dem Genitiv und dem Instr.-Adverbial kurz erörtert. Ich habe die Formen als *-ve/i* bzw. *-ae/i* angesetzt, weil sie gegenüber dem Mit.-Briefe in den Texten aus Boğazköy häufig mit Vokalismus *i* begegnen: Der Genitiv wird oft mit den *i*-haltigen Zeichen BI und PI$_i$ (*-wi*$_i$) – neben PI$_e$ (*-we*$_e$) –, der Instr.-Adverb. oft mit -A-I – neben -A-E – geschrieben. Daß solche Schreibungen nicht nur als graphematisches, sondern auch als phonematisches Phänomen zu deuten sind, ist sehr wahrscheinlich (dazu s. Giorgieri, Wilhelm 1995: 39). Auch der Vokalismus der Instr.-Dimens. *-ne/i* ist nicht eindeutig, weil diese Endung überwiegend mit dem Zeichen NI (*-ni/né*) wiedergegeben ist.

Dagegen habe ich mich der Übersichtlichkeit halber entschieden, den anlautenden Konsonant des Genitivs und des Dativs trotz der in den Boğazköy-Texten häufigen Schreibungen mit Okklusiv (BI bzw. PA) in der Basisform als Frikativ /*v*/ anzusetzen, da die allomorphischen Varianten mit Okklusiv (*-pe* bzw. *-pa*) von bestimmten phonotaktischen Regeln bestimmt sind (s. § 2.5.2: *b* + *-ve* bzw. *-va* > *p=pe/pa*). Auch die in den Boğazköy-Texten häufig zu beobachtenden Schwankungen bei der Wiedergabe der hurritischen Frikative sind auf jeden Fall wohl nicht als rein graphematisches Phänomen zu deuten.

23 Wilhelm 1995a: 132 Anm. 5; 1995b: 140 mit Anm. 26–27.

24 Darüber s. oben § 1.3.5.1.

25 Zu diesem adjektivischen Derivationssuffix s. zuletzt Wilhelm 1995a: 123 f.

darstellt, der unter Auslassung des auslautenden Themavokals *-i* aus dem Derivationsvokal *-o-* und dem adjektivischen Suffix *-ži/-šše*[26] zusammengesetzt ist.

2.2. Auch andere Kasusendungen sind eigentlich als kombinierte Morpheme zu betrachten, die aus zwei verschiedenen, segmentierbaren Elementen entstanden sind.

2.2.1. So ist z.B. der Assoziativ/Äquativ *-nn(i)=a* eindeutig die Kombination des oben besprochenen adjektivisch-adverbialen Suffixes *-nni* mit dem Essiv *-a* (Wilhelm 1995a: 132 Anm. 5; 1995b: 140 Anm. 26). Diese richtige Beobachtung von G. Wilhelm wird m.E. durch die Existenz weiterer ähnlicher adverbialer Bildungen bestätigt, die ebenfalls aus dem Suffix *-nni* bzw. seiner Variante *-ni* und einer Kasusendung oder dem komplizierten, die Essivendung *-a* enthaltenden Morphemkonglomerat *-o=ḫḫ(e)=a* bestehen, wie vorliegendes Schema zeigt[27]:

	Instr.-Adv. *-ae*	Essiv *-(o=ḫḫ(e)=)a*	Instr.-Dimens. *-n(e/i)*
-ni	*-n(i)=ae*[28]	—	*-n(i)=ne=n*[29]
-nni	*-nn(i)=ae*[30]	*-nn(i)=a* *-nn(i)=o=ḫḫ(e)=a*[31]	—

[26] Zu diesem Derivationssuffix s. zuletzt Wilhelm 1995a: 125 f. Vgl. auch G. Wilhelm, *SMEA* 29 (1992) 241.

[27] Dabei ist es zu beobachten, daß die Formen mit dem Suffix *-nni* aus Substantiven, jene mit dem Suffix *-ni* dagegen aus Adjektiven abgeleitet sind. Der adjektivische, derivative Charakter letzterer Bildungen wird durch die Anwesenheit des Derivationsvokals *-o-* gesichert (*-o=n(i)=ae*, *-o=n(i)=ne=n*), der in den Formen mit *-nni* fehlt bzw. erst rechts des Suffixes *-nni* antritt.

[28] Etwa zu *tea/i*? „viel": *te(a/i?)=o=n(i)=ae* „sehr, im großen Maße" (*passim*). Ähnliche adverbiale Formen sind ebenfalls durch die Endung *-ae* auch vom adjektivischen Suffix *-ži/-šše* abgeleitet: z.B. zu *niri* „gut" *nīr(i)=o=ž(i)=ae* „in guter Weise" (*passim*).

[29] Etwa zu *fağri* „schön, fein": *fağr(i)=o=n(i)=ne=n* „in schöner Weise" (Mit. I 81; s. mit anderer Analyse, die m.E. falsch ist, Wilhelm 1995a: 124).

[30] Etwa zu *šēna* „Bruder": *šēnā=nn(i)=ae* „brüderlich (gesonnen)" (Mit. IV 12; s. Wilhelm 1985: 494).

[31] Etwa zu *tiža* „Herz" und (mit Suffixaufnahme) zu *šēna*: *šēn(a)=iffu=ṷe=nē=nn(i)=o=ḫḫ(e)=a tižā=nn(i)=o=ḫḫ(e)=a* wörtl. „in einer Weise, die zu dem, was zum Herzen meines Bruders paßt, gehört" (Mit. II 10). Vgl. die gleiche Wendung mit *-nn(i)=a*: *šēn(a)=iffu=ṷe=nē=n tižā=nn(i)=a* wörtl. „in einer Weise, die zum Herzen meines Bruders paßt" (Mit. IV 34); zu diesen Formen s. zuletzt Wilhelm 1995a: 119 f. Zu erinnern ist auch an die folgende adverbiale Form auf *-o=ḫḫ(e)=a* zu *šēn=ni* (Nebenform mit „individualisierendem Suffix" *-ni* zu *šēna*): *šēn=n(i)=o=ḫḫ(e)=a* „in brüderlicher Weise" (Mit. IV 121; frdl. Hinweis Frau I. Röseler).

2.2.2. Was den Ablativ *-dan(i)* betrifft, so wird diese Endung als die Kombination des Direktivs *-da* mit dem Instrumental-Dimensional *-ni/e* betrachtet, wie bereits oben gesagt (s. Anm. 6 mit einschlägiger Literatur).

2.3. Im Hurritischen konnten die Kasusendungen an Nomina (2.3.1), also an Substantive und Adjektive, sowie an Pronomina (2.3.2), Numeralia (2.3.3), und Verbalnomina (2.3.4) suffigiert werden.

2.3.1. Was ihre Position in der Morphemkette des *Nomens* betrifft, so treten die Kasusendungen im Singular (s. Tab. 2.1, S. 255) normalerweise direkt an die Possessivsuffixe oder den sogenannten Relator *-ne-* an. Einige Kasusendungen, wie z.B. der Essiv *-a*, der Instrumental-Adverbial *-ae/i* oder der Äquativ *-o=ž*, werden aber im Singular fast regelmäßig ohne den Relator direkt an den nominalen Themavokal suffigiert[32], was bei anderen Kasusendungen, wie z.B. dem Ergativ oder dem Genitiv, nur selten geschieht.

Bei den Pluralformen (s. Tab. 2.2., S. 255 und unten § 2.4) wird der Pluralisator *-až-* zwischen das Possessivsuffix bzw. den Relator *-na* und das Kasusgrammem eingefügt.

2.3.1.1. An die Kasusendungen können weitere Enklitika suffigiert werden, wie z.B. die enklitischen Personalpronomina (zu den phonotaktischen Phänomenen, die beim Antritt der enklitischen Pronomina am Ergativ stattfinden, s. unten § 2.5.4).

2.3.1.2. Bei einigen Ethnika wird das Zugehörigkeitssuffix *-ġe* (Nisbe) zur Genitivendung *-ve* hinzugefügt, wodurch sich das Suffixkonglomerat *-p=ḫe* ergibt (z.B. *nīnuu̯a=p=ḫe* „der von Ninua, Niniviter" KBo 32.11 I 10; zu diesen Nisbe-Bildungen s. Wilhelm 1980b: 99; 1992a: 133)[33].

2.3.2. Was die Deklination der *Pronomina* betrifft, verweise ich auf die grundlegenden Beiträge von Wilhelm 1984 und Wegner 1992, deren Ergebnisse in den Tab. 3.1–2 (S. 256 zusammengestellt sind, in denen die Paradigmen der selbständigen Personalpronomina bzw. der deiktischen Pronomina vorgelegt werden).

2.3.3. Die Suffigierung von Kasusendungen an *Numeralia* ist selten bezeugt. Die spärlichen Belege zeigen, daß nicht nur die Ordinalzahlen[34], sondern auch die Kardinalzahlen in Kasuskongruenz mit dem Bezugswort stehen. Dabei ist

---

32 Bei der Suffigierung einer vokalischen Endung (*-a, -ae, -o=ž*) fällt der nominale Themavokal aus, nach der m.W. erst von Wilhelm 1992b: 157 formulierten Regel: Bei morphosyntaktisch bedingtem Zusammenstoß zweier Vokale schwindet meist der erste.

33 Diese Formen sind oft in den Nuzi-Urkunden belegt: etwa *Apapḫe=na, Arrapḫe*(?), *Baqqanupḫe* usw. (s. zu den einzelnen Ortsnamen Fincke 1993).

34 Zur Bildung der Ordinalzahlen s. zuletzt Giorgieri, Röseler 1998: 90 Anm. 13 mit einschlägiger Literatur.

allerdings die Verwendung von Singular bzw. Plural eines Nomens nach einer Kardinalzahl bisher nicht völlig geklärt. Nach den unten angeführten Beispielen stehen anscheinend — besonders beim Absolutiv — niedrige (einstellige) Zahlen mit Plural, große (zwei- und vierstellige) dagegen mit Singular[35]:

(a) Kardinalzahlen:

Absolutiv Sg.: *nūbi pidari* „zehntausend Rinder" (KBo 32.13 I 15, 16);
kungallē kīge nūbi „dreißigtausend Fettschwanzschafe" (KBo 32.13 I 16 f.).

Absolutiv Pl. (*-na*): *kīgē ... ēvren(i)=na* „drei Könige" (KBo 32.19 I 6);
tumni īžiḫḫe=na „vier (Objekte) aus *i.*" (Mit. II 59);
šēžē ... ēvren(i)=na „sechs Könige" (KBo 32.19 I 7 f.);
šinde=na ... šije=na „die sieben Wasser" (ChS I/1 Nr. 5 II 13).

Essiv (*-a*): *tamr(i/a)=a evern(i)=a* „neun Könige" (KBo 32.19 I 4);
kir=(e)man(i)=a šabl(a/i)=a „achtzehn/achtzig Jahre lang" (KBo 32.20 I 5').

Instr.-Dimens.(*-ne=n*?): *nubē=ne=n=an ḫār(i)=re(<ne)=n* „und (*-an*) auf/durch zehntausend Wege(n)" (Mit. I 93).

Instr.-Adverb. (*-ae/i*): *šind=ad(i)=āi sij(e)=āi* „mit je sieben Wassern" (ChS I/1 Nr. 16 II 13'')[36].

(b) Ordinalzahlen:

Dativ (*-va*): *ēmman=ze=ne=va ... fē=va abi=va* „vor dich, den zehnten" (KBo 32.19 I 9 f.)[37].

Essiv (*-a*): *šindi=žūu̯?=a-... šūu̯(a/i)=a* „am siebten Tag" (KBo 32.19 I 22)[38].

Instr.-Dimens. (*-ne/i*)[39]: *kir=(e)mān(i)=zi=ni šabal(a/i)=li(< ni)* „von/nach dem achtzehnten/achtzigsten Jahr" (KBo 32.20 I 11').

2.3.3.1. Belegt sind auch Bildungen des Typs Kardinalzahl + Possessivsuffix + Kasusendung:

(Freischwebender) Genitiv Pl. (*-až=e*):
šin=i=až=e=nā(=mmaman) „die (*-na, scil.* Worte) von ihren (Pl.) beiden (Tontafeln)" (Mit. III 40).

Dativ Pl. (*-až=a* ?):
kīg(e)=i=āž=a tumn(i)=i=až=a „zu ihren(Pl.) drei, zu ihren(Pl.) vier" (ChS I/1 Nr. 4 Rs. 9', Kontext fragmentarisch).

---

35 Dazu s. Wilhelm 1980a: 135 Anm. 6; Giorgieri, Röseler 1998: 91 mit Anm. 17. Solche Faustregel gilt allerdings nicht für die Beispiele im Essiv und im Instr.-Adverb. Das hängt wohl vom besonderen, quasi-adverbialen Status dieser Endungen ab, bei denen Pluralformen selten (beim Essiv) bzw. nie (beim Instr.-Adverb.) belegt sind. Dazu s. unten § 2.4.2–3.

36 S. Wegner 1992: 231 f. Zu den auf *-ad(i)=ae* endenden Distributivzahlen s. unten, § 2.3.3.2*b*.

37 S. Neu 1996a: 378; Wilhelm 1997: 288.

38 S. Haas, Wegner 1996: 287 f.

39 Oder Lokativ(-Dimensional) auf *-ē*: *kir=(e)mān(i)=zi=n(e)=e šabal(a/i)=l(e<ne)=e* „im achtzehnten/achtzigsten Jahr"?

2.3.3.2. Mit dem Essiv, der besonders in den aus dem Zugehörigkeitssuffix *-ġe/-ḫḫe* und der Essivendung *-a* bestehenden Suffixkomplexen *-ġ(e)=a* bzw. *-o=ḫḫ(e)=a* auftritt, und dem Instrumental-Adverbial werden Zahladjektive und Zahladverbien gebildet[40]:

(a) Essiv (*-a*): *šug=a* „als einer; nur", *šug=am=ġ(e)=a* „einfach"[41];
šin=am=ġ(e)=a „zweifach", *šin=z(i)=o=ḫḫ(e)=a* „an zweiter Stelle";
tamr=am=ġ(e)=a „neunfach";
eman=am=ġ(e)=a „zehnfach".

(b) Instr.-Adverb. (*-ae/i*): *šin=ai* „zweimal", *šin=ad(i)=ae* „je zwei";
kig=ad(i)=ae „je drei";
šind=ai „siebenmal", *šind=ad(i)=ai* „je sieben"[42].

2.3.4. Zahlreiche *nominale Verbalformen* sind im Hurritischen belegt[43], die genau wie die Nomina Kasussuffixe tragen können. Hierbei sind einige besondere Bildungen zu besprechen.

2.3.4.1. Jüngst hat E. Neu vorgeschlagen, die gerundialartigen Verbalformen auf *-m=ai* seien wahrscheinlich mit der Instrumental-Adverbialendung *-ae/i* gebildet[44]: *al(=)ˀu=m=ai(=n)* „sprechend" (*passim* in mythologischen Texten)[45]; *ḫāž=ī=m=ai* bzw. *ḫaž=i=m=āi* „hörend" (KBo 32.14 I 8 bzw. I 50, Rs. 38.59); *faž=u=m=ai* „eintretend" (KBo 32.13 I 3); *fur=ī=m=ai=n* „sehend" (Mit. IV 122).

Gerade das zuletzt angeführte Beispiel aus dem Mit.-Brief, das von E. Neu nicht berücksichtigt wurde[46], scheint aber gegen die an sich semantisch sehr plausible Identifizierung des gerundialen Morphems *-ai* mit der Instr.-Adverbialendung *-ae/i* zu sprechen. Im graphischen System des Mit.-Briefes, in dem die Vokalqualität konsequent unterschieden wird, wird der Instr.-Adverb. m.W. immer *-a-e* geschrieben[47]. Dagegen ist die Verbalendung in der Form *fur=ī=m=ai=n* mit dem Zeichen IN geschrieben (*wu-ri-i-ma-in*), das im Mit.-Brief

40 Zu diesen Formen und den Belegstellen s. besonders Wilhelm 1992a: 134; 1998b: 182 f. mit Anm. 19; im Druck: Anm. 2.

41 Die Multiplikativzahlen bestehen aus: Zahlwort + Faktitivsuffix *-am-* + *-ġ(e)=a*.

42 Zu dieser Form s. auch oben, § 2.3.3*a*.

43 Einen Überblick über die bisher bekannten hurr. Verbalnomina mit einschlägiger Literatur bietet Wilhelm 1992a: 149; dazu s. auch Neu 1995b: 49 ff.; Catsanicos 1996: 287 f.

44 S. besonders Neu 1988d: 504 ff., 512 f.; Wilhelm 1992: 140.

45 Eine gerundiale Bedeutung der Form *al(=)ˀu=m=ai(=n)* wurde bereits von Salvini 1977: 77 richtig erkannt. Eine gerundiale Funktion des Morphems *-ae/i* wurde auch von Speiser 1941: 120, allerdings unter falschen Voraussetzungen, vorgeschlagen (seine Analyse der Form *alumain* auf S. 138 ist hinfällig!).

46 Auf die Form *fur=i=m=aī=n* als Gerundium hat m.W. zunächst Salvini 1988: 168 richtig hingewiesen.

47 Etwa: *nīr(i)=ō=ž(i)=ae* Mit. I 55.58.70.82, IV 38; *te(a/i)=ō=n(i)=ae* II 49.55.62.64.112 usw.; *ḫi<a>roḫḫ(e)=ae* III 66; *tād=ar=aš=k(i)=ae* III 51.107; *šēnā=nn(i)=ae* IV 12.

nur für den *i*-Vokal (IN: [in] vs. EN: [en]) verwendet wird. Daraus ergäbe sich, daß wir es mit zwei verschiedenen Morphemen zu tun haben, die im Mit.-Brief graphisch unterschieden werden. Demzufolge erscheint die Verbindung des gerundialen Suffixkomplexes *-m=ai* mit der Instr.-Adverbialendung auf *-ae/i* nicht problemlos zu sein und sollte vorläufig nur mit Vorbehalt vermutet werden.

2.3.4.2. Dasselbe gilt m.E. auch für einige nicht-finite Verbalformen auf *-l=ae/i*, die bisher nur in hurritischen Texten aus Boğazköy beobachtet wurden und nach Auffassung E. Neus ebenfalls mit dem Instr.-Adverbialendung gebildet sind[48]. Sie haben die Funktion entweder *a*) eines untergeordneten Relativsatzes: *naḫḫ=i=l=āi* „den (sein Herr) eingesetzt hat" (KBo 32.14 IV 15, Rs. 25); *[f]ut(=)*[?]*t=i=l=āe* „den (Kumarbi) gezeugt hat" (ChS I/5 Nr. 87 IV 21), oder *b*) eines Konsekutivsatzes: *šid=i=l=āi* „so daß (die Gottheit ihn) verfluchte" (KBo 32.14 I 22, IV 5).

Auch in diesem Falle ist eine instrumentale Herkunft dieser Formen nicht völlig auszuschließen. Ich wäre aber eher geneigt, das Suffix *-ai* sowohl dieser Formen auf *-l=ai*, als auch eventuell der oben besprochenen Formen auf *-m=ai* mit dem Morphem *-ai* zu identifizieren, das bei im Mit.-Brief belegten, nicht-finiten Verbalformen mit finaler bzw. konsekutiver Bedeutung auftritt[49] und das ich von der Instr.-Adverbialendung *-ae/i* wiederum trennen möchte.

Eine eingehende Diskussion des Problems, die eine ausführliche Erörterung der betreffenden Verbalformen aus dem Mit.-Brief im Vergleich zu den besprochenen Verbalnomina aus den Boğazköy-Texten voraussetzen würde, würde jedoch den Rahmen dieses Aufsatzes sprengen. An dieser Stelle sei es genug, auf das Problem solcher Verbalnomina auf *-m=ai* bzw. *-l=ai* und ihrer möglichen Verhältnisse einerseits mit dem Verbalmorphem *-ai* der nicht-finiten Verbalformen des Mit.-Briefes, andererseits mit dem Instr.-Adverb. *-ae/i* hingewiesen zu haben.

2.3.4.3. An den Infinitiv auf *-umme* wird im Hurro-Akkadischen von Nuzi häufig der Essiv *-a* und seltener der Instrumental-Dimensional *-ne/i* – oder der

---

48 S. ausführlich Neu 1988d: 508 ff.

49 Zu den finalen Formen auf *-ai=n/ž* im Mit. s. zuletzt Wilhelm 1998b: 181 f. mit einschlägiger Literatur: z.B. *faž=ai=n(=an)* (Mit. III 33); *itt=ai(=nn(a)=ān)* (IV 53); *itt=ai=ža (=ll(a)=ān)* (IV 52). Formen auf *-l=ai*, die eine ähnliche, finale-konsekutive Bedeutung haben, sind etwa: *tupp=o=l=ai=n* (Mit. III 26); *pal=(i)=l=ai=n* (IV 64); *pal=(i)=l=ai=ža(=lla=man)* (Mit. IV 65). Zum Teil unklar ist die Analyse der wohl hierher gehörigen Form *ḫaž=āž=ill*[?]*= āi=n(=i=ll(a)=ān)* (IV 23).

Davon zu trennen sind die Jussiv-Desiderativformen auf *-l=ae=n/ž* (etwa *pal=(i)=l=āe=n* Mit. IV 56.59; *tag=o=l=aē=ž* ChS I/1 Nr. 10 IV 15').

Zum (nominalisierenden?) Morphem *-l-* in den Verbalnomina auf *-l=ai* s. unten § 2.3.4.5 mit Anm. 56.

Lokativ(-Dimensional) auf *-ē*, wenn man jetzt dem Vorschlag von Wilhelm 1997: 284 f. Anm. 40 folgt – suffigiert[50].

2.3.4.3.1. Der mit der Essivendung versehene Infinitiv begegnet in der in Nuzi gebräuchlichen Konstruktion, die einen hurritischen Infinitiv auf *-umm(e)=a* mit akkadisch *epēšu* „machen" verbindet: z.B. *puġ=ugar=umm(e)=a epēšu* „tauschen" (Fincke 1995: 19 f.); *alad=umm(e)=a epēšu* „begleichen; kaufen" (Wilhelm 1996a: 361 ff.)[51].

2.3.4.3.2. Die seltenen, mit der Endung *-ne/i* oder *-ē* versehenen Infinitivformen werden in Nuzi mit der akkad. Präposition *ana* gebildet und haben die Funktion einer adverbialen Bestimmung des Zweckes: *ana ḫalv=umme=ne/ =n(e)=e* „für das Einfrieden" (Wilhelm 1987: 332); *ana naḫ[la]pta ana ku[ru]$^{?}$mme =ne/=n(e)=e* „für das Herstellen(?) eines Mantels (akkad. *naḫlaptu*)" (Wilhelm 1993: 104 f.).

2.3.4.3.3. Jüngst hat Wilhelm (1996a: 363 f.) sogar auf eine bisher nicht erkannte Infinitivform im Genitiv hingewiesen: *alad=am(m)i=ne=ve*[52] „des Begleichens (dem Vorratsspeicher")."

2.3.4.4. Deklinierte Formen des agens-orientierten resultativen Partizips auf *-i=re/i*[53] sind etwa folgende:

Ergativ (*-ž*): *šad=i=re=ž* „Stellvertreter(?)"[54] (ChS I/1 Nr. 41 II 33, III 18.25, IV 26);

Genitiv (*-u̯i*, nach Possessivsuff. 1. Pers. Sg. *-iffu-*): *pa=i=r(i)=iffu=u̯i* „(die Hand) von demjenigen, der mich gebaut hat (*pa-* 'bauen')" (KBo 32.14 Rs. 37)[55];

Dativ (*-va*): *šad=i=re=va* „dem Stellvertreter(?)" (ChS I/1 Nr. 41 III 5);

Direktiv (*-da*): *šad=i=re=da* „zu dem Stellvertreter(?)" (ChS I/1 Nr. 41 III 16).

2.3.4.5. Besondere Beachtung verdienen die in der Bo.Bil. belegten, in ihren einzelnen morphologischen Elementen leider noch unklaren nominalen Verbalformen auf *-lia/e*, die anscheinend nur im Ergativ (*-ž*) begegnen und

---

50 Zu *-umma* s. Wilhelm 1970: 8; 1987: 336 ff.; Haas, Wilhelm 1974: 132 ff. Zu *-ummene/i* s. Wilhelm 1987; 1993: 102 ff. Die Formen auf *-ummene/i* (s. auch oben, § 1.3.2) könnten als *-umme=ne/i* oder *-umme=n(e)=e* analysiert werden (zum Problem solcher Endungen s. unten, Kapitel 3).

51 Für weitere Beispiele s. etwa *AHw*, 225a; Fincke 1998.

52 Die Form ist im sumerisch-hurritischen ḪAR-ra=*ḫubullu*-Vorläufer aus Ugarit belegt. Dieses Vokabular zeigt häufig einen aberranten Vokalismus der hurritischen Wörter: erwartungsgemäß mußte die Form eher **alad=umme=ne=ve* lauten.

53 S. besonders Wilhelm 1988: 55 ff.

54 Falls zu *šad-* „ersetzen" gehörig.

55 Zu mehreren Formen dieses Typs s. Catsanicos 1996: 203 f., 288 und s. auch unten Anm. 63.

denen die Funktion eines passivischen Partizips zugeschrieben wird[56]. Sie werden in der hethitischen Fassung mit Relativsätzen übersetzt und sind m.E. mit den ergativen, durch das Suffix *-šše* nominalisierten Verbalformen funktionell zu vergleichen, zumal beide Konstruktionen attributiv verwendet werden und der Suffixaufnahme unterliegen: z.B. *pa=i=lia*?*=ne=ž* (... *šuġun*(*i*) *=ne=ž*) „die (von mir) gebaute (Mauer, *šuġuni*)" (KBo 32.14 Rs. 38)[57].

2.4. Fast alle Kasusendungen haben eine *Pluralform*, die ein aus dem Pluralisator *-až-* und dem Kasusmorphem bestehender Suffixkomplex ist.

2.4.1. Beim endungslosen Absolutiv wird der Plural durch verschiedene Suffixe markiert. Bei den Nomina tritt normalerweise der Relator oder Artikel Pl. *-na* auf: z.B. *eni* „Gott" vs. *en*(*i*)*=na* „Götter" (*passim*). Vereinzelt begegnet aber auch das enkl. Pronomen 3. Pers. Pl. *-l*(*la*) als Pluralmarkierung: z.B. *ēni=ll*(*a*)*=an* „die Götter" (Mit. IV 65); *ēlgi=lla* „die glänzenden Applikationen" (KBo 32.14 I 58)[58]; *ḫemza*(< *i*)*=l* „die Bande" (ChS I/5 Nr. 80 I 22)[59].

Bei den selbständigen und deiktischen Pronomina tritt als Pluralisator überwiegend das enkl. Pronomen *-lla* (*fe=lla*, *mane=lla*, *akki=lla*, *andi=lla*) auf, in einem Falle aber auch das Suffix *-na* (*ane=na*; zu diesen Formen s. Tab. 3.1–2, S. 256).

Bei den Possessivsuffixen wird als Pluralmarkierung das Suffix *-až-* verwendet: *attārd(i)=iff=až*^{MEŠ} „unsere Vorväter" (Mit. I 8); *tupp*(*i*)*=i=až* „ihre Tontafeln" (Mit. III 39).

2.4.2. Der Plural fehlt nur bei dem Instrumental-Adverbial auf *-ae/i*, dem Lokativ(-Dimensional) auf *-ē* und dem Äquativ auf *-o=ž*. Das Phänomen ist wahrscheinlich mit dem quasi-adverbialen Charakter dieser Endungen verbunden, die numerusindifferent sind[60].

---

56 Darüber und zu den Belegen s. Neu 1995b: 49 ff.; 1996a: 103, 111, 156, 193, 207 ff.; Catsanicos 1996: 288. Das Element *-l-* ist m.E. wohl dasselbe (nominalisierende?) Morphem, das in den oben besprochenen Verbalnomina auf *-l=ai* (§ 2.3.4.2) auftritt. Davon zu trennen ist das Morphem *-l-*, das bei Wunschformen (etwa: *-l=e*, *-l=ae=n/ž*, *-l=anni*, *-l=eva*(*=ž*)) eine verstärkende Funktion hat (darüber s. Wilhelm 1992a: 139; Giorgieri 1998: 74 Anm. 8).

57 Die heth. Übersetzung dieser Form lautet: *u̯etenun kuin kuttan* „die Mauer, die ich gebaut habe" (KBo 32.14 Rs. 45).

58 Allerdings neben *ēlgi* (Absol. Sg.) *ibid.* I 57. In beiden Fällen hat der hethitische Übersetzer Pluralformen benutzt: *šuppišduu̯arīēš* (*ibid.* II 59, Nom. Pl.) bzw. *šuppišduu̯ariuš* (II 56, Akk. Pl.). Das Wort *ēlgi* „appliques" scheint einen kollektivischen Sinn zu haben; s. Catsanicos 1996: 222; Neu 1996a: 146. Auch bei anderen Substantiven in der Bo.Bil., die aber lexikalisch nicht völlig klar sind, hat das Pronomen *-l*(*la*) die Funktion der Pluralmarkierung: *ārni=l* (KBo 32.14 Rs. 57), *šagarē=lla*(?) (*ibid.* Rs. 62); s. Neu 1996a: 203, 211.

59 Zum Problem des morphophonematischen Wandels *e/i* > *a* vor enklitischen Pronomina s. jetzt ausführlich Wilhelm im Druck: Anm. 9.

60 Nach Giorgieri, Wilhelm 1995: 53 und Wegner 1995c: 124 Anm. 31 liegt ein Instr.-Adverb. Pl. in der Form **ši=n*(*a*)*=āi* (ChS I/1 Nr. 41 I 44; KBo 32.14 I 35, zu *ši* „Auge": „mit den Augen") vor, die daher eine abweichende Konstruktion des Plurals ohne das Suffix *-až-*

2.4.3. Besondere Beachtung verdient die Tatsache, daß der hurr. Essiv manchmal gegenüber der grammatikalischen Kategorie des Numerus indifferent scheint. Das geschieht anscheinend nur, wenn der Essiv nicht in lokativischem Sinn verwendet wird[61]. Das Phänomen, das an dieser Stelle nur kurz erwähnt werden kann, aber einer eingehenden Untersuchung wert wäre, kann besonders in den Texten der Bo.Bil. beobachtet werden, in denen die hethitischen Übersetzer Singularformen des hurritischen Essivs dem Zusammenhang nach mit hethitischen Pluralformen wiedergeben, wie folgende ausgewählte Beispiele zeigen:

(1) KBo 32.13 I 22 *fand=ar=i=nni=nā=ma ag=i=b neġern(i)=a* „Die Köche aber nahmen Brust(stücke) auf" (heth. II 22 f. $^{\text{LÚ.MEŠ}}$MUḪALDIM=*ma=kan* ^{UZU}GABA$^{\text{ḪI.A}}$ *šarā dāir*; zur Syntax des hurr. Satzes s. Wilhelm 1992a: 133; im Druck: Beisp. Nr. 15; Haas, Wegner 1997: 445);

(2) KBo 32.19 I 16 *ōlmi=šši nān=ed=i ad=īr=ġ(e)=a* „euere Waffe wird den Gegner / die Gegner schlagen" (heth. II 16 f. erg. nach III 41′ f. *nu šumenzan=[pat*$^{?}$ ^{GIŠ}TUKUL$^{\text{ḪI.A}}$-*KUNU uizz]i ḫarpanall[iuš ḫullanniwa]n dāi*; s. Neu 1995a: 198 mit Anm. 18; 1996a: 412 f.; Wilhelm im Druck: Beisp. Nr. 17)[62].

---

zeigen würde. Ich wäre dagegen geneigt, in dieser Form eher einen Instr.-Adverb. Sg. zur Nebenform *šini* (s. Haas 1988: 121, 138 Anm. 14 u. Wilhelm 1998d: 175; mit „individualisierendem Suffix" *-ni*: *ši* : *šini* „Auge" wie *tiža* : *tižni* „Herz", *idi* : *idni* „Körper", dazu Giorgieri 1998: 75 Anm. 12) zu sehen: *šin(i)=ae* „mit dem Auge". Demzufolge ist auch die Form *ši-i-na* in KBo 32.14 I 28 *pace* Wegner 1995c: 124 Anm. 31; Catsanicos 1996: 270; Neu 1996a: 137; Wilhelm 1998d: 174 kein Absolutiv Pl. (**ši=na*), was syntaktisch nicht möglich ist (doppelter Absolutiv!), sondern ein Essiv Sg. in lokativischer Funktion (*šīn(i)=a* „im Auge"); für eine Pluralform *šī=l* nach der in 2.4.1 beschriebenen Bildungsweise s. G. Wilhelm 1998d: 174 Anm. 3.

Verdächtig ist auch die in den Boğazköy-Texten oft belegte Form DINGIR^{MEŠ}-*na-a-e* (ChS I/1, S. 474), die tatsächlich an einen Instr.-Adverb. Pl. denken läßt (wieder ohne *-až-*: **en(i)=n(a)=ae* „durch die Götter"). Dabei handelt es sich aber eher um eine fehlerhafte Schreibung für die nach dem attributiven Genit. Pl. aufgenommene Instr.-Adverbialendung. Die Form ist nämlich als *en(i)=n(a)=a<ž>=(e)=ae* „durch das ... der Götter" zu emendieren (so mit Wilhelm 1998a: 179 f.).

61 Die Essivendung im Plural lautet *-až=a* und hat m.W. immer lokativische (lagebezogene) Funktion: z.B. *ašt=ugār(i)=iff=až=a* „in unserer Entsprechung" (Mit. II 76); *ōmīn(i)=n(a)=až=a* „in den Ländern" (Mit. II 96); *tiž(a)=i=až=a* „in ihrem/n Herzen" (Mit. I 78). Nur nach dem Kontext ist es möglich zu entscheiden, ob es sich dabei um einen Essiv Pl. oder eher um einen ebenfalls auf *-až=a* lautenden Dativ Pl. handelt.

62 Es sei bemerkt, daß, wie es auch aus den oben angeführten Beispielen hervorgeht, das Phänomen vor allem bei der sogenannten „Absolutiv-Essiv-Konstruktion" (s. oben § 1.3.5. 3.1) begegnet. Dabei liegt wohl eine Opposition mit der normalen „Ergativ-Absolutiv-Konstruktion" vor, in der die Pluralität des Patiens im Absolutiv dagegen ausgedrückt wird, wie die folgenden beiden Beispiele aus der Bo.Bil. zeigen:

Absol.-Essiv-Konstr.: KBo 32.19 I 4 (= KBo 32.20 IV 16′ f.) *tamr(i)=a evern(i)=a sāz=ol=ōšt=i=ri* „derjenige, der neun Könige verköstigt hat" (heth. KBo 32.19 II 3 f. erg. nach III 28′ f. [*ANA* 9 LUGA]L^{MEŠ} *kuiš adā[nna piškizz]i*); zur Syntax des Satzes s. Wilhelm im Druck: Beisp. Nr. 18.

Erg.-Absol.-Konstr.: KBo 32.19 I 6 (= KBo 32.20 IV 18′) *kīgē sāž=ol=ōž=a ēvren(i)=na* „er verköstigte drei Könige" (heth. KBo 32.19 II 6 erg. nach III 31′ *ANA* 3 LUGAL^{MEŠ} [*adanna*

2.5. Im Rahmen der *Morphophonematik* sind bestimmte phonotaktische Veränderungen zu beobachten, die bei der Kombination einiger Kasusendungen mit dem direkt vorausgehenden bzw. folgenden Suffix auftreten (s. auch § 2.3.1.2).

2.5.1. Die Genitivendung /*ve/i*/ und die Dativendung /*va*/ werden im Sg. nach /*u*/ zu /*u̯e/i*/ bzw. /*u̯a*/. Es sei betont, daß diese Veränderung in dem graphischen System des Mittani-Briefes einen konsequenten schriftlichen Niederschlag findet, wobei die Endungen nicht mit dem Keilschriftzeichen PI (*-we* bzw. *-wa*), sondern mit der Zeichenfolge -Ú-E bzw. -Ú-A wiedergegeben sind: z.B. *u-u-mi-i-in-né-e-we*(PI) „des Landes" (*ōmīn*(*i*)*=nē=ve*; Mit. I 62 u. *passim*) vs. ^{d}*A-ma-a-nu-ú-e* „des Amon" (*Amānu=u̯e*; Mit. II 77); *we-e-wa*(PI) „dir" (*fē=va*; Mit. III 58) vs. *at-ta-íw-wu-ú-a* „meinem Vater" (*atta*(*i*)*=iffu=u̯a*; Mit. III 68)[63].

2.5.2. Beim Genitiv und Dativ Sg. von Konsonantstämmen sind manchmal Assimilationen des anlautenden /*v*/ der Endung zum vorausgehenden konsonantischen Stamm zu beobachten[64]. Dasselbe geschieht beim Antritt der

---

pišk]*it*); so auch KBo 32.19 I 7 f. (= 32.20 19′ f.) *šēžē sāž=ol=ōž=a ēvren*(*i*)*=na* „er verköstigte sechs Könige".

Dazu sei auch an die oben (§ 2.3.3) bereits angeführte Stelle KBo 32.20 I 5′ *kir=*(*e*)*man*(*i*)*=a šabl*(*a/i*)*=a* „achtzehn/achtzig Jahre lang" erinnert, wobei der Essiv Sg. jedoch mit dem Zahlwort achtzehn oder achtzig gebildet ist.

63 Die Schreibung des Genitivs und des Dativs in den hurritischen Texten aus Boğazköy ist dagegen nicht einheitlich. Die hethitischen Schreiber benutzten dafür die Zeichen BI, PI_{e} ($\textit{-we}_{e}$) und PI_{i} ($\textit{-wi}_{i}$) bzw. PA und PI_{a} ($\textit{-wa}_{a}$), ohne dabei bestimmte graphematische Regeln zu berücksichtigen.

Vereinzelt sind jedoch auch in den Texten aus Boğazköy Schreibungen des Typs -U/Ú-E/I belegt, die zur Wiedergabe der allomorphischen Genitivendung /*u̯e*/ nach /*u*/ dienen: *Ḫe-e-pa-a-tu-u-i* „der Ḫebat" (*Ḫēbātu=u̯i* ChS I/1 Nr. 5 II 5, neben *Ḫebat=te* und *Ḫebapte*, s. § 2.5.2), ^{d}*Ni-kal-l*[*u*]-⌜*ú-e*⌝ „der Ningal" (*Nigallu=u̯e* ChS I/1 Nr. 5 II 8); *ta-bi-ri-pu-ú-i* „von demjenigen, der mich gegossen hat; meines Metallgießers" (*tab=i=r*(*i*)*=iffu=u̯i* KBo 32.14 I 47; zu mehreren Formen dieses Typs, die aus einem Partizip auf *-iri*, dem Possessivsuff. 1. Pers. Sg. *-iffu-* und der Genitivendung bestehen, s. Catsanicos 1996: 203 f. mit Anm. 41 und oben § 2.3.4.4). Daß solche Schreibung jedoch bei den heth. Schreibern keine strikte Regel zur Wiedergabe der Lautfolge [uu̯V] geworden ist, zeigt z.B. die Form ^{d}*Ni-ga-lu-u-pa* „zu der Ningal" (für *Nigalu=u̯a* ChS I/1 Nr. 5 III 24). Daneben begegnen auch Schreibungen -Ú-E/I, die entweder unbegründet (z.B. ^{d}UTU-⌜*ke*⌝-[*ú*]-*e* für *Šimige=ve* ChS I/1 Nr. 5 II 9) oder unklar (vielleicht sogar fehlerhaft: z.B. *ke-el-du-ú-i* ChS I/1 Nr. 41 III 6; vgl. Schwemer 1995: 87 Anm. 25) sind.

Die Graphie -U/Ú-E/I für /*u̯e/i*/ ist auch in Nuzi belegt: etwa AN.ZA.GÀR *ša* ^{m}*A-wi-lu-e*, URU *Ku-la-ad-du-ú-i* u. *Ku-lu-ud-du/tu-e*, AN.ZA.GÀR *ša* ^{m}*Mar-du-ku-e*, AN.ZA.GÀR (*ša*) *Nu-ul-lu-e-*(*na-aš-we*), URU ⌜*Ši-bu-e*⌝, URU *Ta-ri-ba-du-e*, URU *Za-al-ma-nu-e*, URU *Za-al-mu-e* (Fincke 1993: 65, 152, 173, 193, 256, 276, 342, 343 f.), neben jedoch etwa URU *Ḫa-ši-ik-ku-we*(PI), URU *Ḫé-er-ru/rù-we*(PI), URU *Ta-ku-we*(PI) (Fincke 1993: 96, 98 f., 269).

64 S. zuletzt Wilhelm 1997: 286 f. Anm. 47 (mit Beispielen und auch zu den nicht-assimilierten Formen). Abgesehen von den ältesten Sprachstufen (Ende 3. Jht.), begegnen konsonantische Stämme im Hurritischen nur bei Götter-, Orts-, Gewässer- und Personennamen.

Genitiv- und Dativendung an das Possessivsuffix 2. Pers. Sg. *-b-*[65]: z.B. ᵈ*Ḫebat* + *-ve* > ᵈ*Ḫebat=te* „der Hebat" (*passim*); *Tēššob* + *-ve* > *Tēššop=pe* „des Teššup" (*passim*); *attai* + *b* + *-va* > *attaī=p=pa* „deinem Vater" (Mit. III 58); *Igingallīš* + *-va* > *Igingallīš=ša* „für Igingalliš" (KBo 32.19 I 5 = 32.20 IV 17').

2.5.2.1. Selten ist auch die Metathese Konsonant + *-ve/-va* > *p* + Konsonant + *-e/a* belegt[66]: z.B. ᵈ*Ḫebat* + *-ve* > ᵈ*Ḫebapte* „der Ḫebat" (Gen.); ᵈ*Kužuġ* + *-va* > ᵈ*Kužupḫa* „dem Kušuḫ".

2.5.3. Beim Genitiv und Dativ Plural verschwindet normalerweise der Anlaut */v/* der Endung nach dem Pluralisator *-až-*: *-až-* + *-ve/i* > *-až=e/i*; *-až-* + *-va* > *-až=a*: z.B. *en(i)=n(a)=až=e* „der Götter" (*passim*); *en(i)=n(a)=až=a* „den Göttern" (*passim*).

Besonders in den Nuzi-Urkunden begegnen aber auch ältere Genitivformen mit erhaltenem */v/* bei Ortsnamen: z.B. AN.ZA.GÀR (*ša*) *Nu-ul-lu-e-na-aš-we* „*dimtu* derer von Nullu" (*nullu=ue=n(a)=aš=fe*; Fincke 1993: 193); URU *Pa-ḫa-(ar)-ra-aš-we-(e)* (zu akkad. *paḫāru* „Töpfer"; *paḫ(ḫ)ar(i)=r(a<na)=aš=fe*, Fincke 1993: 211). Der zuletzt angeführte Ortsname ist wohl auch in der Variante URU *Pa-aḫ-ḫ[a-ra-aš]-še* belegt, die eine assimilierte Form *-aš=še* vermuten läßt (Fincke 1993: 212).

Eine alte Dativform auf *-aš=fa* ist etwa in einer Urkunde altbabylonischer Zeit aus Šušarrā belegt: *a-na ša-al-lu-ur-ra-aš-wa* (*šallur(i)=r(a<na)=aš=fa*; Eidem 1992: 59)[67].

2.5.4. Eine Reihe phonotaktischer Veränderungen findet bei der Suffigierung von den enklitischen Personalpronomina an den Ergativ *-ž* statt:

(a) vor den Pronomina der 1. Pers Sg. *-t/-tta*, 2. Pers. Sg. *-m/-mma*, 1. Pers. Pl. *-dil/-dilla* und 3. Pers. Pl. *-l/-lla* verschwindet die Ergativendung: z.B. *še-e-ni-íw-wu-ú-ul-la-a-an* „und (*-ān*) mein Bruder (Erg.) sie (Absol.)" (*šēn(a)=iffū=(ž)=ll(a)=ān*, Mit. IV 39);

(b) die Langform des Pronomens der 3. Pers. Sg. *-nna* assimiliert sich der Ergativendung: *-ž* + *-nna* > *-šša*: z.B. *še-e-ni-íw-wu-uš-ša-a-an* „und (*-ān*) mein Bruder (Erg.) es (Absol.)" (*šēn(a)=iffu=šš(a)=ān*, Mit. III 13).

Für eine Sammlung weiterer Beispiele sei auf Farber 1971: 47 ff. verwiesen.

---

65 Im Mit. sind die Genitiv- bzw. die Dativendung in diesem Falle immer mit den Zeichen BE bzw. PA konsequent geschrieben: z.B. *še-e-na-a-ab*-BE „deines Bruders" (*šēnā=p=pe*, Mit. I 89); *at-ta-i-ip*-PA „deinem Vater" (*attaī=p=pa*, Mit. III 58). Diesselbe graphematische Regel gilt im Mit. selbstverständlich auch bei der Wiedergabe des Genitivs des auf */b/* auslautenden GNs Teššup: *Te-e-eš-šu-u-ub*-BE „des Teššup" (*Tēššōp=pe*, Mit. II 77). Was die hurritischen Texten aus Boğazköy betrifft, sind auch in diesem Falle Schwankungen bei der Verwendung der Zeichen BI, PI_E (*-we_e*) bzw. PA, PI_a (*-wa_a*) zu beobachten.

66 Darüber und zu den Belegen s. zuletzt Trémouille 1997: 227; Wilhelm 1997: 287 Anm. 47.

67 Frdl. Hinweis G. Wilhelm.

2.6. Ein spezielles *morphosyntaktisches* Phänomen, das bei den Kasusendungen stattfindet, ist die sogenannte *Suffixaufnahme*. Um eine leicht modifizierte Definition von Frans Plank zu verwenden, heißt Suffixaufnahme, daß an genitivischen oder durch das (adjektivierende) Zugehörigkeitssuffix *-ġe/-ḫḫe* und durch das Nominalisierungssuffix *-šše* sowie durch die adjektivischen Suffixe *-ni/-nni* und *-ži* markierten Attributen, in der Regel nach den anaphorischen oder kataphorischen Suffixen *-ne-* und *-na-* (sog. Artikel oder Relator), der Komplex von Numerus- und Kasussuffixen oder auch ein größeres Konglomerat von adverbialen Suffixen des Bezugsnomens wiederholt wird (Plank 1988: 81)[68]. Die Suffixaufnahme dient nämlich zur Kongruenzmarkierung der oben genannten attributiven Bildungen zu ihrem Bezugswort[69].

Für eine Sammlung mehrerer Beispiele verweise ich auf Wegner 1995b und Wilhelm 1995a. An dieser Stelle begnüge ich mich der Klarheit halber mit einem ausgewählten Beispiel für jede attributive Form (die aufgenommenen Kasussuffixe sind durch Fettdruck hervorgehoben)[70]:

(a) beim Genitiv *-ve*: *šēn(a)=iffu=ụe=ne=**ž** ašt(i)=i=**ž*** „meines Bruders seine Frau (*ašti*)" (Erg. Sg. *-ž*) Mit III 7;

(b) beim Suffix *-ġe/-ḫḫe*: *ḫatt(i)=o=ġe=ne=**va** omin(i)=ne=**va*** „dem Land (*omini*) Ḫatti" (Dat. Sg. *-va*) ChS I/1 Nr. 49 II 26;

(c) beim Suffix *-šše*: *tivê=**na** tān=ož=aụ=šše=**na*** „die Dinge (*tive*), die ich gemacht habe" (Absol. Pl. *-na*) Mit. I 73;

(d) beim Suffix *-ni/nni*: *Tušrattā=**ve** Mīttā=n(i)=ne=**ve** evr(i)=ī=**ve*** „des Tušratta, des mittanischen Herrschers" (Gen. Sg. *-ve*) Mit III 103 f.;

(e) beim Suffix *-ži*: *en(i)=n(a)=**āž=a** ... talav(i)=ō=ži=n(a)=**āž=a*** „den großen Göttern" (Dat. Pl. *-āž=a*) ChS I/1 Nr. 41 III 19 f.

Wenn der endungslose Absolutiv Sg. Bezugswort ist, hat auch das Attribut keine Endung: *šēn(a)=iffu=ụe ašti* „die Frau meines Bruders" Mit. III 21.

2.6.1. Ein abweichendes Muster zeigt der Instrumental-Adverbial auf *-ae/i*, der sich insofern anders als die anderen Kasusendungen verhält, als bei der Suffixaufnahme am Genitiv der Relator *-ne* vor der Kongruenzmarkierung regelmäßig fehlt[71]: z.B. *Teššop=p(e)=**āi*** (nicht **Teššop=pe=n(e)=āi*) *tev(e)=**āi*** „durch das Wort des Teššup" ChS I/1 Nr. 10 IV 17'.

Das Fehlen des Relators bei der Kongruenzmarkierung am Rectum hängt wohl damit zusammen, daß auch beim Regens im Instr.-Adverb. der Relator normalerweise nicht erscheint (s. oben § 2.3.1).

---

68 S. bereits auch Bush 1964: 149 ff.; Wilhelm 1983: 110 mit Anm. 51–52 und jetzt Wegner 1995b; Wilhelm 1995a; Haas, Wegner 1997: 449 f.

69 Zu den noch unklaren Verbalnomina auf *-lia/e*, die anscheinend der Suffixaufnahme unterliegen, s. oben § 2.3.4.5.

70 Die Beispiele stammen aus Wilhelm 1995.

71 Diese Auffassung, die auf Albrecht Goetze zurückgeht, wurde von E.A. Speiser und F.W. Bush kritisiert, aber jetzt von Wilhelm 1995a: 119; 1998a als richtig akzeptiert.

2.6.2. Ein ähnliches Phänomen, das allerdings weiterer Untersuchungen bedarf, wurde jüngst auch beim Ergativ im Boğazköy-Hurritischen beobachtet[72]: z.B. *futki=ž Fāzanigar=v(e)=***až** (nicht **Fāzanigar=ve=ne=ž*) *Sāzalla=***ž** „Sazalla, der Sohn des Fazanigar" KBo 32.15 IV 16 f.; *Kummi=ne=ve=***ž** (nicht **Kummi=ne=ve=ne=ž*) *Teššob=***až** *ēvr*[(*i*)=*ie*=**ž** „Teššup, Herr von Kumme" IBoT 2.51+ I 9'.19'.

Dasselbe Muster gilt z.B. auch bei folgender Form im Essiv Sg.: *el*(*i*)=**a** *faġr*(*i*)=*o*=*ž*(*i*)=**a** (nicht **faġr*(*i*)=*o*=*ž*(*i*)=*n*(*e*)=*a*) „ein schönes Fest" KBo 32.13 I 12. Auch in diesem letzten Falle hängt das Fehlen des Relators bei der Kongruenzmarkierung wohl davon ab, daß auch beim Regens im Essiv Sg. der Relator fast regelmäßig nicht auftritt.

3. Ein offenes Problem: Die Endung auf *-ne/i*.

Zusammenfassend kann man sagen, daß sich unsere Kenntnis des hurritischen Kasussystems im Vergleich zu den von Bush, Friedrich, Diakonoff und Khačikyan gebotenen Darstellungen wesentlich verbessert und erweitert hat. Dies steht mit den hervorragenden Fortschritten, die in den letzten fünfzehn Jahren von der Hurritologie erzielt wurden, völlig im Einklang. Es ist aber nicht verwunderlich, daß neben neuen, allgemein akzeptierten Einsichten auch neue strittige Frage aufgetreten sind.

Zum Schluß sei gerade ein in der heutigen Forschung vieldiskutiertes Problem erörtert, das die Funktion des von mir versuchsweise „Instrumental-Dimensional" genannten Kasus auf *-ne/i*[73] sowie sein Verhältnis einerseits mit dem gleichlautenden sog. Relator (oder Artikel), andererseits mit dem von mir als „Lokativ(-Dimensional)" bezeichneten Kasus auf *-ē* betrifft.

3.1. Ausgangspunkt ist die Erwägung G. Wilhelms[74], man könne in den auf *-ne/i* endenden Formen, die eine Richtungskomponente (Direktiv und Ablativ) haben, vielleicht den *ē*-Kasus in defektiver Schreibung isolieren, der dem Relator *-ne* suffigiert ist (*-n*(*e*)=*e*). Die Endung *-ne/i* (mit ihrer Kurzform *-n*), die mit dem urartäischen Ablativ-Instrumental *-ne* zu vergleichen ist, sei dagegen nur auf den Instrumental beschränkt. Mit anderen Worten, wäre die Funktion des Instrumentals auch morphologisch von jener der Richtungsangabe in der Weise zu differenzieren, daß hier tatsächlich das /*n*/ Bestandteil der Endung ist.

Eine andere Meinung vertritt dagegen E. Neu, der einen Ablativ-Instrumental auf *-ne* von dem Relator Sg. auf *-ne* in direktivischer und lokativischer Funktion unterscheidet[75].

---

72 Giorgieri *apud* Wilhelm 1997: 285 Anm. 43; Haas, Wegner 1997: 450. Dazu s. mit weiteren Beispielen M. Giorgieri, „Beiträge zum Boğazköy-Hurritischen I" (demnächst).

73 Wie schon oben (Anm. 22) gesagt, ist der Vokalismus der Endung nicht eindeutig, weil sie überwiegend mit dem Zeichen NI (*-ni/né*) geschrieben wird.

74 Wilhelm 1997: 284 f. Anm. 40; s. oben § 1.3.5.4.2.

75 Zuletzt Neu 1996a: *passim*; s. oben § 1.3.5.4.

3.2. Da die Existenz einer Kasusendung auf *-ne/i*, die oft in der verkürzten Form *-n* auftritt, in instrumentaler Funktion nicht bezweifelt werden kann[76], so soll untersucht werden, ob dasselbe Morphem auch eine räumliche Komponente hat und sowohl von der Endung auf *-ē*, als auch von dem Relator Sg. auf *-ne* unterschieden werden kann.

3.2.1. Wenn man zunächst die allerdings spärlichen Belege aus dem Mittani-Brief, der am besten verständlichen hurritischsprachigen Urkunde neben der Bo.Bil., in Betracht zieht, so ergibt sich, daß jene Formen, die auf *-ne/i* auslauten und in durchsichtigen Zusammenhängen stehen, eine räumliche Komponente haben, die lokativisch, direktivisch und vielleicht auch ablativisch ist. Die instrumentale Funktion ist dagegen auf Formen beschränkt, die auf *-ne=n* (Relator + Kurzform der Endung) enden und in den verständlichen Kontexten keine Funktion eines Ortskasus haben[77]:

(a) Formen auf *-ne/i* (oder *-n(e)=e*?):

(1) *Iġibe=ne/i* I 86 „von Iḫibe her(?)";
(2) *Šimīge=nē=ve=nē=mān* I 86 „und (*-mān*) in die/zur Stadt der Šimige"[78];
(3) *Šimīge=nē=ve=nē=mmaman* I 94 „in die/zur Stadt der Šimige";
(4) *šukkan(i)=ne/i ēže=ne/i* III 30 „in/von/zu(?) einer einzigen Erde"[79];
(5) *šukkan(i)=ne/i=mān šue=ne/i* III 114.118 „und in jedem einzelnen" o.ä.;
(6) *ēže=ne/i* IV 125 „auf der Erde".

(b) Formen auf *-ne=n*:

(1) *pic(i)=o=n(i)=ne=n* I 79 „in erfreulicher Weise";
(2) *faġr(i)=o=n(i)=ne=n* I 81 „in schöner Weise";
(3) wohl auch *pend(i)=o=n(i)=ne[=n]* II 87 „in rechter Weise"[80];
(4) *šukkan(i)=ne=n ... tivē=ne=n* IV 32 f. „durch ein einziges Wort".

Der Befund des Mit.-Briefes scheint daher dem Vorschlag G. Wilhelms, die Formen auf- *ne/i* in der Funktion einer Ortsangabe seien als Relator + *-ē*-Kasus

---

76 Ausschlaggebend dafür sind die zahlreichen Belege, bei denen die Endung entweder an den Relator *-ne* (überwiegend in der Kurzform *-n*: *-ne=n*) oder an ein Possessivsuffix antritt; dazu vgl. Wilhelm 1983; 1997: 285 Anm. 40.

77 Einige Beispiele sind allerdings unsicher, da sie in fragmentarischen bzw. wenig verständlichen Kontexten stehen: z.B. *tīġ=an=ōl=om=ā=šše=ni/e* Mit. III 8 (die Deutung der Form als Absolutiv Sg. mit Relator *-ne* durch Girbal 1994b: 376 finde ich schwierig zu akzeptieren).

Besonders beachtenswert ist folgender Beleg, der nach dem Sinn an die Funktion einer auf *-ne=n* endenden Form als Ortsangabe denken läßt: *Māžriā=n(i)=nē=n [ōmīn(i)]=n[ē]=n* Mit. I 10 f. (ergänzt nach Fincke, Wilhelm 1995: 138) „in/zu/aus(?) dem ägyptischen Land". Das würde meiner obigen Behauptung widersprechen, der Kontext ist aber sehr fragmentarisch, so daß eine sichere Entscheidung zur Bedeutung der Stelle nicht möglich ist.

Ein weiterer unsicherer Beleg ist *nubē=ne=n=an ḫār(i)=re(< ne)=n* Mit. I 93 „ und (*-an*) auf/durch(?) zehntausend Wege(n)", da das *-n* das enkl. Pron. 3. Pers. Sg. sein könnte.

78 Die *Plene*-Schreibung der Endung (*-né-e-*) gibt die Akzentverlängerung wieder.

79 Zum Ansatz des Wortes „einzig" als *šukkani* s. Wilhelm im Druck: Anm. 7.

80 Erg. nach Wilhelm 1995a: 124.

in defektiver Schreibung[81] zu segmentieren (*n*(*e*)=*e*), nicht zu widersprechen. Gleichwohl wäre auch die Deutung des Morphems -*ne/i* bei diesen Formen als Relator Sg. theoretisch möglich.

Die Funktion des Instrumentals ist dagegen durch die Kurzform -*n* ausgedrückt, die dem Relator suffigiert wird.

3.2.2. Wenn man aber die hurritischen Texte aus Mari und Boğazköy berücksichtigt, so steht der durch den Befund des Mit.-Briefes oben dargestellten Situation eine Reihe von Beispielen entgegen, die eindeutig beweisen, daß mindestens im älteren Hurritischen die Form des Morphems nicht nur in instrumentaler, sondern auch in direktivischer und ablativischer Funktion tatsächlich -*ne/i* oder -*n* war. Mit anderen Worten, war das /*n*/ Bestandteil der Endung und nicht der Relator, da das Morphem -*n*(*e/i*) oft in dem Komplex Relator + Endung bzw. Possessivsuffix + Endung auftritt.

Die unten angeführten Beispiele wurden auf Grund ihrer Durchsichtigkeit gewählt, obwohl mehrere Formen belegt sind, die aber in mir völlig unverständlichen bzw. zu fragmentarischen Kontexten stehen[82] (die Endung ist durch Fettdruck hervorgehoben):

(a) Ablativische Funktion:

(1) *timar*(*i*)=*re*(< *ne*)=[***n***] [*eže*=*n*]*e*=***n*** *tūr*(*i*)=*re*(< *ne*)=***n*** „von der dunklen, unteren Erde“ ChS I/5 Nr. 77 III 32′ f.[83];

(2) *Tēššob*=*a*(*ž*)=*m* *Kumme*=*ne*=***n*** „Teššup aus/von Kumme dich (-*m*)“ Mari 1: 34;

(3) *en*(*i*)=*na* *Kumme*=*ne*=***n*** „die Götter aus/von Kumme“ Mari 7 + 6: 13′;

(4) *Tēššob* ... *kešḫi*=*ne*=***n*** *pāl*=*i*=*kka*(< *i*)=*mma* „Teššup, ... aus(?) dem Thron weißt Du nicht“ KBo 12.80 + KUB 45.62 I 7 f.

(Eine weitere Form in ablativischer Funktion, die sich aber in sehr beschädigtem Kontext befindet, ist wohl *faban*(*i*)=*nē*=***n*** „aus dem Berg“ ChS I/5 Nr. 40 Rs. 34′.38′; s. Wilhelm 1983: 104).

(b) Direktivische Funktion:

(5) ChS I/1 Nr. 41 III 47 ss. *ōnnu išti pāġi*=*b*=***ane/i***=*d* *mēġ*=*a* / ... *ōnnu išti fūri*=*b*=*ada*=*d* *mēġ*=*a* „nun trete ich zu deinem Haupt / ... nun trete ich zu deinem Angesicht“ ChS I/1 Nr. 41 III 47 ss.[84];

---

[81] Die sicheren Belege des Kasus auf -*ē* zeigen immer die *Plene*-Schreibung der Endung (z.B. Mit. IV 19.49).

[82] Etwa: ChS I/1 Nr. 2 Vs. 19 *ḫavorni*=***n***; ChS I/1 Nr. 9 II 49 *ḫavōron*(*i*)=*ne*=***ne/i***. Diesen Formen ist m.E. nach dem Sinn her wohl eine räumliche Komponente zuzuschreiben.

Ein weiteres Beispiel, das kurz besprochen werden soll, ist die Form *i-ti-ia-an* ChS I/5 Nr. 2 Vs. 44′. Sie könnte sowohl als Ablativ (*idi*=*ja*=***n*(*e/i*)** „von seinem Körper“), als auch als Instrumental (*idi*=*ja*=***n*(*e/i*)** „mit seinem Körper“) oder sogar als Essiv + enkl. Pron. 3. Pers. Sg. (*id*(*i*)=*i*=*a*=*n* „es in seinem Körper“) gedeutet werden; zum ganzen Zusammenhang s. zuletzt Giorgieri 1998: 80 f.

[83] Zur richtigen Deutung dieser Stelle s. Wilhelm 1996b: 183 *contra* Neu 1996a: 247.

[84] S. mit z.T. abweichender Deutung der Stelle Wilhelm 1991b: 45. Die Form *wu*$_u$-*u-ri-pa-ta-at*, die von Wilhelm versuchsweise als *fūr*=*i*=*bada*(< *e*)=*d* „zu schauen“(?) gedeutet wird,

(6) KBo 32.13 I 25 f. *ammadi=na ēn(i)=na Tēššop=pa=lla naḫḫ=ō=žo fandi=**n*** „die uralten Götter ließ sie (*scil.* Allani) dem Teššup sich zur Rechten[85] setzen".

3.3. Diese Beispiele sind deshalb wichtig, weil sie beweisen, daß auch die Endung in ablativischer und direktivischer Funktion als *-n(e/i)* angesetzt werden kann und nicht als *-n(e)=e* segmentiert werden darf[86]. Demzufolge wäre ich geneigt, an sich nicht eindeutige, direkt nach dem Themavokal auf *-ne/i* endende Formen wie etwa *e-ep-ḫé-e-ni/né* „aus/von einem Ofen" (KBo 32.14 IV 9.10) oder *ši-i-e-ni/né* „ins Wasser/in den Fluß" (KBo 32.14 I 59) als *ēpḫē=ne/i* bzw. *šije=ne/i* zu segmentieren. So möchte ich auch folgendes, auffallendes Beispiel folgendermaßen analysieren: *timer(i)=rē(< nē) eže=ne tūr(i)=re(< ne)* „in die dunkle Erde hinab" (KBo 32.13 I 10), obwohl tatsächlich hier eine anscheinende Opposition zwischen dieser direktivischen Form auf *-nē* und dem ablativischen Beispiel (1) auf *-ne=n* vorliegt.

Gleichzeitig beweist das Beispiel (5) endgültig, daß die Endung *-ne/i* in direktivischer Funktion mit dem Relator nicht identifiziert werden kann, da sie an das Possessivsuffix 2. Pers. Sg. *-b* suffigiert ist. Bei solchen Formen handelt es sich daher nicht um Absolutive mit Relator. Das steht völlig im Einklang mit der Tatsache, daß der Relator Sg. *-ne* anscheinend mit dem Absolutiv nicht kompatibel ist[87].

3.4. Anders ist der Sachverhalt bei der lokativischen Funktion. Dafür kann ich kein sicheres Beispiel nachweisen, das den Ansatz der Lokativendung als *-ne/i* ermöglicht[88], so daß der Kasus auf *-ē* am besten als Lokativ bestimmt werden kann.

---

möchte ich eher als Direktiv auf *-da* zu *fūri=b* „dein Blick/Auge/Angesicht" erklären: *fūr=i=b=ada(=d)*. Die Form ist daher parallel zur Form *pāġi=b=**ane/i**(=d)* und bestätigt deren direktivische Funktion. Allerdings wäre eine Form *fūr=i=b=uda* zu erwarten. Ein Wechsel *a/u* ([o]?) ist aber auch anderswo in hurr. Texten aus Boğazköy belegt: z.B. *ta-la-a-wa$_a$-še* (ChS I/5 Nr. 87 IV 23) und *ta-la-ap-pa-(a-aš)-ša* (KUB 47.78 I 9'.11') statt *talav=o=ži*. Umgekehrt: *Du-ú-du-ḫe-pa* (etwa KBo 2.15 II 2.14 = KUB 25.14 I 28.46, III 10) statt *tād=o-Ḫeba*. Darüber hinaus ist es zu bemerken, daß auch die Ergativendung nach Konsonant eine Schwankung *a/u* zeigt (zu den Allomorphen *-až*, *-už* zuletzt Wilhelm 1998c: 134). Gerade bei der Form *pāġi=b=ane/i(=d)* steht die allomorphische Variante *-ane/i* mit der Pluralform *-až=ane/i* völlig im Einklang, die wohl in *faban(i)=n(a)=až=ane* belegt ist (s. Wilhelm 1983: 112). Vgl. auch die Form *Tēššob=ada* "zu dem Teššup" KBo 27.188, 7'.

85 *Pace* Neu 1996a: 264 ist das Suffix *-n* keine emphatische Partikel, sondern die Kurzform des Instrumental-Dimensionals *-ne/i* in direktivischer Funktion. In der heth. Fassung ist diese Form mit dem üblichen *Ablativus directionis* ZAG-*az* übersetzt (KBo 32.13 II 27).

86 Das ist m.E. auch sprachgeschichtlich insofern berechtigt, als die Endung *–nə* im Urartäischen nicht nur instrumentale, sondern auch ablativische Bedeutung hat und das Element *-n(i)* im hurr. Ablativ *-dan(i)* wohl gerade die hier besprochene Endung ist.

87 Wilhelm 1993: 106 ff.

88 Z.B. könnte die Form *e/i-ki-e-ni* KBo 32.14 I 49, Rs. 37.59 lokativisch als *egi=je=ni* „in seiner Mitte" gedeutet werden. Sie kann aber ebenso ablativisch als *egi=je=ni* „von seiner Mitte" oder sogar adjektivisch als *egēni* „innere" erklärt werden; darüber s. Neu 1996a: 153 f.

Die abweichende Situation des Mittani-Briefes, in dem die Endung *-n(e/i)* auf die instrumentale Funktion beschränkt scheint, könnte einfach zufällig sein, es sei denn, daß sie vielleicht etwas spekulativ dahingehend erklärt werden könnte, daß dieser Text eine jüngere Sprachstufe widerspiegelt, in der einerseits sich die ursprünglich nur lokativische Endung *-ē* zu einem allgemeinen Ortskasus in lokativischer, direktivischer (s. auch oben Anm. 12!) und ablativischer Funktion entwickelt hat, andererseits die ursprünglich dimensional-instrumentale Endung auf *-ne/i* ihre Richtungskomponente zugunsten der instrumentalen Funktion verloren hat.

Bibliographie

Bush, Frederic William

1964 „A Grammar of the Hurrian Language". Unpublished Ph.D. Dissertation, Brandeis University.

Catsanicos, Jean

1996 „L'apport de la bilingue de Ḫattuša à la lexicologie hourrite", in: J.-M. Durand (ed.), *Mari, Ébla et les Hourrites. Dix ans de travaux* (*Amurru* 1), Paris, 197–296.

Diakonoff, Igor M.

1971 *Hurrisch und Urartäisch* (MSS 6), München.

Dietrich, Manfred, und Walter Mayer

1991 „Beiträge zum Hurritischen (I). Einzelfragen zu Grammatik und Lexikon des Mitanni-Briefs", *UF* 23, 107–26.

1993 „Die Deklination des Hurritischen im Mitanni-Brief", *UF* 25, 143–56.

Eidem, Jesper

1992 *The Shemshāra Archives* 2: *The Administrative Texts*, Copenhagen 1992.

Farber, Walter

1971 „Zu einigen Enklitika im Hurrischen (Pronomen, Kopula, syntaktische Partikeln)", *Or*NS 40, 29–66.

Fincke, Jeanette

1993 *Die Orts-und Gewässernamen der Nuzi-Texte* (RGTC 10), Wiesbaden.

1995 „Beiträge zum Lexikon des Hurritischen von Nuzi", *SCCNH* 7, 5–21.

1998 „Beiträge zum Lexikon des Hurritischen von Nuzi. Teil 2", *SCCNH* 9, 41–48.

Fincke, Jeanette, und Gernot Wilhelm

1995 „Notes on the Mittani Letter. MitN no. 7/2: Mit. I 11 and 14", *SCCNH* 7, 137–38.

Friedrich, Johannes

1969 „Churritisch", in: *Altkleinasiatische Sprachen* (HdO I.2.1/2.2), Leiden/Köln, 1–30.

Giorgieri, Mauro

1998 „Die erste Beschwörung der 8. Tafel des Šalašu-Rituals", *SCCNH* 9, 71–86.

Giorgieri, Mauro, und Ingeborg Röseler

1998 „Hurritisch *kirman*(*i*): Ein Beitrag zu den hurritischen Numeralia", *SCCNH* 9, 87–94.

Giorgieri, Mauro, und Gernot Wilhelm

1995 „Privative Opposition im Syllabar der hurritischen Texte aus Boğazköy", *SCCNH* 7, 37–55.

Girbal, Christian

1988 „Der Paragraph 24 des Mittani-Briefes", *ZA* 78, 122–36.

1990 „Zur Grammatik des Mittani-Hurritischen", *ZA* 80, 93–101.

1994a „Kommentare zu einigen Stellen aus dem Mittanni-Brief", *SMEA* 34, 81–86.

1994b „Der hurritische Ausdruck für 'sowohl ... als auch ...'", *AoF* 21, 376–79.

Haas, Volkert

1988 „Die hurritisch-hethitischen Rituale der Beschwörerin Allaituraḫ(ḫ)i und ihr literarhistorischer Hintergrund", in: V. Haas (Hrsg.), *Hurriter und Hurritisch* (Xenia 21), Konstanz, 117–43.

1998 *Hurritische Ritualtermini in hethitischem Kontext* (ChS I/9), Roma.

Haas, Volkert, und Ilse Wegner

1991 Rezension zu: H. Otten, Ch. Rüster, *Die hurritisch-hethitische Bilingue und weitere Texte aus der Oberstadt* (KBo XXXII), in: *OLZ* 86, 384–91.

1996 „Stern, Tag und Segen(?) im Hurritischen", *SCCNH* 8, 285–90.

1997 „Literarische und grammatikalische Betrachtungen zu einer hurritischen Dichtung", *OLZ* 92, 437–55.

Haas, Volkert, und Gernot Wilhelm

1974 *Hurritische und luwische Riten aus Kizzuwatna* (AOATS 3), Kevelaer/ Neukirchen-Vluyn.

Khačikyan, Margarit L.

1985 *Churritskij i urartskij jazyki*, Jerevan.

Laroche, Emmanuel

1968 „Documents en langue hourrite provenant de Ras Shamra", in: *Ugaritica* 5 (MRS 16), Paris, 447–544.

Neu, Erich

1988a „Zum hurritischen 'Essiv' in der hurritisch-hethitischen Bilingue aus Ḫattuša", *Hethitica* 9, 157–70.

1988b „Varia Hurritica. Sprachliche Beobachtungen an der hurritisch-hethitischen Bilingue aus Ḫattuša", in: E. Neu/Chr. Rüster (Hrsg.), *Documentum Asiae Minoris Antiquae. Festschrift für Heinrich Otten zum 75. Geburtstag*, Wiesbaden, 235–54.

1988c *Das Hurritische: Eine altorientalische Sprache in neuem Licht* (AWL Mainz, Abhdl. der geistes- und sozialwiss. Klasse 1988/3), Mainz/ Stuttgart.

1988d „Hurritische Verbalformen auf *-ai* aus der hurritisch-hethitischen Bilingue", in: P. Kosta *et al.* (Hrsg.), *Studia indogermanica et slavica. Festgabe für Werner Thomas zum 65. Geburtstag* (Specimina Philologiae Slavicae, Suppl. 26), München, 503–13.

1988e „Zur Grammatik des Hurritischen auf der Grundlage der hurritisch-hethitischen Bilingue aus der Boğazköy-Grabungskampagne 1983", in: V. Haas (Hrsg.), *Hurriter und Hurritisch* (Xenia 21), Konstanz, 95–115.

1992 „Der hurritische Absolutiv als Ortskasus. Zur Syntax der hurritisch-hethitischen Bilingue aus Ḫattuša", in: H. Otten *et al.* (Hrsg.), *Sedat Alp'a Armağan. Festschrift für Sedat Alp. Hittite and Other Anatolian and Near Eastern Studies in Honour of Sedat Alp*, Ankara, 391–400.

1995a „Futur im Hethitischen?", in: H. Hettrich *et al.* (Hrsg.), *Verba et structurae. Festschrift für Klaus Strunk zum 65. Geburtstag*, Innsbruck, 195–202.

1995b „Miscellanea Hurritica", *SCCNH* 5, 45–52.

1996a *Das hurritische Epos der Freilassung I. Untersuchungen zu einem hurritisch-hethitischen Textensemble aus Ḫattuša* (StBoT 32), Wiesbaden.

1996b „Zu einigen Satzmustern des Hurritischen", *Hethitica* 13, 65–72.

Plank, Frans

1988 „Das Hurritische und die Sprachwissenschaft", in: V. Haas (Hrsg.), *Hurriter und Hurritisch* (Xenia 21), Konstanz, 69–93.

Salvini, Mirjo

1977 „Sui testi mitologici in lingua hurrica", *SMEA* 18, 73–93.

1988 „Die hurritischen Überlieferungen des Gilgameš-Epos und der Kešši-Erzählung", in: V. Haas (Hrsg.), *Hurriter und Hurritisch* (Xenia 21), Konstanz, 157–72.

Schwemer, Daniel

1995 „Das alttestamentliche Doppelritual *ᶜlwt wšlmym* im Horizont der hurritischen Opfertermini *ambašši* und *keldi*", *SCCNH* 7, 81–116.

Speiser, Ephraim A.

1941 *Introduction to Hurrian* (AASOR 20), New Haven.

Thureau-Dangin, François

1931 „Vocabulaires de Ras-Shamra", *Syria* 12, 225–66.

Trémouille, Marie-Claude

1997 *ᵈḪebat. Une divinité syro-anatolienne* (Eothen 7), Firenze.

Wegner, Ilse

1990 „Phonotaktischer *n*-Verlust in Jussivformen des Boğazköy-Hurritischen", *Or*NS 59 (Gs. E. von Schuler), 298–305.

1992 „Die selbständigen Personalpronomina des Hurritischen", *SMEA* 29, 228–37.

1994 „Hurritische Verba *dicendi* mit einfacher und doppelter Absolutiv-Rektion", *AoF* 21, 161–70.

1995a „Der Name der Ša(w)uška", *SCCNH* 7, 117–19.

1995b „Suffixaufnahme in Hurrian: Normal Cases and Special Cases", in: F. Plank (ed.), *Double Case. Agreement by Suffixaufnahme*, New York/Oxford, 136–47.

1995c „Die hurritischen Körperteilbezeichnungen", *ZA* 85, 116–26.

Wilhelm, Gernot

1970 *Untersuchungen zum Ḫurro-Akkadischen von Nuzi* (AOAT 9), Kevaeler/Neukirchen-Vluyn.

1980a „Der Komitativ des Urartäischen", *SMEA* 22, 133–36.

1980b *Das Archiv des Šilwa-teššup*, Heft 2, Wiesbaden.

1983 „Der hurritische Ablativ-Instrumentalis */ne/*", *ZA* 73, 96–113.

1984 „Die Inschrift auf der Statue der Tatu-Ḫepa und die hurritischen deiktischen Pronomina", *SMEA* 24, 215–22.

1985 „Hurritische Lexikographie", *Or*NS 54, 487–96.

1987 „Zum hurritischen Infinitiv in Nuzi", *SCCNH* 2, 331–38.

1988 „Gedanken zur Frühgeschichte der Hurriter und zum hurritisch-urartäischen Sprachvergleich", in: V. Haas (Hrsg.), *Hurriter und Hurritisch* (Xenia 21), Konstanz, 43–67.

1991a „A Hurrian Letter from Tell Brak", *Iraq* 53, 159–68.

1991b „Zur hurritischen Gebetsliteratur", in: D.R. Daniels *et al.* (Hrsg.), *Ernten, was man sät. Festschrift für Klaus Koch zu seinem 65. Geburtstag*, Neukirchen, 37–47.

1992a „Hurritische Lexikographie und Grammatik: Die hurritisch-hethitische Bilingue aus Boğazköy", *Or*NS 61, 122–41.

1992b Rezension zu: *Hethitica* IX, in: *ZA* 82, 156–57.

1993 „Zur Grammatik und zum Lexikon des Hurritischen", *ZA* 83, 99–118.

1995a „Suffixaufnahme in Hurrian and Urartian", in: F. Plank (ed.), *Double Case. Agreement by Suffixaufnahme*, New York/Oxford, 113–35.

1995b „Notes on the Mittani Letter. MitN no. 7/4: Mit. II 71 f.", *SCCNH* 7, 139–40.

1996a „Nuzi Note 28: *aladumma epēšu* 'begleichen; kaufen'", *SCCNH* 8, 361–64.

1996b „L'état actuel et les perspectives des études hourrites", in: J.-M. Durand (ed.), *Mari, Ébla et les Hourrites. Dix ans de travaux* (*Amurru* 1), Paris, 175–87.

1997 „Die Könige von Ebla nach der hurritischen Serie 'Freilassung'", *AoF* 24 (Fs. H. Klengel), 277–93.

1998a „Zur Suffixaufnahme beim Instrumental", *SCCNH* 9, 177–80.

1998b „Notes on the Mittani Letter. MitN no. 9/1: Mit. IV 52", *SCCNH* 9, 181–85.

1998c „Die Inschrift des Tišatal von Urkeš", in: G. Buccellati, M.K. Kelly-Buccellati, *Urkesh and the Hurrians. Studies in Honor of Lloyd Cotsen* (Bibliotheca Mesopotamica 26), Malibu, 117–43.

1998d „Hurr. *šinussi* 'Scheuklappe'?", *SCCNH* 9, 173–76.

im Druck „Die Absolutiv-Essiv-Konstruktion des Hurritischen", in: *Festschrift für R. Schmitt-Brandt*.

Tab. 1. Das Paradigma der hurritischen Kasusendungen

	Singular	Plural	Syntaktische Funktion und Bedeutung
Absolutiv	*-ø*	*-na, -l(la), -až*[1]	– Subjekt eines intrans. Verbs bzw. eines trans. nicht-ergat. Verbs („Antipassiv") bzw. eines Zustandsverbs – Objekt eines trans. ergat. Verbs – *Casus pendens* / Vokativ[2]
Ergativ	*-ž*[3] nach Konsonant: *-až, -už*[4]	*-až=u/ož*[5]	– Subjekt eines trans. ergat. Verbs
Genitiv	*-ve/i* Allomorphe[6]: *-u̯e/i, -pe, -te, -p-*	*-až=e/i* *-aš=fe*[7]	– attributive Funktion – Ausdruck der Zugehörigkeit
Dativ	*-va* Allomorphe[8]: *-u̯a, -pa*	*-až=a* *-aš=fa*[9]	– destinativische Funktion
Komitativ	*-ra* nach Konsonant: *-ura*	*-až=ura*	– „zusammen, mit"
Essiv[10]	*-a, (-ja)*[11]	*-až=a*	– Lokativ – Essiv – Destinativ – Objekt eines trans. nicht-ergat. Verbs („Antipassiv") – Adverb zu Zahladjektiven – Ausdruck des Zustandes
Assoziativ/Äquativ (auch Adverbialis)	*-nni* .... *-nn(i)=a* Kurzform[12]: *-n*	— .... *-až=onn(i)* *=a*[13]	– „wie" – „als"
Direktiv	*-da* nach Konsonant: *-uda, -ada*	*-aš=ta*	– Richtungsangabe – postpositionelle Funktion bei den Substantiven *āi/abi, edi, egi, furi* (mit Dativ)[14]
Ablativ	*-dan(i)*[15]	*-aš=tan*	– separativische Funktion – mit *tiššan, tea* „mehr als"[16]
Instrumental-Dimensional (bisher: „Ablativ-Instrumentalis")	*-ne/i*[17] Kurzform: *-n* nach Konsonant: *-ane/i*	*-až=ane/i*	– Instrumental .... – Ablativ („woher?")
Lokativ (-Dimensional) (bisher: „*e*-Kasus")	*-ē*	—	– Direktiv („wohin?") .... – Lokativ („wo?") – „in bezug auf, betreffs, über"

Instrumental-Adverbial[18]	*-ae/i*	—	– bei Nomina: instrumentale Funktion – bei Adjektiven: adverbiale Funktion – bei Numeralia: Zahladverbien (– bei Verbalnomina: gerundiale Funktion)?[19]
Äquativ[20]	*-o=ž*	—	– „wie“

ANMERKUNGEN ZU TAB. 1

1: s. § 2.4.1.
2: s. § 1.3.5.3.2 mit Anm. 17.
3: *-ž* + *-nna* (enkl. Pron. 3. Pers. Sg.) > *-šša*; *-ž* vor *-tta* (enkl. Pron. 1. Pers. Sg.), *-mma* (enkl. Pron. 2. Pers. Sg.), *-dilla* (enkl. Pron. 1. Pers. Pl.), *-lla* (enkl. Pron. 3. Pers. Pl.) fällt aus. S. § 2.5.4.
4: zu den Varianten *-až*, *-už* s. Wilhelm 1998c: 134 mit Anm. 96–97.
5: die Vokalfarbe (/*u*/ oder /*o*/) ist unbestimmbar.
6: s. § 2.3.1.2 und 2.5.1–2.
7: s. § 2.5.3.
8: s. § 2.5.1–2.
9: s. § 2.5.3.
10: zu den verschiedenen syntaktischen Funktionen des Essivs s. jetzt Wilhelm im Druck: Anm. 2. S. auch § 2.2.1, 2.3.3.2, 2.3.4.3.1, 2.4.3.
11: Eine von Speiser und Bush angesetzte lokativische Endung auf *-ja* begegnet anscheinend nur in ChS I/5 Nr. 1 Rs. 25' *ḫa-ur-ni-ia* und im Paralleltext ChS I/5 Nr. 2 Rs. 62' *ḫa-u-ru-un-ni-ia* („im/in den Himmel“).
12: nur bei der Suffixaufnahme; s. Wilhelm 1995a: 119.
13: s. z.B. KBo 32.20 I 2' *ēvren(i)=n(a)=āž=ōnn(i)=a*.
14: *ā(i)/ab(i)=i=da* „zu seinem Angesicht“ > „vor“ mit Dat.: Mit. III 98 *ên(i)=iffu=ụa â(i)=î=da* „vor meiner Gottheit“ (wörtl. „meiner Gottheit, zu ihrem Angesicht“).
ed(i)=i=da „zu seiner Person“ > „betreffs, für“ mit Dat.: Mit. III 52 f. *attaī=p=pa ed(i)=î=da* „für deinen Vater“ (wörtl. „deinem Vater, zu seiner Person“).
eg(i)=i=da „in“ mit Dat.: ChS I/1 Nr. 9 IV 16 *išḫuni=va eg(i)=i=da* „im Silber“.
fur(i)=i=da „zu seinem Blick/Auge“ > „in Anbetracht“ mit Dat.: Mit. I 91 *tažē=nē=va fur(i)=ī=da* „in Anbetracht des Geschenks“ (wörtl. „dem Geschenk, zu seinem Blick“).
15: Die Form *-dani* ist in der Bo.Bil. belegt (KBo 32.14 I 18 *a-ar-ti-i-ta-ni*: *ārd(i)=ī=dani* „von seiner Stadt“). Bei Antritt des enkl. Pron. 3. Pers. Pl. *-lla* an die Endung *-dan* tritt ein Stützvokal *-i-* zwischen den Auslaut *n* und das enkl. Pronomen: Mit. III 47 *ed(i)=ī=dan=i=lla=man*. Bei Antritt des enkl. Pron. 3. Pers. Sg. *-nna* gilt diese Regel nicht: Mit. III 46 *ed(i)=ī=da(n)=nna=man*.
16: z.B. Mit. III 50 *attard(i)=iffu=dan tišša(n)=nna=man* „mehr als meine Vorväter“.
17: s. Kapitel 3. Bei Suffigierung des *ne/i*-Kasus an Stämme, die auf *-l/n/ri* enden, gilt die folgende Assimilationsregel: *-li* + *-ne/i* > *-l(i)=le/i*; *-ni* + *-ne/i* > *-n(i)=ne/i*; *-ri* + *-ne/i* > *-r(i)=re/i* (s. z.B. KBo 32.13 I 10 *timer(i)=rē(< nē) eže=ne tūr(i)=re(< ne)* „in die dunkle Erde hinab“).
18: s. § 1.3.5.2, 2.2.1, 2.3.3.2, 2.4.2 mit Anm. 60.
19: s: § 2.3.4.1–2.
20: s. § 2.1.1. Bisher nur in Mari und Boğazköy beobachtet.

Tab. 2. Die Position der Kasusendungen in der nominalen Morphemkette

1	2	3	**4**	5
Wurzelkomplex (Wurzel + Wurzelerweiterungen + Wortbildungssuffixe + Themavokal)	Relator (Sg. *-ne*, Pl. *-na*) bzw. Possessiv- suffixe (1. Pers. *-iffu-*, 2. Pers. *-v-*, 3. Pers. *-i-*)	Pluralisator (*-až-*) (beim Relator: *-n(a)=až-*) (bei den Possessiv- suffixen: 1. Pers. *-iff=až-*, 2. Pers. *-(š)š-*, 3. Pers. *-ij=až-*)	**Kasusen- dungen**	enkl. Pronomina (z.B.: 1. Pers. Sg. *-d/-tta*, 2. Pers. Sg. *-m/-mma* 3. Pers. Sg. *-n/-nna* usw.) bzw. weitere Enklitika oder Konnektive (z.B. *-an*, *-man*, usw.) bzw. Derivationssuffix *-ġe* (nur nach dem Geni- tiv)

Tab. 2.1. Beispiele im Singular:

	1	2	3	4	5
Direkt nach dem Themavokal: *magann(i)=a* „als Geschenk" Mit. III 58	*maganni* „Geschenk"			***-a*** (Essiv)	
Nach dem Relator: *Šimīge=nē=va=mān* „und der Sonnengottheit" Mit. I 87	*Šimīge* „Sonne(ngottheit)"	*-nē-* (Relator Sg.)		***-va-*** (Dativ)	*-mān* „und"
Nach dem Possessivsuffix: *šēn(a)=iffu=šša=man* „mein Bruder ihn" Mit. II 58	*šēna* „Bruder"	*-iffu-* „mein" (Possessivsuffix 1. Pers. Sg.)		***-ž-*** (Ergativ: *-ž* + *-nna* > *-šša*)	*-nna=man* (enkl. Pron. 3. Pers. Sg., Partikel)

Tab. 2.2. Beispiele im Plural:

	1	2	3	4	5
Nach dem Relator: *en(i)=n(a)=až=a* „den Göttern" *passim*	*eni* „Gott"	*-na-* (Relator Pl.)	*-až-*	***-va*** (Dativ)	
Nach dem Possessivsuffix: *ež(e)=iff=aš=tan* „von unseren Erden" Mit. II 11	*eže* „Erde"	*-iff-* (Possessivsuffix 1. Pers.)	*-aš-*	***-tan*** (Ablativ)	

3. Die Deklination der hurritischen Pronomina

Tab. 3.1. Die selbständigen Personalpronomina
(nach Wegner 1992 mit Ergänzungen):

	1. Person	2. Person	3. Person
Singular			
Absolutiv	*ište(=n)*	*fe*	*man(n)i*
Ergativ	*iž=až*	*fe=ž*	*manu=ž*
Genitiv	*šo=ve*	*fe=ve*	—
Dativ	*šo=va*	*fe=va*	—
Direktiv	*šu=da*	—	—
Ablativ	—	—	*manu=dan*
Komitativ	*šu=ra*	—	*manu=ra*
Äquativ/Assozitiv	*šo=nn(i)=a*	—	*manu=nn(i)=a*
Plural			
Absolutiv	*šatti(=lla)*	*fe=lla*	*mane=lla*
Ergativ	*šije=ž*	*fe=ž=už*[?]	*man=ž/z=ož*
Genitiv	—	—	—
Dativ	*š(o)=až=a*[?]	*fe=ž=a*	*man=z=a*
Direktiv	*š(u)=až=uda*[?]	—	—
Komitativ	—	—	*man= ž/z=o/ura*

Tab. 3.2. Die deiktischen Pronomina
(nach Wilhelm 1984 mit Ergänzungen):

	demonstrativ		anaphorisch-kataphorisch		alternativ	
	hier	dort? ←	— dort	hier	hier	dort
Singular						
Absolutiv	*anni*		*ani*[?]	*andi*[1]	*akki*	*agi*
Ergativ	—		—	—	*akku=ž*	—
Genitiv	—		—	*andu=u̯e*	—	—
Dativ	—		*anu=u̯a*	*anu=u̯a*	—	*agu=u̯a*
Ablativ	*annu=dan*		*anu=dan*	—	*akku=dan*	—
Lok.(-Dim.)	—		—	*andū=ê*	—	—
Direktiv	—		—	—	—	*agu=da*
Plural Absolutiv	*anni=lla*		*ane=na/lla*	*andi=lla*	*akki=lla*	—

Anmerkungen zu Tab. 3

1: Im Althurritischen (Tišatal-Inschrift, Ende 3. Jht.) befindet sich die Form *'alli* als anaphorisches Pronomen (Wilhelm 1998c: 133 f.).

The Hurrian Verb Revisited

MARGARIT L. KHAČIKYAN
Yerevan, Armenia

The understanding of the Hurrian verbal system has progressed substantially over the past decade. This article takes into account the recently published Hurro-Hittite bilingual along with the most recent scholarship on the verbal system to provide a new description of the structure of the Hurrian verbal system.

The Hurrian verbal system is comprised of the following subsystems:

- Ergative conjugation
- Non-ergative (absolutive) conjugation
- Oblique moods
- Participles and gerunds

The ergative conjugation was characteristic of transitive verbs of the indicative mood. It was formed by attaching personal endings of the ergative range, which originated as possessive pronouns, cf. Table I.

TABLE I

		Ergative endings	Possessive pronouns
Sg.	1p.	*-af(fu)/-o*	*-iff(u)*
	2p.	*-o/u/w*	*-v*
	3p.	*-(y)a* [a)]	*-ye/a-*
Pl.	1p.	*-af-ša*	*-iff-aš*
	2p.	*-aššu*	*-šši-*
	3p.	*-d-a* [b)]	*-iy-aš*

a) *-ya* was used only in the forms of the present tense (*paliya* "he knows," Mit. I_{74}; *kadiya* "he says" KBo 32 11 IV_{13}); *-a* is attested in the forms of the past and the future tenses, as well as in a number of forms of the

Studies on the Civilization and Culture of Nuzi and the Hurrians - 10

present tense (*ar-ož-a* "he gave," Mit. I_{46}; *ar-ed-a* "he will give," *ibid.*, I_{106}; *šidar-a* "he curses," KBo 32 14 I_{11}).

b) *favanažuš ad-o-d-a šewenažuž nud-o-d-a Šimigenewena šinde šalarde* "the mountains are *ad*-ing, the rivers are *nud*-ing Šimige's seven daughters," *Mari* 5_{8-11}.

The case of the subject in the ergative conjugation was the ergative, that of the object—the absolutive.[1] The absolutive conjugation, unlike the ergative one, covered the entire spectrum of Hurrian verbs:

1) transitives, with the subject in ergative and the object in absolutive (*kazi tavalle-š...tavašt-o-m* "a smith cast a jug," KBo 32 14 I_{42-43});
2) semantically transitives, with the subject in absolutive and the object in essive (*el-a ... tant-i-b ...* ᵈ*Allani* "Allani made a feast (lit.: as a feast)," *ibid.*, 13 I_{12}) or with no object at all (*pašš-i-n-an eniffe šuda* "my brother sends to me," Mit. III_{112-13});
3) semantically middle verbs *ḫimzatḫož-i* ᵈ*Allani* "Allani girded up," KBo 13 I_{10}; *Megi* ... ᵈ*Teššoffa ugulgari uri* "Megi bent down in front of Teššob's feet," *ibid.*, 15 IV_{10});
4) intransitives (*naḫḫab* ᵈ*Teššob* ... *kešḫine* "Teššob sat down on the throne," *ibid.*, 13 I_4);
5) verbs of state (*favani ḫažimai paru Ištaniy(e)da* "on hearing [this] the mountain felt ill in his heart"), *ibid.* 14 I_8).

The absolutive conjugation was formed by adding the personal suffixes of the absolutive range (cf. Table II) to the verbal stem, ending in the thematic vowels *-a*, *-i*, *-o* (denoted by the sign U),[2] *-u* (graph Ú).

TABLE II

	Singular	Plural
1p.	*-t(ta/e)*	*-di-l(la)*
2p.	*-m(ma)/-b*[a)]	*-ppa*
3p.	*-m/b*[b)], *-n(na)*	*-l(la)*

---

1 An exception to this rule is the verb *kad-*, "to say," the subject of which, as well as the object, stands in the absolutive case: ᵈ*Teššoffa tiwena* ᵈ*[Išḫara] [ka]diya* "Išḫara says words to Teššob," KBo 32 11 $IV_{12'-13'}$.

2 On the quality of this vowel, cf. G. Wilhelm, "Zum hurritischen Verbalsystem," in: *Texte, Sätze, Wörter und Moneme* (Festschrift für Klaus Heger zum 65. Geburtstag, Heidelberg 1992) 667.

a) The expression of the 2nd and 3rd person pronouns by the same graphemes (*b/m*) attests to their labial character, but does not allow us to obtain more information on their phonetics.

b) The 3rd person pronoun *-m/b* is attested in archaic dialects and in personal names.

The use of this pronoun was different from that of all the other absolutive pronouns that functioned as subjects of intransitive and objects of transitive verbs: it was used as the subject of transitive and intransitive verbs, but is not attested with verbs of state. This circumstance allows us to assume that this pronoun expressed the subject of action as opposed to the subject of state and, hence, should be considered as a residual feature, typical of the active typology.[3] The residual and recessive character of this pronoun is corroborated by the fact that it is sometimes omitted in the Hurro-Hittite bilingual (*šeḫl-o* "he entered the palace," KBo 32 13 I_1; *naw-a* "he is grazing/grazes," *ibid.*, 14 I_{26}, *ḫill-i* "he says," *ibid.*, 14 IV_{38}.

The alternation *-b/-m* not only in transitive, but also in intransitive forms argues against distinguishing between a subject pronoun *-b* ("he") and a bipolar pronoun *-m* ("he-him").[4]

From the fact that verbs with the pronominal ending *-b/m* are attested with both singular and plural subjects, E. Neu concluded that it was indifferent to number.[5] However, taking into consideration that

a) *-b/m* was absent in the forms with the pluralizing suffix -(*i*)*d*- (*kiwud-o*, KBo 32 13 I_2, *naḫed-o*, *ibid.*, 14 I_{34}) and

b) agreement in number was often optional in archaic languages (cf. *ir* [sg.] *bebti-p* [pl.] "they rebelled," DB II_2, in Elamite),

we are inclined to interpret it as an originally singular pronoun, which was neutralized in certain positions.

The thematic vowel *-a* was used, as a rule, with semantically intransitive verbs (*un-a* "he comes," Mit. II_{14}; *ittošt-a* "he went," *ibid.*, I_{90}; *naḫḫ-a-b* "he sat down," KBo 32 14 IV_{25}, *teḫešt-a-b* "he grew up," *ibid.*, IV_3; *ḫaban-a-b* "he set off," *ibid.*, I_3). It is also attested in the Hurro-Hittite bilingual:

a) in a verb of middle semantics: *naw-a* "it grazes," KBo 32 14 I_{26}, and

b) in some forms which expressed state: *ḫenz-a* "(if) he is in trouble," *ibid.*, 15 I_5'; *fett-a* "(if) he is hungry," *ibid.*, $I_{8'}$.[6]

---

[3] The active typology is characterized by the opposition of verbs of action to verbs of state, cf. G.A. Klimov, *Tipologia iazykov aktivnogo stroia* (Moscow 1977) 84.

[4] On the interpretation of the pronoun *-m* as a bipolar grammeme, cf. G. Wilhelm, *op. cit.*, 666.

[5] E. Neu, *Das Hurritische: Eine altorientalische Sprache in neuen Licht* (Akademie der Wissenschaften und der Literatur, Abhandl. der geistes- und sozialwiss. Klasse Jg. 1988/3; Mainz-Stuttgart 1988) 7 n. 11.

[6] Were it not for the pronoun *-b* being present in the form *tapš-ab* (meaning unknown),

The thematic vowel *-i-* was typical

a) of detransitivized verbs of the antipassive construction, that is of semantically transitive verbs, the direct object of which was either omitted or stood in essive, whereas the subject was in absolutive: *farinina muž-i-b* "the bakers tidied up," KBo 32 13 I_{21}; *fandarinina ag-i-b neḫirna* "the cooks brought (of) brisket," *ibid.*, 13 I_{22}.

b) of semantically reflexive or middle verbs: *ḫimzatḫož-i* "she girded up," *ibid.*, 13 I_{10}; *ugulgar-i* "he bent down," *ibid.*, 15 IV_{10}.

Cases are attested when the subject and the object of the verb with the thematic vowel *-i-* stood in the absolutive.

The vowel *-i-* (or, maybe, *-e*?) is attested also at the end of some verbs of state: *manni/e* "he is," *tuppi/e* "are/is available/at (his) disposal," Mit. III_{115}.

The thematic vowel *-o-* was used in transitive forms with the subject in ergative and the object in absolutive: *Kumarwene-ž un-o-b* "Kumarve gave birth (to you)," KUB XLVII 78 I_{14}. This vowel is attested only in Old Hurrian. It fell into disuse in later dialects.

Among the forms ending in C*u* there are also verbs of state: *paru* "he felt ill," KBo 32 14 I_8. Thus, the forms expressing state were formed by means of the vowels *-i*, *-a* and the graph. C*u*. The presence of markers of the intransitive and detransitivized verbs *-a-* and *-i-* in verbs of state is quite normal for Hurrian, which was a language of the ergative typology. The use of the transitive marker *-o-*, on the other hand, was absolutely impossible in the frames of the ergative or active typology. Hence, the vowel *u* (evidently [*u*]) attested in the verbs of state cannot be identical to the thematic vowel present in transitive forms.

An identical distribution of thematic vowels seems to be found in personal names of the type verb-noun. Of these names the easiest to interpret are those of types:

a) V-*a-b*-DN/N: *Un-a-b-elle* "the sister came," *Un-a-b-Teššob* "Teššob came" and

b) V-*i-b*-DN/N: *Tad-i-b-Teššob* "Teššob loves/loved," *Ar-i-b-Ebla* "Ebla gave."

Less transparent is the structure of names with the thematic vowel *-o-* (*Haš-o-m-allai*, *Šar-o-m-elle*).

As sentences with transitive verbs ending in *-o-* were tripartite and implied the presence of both the subject and the object (the agent and the goal), and as the DNs were evidently the subjects of these sentences, their objects were expressed by the pronominal element *-m/b*. This element could not be the 3rd person pronoun *-m/b*, since, being a relic of the active stage of the language (cf.

---

parallel to *ḫenza*, these forms might be interpreted as those of the oblique mood in *-ai/e>â*. As to the presence of the subject of action in *tabš-a-b* (presumably a verb of state), it may be explained by the fact that *tabšab* was conjugated here according to the pattern of intransitive verbs, which usually ended in *-b*.

supra), this pronoun functioned as the active subject of the sentence. For this reason, we are inclined to interpret the element *-m/b* as the 2nd person pronoun and translate these forms as "the Lady heard you," "the sister wanted you."[7]

In some PNs with the thematic vowel *-u* in the verbal member this vowel may be interpreted as the marker of state [*-u-*]: *Madu(š)-Šawuška* "wise is Šawuška(?)."

In the PN cited above, as well as in a number of others, the verbal member ended in *-š: Hai-š-Teššob* "Teššob-heard." This formant seems to be identical to the element *-š*, which is attested in the Sumerian-Hurrian bilingual in verbal forms ending in –VšV.[8] The latter corresponded to the 3rd person singular forms of the Sumerian version: [in]-gar = *ki-ba-šu* "he put" Rs. 8+11 II_{31}, in-dadag = *ša-ḫa-la-šu* "he cleaned," *ibid.* II 31. The 3rd person plural verbs in the Sumerian version of this text were translated into Hurrian by forms ending in the 3rd person absolutive pronominal suffix *-lV*: in-gar-e-meš = II-*ša-*[*la*] "they put," I_{32}; in-dadag-e-meš = II-*ša-*[*la*] "they cleaned," *ibid.* II_{32}.

In the same text, Hurrian forms ending in –VšV-*te* are also attested. These forms are parallel to the Sumerian verbs with the suffix *mu-*. As the latter expressed an action oriented towards the locutor, the Hurrian particle *-te* may be interpreted as the 1st person singular personal suffix *-tta.*[9]

The meaning of the element *-š* is unknown. But it is quite clear that this element and the pronoun *-b* in the verbal members of PNs are comparable. As one of the functions of the personal pronominal suffixes may be defined as correlative/copulative (they correlated the subject with the predicate), it is possible that *-š* was a correlative particle, indifferent to person and number. This particle should probably be connected with the correlative-nominalizing particle *-šše-*, by means of which the verb of the subordinate clause was substantivized and agreed with the antecedent: *tiwe-na tanoža-šše-na* "the things that I have done," Mit. I_{73}.

The distribution of the thematic vowels presented above is characteristic only of the affirmative forms of the absolutive conjugation. The situation is different with the negative forms. Of the negative suffixes *-ud-*, *-ma, w*(*a*)-, and -*VkkV* (*mannuwur* "is not" KBo 14 I_{17}; *fur-ud-o-m* "he does not/did not see," *ibid.*, I_{38}; *kuliya-ma* "he does not say," Mit. $II_{105, 106}$; *ur-ikki* "(we) do not want," *ibid.*, II_{74}), we shall consider -*VkkV*, which is of special interest for our purposes. This suffix is attested in two variants: *-ikki* and *-ukku/a* (*u* is changed into *a*

---

7 A different interpretation of these names, based on the assumption that *-m* was a 3rd person bipolar pronoun, different from *-b* ("he-him"), was presented by G. Wilhelm, *op. cit.*, 667.

8 Cf. the author's article "On Some Models in Hurrian Onomastics," *SCCNH* 2 (1987) 154.

9 The identification of the particle *-te* with *-t*(*ta*) seems more convincing than the author's former attempt to ascribe to it a centripetal function, cf. "Towards the Categories of Aspect and Version in Hurro-Urartian," *ZA* 74 (1984) 96.

before the personal suffixes of the absolutive range: *mann-ukka-lla-* "they are not," Mit. IV_2).

The vocalization *-ikki* was typical of the verbs with the thematic vowel *-i-* (*an-ikki* "[the heart] doesn't rejoice," KBo 32 15 $I_{22', 23'}$), whereas *-ukku/a* was particular to those that had the vowels *-a-* or *-u-* in the affirmative forms (*unukka-lla* "they do not come" Mit. I_3, *tupp-ukku* "[the tablets] are not available," *ibid.*, III_{45}). The fact that the vowel *-u-* is present in the negative forms of verbs of state (with the thematic vowel *-u-*), as well as in intransitive verbs (with the vowel *-a-*), indicates that the marker of state *-u-* was generalized in the negative forms as the marker of intransitive, but not detransitivized(!) verbs. The latter had preserved their thematic vowel *-i-* in the negative forms.

Such merging of verbs of state with intransitive verbs is quite normal for an ergative language, unlike those of the active typology with their opposition action : state.

The distribution of the thematic vowels is different in the imperative mood, as well. The imperative was expressed in the verbal stem with the thematic vowels *-i, -a, -u,*[10] followed occasionally by the 2nd person singular pronominal suffix *-b/m*.

The thematic vowel *-a-* is attested in the intransitive verbs (*una-mma* "may you come," KBo 21 33 I_{24}; *šalḫol-a* "listen!," KBo 32 14 IV_7), *-i-* in the transitives (*ar-i* "give!," Mit. I_{51}) and *-u-* in verbs of state (*kelu-mma* "may you be well," KUB 32 44 Vs. II_2), of involuntary action (*kud-u* "may it fall down," KBo 32 14 I_{57}), and in those of state resulting from a transitive action, i.e., in forms of passive semantics (*kir-u-n*(*na*) "may he/she be set free," *ibid.*, 15 $IV_{2,3}$; *pind-u-n* "may she be sent off," *ibid.*, IV 6).[11]

The plural imperative was expressed by means of the suffix *-š*: *kole-š* "leave!" (pl.), KBo 32 11 IV_6, *sammalaštu-š* "may they be broken," *ibid.*, 14 I_{58}. This suffix is evidently connected with the element -š- of the pluralizing suffix *–aš/ša* and should not be confused with the correlative particle *-š* discussed above.

Thus, the imperative forms reveal a distinction between (a) transitive and detransitivized verbs, (b) intransitive verbs, and (c) verbs of state.

Oblique moods in Hurrian were formed by means of the suffixes -i/*e*, *-ai/e*, and *-i/ewa* often combined with the element *-l*(*l*)-: *talmašt-i-l-i* "may I glorify," KBo 32 11 I_2; *ittid-i/e-n* "may they come," Mit. III_{23}; (*ai*) ... *id-i-l-â*(<*ai*)*-nni* "if only (Teššob) would break (it)," KBo 32 14 I_6; *fež-ewa* "if (an enemy) happens to be," Mit. IV_{112}.

The element *-l*(*l*) was usually preceded by the vowels *-i-* or *-u-*. But it is often unclear whether we are dealing with the thematic vowel followed by *-l*(*l*)-, or

---

10 Cf. G. Wilhelm, "Der hurritische Ablativ-Instrumentalis /ne/," *ZA* 73 (1983) 108ff. The author's objections to Wilhelm's conception on this issue in *Khurritskii i urartskii iazyki*, (Yerevan 1985) 108, are not convincing.

11 These forms might be interpreted as active forms with the thematic vowel *-o-*: "let (him/her) free," "send (her) off." But since the transitive imperative was expressed by the vowel *-i-*, it seems more appropriate to interpret these forms as passives.

the suffixes *-il-* or *-ol-*. A form with the thematic vowel *-o-* before the cohortative suffix *-i/e-*, instead of *-i* in later dialects, is attested in the Tišadal-inscription: *tašp-o-i/e/n* "may (the god) annihilate (him)," Urk_{14}.

Participles in Hurrian were formed by means of the following suffixes:

a) *-ire*, used for building active participles: *pa-ire* "builder," *tav-ire* "smith."

b) *-aure*, used for building passive participles: *ḫuž-aure* "tied up, captured."[12]

c) *-ure*: *kiw-ure* "placed(?)." The function of this suffix is not quite clear, since participles ending in *-ure* are attested in obscure contexts. However, as this suffix is also attested in the negative participle of the verb *manni/e* "to be" (*mannuwur* "not being"), we may assume that, at least in the Hurro-Hittite bilingual, this suffix was used for forming participles from verbs of state, as well as passive participles (cf. the imperative forms, where *-u-* is attested in verbs of state, of involuntary action, as well as in passive forms).

d) *-iliya-*, used for building passive participles: *pailiya-* "built," *šeduiliya-* "reared." The passive semantics in this suffix was, perhaps, expressed by the element *-l-* as opposed to *-r-* in *-ire*.

In Hurrian adverbial participles/gerunds with the suffixes *-uwa*, *-mai*, and *-kai* are attested: *kazi taballiž ... tavaštom ... agurna agul-uwa* "the smith cast a jug ... having glossed (it) with gloss(?)," KBo 32 14 I_{42-44}; *tabrenni ḫaž-i-mai paru ištaniy(e)da* "on hearing (this) the smith felt ill in his heart," *ibid.*, 10_{50-51}; *tunidu pudangai* (*<pud-an-i-kai?*) *abi ewriwa* "they succeeded to present him before his master," *ibid.*, 14_{17-18}.

The forms with the suffix *-uwa* do not seem to reveal any thematic vowels. In participles with *-mai*, on the contrary, this suffix is preceded by the vowel *-i-* in the forms of transitive—or middle semantics (*ḫaž-i-mai* "on hearing," KBo 32 14 I_{50}; *kunz-i-mai* "bending down," *ibid.*, 15 IV_{13}) and *-u-* in those of intransitive semantics (*faž-u-mai* "coming in," *ibid.*, 13 I_3).

Thus, of the four thematic vowels revealed in Old Hurrian dialects, three belong to the sphere of verbs of action (transitive, intransitive, detransitivized) and one to that of verbs of state.

In all probability, in the pre-ergative period of Hurrian, when the opposition action vs. state was dominant, the thematic vowel *-o-* expressed a centrifugal action, the vowel *-i-* a centripetal action,[13] *-a-* was the marker of *verba movendi*, and *-u-* that of the verbs of state.

The change in the typology of Hurrian from active to ergative resulted in blurring the distinction among the aforementioned subgroups of verbs, cf. the

---

12 Cf. G. Wilhelm, "Gedanken zur Frühgeschichte der Hurriter und zum hurritisch-urartäischen Sprachvergleich," Xenia 21 (1988) 57–63.

13 The category of version with the opposition of extrovert (centrifugal) and introvert (centripetal) action was typical of languages of active typology, cf. G.A. Klimov, *op. cit.*, 141ff. The data provided by the Hurro-Hittite bilingual argue against the author's former

presence of the intransitive marker *-a-* in verbs with middle semantics, instead of the marker *-i-* (*naw-a* "it grazes"), or of the marker of state *-u-* in the negative forms of the intransitive verbs, instead of the marker *-a-* (*un-u-kkallan* "they do not come"), or of the marker of the detransitivized or middle verbs *-i-* in transitive imperatives, instead of *-o-* (*ar-i* "give!").

The late Hurrian dialects distinguished three tenses: the present tense with no marker, the past tense, denoted by the suffix *-ož-*, and the future with the marker *-ed-*: *tad-av* "I love," Mit. I_{75}; *un-a* "he comes," *ibid.*, II_{14}; *ar-ož-av* "I gave," *ibid.*, III_{2}; *ar-ed-a* "he will give," *ibid.*, I_{106}.

The situation was different in the Old Hurrian dialects. In the dialect of the Hurro-Hittite bilingual, forms of the present and future (but not the past) tenses of the ergative conjugation are attested: *kad-iya* "he says" KBo 11 $I_{11,12}$; *paḫ-ed-av* "I shall destroy," *ibid.*, 19 I_{24}.

The past tense of transitive verbs was expressed by forms of the absolutive conjugation: *ulan-o-m* "(the dog) ate," KBo 32 14 $IV_{12,24}$; *pašt-o-m* "he built," *ibid.*, 14 IV_{23}. The absolutive conjugation in this dialect does not reveal temporal distinctions. The forms with no special temporal markers functioned as those of the present and past tense: *nav-a* "(it) grazes," *ibid.*, 14 I 26; *naḫḫ-a-b* "he sat down," *ibid.*, 13 I_{4}.

The future tense was expressed by forms of oblique moods, which were translated into Hittite by forms of the present-future tense: *kadul-(i)-i/e* = *memiškimi* "I will tell," *ibid.*, 14 IV/III_{21}; *kapp-i-l-ewa-š* = *piweni* "we will pour," *ibid.*, 15 $I/I_{19'}$.

The suffix *-ož-* (the past tense marker in later dialects) was, as a rule, absent in the forms, which corresponded to the Hittite past tense forms. However, it is attested in a few forms of the absolutive conjugation: *šiyal-ož-o-m* "(he) put," *ibid.*, 14 IV_{56}; *ḫimzatḫ-ož-i* "(Allani)" girded up," *ibid.*, 13 I_{10}.

From this we may conclude that the suffix *-ož-* was not originally a temporal marker. Its presence, as well as the occasional absence of the subject marker *-b/m* in forms of the absolutive conjugation (*nav-a*, *ḫimzatḫ-ož-i*, *ugulgar-i*), facilitates the interpretation of the form *naḫḫožo* "she seated (them)" KBo 32 13 I_{26}. It is seemingly an absolutive conjugation form of the transitive verb *naḫḫož-* with the subject marker *-b/m* omitted.[14]

From this survey, it is obvious that a developed system of tenses was not peculiar to the Old Hurrian dialects, especially in the sphere of the absolutive conjugation. This is quite normal since the category of tenses was not typical of languages of the active typology[15] and since the absolutive conjugation was older than the ergative and reflected the active stage of Hurrian (or, rather,

---

attempt to ascribe to the thematic vowels *-o-* and *-i-* an aspectual distinction, cf. *ZA* 74 (1984) 92–95.

14 The absence of *-b/m* in this form may have resulted from the labial character of the initial consonant of the following word (*fandin*).

15 Cf. G.A. Klimov, *op. cit.*, 144.

Proto-Hurrian)—cf. the residual use of *-b/m* as the subject of both transitive and intransitive action.[16]

It should, however, be noted that in the Hurro-Hittite bilingual the temporal system was not completely formed in the block of the ergative conjugation, either. This follows from the fact that forms with the future tense suffix *-ed-* and those with the suffix –V*št*- are attested in parallel sentences: … *paḫ-ed-av* … *ḫub-ušt-av* "I shall destroy … I shall break," KBo 19 $I_{24...27}$. Therefore, perhaps we may ascribe to –V*št*- the function of a future tense marker. Yet, the fact that this suffix is attested in forms of the past tense (*pa-ašt-o-m* "he built," *ibid.*, 14 IV 23) argues against its being a future tense formant. It is likely that this suffix belonged to the sphere of Aktionsart formants and was semantically close to the suffix *-ed-*. The latter was later reinterpreted as a future tense marker. Obviously the suffix *-ož-* underwent a similar development, functioning as the past tense formant.

16 Note that in Urartian, the verbal system of which was closer to that of Old Hurrian (cf. the presence of the thematic vowel *-o-* in transitive verbs and the use of the personal suffix *-be* in intransitives: *amašt-o-ve* "I set on fire," *nun-a-be* "he came"), the suffix *-ož-* was absent.

A New Trilingual Vocabulary from Ras Shamra and the Relationship between Hurrian and Urartian

BÉATRICE ANDRÉ-SALVINI and MIRJO SALVINI
Paris / Rome

Our recent publication of the trilingual vocabulary, RS 94-2939 (*SCCNH* 9 [1998] 3–40) has provided ca. one hundred Hurrian entries with translations into Sumerian and Akkadian. Of these, 54 items were added to the existing Hurrian lexicon. The current article, utilizing newly published or collated Urartian inscriptions, examines new data for Hurrian lexicography with particular emphasis on their relationship to Urartian.

In 1994, during the archaeological campaign of the French mission at Ras Shamra/Ugarit, an incomplete cuneiform tablet inscribed with a trilingual vocabulary of the type S^{a}[1] was discovered. The tablet is 12.7 cm high, 17.8 cm wide, and 4.5 cm thick. Its shape and convexity show that it actually represents half of the original tablet. The text presents five columns, three on the obverse and two on the reverse; it is certain that it had also a sixth column, but the inscribed part has been lost with the missing part of the tablet.

Recently we published the text edition,[2] and wish to present here a few remarks showing the importance of the new document, which, to a large degree, can be integrated within the already known "Syllabary A Vocabulary" published twelve years ago by John Huehnergard.[3]

In the context of the XLVe Rencontre assyriologique internationale and its Hurritological section, our attention turns mainly to the acquisition of new data for the lexicography of Hurrian and particularly to its relationship to Urartian. The morphology and structure of both languages have been investigated extensively in recent years (e.g., the phenomena of ergativity[4] and "Suffixaufnahme"[5]) and will not be the subject of this paper.

---

1 Cf. MSL III 51–87.

2 Béatrice André-Salvini et Mirjo Salvini, "Un nouveau vocabulaire trilingue sumérien-akkadien-hourrite de Ras Shamra," *SCCNH* 9 (1998) 3–40. See also *idem*, SMEA 41/1 (1999) 145–46.

3 John Huehnergard, *Ugaritic Vocabulary in Syllabic Transcription* (HSS 32), Atlanta, 1987.

4 G. Steiner, "The Intransitive-passival Conception of the Verb in Languages of the Ancient Near East," in: *Ergativity. Towards a Theory of Grammatical Relations* (ed. by Frans

Studies on the Civilization and Culture of Nuzi and the Hurrians - 10

The new text from Ugarit offers approximately one hundred entries with Sumerian and Akkadian translations of Hurrian words, the majority of which were not attested in existing exemplars of the S^a polyglot vocabulary. Some correspondences are missing in lacuna so that we do not have all the values of the new Hurrian words. Nevertheless, thanks to the new tablet, the increase in both our Hurrian thesaurus and vocabulary is very significant.

A noteworthy aspect is that the vocabulary confirms some meanings that were previously conjectured with the combinatory method of linguistic analysis. It is the case, for instance, of the Hurrian word *irate*, which corresponds in I 11 to Sumerian MUŠEN and to Akkadian *iṣṣūru* "bird";[6] this is a happy solution to an unfortunate circumstance of the Hurrian-Hittite bilingual texts from Boğazköy, where the Hittite correspondence of Hurrian *erate* is missing. But Volkert Haas and Ilse Wegner,[7] the Hurritologists of Berlin, had already guessed the correct meaning of *erate* on two different occasions on the basis of an *itkalzi*-text:[8] *naunneš ḫawurunnibineššа eratineš* seems to relate "birds" with the "pastures of heaven."

We note also the word for "dog," Hurrian *erwi*, which translates Sumerian UR and Akkadian *kalbu* (II 11). The new Ras Shamra tablet thus confirms the data of the Boğazköy bilingual, in which Hurrian *erbi* corresponds to UR.GI_7,[9] thereby enabling us to recognize the same word in the Hurrian tale of the hunter Kešši (dat. pl. *e-er-bi-i-na-a-ša*, KUB XLVII 2 lk. Rd. 4). In connection with this, it is worthy of note that the Hurrian word for hunter, *kebli*,[10] in the same cycle of texts, was independently established by M. Salvini with the combinatory method and by E. Neu by interpretation of the bilingual. Such a coincidence of results between the two methods was satisfactorily established at the hurritological symposium of Konstanz.[11]

Another case is *ḫani*, the Hurrian word for "baby," which corresponds in our text to Akkadian *š]e-ru* (= *šerru*).[12] This confirms the interpretation obtained

---

Plank), London-New York etc.: Academic Press, 1979, 185–216; F. Plank, "Das Hurritische und die Sprachwissenschaft," in: V. Haas (ed.), *Hurriter und Hurritisch* (Xenia 21), Konstanz: Universitätsverlag, 1988, 69–93.

5 Cf. G. Wilhelm, "Suffixaufnahme in Hurrian and Urartian," in: Frans Plank (ed.), *Double Case Agreement by Suffixaufnahme*, New York-London: Oxford University Press, 1995, 113–35.

6 RS 94-2939, I 11: MUŠEN = *iṣ-ṣú-ru* = *i-ra-te*.

7 V. Haas, *ZA* 79 (1989) 266; I. Wegner, *Or*NS 59 (1990) 303 n. 13.

8 *ChS* I/1, no. 3, obv. 21f.

9 KBo XXXII 14 IV 13 *e-er-bi* (Hurr.) = III 13 UR.GI_7-aš (Hitt.), E. Neu, StBoT 32, 1966, 170–71.

10 *ke-e-eb-li*, KUB XLVII 1 (Kešši) I 10′.

11 V. Haas (ed.) *Hurriter und Hurritisch* (Xenia 21), Konstanz: Universitätsverlag, 1988: cf. E. Neu, p. 102 and n. 18; M. Salvini, *ibid*. 164.

12 RS 94-2939, II 22: [= *š]e-ru* = *ḫa-a-ni*.

by the combinatory method by Chr. Girbal, who translated *ḫani* as "child" in a fragment of the Ullikummi myth.[13]

Confirmation of an important morphological acquisition concerns the negative value inherent to the nominal suffix *-ubad-*, which was first analyzed by Emmanuel Laroche.[14] Some scholars (Neu, Wegner, and now Giorgieri[15]) interpreted the substantives with this suffix to have a negative meaning. The entry ḪUL = *masku* = *nirupate*[16] now shows their analyses to be correct.

The verb *zul=ud=umme* = Akkadian *paṭāru* "to deliver"[17] is a good example of a different negation suffix, *-ud-*, which occurs in verbs (e.g., *am=ud-* "not to reach," *bur=ud-* "not to see") and was determined thanks to the Hurrian-Hittite Boğazköy bilingual.[18]

The entry in II 10 ḪAL = *ba-a-ru* = *wu-ru-ul-li-ni*, which corresponds to S[a] No. 46.2?,[19] gives us the name of the diviner and confirms also for Hurrian the etymological connection between the profession *bārû* and the verb *barû*, "to look upon." In Hurrian the family of words is larger, since, besides the verbal root *wur-* "to look," we have also *wu-ri* "the eye:" col. II 1 IGI = *e-nu* (i.e., Akkadian *īnu*, Assyrian *ēnu*), and the well-known *wuri* "sight." The morphological analysis of this word is *wur=ul(l)=i=nni* and it is analogous to other substantives designating professions, such as *urb=ar=i=nni* "butcher" and *itt=ar=a=nni* "runner, courier."[20] The function of the suffix *-ul-* is not clear, but it could be an intensive or frequentative. The diviner, or haruspex, is a man who exercises the profession of making frequent observations.

The present vocabulary from Ras Shamra offers also new elements that confirm the close connection with the Urartian language. The personal 3rd person sg. pronoun is *manni* "he," as we definitely read in V 6′, where it translates Sumerian LÚ and Akkadian *šú-ú*. This confirms the proposal of Wegner and Girbal[21] and corroborates the Boğazköy bilingual.[22] We now can

---

13 See the sequence: *un-nu an-ni ḫa-a-ni* "nun dieses Kind" KUB XLV 61, II? 9 (Ullikummi), Chr. Girbal *apud* V. Haas, *ZA* 79 (1989) 267, n. 27.

14 *SMEA* 22 (1980) 83–86.

15 All are cited in our article, *SCCNH* 9 (1998) 14, s.v. *nirupate*.

16 RS 94-2939, V 11′: ḪUL = *ma-às-*⸢*ku*⸣ = ⸢*ni-ru-pa-te*⸣ "bad" (=*ubad*=).

17 RS 94-2939, V 19′: GAB = *pa-ṭá-ru* = ⸢*zu*⸣*-lu-du-um-mi* "deliver" (=*ud*=).

18 E. Neu, "Neue Wege im Hurritischen," XXIII. *Deutscher Orientalistentag*, Stuttgart: Franz Steiner Verlag, 1989, 301; *idem*, *Das Hurritische: Eine altorientalische Sprache in neuem Licht* (Akademie der Wissenschaften und Literatur, Mainz), Stuttgart: Franz Steiner Verlag, 1986, 24 n. 71. Cf also G. Wilhelm, *Iraq* 53 (1991) 164; *idem*, *SMEA* 29 (1992) 211f.

19 Huehnergard (cf. note 3), 28.

20 *GLH* 128. But see also F. Starke, StBoT 31, 1990, 500–1, who interprets it as a Luvian word.

21 I. Wegner, *SMEA* 29 (1992) 234f.

22 KBo XXXII 14 I 18 and 32 (Hurr.) *ma-a-an-ni* = II 18 (Hitt.) *a-pa-a-aš* ... *ku-iš*, 32 *a-pa-a-aš* ... *ku-in*.

be sure that Urartian *mani* "him" is the same word. In general we have in Urartian a single consonant, whereas in Hurrian it is often doubled. Urartian *mani* was independently translated, since it is attested only in formulaic curses, such as *turinini* ^{D}*Ḫaldi=še* ^{D}IM(=*še*) ^{D}UTU(=*ni*)(=*še*) *mani* ...[23]

A greater appreciation of our increased knowledge of the Hurrian lexicon as a result of the discovery of this tablet can be gained by organizing the material according to nomenclature. Utilizing the translations, we placed the words in the following categories: (1) verbs; (2) substantives; (3) adjectives; (4) adverbs; and (5) pronouns. The substantives were assigned to the following sub-categories: (2a) abstract concepts; (2b) concrete objects; (2c) human beings (age categories, sex, family relationships, functions, professions); and (2d) parts of the anatomy. Of course, additional categories can be introduced, but by this method we can at least check our current knowledge of the Hurrian lexicon.

Unfortunately we are limited by the fact that many words, both verbs and substantives, are attested only here or in similar polyglot vocabularies. Also these new Hurrian words are, at times, incomplete or difficult to read so that they do not always help to translate sentences of rituals or mythological tales. Nevertheless, among the more than fifty new words, we found keys to the understanding of Hurrian texts. One such "key" is worthy of mention here: the vocabulary contains the Hurrian word for "snake," *apše*, which, in our text, corresponds to Sumerian MUŠ and Akkadian *ṣēru*.[24] Since *apše* occurs also in a mythological text, this equation allows us to identify the Hurrian version of the Ḫedammu Myth, whereas, previously, it was attributed to Ullikummi.[25]

The comparison of these two sister languages sometimes takes a step backwards, necessitating a rejection of apparently established facts. This is the case for the word for "earth" and the proposed correspondence between Hurrian *ḫawurni* and Urartian *qiura=ni*, a comparison that already seemed somewhat forced. Urartian *qiura* really does mean "earth." Building inscriptions contain sentences, for example, such as that on Rusa II's stela in Zwartnots, near Ečmiadzin:[26]

> (7) *qiurani šulie manu* (8) *ui giei ištini manuri* (9) *šuki* ^{D}*Ḫaldiše ubarduduni* (10) *ieše ini* ^{GIŠ}*uldie* (11) *terubi...*
>
> the earth was waste/empty/undeveloped, nothing existed here (before); when/as soon as(?) Ḫaldi ordered, I founded this vineyard ...

The word *šuki* in the above sentence enables us to suggest another lexical connection between Hurrian and Urartian. Loosely translated, *šuki* could mean something like "when/as soon as." But there is also a possible etymological

---

23 An analysis of Urartian cursing formulas was made by W.C. Benedict, *JAOS* 81 (1961) 383–85.

24 RS 94-2939 IV 6′: MUŠ = *ṣí-ru* = ⸢*ap-še*⸣ "snake."

25 See literature in *SCCNH* 9 (1998), 8, s.v. *apše*.

26 *UKN* 281 = *HchI* 126, lines 7–10.

connection with a Hurrian word. The Boğazköy bilingual presents the following equation: Hurrian *šu-uk-ki* = 1-*ŠU* "once," in the Hittite version.[27] In fact, we already have a word meaning "when"; it is *iu*.[28] *šuki* could signify that the supreme god Ḫaldi gives his order only "once," and immediately his "servant" Rusa carries it out.

From the Hurrian side, the frequently attested couple *eše ḫawurni* was traditionally translated: "heaven and earth." But, after the discovery of the Hurrian-Hittite Boğazköy bilingual and its study by Erich Neu, it has been definitely established that it is the inverse: "earth and heaven." Our vocabulary confirms this with the equation *ḫaurni* = AN = *šamû*, i.e., "heaven."[29] This revelation was not only the cause of some difficulty among the handful of Hurritologists who were forced to "move heaven and earth,"[30] but it also proved that any equation with Urartian *qiura=ni* is groundless.[31]

Diakonoff reconstructed an original **qawrV-* in order to reconcile Hurr. **k/ḫawri/a* with Urart. *qəwrā*; and this Hurro-Urartian proto-word was, in turn, connected to some Eastern Caucasian words meaning "field." Together with many other etymologies, this supposed correlation supported the theory that Hurro-Urartian belonged to the Eastern Caucasian family of languages.[32] Diakonoff also[33] posited an Urartian word *eši-* "heaven," from a locative *e-ši-a*, evidently influenced by the supposed Hurrian *eše* = "sky."[34] The passage is in the same stela of Zwartnots, by Rusa II, quoted below: (line 22) *a-še* A^{MEŠ} *e-ši(-)a(-)ṣi-ú-li* and was translated by Diakonoff as: "when the water runs from heaven(?)."

After reversing the meanings and by maintaining an etymological approach, we can now cautiously propose the translation: "when the waters irrigate the earth(?)." Unfortunately, the whole sequence is attested only here and we cannot even separate the two words *ešia ṣiuli* or *eši aṣiuli*; in any case, the second seems to be a verbal form. (A different equation could be proposed, between Hurrian *eše* "earth" and Urartian *eši* "place," but this is far from convincing.)

---

27 KBo XXXII 15 I 22′ = II 22′. See also E. Neu, *Hethitica* 9 (1988) 163.

28 Cf. the sentence *iu Ḫaldi=š(e)=me* LUGAL-*TÚ-ḫi aru=ni* "when Ḫaldi gave me the kingship" (*UKN* 155 G 1 = *HchI* 103 2).

29 RS 94-2939 II 6: AN = *ša-mu-ú* = *ḫa-ur-ni*.

30 See the fragment RS 20.189 A+B, published by E. Laroche in *UF* 11 (1979) 478, and collated by W.H. van Soldt, *UF* 21 (1989) 365–68. Line 29 establishes the right equation: [AN = *ša-mu-ú* = *ḫa*]-*bur-ni* = Ugaritic [*š*]*a*-⌜*mu*⌝-*ma* "sky."

31 Cf. I.M. Diakonoff, *Hurrisch und Urartäisch* (= *HuU*), München: Kitzinger, 1971, 59, who reconstructed an original **qawrV-* (hurr. **k/ḫawri/a*, urart. *qəwrā*); p. 60 he registered an Urartian word *eši-* "Himmel," Lok. *e-ši-a*, evidently influenced by the supposed Hurrian *eše* = "sky"; cf. also M.L. Khačikyan, *Churritskij i urartskij jazyki*, Erevan 1985, 43, 46, 50.

32 I.M. Diakonoff / S.A. Starostin, *Hurro-Urartian as an Eastern Caucasian Language*, (MSS Bh. 12, N.F.), München: Kitzinger 1986, 58f.

33 Ibid., 60.

34 For an Eastern Caucasian etymology also for *eše*, see again Diakonoff / Starostin, *ibid.*, 24.

We have cited this intriguing episode in order to show how far linguistic speculation can sometimes go.

We know at present 13 words designating different parts of the body, and half occur in the new tablet: lungs, foot, anus, thigh, tooth, breast, sex (both in concrete and abstract meaning[35]). Interesting and perhaps most "ennobled" among these new terms is Hurrian *urmi*, which corresponds to Akkadian *kabittu*, and which means "inside of the body, liver," and also "emotions, thoughts, mind, spirit."

Our trilingual vocabulary offers also *ur-ni*, which corresponds to Sum. ÚR and Akk. *pēnu* "foot, leg."[36] The tradition of the Hurrian word for "foot" becomes even more complex, because we knew already that *ugri* designated the leg of a table,[37] which was connected by J. Friedrich with Urartian *kuri* "foot."[38] Moreover, the Hurrian-Hittite bilingual[39] offers another writing for the same word: *uri*, which is considered to be a secondary form of *ugri*.[40] It has also been suggested that Hittite *urgi-* "track" and the verb *urgija-* "to track down" are derivations from the Hurrian word with metathesis.

Some divination texts in Boğazköy and in Meskene contain the word *urnirni*.[41] Laroche interpreted[42] them as a "partie omineuse" and suggested a correspondence with Akkadian *ubānu* "finger," as a part of the liver. It is clear that *urni* has to be connected with *urnirni*. The problem of this word family, in any case, remains open.

It has been established that the frequent verbal form in Urartian annals *am=ašt=u=bi*, "I burned off," (the object is the enemy country or fortresses and settlements)[43] is an expansion by means of the suffix *-ašt-* of a root *am-*, which also in Hurrian means "to burn." We know this also from the Boğazköy bilingual, in which the verbal form *amelanni* is attested, meaning: "may he burn off completely."[44] In a former article I suggested that the simple root *am-* was probably attested in Urartian too, in the form *am=u=bi*, in the Annals of Argišti I.[45] We can

---

35 "Sexual parts" and "sexual power"; but see the opposite meaning of *CAD*, B 144a.

36 RS 94-2939 IV 9′: ÚR = *pè-e-ni* = *ur-ni* "foot, leg."

37 E. Laroche, *GLH*, 277.

38 J. Friedrich, "Beiträge zu Grammatik und Lexikon des Chaldischen 2. Teil," *Caucasica* 8, 1931, 147, *idem*, "Zwei churritisch-urartäische Wortgleichungen," *Handes Amsorya* 75 (1961) 512, Nr. 10–12.

39 KBo XXXII 15 IV 9–10 = III 9–10.

40 See the discussion by E. Neu, *StBoT* 32, 1996, 243, 355, 356.

41 See St. de Martino, *ChS* I/7, p. 156.

42 E. Laroche, *RA* 64 (1970) 138, and *GLH*, p. 286.

43 E.g., in the Annals of Argišti I, *UKN* 127 IV 58: [KUR] *e-ba-a-ni a-ma-áš-tú-bi* "I burnt off the country."

44 E. Neu, *StBoT* 32, 1996, 105, 106. KBo XXXII 14 I 6 (Hurr. *a-me-la-a-an-ni*) = II 7 (Hitt. *ar-ḫa wa-ar-nu-zi*).

45 M. Salvini, "Ein Beitrag zur hurritisch-urartäischen Morphologie," *Or*NS 59 (1990) 243–50, see esp. 245.

now confirm this thanks to a neglected short text from Kefkalesi, a site dominating the northern shore of Lake Van. The same inscription is repeated on each of nine carved blocks unearthed in Kefkalesi; but the text has not been published in a satisfactory way. Only the first quarter of the text, corresponding to one of the four faces, was copied by the excavators. We can now offer a complete transcription[46] that has very few assured restorations of single signs:

1. ᴰ*ḫal-di-ni-ni al-su-i-ši-ni* ᵐ*ru-sa-a-še* ᵐ*ar-giš-te-ḫi-ni-še i-ni*
2. É *a-ši-ḫu-si-e za-du-ni qar-bi-e šú-li ma-nu ú-i a-i-še-e-i*
3. LUGÁL-*še za-da-la-ni šú-ki* ᴰ*ḫal-di-i-še i-zi-du-ú-ni i-e-še za-du-bi*
4. ᵐ*ru-sa-a-*[*še*] *a-li a-lu-še i-n*[*i* DUB-*t*]*e tú-li-e a-mì-ni-ni* ᴰUTU-*ni-še*

> By the power of Ḫaldi, Rusa, the son of Argišti, built this *ašiḫusi* House. The rock was untouched(?), a (prior) king had built nothing (before). When/as soon as(?) Ḫaldi ordered, I made (it). Rusa says: whoever destroys this [inscrip]tion, may the sun-god burn him (off).

The form *am=ini=ni* is new in formulaic curses and, indeed, in general. It is an imperative of *am-*, "to burn off," in which *-ini-* expresses the imperative mode and *-ni* the object suffix, "him." Compare the frequent *tu-ri-ni-ni* (*tur=ini=ni*) "may annihilate him."[47] Moreover, this form confirms the phonetic value *mì* for the sign ME. The connection between the sun-god (ᴰUTU) and his action is logical, but it is attested in Urartian texts here for the first time.

We now offer examples of an experimental method or perhaps practice that establishes a link between clay tablets found in Boğazköy or Ugarit and Urartian rock inscriptions, and particularly with respect to their archaeological context and surrounding landscape.

Confirmation of the correctness of the etymological connection between Hurrian *tarmani* "spring"[48] and Urartian *tarmani=li*, proposed by Diakonoff,[49] was made by M. Salvini on his first visit to Van Kalesi,[50] the site of the Urartian capital Ṭušpa. At the base of its northern slope there is hollow with three inscriptions of King Minua.[51] This place and the stagnant water on the ground showed that originally it must have been a spring, which are common at the foot of Van Rock.

The crucial information is in the word *tarmanili*, which occurs only in these rock inscriptions, and which was not translated in the corpora of Melikišvili and

---

46 M. Salvini, "The Inscription of the Urartian King Rusa II at Kefkalesi (Adilcevaz)," *SMEA* 40/1 (1998) 123–29.

47 See W.C. Benedict, *JAOS* 81 (1961) 385.

48 RS quadr. 137 III 8: IDIM = (Hurr.) *tar-*⌜*ma*⌝*-ni* = (Ugar.) *nap-ku*; see *GLH*, 257.

49 Diakonoff, *HuU*, 66.

50 M. Salvini, *Or*NS 39 (1970) 410–11.

51 *UKN* 92 a-c = *HchI* 59a-c = *CICh* 87a-c.

König—but neither scholar had ever been to Van. The sentence on lines 2–4 *ini=li tarmani=li atḫu=ali šidištu=ali* should be translated: "he excavated and constructed these springs/fountains." In any case, it is understandable why two verbs are used here: the uncommon *atḫu-* and the well-known *šidištu-*. The second one means "to construct" and is frequently attested in building inscriptions, but the first must mean a preceding action, "to excavate" or the like. It is possible that in Urartian times a monumental fountain stood there—one may think of something like the "çeşme" of the Sultans.

This small discovery, which should be checked by archaeological excavation, helped to interpret another place in Iranian Azerbaijan, with its almost destroyed inscription. East of the Zagros, on a natural road linking the plain of Urumiyeh with the valley of Ushnaviyeh, American archaeologists of the Hasanlu excavation team, lead by R.H. Dyson, first noticed this niche, which was described and published by W. Kleiss.[52] The faint traces of some cuneiform signs were interpreted as the remains of a great inscription covering the whole niche. But the condition of the rock does not give the impression of destruction, rather of having been washed away by water. It is probably the path of an ancient rock spring, which now is located 20 meters lower down. In fact, it is possible to reconstruct four separate short inscriptions, all duplicates, which celebrate a *taramanili*, a spring of King Minua.[53] The place is named Ain-e Rum, "Spring of the Romans, Byzantines," or the like.

Our last, short example is the "story" of the woman Tariria. The story begins and ends with a rock inscription. The first is the inscription of Minua near Katepants, in the region of Van, near the old so-called "Canal of Semiramis," actually the Canal of Minua:

(1) *Minua=i=ni=ei* ^{MUNUS}*sila=ie* (2) ^{MUNUS}*Tariria=i ini* ^{GIŠ}*uldi*
(3) ^{MUNUS}*Tariria=ḫi=ni=li tini*

This vineyard belongs to Tariria, the *sila* of Minua, foundations of Tariria is its name.

Independent of all other considerations, it is an interesting monument because it reveals the important role played by a woman of the Urartian royal family.

The word *sila* is clearly a term designating a family relationship, and it has usually been translated "daughter" because of a proposed connection with Hurrian *šala/i* "daughter."[54] And, on this basis, an *a/i*-interchange between Hurrian and Urartian has been proposed.[55]

---

52 W. Kleiss, "Bericht über Erkundungsfahrten in Iran im Jahre 1971," *AMI* NF 5 (1972) 149–51, with figs. 22 and 23, and pls. 37,3 and 38,1.

53 M. Salvini, in: P.E. Pecorella and M. Salvini, *Tra lo Zagros e l'Urmia*, Roma: Edizioni dell'Ateneo, 1984, 71–78.

54 See especially G.A. Melikišvili, *VDI* 1951/4, 35 n. 2; *idem*, *UKN*, p. 405; *idem*, *USpr* 9 and 86; I.M. Diakonoff, *HuU*, 46, 61; J. Friedrich, "Hurritisch," in: *Altkleinasiatische Sprachen* (HdO), Leiden, 1969, 47. See also the literature quoted by G. Wilhelm, *ZA* 66 (1976) 107, n. 17.

55 Diakonoff, *HuU*, 56.

But another rock inscription was recently discovered in the territory of Nachičevan,[56] according to which the meaning of *sila* is clearly "wife," not "daughter." Consequently, this negates any proposed connection with Hurrian *šala*. It relates of a conquest of Išpuini and Minua at the time of their co-regency. The last two sentences of this very damaged text are interesting in our present context:

> (4) ^{D}*ḫal-di-e-i pu-lu-si* (^{D}*Ḫaldi=ei pulusi*) ^{KUR}*pu-lu-⸢ú-a?-di?-ni?-e?⸣ te-ru-n[i]* (5) ⸢*ar?-di?*⸣-[*še?* (x x) x GU]$_4$? ^{D}*ḫal-di-e ur-pu-li-ni* GU_4.ÁB ^{D}*ḫal-di-*⸢*i?*⸣(or ⸢^{MUNUS}⸣)*si-la-i-e* ^{KUR}*p[u?-*
>
> an inscription of Ḫaldi they set in the Land of Puluadi, they established as an order: [one goat one o]x must be sacrificed to Ḫaldi, one cow to Ḫaldi's *sila* (in the) Land of Pu[luadi(?)].

It is clearly an offering to Ḫaldi's wife Uarubani, whose name is here replaced by her status. We already know from the rock niche of Meher Kapısı that the list of goddesses begins with an offering of a cow (GU_4.ÁB) to Arubani.[57] (In that same line there is epigraphic evidence disproving the supposed Urartian correspondence of Hurrian Ḫebat with Ḫuba. In reality we have to read ^{D}*ba!-ba*[58] and not *^{D}*ḫu-ba*,[59] who would be the wife of the weather-god Teišeba.)

These final remarks are, of course, a *pars destruens*, but a necessary contribution of "rock philology" for the reconstruction of language connections.

[See below Nuzi Note 62, page 434 for supplementary remarks.]

Special Abbreviations

ChS = *Corpus der Hurritischen Sprachdenkmäler* (ed. V. Haas, M. Salvini, I. Wegner, G. Wilhelm), Rome 1984 ss.

CICh = C.F. Lehmann-Haupt, *Corpus Inscriptionum Chaldicarum*, Berlin 1928–35.

GLH = E. Laroche, *Glossaire de la langue hourrite*, Paris: Éditions Klincksieck, 1980 (also: *RHA* XXXIV–XXXV, 1977–78).

HchI = F.W. König, *Handbuch der chaldischen Inschriften* (AfO Beiheft 8), Graz 1955–57.

HuU = I.M. Diakonoff, *Hurrisch und Urartäisch*, München: Kitzinger, 1971.

UKN = G.A. *Urartskie Klinoobraznye Nadpisi*, Moskva: Izdatel'stvo Akademii Nauk, 1960.

USpr = G.A. Melikišvili, *Die urartäische Sprache* (Studia Pohl 7), Rome: Biblical Institute Press, 1970.

---

56 S.G. Hmayakyan, V.A. Igumnov, H.H. Karagozyan, "An Urartian Cuneiform Inscription from Ojasar-Ilandagh, Nachičevan," *SMEA* 38 (1996) 139–51. See also the new edition of this text by M. Salvini, "Eine urartäische Felsinschrift in der Region Nachičevan," *ZA* 88 (1998) 72–77.

57 *UKN* 27 = *HchI* 10, 21//68 = *CICh* 18.

58 We have to remember that already W.C. Benedict, *JAOS* 80 (1960) 103 n. 22, preferred to read ^{D}*Ba-ba-a* on the basis of Lehmann-Haupt's squeeze of *CICh* 18.

59 We have to correct G.A. Melikišvili, *Or*NS 34 (1965) 444 (Ḫuba = Ḫepat), and I.M. Diakonoff, *HuU*, 62 (^{D}*ḫu-ba-a*, die Gemahlin des Teišeba, hurr. Ḫeba[t]).

La religion des Hourrites: état actuel de nos connaissances

MARIE-CLAUDE TRÉMOUILLE
CNR, Istituto per gli Studi Micenei ed Egeo-Anatolici

The author provides a survey of the results of research in Hurrian religion during the last 25 years. She outlines the areal distribution and ethno-linguistic origins of the Hurrian gods, the characteristic practices of Hurrian ritual, and the latest attempts to analyze Hurrian prayers, hymns, and omens. In a comment on Hurrian rulers and the ideology of kingship, she suggests the equation of the well-attested name element *–adal* with the god Nergal. She also suggests the abandonment of the concept of a division between a western and an eastern Hurrian pantheon.

1. Pour mieux apprécier les acquis nouveaux et cerner les domaines où la recherche stagne encore, il convient, dans n'importe quelle matière, de prendre un certain recul. En ce qui concerne la religion des Hourrites, une date s'impose: 1974, quand, au cours de la XXIe Rencontre Assyriologique Internationale, tenue à Rome sur le thème „Panthéon systématique et panthéons nationaux", deux maîtres—A. Kammenhuber et E. Laroche—présentèrent des contributions fondamentales[1]. Ces deux spécialistes appréhendaient le problème des conceptions religieuses des Hourrites certes de façon différente, mais leurs études ouvrirent la voie à une unique et nouvelle approche scientifique. On ressentit alors que le système religieux hourrite n'était pas homogène, mais qu'il dépendait en grande partie du contexte culturel dans lequel les Hourrites étaient insérés.

Une Rencontre Assyriologique de peu postérieure, consacrée exclusivement aux Hourrites—celle de 1977 à Paris—mit au clair l'existence de situations spécifiques à l'Ouest, d'où provient la plupart de notre documentation, et à l'Est, dans la région que l'on considère traditionnellement comme l'ancien habitat des populations hourrites. On distingua alors, principalement sur la

---

[1] A. Kammenhuber, „Neue Ergebnisse zur hurrischen und altmesopotamischen Überlieferung in Boğazköy", *Or*NS 45 (1976) 130–46; E. Laroche, „Panthéon national et panthéons locaux chez les Hourrites", *Or*NS 45 (1976) 94–99. V. aussi la communication de K. Deller, „Materialen zu den Lokalpanthea des Königreiches Arrapḫe", *Or*NS 45 (1976) 33–45.

Studies on the Civilization and Culture of Nuzi and the Hurrians - 10

base de la présence et de la fréquence de certains théonymes dans la documentation, entre un panthéon occidental et un panthéon oriental, avec éventuellement des variétés locales. Seuls quelques dieux—Teššub, Šauška, Šimige—se voyaient reconnus comme divinités pan-hourrites. Parmi les contributions de cette Rencontre dédiées à la religion rappelons en particulier celles de V. Haas[2] et de W. Lambert[3], dont les titres sont significatifs, mais on doit souligner que presque toutes les communications présentées touchèrent, de près ou de loin, au problème de la religion des Hourrites. M.C. Astour[4], par exemple, relevait les éléments syriens dans la religion hourrite, tandis que J.R. Kupper[5] traitait de la présence hourrite à Mari et remarquait combien les traces laissées par les Hourrites dans la religion de Mari étaient faibles. Pour leur part C. Grottanelli[6] et P. Xella[7] s'attachaient à des problèmes de mythologie.

2. A plus de vingt ans de ces deux Rencontres, bien peu de sources nouvelles, d'un point de vue épigraphique, sont venues s'ajouter à la documentation dont ces savants disposaient.

Seule la série de textes découverts sur le site de l'ancienne capitale hittite Ḫattuša, que l'on appelle couramment „la Bilingue", apporte quelques éléments nouveaux, même si dans son ensemble il ne s'agit pas d'un document à caractère religieux[8]. Une unique tablette, KBo 32.13, a un contenu mythologique[9], mais elle est malheureusement fragmentaire. On y raconte que le dieu de l'orage Teššub, accompagné selon la version hittite par le dieu Šuwaliyat[10],

---

2 „Substratgottheiten des westhurrischen Pantheons", *RHA* 36 (1978) 59–69.

3 „The Mesopotamian Background of the Hurrian Pantheon", *RHA* 36 (1978) 129–34.

4 „Les Hourrites en Syrie du Nord: rapport sommaire", *RHA* 36 (1978) 1–22, en particulier 7 s., 14 s., 16.

5 „Les Hourrites à Mari", *RHA* 36 (1978) 117–28, en particulier 117 ss.

6 „Observations sur l'histoire d'Appou", *RHA* 36 (1978) 49–57.

7 „Remarques comparatives sur le <<roman de Kešši>>", *RHA* 36 (1978) 215–24.

8 V. E. Neu, „Knechtschaft und Freiheit. Betrachtungen über ein hurritisch-hethitisches Textensemble aus Ḫattuša", in: B. Janowski, K. Koch, G. Wilhelm (eds.), *Religionsgeschichtliche Beziehungen zwischen dem Alten Testament, Nordsyrien und Anatolien* (OBO 129), Freiburg/Schweiz: Universitätsverlag, 1993, 329–61; *id.*, *Das hurritische Epos der Freilassung* (StBoT 32), Wiesbaden: Harrassowitz Verlag, 1996; *id.*, „La bilingue hourro-hittite de Ḫattuša, contenu et sens", in: J.-M. Durand (ed.), *Mari, Ebla et les Hourrites. Dix ans de Travaux* (Amurru 1), Paris 1996, 189–95. V. aussi, dernièrement, H.A. Hoffner, Jr., „Hurrian Civilization from a Hittite Perspective", in: G. Buccellati, M.K. Kelly-Buccellati, *Urkesh and the Hurrians. Studies in Honor of Lloyd Cotsen* (Bibliotheca Mesopotamica 26), Malibu 1998, 178–83.

9 Selon V. Haas - I. Wegner, *OLZ* 86 (1991) 385–96, KBo 32.11 Vo IV aussi pourrait contenir une narration à caractère mythologique.

10 On pouvait s'attendre à trouver, dans le texte hourrite correspondant, le nom du dieu Tašmišu qui sert d'acolyte au dieu de l'orage dans le „Chant de Ullikummi". Or il n'en est rien: on rencontre ici, au contraire, un terme de sens inconnu *šatta(-)ḫamura*. Toutefois, vu que ce mot semble contenir le suffixe de comitatif *-ra*, il indique vraisemblablement bien quelqu'un qui „accompagne" Teššub.

rend visite à la déesse des Enfers Allani et que celle-ci fait préparer pour lui un grand festin, auquel participent également les „dieux antiques". Inutile de souligner que le contenu de cette tablette est peu significatif pour une reconstruction de la religion des Hourrites!

D'autres archives, nous dit-on, ont été découvertes ailleurs en Anatolie[11] il y a une dizaine d'années; il y figurerait des tablettes en langue hourrite et de contenu religieux—en particulier des rituels, comme le rituel *itkalzi* -, mais cette documentation est inutilisable puisqu'on attend encore sa publication.

Ce qui apparait plus significatif pour les études sur la religion des Hourrites, c'est d'une part la publication des documents épigraphiques provenant d'Ebla, qui nous fournissent un tableau des croyances dans la Syrie du nord à la fin du IIIème millénaire, mais aussi la révision des documents et l'étude des textes relatifs au Moyen-Euphrate et à la Syrie. Celles-ci sont à la base du changement de perspective sous laquelle on considère le rôle de ces régions à l'âge du Bronze moyen et récent. Cette meilleure connaissance des caractères spécifiques de la culture syrienne et moyen-euphratique, à travers l'étude des documents de Mari, Emar, Ugarit, etc. est essentielle car c'est elle qui permet précisément de comprendre dans quel contexte culturel se sont formés les documents en langue hourrite qui nous sont parvenus.

Comme bref *excursus*, rappelons maintenant, en les ordonnant de façon chronologique, quelles sont les sources dont nous disposons aujourd'hui pour esquisser un tableau de la religion des Hourrites. On l'observera immédiatement, celles-ci sont de nature et de quantité bien inégales. De plus, il s'agit presque toujours de documents secondaires, j'entends par là des textes qui proviennent de sites où la population hourrite n'était pas prédominante et qui, par conséquent, ressentent de la culture „hôte", que ce soit la Paléo-Babylonie, Mari, la Syrie septentrionale ou encore l'Anatolie hittite. Je reviendrai ensuite sur l'importance, à mon avis fréquemment sous-évaluée, que cet élément revêt pour une plus exacte reconstruction des croyances religieuses des Hourrites.

Les documents les plus anciens proviennent de la Mésopotamie du Nord[12]: il s'agit en l'occurence des deux documents de fondation bien connus de rois d'Urkiš, le premier de Atalšen (tablette de bronze de Samarra: AO 5678), datable selon G. Wilhelm au tout début de la dynastie d'Ur[13], l'autre de Tišatal[14] (tablette de pierre: AO 19937-38), qui remonte à l'époque des Goutis.

---

11 Sur la trouvaille épigraphique de Ortaköy v. A. Süel, „Ortaköy: Eine hethitische Stadt mit hethitischen und hurritischen Tontafelentdeckungen", in: *Festschrift Sedat Alp*, Ankara 1992, 487–91; *ead.*, „Ortaköy - Šapinuwa tabletlerinin tarihlendirilmesi", in: S. Alp / A. Süel, *Acts of the IIIrd International Congress of Hittitology*, Ankara 1998, 551–58.

12 Pour un panorama de la documentation pré-mittannienne v., dernièrement, M. Salvini, „The Earliest Evidences of the Hurrians before the Formation of the Reign of Mittanni", in: *Urkesh and the Hurrians. Studies in Honor of Lloyd Cotsen* (BibMes 26), Malibu 1998, 101–15.

13 G. Wilhelm, „Gedanken zur Frühgeschichte der Hurriter und zum hurritisch-urartäischen Sprachvergleich", in: V. Haas (ed.), *Hurriter und Hurritisch* (Xenia 21), Konstanz: Universitätsverlag, 1988, 46 ss.

14 Une étude exhaustive de cette inscription est présentée par G. Wilhelm, „Die Inschrift

Viennent ensuite des textes d'époque paléo-babylonienne, en particulier les tablettes de Mari contenant des conjurations et mentionnant dans un cas le souverain Zimri-Lim[15], ainsi que des conjurations „dans la langue de Subir" provenant de la Mésopotamie méridionale[16].

Puis une tablette d'Alalaḫ contenant des indications pour un sacrifice[17].

Ensuite toute la masse des documents provenant de Ḫattuša[18]. Il ne s'agit souvent que de copies impériales, mais pour un grand nombre il est certain que les originaux remontent à la période moyen-hittite. A l'intérieur de ceux-ci il convient de distinguer entre:

des documents provenant de la Syrie septentrionale (la „Bilingue"[19], avec la mention d'Ebla, et les rituels magiques du Mukiš[20])
des documents relatifs à Alep (listes d'offrandes, rituels, fêtes)[21]
des documents provenant de Kizzuwatna (rituels magiques et de fête)[22]
des documents provenant de Šapinuwa (principalement des rituels magiques)[23]

---

des Tišatal von Urkeš", in: *Urkesh and the Hurrians. Studies in Honor of Lloyd Cotsen* (BibMes 26), Malibu 1998, 117–43.

15 F. Thureau-Dangin, „Tablettes hurrites provenant de Mari", *RA* 36 (1939) 1–28.

16 J.A. van Djik, *Nicht-kanonische Beschwörungen und sonstige literarische Texte* (VS NF 1), Berlin 1971, Nr. 5–7, 20, 22, 26.

17 *AT* 126, v. D.J. Wiseman, *The Alalakh Tablets*, London 1953.

18 Tous les textes en langue hourrite provenant de Ḫattuša sont en cours de publication dans la série *Corpus der hurritischen Sprachdenkmäler, Abteilung I: Die Texte aus Boğazköy* (= ChS I), Roma 1984 ss.

19 Cf. note 8.

20 V. Haas - H.-J. Thiel, *Die Beschwörungsrituale der Allaituraḫ(ḫ)i und verwandte Texte*, AOAT 31, Neukirchen-Vluyn 1978; V. Haas, „Die hurritisch-hethitischen Rituale der Beschwörerin Allaituraḫ(ḫ)i und ihr literarhistorischer Hintergrund", in: V. Haas (ed.), *Hurriter und Hurritisch* (Xenia 21), Konstanz: Universitätsverlag, 1988, 117–43; V. Haas - I. Wegner, *Die Rituale der Beschwörerinnen* ^{SAL}ŠU.GI (ChS I/5), Roma: Multigrafica Editrice, 1988, Nr. 1–39; M. Salvini - I. Wegner, *Die Rituale des AZU-Priesters* (ChS I/2), Roma: Multigrafica Editrice, 1986, Nr. 40–42.

21 V. M. Salvini - I. Wegner, ChS I/2 *cit.*, Nr. 1–14 (*CTH* 701); v. aussi *CTH* 698. Sur le culte d'Alep v. V. Haas, *Geschichte der hethitischen Religion* (HdO), Leiden etc.: Brill, 1994, 553–56. Pour un panorama des fêtes pour les dieux d'Alep v. M.-Cl. Trémouille, ^{D}*Ḫebat. Une divinité syro-anatolienne* (Eothen 7), Firenze: LoGisma editore, 1997, 93–102 avec bibliographie.

22 V. M. Salvini - I. Wegner, Die hethitisch-hurritischen Rituale des (ḫ)išuwa-Festes, *SMEA* 24 (Gs. Piero Meriggi, 1984), 175–85; I. Wegner - M. Salvini, *Die hethitisch-hurritischen Ritualtafeln des (ḫ)išuwa-Festes* (ChS I/4), Roma: Multigrafica Editrice, 1991. V. aussi *CTH* 471–500, *CTH* 699–700, *CTH* 702–6.

23 V. V. Haas, *Die Serien itkaḫi und itkalzi des AZU-Priesters, Rituale für Tašmišarri und Taduḫepa sowie weitere Texte mit Bezug auf Tašmišarri*, ChS I/1, Roma: Multigrafica Editrice, 1984. D'autres textes provenant de cette même localité sont publiés dans M.-Cl. Trémouille, *Texte verschiedenen Inhalts* (ChS I/8) (sous presse). V. aussi M.-Cl. Trémouille, „Quelques observations sur KBo 23.27+ et ses relations avec *CTH* 776", in: Studi e Testi II (Eothen 10), Firenze (1999), 193–211.

les textes mythologiques[24]
les textes de divination[25]

D'autres documents encore—textes divinatoires, rituels et listes d'offrandes—proviennent d'Emar[26] et d'Ougarit[27].

A cela s'ajoute l'anthroponymie. Le corpus des noms propres hourrites—des *Satznamen* à élément théophore dont l'analyse est un outil fondamental pour la recherche historico-religieuse—s'est accru, mais aucun élément nouveau n'est venu vraiment bouleverser nos connaissances[28].

3. Le problème de la constitution des divers panthéons[29] et l'évaluation du rôle joué par le substrat dans cette constitution ont été le sujet principal de bon nombre des articles consacrés à la religion des Hourrites au cours des vingt-cinq dernières années. Les pratiques cultuelles ont été, elles aussi, soumises à examen. Par contre, la mythologie et la divination n'ont guère été prises en considération, aussi parce que la documentation récemment acquise n'a pas apporté d'éléments significatifs en ce qui les concerne.

3.1. Le panthéon

L'intérêt des chercheurs s'est principalement concentré sur le panthéon occidental[30]. Ceci s'explique facilement si l'on considère que presque toutes les sources utiles proviennent de Ḫattuša et, secondairement, d'un point de vue quantitatif, d'Ougarit, d'Emar et de Mari.

Les textes religieux en langue hourrite ou en langue hittite avec des passages en hourrite trouvés dans la capitale hittite contiennent un nombre impressionnant de divinités[31] que l'on peut subdiviser approximativement en

---

24 V. M. Salvini, *Die mythologischen Texte* (ChS I/6), Roma (sous presse).

25 V. St. de Martino, *Die mantischen Texte* (ChS I/7), Roma: Bonsignori Editore, 1992.

26 V. M. Salvini, *Les textes hourrites de Meskéné/Emar* (ChS II/3) [EMAR VII], Roma (sous presse); Th. Richter, „Die Lesung des Götternamens AN.AN.MAR.TU", *SCCNH* 9 (1998) 135–37.

27 V. M. Salvini - J. Sanmartín - G. Wilhelm, *Die hurritischen Texte aus Ugarit*, Roma (en cours de préparation).

28 Sur l'onomastique hourrite v. en particulier G. Wilhelm, „Zum hurritischen Verbalsystem", in: S.R. Anschütz (d.), *Texte, Sätze, Wörter und Moneme. Festschrift für Klaus Heger zum 65. Geburtstag*, Heidelberg 1992, 659–71; *id.*, „Zu den hurritischen Namen der Kültepe-Tafel kt K/k 4", *SCCNH* 8 (= Gs.R.F.S. Starr, 1996), 335–43; *id.*, entrée „Name, Namengebung. D. Bei den Hurritern", in: *Reallexikon der Assyriologie* IX, Berlin - New York 1998, 121–27.

29 Cf. I.M. Diakonoff, „Evidence on the Ethnic Division of the Hurrians", *SCCNH* 1 (1981) 77–89, en particulier 80 ss.

30 V., par exemple, A. Archi, „Substrate: Some Remarks on the Formation of the West Hurrian Pantheon", in: *Festschrift Sedat Alp*, 7–14.

31 Pour une récolte de tous les théonymes mentionnés dans les textes de Ḫattuša/Boğazköy v. B.H.L. van Gessel, *Onomasticon of the Hittite Pantheon* (HdO), Leiden etc.: Brill, 1998.

trois groupes: des divinités mésopotamiennes, des divinités hourrites, des divinités du substrat.

L'attribution d'un dieu ou d'une déesse aux deux premiers groupes peut se faire en se basant principalement sur le nom de la divinité, qui laisse souvent deviner son origine. Ainsi, on reconnait bien sûr Ningal derrière Nikkal ou Damkina derrière Tapkina. Quelquefois le théonyme est plus estropié: Pendigalli par exemple recouvre un Bēlat ekalli, et Peltimāti sans doute un Bēlat māti. Quant à Teššub, Šimige, Kušuḫ, aucun doute sur eux, ce sont „les" dieux hourrites. Je reviendrai ensuite sur les théonymes hourrites.

La présence dans des textes d'Ebla de noms divins comme Adamma ou Aštabi, théonymes bien attestés dans les textes religieux hourrites de Ḫattuša et d'Ougarit, avait mené à la conclusion qu'il existait un noyau de divinités hourrites—Išḫara ou Ḫebat par exemple—déjà en Syrie du Nord à l'époque des Archives. Il s'agit au contraire, comme l'a démontré A. Archi, de divinités appartenant au substrat que les Hourrites ont intégré à leur panthéon lors de leur installation dans la région[32].

Dans certains cas, l'abondance de documentation a permis la mise en place de dossiers sur quelques-unes de ces divinités. Ištar/Ša(w)uška a été l'objet d'une étude de I. Wegner[33] et, récemment, la même spécialiste a proposé une intéressante analyse du nom de cette divinité (v. § 4.1). D. Prechel a dédié une monographie à la déesse Išḫara[34], une divinité du subtrat bien attestée dans les textes éblaïtes—A. Archi aussi lui a consacré un article[35]—et dont le culte s'étendit jusqu'en Mésopotamie méridionale d'une part et en Anatolie de l'autre. J'ai moi-même traité d'une autre déesse, Ḫebat, que les Hourrites ont vénérée principalement comme déesse poliade d'Alep et dans sa fonction de distributrice de royauté qu'elle partage avec son parèdre, le dieu de l'orage d'Alep[36]. Rappelons encore les travaux de A. Archi sur le nom de la déesse

---

32 A. Archi, in: *Festschrift Sedat Alp*, 10 s.; *id.*, „How a Pantheon Forms", in: B. Janowski, K. Koch, G. Wilhelm (eds.), *Religionsgeschichtliche Beziehungen zwischen dem Alten Testament, Nordsyrien und Anatolien* (OBO 129), Freiburg/Schweiz: Universitätsverlag, 1993, 129 *cit.*, 1–18; *id.*, „Studies on the pantheon of Ebla II", *Or*NS 66 (1997) 414–25, en particulier 416–18; *id.*, „The Former History of Some Hurrian Gods", in: S. Alp / A. Süel, *Acts of the IIIrd International Congress of Hittitology*, 39–44.

33 I. Wegner, *Gestalt und Kult der Ištar-Šawuška in Kleinasien* (AOAT 36), Neukirchen-Vluyn: Neukirchener Verlag, 1981; v. aussi *ead.* „Der Name der Ša(w)uška", *SCCNH* 7 (1995) 117–20.

34 D. Prechel, *Die Göttin Išḫara. Ein Beitrag zur altorientalischen Religiongeschichte*, Münster 1996.

35 A. Archi, „Divinités sémitiques et divinités de substrat. Le cas d'Išḫara et d'Ištar à Ebla", *M.A.R.I.* 7 (1993) 71–78.

36 M.-Cl. Trémouille, ^{D}*Ḫebat* cité à la note 21.

Ḫebat[37] et sur la déesse Šalaš, parèdre de Dagan/Kumarbi[38], et l'article de V. Haas sur le taureau divin Tilla[39].

Une étude récente a été consacrée par I. Wegner aux listes, ou *kaluti*[40], qui énumèrent les divinités en deux séries: d'un côté les dieux, de l'autre les déesses, selon le schéma représenté iconographiquement à Yazılıkaya[41]. Tout comme le nom *kaluti*[42], qui dérive vraisemblablement de l'akkadien *kalû* „tout", „totalité", il est possible que le concept soit lui aussi d'ascendance mésopotamienne, puisque, comme l'observait déjà E. Laroche en 1974, le système de parédries que représentent les *kaluti* masculins opposés aux *kaluti* féminins n'est qu'un „démarquage à peine voilé des parédries babyloniennes"[43].

3.2. Le culte

C'est surtout dans le domaine du culte que les nouvelles approches ont donné les résultats les plus sensibles. Les archives de Ḫattuša avaient livré depuis longtemps un lot important de tablettes sur lesquelles la recherche a pu se fonder. Cette documentation provient, à l'origine, principalement de Kizzuwatna, région qui gravite culturellement—et probablement aussi géographiquement—sur la métropole d'Alep. Pour la connaissance des pratiques religieuses de Kizzuwatna je rappellerai l'important travail en commun de V. Haas et de G. Wilhelm dans la série AOATS, où sont rassemblés la plupart des rituels d'évocation[44]. On mentionnera aussi les éditions de certains textes religieux de la part de R. Lebrun.[45] En ce qui concerne le lexique particulier à l'ensemble de cette documentation, rappelons les travaux de A. Kammenhuber[46] et V. Haas[47];

---

37 A. Archi, „Studies on the pantheon of Ebla", *Or*NS 63 (1994) 249–52.

38 A. Archi, „Šalaš Consort of Dagan and Kumarbi", in: Th.P.J. van den Hout / J. de Roos (eds.), *Studio historiae ardens. Ancient Near Eastern Studies Presented to Philo H.J. Houwink ten Cate*, Istanbul 1995, 1–6.

39 V. Haas, „Betrachtungen zum Gotte Tilla", *SCCNH* 1 (1981) 183–88.

40 I. Wegner, *Hurritische Opferlisten aus hethitischen Festbeschreibungen. Teil I: Texte für IŠTAR-ŠA(W)UŠKA* (ChS I/3–1), Roma: Bonsignori Editore, 1995.

41 Le même schéma se retrouve peut-être aussi dans le temple découvert récemment dans la citadelle d'Alep, dont on a déjà dégagé la théorie des divinités masculines.

42 V. J. Puhvel, *Hittite Etymological Dictionary* Vol. IV, Berlin - New York: Walter de Gruyter, 1997, 33 s.

43 E. Laroche, *Or*NS 45 (1976) 97.

44 V. Haas - G. Wilhelm, *Hurritische und luwische Riten aus Kizzuwatna* (AOATS 3), Neukirchen-Vluyn: Neukirchener Verlag, 1974.

45 R. Lebrun, „Textes religieux de la fin de l'empire", *Hethitica* 2 (1977) 93–153; *id.*, „Les rituels d'Ammiḫatna, Tulbi et Mati contre une impureté = *CTH* 472", *Hethitica* 3 (1979) 139–64; *id.*, „L'aphasie de Muršili II = *CTH* 486", *Hethitica* 6 (1985) 103–38, *id.*, „Rituels de Muwalanni, à Manuzziya = *CTH* 703", *Hethitica* 13 (1996) 49–64.

46 A. Kammenhuber, „Hethitische Opfertexte mit *anaḫi-*, *aḫrušḫi-*, und *ḫuprušḫi-* und hurrischen Sprüchen", *Or*NS 55 (1986) 105–30; 390–423.

47 V. Haas, *Die hurritischen Ritualtermini in hethitischem Kontext* (ChS I/9), Roma: CNR, Istituto per gli Studi Micenei ed-Egeo-Anatolici, 1998.

j'ai moi-même publié quelques études sur des termes techniques utilisés dans ces rituels[48].

L'appartenance d'une tablette au noyau des textes religieux de Kizzuwatna est assurée non seulement par la présence d'un vocabulaire technique particulier, ou de théonymes et de toponymes spécifiques, mais aussi et surtout par des actions rituelles typiques. C'est pourquoi la documentation de Kizzuwatna est particulièrement importante, car, tout comme les textes d'Emar nous documentent les pratiques cultuelles pour le Moyen Euphrate, celle-ci permet de dresser un tableau des pratiques religieuses officielles et populaires de la Syrie du nord du IIème millénaire. L'étude de ces pratiques et leur rapprochement avec les prescriptions rituelles décrites par exemple dans certains textes ougaritiques ou dans des livres vétérotestamentaires comme le Lévitique ont porté à relever des persistances.

Parmi les rites qui ont été soumis à examen rappelons d'abord les sacrifices du sang, *uzi(ya) zurki(ya)*, étudiés par V. Haas[49], qui consistent à immoler des animaux et à répandre leur sang sur l'autel et sur les objets sacrés servant au sacrifice (on les a rapprochés des rites *ḥaṭṭaʾt ʾašam*), puis les rituels *keldi(ya) ambašši(ya)*, c'est-à-dire un sacrifice offert pour s'attirer la bienveillance de la divinité et qui consiste principalement en un holocauste. A ces rites parallèles aux rituels hébraïques *ʿlwt wšlmym* D. Schwemer a consacré un article important[50]. Les rites d'élimination qui consistent dans le transfert de l'impureté d'un individu sur un animal, le „bouc émissaire", et qui trouvent un parallèle intéressant dans les rites „pour Azazel" ont été l'objet d'une étude de B. Janowski—G. Wilhelm[51]. C. Kühne a pour sa part analysé les rites préparatoires au sacrifice proprement dit[52].

Tout dernièrement H.A. Hoffner[53] a proposé un rapprochement entre le rite exprimé par le verbe hittite *waḫnu-* „agiter, tourner, entourer" et celui dont

---

48 M.-Cl. Trémouille, „Il *tabri* e i suoi addetti nella documentazione ittita", in: F. Imparati (ed.), *Quattro Studi Ittiti* (Eothen 4), Firenze: Elite, Edizioni Librarie Italiane Estere, 1991, 77–105; *ead.*, „Note sur le terme *ḫurtišši* dans les textes de Boğazköy", in: O. Carruba, M. Giorgieri, C. Mora (eds.), *Atti del II Congresso Internazionale di Hittitologia* (StMed 9), Pavia: Gianni Iuculano Editore, 1995, 369–80; *ead.*, „Un objet cultuel: le *šeḫelliški*", *SMEA* 38 (1996) 73–93. Une recherche spécifique est actuellement en cours: elle prévoit entre autres la publication en traduction commentée de tous ces rituels de Kizzuwatna.

49 V. Haas, „Ein hurritischer Blutritus und die Deponierung der Ritualrückstände nach hethitischen Quellen", in: B. Janowski, K. Koch, G. Wilhelm (eds.), *Religionsgeschichtliche Beziehungen*, 1993, 67–85; *id.*, ChS I/9 cité à la note 47.

50 D. Schwemer, „Das alttestamentliche Doppelritual *'lwt wšlmym* im Horizont der hurritischen Opfertermini *ambašši* und *keldi*", *SCCNH* 7 (1995) 81–116.

51 B. Janowski - G. Wilhelm, „Der Bock, der die Sünde hinausträgt", in: B. Janowski, K. Koch, G. Wilhelm (eds.), *Religionsgeschichtliche Beziehungen*, 1993, 109–69.

52 C. Kühne, „Zum Vor-Opfer im alten Anatolien", in: B. Janowski, K. Koch, G. Wilhelm (eds.), *Religionsgeschichtliche Beziehungen*, 1993, 225–83.

53 H.A. Hoffner, Jr., in: G. Buccellati, M.K. Kelly-Buccellati, *Urkesh and the Hurrians* (BibMes 26), 1998, 187 s.

parle par exemple le Lévitique 23, 20: „Le prêtre agitera rituellement[54] les agneaux avec le pain des prémisses comme offrande à agiter (offrande *tenûfa*) devant le Seigneur". Toutefois, il me semble que le geste exprimé par le verbe *waḫnu-*, geste qui comparait par ailleurs non seulement dans les textes d'ascendance hourrite mais déjà dans le rituel ancien-hittite KBo 17.1[55], indique plutôt l'acte magique qui consiste à entourer ou la personne à purifier, ou le simulacre divin[56], ou encore le temple[57], en quelque sorte la création d'un „cercle magique".

Par contre, d'autres procédures rituelles peuvent être mises en comparaison; j'en rappellerai deux:

D'abord, l'imposition de la main. L'imposition de la main est un geste attesté dans les rituels magiques anatoliens, où il indique le transfert de l'impureté du „patient" à son substitut, principalement un animal, qui sera ensuite éliminé ou en l'abattant dans une fosse ou en l'éloignant. Dans les textes kizzuwatniens, dont le rituel *CTH* 701 „Libations au trône de la déesse Ḫebat" ou encore le rituel de Allaituraḫ(ḫ)i de Mukiš, tous deux publiés dans la série ChS[58], pourront servir d'exemples, le geste de l'imposition de la main a un tout autre sens, le même qu'a ce geste par exemple dans le Lévitique 1, 4; 4, 4, etc. Ici, il n'a pas le but de faire passer le péché de l'homme sur l'animal, car si cela était le cas, il serait impensable d'offrir ensuite cet animal en sacrifice d'offrande (*keldiya*) à la divinité, l'impureté acquise le rendant impropre à son sacrifice. Ce geste exprime plutôt, à mon avis, une certaine identification de la victime à l'offrant: au travers de la victime, c'est l'offrant lui-même qui se donne à la divinité.

Ensuite, l'oiseau dont on „serre" les ailes. Le même rituel *CTH* 701 contient des indications qui correspondent ponctuellement à des prescriptions du Lévitique. Ici, par exemple, on recommande de ne pas séparer les ailes des tourterelles après que l'oiseau a été fendu en deux (Lév. 1,17). Là, on recommande de „serrer" les ailes de l'oiseau[59], probablement ici aussi une colombe puisque dans une des déclamations en langue hourrite qui accompagne ce sacrifice figure le terme *zinzabu* que l'on interprète normalement comme „colombe"[60], „tourterelle".

---

54 Le verbe hébraïque est *henîf.*

55 Ro II 30–32. Le texte est publié par H. Otten - V. Souček, *Ein althethitisches Ritual für das Königspaar* (StBoT 8), Wiesbaden: Verlag Otto Harrassowitz, 1969.

56 KBo 9.115(+) IV 9–12.

57 KUB 54.36(+) Vo 37'–38'. Pour ce texte v. M.-Cl. Trémouille, „Une 'fête du mois' pour Teššub et Ḫebat", *SMEA* 37 (1996) 79–104.

58 *CTH* 701 est publié dans ChS I/2 *cit.*, le rituel d'Allaituraḫ(ḫ)i dans ChS I/5 *cit.*

59 KBo 21.33+ Vo III 26–27.

60 V. par exemple KBo 21.33+ Vo III 45. Sur la signification de ce terme v. E. Laroche, *Glossaire de la langue hourrite*, Paris: Librairie Klincksieck, 1980, 305.

En l'absence de tout élément de comparaison dans les régions orientales du Proche-Orient il est impossible à ce jour de dire si ces pratiques ont été introduites dans la Syrie du Nord par quelque groupe ethnique—comme pourraient l'être les Hourrites—ou s'il s'agit de rites indigènes communs à un moment donné à diverses populations et que les Hourrites ont assimilés. Rappelons qu'un texte d'Alalaḫ VII—AT 126—contient déjà des prescriptions identiques à celles que l'on trouve dans les rituels kizzuwatniens, rituels qui, pour la plupart, sont datables des XV–XIVèmes siècles. Les textes hourrites de Mari qui remontent, comme nous l'avons dit, à l'époque paléo-babylonienne n'apportent malheureusement aucun élément utile, car ils ne mentionnent, à l'exclusion des noms de divinités, aucun des termes figurant dans les rituels en question.

D'autres aspects du culte ont été également examinés, en particulier les prières. Tandis que H. Güterbock[61] publiait un hymne hourrito-hittite à la déesse Ištar, dont le début du texte conservé rappelle la formule initiale de la Bilingue „Je veux exalter ...[62], G. Wilhelm traçait un panorama des prières hourrites et soulignait les éléments hymniques qui s'y retrouvent et sont de probable dérivation mésopotamienne[63].

3.3. Pour ce qui est de la divination, peu de travaux y ont été consacrés. Outre, bien sûr, l'édition des textes mantiques de Boğazköy par St. de Martino[64], on retiendra surtout l'étude de G. Wilhelm sur quelques *danānu*-Omina[65] en langue hourrite découverts dans la capitale hittite. Avec la prochaine publication des textes hourrites d'Emar[66], dont un grand nombre est constitué de textes divinatoires, les spécialistes disposeront de nouveaux matériaux d'étude sur les techniques de divination utilisées par les Hourrites, en particulier sur l'hépatoscopie[67]. Quant à la divination effectuée à l'aide de l'oiseau *ḫurri*, il est

---

61 H.G. Güterbock, „A Hurro-hittite Hymn to Ishtar", in: J.M. Sasson (ed.), *Studies in Literature from the Ancient Near East Dedicated to Samuel Noah Kramer* (JAOS 103/1, 1983) 155–64, avec bibliographie; G. Wilhelm, „Hymnen der Hethiter", in: W. Burkert / F. Stolz, *Hymnen der Alten Welt im Kulturvergleich* (OBO 131), Freiburg/Schweiz: Universitätsverlag, 1994, 70–73.

62 La forme verbale hittite est *wallaḫḫi* que H.G. Güterbock traduit par „I shall praise"; dans la Bilingue la forme verbale hourrite est *talmaštili* que E. Neu rend par „ich will preisen".

63 G. Wilhelm, „Zur hurritischen Gebetsliteratur", in: D.R. Daniels, U. Gleßmer, M. Rösel (eds.), *Ernten, was man sät, Festschrift für Klaus Koch zu seinem 65. Geburtstag*, Neukirchen: Neukirchener Verlag, 1991, 37–47; *id.*, „Hymnen der Hethiter", 59–77, en particulier 74.

64 V. note 25.

65 G. Wilhelm, „Eine hurritische Sammlung von *dananu*-Omina aus Boğazköy", *ZA* 77 (1987) 229–38.

66 V. note 26.

67 V.A. Archi, „Hethitische Mantik und Ihre Beziehungen zur mesopotamischen Mantik", in: H.-J. Nissen / J. Renger (eds.), *Mesopotamien und seine Nachbarn* (BBVO 1), Berlin: Dietrich Reimer Verlag, 1987, 288.

bon de remarquer qu'elle est déjà attestée dans les textes de Mari[68]. Une autre technique divinatoire attribuée généralement au milieu hourrite de Kizzuwatna, qui consiste à étudier les mouvements de certains poissons, pourrait avoir eu une longue tradition en milieu nord-syrien, puisqu'elle semble être mentionnée dans le texte attribué à Lucien de Samosate sur la Dea Syria de Hierapolis.

3.4. En ce qui concerne la mythologie, à part les travaux cités aux notes 6 et 7, et en dehors des présentations générales des mythes hittites[69], aucune étude spécifique n'a été consacrée à la mythologie hourrite dans son ensemble. Par contre, d'importantes contributions à des précises compositions mythologiques ont été élaborées par H.A. Hoffner[70], E. Neu[71] et M. Salvini[72] qui prépare, entre autres, une édition complète des textes mythologiques en langue hourrite[73]. D'une part, il serait nécessaire d'identifier les divers mythologèmes qui s'y retrouvent, de l'autre, une comparaison systématique avec les éléments mythiques analogues dans la documentation mésopotamienne ainsi que dans l'iconographie[74] permettrait peut-être de reconnaître une certaine stratification dans les textes mythologiques hourrites. Il est en effet possible que l'empreinte suméro-akkadienne que l'on note dans la mythologie hourrite provienne directement de contacts à haute époque (fin du IIIème et début du IIème millénaire) ou bien qu'elle soit à attribuer à l'influence de la culture nord-syrienne, elle-même imbue de culture mésopotamienne[75]. En faveur d'une réponse affirmative à la première alternative parlent des mythes comme celui de Gurparanzaḫ, ou encore un rituel comme celui étudié dernièrement par St. de Martino[76]. Par contre, des mythes où figure la mer, comme celui de Ḫedammu ou celui de Ullikummi, ont probablement été élaborés dans un contexte syrien.

---

68 V. J.-M. Durand, „Introduction générale sur les devins", *ARMT* XXVI/1,1988, 38; *id.*, „La divination par les oiseaux", *M.A.R.I.* 8 (1997) 273 s. avec note 4.

69 H.A. Hoffner, Jr. , *Hittite Myths*, Atlanta: Scholars Press, 1990; F. Pecchioli Daddi - A.M. Polvani, *La mitologia ittita*, Brescia: Paideia Editrice, 1990.

70 H.A. Hoffner, „The Hurrian Story of the Sungod, The Cow and the Fisherman", *SCCNH* 1 (1981) 189–94; *id.*, „The Song of Silver: A Member of the Kumarbi Cycle of 'Sings'", in: E. Neu / Ch. Rüster (eds.), *Documentum Asiae Minoris Antiquae. Festschrift für Heinrich Otten zum 75. Geburtstag*, Wiesbaden: Otto Harrassowitz, 1988, 143–66.

71 E. Neu, „Kešše-Epos und Epos der Freilassung", *SMEA* 31 (1993) 111–20.

72 M. Salvini, „Die hurritischen Überlieferungen des Gilgameš-Epos und der Kešši-Erzählung", in: V. Haas (ed.), *Hurriter und Hurritisch*, 157–72.

73 V. M. Salvini, „Sui testi mitologici in lingua hurrica", *SMEA* 18 (1977) 73–91; *id.*, ChS I/6 cité à la note 24.

74 D. Stein, „Mythologische Inhalte der Nuzi-Glyptik", in: V. Haas (ed.), *Hurriter und Hurritisch*, 173–209.

75 On rappellera à ce propos les observations de G. Wilhelm, in: J.-M. Durand (ed.), *Mari, Ebla et les Hourrites*, 180 s. avec note 70.

76 St. de Martino, „KUB XXVII 38: Ein Beispiel kultureller und linguistischer Überlagerung in einem Text aus dem Archiv von Boğazköy", *SMEA* 31 (1993) 121–34.

4. Après ce rapide tour d'horizon sur les principales recherches historico-religieuses de ces dernières années, je me permetterai maintenant quelques reflexions.

4.1. Je m'arrêterai tout d'abord sur les théonymes hourrites.

Récemment I. Wegner, dans un brillant article[77], a démontré que le nom de la déesse hourrite Ša(w)uška est dérivé de l'adjectif *šav=o=ži*, avec l'ajout d'un suffixe /k/, un „honorificum", et une terminaison *-a* assez fréquente pour les noms de dieux (on retrouve peut-être ces deux derniers dans le nom du dieu Soleil Šimika[78]). Selon cette analyse, Šauška est donc en réalité une épithète signifiant „la Grande". La similitude de caractères que l'on remarquait entre la déesse Šauška et la déesse Ištar n'est, par conséquent, pas due à un syncrétisme mais s'explique par leur identité[79].

Les résultats de l'étude de I. Wegner invitent à réflechir sur l'ensemble des théonymes hourrites. Or, si l'on considère les noms de dieux attestés dans les textes hourrites, quelle que soit leur origine, un élément semble spécifique, péculier des Hourrites dans leurs rapports avec la sphère du divin: la tendance à donner aux divinités non pas un „nom" mais une épithète qui fonctionne comme nom. Cette épithète peut être constituée

par un substantif: on a ainsi Allani „la Dame";

par un adjectif substantivé indiquant une caractéristique de la divinité: Mušuni „la juste", „l'ordonnatrice"[80],

une phrase: Tiyabenti „celui/celle qui parle de façon juste"[81]; Ebrimuša „le Seigneur est juste"[82],

ou encore un ethnique, et ce sont les plus nombreux: Kumarbi „(celui) de Kumar"[83], „Nabarbi „(celle) de Nawar"[84], Pišanuḫi „(provenant) de Pišanu", Pišaišapḫi „(provenant) de Pišaiša", Pidenḫi

---

[77] Article cité à la note 33.

[78] Cette forme du théonyme alterne en effet avec Šimige. On observera qu'une forme ancienne de ce nom (dans le texte de Mari 2: 12, 16) est Šimia, sans *-k-*, tout comme la forme la plus ancienne du nom Šauška est Šauša.

[79] G. Wilhelm, in: J.-M. Durand (ed.), *Mari, Ebla et les Hourrites*, 180 s.

[80] V. G. Wilhelm, entrée „Mušun(n)i, Mušni", in: *Reallexikon der Assyriologie* VIII, Berlin - New York 1993–1997, 498 s.; M.-Cl. Trémouille, ^{D}*Ḫebat* cité à la note 21, 185–89.

[81] V. M.-Cl. Trémouille, ^{D}*Ḫebat* cité à la note 21, 207–10.

[82] H. Otten, entrée „Ibrimuša", *Reallexikon für Assyriologie* V, Berlin - New York 1976–1980, 23.

[83] V. G. Wilhelm, „Kumme und *Kumar: Zur hurritischen Ortsnamenbildung", in: P. Calmeyer e.a., *Beiträge zur Altorientalischen Archäologie und Altertumskunde, Festschrift für Barthel Hrouda zum 65. Geburtstag*, Wiesbaden: Harrassowitz Verlag, 1994, 315–19.

[84] Sur la „Dame de Nawar/Nagar", l'une des plus anciennes divinités hourrites mentionnées dans les textes et élément de noms théophores dès la période d'Ur III, v. dernièrement M. Guichard, „Zimrî-Lîm à Nagar", *M.A.R.I.* 8 (1996) 329–37 avec bibliographie. V. aussi V. Haas, entrée „Nabarbi", *Reallexikon für Assyriologie* 9, 1997, 1 s.

„(provenant) de Piden", peut-être aussi Kušuḫ(e) „(provenant) de Kuzi(na)"[85], etc.

Il est donc bien possible que ces „théonymes" hourrites masquent en réalité des entités divines connues par ailleurs, mais sous un autre nom. L'étude systématique de leurs péculiarités et leur comparaison avec d'autres divinités qui présenteraient les mêmes caractéristiques et dont l'un des lieux de culte, si ce n'est le principal, correspondrait avec le toponyme à la base de ces ethniques pourraient permettre de les identifier.

4.2. Je prendrai ensuite en considération les rapports entre les souverains hourrites et l'idéologie de la royauté.

Dans la Mésopotamie du Nord, on le sait, l'idéologie en vigueur est celle du roi „fort", dont la vaillance et le courage sont preuve de l'appui des dieux. En Syrie, au contraire, l'idéologie royale est liée au concept de „justice", en particulier sous l'égide du dieu de l'orage d'Alep et de sa parèdre. On peut donc, en quelque sorte, parler de deux systèmes idéologiques différents. Or, il apparait clairement que les rois hourrites se conformaient à l'une ou l'autre de ces idéologies selon la région où ils habitaient et quelle que soit la dimension du territoire sur lequel ils imposaient leur souveraineté.

Ainsi les rois hourrites Adalšen et Tišadal suivent l'idéologie nord-mésopotamienne du roi „fort". Il est en effet significatif, à mon avis, qu'ils dédient chacun un temple à Ner(i)gal, le dieu „fort" par excellence auquel par exemple Naram-Sin attribue le mérite de ses propres victoires[86].

Dans ce sens va également, selon moi, le choix des noms des souverains des plus anciens royaumes hourrites orientaux: Taḫiš-atili de Azuḫinum, Puttim-adal de Šimurrum, Talpuš-atili di Nagar, Adal-šen d'Urkiš et de Nawar, Tiš-adal et Ann-atal d'Urkiš, contiennent tous l'élément *-adal* qui signifie „le Fort"[87], c'est-à-dire l'épithète qui indique le dieu Nergal. Encore en appui à cette hypothèse on soulignera la fréquence du terme ugur dans l'onomastique de Nuzi, ugur étant l'équivalent de l'akk. *namṣaru* „l'épée", symbole divinisé[88] et autre appellatif du dieu Nergal.

---

85 V. G. Wilhelm, *Grundzüge der Geschichte und Kultur der Hurriter*, Darmstadt: Wissenschaftliche Buchgesellschaft, 1982, 75.

86 Cf. par exemple le texte gravé sur la base de statue découverte à Bassetki.

87 Cf. M. Salvini, in: G. Buccellati, M.K. Kelly-Buccellati, *Urkesh and the Hurrians*, 99–115, qui cite encore d'autres noms en *-adal* p. 112. Il est significatif, à mon avis, que le roi de Tikunani, auquel s'adresse le Labarna hittite dans la lettre publiée par M. Salvini, „Una lettera di Ḫattušili I relativa alla spedizione contro Ḫaḫḫum", *SMEA* 34 (1994) 61–80, ne porte pas un nom en *-adal*. Cela indique, selon moi, qu'il ne participe pas de l'idéologie du roi „fort", mais qu'il suit au contraire l'idéologie „syrienne", comme les rois de Mari. En conséquence, il est probable que le territoire de Tikunani sur lequel règne Tunip-Teššub soit à chercher dans la partie occidentale de la Mésopotamie septentrionale, puisqu'il gravite idéalement sur Alep.

88 A ce propos on rappellera la représentation de cette divinité, sous forme d'une épée, dans la chambre B de Yazılıkaya. Le choix de cette iconographie dans ce que l'on considère

Les attestations concernant le rôle du dieu de l'orage d'Alep dans l'idéologie royale de la Syrie sont nombreuses et bien connues. Je n'y insisterai pas. Ce que je voudrais souligner ici, c'est le rôle identique joué par le dieu de l'orage de Kumme, comme le montre bien à mon avis le texte de la Bilingue relatif à Ebla.

Selon les mots de J.-M. Durand, „le dieu de l'orage d'Alep est un dieu ... qui attache une attention exclusive à la justice, tout particulièrement celle due aux faibles"[89]. Ainsi, dans un oracle prononcé par le prophète d'Addu d'Alep à propos d'un édit de restauration, c'est à dire de remise des dettes (*andurārum*) le dieu déclare „... rends-leur justice. ... Si tu fais ce que je viens de t'écrire, et si tu prêtes attention à ma parole, alors je te livrerai ton pays d'Est en Ouest..."[90]. De même dans une lettre à Zimri-Lim on peut lire: „Si tu laisses libre cours à l'Edit de restauration, alors ta royauté sera éternelle"[91].

On ne peut manquer de rapprocher ces paroles de celles de Teššūb de Kumme dans le texte de la Bilingue, texte que son colophon indique précisément comme „chant de la restauration", le hourrite *kirenzi* (hittite *para tarnumar*) étant l'équivalent de l'akk. *andurārum* et de l'hébreu *dêrôr*[92]: „Mais si dans Ebla, la ville du trône, vous donnez libre cours à (l'édit de) [la] restauration, alors je bénirais vos armes comme [...] et il arrivera que vos armes vainqueront vos adversaires"[93].

Le dieu de l'orage de Kumme/i(ya) et le dieu de l'orage d'Alep, qu'on les appelle Teššub, Addu ou Adad, ont donc des caractéristiques communes, en particulier en ce qui concerne l'idéologie de la justice. Il en découle que la présence du dieu de Kumme dans la Bilingue n'indique pas nécessairement qu'Ebla à l'age du bronze moyen ait été particulièrement marquée par la religion hourrite.

---

généralement comme la chambre sépulcrale de Tudḫaliya IV s'accorde avec le vaste programme de construction de ce même souverain („la Ville de Tudḫaliya") en regard de la nouvelle fondation de son antagoniste assyrien, Kār-Tukultī-Ninurta. Les deux épisodes peuvent être interprétés comme la volonté du souverain hittite de se battre avec les mêmes armes de propagande que son ennemi oriental.

89 J.-M. Durand, „Le combat entre le Dieu de l'orage et la Mer", *M.A.R.I.* 7 (1993) 60.

90 B. Lafont, „Le roi de Mari et les prophètes du dieu Adad", *RA* 78 (1984) 7–18; et *ARMT* XXVI/3.

91 *ARMT* XXVI/1 194, [A.4260] 38–43, v. J.-M. Durand, „Echange de lettres avec les dieux", *ARMT* XXVI/1, Paris 1988; *id.*, „Les textes prophétiques", *ARMT* XXVI/1, Paris 1988, 404 s. Pour d'autres données analogues v. A. Lemaire, „Les textes prophétiques de Mari", in: J.–M. Durand (ed.), *Mari, Ebla et les Hourrites*, 433 s.

92 Une *andurārum* est attestée pour Zimri-Lim (peut-être au début de son règne). V. D. Charpin, „L'andurârum à Mari", *M.A.R.I.* 6 (1990), 253–70. Doit-on mettre cette pratique en rapport avec la mention d'une „année d'Adad d'Alep", qui pour P. Villard, „La place des années de «Kaḫat» et d'«Adad d'Alep» dans la chronologie du règne de Zimri-Lim", *M.A.R.I.* 7 cit, 315–28, serait à placer en ZL 1'?

93 E. Neu, *Das hurritische Epos der Freilassung* (StBoT 32), 221, 381.

4.3. Pour terminer, l'opposition „panthéon oriental : panthéon occidental" ne doit pas être exagérée. Elle n'est sans doute qu'apparente et due à une consistance inégale de la documentation religieuse, réduite à l'Est à deux inscriptions dédicatoires, abondante à l'Ouest avec toute la gamme des textes que l'on peut qualifier de religieux: récits mythologiques, rituels magiques et de fête, textes divinatoires, listes de divinités et d'offrandes. Une comparaison entre les anthroponymes hourrites provenant de tout le Proche-Orient ancien montre que ce sont, dans l'ensemble, les mêmes dieux qui fournissent l'élément théophore entrant dans la composition de ces noms. Par conséquent, à mon avis, la vision d'une religion des Hourrites subdivisée *grosso modo* en deux blocs doit être abandonnée.

Certes, la situation documentaire la plus favorable se trouve à l'Ouest, avec les tablettes provenant de Ḫattuša, mais c'est aussi celle qui est la plus compromise, car on y trouve des éléments mésopotamiens, auxquels s'ajoutent des éléments syriens (dans lesquels sont probablement déjà confondus des éléments mésopotamiens), auxquels s'ajoutent des éléments anatoliens. Il en résulte un amalgame dont il est bien difficile de démêler les composantes et dans de telles conditions l'identification des éléments hourrites originels est pratiquement impossible.

En guise de conclusion

La documentation que nous possédons à ce jour montre que les Hourrites vénéraient les mêmes dieux et suivaient les mêmes pratiques religieuses que les autres populations contemporaines du Proche-Orient. Poussé à l'extrême, on pourrait même arriver à se demander si une „religion des Hourrites" a jamais existé.

C'est dans les premières localités qui nous sont connues comme habitat des Hourrites, à l'Est, que pourraient s'être conservés des caractères spécifiques. Il faut donc attendre—et espérer—qu'Urkeš et Nagar, Tell Mozan et Tell Brak, nous apportent quelques lumières plus vives.

Ausgewählte Kapitel zur hurritisch-hethitischen Bilingue*

ERICH NEU†
Ruhr-Universität Bochum

The author refers to various points of disagreement between his and other scholars' positions concerning the Hurro-Hittite bilingual series *kirenzi*, "manumission" from Boğazköy. He discusses some entries from the new trilingual wordlist from Ugarit (see *SCCNH* 9 [1998] 3–40) that are relevant to the Boğazköy bilingual, and lists some Luwian forms in the Middle Hittite version of the text. Some fresh collations yield confirmation of or corrections to the author's edition.

ZUR BILINGUE ALLGEMEIN

1.1. Die in KBo 32 (1990) von H. Otten und Chr. Rüster edierte hurritisch-mittelhethitische Bilingue[1], für die wir in StBoT 32 (1996) eine Bearbeitung vorgelegt haben, findet jetzt erfreulicherweise immer häufiger Erwähnung und Berücksichtigung in der hurritologischen Sekundärliteratur. Damit nehmen allgemein die Bemühungen um das richtige Verständnis von Grammatik und Lexikon des Hurritischen wie auch um die inhaltliche Deutung des gesamten zweisprachigen Textensembles, das man ohne Übertreibung zur Weltliteratur zählen darf[2], zu. Da der aus Nordsyrien nach Ḫattusa verbrachte hurritische (hurr.) Text hinsichtlich seiner Entstehungszeit wesentlich älter ist als der

---

* Für die XLVe Rencontre assyriologique internationale hatten wir als Vortragsthema „Ausgewählte Kapitel zum Inhalt und zur sprachlichen Form der hurritisch-hethitischen Bilingue" angekündigt. Die jetzige gekürzte Formulierung ist durch die Änderung des ursprünglichen Konzepts bedingt. Leider ließ sich meine Teilnahme an dem Kongreß aus verschiedenen Gründen nicht verwirklichen. Für die Aufnahme dieses Beitrags in die Akten des Hurriter/Nuzi-Treffens danke ich sehr herzlich den Veranstaltern der Rencontre und zugleich dem Herausgeber Herrn Prof. Dr. G. Wilhelm.

† Prof. Neu died on December 31, 1999.

1 Sämtliche Belege der Bilingue werden in diesem Beitrag in der Regel ohne Sigel und Bandzahl der Editionsreihe zitiert. So meint z.B. „19 I 4" die ausführlichere Zitation „KBo 32.19 I 4". Nur dann, wenn sich dadurch Unklarheiten ergeben könnten, wird „KBo 32" hinzugefügt.

2 So jetzt auch Otto 1998: 295.

Studies on the Civilization and Culture of Nuzi and the Hurrians - 10

Mittani-Brief, der bisher die Grundlage für Darstellungen der hurr. Grammatik abgab, und beide Textzeugnisse unterschiedlichen Dialektarealen zugehören, bereichert das immer tiefere Eindringen in die Sprachform des hurr. Textes, der in Ḫattuša um 1400 v. Chr. mit einer recht verläßlichen hethitischen (heth.) Übersetzung versehen worden war, erheblich unsere Kenntnisse der hurr. Grammatik wie übrigens auch des hurr. Lexikons. Schon jetzt zeichnen sich zarte Konturen einer sprachlichen Entwicklung innerhalb des Hurritischen ab (StBoT 32, 5f.). Inzwischen lassen sich auf der grammatischen und lexikalischen Ebene auch immer mehr überzeugende Beziehungen und Verknüpfungen zwischen dem Hurritischen und dem viel später bezeugten Urartäischen aufzeigen, was für die Frage nach dem genauen Verwandtschaftsverhältnis dieser beiden Sprachen von Bedeutung ist (vgl. dazu Wilhelm 1995: 113f.; Verf., StBoT 32, 16 Anm. 29). Der hurr. Text der Bilingue hat auch den Anstoß gegeben, erneut der Frage nach einer eventuellen genetischen Verwandtschaft von Hurritisch (einschließlich Urartäisch) und bestimmten kaukasischen Idiomen nachzugehen (Ivanov 1998)[3].

1.2. Unter sprachtypologischem Gesichtspunkt stellt das Hurritische eine suffigierende Ergativsprache mit agglutinierender Morphologie dar (Plank 1988: 69ff.). Ein besonderes Satzmuster des Hurritischen bildet das sogenannte Antipassiv[4]. Die für das Hurritische behauptete „Split Ergativity" („gespaltene Ergativität")[5] läßt sich nach unserem Verständnis der hurr. Grammatik aber nicht bestätigen.

1.3. Dank der beigefügten heth. Übersetzung, die uns die hurr. Sprachform der Bilingue im wesentlichen erschließen hilft, vermag das Hurritische umgekehrt trotz typologischer Verschiedenheit aber auch Informationen für unsere Kenntnis des Hethitischen zu liefern. So hat, um hier nur ein Beispiel zu erwähnen, ein typologischer Sprachvergleich zweifelsfrei ergeben, daß die in der Sekundärliteratur vertretene Auffassung, wonach die Herausbildung der in heth. Texten häufig gebrauchten enklitischen Ortsbezugspartikeln durch das Hurritische bedingt sei, unhaltbar ist[6].

1.4. So stellt also die hurritisch-mittelhethitische Bilingue in vieler Hinsicht ein bisher einzigartiges literarisches Sprachdenkmal dar, das es mit gemeinsamen Anstrengungen weiter zu erforschen gilt.

---

3 Herrn Prof. Ivanov danke ich sehr herzlich, daß er mir seine diesbezügliche Untersuchung bereits im Druckmanuskript zur Kenntnis gegeben hat.

4 Girbal 1992: 171ff.; Haas, Wegner 1991: 390f.

5 So Haas, Wegner 1997: 444.

6 Neu 1988: 248ff.— Auch das Hattische kommt dafür nicht in Frage, wie man sich für die Ortsbezugspartikeln *-kan* und *-šan* jetzt auch an der hattisch-hethitischen Bilingue (Klinger 1996: 638f.) überzeugen kann.

EPOS DER FREILASSUNG ODER SERIE „FREILASSUNG"?

2.1. Mit der in StBoT 32,7f. gegebenen Begründung hatten wir das zweisprachige Textensemble entsprechend dem bereits im Kolophon der Proömiumstafel (11 IV 22') bezeugten Schreibervermerk SÌR *parā tarnumaš* als „Epos der Freilassung" bezeichnet, wohl wissend um die Problematik einer adäquaten deutschen Übersetzung des Sumerogramms SÌR (vgl. engl. „The Song of Release", franz. „Epos de l'affranchissement"). Unsere Intention war es, den gesamten Schreibervermerk in deutscher Übersetzung darzubieten, um auch demjenigen Leser, dem der sumerische Begriff fremd ist, die vollständige Information der Textvorlage zu vermitteln. Der Ausdruck SÌR *parā tarnumaš* erschien den heth. Schreibern als inhaltliche Kennzeichnung der zweisprachigen Textgruppe angemessen, und daher war der Philologe gefordert, nach einer passenden, zugleich auch griffigen deutschen Übersetzung zu suchen. Den Begriff SÌR davon auszunehmen, dafür sahen wir keinen Grund. Daher haben wir uns schließlich unter Zurückstellung philologischer und literaturtheoretischer Bedenken für dessen Wiedergabe mit dem von uns mehr etikettartig verstandenen Ausdruck „Epos" entschieden, der z.B. von H.G. Güterbock bereits für die Übersetzung der zur hurr. Erzählung vom Jäger Kešše gehörenden Tafelunterschrift SÌR ^{m}Kešše gebraucht worden war (StBoT 32, 7 mit Anm. 13; 33f. mit Anm. 2).

2.2. Nun hat sich aber Wilhelm 1997: 277f. entschieden gegen die Verwendung des Gattungsbegriffes „Epos" für die zweisprachige Textgruppe ausgesprochen und übernimmt stattdessen den viel später in der Assyriologie bezeugten neutralen Begriff „Serie". Somit bezeichnet er das hurritisch-hethitische Textensemble als Serie „Freilassung" und läßt das Sumerogramm SÌR unübersetzt.

Der Begriff „Serie" bietet sich jedoch als Ordnungsschema auch ohne Rückgriff auf assyriologische Gegebenheiten geradezu an, haben doch die Schreiber die einzelnen Tafeln auch mit Zahlangaben versehen, von denen uns leider nur wenige erhalten geblieben sind („1. Tafel", „2. Tafel, „5. Tafel"), was die Feststellung der genauen Reihenfolge erheblich erschwert. Schon vor Erscheinen des oben erwähnten Aufsatzes von G. Wilhelm haben wir in unserer Bearbeitung immer wieder von Serie, Tafelserie(n) oder Seriennummer gesprochen (StBoT 32, 2, 16f., 483 *et passim*), ja, wir haben mit Blick auf die vorhandenen Duplikattexte wiederholt darauf hingewiesen, daß es mehrere Serien vom „Epos der Freilassung" gegeben haben muß. Um den Zahlangaben der Schreiber Rechnung zu tragen, gebrauchten und gebrauchen wir also den Ordnungsbegriff Serie, während der von uns mit „Epos der Freilassung" wiedergegebene Ausdruck ebenso entsprechend der Kennzeichnung durch die Schreiber auf den Inhalt der Tafeln Bezug nimmt. Daher schließen sich diese beiden Bezeichnungen formaler und inhaltlicher Art auch nicht gegenseitig aus. Dies als Antwort auf die als Frage formulierte Kapitelüberschrift.

2.3. In der Regel notierten die Schreiber in den Tafelkolophonen auch, ob der Text einer Tafel „fertig" oder „nicht fertig" war, der Text also auf einer weiteren Tafel fortgesetzt wurde. Auch von diesen Hinweisen haben sich nur wenige erhalten. Daß ein solcher Schreibervermerk vereinzelt auch zur Bestimmung der Tafelreihenfolge beizutragen vermag, soll hier an einem Beispiel erläutert werden.

Die nur sehr bruchstückhaft erhaltene 2. Tafel (= KBo 32.12) trägt den Schreibervermerk „Nich[t fertig]", und tatsächlich endet der Text dieser mit Parabeln beschrifteten Tafel mit dem sogenannten Übergangsparagraphen, der von einer Parabel zu einer anderen überleitet. Demnach muß die folgende Tafel mit dem Text einer Parabel begonnen haben. Dies aber trifft genau für die als Nr. 14 edierte Tafel, die insgesamt sieben Parabeln enthält, zu. Mit dieser Tafel, die wir als „3. Tafel" der gleichen Serie betrachten, endet dann auch für diese Serie die Darbietung der Parabeln; denn der betreffende Schreiber hat sogar den unteren und linken Tafelrand dicht beschrieben, um auf diese Weise auch die letzte Parabel noch auf dieser Tafel unterzubringen (StBoT 32, 17f., 59). Dieses Bemühen zeigt sich auch schon daran, daß er bereits auf der Tafelrückseite (ab Zeile 23) die raummäßig großzügigere Zwei-Kolumnen-Beschriftung (linke Kolumne Hurritisch, rechte Kolumne Hethitisch) zugunsten eines über die gesamte Tafelbreite (unter Weglassen des Kolumnentrenners) fortlaufenden Textes aufgegeben hat (vgl. StBoT 32, 1 Anm. 2)[7].

Die neue Trilingue RS 94-2939 und die Bilingue aus Ḫattuša

3.1. In *SCCNH* 9 (1998) 3ff. haben B. André-Salvini und M. Salvini eine 1994 in Ugarit gefundene Trilingue (Sumerisch, Akkadisch, Hurritisch) in einer vorbildhaften Bearbeitung vorgelegt. Dafür wie auch für die rasche Publikation gebührt den Autoren ein herzliches Dankeschön. Mehrere Einträge dieses dreisprachigen, leider nicht vollständig erhaltenen Vokabulars tangieren auch die hurritisch-mittelhethitische Bilingue aus Boğazköy-Ḫattuša, worauf teilweise auch schon die beiden Autoren hingewiesen haben. Im Folgenden werden wir auswahlweise einige uns besonders beachtenswerte Bezüge herausstellen und besprechen. Dabei folgen wir der alphabetischen Anordnung (*SCCNH* 9, 8ff.), auf die wir mit der Abkürzung LA (= Liste Alphabétique) und Seitenzahl verweisen.

3.2. Es fällt auf, daß innerhalb der Bilingue dem hurr. Wort für „Baumeister" (*i-te-en-ni*), das dem akkadischen (akkad.) *itinnu/etennu* entlehnt ist (StBoT 32, 183f.), in der heth. Übersetzung das Sumerogramm ^{LÚ}NAGAR eigentlich „Zimmermann" entspricht (für Einzelheiten Neu 1993: 59f). In der Trilingue

---

7 Daher können wir uns auch nicht der Auffassung von Wilhelm 1997: 292f. anschließen, der auf die „2. Tafel" (Text Nr. 12) den Text Nr. 20 als „3. Tafel" folgen lassen und Nr. 14 (unsere „3. Tafel") als nicht zu dieser Serie gehörig betrachten, sondern das darin „zusammengestellte Weisheitsmaterial ... als Paralipomena" werten möchte.—Um einem möglichen Mißverständnis (Haas, Wegner 1997: 437f.) vorzubeugen, sei angemerkt, daß die Reihenfolge, in der wir in StBoT 32 die einzelnen Texte abhandeln, zwar die überlieferten Tafelnummern berücksichtigt, letztlich aber nach inhaltlichen Kriterien die Abfolge der Bearbeitung meint.

(LA 8) ist vom hurr. Eintrag nur noch *a*[- erhalten, und in der sumerischen (sumer.) Spalte steht TIN. Immerhin zeigt der hurr. Eintrag aber eine deutliche lexikalische Abweichung von der Bilingue.

3.3. Auch die Bilingue bezeugt entsprechend der Trilingue (LA 8) den Namen der Unterweltsgöttin als Allani, wenn auch in unterschiedlicher Graphie als *A-al-la-a-ni*, mit Richtungskasus dann *A-al-la-a-an-ni* (StBoT 32, 590).

3.4. Schon aufgrund der inhaltlichen Logik des Kontextes hatten wir den hurr. Ausdruck *ta-a-ti-i̯a-aš-ši* der Bilingue (13 I 28), der in der heth. Übersetzung keine Entsprechung hat, dahingehend verstanden, daß Allāni, die Sonnengöttin der Erde, Zuneigung für Teššub, den bei ihr als Gast weilenden Herrschergott des hurr. Pantheons, empfindet (StBoT 32, 267; entsprechend Catsanicos 1996: 209, 269). Haas, Wegner 1997: 449 hingegen—wohl basierend auf der Grammatik des Mittani-Briefes—haben unsere Interpretation als fehlerhaft verworfen und die Meinung vertreten, daß Teššub die Göttin Allāni liebt, Teššub also Allāni zugeneigt ist. Nun zeigt aber die Trilingue (LA 9, vgl. 22) mit hurr. *a-mu-*⸢*mi-i̯a-aš-še*⸣ (*am=om=i=a=šše*) „erstrangig", daß mit *tād=i=a=šše* vergleichbare Bildungen auf *-(a)šše* auch adjektivischen Charakter („une valeur adjectivale") haben können, so daß unsere Auffassung von *tād=i=a=šše*, wonach Allāni für Teššub Zuneigung empfindet, sehr wohl möglich ist. Der betreffende Ausdruck stünde dann in der Bedeutung „Liebende" oppositionell neben Allāni[8].

3.5. Bezüglich der durch die Trilingue (LA 11) bezeugten Wortgleichung hurr. *e-we-er-ni* = sumer. LUGAL = akkad. *šar-ru* verdient aus der Bilingue die Ausdrucksweise ᴰIM-*ub* ᵁᴿᵁ*Kum-mi-ni-bi da-la-a-u̯u*ᵤ̈*-ši ib-ri* (15 IV 14, vgl. 11 1 1 f.; StBoT 32, 30, 296/297) Beachtung, der in der heth. Übersetzung ᴰIM-*aš* ᵁᴿᵁ*Kum-mi-i̯a-aš* LU[GA]L GAL entspricht und die wir daher mit „Teššub, großer König von Kummi!" übersetzt haben (s. auch StBoT 32, 360). Damit weichen wir—gestützt auf die heth. Übersetzung—von der in der Sekundärliteratur anzutreffenden Unterscheidung, wonach *evri* „Herr" und *everni* „König" (mit ‚individualisierendem' Suffix *-ni*; vgl. StBoT 32, 401 Anm. 17) bedeuten soll, ab. Nach den Bearbeitern der Trilingue stellt *evri* das eigentliche hurr. Wort für „König" dar („determiné ewir=ni"), während *šarri* bekanntlich dem Akkadischen entlehnt ist[9]. In diesem Zusammenhang sind die innerhalb der Bilingue im gleichen Text auftretenden Pluralformen *e-bi-ir-na* und *e-eb-ri-in-na* bemer-

---

[8] Sehr herzlich danke ich Herrn Kollegen Wilhelm, der mich auf meine Frage nach der Interpretation von *ta-a-ti-i̯a-aš-ši* unter Bezugnahme auf den hier genannten Beleg der Trilingue freundlicherweise wissen ließ (Brief vom 17.8.1998), daß sich mein Verständnis des betreffenden Ausdrucks der Bilingue sachlich wie auch grammatisch rechtfertigen ließe, sofern man für dieses Phänomen von nominalisierten Verbalformen, die Lexikalisierung erfahren haben, ausgehen darf. Vergleichsweise führt er noch *ašḫ=i=a=šše* „Opferherr" an.

[9] Doch s. auch die von den beiden Autoren (*ibidem*) zitierten Vokabulareinträge mit akkad. *bēlu* = hurr. *e-wi-ri* und akkad. *šarru* = hurr. *i-wi-ir-ni*.

kenswert, die beide in der heth. Übersetzung durch LUGAL^{MEŠ} wiedergegeben werden (19 I 4, 6, 8, StBoT 32, 378/379)[10].

3.6. Durch die Trilingue (LA 12) wird der Befund der Bilingue (und auch darüber hinaus), wonach *ḫa-ur-ni* „Himmel" (und folglich *eše* „Erde") bedeutet, bestens bestätigt (vgl. StBoT 32, 187f. *et passim*).

3.7. Mit dem Eintrag *ma-an-ni* in der Bedeutung „er" sichert die Trilingue (LA 13f.) für diese Pronominalform nun auch die Doppelschreibung *-nn-* (dies ergänzend zu StBoT 32, 37 Anm. 15; 132; s. schon Haas, Wegner 1991: 389).

3.8. Abweichend von der Schreibung *pu-ra-mi* „Sklave, Diener" der Trilingue (LA 15) findet sich in der Bilingue die Graphie *pu-ra-am-mi* (StBoT 32, 344f.).

3.9. Die in der Trilingue (LA 15) bezeugte hurr. Vokabel *šal-mi* „Asche" (akkad. *dikmēnu*) stützt indirekt die Interpretation der innerhalb der Bilingue mehrfach auftretenden heth. Akkusativform (Sing.) *ḫaššan* als „Herd, Feuerstelle" mit der hurr. Entsprechung *ḫumni,* wäre doch sonst für das heth. „Asche"-Wort *ḫašš*(*a*)- (mit langem oder kurzem Wurzelvokal) gemäß der Trilingue hurr. *šalmi* als lexikalisches Pendant zu erwarten gewesen (vgl. zur Diskussion StBoT 32, 428ff.).

3.10. Für die hurr. Verbalwurzel *šatt-* erweist jetzt die Trilingue (LA 15) die Bedeutung „ergreifen" (akkad. *ṣabātum,* sumer. DIB), der im Hethitischen das Verbum *ep-/app-* entsprechen sollte. Für die in der Bilingue überlieferte prädikative Partizipialform *ša-at-tu-ub*[11] bzw. *ša-ad-du-u*[*b* ist die heth. Übersetzung an beiden Belegstellen nicht erhalten (StBoT 32, 299, 520). Von diesem Verbum hat man die verbale Wortgleichung hurr. *ḫā-* = heth. *dā-* „(weg)-nehmen" zu unterscheiden (StBoT 32, 113ff. und schon Laroche 1980: 89).

3.11. Von dem hurr. Eintrag für „Sklavin, Dienerin" ist in der Trilingue (LA 20) nur der Wortanfang *ul*[- erhalten, doch bestätigt dieser, daß die betreffende

---

10 Obwohl für *e-bi-ir-na* in 20 IV 17' durch 19 I 4 die Bedeutung „Könige" gesichert ist, analysieren Giorgieri, Röseler 1998: 88 im Anschluß an Wilhelm 1997: 290 die betreffende Wortform auf der Vorderseite von Nr. 20 als Essive zu *ever=ni* „König" (anders Neu 1996b: 69 sowie StBoT 32, 304, 443f.). Nicht anfreunden können wir uns mit der Vorstellung (Wilhelm 1997: 291), daß die in 20 Vs. I genannten Könige zu insgesamt sechs Vorgängerkönigen von Mēgi, dem König von Ebla, gehören sollen, die alle schon von Purra verköstigt worden seien. Problematisch erscheint uns auch die Deutung von *I-ki-in-kal-i-iš-ša* 19 1 5 als Dativ (G. Wilhelm, a.a.0. 286f.), die der heth. Übersetzung (StBoT 32, 379 Anm. 3) entgegensteht. Da sich Purra, wohl eine führende Persönlichkeit der Stadt lkinkalis, zusammen mit „Söhnen der Stadt lkinkališ" in eblaitischer Gefangenschaft befindet, erscheint es nicht ungewöhnlich, wenn diese Stadt (in 19 1 5 grammatisches Subjekt) zur Versorgung in Ebla herangezogen wird (vgl. auch Otto 1998: 293 mit Anm. 9). Für die Diskussion um den Namen Mēgi sei über die in StBoT 32, 406f. besprochene Sekundärliteratur hinaus noch Kühne 1998: 311ff. genannt.

11 Der Lesung und Interpretation von Haas, Wegner 1997: 450 vermögen wir nicht zu folgen.

hurr. Vokabel nicht als *nulmi,* sondern als *ulmi* anzusetzen ist (zur Diskussion StBoT 32, 346 *et passim*).

3.12. Mit Blick auf den in der Trilingue (LA 22) bezeugten hurr. Getreideterminus *ut-te* „épeautre" (akkad. *ku-un-šu,* sumer. ZÍZ) hat man jetzt diesen Ausdruck erneut mit den in der Bilingue überlieferten Getreidebezeichnungen zu diskutieren, wo z.B. halblogographisches ZÍZ-*tar* der heth. Übersetzung dem hurr. Wort *i-zu-u-zi* entspricht (StBoT 32, 310f., vgl. Hoffner 1974: 65ff.).

3.13. Für das hurr. „adjectif élargi" *wa-aḫ-ru-še* „bon, sain" der Trilingue (LA 22) sei auf das Essiv-Syntagma *e-la* wa_{a}*-aḫ-ru-ša* aus dem als Antipassiv konstruierten Satz der Bilingue 13 I 12f. hingewiesen (StBoT 32, 220, 252).

Luwismen im mittelhethitischen Text der Bilingue

4.1. Mit einem gewissen Erstaunen nahmen wir bei unserer Bearbeitung der Bilingue zur Kenntnis, daß ganz unerwartet im mittelheth. Text eine luwische Infinitivform auftritt: *a-ar-šu-u-na* (*arš=ūna*). Aber auch außerhalb der Bilingue begegnet ganz überraschend in der heth. Wiedergabe des hurr. Märchens vom Fischerehepaar ein luwischer Infinitiv (StBoT 32, 515)[12].

4.2. Falls die Lesung *t*]*ar-pa-aš-ša-a-aš* 19 III 14' und 69,5' (s. unten 5.3) in der Bedeutung „Personalersatz" richtig ist, hätte man einen weiteren Luwismus für die Bilingue zu verzeichnen (vgl. Melchert 1993: 215; Tischler 1993: 211f.).

4.3. Luwische Herkunft dürfte auch der reduplizierten Verbalform *za-az-ga-a-i* (3. Pers. Prs.-Fut. Akt., mit schwundstufiger Wurzel und heth. Flexion) zukommen, die sich über das gemeinsame Wurzelelement **za=zg(V)-* mit dem ‚Glossenkeil'-Wort und Nomen actoris *zazkitalla-* (noch unbekannter Bedeutung) in Verbindung bringen läßt (StBoT 32, 214ff.; Melchert 1993: 282).

Zur Lesung und Textherstellung

5.1. Im Sommer 1997 war es mir möglich, erneut Kollationen an den Textoriginalen der Bilingue vorzunehmen[13]. Einige davon teilen wir im folgenden mit. Wir beginnen mit KBo 32.14. Für diesen Text sei zugleich auf das Textphoto in StBoT 32 Tafeln III und IV (am Ende des Heftes) verwiesen.

I 47: Von Haas, Wegner 1995: 28f.; 1993: 55 und Catsanicos 1996: 203f. wird die hurr. Wortform *pu-ú-i* bzw. $wu_{ú}$*-ú-i* als Genitiv des enklitischen Possessivpronomens der 1. Pers. Sing. verstanden und dabei auf mehrfaches Fehlen eines deutlichen Abstands zu dem jeweils vorhergehenden Wort hingewiesen. Für I 47 bemerken die betreffenden Autoren jedoch zu Recht, daß

---

12 Da das Fragment KBo 32.47a Teil einer Tafel mit Parabeln ist, kann es entgegen Haas, Wegner 1995: 183 nicht Duplikat zu 19 II 27ff. sein.

13 Dafür danke ich sehr herzlich dem Grabungsleiter von Boğazköy-Ḫattuša Herrn Dr. J. Seeher und dem damaligen Vertreter der türkischen Generaldirektion der Denkmäler und Museen Herrn H. Şahin vom Museum Boğazkale.

dort zwischen *ta-bi-ri* und *pu-ú-i* ein klarer Wortabstand gegeben ist. Zieht man den Beleg *wu*$_{\text{ú}}$*-ú-i* von außerhalb der Bilingue heran (KUB 32.19+ I 15), muß man auch dort einen deutlichen Abstand zum vorangehenden Wort feststellen. Da im hurr. Text der Bilingue wiederholt Wortabstände dort, wo man sie aus grammatisch-syntaktischer Sicht erwartet, nicht durchgeführt sind, wiegen nach unserem Verständnis die beiden Belege (darunter ein externer) mit deutlichem Wortabstand mehr als diejenigen ohne eine derartige Pausa-Markierung. Hinzu kommt, daß der heth. pronominale Ablativ *am-me-ta-az* 19 II 35 entgegen Haas, Wegner 1993: 55 Anm. 5; 1995: 28f. keine Handhabe für die Deutung der fraglichen hurr. Wortform abgibt. Bei heth. *ammedaz* handelt es sich um einen komitativen Ablativ im Sinne von „mit mir"; dieser stellt einen konstitutiven inhaltlichen Bestandteil für die heth. Wiedergabe der hurr. Verbalform *ta-la-aš-ta-a-ú* „ich werde (mit mir) hinfortnehmen" dar (StBoT 32, 384, 385), wobei das entsprechende heth. Verbum leider nur bruchstückhaft erhalten ist. So tun sich erwartungsgemäß die beiden Autoren auch sehr schwer, in dem kurzen Satz der hurr. Vorlage (I 35) das vermeintliche enklitische Possessivum der 1. Pers. Sing. inhaltlich und syntaktisch sinnvoll unterzubringen. Keiner ihrer Deutungsversuche ist auch nur annähernd überzeugend. Wir selbst möchten die fragliche Wortform versuchsweise als selbständigen pronominalen Genitiv *fu=ve* mit possessivischer Funktion (3. Pers. Sing.) verstehen, vergleichbar der pronominalen Genitivform *šo=ve* bzw. *šo=ve* „meiner" (StBoT 32, 152, 428)[14]. Eine abschließende Beurteilung ist vorerst nicht möglich.

II 1: Schon im Vorfeld unserer Textbearbeitung stellte sich uns die Frage, ob am Zeilenende heth. *tu-e-eg-ga-a*[*z-* oder eher *tu-e-eg-ga-a*[*š-* zu lesen sei. Catsanicos 1996: 229 bietet unter Hinweis auf den Ablativ *tar-na-aš-ši-it* „aus seinem Schädel" (bei Tischler 1993: 191) die zweite Lesung. Die Tafel ist genau an der oberen Schrägung des Keilkopfes ausgebrochen. Vergleicht man das zunächst fragliche Zeichen mit der Zeichenform AŠ (*ibidem* I 7), so fällt auf, daß diese größer ist und kaum über einen nach rechts auslaufenden Keilstrich verfügt. Dies läßt sich auch noch sonst auf der gleichen Tafel beobachten. Schließlich sei auch noch auf den Wortausgang *-a*]*z-še-et* 99, 1' verwiesen (StBoT 32, 100, 540). Dies alles zusammengenommen ließ uns die Lesung *tu-e-eg-ga-a*[*z-še-et*] bevorzugen.

5.2. Wir kommen zu KBo 32.15:

II 8': Hier entfällt in unserer Umschrift aus Raumgründen die in Klammern stehende Pronominalform *ku-iš-ša* (StBoT 32, 289; mit Wilhelm 1997: 280 Anm. 16). In II 7' der deutschen Übersetzung muß es „einen halben Schekel" heißen. Der Text der Zeile I 16' ist in der deutschen Übersetzung

---

14 Zu den selbständigen Personalpronomina des Hurritischen s. Wegner 1992: 227ff. Vom Pronomen *man(n)e* „er" scheint ein Genitiv **man=ve* bisher nicht bezeugt. Zu diesem Pronomen der 3. Pers. Sing. stellt der Genitiv *fu=ve* vielleicht eine Neben- oder Suppletivform dar.

(StBoT 32, 290) noch folgendermaßen zu ergänzen: ... aus (seiner) *Not*[*lage*.– Ein Gott (ist) Mensch!][15].

III 15: Für die Lesung der heth. Verbalform als *pé-e*[*-ḫu-t*]*e-mi* s. bereits Neu 1997a: 131.

IV 1: Hier liegt der Genitiv *pí-ta-ri-we*$_e$ „eines Rindes" vor[16].

IV 18: Zwischen der negierten Verbalform *a-ri-ia-am-ma* und dem Personendeterminativ dürften nur noch zwei Keilschriftzeichen gestanden haben. Vor dem Personenkeil scheint nämlich ein normales Spatium als Wortabstand vorzuliegen. Die Zeichenreste ähneln ungefähr einer Lesung [B]I.U[M], ohne daß sich daraus durch Kombinieren oder durch Rückgriff auf damit vergleichbare Zeichenformen eine sinnvolle Deutung gewinnen ließe[17].

5.3. Kollationsergebnisse zu KBo 32.19 schließen sich an:

II 9: Hier können wir es bei unserer Lesung *ki-nu-un-ma-aš* ^{D}[IM*-aš*, in StBoT 32, 379 belassen (anders Wilhelm 1997: 288 Anm. 49). Im Gegensatz zur hurr. Vorlage, wo der Subjektwechsel nicht angezeigt ist, fügt der heth. Übersetzer erläuternd das neue Satzsubjekt, nämlich: Wettergott (= Teššub), hinzu, entsprechend auch III 33'f. mit heth. Redepartikel. Der proleptische Gebrauch des heth. Pronomens *-aš* / *-an* läßt sich häufig in heth. Texten der hurr. Übersetzungsliteratur beobachten.

II 50: Bei einer jetzt uns möglich erscheinenden Lesung *mu-u*[*n-* könnte man an eine Form des heth. Verbums *munnai-* „verbergen, verstecken" denken (StBoT 32, 387).

III 14': Am ehesten ist *t*]*ar-pa-aš-ša-a-aš* zu lesen. Bei dem nur bruchstückhaft erhaltenen Zeichen scheint es sich um eine althethitische Form von TAR zu handeln, wobei der etwas breite Kopf des senkrechten Keilchens weit nach rechts ausschwingt (zur Wortbedeutung s. oben unter 4.2).

5.4. Auch wenn in KBo 32.20 I 18 am Zeilenanfang vor *ša-ar-r*]*i* noch etwas Raum zu sein scheint, erweist sich doch unsere nach *ibid.* I 6' vorgenommene Ergänzung *ki-iš-ḫi-ni* (StBoT 32, 438) dort als zu lang (vgl. Wilhelm 1997: 290).

---

15 Für die in ihrer Interpretation umstrittene Zeichenkombination AN UŠ UN (StBoT 32, 314ff.) schlagen Güterbock, Hoffner 1994: 62a die durch nichts abgesicherte, innerhalb der Bilingue sich höchst merkwürdig ausnehmende Lesung ^{D}ÚS*-un* vor, während Wilhelm 1997: 280 mit dem Hinweis „Unklar" die ungewöhnliche Umschrift DINGIR.UŠ*-un* bietet.

16 Dies auch zur Umschrift von Wilhelm 1997: 283, dessen Übersetzung von IV 1 uns im Rahmen des Kontextes unverständlich bleibt. Schon die heth. Übersetzung weist mit der Pluralform *malkianzi* „sie spinnen" darauf hin, daß von einer Spinnerin nicht die Rede sein kann, es sich vielmehr auch in der hurr. Vorlage um eine Tätigkeit der schon zuvor genannten Gefangenen (bzw. Schuldsklaven) handelt. Zu unserem eigenen Übersetzungsvorschlag s. StBoT 32, 294/295, 341 sowie Neu 1997b: 262 Anm. 22.

17 G. Wilhelms (a.a.0. 286) mit Fragezeichen versehener Lesungsvorschlag *i?-te?-i?*, den wir am Original überprüft haben, erscheint uns raummäßig zu groß und entspricht schwerlich den erhaltenen Zeichenresten (s. dazu das Textphoto in StBoT 32 Tafel VI). Zur Textherstellung der heth. Übersetzung (15 III 19–20) s. aber auch StBoT 32, 297.

BIBLIOGRAPHIE

André-Salvini, Béatrice, Salvini, Mirjo

1998 „Un nouveau vocabulaire trilingue sumerien-akkadien-hourrite de Ras Shamra", *SCCNH* 9, 3–40.

Catsanicos, Jean

1996 „L'apport de la bilingue de Ḫattuša à la lexicologie hourrite", in: J.-M. Durand (Hrsg,), *Mari, Ébla et les Hourrites, dix ans de Travaux, I* (Amurru 1), Paris, 197–296.

Giorgieri, Mauro / Röseler, Ingeborg

1998 „Hurritisch *kirman(i):* Ein Beitrag zu den hurritischen Numeralia", *SCCNH* 9, 87–94.

Girbal, Christian

1992 „Das hurritische Antipassiv", *SMEA* 29, 171–81.

Güterbock, Hans Gustav / Hoffner, Harry A., Jr.

1994 *The Hittite Dictionary of the Oriental Institute of the University of Chicago.* Volume P, Fascicle 1.

Haas, Volkert / Wegner, Ilse

1991 (Rezension von) H. Otten - Chr. Rüster, *Keilschrifttexte aus Boghazköi,* 32. in: *OLZ* 86, 384–91.

1993 [1994] „Baugrube und Fundament", *IstMitt* 43, 53–58.

1995 „Stadtverfluchungen in den Texten aus Boğazköy sowie die hurritischen Termini für ‚Oberstadt', ‚Unterstadt' und ‚Herd'", in: U. Finkbeiner - R. Dittmann - H. Hauptmann (Hrsg.), *Beiträge zur Kulturgeschichte Vorderasiens. Festschrift für Rainer Michael Boehmer,* Mainz, 187–94.

1997 „Literarische und grammatikalische Betrachtungen zu einer hurritischen Dichtung", *OLZ* 92, 437–55.

Hoffner, Harry A., Jr.

1974 *Alimenta Hethaeorum. Food Production in Hittite Asia Minor* (AOS 55). New Haven, Conn.

Ivanov, Vyacheslav Vs.

1998 *Comparative notes on Hurro-Urartian, Northern Caucasian and Indo-European* (Druckmanuskript).

Klinger, Jörg

1996 *Untersuchungen zur Rekonstruktion der hattischen Kultschicht* (StBoT 37), Wiesbaden.

Kühne, Cord

1998 „Meki, Megum und Mekum/Mekim", *IOS* 18, 311–22.

Laroche, Emmanuel

1980 *Glossaire de la langue hourrite,* Paris.

Melchert, H. Craig

1993 *Cuneiform Luvian Lexicon* (Lexica Anatolica Vol. 2). Chapel Hill, N.C.

Neu, Erich

1988 „Varia Hurritica. Sprachliche Beobachtungen an der hurritisch-hethitischen Bilingue aus Ḫattuša", in: E. Neu - Chr. Rüster (Hrsg.), *Documentum Asiae Minoris Antiquae. Festschrift für Heinrich Otten zum 75. Geburtstag*, Wiesbaden, 235–54.

1993 [1994] „‚Baumeister' und ‚Zimmermann' in der Textüberlieferung aus Ḫattuša", *IstMitt* 43, 59–62.

1996a *Das hurritische Epos der Freilassung. Untersuchungen zu einem hurritisch-hethitischen Textensemble aus Ḫattuša* (StBoT 32), Wiesbaden.

1996b „Zu einigen Satzmustern des Hurritischen", *Hethitica* 13, 65–72.

1997a „Zum Alter von hethitisch *piški-* und *peški-*", *NABU* 1997/4, 131.

1997b „Akkadisches Lehnwortgut im Hurritischen", *Archivum Anatolicum* 3, 255–63.

Otten, Heinrich / Rüster, Christel

1990 *Die hurritisch-hethitische Bilingue und weitere Texte aus der Oberstadt* (Keilschrifttexte aus Boghazköi [KBo] 32). Berlin.

Otto, Eckart

1998 (Rezension von) E. Neu 1996a, *ZAR* 4, 290–95.

Plank, Frans

1988 „Das Hurritische und die Sprachwissenschaft", in: V. Haas (Hrsg.), *Hurriter und Hurritisch* (Xenia 21), 69–93.

Tischler, Johann

1993 *Hethitisches etymologisches Glossar.* Mit Beiträgen von Günter Neumann und Erich Neu, Teil III, Lieferung 9, Innsbruck.

Wegner, Ilse

1992 „Die selbständigen Personalpronomina des Hurritischen", *SMEA* 29, 227–37.

Wilhelm, Gernot

1995 „Suffixaufnahme in Hurrian und Urartian", in: F. Plank (ed.), *Double Case. Agreement by Suffixaufnahme*, New York - Oxford, 113–35.

1997 „Die Könige von Ebla nach der hurritisch-hethitischen Serie ‚Freilassung'", *AoF* 24, 277–93.

KEILSCHRIFTEDITIONEN

KBo *Keilschrifttexte aus Boghazköi*, Leipzig - Berlin 1916ff.

KUB *Keilschrifturkunden aus Boghazköi*, Berlin 1921ff.

Part II
General Studies

More Joins from the Collection of the British Museum Arrapḫe Texts

JEANETTE FINCKE
Julius-Maximilians-Universität, Würzburg

The publication of 163 'Nuzi'-texts in the British Museum by Gerfrid G.W. Müller (*Londoner Nuzi Texte*, [SANTAG 4]) made possible two more joins among the tablets and fragments from Arrapḫa (Kirkūk). The transliterations of these still fragmentary texts are provided in this article.

The British Museum is in possession of more than 360 tablets and fragments deriving from accidental finds at Kirkūk (Arrapḫe) and Nuzi (Yorġān Tepe),[1] made chiefly early in this century.[2] Although several scholars studied this collection over the last few decades, less than half of the material had been published in copy[3] and/or[4] transliteration.[5] Recently, Gerfrid G.W. Müller

---

1 M.P. Maidman published a catalogue of these tablets that includes a short description of the contents of each text in "The Nuzi Texts of the British Museum," *ZA* 76 (1986) 254–88. Subsequently, about ten additional texts have been identified as belonging to this collection, cf. G.G.W. Müller, SANTAG 4 (1998), p. 15, n. 4.

2 Information about these accidental finds is summarized by J. Fincke, *SCCNH* 9 (1998) 49–51. See also O. Pedersén, *Archives and Libraries in the Ancient Near East 1500–300* B.C. (Bethesda, Md., 1998), pp. 30–31.

3 CT 2 no. 21 (Bu. 91-5-9, 296; 1896; copied by T.G. Pinches); CT 51 nos. 1–14 (1972; copied by H.H. Figulla, L., and C.B.F. Walker).

4 C.J. Gadd, "Tablets from Kirkuk," *RA* 23 (1926) 49–161 (49 tablets and fragments from the BM); A.R. Millard, "Strays from a 'Nuzi' Archive," *SCCNH* 1 (1981) 433–39 (3 tablets); M.P. Maidman, "A Unique Teḫip-tilla Family Document from the British Museum," *SCCNH* 7 (1995) 57–63 (1 tablet).

5 K. Grosz, *The Archive of the Wullu Family* (CNI Publications 5; Copenhagen, 1988), pp. 159–82 (about 40 texts); M.P. Maidman, "Some Late Bronze Age Legal Tablets from the British Museum: Problems of Context and Meaning," in B. Halpern and D.W. Hobson, eds., *Law, Politics and Society in the Ancient Mediterranean World* (Sheffield Academic Press, 1993), pp. 42–89 (11 texts); G.G.W. Müller, *Studien zur Siedlungsgeographie und Bevölkerung des mittleren Osttigrisgebietes* (HSAO 7; Heidelberg, 1994), pp. 235–71 (41 texts); J. Fincke, "Noch einmal zum mittelassyrischen *šiluḫli*," *AoF* 21 (1994) 339–51 (1 text pp. 344f.); *idem*, "Einige Joins von Nuzi-Texten des British Museum," *SCCNH* 7 (1995) 23–36 (6 joined texts—the

Studies on the Civilization and Culture of Nuzi and the Hurrians - 10

made available 163 more texts from this corpus by publishing them in copy, transliteration, translation, and with commentary. In addition, he carefully documented the seal impressions (*Londoner Nuzi-Texte*, SANTAG 4, [Wiesbaden, 1998]). My study of Müller's fragment copies has enabled me to make two pairs of joins. Dr. C.B.F. Walker kindly checked and verified these joins at the British Museum. In his letter, he drew attention to the clean breaks on each fragment, which indicate a high probability of identifying the remaining parts of the tablets.[6] The transliterations of both texts are presented here, albeit the tablets are still fragmentary.

1. BM 23716 (G. Müller, SANTAG 4 no. 6) + BM 95435 (G. Müller, SANTAG 4 no. 151) (join: Febr. 11. 1999)

   This text is a fragmentary *ṭuppi mārūti* belonging to the archive of Šurki-tilla, son of Teḫip-tilla. He adopts *Ṣi-ni-k/ge*, son of Eḫli-teššup, and receives a field in the northern part of a *dimtu*, west of the street going to the town Uḫina, and south of the wadi (*naḫli*). Among the witnesses are men from the town of Šunari. [Zini], son of [Kia]nnipu, is the scribe.

obv.

1 [*ṭup-p*]*í ma-ru-ti ša* ^{m}*Ṣi-*[*n*]*i-g*[*e*]
2 [DUMU *E*]*ḫ-li-te-šup* ^{m}*Šur-ki-til-la*
3 [DUMU *Te*]-*ḫi-ip-til-la a-na ma-ru-ti*
4 [*i-t*]*e-pu-uš ki-ma* ḪA.LA-*šu*
5 [n ANŠE] A.ŠÀ *i+na il-ta-na-an* AN.ZA.GÀR
6 [*ina šu*]-*pa-al* KASKAL *ša* URU *Šu-ḫi-na*
7 [*i-na sú*]-*ta-na-an na-aḫ-li*
8 [*a-na* ^{m}*Šu*]*r-ki-til-la in-dì-in*
9 [*ù* ^{m}*Šu*]*r-ki-til-la a-na* ^{m}*Ṣi*$^{!}$*(ad)-ni-ge*
10 [*ki-ma* NÍ]G.BA-*šu* 30 MA.NA URU[DU] 15 ANŠE ŠE.ME[Š]
11 [n *na-a*]*ḫ-la-ap-tu*$_{4}$ 1 GÌ[R n] MA.NA URUDU.ME[Š]
12 [__ __ _]_.MEŠ ^{m}*Šur-ki-til-l*[*a* <*a-na*>] ^{m}*Ṣi*$^{!}$*(ad)-ni-ki i-*[*din*]
13 [*šum-ma*] ⸢A⸣.ŠÀ GAL *la i-*[*na-ak*]-*ki-is*
14 [*šum-ma*] ⸢A⸣.ŠÀ *pa-qí-ra-*[*na ir-t*]*a-ši*
15 [A.ŠÀ-*šu*]-*ma* ^{m}*Ṣi-*[*ni-ki*] ⸢*ú*⸣-*za-ak-ka*$_{4}$-*m*[*a*]
16 [*a-na* ^{m}*Šur-ki-ti*]*l-l*[*a in-d*]*ì-in*
17 [*il-ka*$_{4}$ *ša* A.ŠÀ ^{m}*Ṣi-ni-k*]*i-ma*
18 [*na-ši ù* ^{m}*Šur-ki-til-la la n*]*a-ši*

fragments of two of these had already been published by K. Grosz, CNI 5); *idem*, "Beiträge zum Lexikon des Hurritischen von Nuzi," *SCCNH* 7 (1995) 5–21 (1 text pp. 6–7).

6 I thank Dr. Christopher Walker for kindly responding to each of my several requests.

19 [*ma-an-nu ša i+na be-ri-šu-nu* KI.BAL]*-at*
20 [__ __ __ __ __ __ __ __]__
21 [__ __ __ __ __ __ __ __ n M]A.NA KÙ.SIG$_{17}$
22 [__ __ __ __ __ __ *i+na-an*]*-din*

---

lower edge
23 [IGI __ __ __ __ __ __ __ __]*-ki*$^!$*(ku)-in-tar*
rev.
24 [IGI __ __ __ __ __ __ __ __]*-iạ*
25 [IGI __ __ __ __ __ __ __*-l*]*a*$^?$
26 [IGI __ __ __ __ __ __ __*-n*]*a*
27 [IGI __ __ __ __ __ __ __ __]
28 [IGI __ __ __ __ __ __ __ __]
29 [n LÚ.MEŠ *an-nu-tu*$_4$ *ša* U]RU *Šu-na-ri*
30 [ŠU *Zi-ni* DUB.SAR DUMU *Ki-a*]*n-ni-pu*
32 [*an-nu-tu*$_4$ LÚ.MEŠ *mu*]*-še-el-wu*
33 [__ __ __ __ __ __]*-la/-a*]*d ap/du* ⌜*ḫé/ú*⌝ [
34 [__ __ __ __ __ __.M]EŠ
35 [*ṭup-pu i+na* EGIR*-ki šu-du-t*]*i*
36 [*i+na* KÁ.GAL *ša* URU __ __ (__) *ša-ṭ*]*ì-ir*
37 [__ __ __ __ __ __ __ __ (__) __ _]_
(rest of reverse is broken off)

Comments

l. 1, 9: *Ṣi-ni-ge*, ll. 12, 15, 17: *Ṣi-ni-ki.*

The use of the cuneiform sign ṢI instead of ZI to represent an initial sibilant of a personal name is uncommon in the Nuzi texts. Apart from this, the personal name might be compared to the name written *Zi-ni-ke* in *RA* 23 (1936) 22:11. I.J. Gelb and A.A. MacRae, *NPN* 180a and 313a, considered this writing as a mistake for Sîn-iqīša: *Zi-ni-ki-*<*ša*>. However, to my knowledge, the name Sîn-iqīša is never written with the sign GE in the Nuzi texts.

l. 6: KASKAL *ša* URU *Šu-ḫi-na*

We know about the road of Uḫina (see RGTC 10, 316; G.G.W. Müller, HSAO 7, p. 134) leading through the northern part of the *dimtu* Arip-ḫurra (EN 9/1, 183, 197) and the *dimtu* Malašu (EN 9/1, 183). If we assume that the *dimtu* Malašu is named for the canal Malašu, and, additionally, that this canal (the Malašu is called *atappu*, *jarru*, and *naḫlu*; see RGTC 10, 380) is the same *naḫlu* the scribe of our text is hinting at (l. 7), the field might be located in the area west of Unap-še(we) (see RCTC 10, 380).

l. 11: 1 GÌ[R n] MA.NA URUDU.ME[Š]

The description "one dagg[er/kni[fe, (and) n] minas of copper" as part of the gift (l. 10: NÍG.BA-*šu*) is rather puzzling because of the "30 minas of copper" that already are mentioned in the previous line (l. 10: 30 MA.NA URU[DU]). As one of the last metal items in a list of objects that is part of a gift or a share in a Nuzi transaction, one would expect to find tin (AN.NA, *annaku*) because lists like these are arranged according to the value of each item, the most valuable item being listed first. Sometimes the value of all items is summarized as *annû* KÙ.BABBAR.MEŠ, "this silver" (e.g., EN 9/2, 189:8'; 9/1, 252:13) or *annû* KÙ.BABBAR.ḪI.A (e.g., BM 85218 = G.G.W. Müller, HSAO 7, no. 20:6: *annûti* ...).

l. 30: [ŠU *Zi-ni* DUB.SAR DUMU *Ki-a*]*n-ni-pu*

Restored according to CT 2, 21:29: *Zi-ni* DUMU *Ki-an-ni-pu* DUB.SAR (archive of Šurki-tilla, son of Teḫip-tilla). There are two other documents from the same archive that mention this scribe: *Zi-ni* DUB.SAR-*rù* (BM 26600 l. 8 = G.G.W. Müller, HSAO 7, no. 16) and *Zi-ni* DUMU *Ki-an-ni-pu* (Jank. 28 rev. 5'). BM 17605 is a *ṭuppi mārūti* of Zike, son of Šurki-tilla, that is written by the same scribe; see M.P. Maidman, *ZA* 76 (1986) 264.

2. BM 95234 (G. Müller, SANTAG 4 no. 95) + BM 95316 (G. Müller, SANTAG 4 no. 115) (join: Febr. 12. 1999).

This fragmentary tablet is a receipt. Nine men (l. 11') are listed by name (ll. 2'-10'). They each received (l. 12': *ilqû*) an equal share (? l. 11') of an unknown item. After receiving the item, the men gave (l. 13': *iddinū*) the same or another item to someone else (l. 12': *ù* [...]). None of the individuals mentioned in this fragment is known from other texts. Unless the remaining part of the tablet is found, I cannot identify the archive to which this document belongs (obv. ll. 0'-1' ?).

obv. (beginning of obverse is broken off)

1' DUM[U$^{?}$

2' ^{m}*Un*-[

3' ^{m}*A-kip-til-la* ⸢DUMU⸣ [_]_-⸢__⸣-_[_

4' ^{m}*Ul-mi-ia* DUMU *Ni-ir-ḫi-*_[_

5' ^{m}*Ḫa-ši-ip-til-la* DUMU *Ku-la-ḫu-b*[*i*]

6' ^{m}*Ḫa-ni-ku* DUMU *Tup-ki-til-la*

7' ^{m}*El-ḫi-ip*-LUGAL ⸢DUMU⸣ *Ša-du-ge-we*

8' ^{m}*Al-ki-til-la* DUMU ⸢*A*⸣*-ta-te*

9' ^{m}*Al-ki-te-šup* DUMU ⸢*Šur*⸣*-ki-til-la*

10' ^{m}*Tar-mi-til-la* DUMU [_]_-*ri-til-la* // [*A*]*r*$^{?}$*-til-la*

11' 9 LÚ.MEŠ *an-nu-tu*$_4$ [__ T]A$^?$.À[M$^?$
12' *il-qú-ú ù* [
13' *id-dì-nu* [
(rest of obverse is broken off)
rev. (beginning of reverse is broken off)
14' NA$_4$ ^{m}*Tar-*[*mi-til-la*
15' NA$_4$ ^{m}*U*[*n*$^?$-.../*A*[*l*$^?$-*ki*$^?$-*til*$^?$-*la*$^?$
(seal impression SANTAG 4 no. 95.A)
16' NA$_4$ ^{m}*A-*[*kip-til-la*
(rest of reverse is broken off)
left edge
17' [... NA$_4$ ^{m}*Al-ki*]-*te-šup* DUMU *Šur-ki-til-la*
(seal impression SANTAG 4 no. 95.B)

L'*andurāru* à l'époque médio-babylonienne, d'après les documents de Terqa, Nuzi et Arrapḫa *

BRIGITTE LION
Université Paris I-Panthéon-Sorbonne

Andurāru(m) has been considered as a royal decree cancelling debts or manumitting slaves typical of the Old Babylonian period. Nevertheless, it is attested during Middle Babylonian times as well. According to the chronology suggested by A. Podany for the Terqa tablets, the term *andurāru(m)* existed in Syria between 16th and 13th centuries B.C. Data from Arrapḫa and Nuzi, dating from 14th century, provide six additional references to *andurāru(m)* and two to *kirenzi*, the Hurrian equivalent of *andurāru(m)*, demonstrating that the *andurāru(m)/kirenzi* was enacted also in the transtigridian kingdom of Arrapḫa. This paper discusses the evidence for *andurāru(m)* in texts from the kingdom of Arrapḫa.

Les *andurāru* sont des décisions royales permettant, par une abolition des dettes et de leurs conséquences directes, le retour d'un bien aliéné ou d'une personne asservie à son statut antérieur. Le phénomène est surtout connu pour l'époque paléo-babylonienne et, sur ce point, la magistrale synthèse de F.R. Kraus fait autorité[1]. Les travaux de D. Charpin[2] ont apporté des informations nouvelles pour la connaissance de cette pratique dans la Syrie amorrite. Néanmoins, deux groupes de documents d'époque médio-babylonienne, les tablettes de Terqa d'une part, celles de Nuzi d'autre part, montrent que les *andurāru* étaient toujours décrétées par les souverains à des époques plus récentes, allant du XVIe au XIIIe s. av. J.-C. pour la documentation de Terqa et de sa région, correspondant au XIVe s. pour les archives de Nuzi.

---

* Mes remerciements vont à D. Charpin, S. Lafont, C. Michel et G. Wilhelm, pour leurs relectures, conseils et suggestions, ainsi qu'à Madame G. Dosch, qui m'a très aimablement transmis le manuscrit de son Magister-Arbeit inédit, *Die Texte aus Room A 34 des Archivs von Nuzi*, Heidelberg 1976. Je reste évidemment seule responsable des idées développées dans cet article.

1 *Königliche Verfügungen in altbabylonischer Zeit*, SD 11, Leiden 1984.

2 «L'*andurârum* à Mari», *M.A.R.I.* 6 (1990) 253–70.

Studies on the Civilization and Culture of Nuzi and the Hurrians - 10

I. Les textes de Terqa

La nouvelle chronologie des tablettes de Terqa proposée par A.H. Podany[3] place au début de la période médio-babylonienne plusieurs souverains qui étaient considérés jusque-là comme ayant régné à l'époque paléo-babylonienne. Il s'agit d'Iddin-Kakka, Išar-Lîm, Iggid-Lîm et Isiḫ-Dagan, quatre rois qui se sont succédé, dans cet ordre, de père en fils; A. Podany situe leurs règnes «probably during the 16th century». Après une période de soumission au Mittani, Hammu-rabi aurait régné au XVe ou au XIVe s. av. J.-C.[4] Ces souverains d'époque médio-babylonienne sont les seuls à porter le titre de «roi de Ḫana», qui figure sur leurs sceaux[5].

Les tablettes rédigées sous ces règnes étaient jusqu'alors considérées comme paléo-babyloniennes; la permanence des formulaires juridiques renforçait cette impression[6]. Elles doivent désormais se voir attribuer une date plus basse. Plusieurs d'entre elles évoquent des *andurāru*. Certaines étaient déjà connues par F.R. Kraus[7] mais rangées parmi la documentation paléo-babylonienne. De fait, il est même possible que ces mentions d'*andurāru* aient contribué à influencer les divers auteurs qui ont proposé de dater les contrats dits «de Ḫana» de la première moitié du second millénaire av. J.-C. Les entrées des dictionnaires ayant été écrites antérieurement aux propositions d'A. Podany, le *CAD* A/2, «andurāru», p. 116a, mentionne deux de ces textes[8], mais sous la rubrique générale «Ḫana texts»; le *AHw*, «andurāru(m)», pp. 50b–51a, classe ces deux mêmes documents[9], l'un sous la rubrique «aB», l'autre sous «aB in Ḫana».

A ce jour, on compte six documents datant du début de l'époque médio-babylonienne qui mentionnent l'*andurāru*. Ils permettent de voir quelles

---

3 «A Middle Babylonian Date for the Ḫana Kingdom», *JCS* 43–45 (1991–93) 53–62, et «Some Shared Traditions between Ḫana and the Kassites», dans G.D. Young, M.W. Chavalas et R.E. Averbeck (éds.), *Crossing Boundaries and Linking Horizons, Mél. M. C. Astour*, Bethesda 1997, 417–32. Cf. aussi D. Charpin, *NABU* 1995/23.

4 *Mél. M. C. Astour*, 428.

5 L'Etat que gouvernent alors ces rois se situe sur le Moyen-Euphrate et s'étend également le long du Ḫabur; Terqa n'en est sans doute pas la capitale, celle-ci devrait plutôt être cherchée à Bidah. Pour la localisation géographique de cet Etat et son extension, cf. A. Podany, *JCS* 43–45 (1991–93), 60–61. Il est possible aussi que le terme de «Roi de Ḫana» corresponde à une domination sur des hommes attachés à un mode de vie, en l'occurrence les bédouins semi-nomades de ces régions, et non sur un espace géographique très précisément défini, comme c'est le cas dans les textes de Mari: cf. D. Charpin, *NABU* 1995/23.

6 O. Rouault, «Cultures locales et influences extérieures: le cas de Terqa», *SMEA* 30 (1992) 247–56, montre bien la continuité des pratiques et formulaires juridiques dans les tablettes de Terqa.

7 *Königliche Verfügungen in altbabylonischer Zeit*, SD 11, Leiden 1984, 99–100.

8 Cités TCL 1, 237 et *RA* 34 (1937) 184.

9 Cités *RA* 34 (1937) 186 et VAB 5, 219.

opérations risquaient d'être annulées par cette mesure et, par conséquent, d'estimer le champ d'application des édits royaux à cette époque.

1. *Le statut des biens immobiliers*

Trois contrats de transferts de biens immobiliers précisent que le bien aliéné ne peut être soumis à l'*andurāru*. Deux d'entre eux, et peut-être même les trois, portent une clause déjà amplement documentée par les contrats paléo-babyloniens de Terqa, stipulant que le bien concerné est *naṣbum ša lā baqrim u lā andurārim*, «irrévocable, ne pouvant faire l'objet d'une contestation ni être soumis à l'*andurāru*»[10]. Ces trois tablettes concernent:

— une donation de maison par le roi Išar-Lîm, TCL 1 237: 14-16[11]: é *na-aṣ-bu-um ša la-a ba-aq-ri-im ù la an-du-ra-ri-im*.

— une vente de champ à l'époque d'Iggid-Lîm: TPR 7, n° 4: 2'-3'[12]: a-šà *ù* [...] *ša la ba-a*[*q-ri(-im)*] *ù la an-d*[*u-ra-ri(-im)*]. Le texte est fragmentaire; un autre bien est aliéné en même temps que le champ. Il semble s'agir d'une vente, car quelques traces évoquent peut-être le versement d'une somme correspondant au prix d'achat.

— une vente de verger datée de l'année d'accession de Hammu-rabi, *Syria* 37 (1960) 206: 16-17[13]: ^{giš}kiri$_6$ *na-aṣ-bu-um ša la ba-aq-ri ù la* ama-gi-*ri*.

A ces trois documents, datables selon A. Podany des XVIe et XVe, voire XIVe s. av. J.-C., il faut ajouter un contrat, provenant probablement lui aussi de la région de Terqa, qui comporte le même type de formulaire, mais qui est rédigé en écriture médio-assyrienne. Il est daté par un éponyme, Libūr-zānin-Aššur; s'il ne s'agit pas d'un homonyme, mais du *līmu* ayant exercé cette fonction sous le règne de Salmanazar I ou de Tukulti-Ninurta I, la rédaction du texte se placerait au XIIIe s. av. J.-C.[14] Cette tablette enregistre là encore une vente de champ. Les l. 22-24 indiquent: *ṭup-pu na-aṣ-bu ša* ⌜*la*⌝*-a ba-aq-ri ù l*[*a*]-⌜*a*⌝ ama-ar-gi. Cette expression est inhabituelle, puisque la clause qui s'applique ordinairement au bien vendu porte ici sur la tablette. Sans doute faut-il entendre, puisque

10 Sur le terme *naṣbum*, cf. M.W. Chavalas, «*Naṣbum* in the Khana contracts from Terqa», dans G.D. Young, M.W. Chavalas et R.E. Averbeck (éds.), *Crossing Boundaries and Linking Horizons, Mél. M. C. Astour*, Bethesda 1997, 179–88, avec la bibliographie antérieure.

11 Transcription et traduction: M. Schorr, VAB 5, n° 219, pp. 302–3. Cf. aussi J. Lewy, «The Biblical Institution of *d^{e}rôr* in the Light of Akkadian Documents», *Eretz-Israel* 5 (1958) 23–24. Sur les donations royales, cf. O. Rouault, *SMEA* 30 (1992) 254–55.

12 O. Rouault, *Terqa Preliminary Reports* 7. *Les documents épigraphiques de la troisième saison*, (*SMS* 2/7) 9–10.

13 J. Nougayrol, «Documents du Habur. 1. Une nouvelle tablette du Ḫana», *Syria* 37 (1960) 205–9.

14 H.M. Kümmel, «Ein Kaufvertrag aus Ḫana mit mittelassyrischer *līmu*-Datierung», *ZA* 79 (1989) 191–200.

ladite tablette tient lieu de titre de propriété, que c'est la transaction décrite par la tablette qui ne peut être soumise à *andurāru*[15].

La clause vise à soustraire les terrains aux effets d'une éventuelle *andurāru*, qu'il s'agisse de ventes entre particuliers ou, dans un cas, d'une donation royale. Si le terme *andurāru* a le même sens qu'à l'époque paléo-babylonienne, cela signifie que certains biens immobiliers, aliénés par nécessité et dans des circonstances économiques particulièrement dures pour le vendeur, pouvaient, à la proclamation d'un édit royal, revenir à leur premier propriétaire. Mais le sens exact de cette mention fait problème. On pourrait comprendre que des vendeurs, pressés par la nécessité, acceptent de renoncer à l'éventuel bénéfice d'une *andurāru* à venir, quitte à refuser d'appliquer un édit royal; cette solution est cependant douteuse dans la mesure où, ici, l'un des textes concerne une maison donnée par le souverain lui-même. Une autre proposition a été faite par G. Buccellati[16], qui distingue deux types de terrains: les propriétés familiales, héritées des parents et transmises de génération en génération, que leurs propriétaires répugnent à aliéner, d'une part; et d'autre part, des biens immobiliers n'appartenant pas à un patrimoine familial, qu'il est loisible de vendre ou d'acheter. Seuls les biens relevant de cette seconde catégorie seraient qualifiés de *naṣbum*, ce terme indiquant qu'ils peuvent faire l'objet de spéculations. Ils ne pourraient être revendiqués en tant que biens patrimoniaux, ce qu'exprime la mention *ša lā baqrim*. Enfin, ils échapperaient aux effets d'une éventuelle *andurāru*: *lā andurārim*.

G. Buccellati développe peu ce dernier point, qui est cependant extrêmement intéressant et qui apporte un argument supplémentaire à son hypothèse. Les édits de *mīšarum* des souverains paléo-babyloniens montrent qu'il existe deux types de dettes[17]: les prêts de nécessité, contractés pour survivre, qui sont annulés par une mesure d'*andurāru*; et les prêts commerciaux, qui échappent à l'*andurāru*, car celle-ci, visant à rétablir un semblant de justice sociale, ne cherche pas pour autant à désorganiser l'économie ni à ruiner les bailleurs de fonds des marchands. La même distinction s'appliquerait ici aux terres. Le domaine familial, hérité des ancêtres et considéré comme une propriété inaliénable, n'est vendu qu'en cas d'absolue nécessité; sa mise en vente seule suffit à témoigner que le propriétaire se trouve dans une situation dramatique. L'*andurāru* interviendrait donc pour permettre à une personne appauvrie de reprendre un terrain de ce type. En revanche, les terrains passant de mains en mains, au gré des stratégies financières de riches propriétaires terriens, échapperaient par leur nature même à cette mesure, leur vente n'ayant pas pour cause une nécessité économique pressante. Les terrains mentionnés ci-dessus, y compris la maison donnée par le roi, entreraient dans cette seconde catégorie.

---

15 H.M. Kümmel, *ZA* 79 (1989) 195, traduit ainsi ces lignes: «Die Tafel ist unanfechtbar (?). Das Feld (ist) frei von einem Vindikation(sanspruch) und (unterliegt) nicht einer (etwaigen) Lastenbefreiung».

16 «A Note on the *muškēnum* as a "Homesteader"», *MAARAV* 7 (1991) 91–100.

17 Cf. l'édit «de X», § A, B et C, et l'édit d'Ammiṣaduqa, § 5 à 9.

2. *Le statut des personnes*

Un contrat d'adoption du règne d'Iggid-Lîm, RBC 779[18], comporte exactement la clause qui s'applique ordinairement aux biens aliénés. Il y est en effet précisé au sujet du fils adoptif, l. 11′-12′: dumu *na-aṣ-bu ša la ba-aq-ri ù la an-dá-ra-ri*.

Comme c'était déjà le cas à l'époque paléo-babylonienne, les mesures décrétées lors d'une *andurāru* concernent donc non seulement les biens fonciers, mais également les personnes: l'enfant adopté dans RBC 779 ne doit pas changer de statut même si une *andurāru* est proclamée. Le début de ce document étant cassé, on ne connaît pas les conditions exactes de l'adoption; en particulier, le statut initial de l'adopté est perdu, ce qui ne permet plus de comprendre à quel résultat précis aurait abouti une *andurāru*, si elle avait été appliquée — résultat que les adoptants tenaient à éviter. Les éditeurs du document commentent ainsi ce passage: «In any event, the general purpose of the phrase seems to be to secure the new parents against claims by the original parents or other guardians of the boy»[19]. Si la clause a le même sens que dans les contrats de ventes de terrains, où elle indique qu'un bien, par sa nature même, échappe à l'*andurāru*, elle pourrait signifier que la personne adoptée n'est pas concernée par une mesure de ce type, de par son statut au moment de l'adoption: peut-être s'agit-il simplement d'une personne libre, qui reconnaît ainsi ne pas avoir accepté son adoption sous l'effet de contraintes économiques. Une autre possibilité serait celle d'une adoption accompagnant un affranchissement d'esclave, la clause indiquant alors que, même en cas d'*andūraru*, l'esclave affranchi ne sera pas à nouveau asservi. L'état du document et l'absence, pour le moment, de textes parallèles dans la documentation de Terqa ne permettent guère que des hypothèses.

La suite du contrat prévoit que l'adopté doit recevoir une partie de l'héritage, mais il existe au moins un autre héritier (l. 7′-10′). Le couple adoptant avait donc déjà une descendance. De ce fait, l'opération ne visait pas à procurer un fils à un couple stérile; son caractère premier ne devait pas être familial, mais économique. La fin du contrat étant elle aussi perdue, on ne peut comprendre les visées précises de cette adoption. Mais une éventuelle *andurāru*, en annulant l'adoption, aurait également réduit à néant ses conséquences dans la stratégie économique familiale. Faire insérer une clause spécifique dans le contrat permettait de préserver à la fois l'adoption et ses conséquences pour la transmission des biens immobiliers.

3. *Mention de l'*andurāru *dans un nom d'année*

La clause précisant qu'un bien foncier, ou dans un cas un enfant adopté, ne peut être soumis à l'*andurāru* est très fréquente dans les contrats de Terqa plus

---

18 A.H. Podany, G.M. Beckman, G. Colbow, «An Inheritance Contract from the Reign of Iggid-Lim of Ḫana», *JCS* 43–43 (1991–93) 39–51.

19 *Ibid.*, p. 49.

anciens, datant de l'époque paléo-babylonienne. De ce fait, on pourrait tenir sa présence dans les contrats médio-babyloniens pour l'effet d'une pure tradition, les scribes se contentant de recopier un formulaire archaïque et vide de sens.

Or l'*andurāru* est au contraire une réalité vivante, puisqu'il existe un nom d'année de Hammu-rabi évoquant sa proclamation par le roi: mu *am-mi-ra-bi-iḫ* lugal *an-du-ra-ra i-na* kur-*šu iš-ku-nu*, «année où le roi Hammu-rabi a placé l'*andurāru* dans son pays»[20]. On comprend alors d'autant mieux les clauses établissant qu'un bien ou une personne échappe à cette mesure.

L'une des transactions concernées, la vente de verger mentionnée plus haut, est précisément datée de l'année d'accession de ce même roi Hammu-rabi: mu *am-mi-ra-pi* lugal *a-na* ^{giš}g[u-za *a-b*]*i-šu e-lu-ú*, «année où le roi Hammu-rabi est monté sur le trône de son père»[21]. Or les toutes premières années d'un règne étaient particulièrement indiquées pour les mesures de rémission, cadeau de joyeux avènement qui soulageait un moment les plus pauvres et laissait croire à un assainissement économique. De ce fait, les acheteurs du verger, prévoyant peut-être l'imminence d'une *andurāru*, faisaient preuve de pragmatisme en précisant qu'elle ne s'appliquerait pas au terrain qu'ils venaient d'acquérir.

4. *Bilan*

Les textes de Terqa montrent ainsi que l'*andurāru* correspond à une réalité toujours vivante entre le XVIe et le XIIIe s. Outre un nom d'année, toutes les attestations visent à préciser le statut exact des biens qui changent de propriétaire ou, dans un cas, de la personne adoptée. L'insertion d'une clause indiquant qu'un bien ne peut être soumis à *andurāru* était déjà connue non seulement par les contrats paléo-babyloniens de Terqa, mais encore par les textes paléo-assyriens de Cappadoce, ceux de Mari et plusieurs textes d'Alalaḫ VII[22]; il faudrait, en tenant compte des propositions de G. Buccellati, réexaminer ces documents.

A Terqa, la documentation des époques amorrite et médio-babylonienne témoigne d'une remarquable permanence, du point de vue des contenus et des formulaires; ce fait a d'ailleurs, pendant longtemps, rendu difficile la datation des tablettes. Les habitudes scribales, tout comme les pratiques économiques et sociales ont perduré; il en va en partie de même des pratiques politiques. L'*andurāru* s'inscrit dans un contexte d'héritage direct des usages paléo-babyloniens, qui se sont maintenus durant plusieurs siècles sans solution de continuité.

---

20 F.J. Stephens, «A Cuneiform Tablet from Dura-Europos», *RA* 34 (1937) 184, l. 14–16. Cette tablette enregistre une transaction immobilière qui, du simple fait qu'elle est conclue l'année suivant l'*andurāru*, n'est pas concernée par cette mesure; mais le formulaire ne donne aucune indication sur ce point.

21 *Syria* 37 (1960) 206, CG, l. 32–33.

22 D. Charpin, *M.A.R.I.* 6 (1990) 258–63, édition et commentaire du texte de Mari A.2654, avec bibliographie; cf. aussi pp. 266–67, à propos d'ARM 8 33.

II. Les Textes du Royaume d'Arrapḫa

Bien loin des rives de l'Euphrate et du Ḫabur, au-delà du Tigre, le petit royaume d'Arrapḫa, documenté par les textes de sa capitale Arrapḫa (Kirkouk), ainsi que par ceux des villes de Nuzi (Yorgan-Tepe) et Kurruḫanni (Tell al-Faḫḫār), connaît également, à l'époque médio-babylonienne, des mesures d'*andurāru*. Même s'il demeure difficile d'insérer très précisément ces textes dans la chronologie générale du Proche-Orient, D. Stein a montré qu'il fallait les dater du XIVe s. av. J.-C.[23]

1. andurāru *et* kirenzi

Le terme d'*andurāru* figure dans plusieurs tablettes de Nuzi. Le mot hourrite *kirenzi*, qui apparaît aussi dans ce corpus, évoque la même réalité. Le sens de *kirenzi* a été clarifié par E. Neu, grâce à l'étude de la bilingue hurro-hittite de Boğazköy[24], dans laquelle *kirenzi* est l'équivalent du hittite *para tarnumar*, «affranchissement». On trouve à Nuzi quatre attestations d'*andurāru* et deux de *kirenzi*. Les documents d'Arrapḫa, contemporains de ceux de Nuzi, montrent également deux occurrences du terme *kirenzi*.

Une autre formule a souvent été associée à ces mesures, celle qui précise qu'une tablette *ina arki šūdûti šaṭir*, «a été écrite après *šūdûtu*». *šūdûtu* est le terme employé pour désigner un édit royal[25] et de ce fait, cette clause a parfois été considérée comme l'équivalent de l'expression *ina arki andurāri*[26]. Néanmoins, les deux formules sont à distinguer, pour plusieurs raisons:

— Un édit royal, AASOR 16 51, retrouvé dans le palais[27], est défini dès sa première ligne comme *šūdûtu*; il contient des mesures concernant les

---

23 «A Reppraisal of the "Sauštatar Letter" from Nuzi», *ZA* 79 (1989) 36–60.

24 «Zur Grammatik des Hurritischen auf der Grundlage der hurritisch-hethitischen Bilingue aus Boğazköy-Grabungskampagne 1983», dans V. Haas (éd.), *Hurriter und Hurritisch*, Xenia 21 (1988) 97–99, et *Das Hurritische: Eine altorientalische Sprache in neuem Licht*, Mainz 1988, 10–15. Cf. G. Wilhelm, «Hurritische Lexikographie und Grammatik: Die hurritisch-hethitische Bilingue aus Boğazköy», *Or*NS 61 (1992) 131; J. Catsanicos, «L'apport de la bilingue de Ḫattuša à la lexicologie hourrite», *Amurru* 1 (1997) 252–53, § 14.3.

25 Sur les édits royaux, cf. E.R. Lacheman, «The Word *šudutu* in the Nuzi Tablets», *ACIO* 25 (Moscou 1960), 1962, 233–38; M. Müller, *Die Erlässe und Instruktionen aus dem Lande Arrapḫa. Ein Beitrag zur Rechtsgeschichte des Alten Vorderen Orients*, Phil. Diss., Universität Leipzig 1968, en particulier pp. 43–88 et «Sozial- und wirtschaftspolitische Rechtserlässe im Lande Arrapḫa», dans H. Klengel (éd.), *Beiträge zur Sozialen Struktur des alten Vorderasien, Schriften zur Geschichte und Kultur des alten Orients* 1, Berlin 1971, 53–60. Voir aussi M.P. Maidman, «"Privatization" and Private Property at Nuzi: The Limits of Evidence», dans M. Hudson et B.A. Levine (éds.), *Privatization in the Ancient Near East and Classical World*, Cambridge 1996, 157 et n. 18 p. 172, avec la bibliographie antérieure.

26 Pour la discussion de ce point, cf. B.L. Eichler, *Indenture in Nuzi: The Personal Tidennūtu Contract and its Mesopotamian Analogues*, New Haven et Londres 1973, 32–34; N.P. Lemche, «*Andurārum* and *mīšarum*: Comments on the Problem of Social Edicts and Their Application in the Ancient Near-East», *JNES* 38 (1979) 11–22 et spécialement pp. 18–20.

27 Dans la pièce R 76, cf. W. Mayer, *Die Archive des Palastes und die Prosopographie der*

esclaves du palais. D'autres proclamations royales sont connues, comme HSS 15 1[28], HSS 14 9 ou JEN 195[29]. Aucun de ces textes ne mentionne des mesures qui puissent évoquer de près ou de loin une *andurāru*.

— Les deux expressions, *ina arki šūdûti ina arki andurāri*, figurent côte à côte dans le même document, HSS 9 102, ce qui indique qu'elles ne sont pas exactement équivalentes (voir ci-dessous § II.2.1). Une autre tablette, EN 9/1 195, est écrite *ina arki šūdûti ina šatti ša kirenzi* (voir ci-dessous § II.2.3).

— Enfin, la formule *ina arki šūdûti* est extrêmement fréquente dans les documents d'Arrapḫa, Nuzi et Kurruḫanni et apparaît à la fin de contrats de natures très diverses; or les *andurāru* devaient être, au contraire, des mesures relativement rares.

Cela fait penser que la proclamation d'une *andurāru* pouvait prendre la forme d'un édit royal de type *šūdûtu*[30], mais que toutes les *šūdûtu* ne concernaient pas forcément une *andurāru*. Pour cette raison, les très nombreuses mentions de *šūdûtu* ne sont pas prises en compte ici, mais uniquement les attestations d'*andurāru* ou de *kirenzi*.

2. *Les transactions effectuées après* andurāru *ou* kirenzi

Un certain nombre de contrats sont rédigés après une mesure d'*andurāru* (ou *kirenzi*), cette mention intervenant en général à la fin du contrat. Cette précision peut se comprendre de deux façons. Soit il s'agit d'une formule de datation, comme il en existe quelques-unes, fort rares à Nuzi, se référant à un événement marquant, mais sans rapport direct avec le contenu du contrat. Soit, au contraire, cette précision vise à établir que les termes du contrat, rédigé après l'*andurāru*, échappent à cette mesure, puisqu'elle est exclusivement rétroactive.

Pour en décider, il faut considérer le contenu des contrats portant ces mentions.

Berufe, AOAT 205/1, Neukirchen-Vluyn 1978, 65. Pour l'étude de ce texte, cf. M. Müller, *Die Erlässe und Instruktionen aus dem Lande Arrapḫa…*, pp. 7–42.

28 Il s'agit d'ordres royaux adressés au *ḫazannu* de Tašuḫḫe, au sujet de la mise en défense du territoire; le terme *šūdûtu* est employé l. 41. K. Deller, «Gab es einen König von Arrapḫe Namens Muš-Teja?», *Assur* 3 (1983) 154–63, donne l'abondante bibliographie afférente à ce document; il faut ajouter C. Zaccagnini, *BiOr* 41 (1984) 130–31 et G. Wilhelm, «Mušteja», *RlA* 8 (1997) 498.

29 Ces textes ne contiennent pas le substantif *šūdûtu*, mais la formule lugal *ul-te-dì-mi*, (JEN 195: 12) ou *ki-na-an-na* lug[al] (…) *uš-te-dì* (HSS 14 9: 1–3), «le roi a fait la proclamation (suivante)», sur la même racine, cf. *CAD* I, *idû*, 33b et *AHw*, *edû(m)* 188b. Ces proclamations concernent, dans JEN 195, les rachats de prisonniers arraphéens et dans HSS 14 9, l'*ilku* dû par les habitants de certaines villes; cf. M. Müller, *Die Erlässe und Instruktionen aus dem Lande Arrapḫa…*, pp. 89–174 (HSS 14 9) et 175–94 (JEN 195).

30 Cf. E. Neu, *Das Hurritische: Eine altorientalische Sprache in neuem Licht*, Mainz 1988, 14, n. 30: «Wie G. Wilhelm (brieflich) zu überlegen gibt, könnten sich die Ausdrücke *šūdûtu* und *andurāru* semantisch zueinander verhalten wie Form und Inhalt, indem nämlich *šūdûtu* "Edikt, Proklamation", *andurāru* aber die konkrete Ausführung des Erlasses, die tatsächliche "(Schulden)-Befreiung" bedeutet haben mag».

2.1 *Après* andurāru

Deux contrats portent cette mention, HSS 5 25 et HSS 9 102. Tous deux proviennent de la maison ouest du petit tell dit «A», au nord-est du tell central de Nuzi.

Dans HSS 5 25[31], Akkul-enni déclare avoir donné sa sœur, Bēlt-Akkadi-ummi, en mariage à Ḫurazzi, et avoir reçu de ce fait 40 sicles d'argent. Bēlt-Akkadi-ummī déclare à son tour que son frère la donne en mariage à Ḫurazzi avec son consentement. La tablette est rédigée à la porte de la ville de Matiḫa, *ina* egir *an-du-ra-ri* (l. 24).

Ce contrat est en fait le troisième d'une série impliquant les mêmes personnes. Dans HSS 5 69, Akkul-enni remet sa sœur Bēlt-Akkadi-ummī à Ḫurazzi en tant que sœur (*ana aḫāti ittadin*), et reçoit 40 sicles d'argent. HSS 5 80 est le contrat de mariage par lequel Akkul-enni donne Bēlt-Akkadi-ummī en mariage à Ḫurazzi; celui-ci fournit comme *terḫatu* un bœuf et 10 sicles d'argent; la dot (*mulūgu*), qui constitue en fait une partie non précisée de la *terḫatu*, est remise à la jeune femme par Akkul-enni. En outre, Akkul-enni donne une autre de ses sœurs, Kapulanza, comme fille adoptive à Ḫurazzi, à charge pour lui de lui trouver un époux.

Cette affaire compliquée, qui se règle en trois étapes, montre qu'Akkul-enni, en tant que frère, organise le mariage de ses sœurs, probablement après la mort de leur père. Il s'en remet par deux fois à Ḫurazzi, lui faisant adopter Bēlt-akkadi-ummī comme «sœur», puis Kapulanza comme «fille». Ḫurazzi épouse la première s'engage à trouver un époux pour la seconde. Ce transfert des droits doit correspondre à une situation économique assez peu brillante de la famille d'Akkul-enni; il est fort probable qu'il accepte de transférer une partie de son autorité sur ses sœurs à une tierce personne parce qu'il éprouverait des difficultés à les doter décemment. HSS 5 80 précise ainsi que lorsque le mariage de Kapulanza aura été consommé, Ḫurazzi donnera 20 sicles d'argent à Akkul-enni, alors que la somme habituelle versée par la famille de l'époux correspond plutôt à 40 sicles; dans ce cas, cela pourrait indiquer que Ḫurazzi compte garder la moitié du contre-don.[32]

HSS 9 102 fait partie des archives d'Ilānu fils de Tayuki trouvées dans la pièce A 34[33]. Par ce contrat de *titennūtu*, Turari engage un champ auprès d'Ilānu;

---

31 Les tablettes HSS 5 25, 69 et 80 ont été transcrites et traduites par E.A. Speiser, «New Kirkuk Documents Relating to Family Law», *AASOR* 10 (1928/29) 59–62 (commentaire pp. 21–27) et par S. Greengus, «Sisterhood Adoption at Nuzi and the "Wife-Sister" in Genesis», *HUCA* 46 (1975) 28–31. Cf. aussi K. Grosz, «Dowry and Brideprice in Nuzi», *SCCNH* 1 (1981) 176. Réputées provenir de la pièce A 34, ces trois tablettes sont transcrites par G. Dosch, *Die Texte aus Room A 34 des Archivs von Nuzi,* Magister-Arbeit, Heidelberg 1976, mais selon les indications figurant dans ce manuscrit, elles proviendraient en fait de la pièce A 30; elles ne se rattachent pas aux lots d'archives trouvés en A 34.

32 K. Grosz, «On Some Aspects of the Adoption of Women in Nuzi», *SCCNH* 2 (1987) 131–52, et en particulier, sur ces trois textes, pp. 151–52.

33 Ce texte est transcrit par G. Dosch, *Die Texte aus Room A 34 des Archivs von Nuzi,* Magister-Arbeit, Heidelberg 1976, n° 117, pp. 184–85.

en échange, il obtient 10 mines d'argent et un *imēr* de grain. La durée du contrat est de 3 ans, à l'issue desquels Turari doit rendre étain et grain, pour pouvoir reprendre son champ. La tablette est rédigée *ina* egir-*ki šu-du-ti i+na* egir-*ki an-du-ra-ri* (l. 30–31).

2.2. *Après* kirenzi

HSS 19 118[34] provient des archives sud-ouest, de V 428 ou P 401[35]. C'est une déclaration de Šennaya, qui a reçu d'Artaya un esclave; il s'engage à le rendre, ou à le remplacer par une esclave, ou encore, s'il dépasse l'échéance à laquelle il doit fournir l'esclave, à verser un montant en grains. La tablette est rédigée à Nuzi *ina* e[gi]r-*ki ki-re-en-zi* (l. 16–17). L'esclave fourni sert de gage[36], sans doute d'une dette contractée par Artaya envers Šennaya.

Parmi les documents trouvés dans les fouilles clandestines d'Arrapḫa, BM 104828+104830+104836 offre la même formule [*ina* eg]ir-*ki ki-re-en-z*[*i*] (l. 23')[37]. Il s'agit d'un contrat de *tidennūtu*, assez abîmé, par lequel Šunšu-naya avance à Akap-šenni des biens dont la nature exacte est perdue, et reçoit en gage le champ de ce dernier. Ce contrat n'a pu être rattaché à aucun lot d'archives précis.

2.3. *L'année de la* kirenzi

EN 9/1 195[38], issu du quartier sud-ouest de Nuzi (P 466), relève des archives d'Eḫel-Teššup fils de Taya[39]. Ce contrat de *titennūtu* engage un champ, appartenant à Ḫawinnaya, auprès d'Eḫel-Teššup; celui-ci fournit du grain et du cuivre à Ḫawinnaya. A la fin de la transaction, aux l. 21–24, le scribe note: [*ṭup-pu*] *i+na* [egi]r *šu-du-*[*t*]*i* ⌜*i+na*⌝ k[á ká-gal] *ša šu-pa-l*[*i*] *i+na* mu *š*[*a ki-r*]*e-en-zi ša*$_{10}$-*ṭì-ir*, «[la tablette] a été rédigée [aprè]s proclamation à la [grand] po[rte] de l'ouest, l'année d[e la *kir*]*enzi*». L'événement qui donne son nom à une année ne pouvant qu'être antérieur au commencement de celle-ci, il faut comprendre que la *kirenzi* a eu lieu l'année précédente.

---

34 Transcription, traduction, commentaire: A Shaffer, «Hurrian **kirezzi*, West-Semitic *krz*», *Or*NS 34 (1965) 32–34.

35 V 428 est le lieu de provenance indiqué par HSS 19, p. vii; cette tablette serait la seule à en provenir. En revanche, M. Morrison, dans *SCCNH* 2 (1987) 198, la rattache aux archives sud-ouest, groupe 2, et donne comme lieu de provenance P 401, ce qui permettrait de l'intégrer aux archives d'Artaya fils de Pui-tae; HSS 19 118 ne mentionne aucun patronyme pour Artaya, mais puisque le présent document lui sert de garantie, celui-ci devait être conservé parmi ses archives, ce qui rend cette hypothèse d'autant plus légitime.

36 l. 4: ìr *ši-pí-ir-ta-šu*, cf. *CAD* Š/3, «šipirtu B», p. 69a, qui cite le passage.

37 Ce contrat est transcrit par K. Grosz, *The Archive of the Wullu Family*, Copenhagen 1988, 174–75 et traduit p. 147. L'éditrice a donné la copie de la ligne 23'; la lecture *kirenzi* a été vue par J. Fincke, «Einige Joins von Nuzi-Texten des British Museums», *SCCNH* 7 (1995) 36.

38 SMN 2649; cette tablette est évidemment citée par son numéro d'inventaire dans les articles antérieurs à *SCCNH* 2 (1987), volume où ont été publiées les copies de EN 9/1.

39 Sur cette archive familiale, cf. M. Morrison, *SCCNH* 2 (1987) 169–74.

2.4. *Formules de datation, formules de protection*

La mention, dans chacun de ces actes, d'une mesure de rémission légèrement antérieure à leur rédaction, peut dans tous les cas entretenir un rapport direct avec leur contenu. Les mesures d'abolition des dettes ne portent que sur le passé et préciser qu'une *andurāru* ou *kirenzi* vient d'avoir lieu est une façon de souligner que la transaction enregistrée échappe à ses effets.

Les contrats de *titennūtu* correspondent à des prêts avec prise d'un gage antichrétique par le créancier. L'emprunteur place ses terres, voire un membre de sa famille ou lui-même, à la disposition de son créancier; les revenus de la terre ou le travail de la personne constituent l'intérêt du prêt. Ces mises en gage ont en général pour origine les difficultés économiques de l'emprunteur, qui s'adresse à une personne beaucoup plus riche que lui, pouvant lui fournir immédiatement les biens dont il manque. La vérification peut en être faite pour les protagonistes de HSS 9 102: Turari, qui engage son champ, n'est pas connue par ailleurs, indice probable d'une situation sociale peu élevée. En revanche, Ilānu fils de Tayuki a laissé une archive relativement importante, comprenant de nombreux contrats de *titennūtu*, qui témoigne de sa richesse. Il en va de même pour EN 9/1 195: Eḫli-Teššup fils de Taya est connu par une quinzaine de contrats de *titennūtu*, qui correspondent à des investissements fonciers; Ḫawinnaya et son frère Katiri sont aussi attestés dans des contrats de *titennūtu*, mais toujours comme emprunteurs mettant en gage leurs terres, ce qui indique une paupérisation de cette famille. Les *andurāru*, si elles annulaient non seulement les dettes mais aussi leurs effets, devaient rendre caducs les contrats de *titennūtu*. Logiquement, les biens prêtés devaient demeurer acquis à l'emprunteur, qui pouvait en outre reprendre son gage.

HSS 19 118, accord lié à la mise en gage d'un esclave, fait également partie des opérations qui pourraient être annulées par une *kirenzi*. La clause précisant que l'accord a lieu après la *kirenzi* met le créancier à l'abri d'une revendication du débiteur, premier propriétaire de l'esclave[40].

40 Il faut cependant noter qu'un paragraphe mal conservé de l'édit de Samsu-iluna, le § 3', précise que l'*andurārum* ne s'applique pas à un esclave donné en gage. L'édit de *mīšarum* d'Ammi-ṣaduqa, § 20–21, distingue deux cas: l'habitant du Numḫa, de l'Emutbal, de l'Idamaraṣ, d'Uruk, d'Isin, de Kisura ou de Malgium qui a dû se donner lui-même en gage pour dette, ou donner un membre de sa famille, obtient son *andurārum* en cas d'édit royal, c'est-à-dire qu'il revient à son statut antérieur de personne libre (§ 20); en revanche, si un habitant de ces mêmes régions ou villes a donné en gage un esclave, l'*andurārum* de ce dernier n'est pas effectuée (§ 21) et l'esclave demeure au service du créancier. Pour l'interprétation de ces paragraphes, je suis D. Charpin, «Les Décrets Royaux à l'Epoque Paléo-Babylonienne, à Propos d'un Ouvrage Récent», *AfO* 34 (1987) 36–37. HSS 19 118 évoquerait plutôt le § 21 de l'édit d'Ammi-ṣaduqa, qui stipule que le statut de l'esclave donné en gage n'est pas affecté par décret royal. Néanmoins, le contenu précis des édits, qui se perpétue avec une grande stabilité sous la première dynastie de Babylone, n'avait pas forcément trouvé un prolongement exact dans le royaume d'Arrapḫa. En l'absence de tout texte d'édit royal sur ce point, il est impossible de trancher. A Mari, au moins deux textes mentionnant des *andurārum* font référence aux esclaves, mais leur état fragmentaire ne permet pas de savoir exactement quels

HSS 5 25 est plus complexe et il demeure difficile d'estimer les effets exacts d'une *andurāru* pour des adoptions et un mariage. Akkul-enni pourrait être tenté de rétablir l'intégralité de ses droits sur ses sœurs, en arguant du fait que seules les circonstances économiques l'ont conduit à s'en remettre, pour leur mariage, à Ḫurazzi. Si une éventuelle *andurāru* annulait toute l'affaire, elle pourrait casser deux actes d'adoption, un mariage et les transferts de biens meubles liés à ces circonstances.

Si ces hypothèses sont exactes, les mentions d'*andurāru* ou de *kirenzi* auraient pour but premier d'insister sur le fait que l'opération décrite dans le contrat, intervenant après une mesure royale, échappe à ses effets. Cela n'exclut pas qu'il s'agisse également de formules de datation, EN 9/1 195 évoquant même un nom d'année. Les tablettes de Nuzi ne portent quasiment jamais de date: de ce fait, situer un acte juridique, et tout spécialement les prêts et les *titennūtu*, par rapport à une *andurāru* ou *kirenzi*, est le plus sûr moyen d'échapper aux tentatives de fraude du débiteur.

On peut rappeler qu'une tablette de Mari datant de l'époque de Yaḫdun-Lîm, M.11264, précise qu'un prêt d'argent est effectué après *andurāru* (l. 15: *wa-ar-ki ú-du-ra-ri*); cette clause «signifie que le prêt a eu lieu peu après la proclamation d'une telle mesure par le roi et a pour but de protéger le créancier contre une éventuelle contestation du débiteur»[41]. Il en va de même, en Babylonie, pour les contrats conclus *warki ṣimdat šarrim*[42], les parties voulant indiquer par là qu'une transaction effectuée après les mesures de *mīšaru* ou d'*andurāru* contenues dans cet édit ne saurait y être soumise. Les cinq textes présentés ci-dessus correspondraient à des situations comparables.

En outre, ces cinq contrats appartiennent à des archives privées et confirment le rôle des édits royaux, promulgués par les souverains d'Arrapḫa, dans les transactions entre particuliers.

3. *Renoncement aux effets de la* kirenzi *dans un contrat d'adoption*

Dans un contrat d'Arrapḫa[43], une femme, Untuya, se fait «adopter en tant que sœur» (*ana ahatūti*) par Wantiya. Wantiya lui remet des maisons dans la ville d'Arrapḫa, et Untuya verse à Wantiya 24 sicles d'argent. Cette adoption a un caractère économique: elle permet à Untuya de disposer de maisons contre une somme d'argent. Elle entre donc dans le schéma général des «adoptions-ventes», même si la bénéficiaire se fait adopter en tant que sœur par la personne

---

esclaves sont concernés par cette mesure: M.11009+11010 et M.14033, D. Charpin, *M.A.R.I.* 6 (1990) 263–65 et 267–69.

41 D. Charpin, *M.A.R.I.* 6 (1990) 256–57.

42 Cette formule se présente avec diverses variantes, cf. F.R. Kraus, *Königliche Verfügungen in altbabylonischer Zeit,* SD 11, Leiden 1984, 51–69.

43 J. Fincke, «Einige Joins von Nuzi-Texten des British Museums», *SCCNH* 7 (1995) nº 6 = BM 104822+104835, pp. 35–36. Les deux morceaux avaient été publiés séparément par K. Grosz, *The Archive of the Wullu Family,* Copenhagen 1988, 172 et 177 (transcriptions), 128 et 132 (traductions).

qui lui cède son bien, et non en tant que fille. Untuya est la mère de Šekar-Tilla, qui a laissé un petit lot de tablettes[44]; celle-ci a dû être conservée dans les archives de Šekar-Tilla, comme titre de propriété, lorsque celui-ci a hérité des maisons mentionnées dans le contrat.

La l. 9 comporte une clause inhabituelle: [mu-m]eš *ki-re-en-zi la i-*⌜*il*⌝-[*la-ku-ú*], «ils ne tiend[ront pas compte] des années de *kirenzi*», les deux contractants s'engageant ainsi à renoncer aux effets d'une telle mesure. Ces effets, s'ils sont demeurés les mêmes qu'à l'époque paléo-babylonienne, pourraient consister dans l'annulation de l'«adoption-vente», ou éventuellement contraindre Untuya à verser à Wantiya une somme d'argent complétant les 24 sicles, si ceux-ci ne représentent pas la valeur réelle des maisons. A ma connaissance, il s'agit de la seule clause de ce type contenue dans un contrat d'adoption[45].

4. *Libérations de personnel palatial liées à l'*andurāru

Deux textes provenant du palais de Nuzi, trouvés dans la pièce R 76[46], témoignent de libérations de personnel liées à l'*andurāru*.

HSS 16 354 est une liste de noms propres féminins. Après les cinq premiers noms, le scribe a précisé: 5 mí-meš *an-nu-tu*$_4$ *i-na an-du-ra-ri i-te-lu*, «ces 5 femmes sont parties de fait de l'*andurāru*» (l. 6-7); après les huit suivants: 8 mí-meš *an-nu-tu' mi-tù-ú*, «ces 8 femmes sont mortes» (l. 16). Le palais compte donc les pertes subies parmi la population féminine, une *andurāru* ayant pour conséquence un départ de personnel.

HSS 13 149 est une lettre envoyée par Kuwari à Erwi-Talma; l'expéditeur s'y fait l'écho des doléances d'un certain Kaite et termine ainsi son message: *i-na-an-na* mí *i-na in-du-ra-ri i-te-e-li*$^!$ *ù ša-a-na-am-ma* mí-meš $^{[I]}$*ka*$_4$*-i-te i-ri-iš-mi*, «Maintenant, une femme est partie du fait de l'*andurāru* et Kaite a réclamé d'autres femmes». Là encore, l'effet de la mesure d'*andurāru* a permis à une personne de revenir à son statut antérieur, et par là-même de sortir du service auquel elle était affectée.

Aucune indication n'est donnée sur le statut premier de ces femmes, auquel elles reviennent probablement. Peut-être s'agit-il de femmes prises en gage par le palais, ou réduites en servitude en remboursement d'une dette, qui recouvrent leur liberté.

---

44 K. Grosz, *The Archive of the Wullu Family*, 128–38.

45 La plupart des adoptions conclues à Nuzi semblent l'avoir été sous la pression de circonstances économiques très peu favorables pour l'adoptant, qui par le contrat cédait des biens-fonds à l'adopté. Si une *andurāru* (ou *kirenzi*) pouvait affecter ce type de transfert de biens, il pourrait y en avoir des traces dans la documentation du royaume d'Arrapḫa; mais celles-ci n'ont pas, pour autant que je le sache, été repérées.

46 Sur les tablettes trouvées dans cette pièce, cf. W. Mayer, *Die Archive des Palastes und die Prosopographie der Berufe*, AOAT 205/1, Neukirchen-Vluyn 1978, 65–82.

5. *Bilan*

Les attestations d'*andurāru* ou de *kirenzi* à Nuzi et Arrapḫa apparaissent ainsi de trois façons différentes:

— dans des formules de datation, qui servent vraisemblablement à insister sur le fait que la transaction, effectuée après *andurāru* ou *kirenzi*, y échappe;

— dans un engagement pris entre particuliers, la personne aliénant son bien accepte de renoncer aux effets éventuels d'une proclamation de *kirenzi*;

— dans des tablettes du palais qui montrent que des libérations de personnel ont été effectuées suite à une *andurāru*.

D'une part, ces textes indiquent que ces mesures, tout comme à l'époque paléo-babylonienne, concernent à la fois le domaine royal (ici des servantes du palais) et les biens des particuliers. D'autre part, l'*andurāru* ou *kirenzi* semble pouvoir annuler les mêmes opérations qu'à l'époque paléo-babylonienne, celles découlant directement de la paupérisation d'une partie de la population; il s'agit ici tout spécialement des dettes avec prise de gage (*titennūtu*), des adoptions-ventes et peut-être de l'asservissement pour dettes.

L'héritage paléo-babylonien est clair, même s'il est très difficile d'établir par quelles voies il a pu se transmettre[47]. Mais l'existence d'un terme hourrite, *kirenzi*, complique les données du problème, en indiquant que cette pratique pouvait avoir également d'autres origines; l'étude de la bilingue hourro-hittite devrait apporter des précisions sur ce point.

Néanmoins, si les souverains d'Arrapḫa voulaient éviter qu'une partie de la population ne tombe dans une misère trop désespérante, ces mesures s'avéraient insuffisantes; elles n'empêchèrent pas la concentration des biens, et surtout des biens fonciers, aux mains de quelques riches familles, celles, précisément, qui ont laissé des archives. Comme l'a noté M.P. Maidman, «General pauperization within the private economy appears to have taken place. Government attempts at general debt remission or land reform to reverse the trend met with no apparent success»[48].

Conclusion

Si les mentions d'*andurāru* apparaissent de façon bien différente dans les documents de Terqa et dans ceux du royaume d'Arrapḫa, on observera cependant qu'il s'agit toujours de documents de la pratique. Cela peut expliquer que ce phénomène ait jusqu'alors peu attiré l'attention, dans la

---

[47] Ce point a déjà été vu, cf. M. Müller, «Sozial- und wirtschaftspolitische Rechtserlässe im Lande Arrapḫa», dans H. Klengel (éd.), *Beiträge zur Sozialen Struktur des alten Vorderasien, Schriften zur Geschichte und Kultur des alten Orients* 1, Berlin 1971, 59–60 et n. 26.

[48] «Nuzi: Portrait of an Ancient Mesopotamian Provincial Town», dans J.M. Sasson (éd.), *Civilizations of the Ancient Near East*, New York 1995, t. 2, p. 946.

mesure où aucun édit royal n'a été retrouvé, alors que la Babylonie d'époque amorrite en a livré plusieurs exemples. Cependant, de tels édits existaient probablement. La référence à une décision royale dans un nom d'année de Hammu-rabi, roi de Ḫana, a toutes chances de renvoyer à un document écrit qui ne nous a pas été conservé. A Nuzi, des édits royaux (*šūdûtu*) ont été retrouvés; même si aucun ne concerne les mesures d'*andurāru*, rien n'interdit de penser que l'*andurāru* pouvait, elle aussi, faire l'objet d'une proclamation qui n'était pas uniquement orale.

On peut ajouter à ces références d'époque médio-babylonienne le texte littéraire MAH 15922, republié par W. Sommerfeld[49]. Ce document fait l'éloge du roi Kurigalzu, probablement Kurigalzu II, et doit donc se placer au XIVe s. av. J.-C. Il compte parmi les bienfaits du roi l'établissement de l'*andūrarum* à Babylone: le souverain y est en effet appelé *ša-ki-in an-du-ra-ar ni-ši* ká-dingir-ra^{ki} (l. 13).

Ce dossier indique donc clairement que la pratique de l'*andurāru* ne s'est pas du tout limitée à l'époque paléo-babylonienne. Au contraire, elle a perduré dans la seconde moitié du IIe millénaire avant J.-C., tant en Syrie qu'en Transtigrine, avec des évolutions diverses. Il est fort possible qu'elle ait fait l'objet d'une tradition continue dans le Proche-Orient ancien, puisqu'elle est encore mentionnée à plusieurs reprises à l'époque néo-assyrienne. L'établissement de la chronologie des tablettes de Terqa et le réexamen des tablettes de Nuzi fournissent ainsi quelques «maillons manquants» dans l'histoire de cette mesure royale.

49 «Der Kurigalzu-Text MAH 15922», *AfO* 32 (1985) 1–22.

JEN 781–789: The Text Editions

M. P. MAIDMAN
York University

For David I. Owen, First Incumbent of the Bernard and Jane Schapiro Professorship in Ancient Near Eastern and Judaic Studies, Cornell University

As indicated in an earlier article (*SCCNH* 9 [1998] 95), plans to publish the text editions of JEN VII in a pair of volumes have been modified. Following the first volume (*SCCNH* 6 [1994]) in which text editions of the first one hundred tablets appeared, it was decided that the editions of the remaining one hundred tablets would appear in a series of articles. The first article presented six editions (SCCNH 9 [1998]). The current article continues with nine more text editions.

This article continues the publication of the text editions of the Nuzi tablets from the Oriental Institute of the University of Chicago published in JEN VII (Lacheman and Maidman 1989).[1] The first one hundred editions were published as *SCCNH* 6 (Maidman 1994) and six more appeared as an article in *SCCNH* 9 (Maidman 1998). I present here an additional nine text editions, culminating with JEN 789, which makes direct reference to three other texts also edited here (JEN 785–787) and is relevant to a fourth (JEN 784). It is an especially interesting group of documents.

For details regarding the presentation of these texts, certain typographical idiosyncrasies, and unannotated references to named and unnamed scholars, the reader is referred to earlier comments on these matters (Maidman 1994, 3–8; 1998, 95).

[1] I wish to acknowledge with gratitude the continuing support of the Social Sciences and Humanities Research Council of Canada, most recently with a Research Grant for 1998–2001. I also thank my former student Mr. John King for his help in entering unpublished Chicago Nuzi texts into an electronic data base used in the preparation of this article.

Studies on the Civilization and Culture of Nuzi and the Hurrians - 10

JEN 781

OBVERSE

1 ṭup-pí t[i-de$_4$-en-nu-ti]
2 ša ^{f}Ḫu-uš-ḫu-šu aš?-ša-*⸢ti⸣?
3 ⸢ša⸣!? $^{m!}$Ḫa-na-a-a [(?)]
4 8 ^{GIŠ}APIN ⸢A⸣.[ŠÀ]
5 [i?]-⸢na⸣? URU Nu-z⸢i⸣ [ ]
6 [(x) URU] •A!-ta-ak-k[ál?]
7 *⸢x x⸣ ša URU •N[u?-zi?]
8 ⸢i-n⸣a il-ta-[na-an]
9 i+⸢na x x⸣ [ ]
10 ⸢i⸣?-[na?]
11 ⸢x⸣ [ ]
12 ⸢a⸣?-[na? ti?]-⸢de$_4$?-en?-nu⸣?-[ti? a?-na? n? MU?.MEŠ?]
13 [a-na ^{m}Ta]r-mi-til-la DUMU Šur-ki-til-la
14 [it-ta-di-i]n? ù ^{m}Tar-•mi-til-la
15 [ ] ⸢x⸣ ù 2 [M]A.NA SÍG
16 [a?-na? $^{f?}$]Ḫ[u?-uš?-ḫu?-š]u? it-ta-⸢din⸣
17 [im?]-⸢ma?-ti⸣?-[me?-e? n? MU?.MEŠ? im?-ta?-lu?(-ú?)]
18 [KÙ.BAB]BAR.MEŠ ša KA ṭ⸢up⸣-pí
19 $^{[f]}$Ḫu-uš-ḫu-šu a-na

LOWER EDGE

20 [^{m}Tar]-mi-til-la •GUR!-ru
21 *⸢ù⸣ *A.ŠÀ-šu i-leq-qè
22 •um-ma ^{f}•Ḫu-uš-ḫu-šu-ma

REVERSE

23 •[m]u? ⸢x x⸣ NI RU •BU MEŠ?
24 DUMU [ ] ⸢x⸣ UD? ⸢x⸣
25 [ ] ⸢x x⸣ [ ]
26 [ ] ⸢x⸣? [ ]
27 [ ] ⸢x x⸣? [el-te]-qè-mi
28 [ ] Q[A] lu-ú ⸢šum-ma A.ŠÀ⸣
29 [pa$_{(1/2)}$]-qí-⸢ra⸣-[na TUK-ši] ù A.ŠÀ ša-a-šu-ma
30 $^{⸢+f⸣}$Ḫu-u⸢š⸣-[ḫu]-šu ú-za-ak-ka$_4$-$^{+}$ma
31 ṭup-pu AŠ [EGIR^{-ki}] šu-du-ti
32 a-na pa-ni [ ] ⸢x⸣ [ ] A.ŠÀ GUR-⸢•ru⸣
33 um-ma ^{f}Ḫu-[uš-ḫu]-šu-ma [ ]
34 [I]GI Ut-ḫap-ḫa-[a-a DUMU] Eḫ-l[i-te-šup]
35 IGI Zi-k[é DUMU] Ḫa-na-a-a
36 IGI Ḫa-ši-i[p-•ti]l-•la DUMU Zi-l[i?-]
37 IGI E[r?-wi?-LU]GAL? DUMU En-rù-šúk

38 IGI ˹x˺ -[ ]-•˹*x*˺-*e* DUMU *A-kip-ta-še-*[*en-ni*]
39 IG[I] *Ša-ta-am-mu-uš-ni* DUMU *Ú-n*[*a-a-a*]
40 IGI *Tu-ra-ar-te-šup*
41 DUB.SAR$^{-rù}$ DUMU *It-ḫa-pí-ḫe*

S.I. S.I.

42 NA$_4$ DUB.SAR$^{-rù}$ NA$_4$ ^{m}*Er-wi-*•LUGAL
43 NA$_4$ ^{m}*Ut-ḫap-ḫa-a-a* NA$_4$ ^{m}[ ]-˹x˺-[ ]

UPPER EDGE

S.I.

LEFT EDGE

44 •N[A$_4$? ^{m}]-•˹*x*˺ -*ta-e*

S.I.

45 [N]A$_4$ ^{m}*Šá-ta-a*[*m-m*]*u-uš-ni*

TRANSLATION

(1–3) Antichretic loan tablet of Ḫušḫušu wife of Ḫanaya.

(4–14a) .... gave [to] Tarmi-tilla son of Šurki-tilla as(?) an antichretic(?) loan(?) [for? n? years?] a .8 homer ... field in(?) the town of Nuzi ... [the town of] Atakkal ... of the town of Nuzi(?) ..., to the north of ..., to the ..., to the ..., ...

(14b–16) And Tarmi-tilla gave [to?] Ḫušḫušu(?) ... and two minas of wool.

(17–21) When(?) [n? years? are? complete?] (and) Ḫušḫušu returns to Tarmi-tilla the silver (i.e., the goods) as per (the stipulations of this) tablet, then(?) she shall retrieve her field.

(22–27) Thus Ḫušḫušu: "I have received .... ."

(28a) .... (See, however, below, note to line 28.)

(28b–30) Should the field [have] claimants, Ḫušḫušu shall clear (it [i.e., the land]);

(31–33) (this) tablet [after] the proclamation; before (i.e., in the presence of) ... he shall(?) return the field; thus Ḫušḫušu ... .

(34–41) Before Utḫap-ḫaya [son of] Eḫli-tešup; before Zike [son of] Ḫanaya; before Ḫašip-tilla son of Zi-li(?)-...; before Erwi(?)-šarri(?) son of En-šukru; before ...-e son of Akip-tašenni; before Šatam-mušni son of Unaya; before Turar-tešup, the scribe, son of Itḫ-apiḫe.

(42–45) (*seal impression*) Seal impression of the scribe; (seal impression) seal impression of Erwi-šarri; seal impression of Utḫap-ḫaya (*seal impression*) seal impression of ...; seal(?) impression(?) of(?) ...-tae (*seal impression*) seal impression of Šatam-mušni.

COMMENTS

This tablet has deteriorated somewhat since it was first copied.

The text and seal impression on the left edge face the obverse.

A small segment appearing to represent the first sign(s) of lines 6–10 has been misplaced in the copy. These signs clearly represent parts of lines 7–11.

Note that the upper edge and the left edge contain one seal impression each, though one might expect two in each place given the legends on lines 43, 44, and 45.

Although the tablet has sustained considerable damage, enough of the text survives to reveal elements (when combined) of the telltale terminology of the *ṭuppi tidennūti*: *ṭuppi* (l. 1), *ša pī ṭuppi* (l. 18), *utarru* (ll. 20, 32), *ileqqe* (l. 21). Once the type of document is identified, one can, for the most part, trace the sequence of clauses associated with the real estate *ṭuppi tidennūti*. The range of clauses associated with this text type, their phraseology, and their typical sequence are spelled out by Jordan (1990, 77–79).

The following clauses may consequently be identified in JEN 781, using Jordan's typology of the contract type.

ll. 1–14a: contract title / field description.
    1–3: title and principal parties
    4–10/11: field description
    11/12–14a: the field is given by one of the principals *ana tidennūti*

ll. 14b–16: moveable property description.
    14b: donor
    15: commodity
    16: recipient

ll. 17–21: contract duration clause.

ll. 22–27: a declaration by the debtor probably averring her receipt of the mobilia.

The last clause, unlike the previous three, is not recognized in the analysis of Jordan. If these very broken lines are correctly interpreted, a possible problem arises in the interpretation of line 33. That line appears to be a (further) statement by Ḫušḫušu. In light of the present clause, a declaration further on would seem superfluous. However, note a similar pair of statements appearing in JEN 300:29–31, 42–43. The explanation for the repetition there too eludes me.

l. 28a: obscure.

ll. 28b–30: clear title clause.

ll. 31–33: this appears to be a phraseological "*Mischwesen*":
    31: the start of a proclamation clause
    32: perhaps a fragment of a declaration regarding return of the field
    33: the start of a statement by Ḫušḫušu

ll. 34–45: witnesses, sealers, and sealings (a section neglected in Jordan's analysis).

For specific suggestions and restorations made below in the notes, use has been made of suggestive comparative material, especially another real estate antichretic loan tablet of the lender in this text (albeit written by a different scribe), Tarmi-tilla son of Šurki-tilla: JEN 294. See also, JEN 826, another text of this genre written by the scribe of the present tablet. On occasion, other tablets of this type are cited to elucidate JEN 781. Other restorations follow from patterns characteristic of the *ṭuppi tidennūti*. Resulting restorations appear in square brackets. See also notes to the specific lines.

At another level, JEN 549 bears a certain contextual resemblance to JEN 781. That text describes a loan of barley made by the same Tarmi-tilla son of Šurki-tilla to six men. The scribe of that tablet, Turar-tešup son of Itḫ-apiḫe, is the scribe of this tablet as well. Now, the first of the borrowers in that text is one Ḫanaya son of Akku-tešup (JEN 549:2). It is possible that the borrower in JEN 781, Ḫušḫušu "wife" of Ḫanaya, is the widow of the son of Akku-tešup. If so, the current text attests to a continuing dependence of that family on Tarmi-tilla. See also, below, note to line 35.

NOTES

l. 1: *t*[*i-de*$_4$*-en-nu-ti*]. Or the like.

ll. 2–3: *aš?-ša-**⸢*ti*⸣? // *ša*!? $^{m!}$. Line 3 appears to start with ⸢*ù*⸣. However, in the continuation of the text, only Ḫušḫušu appears as the subordinate party, never Ḫanaya. See lines 19, 22, 30, 33. Therefore the interpretation of the start of line 3 adopted here, however tentative, seems preferable. For the same reason, *aš-ša-ti*, or the like, is demanded at the end of line 2 (Lacheman once read, at this point, *aš-ša-at*; cf. JEN 840:3). Though partially effaced, the third sign from the end of line 2 appears as AŠ, not as depicted in the copy. The last sign on line 2 is completely effaced.

l. 4: ⸢A⸣.[ŠÀ]. The restoration is assured by identification of the same property in line 21.

ll. 5–7. JEN 137:8–9 notes the presence of a route to the town of Atakkal with a terminus in Nuzi. Lines 5 and 6 of the present text likely name these same two towns in close juxtaposition. If the connection is correct, then the end of line 5 and the start of line 6 should be restored: AŠ/*i-na* KASKAL *ša*. But if this connection is correct, the possible presence of the toponym "Nuzi" in line 7 remains to be explained.

l. 6: *A*!. The sign appears as  , not as depicted.

l. 7: *N*[*u?-zi?*]. A guess.

ll. 8–11. These lines probably describe the borders of the field in terms of the four sides or cardinal points. Cf. JEN 294:3–6 and—even more detailed—JEN 840:5–13.

l. 8: [*na-an*]. Or the like.

l. 9: ⸢0x x⸣ . A direction could well be called for here. Cf., for example, JEN 294:5–6.

l. 11: ⸢x⸣ . The trace appears as  , not as depicted.

l. 12. For these restorations, cf. JEN 294:7.

l. 13: [^{m}*Ta*]*r*. The restoration is assured by the appearance of the same PN in the next line.

l. 14: [*it-ta-di-i*]*n*?. Or the like (Lacheman once restored [*it-ta*]-*din*). The parallel clause, defining the *quid pro quo*, concludes with the same verb (l. 16).

l. 15. For commodities at this point in the text, cf. JEN 294:10.

l. 16: [*a*?-*na*? $^{\text{f?}}$]*Ḫ*[*u*?-*uš*?-*ḫu*?-*š*]*u*?. Cf. JEN 294:10–11. The traces do not support this very well.

ll. 17–21. Cf. JEN 294:17–20.

l. 17: ⸢*ma*?-*ti*⸣?. Regarding the second trace, the horizontal wedge is not there; the surface is preserved and blank at this point. The extended tail of the *Winkelhaken* may be a gash instead.

Lacheman, unpublished papers, interpreted these traces as [ ] ^{m}*Tar*-[*mi-til-la*]. But cf. JEN 294:17–18a for a more likely reconstruction.

l. 18: [KÙ.BAB]BAR. So too Lacheman. Cf. JEN 294:18b. For this word as a summary term for various commodities, cf. JEN 606:4–8.

l. 19. It is possible that the line begins with *ša*.

l. 20: GUR!-*ru*. This interpretation is supported, not only by the wording of similar texts (see, e.g., JEN 294:20), but by the reappearance of the word, and spelling, further on in this text, in l. 32. For the spelling ending in -*ru*, cf. JEN 825:10; 310:27 (-*rù*).

l. 23: NI RU BU. So too Lacheman. The meaning is wholly obscure to me.

l. 24. After DUMU, Lacheman once thought he saw traces of signs. These are, rather, random lines. Realizing this, Lacheman simply scribbled over the signs he copied. These scribblings remain in the published copy (Lacheman and Maidman 1989, 186).

l. 26. The single remaining trace, the head of the vertical, may not be part of a sign at all.

l. 27: ⸢x x⸣? The former sign does not appear as depicted (i.e., as DÙ, KAK) but, rather, as  . One expects here the mention of the mobilia taken by the debtor.

l. 27: [*el-te*]-*qè-mi*. Cf. JEN 294:24; 300:31.

l. 28: *lu-ú*. These signs are clear and typical, not as depicted.

It is possible that [*ú*]-*k*[a_4-*al*]-*lu-ú* is to be restored here. This might represent a continuation of Ḫušḫušu's statement wherein she notes Tarmi-tilla's possession of her land in exchange for the mobilia. For analogous uses of *kullû*, see JEN 297:30; 300:4; 315:13. In none of those cases, though, is a declaration made to this effect.

ll. 28b–30. Cf. JEN 294:12–14 for a better preserved example of this clause.

l. 29: [TUK-*ši*]. Or the like. The gap allows for the restoration of two signs.

l. 29: *ma*. The spacing is correct as depicted.

l. 30: ⸢^{f}⸣. The sign appears as  , not AŠ, as depicted.

l. 30: *ma*. The sign is a clear MA, not as depicted.

l. 32: *a-na pa-ni*. For another example of "disembodied" *ana pāni*, see JEN 300:30.

l. 32: ⌜x⌝ . The trace appears as , not as depicted.

l. 33: [*uš-ḫu*]. Lacheman once saw these signs as preserved.

l. 34: *Ut-ḫap-ḫa-*[*a-a*]. The restoration is assured by comparison with line 43. No other Nuzi PN beginning "Utḫap-ḫa-[ ]" is known to me.

l. 34: *Eḫ-l*[*i-te-šup*]. This restoration is strongly suggested by JEN 120:35, where one Utḫap-ḫaya son of Eḫli-tešup appears as a witness. This is the only other place in the Nuzi texts where an Utḫap-ḫaya appears. As for the dating of these two attestations, both Utḫap-ḫaya texts involve grandsons of Teḫip-tilla.

l. 35. Might this witness be a son of Ḫušḫušu?

l. 36: *Ḫa-ši-i*[*p-ti*]*l-la*. No other restoration seems possible on the basis of the Nuzi onomasticon. See *NPN*, pp. 214b–215a; and the next note.

l. 36: *Zi-l*[*i*?-]. The signs do not appear as depicted. ZI is clear. The following traces appear as  . The resulting witness, Ḫašip-tilla son of Zili-[ ], may be compared with Ḫašip-tilla son of Zilip-apu and with the like-named son of Ziliya. See *AAN*, p. 55a.

l. 37: *E*[*r*?-*wi*?-LU]GAL?. This reading is supported by the identity of a sealer, Erwi-šarri, on line 42. Lacheman offers the same restoration.

l. 37: *En-rù-šúk*. No such PN is otherwise attested at Nuzi. It appears to be a metathetical spelling for *En-šúk-rù* (representing the common PN, En-šukru), possibly arising from the identical beginnings of the last two signs.

l. 38: ⌜*x*⌝-*e*. What appears in the copy as ḪÁP is no longer preserved, if it was ever there in the first place; [ ]-*ḫáp-e* yields no PN element with which I am familiar. What is preserved is , perhaps yielding [-*t*]*a-e*. Compare the end of the PN on line 44.

Lacheman reads this PN as *Ut-ḫap-ta-e*, comparing the name to that appearing in line 44. There, both he and Porada, unpublished papers, read [*Ut-ḫap*]-*ta-e*.

l. 38: [*en-ni*]. No other restoration of this PN appears possible. Lacheman, at this point, once saw these signs as preserved. If Lacheman's restoration of the personal name is correct, then this patronymic identifies the witness as a principal and witness in other Tarmi-tilla texts. See *NPN*, p. 168b, *sub* UTḪAP-TAE 1).

l. 39: *Ú-n*[*a-a-a*]. The first sign is a clear Ú; the second is the last sign drawn in the copy. The wedges in between do not appear on the tablet.

The restoration yields the identity of a witness attested in other Tarmi-tilla texts. See *NPN*, p. 126a *sub* ŠATAM-MUŠNI 1). "Šatam-mušni" is a name that appears with no other patronymic in the Nuzi texts.

ll. 43–45. See above, comments.

l. 43: ⸢x⸣ . Porada once read this PN as "Ta-[ ]".

l. 44. See above, note to line 38.

JEN 782

OBVERSE

1 [(ù) ^{m}Ka-na-a-a D]UM[U]? ⸢X⸣-[ ]
2 [^{m}Ut-ḫap-t]a-⸢e⸣ DUMU Mu-u⸢š⸣-[te-e]
3 [a-na ma]-•⸢ru⸣-ti e-pu-u[š(-ma)]
4 [2 ANŠ]E A.ŠÀ mi-ṣí-ir-šu ú-[ka-al]
5 [i-na s]u-ta-an A.ŠÀ ša ^{m}Aš-š[u-ra-]
6 [i-na] ša-ad-dá-an mi-iṣ-ri [ša URU KÙ?.SI]G$_{17}$?-GAL
7 [i-n]a šu-pa-al A.ŠÀ ša ^{m}Ḫu-i-t[e-e]
8 [i]-n[a] il-ta-an-ni A.ŠÀ ša ^{m}Tar-mi-⸢y⸣a
9 [k]i-m⸢u⸣ ḪA.LA-šu ^{m}Tù-ra-ri-i-a
10 [ù] $^{*m+}$K⸢a⸣-$^{+}$na-⸢a⸣-a a-na ^{m}Ut-ḫap-ta-e DUMU Mu-uš-te-e it-ta-[di]n
11 ù ^{m}Ut-⸢ḫáp⸣-ta-e 1 GUD.SAL 9 MA.NA AN.NA
12 [n? +] 1 UDU 2 en-zu 15 ANŠE ŠE ki-ma NÍG.BA a-na ^{m}Ka-<na>-a-a
13 ù ⸢a-n⸣a ^{m}Tu-$^{+}$ra-ri-i-a it-ta-din
14 šum-ma A.ŠÀ [pí]-•⸢ir⸣-qà •i-ra-aš-ši
15 ù ^{m}Ka-n⸢a-a⸣-[a it?-t]i? ^{m}Tu-[r]a-ri-i-[a]
16 ú-za-ka-ma •⸢a⸣-[na ^{m}]⸢Ut⸣?-[ḫap-ta-e i-na-an-din]
17 ⸢ù⸣? il!-ka ⸢ša⸣ [A].ŠÀ [ ]⸢x⸣[ ]
18 [ù?] •a-na ^{m}Tu-ra-ri-y⸢a⸣ ù a-na
19 ^{m}Ka-na-a-a ⸢na?-ši!? x⸣
20 ù ^{m}Ut-ḫap-ta-e ⸢la⸣ •na-š[i?]

LOWER EDGE

21 ma-an-nu-um-me-e
22 i-na bi$_{4}$-ri-šu-nu i-$^{+}$⸢bala⸣-$^{+}$ka-$^{+}$tu

REVERSE

23 1 MA.NA KÙ.BABBAR 1 MA.NA KÙ.SIG$_{17}$
24 ú-ma-al-•la-šú
25 ṭup-pu a[n-nu-ú i-n]a EGIR^{-ki} šu-du-ti
26 •i+•na K[Á.GAL š]a URU Ar-ša-$^{+}$li-$^{+}$pè
27 [š]á-⸢ṭì⸣-[ir]
28 IGI E⸢n⸣-[DUMU]-⸢a⸣?-ya ⸢x⸣?
29 [IGI] ⸢x x⸣ [ ] ⸢x x⸣-ku
30 [IGI Ši]-la-ḫi? DUMU ⸢X⸣ [ ]-LUGAL
31 [IGI]-ki-y[a DUMU]-en-ni
32 [IGI]⸢DUMU⸣?
33 [(?)] Pu-un-ni-⸢y⸣a!
34 [IGI]-⸢x-a⸣-a DUMU It-ḫi-ip-LUGAL

35 [*an-nu-tu* LÚ.MEŠ *š*]*a mu-še-el-wu* A.ŠÀ
36 [IGI DUM]U *Ar-ta-še-e*[*n-ni*]
37 [IGI?] ⸢x⸣ [ ]
38 [IGI?] ⸢x x⸣ [ ]

LEFT EDGE

39 [^{NA4}KIŠIB] ⸢x⸣ [ ]
S.I.

TRANSLATION

....

(1–3)[(and) Kanaya] son of … . They (lit. "He") adopted Utḫap-tae son of Muš-teya.

(4–10) Turariya [and] Kanaya gave (lit. "[he] gave") to Utḫap-tae son of Muš-teya as his inheritance share a [2] homer field; they (lit. "he") own (it up to) its border: [to] the south of the field of Aššur-a-…, to the east of the border [of the town of] Ḫurāṣina(?)-rābu, to the west of the field of Ḫui-te, to the north of the field of Tarmiya.

(11–13) And Utḫap-tae gave to Kanaya and to Turariya as a gift 1 cow, 9 minas of tin, …?+1 sheep, 2 goats, (and) 15 homers of barley.

(14–16) Should the field have a claim, then Kanaya with(?) Turariya shall clear (the field and) [give (it)] to Utḫap-tae.

(17–20) And(?) the *ilku* of … field is for Turariya and for Kanaya to bear(?); Utḫap-tae shall not bear (it).

(21–24) Whoever amongst them abrogates (this contract) shall pay to him (i.e., to the other party) 1 mina of silver (and) 1 mina of gold.

(25–27) This tablet was written after the proclamation at [the gate] of the town of Ar-šalipe.

(28–38) Before En-… [son of] …-aya(?); [before] … [son of] …-ku; [before] Šilaḫi son of …-šarri; [before] …-kiya [son of] …-enni; [before] … son(?) of(?) […?] Punniya; [before] …-aya son of Itḫip-šarri . [These are the men] who are the measurers of the field. [Before] … son of Artašenni ; [before?] …; [before?] … .

(39–40) [seal impression of] … (*seal impression*); seal impression of Šu?-ul-… [(*seal impression*?)].

COMMENTS

The document (JEN*u* 28a) seems to have suffered only minor deterioration since it was copied. However, in the same box with this tablet there are eleven small inscribed fragments (JEN*u* 28b–28l). These appear as if they could have come from the tablet. None is an obvious join.

Some restorations of this text are based on comparable passages in JEN 599, a document directly related to JEN 782.[2] The detailed description of the borders

2 The description of landscape in JEN 782 may also be reflected in JEN 300, but the relationship of the contents of these two texts remains to be elucidated.

of the land being transferred is the same in both texts (JEN 599:5–9; 782:4–8) as is the identity of one of the principal parties, Utḫap-tae son of Muš-teya (JEN 599:2, 18; 782:10). That Utḫap-tae is the purchaser of the land in JEN 782 and its vendor in JEN 599 demonstrates that the former text records a transaction anterior to that described in the latter. The findspot of JEN 782, room 13—the archive chamber of Tarmi-tilla son of Šurki-tilla, accords well with the fact that Tarmi-tilla was the eventual purchaser of that land from Utḫap-tae (JEN 599:3, 11), though Tarmi-tilla's name does not appear (nor should such an appearance be expected) in JEN 782; he will have acquired documentation regarding that land, including its history prior to his acquisition of it.[3]

Such pairs, "live" texts together with their "background" texts, have already been noted for the Teḫip-tilla Family (of which Tarmi-tilla was a member) and elsewhere at Nuzi (Maidman 1979, 183 with n. 14; the present pair was overlooked there as is the pair JEN 707, 206 [see Maidman 1994, 130]). In the present instance, JEN 782 itself is strikingly mentioned in JEN 599:24–26 (cf. JEN 782:3–4, 12–13). A comparable reference to a "background" text is to be found in JEN 662:68–69, where JEN 144 is mentioned (Maidman 1979, 7, n. 21).[4]

This pair of texts demands attention for yet another reason. In the first of the two transactions, it most likely is stated that the vendors, Turariya and Kanaya, both bear the *ilku*; Utḫap-tae, the buyer, does not (JEN 782:17–20). But in the second transaction, the same Utḫap-tae, now acting as vendor, is identified as the *ilku*-bearer; Tarmi-tilla, the buyer, is said not to bear this burden (JEN 599:20–21). Thus, despite the explicit claim of the first document, the *ilku* passes from Turariya and Kanaya to Utḫap-tae. Clearly, an apparent disclaimer notwithstanding, legal responsibility for the *ilku* shifts with title to the real estate to which the *ilku* attaches. Such a shift of *ilku*-bearing, demonstrated by a pair of texts in seeming contradiction to the *ilku*-clause itself, is now attested in at least three instances: JEN 782:17–20 with JEN 599:20–21 (the present case); JEN 467:35–36 with JEN 699:46–47 (see Maidman 1976, 321, n. 84; Maidman 1994, 100–2); and JEN 707:14–15 with JEN 206:25–29 (not noted heretofore, but cf., indirectly, Maidman 1994, 127–30).[5]

It appears that the first line of the text is missing. It will probably have read: *ṭup-pí ma-ru-ti ša* ^{m}*Tù-ra-ri-ya/i-a* DUMU PN, assuming different paternity for each vendor.

Lines 21 and 22 are on the lower edge; line 23 begins the reverse. The copy is inaccurate in this regard.

---

3 According to this understanding, JEN 599 should also have been found in room 13, and perhaps it was. There is some confusion regarding its findspot: different records note its findspot as room 15 (Chiera's field notes), room 16 (in a record whose source I can no longer trace), and "no room no." (Lacheman 1939, [viii]).

4 For other "background" texts, see below, JEN 789, Comments.

5 For further on the transfer of the *ilku* with the shift of title to real estate, see below, JEN 789, Comments.

Notes

ll. 1–2. The restoration of the PNs is assured by line 10.

l. 4: [2]. The number is restored from JEN 599:25, which indirectly refers to this very line.

l. 4: *ú*-[*ka-al*]. The restoration is based on JEN 599:5.

l. 5: *Aš-š*[*u-ra-*]. Cf. JEN 599:6.

l. 6: *ša-ad-dá-an*. Cf. JEN 599:7: *e-le-ni*, a synonym.

l. 6: [*ša* URU KÙ?.SI]G$_{17}$?-GAL. Lacheman restores: [*i-na ta-a-a*]-*ri* GAL. This fits the traces nicely, but mention of a standard of measure in the middle of describing the borders of the field (leaving the western border effectively undefined) makes little contextual sense. On the other hand, *ša* URU *is* preserved in JEN 599:7.[6] Of town names ending in GAL at Nuzi, Atakkal and Ḫurāṣina-rābu come to mind. The trace before GAL fits [SI]G$_{17}$ somewhat more probably than TAK$_{2/3}$. Cf. also, perhaps, JEN 300:11, 34, where Ḫurāṣina-ṣeḫru appears. Those two towns are near each other (Fincke 1993, 106–7). On the possible relevance of JEN 300 to the present text, see above, note 1.

l. 7: -*t*[*e-e*]. Cf. JEN 599:8.

l. 8: *n*[*a*]. This trace, despite its placement in the copy, belongs to line 8.

l. 9: *i-a*. These signs are quite distinct, not joined (i.e., *ya*) as appears in the copy. Cf. line 13 for the same signs.

l. 10: *K*˹*a*˺-*na*. These signs are clear and typical, not as depicted in the copy.

l. 11: GUD.SAL. This spelling of what is probably *littu* appears elsewhere at Nuzi. See the dictionaries.

l. 12: [n? +] 1 UDU. Lacheman reads: 1 UDU.

l. 14: [*pí*]. Lacheman once saw this sign preserved.

l. 14: ˹*ir*˺. This trace appears as  , not as depicted.

l. 15: [*it?-t*]*i*?. Lacheman once saw *it-ti* here.

l. 16: [m]˹*Ut*˺?-[*ḫap-ta-e*]. Whether or not the trace is correctly interpreted, the underlying PN is not in doubt.

l. 16: [*i-na-an-din*]. So too Lacheman.

ll. 17–19. The locution *ilka ša eqli ana* PN *naši* is rare. See below, JEN 785:18–19; 789:20–21; and Maidman 1994, 306–7 for two further examples. But in light of these several examples, perhaps the formulation is no mistake.

l. 17. Lacheman interpreted the traces of this line as: *il-ka-šu ša* A.ŠÀ.

l. 18: [*ù*?]. Lacheman saw no sign before the first *a-na*.

---

[6] This renders impossible Fincke's proposed restoration *mi-iṣ-ri* [*ša*] ˹É˺!.GAL (Fincke 1993, 48).

l. 19: ⌜*na*?-*ši*!? x⌝. Lacheman read here: *la na-aš*-[*ši*]. This reading, especially in light of line 20, makes no logical sense.

l. 20: *na*-*š*[*i*?]. Lacheman reads: *na-aš*-[*ši*].

l. 26: K[Á.GAL *š*]*a*. Cf., e.g., JEN 403:30, for the gate of Ar-šalipe and Fincke 1993, 48.

l. 26: *li-pè*. These signs are clear and completely preserved. Fincke's spelling of this GN in this line (1993, 47) is to be corrected accordingly.

l. 27. Or the like. Cf. JEN 403:31.

l. 28: *En*. Lacheman once saw here: *Ak*.

l. 28: ⌜x⌝?. The trace is not as depicted. Rather, it is the tail of a single vertical wedge.

l. 29. Lacheman once reconstructed this line as: [IGI *T*]*e-ḫi*-[*ya*] ⌜DUMU *Ak*⌝-*ku*-*š*[*e-ni*].

As regards chronology, the individual so defined is a member of Teḫip-tilla's generation (see, e.g., JEN 260:13; 265:9; 689:21). Now the present text reflects a time that could well be prior to that of Teḫip-tilla's grandson Tarmi-tilla (he appears in JEN 599, a text later than JEN 782). So that individual from Teḫip-tilla's generation could in theory appear as a witness here.[7]

l. 29: [IGI] ⌜x x⌝. The second trace does not appear as depicted but, rather, as a *Winkelhaken*.

l. 30: [*Ši*]. So too Lacheman. This appears to be the only possible restoration, if the sign after LA is ḪI.

l. 30: ⌜X⌝ [ ]. Lacheman once asserted, for this segment: *Šúk-ri-ip*-. Cf. JEN 625:1–2 and, below, comments to JEN 783.

ll. 32–33. Line 33 appears to consist of only one PN, and it is to be doubted for reasons of space that IGI once appeared before "Punniya." If this is the case, the last trace on line 32 should be a remnant of DUMU.

l. 34. This line curves upward because lines running over from the obverse appear in the space where line 34 would normally have continued.

l. 34: LUGAL. The sign is typical, not as depicted.

l. 35: [*an-nu-tu* LÚ.MEŠ]. Or the like.

l. 35: *mu-še-el-wu* A.ŠÀ. One might posit <*ša*> between these two words.

l. 36: *e*[*n-ni*]. Lacheman once saw these signs as completely preserved.

---

7 However, see below, next note , for implicit evidence that JEN 782 involves a person mentioned in JEN 783 and is, therefore, close in time to the generation of Tarmi-tilla.

JEN 783

OBVERSE

1 [ ]⸢x⸣ *šu* [W]A?
2 [ ] *a-na* [ ]-PA
3 [ ] *ù* ^{m}*Tar-*⸢*mi*⸣*-til-la*
4 [n ANŠ]E GIG 1 UDU.NITA
5 [*ki?-ma?* NÍG?.BA?-*šu? a-na* ^{m}] •*Ši-la-ḫi* SUM^{-nu}
6 [*šum-ma* A.ŠÀ.MEŠ *pa*]*-qí-ra-na i-ra-aš-ši*
7 ^{m}⸢*Ši*⸣-[*la-ḫi*] *ú-za-ka-ma a-na*
8 $^{[m]}$*Tar-*•*mi-*•*til-la i+na-an-di-in*
9 *il-ku ša* +A.ŠÀ.MEŠ ^{m}*Ši-la-ḫi*
10 *na-ši-i* ⸢*ù*⸣ ^{m}*Tar-mi-til-la*
11 •*la na-ši-*⸢*i*⸣ *ma-an-nu-um-*<*me*>*-e*
12 *ša i-na bi*$_{4}$*-r*⸢*i*⸣*-šu-nu* KI.BAL-*tu*$_{4}$
13 2 MA.NA KÙ.[BABBAR] 2 [M]A.⸢N⸣A K⸢Ù⸣.[SI]G$_{17}$
14 [*ú*]*-m*⸢*a*⸣*-*[*al-la*]

LOWER EDGE

15 [*šu*]*-*•*du-ti* ⸢x x x⸣
16 [URU] ⸢*Nu*⸣?-[*z*]*i* [ ]

REVERSE

S.I.

17 NA$_{4}$ ^{m}*Ḫu-ti*$_{4}$*-y*⸢*a*⸣ ^{LÚ}*a-bu-ul-ta-an-nu*
18 IGI *Ḫu-pí-ta* DUMU *Nam-ḫe-na-tal*
19 •IG[I] ⸢*E*⸣*-en-na-ma-ti* DUMU *Ar-te-eš-še*
20 [IGI] ⸢*x*⸣*-ip-te-šup* DUMU *Nam-ḫe-na-tal*
21 [IGI]-⸢*x*⸣*-til-la* DUMU *E-en-na-pa-li*
22 [IGI DUMU] ⸢*x*⸣*-kip-til-la*
23 [IGI DUMU] *E-en-na-ma-ti*
24 [IGI DUMU]-⸢x⸣-*na*
25 [IGI DUMU]-*e*
26 [IGI DUMU]-⸢x⸣-*ta*
27 [IGI DUMU -*t*]*il?-*[*la?*]

LEFT EDGE

28 NA$_{4}$ ^{m}*Ḫu-pí-*[*ta?*]
[S.I.?]

TRANSLATION

(1–3a) … to … .

(3b–5) And Tarmi-tilla gave [to] Šilaḫi [as? his? gift?] … homer(s) of wheat, (and) 1 ram.

(6–8) [Should the field] have claimants, Šilaḫi shall clear (it) and give (it) to Tarmi-tilla.

(9–11a) Šilaḫi shall bear the *ilku* of the field; Tarmi-tilla shall not bear (it).

(11b–14) Whoever between them abrogates (this contract) shall pay 2 minas of silver (and) 2 minas of gold.

(15–16) … proclamation … (town of) Nuzi(?) … .

(17) (*seal impression*) Seal impression of Ḫutiya, the gatekeeper.

(18–27) Before Ḫupita son of Namḫen-atal; before Enna-mati son of Ar-tešše; [before] …-ip-tešup; son of Namḫen-atal; [before] …-tilla son of Enna-pali; [before] … [son of] …-kip-tilla; [before] … [son of] Enna-mati; [before] … [son of] …-na; [before] … [son of] …-e; [before] … [son of] …-ta; [before] … [son of] …-tilla(?).

(28) Seal impression of Ḫupi-ta(?) [(*seal impression*?)].

Comments

This tablet has deteriorated very little since it was copied.

The document is a tablet of real estate adoption—identifiable as such from the surviving formulations (see, e.g., ll. 4–6, 9–11). It stems from room 13, the archive of Tarmi-tilla son of Šurki-tilla; he is the purchaser of land in this contract (ll. 3, 8, 11).

Notes

ll. 2–3. The end of line 2, after *a-na*, might be restored: [^{m}*Tar-mi-til*]-⌜*l*⌝*a* If so, the start of line 3 would likely read SUM^{-nu} (cf. l. 5) or the like.

l. 5: *Ši-la-ḫi*. There is a fair likelihood that this vendor of real estate is Šilaḫi son of Šurkip-šarri, elsewhere identified as belonging to the charioteer class (HSS, XIII, 212:3, 22). The son of Šurkip-šarri is elsewhere also linked to real estate interests in JEN 625 (see ll. 1–2). Also involved there is one Enna-mati son of Ar-tešše (JEN 625:6–7) who reappears in the present text as a witness (JEN 783:19).[8]

l. 6: [A.ŠÀ.MEŠ]. Cf. l. 9.

l. 7: [*ḫi*]. According to Lacheman and the Nuzi files of the Oriental Institute, this sign was once preserved.

l. 8: *di-in*. Contrary to the copy, these two signs are separate and typical in their appearance. The "*din*" of the Oriental Institute file is not correct.

l. 9: *ša*+A. This most unusual ligature is correct as copied.

---

[8] It is also to be noted that Šilaḫi son of Šurkip-šarri may reappear as a witness in JEN 782:30. (See above, second note to JEN 782:30.) Now JEN 782 was written at the "Ar-šalipe Gate" (l. 26); and the land described in JEN 625 is located in the town of Ar-šalipe (l. 4).

JEN 625, 782, and 783 all come from room 13. Thus there are several faint, but distinct, points of contact among all three of these texts.

l. 10: *na-ši-i*. This is correctly copied. The *na-a-ši-i* of Lacheman and the Oriental Institute is mistaken.

l. 11: *-um-<me>-e*. This scribal lapse is correctly reflected in Lacheman's notes and the Oriental Institute files, as well as in an early version of Lacheman's hand copy. The *me* of the published copy must be Lacheman's hypercorrection.

ll. 15–16. These lines likely once contained a *šūdūtu*-clause. However, considerations of space, to judge from where the surviving words appear, suggest this is not a typical example of the clause. Cf. examples in *CAD*, Š/III, p. 195.

l. 17. The seal impression above this line is clear. The suggestion of the copy that the tablet is damaged here is incorrect. In her unpublished papers, Porada, perhaps on the basis of this seal impression, identified this Ḫutiya the gatekeeper with the gatekeeper, Ḫutiya son of Ila-nîšū.[9]

l. 19. See above, note to l. 5.

l. 20: ⸢*x*⸣-*ip*. The Oriental Institute files restore: [*Wu*]-⸢*ur*⸣. But even if the reading *ur* were possible, *Šu* or *Wu* might have preceded this sign. Neither a "Šur-tešup" nor a "Wur-tešup" son of Namḫen-atal is, to my knowledge, elsewhere attested in the Nuzi texts.

ll. 26–27. These last lines—even some of the preceding lines—could have contained identities of sealers together with seal impressions.

l. 28: [*ta*?]. Cf. l. 18.

JEN 784

OBVERSE

1 *ṭup-pí ma*-[*ru*]-⸢*ti*⸣ *š*[*a* ^{m}*Še-še-er-pa*]
2 DUMU *It*-[*ḫ*]*a-pu* ⸢*ù*⸣? [^{m}*Ḫu-i-te*(*-e*) DUMU *Mu-še-ya*]
3 ⸢*a*⸣-*na m*[*a-ru-ti i*]-⸢*pu-uš*⸣?-[*ma*]
4 [É *i-na*] *ṣé-re-ti* $^{+}$*ša* URU KÙ.SIG$_{17}$-*n*[*a*-TUR]
5 [*i-na*] ⸢x⸣ [ ]
6 [*i-na*] ⸢TI? x⸣ AN [I]K? LU
7 [*i-na*] ⸢x x⸣ [*š*]*a*?-*a*
8 [*i-na i*]*l-ta-an-ni* KASKAL^{-ni} [ ]
9 ⸢*šum*⸣-*ma* É GAL *la i-na-k*[*i-is-sú*]
10 [*š*]*um-ma* É TUR *la ú–ra*-[*ad-dì*]
11 [(?)] ⸢*i*⸣-*na* URU KÙ.SIG$_{17}$-*na*-TUR *ki-i* [ḪA.LA-*šu*]
12 [^{m}*Š*]*e-še-er-pa a-na* ^{m}*Ḫu-i-•te*[(*-e*)]
13 [ ] *še še ma-*a it-ta-•din*
14 [*ù*] ^{m}*Ḫu-i-te*-⸢*e*⸣ 13 MA.N[A *an*?-*na*?-*ku*?]
15 [*ù*? (?)] 3 BÁN ŠE *ki*-⸢*ma*⸣ NÍG.BA-•*šu*

---

9 An Ila-nîšū was himself a gatekeeper. See *NPN*, p. 68 *sub* ILA-NÎŠŪ 29).

16 [ ] ⸢x *a*⸣-[*n*]*a* ^{m}*Še-še-*⸢*er*⸣-[*pa*]
17 [*i-lik*]-*šu ša* É *an-nu-*[*ú* ^{m} *Ḫu-i-te(-e) la*] *na-ši*
18 [*ù* ^{m}]*Še-še-er-pa na-š*[*i*]
19 [*šu*]*m-ma* É.ḪI-*šu pí-ir-*[*qa*]
20 [*i?-ra?-aš?*]-*ši ù* ^{m}*Še-**⸢*še*⸣-[*er-pa*]
21 [ ] ⸢x x x⸣ [ ]

.

.

.

LOWER EDGE

22 [*a-na* ^{m} *Ḫu-i-te(-e)*] ⸢*ú*⸣-*ma-a*[*l-la*]
23 [*ṭup-pu an-n*]*u*!-⸢*ú*⸣! *i-na* EGIR$^{-k[i]}$

REVERSE

24 [*šu-du-t*]*i a-na pa-ni a-b*[*u-ul-li*]
25 [*i-na* URU] ⸢KÙ.SIG$_{17}$-*n*⸣*a-**TU[R]
26 [*šá*]-*ṭì-ir an-nu-t*[*u*$_4$ LÚ.MEŠ]
27 [*ša?*] É.ḪI-*šu mu-šal-wu*
28 [*ù?* ŠE].MEŠ *an-na-ku a-*[*na*] ^{m}*Še-še-er-pa*
29 [IGI] ⸢x •x x⸣ [DUMU *Te?-e*]*š-šu-a*
30 [IGI]-*mi-ya* DUMU [ ]-*a-a*
31 [IGI *A*]-*ri-ḫa-ma-an-n*[*a*] DUMU *Me-li-*⸢*ya*⸣
32 [IGI *K*]*i-li-ip-še-ri* DUMU *Na-aš-*•*wi*
33 [IGI *G*]*i*$_5$*-mi-il-la-dá* [DUMU] *Zu-me*!-⸢*e*⸣
34 •IGI ^{d}XXX-GAL DUMU *Be-*[*li-y*]*a*
35 IGI *Ki-ka*$_4$*-pu* D[UMU]
36 IGI *Iz?-za-ak-ka*$_4$ D[UMU ⸢x x⸣-[ ]-⸢x⸣
37 IGI *A*⸢*r*⸣-[ ]-*e* DUMU *Ḫi-*[ ]-⸢x⸣
38 ŠU ^{m}⸢*I*⸣-[*ri*]-*ri* DUB.SAR D[UMU?]
39 *qa-an-*[*na*]-*šu ša* ^{m}*Ḫu-*⸢*i*⸣-[*te(-e)*]
40 *a-na* [*pa-ni*] *ši-bu-*[*ti im-ta-šar*]
41 *ù* [ ] ⸢x⸣ IM ⸢*m*⸣*a* [ ]⸢•x *x⸣ [ ]
42 [N]A$_4$ ^{m}*Še-še-er-pa*

S.I.

43 NA$_4$ ^{m}*Ki-ka*$_4$*-pu*

S.I.

UPPER EDGE

S.I. S.I.

44 N[A$_4$ ^{m}]-⸢x⸣-^{d}UTU? N[A$_4$ ⸢x⸣-[ ]

Translation

(1–3) Tablet of adoption of [Šešerpa] son of Itḫ-apu. Now(?) he adopted [Ḫui-te son of Mušeya.]

(4–13) Šešerpa gave to Ḫui-te as [his inheritance share a] ... [structure] in the town of Ḫurāṣina-ṣeḫru, [in] the suburbs of the town of Ḫurāṣina-[ṣeḫru, to the] ..., [to the] ..., [to the] ..., [to] the north of the road .... If it transpires that the structure is large(r than calculated), it shall not be diminished (lit. "he shall not cut it"), if it transpires that the structure is small(er than calculated), it shall not be enlarged (lit. "he shall not add").

(14–16) [And] Ḫui-te (gave) to Šešerpa as his gift 13 minas [of tin? and?] ...(?) .3 homers of barley.

(17–18) [Ḫui-te shall not] bear the [*ilku*] of this structure; [rather] Šešerpa shall bear (it).

(19–21) Should his (i.e., Šešerpa's) structure have a claim (against it), then Šešerpa [shall clear (the structure) and then] ... to Ḫui-te.

(22) .... and he shall pay [to Ḫui-te] ... .

(23–26a) This [tablet] was written after the proclamation before the gate [in the town of] Ḫurāṣina-ṣeḫru.

(26b–38) These are [the men who? are] the measurers of his structure [and? who are the givers? of the barley] (and) the tin to Šešerpa: [before] ... [son of] Teššuya(?); [before] ...-miya son of ...-aya; [before] Ariḫ-ḫamanna son of Meliya; [before] Kilip-šeri son of Našwi; [before] Gimill-Adad [son of] Zume; before Sin-rabī son of Bêliya; before Kikk-apu son of ...; before Iz(?)-zakku son of ...; before Ar-...-e son of Ḫi-... . Hand of Iriri the scribe, son(?) of(?) ... .

(39–40) He (i.e., Ḫui-te) pressed Ḫui-te's hem (onto this clay) before (these) witnesses.

(41) And ... .

(42–44) Seal impression of Šešerpa (*seal impression*); seal impression of Kikk-apu (*seal impression*); (*seal impression*) seal impression of ...-Šamaš(?); (*seal impression*) seal impression of ... .

Comments

I have read this tablet from a pair of casts only. The original artifact was returned to Baghdad from the Oriental Institute on November 30, 1982. The casts are an inadequate substitute for the original, and, as with other such texts, collation is approximate only. The copy is, *faute de mieux*, assumed to be correct where the casts are indistinct.[10] This circumstance is particularly unfortunate in this case, since parts of the text were not copied by Lacheman. Where I could discern the signs, I added them to Lacheman's copy. Probably, a join was made subsequent to Lacheman's copying the text. As far as one can judge on the basis

---

10 For amplification on the difficulties of such a situation and the procedure adopted, see Maidman 1994, 192, comments to JEN 726. The procedure adopted there is employed here as well.

of these casts, the tablet appears not to have suffered very much damage since it was copied.

JEN 772b–772d are inscribed scraps found in the same box with the casts (= JEN 772a).

The Oriental Institute transliteration of JEN 784 was made by Lacheman. For the most part, then, the reading of the Oriental Institute and of Lacheman represent a single source.

The vendor and purchaser in this contract, Šešerpa son of Itḫ-apu and Ḫuite son of Mušeya, appear together in five or six other texts: JEN 189, 300, 789 (*q .v.*), 821=822, 824, JEN*u* 1158?.[11] In all (probably including JEN*u* 1158), he is the ceder of real estate, once by real estate adoption (JEN 789), otherwise by antichretic loan (possibly excepting JEN*u* 1158). The identity of the principal parties in all these instances, the approximate contemporaneity of the contracts, the general geographical proximity of the real estate described in these texts, and the employment of a single scribe, Iriri, in at least three of these texts (JEN 300, 789, 824[12])—and by extension in this text, since part of his name survives—allow reconstructions in the present text to be made on the basis of the larger body of documents.

NOTES

l. 1: [*ru*]. The Oriental Institute files record this sign as preserved.

l. 1: [^{m}*Še-še-er-pa*]. For this restoration, see lines 12, 16, 18.

l. 2: [*ḫ*]*a*. The Oriental Institute files record this sign as preserved.

l. 2: ⌜*ù*⌝?. The trace appears as:  .The Oriental Institute files record here: *ù*.

l. 2: [^{m}*Ḫu-i-te(-e)* DUMU *Mu-še-ya*]. For the restoration of the first name, see lines 12 and 14. That this individual is the son of Mušeya is demonstrated by his involvement with Šešerpa in five or six other transactions. For details, see above, comments.

ll. 4–7. These four lines, or perhaps the last three, should describe the western, eastern, and northern borders (not necessarily in that order) of the real estate, just as line 8 describes the southern border of the structure.

l. 4: [É]. For this restoration, see lines 9, 10, 17, 19, 27.

ll. 9–10. This clause is peculiar: it intrudes here into the midst of the clause establishing the "inheritance share," ll. 4–8, 11–13, which would read well without ll. 9–10. The same scribe has done this again in JEN 300:9–10. Clauses such as this one usually appear later in the text and apart from other clauses. See, for example, JEN 779:14–17; 780:17–19. This peculiarity is instructive: clearly intrusive elements in ancient documents—even prosaic ones—can have been inserted by an original scribe, not only by an editor.

11 Ḫui-te's acquisitive activities are well attested. See *NPN*, p. 62a, *sub* ḪUI-TE 4). Šešerpa also appears as a principal in JEN 823 and 825.

12 Only JEN*u* 1158 is clearly written by another scribe.

l. 9: -*k*[*i-is-sú*]. Or the like. See JEN 300:9, written by the same scribe.

l. 10: -[*ad-dì*]. Or the like. See JEN 300:10, written by the same scribe.

l. 11: [(?)]. According to the Oriental Institute files, the lines begins: *i-na*.

l. 12: [ᵐ*Š*]*e*. The Oriental Institute files record these signs as preserved.

l. 13: [ ] *še še ma-a*. Cf. Lacheman's *še-še-ba-a* in an isolated manuscript sheet. Otherwise, Lacheman (and hence the Oriental Institute files) seems to have inadvertantly skipped line 13 in (subsequent) transliterations and studies.

The meaning of this half line eludes me entirely. No word(s) or idea, in fact, seem missing between *Ḫui-te* (l. 12) and *ittadin* (l. 13), the words bracketing this gap and these signs. Cf., below, note to line16.

l. 14: 13. This is correct. Lacheman once mistakenly typed "23" but (much?) later corrected this error. In the interim, "23" entered the Oriental Institute transliteration of this line.

l. 14: [*an*?-*na*?-*ku*?]. Cf. l. 28.

l. 15: ⸢*ma*⸣. What is drawn as a vertical on the copy actually appears more like a *Winkelhaken*.

l. 16: [ ] ⸢x⸣. I do not know what this gap contained. As in the case of the start of line 13, nothing obvious is missing from the text here. The Oriental Institute files here suggest [ᵐ*Ḫu-i-te-e*]. This is possible but involves an unusual resumption of the PN from line 14.

l. 17: [*i-lik*]-*šu*. Or the like. For this unusual spelling, I rely on JEN 789:20. *šu* is clear. Neither [*il-k*]*a* (Lacheman) nor [*il*]-ka_4 (Oriental Institute) is to be preferred.

l. 17: [*ú*]. Or the like. Lacheman here suggests: [*tu*].

l. 19: É.ḪI. The scribe has not inadvertantly omitted the A-sign. Cf. l. 27 and JEN 789:31.

l. 20: [*i*?-*ra*?-*aš*?]-*ši*. This restoration is offered, if tentatively, because of the size of the gap to be bridged. However, Lacheman restores [*ir-ta*]-*ši*, an attractive alternative supported by [*ir-t*]*a-ši* in JEN 789:24.

ll. 21–22. These two lines appear to be separated by a gap of several lines. Line 21 possibly concludes the clear-title clause beginning on line 19 (the verb, *inandin* or the like, might have appeared on the line after line 21). Cf., for this clause, JEN 789:23–26. Line 22 concludes with the characteristic verb used for the penalty clause. Cf. JEN 789:36–38. The beginning of this clause may have occupied the two prior lines.

l. 22: *a*[*l*]. The trace does not appear as *i*, as copied, but, rather, as  .

l. 24: *a-na pa-ni a-b*[*u-ul-li*]. This unusual locution is used by the same scribe in JEN 300:33. See *CAD* A/1, p. 89a for other examples of this and similar phrasing, as well as for the more common *ina bāb abulli*.

l. 25: [*i-na*]. Cf. JEN 300:34; 789:43. The Oriental Institute files restore: [*ša*].

l. 26: [*šá*]. Cf. JEN 300:34; 789:43.

l. 26: -*t*[u_4 LÚ.MEŠ]. Or the like. The Oriental Institute files restore: [IGI.MEŠ].

l. 27: É.ḪI-*šu*. See above, note to line 19.

l. 28. As implied by the translation, one expects *nādinānu*, or the like, to appear at the end of the line. There appears to be insufficient space for such a reconstruction. This may represent an accidental omission by the scribe.

l. 29: ⌜x x x⌝. Only the third trace, a horizontal wedge, is correctly copied. The second trace lacks the vertical of the copy and so looks something like BI. The first appears, not as depicted, but, rather, as: . In this light, Lacheman's reading, *Ar-pí-ḫe*, seems plausible. However, he seems to have abandoned this idea (influenced by his subsequent inaccurate copy?); the idea is nowhere reflected in *NPN*. The traces cannot support "*Ḫu-ti-ya*"; one Ḫutiya son of Teššuya appears as a witness in JEN 300:36.

l. 30: [IGI]. Lacheman restores: *Tar*.

l. 30: [ ]-*a-a*. The Oriental Institute Nuzi files reflect a completely preserved *Ta-a-a*. See *NPN*, pp. 143b, *sub* TAI̯A 106); 148b *sub* TARMII̯A 29).[13]

l. 31: [*A*]. The Oriental Institute files indicate this sign as preserved.

l. 33: *me*!. The sign appears, not as depicted, but, rather, as MAŠ.

l. 36: *Iz*?. Lacheman variously suggested *Pa* and Ka_4. No "Izzaka," "Pazakka," or "Kazakka" is, to my knowledge, elsewhere attested among the Nuzi texts.

l. 36: ⌜x x⌝. The second trace appears, not as depicted (i.e., as ⌜NÍG⌝), but, rather, as:  .

l. 37. Lacheman once restored this witness's names as, in effect, *Ar-teya mār Ṭâb-šarru*.

l. 38: ^{m}⌜*I*⌝-[*ri*]-*ri*. This restoration is assured. See above, comments.

l. 38: D[UMU?]. This scribe nowhere else identifies his father.

ll. 39–40. Enough of this clause survives to ensure its correct reconstruction. Cf., for example, HSS, XVI, 452:9–11.

l. 41. I do not understand the gist of this line.

l. 41: ⌜x x⌝. The second last trace appears, not as depicted, but, rather, as:

l. 43. The seal impression below this line is identified by Lacheman as Po 164.

---

13 The reference on those pages (and elsewhere) to "JEN*u* 722a" is to this text, which is actually JEN*u* 792. I shall elsewhere describe the basis of this confusion, which ultimately stems from a misreading.

JEN 785

OBVERSE

1 *ṭup-pí m[a-ru-ti]*
2 *ša* ^{m}*Tù-[ra-r]i* [DUM]U [DINGIR-*ni-šu*]
3 *ù* ^{m}*I[t]-ḫa-pu* D[UMU *Ḫa-ši-ya*]
4 *a-na ma-⸢r⸣u-ti i-pu-[uš]*
5 3 ANŠE 5 ^{GIŠ}APIN A.ŠÀ *iš-t[u?* URU K]Ù.SIG$_{17}$-*na*-TUR
6 *i+na l⸢e⸣-et ša I-te-ya*
7 *i-na •le-et ša* ^{m}*Me-le-en-za-a[ḫ]*
8 *i+na šá-pat* KASKAL^{-ni} *i+na* URU *Ta-ku-we*
9 *ki-ma* ḪA.LA-*šu!* ^{m}*Tù-ra-ri*
10 *a-na* ^{m}*It-ḫa-⸢p⸣u* DUMU *Ḫa-ši-ya it-ta-din*
11 *⸢ù⸣* ^{m}*It-ḫa-pu* 3 GUN 30 MA.NA URUDU
12 *ki-mu* NÍG.BA-*šu a-na* ^{m}*Tù-r⸢a-ri⸣*
13 DUMU DINGIR-*ni-šu at-ta-di[n]*
14 *šum-ma* ⸢A⸣.ŠÀ *pí-ir-[qa]*
15 *ir-ta-ši* ^{m}*[T]ù-r[a-ri]*
16 *ú-za-ka$_4$-ma [a-n]a*

LOWER EDGE

17 ^{m}*It-ḫa-pu [i-na-(ad-)di-nu]*
18 *il-ka$_4$-šu a-na* ^{m}*T[ù-ra-ri]*
19 *na-ši! ù* ^{m}*I[t-ḫa-pu]*

REVERSE

20 *⸢ul⸣ na-ši-ma*
21 *ša i-bala-k[a$_4$?-tu?* 1 MA.NA KÙ.BABBAR (*ù*)]
22 1 MA.NA KÙ.SIG$_{17}$ [*ú-ma-al-la*]
23 ^{NA4}KIŠIB *E-ké-ké*
S.I.
24 ^{NA4}KIŠIB *Tù-ra-ri*
S.I.
25 IGI *Ma-[a]t-wa* DUMU *Ši-en-za-aḫ*
26 IGI *A-k[a-a]p-še-en-ni* DUMU ^{d}UTU-[*ri-ma-ni*]
27 IGI *Ke-li-⸢i⸣p*-LUGAL DUMU *Ši-⸢x⸣-*[ ]
28 IGI *Nu-i-še-r[i]* DUMU *Ku-za?-*[ ]
29 IGI *E-ké-[ké* DUMU]
30 IGI ^{d}IM-[*na-ṣir* DUB.SAR]

LEFT EDGE

31 ^{NA4}KIŠIB *Ma-⸢at⸣!-wa* S.I.
32 S.I. ^{NA4}KIŠIB *Ké-li-ip*-LU⸢GAL⸣

Translation

(1–4) Tablet of adoption of Turari son of [Ila-nîšū]. Now he adopted Itḫ-apu son of [Ḫašiya].

(5–10) Turari gave to Itḫ-apu son of Ḫašiya as his inheritance share a 3.5 homer field from(?) (i.e., "in"?) …(?) [the town of] Ḫurāṣina-ṣeḫru, adjacent to Eteya's (field), adjacent to Melen-zaḫ's (field), abutting the road, in the town of Takuwe.

(11–13) And Itḫ-apu gave (lit. "I gave" for the expected "he gave") to Turari son of Ila-nîšū as his gift 3.5 talents of copper.

(14–17) Should the field have a claim (against it), Turari shall clear (the field) and [give] (it) to Itḫ-apu.

(18–20) Its *ilku* (i.e., the field's) is for Turari to bear(?); and Itḫ-apu shall not bear it.

(21–22) Who(ever) abrogates (this contract) [shall pay 1 mina of silver (and)] 1 mina of gold.

(23–24) Seal impression of Ekeke (*seal impression*); seal impression of Turari (*seal impression*).

(25–30) Before Watwa son of Šien-zaḫ; before Akap-šenni son of Šamaš-[rîmânni]; before Kelip-šarri son of Ši-…; before Nui-šeri son of Ku-za?-…; before Ekeke [son of] …; before Adad-[nāṣir, the scribe].

(31–32) Seal impression of Watwa (*seal impression*); (*seal impression*) seal impression of Kelip-šarri.

Comments

This tablet has suffered virtually no deterioration since it was first copied.

This text has a direct relationship to JEN 789, especially line 17 of that text. This was already implicitly recognized by Lacheman in his close juxtaposition of JEN 785 and 789 in his planned publication of Nuzi tablets. The connection was explicitly noted by Carlo Zaccagnini (1984, 714 with n. 59). For more on the nature of this connection, see below, comments to JEN 789.

The Oriental Institute Nuzi files and one Lacheman manuscript have, after line 30, ten more lines of text. But the top and bottom of the tablet are preserved. These lines must come from another artifact. Subsequently, someone at the Oriental Institute, realizing this, crossed out these ten lines from the file.

The text of the left edge (i.e., ll. 31–32) faces away from the obverse, not toward it, as depicted in the copy.

Notes

l. 2. For the reconstruction of the PNs of this line, see ll. 9, 13.

l. 3: [*Ḫa-ši-ya*]. For this restoration, cf. l. 10.

l. 4: [*uš*]. Cf. JEN 47:4; 89:5; 216:4, all written by the scribe who probably wrote this tablet. For further on this point, see below, note to l. 30.

l. 5: *t*[*u*?]. Lacheman here reads: [*tu*].

ll. 6, 7. *i-na le-et ša*. The absence of a substantive (presumably a form of *eqlu*) in the genitive of the *status rectus* following the substantive in the *status constructus* (also in the genitive) is either a mistake or a kind of ellipsis. Given the appearance of this phenomenon in consecutive lines, the latter alternative is perhaps to be preferred.

l. 6: *I-te-ya*. The male determinative, contrary to the Oriental Institute Nuzi file, is absent, as was already perceived by Lacheman.

l. 8: *i+na* (second). These signs are very faint. *ša* is possible. The Oriental Institute Nuzi file has: "*ša*?".

l. 9: *šu*!. Correct as copied.

l. 11: 30. This is correct, not "31" as in the Oriental Institute Nuzi file.

l. 17: [*i-na-(ad-)di-nu*]. Cf. JEN 89:15; 216:19. On the relevance of JEN 89 and 216 to the present document, see below, note to l. 30.

l. 18: *a-na*. These signs are clear and distinct on the tablet.

l. 19: *ši*!. Though DIN is written, *ši* is meant. See above, note to JEN 782:17–19 for this form of the *ilku* clause. The Oriental Institute Nuzi file reads: *din*. Lacheman reads *ši* and indicates the anomalous form by placing small circles on either side of the sign in the hand copy.

l. 21: *ša i-*. No sign intervenes between these signs.

l. 21: *k*[*a*$_4$?-*tu*?]. Or the like.

l. 21: [1 MA.NA KÙ.BABBAR (*ù*)]. Cf. JEN 89:17; 47:16 (approximately); 216:20; 221:23 (2 minas each instead of 1); 807:18. For the relevance of those texts to this one, see below, note to l. 30.

The resulting reconstruction assumes that scribal habit affects the wording and—to an extent—the content of the penalty clause.

l. 23. The space before (i.e., to the right of) this line is preserved and blank.

l. 24. My collation of the seal impression after this line confirms that it is Po 180. See also Maidman, 1994, 341, note to JEN 768:22.

l. 26: [*ri-ma-ni*]. Or the like. This restoration is based on a suggestion of Lacheman. This witness appears in JEN 216:40 and 221:29, 36.[14] There are several points of contact between those texts and JEN 785, including a common scribe. See, further, below, note to l. 30.

l. 27: *Ši*-⌜*x*⌝-[ ]. See below, note to JEN 786:25.

l. 28: *za*?. Lacheman here reads: *za*.

l. 30: [*na-ṣir*]. This restoration follows the persuasive suggestion of Lacheman. It persuades because Adad-nāṣir the scribe is the writer of JEN 47, 89, 216, 221,

---

14 For the readings, see *NPN*, p. 12b, *sub* AKAP-ŠENNI 13).

and 807. Several threads attach those texts to this one. Itḫ-apu son of Ḫašiya, the purchaser in the present text, is also the buyer in JEN 47 and 89. One Mušeya son of Ḫašiya is the purchaser of land in JEN 216 and 221 and is involved in a real estate exchange in JEN 807. It appears plausible that this Mušeya and Itḫ-apu were brothers.[15] The other principal in the present text, the vendor Turari son of Ila-nīšû, appears as a witness and sealer in JEN 47.[16]

ll. 31–32. Following customary Nuzi practice, the legends in these lines are to be linked to the impressions above/below, not to the impressions alongside. This is clearer where the scribe has placed vertical lines separating the several legends (together with their associated impressions) from each other. See, for example, JEN 817, left edge; 830, left edge.

l. 31: ⸢*at*⸣!. The sign appears, not as copied, but, rather, as:  .

JEN 786

OBVERSE

1 *ṭup-pí ma-r*⸢*u*⸣*-ti ša* ^{m}*A-ri-ka*$_4$*-ma-ri*
2 DUMU *Pu-ra-mi-sú*
3 ^{m}*It-ḫa-pu* •DUMU *Ḫa-ši-ya*
4 *a-na ma-ru-ti* •⸢*i*⸣*-pu-sú*
5 *ki-ma* ḪA.L⸢A⸣-*š*[*u*] ⸢1⸣ $^{[GI]Š}$APIN A.ŠÀ ⸢x⸣?
6 *i-na* ⸢URU⸣ [*Ḫu*]*-ra-*[*ṣí*]*-na*-TUR
7 *i+na le-*⸢*et*⸣ KASKAL^{-ni} *š*[*a*]
8 *i-na le-et* A.ŠÀ *ša* ^{m}⸢x⸣-[ ]
9 *i+na le-et ti-le-e* [ ]
10 ^{m}*A-ri-ka*$_4$*-ma-*⸢*ri*⸣ •*a-***na* ^{m}[*It-ḫa-pu* SUM]
11 *ù* ^{m}*It-*[*ḫa-pu a-na*] ^{m}*A-*[*ri-ka*$_4$*-ma-ri*]
12 8 BÁN *ku-*•*n*[*i*!?*-šu*/*ši ki-ma* NÍG.BA-*šu*]
13 *it-*⸢*ta?-din*⸣? [(*ù*) *šum-ma* A.ŠÀ]
14 *pí-i*[*r-qa ir-ta-ši*]
15 ^{m}*A-*•*ri-*⁺⸢*ka*$_4$*-*⁺*ma*⸣*-*[*ri ú-za-ak-ka*$_4$*-ma*]
16 *a-na* ^{m}*It-ḫa-p*[*u i-na-an-din*]
17 *il-ka ša* A.Š[À ^{m} *na-ši*]

.
.
.

[15] See also, below, n. 42. Another thread: all these texts come from room 1 (JEN 47, 89, 785) or room 4. For the significance of this, see Lacheman (1958, vi), and cf.—again—below, n. 42.

[16] One might note that Akap-šenni son of Šamaš-rîmânni appears as a witness both in this text (l. 26) and in JEN 216 and 221. However, part of the reason his name is restored here is the presumed presence in this text of Adad-nāṣir as scribe. Therefore, the assumed presence of Šamaš-rîmânni has, at best, limited evidentiary value.

LOWER EDGE

18 <*ša*>? *i-na bi*$_4$*-ri-šu-n*[*u* BAL^{-tu}]

19 1 MA.NA KÙ .BABBAR 1 M[A.NA KÙ .SIG$_{17}$]

20 Ì.LÁ.E

REVERSE

+———————————————————————

21 *IGI •*Be-la-nu* DUMU [ ]

22 [IGI] ⸢*x*⸣*-x-pu* [DUMU]

.

.

.

23 IGI [DUMU]

24 IGI *Mi-kí-y*[*a*] D[UMU] ⸢x x⸣ [ ]

25 IGI *Ke-li-ip*-LUGAL DUMU [ ]-⸢*x*⸣*-za-*$^{+}$*a*⸢*ḫ*⸣

26 IGI ŠEŠ-*wa-qar* DUMU *Šal-lu-*⸢*x*⸣-[(?)]

27 IGI *A-ri-*⸢*i*⸣*p-ú-r*[*a*]*-aš-še*

28 DUB.SAR

+———————————————————————

S.I.

29 ^{NA4}KIŠIB ^{m}*A-ri-ka*$_4$*-ma-ri*

S.I.

30 ^{NA4}KIŠIB ^{m}*Ḫa-ši-na-wa-ar*

UPPER EDGE

S.I.

31 ^{NA4}KIŠIB ^{m}*Na-aš-*[*wi*]

LEFT EDGE

32 ^{NA4}KIŠIB ^{m}⸢x x⸣[ ] ^{NA4}KIŠIB ^{m}*Šúk-*•*ra-pu*

S.I. S.I.

TRANSLATION

(1–4) Tablet of adoption of Arik-kamari son of Puramizi. He adopted Itḫ-apu son of Ḫašiya.

(5–10) As his inheritance share, Arik-kamari [gave] to Itḫ-apu a …(?).1 homer field in the town of Ḫurāṣina-ṣeḫru, adjacent to the road of …, adjacent to the field of …, adjacent to the tel … .

(11–13a) And Itḫ-apu gave [to] Arik-kamari .8 homers of emmer [as his gift].

(13b–16) [Should the field have] a claim (against it), Arik-kamari [shall clear (the field) and give(it)] to Itḫ-apu.

(17) … [shall bear] the *ilku* of the field …. .

(18–20) Who(ever) between them [abrogates (this contract)] shall weigh out 1 mina of silver (and)] 1 mina of gold.

(21–28) Before Bêlānu son of . . .; [before] . . .-pu [son of] . . .; . . . .; before . . . [son of] . . .; before Mikkiya son of . . .; before Kelip-šarri son of . . .-zaḫ; before Aḫu-waqar son of Šallu-. . .; before Arip-urašše, the scribe.

(29–32) (*seal impression*) Seal impression of Arik-kamari; (*seal impression*) seal impression of Ḫašin-nawar; (*seal impression*) seal impression of Našwi; seal impression of . . . (*seal impression*); seal impression of Šukr-apu (*seal impression*).

COMMENTS

This tablet has suffered little deterioration since it was copied.

Line 32 appears on the left edge (together with its associated seal impressions), not on the reverse, as depicted in the copy.

As with JEN 785, Lacheman links the present text with JEN 789, specifically with JEN 789:15. However, Zaccagnini (1984, 714 n. 58) suggests that JEN 89 is the referent in JEN 789:15. This is very possible: JEN 89 and 786 are both real estate adoption contracts from room 1, in which Arik-kamari son of Puramizi cedes real estate to Itḫ-apu son of Ḫašiya. See further, JEN 789, Comments.

The scribe of JEN 786 also wrote HSS, V, 96; XIII, 163. Appeal has occasionally been made to the latter text (closer in content to JEN 786 than is HSS, V, 96) in restoring broken passages in the present document. Note, however, below, note to l. 20, that such a procedure for restoration involves some uncertainty.

NOTES

l. 2: *ra*. Or *r*[*a*]. The sign appears, not as depicted, but, rather, as  .

l. 5: *ma*. The sign is clear. It is not MU, as copied.

l. 6: ⸢URU⸣ [*Ḫu*]-*ra*-[*ṣí*]-*na*-TUR. For the syllabic spellings of this GN, see Fincke (1993, 107). The sign, RA, appears, not as depicted, but rather as a normal RA. Cf. the same sign in line 32, although the sign here is somewhat more elongated.

l. 8: ⸢x⸣. Lacheman interprets: *T*[*a*]. The sign appears, not as depicted, but, rather, as .

l. 9: *ti-le-e*. Although the spelling *ti-li-i* is attested at Nuzi (see *AHw*, p. 1359b), I cannot cite other examples of *ti-le-e*.

l. 10: [SUM]. Or the like. Lacheman once recorded "[*i*]*ddin*."

ll. 11–13. Or the like. The restoration of this clause is based on somewhat ambiguous traces.

l. 12: 8 BÁN. For this peculiar way of writing this quantity, see Maidman 1994,123, note to l. 8. Other instances of this scribal practice include JEN 687:8; 705:8; 728:7; and 788:9. Note that my interpretation of JEN 687:8 (Maidman 1994, 61, first note to l. 8) is wrong, and the wonderment expressed there no longer exists. The trace represents B[ÁN], not S[ILA$_3$]; 4.8 homers is meant, not 4.1.

l. 14: [*ir-ta-ši*]. Cf. HSS, XVI, 163:14. For the relevance of that text to the present one, see above, Comments.

l. 15: [*ú-za-ak-ka*$_4$*-ma*]. Cf. HSS, XVI, 163:15 and the previous note.

l. 16: [*i-na-an-din*]. Cf. HSS, XVI, 163:16 and, above, note to line 14.

l. 17. The bearer of the *ilku* is likely to have been Arik-kamari.

l. 18: <*ša*>?. As alternatives to this suggestion, the word may have appeared at the end of line 17 or in the gap in line 18. The suggestion here adopted and the restoration of the rest of this line is based on HSS, XVI, 163:17, written by the scribe who wrote the present text.

l. 19: MA.NA. In the copy, a vertical wedge appears between these signs. This wedge does not appear on the tablet.

l. 20. Cf. HSS, XVI, 163:19: *ú-ma-al-la* in a comparable context. The same scribe thus exhibits variation in his writing habits.

l. 21. The Oriental Institute Nuzi files restore the patronymic, Akit-tirwi. This is an attractive suggestion, since the resulting individual appears as a witness in JEN 89, a text involving the same principal parties as this document.

ll. 22–23. The lines between these two are entirely effaced.

l. 23. Cf. ll. 30–32 for the possible identity of the witness whose name once appeared in this line.

l. 24: *y*[*a*]. The trace appears, not as depicted, but, rather, as  .

l. 24: ⸢x x⸣. The patronymic may be Šien-zaḫ. See below, JEN 787:27 and note. See also below, the very next note. Arguing in favor of the possibility are (1) the close relationship of these two contracts (same purchaser; both resurface in JEN 789); and (2) the rarity of the name Mikkiya (see *NPN*, p. 97b).

l. 25: [ ]-⸢*x*⸣-*za-a*⸢*ḫ*⸣. The last trace appears, not as depicted, but, rather, as  . Regarding the resulting "Kelip-šarri son of ...-zaḫ," note that JEN 785:27, a text involving the same purchaser, identifies a witness as "Kelip-šarri son of Ši-...". It may be that the Kelip-šarris who witnessed both texts are the same and that the common patronymic (reconstituted from both attestations) is *Ši-e*[*n*]*-za-aḫ*. Note further that in JEN 785:25, the patronymic of the first witness, Watwa, is Šien-zaḫ. If the suggestion regarding Kelip-šarri's paternity is correct, it is likely that he is the brother of Watwa: "Šien-zaḫ" is a very rare name at Nuzi.[17] See also the preceding note for the possibility of a third brother.

l. 26: DUMU *Šal-lu-*⸢*x*⸣-[(?)]. Lacheman restores *–ya*, as does *NPN*.[18] Cf. JEN 88:18, where the patronymic of one Aḫu-waqar (the name of the witness in this

17 See *NPN*, p. 133a *sub* ŠIEN-ZAḪ. Indeed, it is quite possible that there was but one Šien-zaḫ attested in the Nuzi texts. Note that JEN 787:27 is likely an attestation of the same name (and person?); it does not appear in *NPN*.

18 *NPN*, p. 11a *sub* AḪU-WAQAR 3).

line) appears as [*Š*]*a?-li-lu-a*.[19] Note also JEN 789:12, which mentions a tablet of one *Ša-al-*[*l*]*u?-ya*. For the relevance of JEN 789 to the present text, see above, Comments.

l. 31: [*wi*]. This is the most likely restoration.

l. 32: ⸢x x⸣. The traces appear, not as depicted, but, rather, as 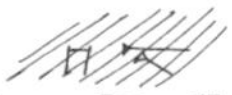 . Lacheman once read here: [ ]-*ma-nu*. In another manuscript he has: [*Be-l*]*a-nu*.[20] This last reading is also adopted in a manuscript of Porada (probably following the Oriental Institute reading: she identifies this individual as the son of Akittirwi; cf. above, note to l. 21). However, the traces do not appear to support either of these readings.

JEN 787

OBVERSE

1 *ṭup-pí ma-ru-ti*$_7$ *ša Zu-ú-mé* DUMU *Mu-ut-ta*
2 ^{m}*It-ḫa-pu* DUMU *Ḫa-ši-*[*ya*]
3 *a-na ma-ru-ti*$_7$*-i-šu-nu i-*⸢*pu-x*⸣*-šu*
4 2 [AN]ŠE 5 ^{GIŠ}APIN A.ŠÀ *i-*[*na*] *ta-a-a-ru?* GAL
5 *i-*[*n*]*a* URU KÙ.SIG$_{17}$*-na-*T[UR] *ṭe*$_4$*-ḫi* ^{md}XX-DINGIR
6 •*ù* [*ṭ*]*e*$_4$*-ḫi* ^{m}*A-ku*$_8$*-*⸢*ya*⸣! *ù ṭe*$_4$*-ḫi* ⸢*Na*⸣*?-aš-*•*wi!?*
7 [(?)] KASKAL^{-ni} *ša* URU *Zi?-pu-ša?/zu?*
8 •⸢*ṭ*⸣*e*$_4$*-ḫi* ^{m}*I-bi-*DINGIR *ù ṭe*$_4$*-ḫi* ^{m}[*N*]*a-aš-wi*
9 *ki-ma* ḪA.LA*-šu a-na It-ḫa-pu* DUMU *Ḫa-ši-ya*
10 *i-ta-ad-nu-ni-šu*
11 *ù It-ḫa-pu*! DUMU *Ḫa-ši-ya*
12 *a-na Zu-ú-mé* DUMU *Mu-ut-ta*
13 3 GUN URUDU *a-na* NÍG.⸢B⸣A*-šu* ⸢*i-t*⸣*a-*[*ad-na*]*-šu*
14 *šum-ma* A.ŠÀ *pá-*⸢*qí*⸣*-ra-na ir-t*[*a-ši*]
15 ^{m}*Zú-mé-e-ma* DUMU *Mu-ut-ta*! *ú-*⸢*za*⸣*-a*[*k-ka-ma*]
16 ⸢*a-na It-ḫa*⸣*-pu* ⸢DUMU⸣ *Ḫa-ši-ya i+na-din*
17 ⸢*šum-m*⸣*a* ⸢*Zu*⸣*-*[*ú-mé* DUMU *Mu-u*]*t-t*[*a*]
18 *i-ba-la-k*[*a*$_4$*-at ù?*]

LOWER EDGE

19 *i+na* E[GI]R$^{-k[i]}$ *It-ḫa-pu*
20 DUMU *Ḫa-ši-ya il!?-ta-s*[*í*]
21 2 MA.*NA *KÙ.*BABBAR *ù* 2 MA.NA K[Ù.SIG$_{17}$]

REVERSE

22 Ì.LÁ.E *ir!-wi!-ša ša* ⸢A⸣.[ŠÀ]
23 ⸢^{m}*Zu-ú-m*⸣*é na-*⸢*š*⸣*i*

---

19 As noted by *NPN*, *ibid.*

20 See line 21.

S.I.

24 NA$_4$.MEŠ [*š*]*a*? ^{m}*Ḫa-iš-te-y*⸢*a*⸣

25 IGI DINGIR-*na-me-*⸢*er* DUMU *A*⸣?-*bi*-DINGIR!?

26 IGI *Wu-ul-*⸢*lu*⸣? DUMU ⸢*Ú*⸣?-*še-ya*

27 IGI ⸢*Mi*⸣-*k*⸢*í*⸣-*ya* DUMU *Še-za-aḫ*

28 IGI *Ta-*⸢*a*⸣-*a* DUMU NÍG.BA-*ya*

29 IGI *Ḫa-*⸢*iš*⸣-*te-ya* DUMU *Šum-ma*-DINGIR

30 IGI *D*[*á*]-*a-ni* DUMU *Na-ka*$_4$-*ta*

31 IGI *Ip-ša-ḫa-lu* DUMU *A-ki-ya*

32 [I]GI *T*[*e*?-*ḫ*]*i*?-*ip*-LUGAL DUMU *Pa-li-ya*

33 IGI *A-*⸢*r*⸣*i-pár-ni* DUMU *Mi-il-ku*$_8$-*ú-a*

34 IGI ^{d}UTU-ME.ZU DUB.SAR$^{-rù}$

S.I.

35 NA$_4$.MEŠ ^{m}*Mi-kí-ya*

LEFT EDGE

S.I. S.I.

36 NA$_4$.MEŠ ^{m}*A-ri-pa?-ni* NA$_4$.[MEŠ] ^{m}*Ip-*⸢*š*⸣*a-ḫa-l*[*u*]

TRANSLATION

(1–3) Tablet of adoption of Zume son of Mutta. He adopted Itḫ-apu son of Ḫašiya.

(4–10) He gave to Itḫ-apu son of Ḫašiya as his inheritance share a field, 2.5 homers by the large standard, in the town of Ḫurāṣina-ṣeḫru, contiguous with (the field of) Šamaš-ilu and contiguous with (the field of) Akkuya and contiguous with (the field of) Našwi(?) [on?] the road to the town of Zipuša(?), contiguous with (the field of) Ibbi-ilu and contiguous with (the field of) Našwi.

(11–13) And Itḫ-apu son of Ḫašiya gave to Zume son of Mutta as his gift 3 talents of copper.

(14–16) Should the field have claimants, then Zume shall clear (it) [and] give(it) to Itḫ-apu son of Ḫašiya.

(17–22a) Should Zume [son of] Mutta abrogate (this contract) [and?] hail Itḫ-apu son of Ḫašiya (into court), he (i.e., Zume) shall weigh out 2 minas of silver and 2 minas of gold.

(22b–23) Zume shall bear the *irwiššu* of the field.

(24) (*seal impression*) Seal impression of Ḫaiš-teya.

(25–34) Before Ilu-namer son of Abi-ilu(?); before Wullu(?) son of Ušeya(?); before Mikkiya son of Šien-zaḫ; before Taya son of Qîšteya; before Ḫaiš-teya son of Šumma-ilu; before Dayyānu son of Nakata; before Ipša-ḫalu son of Akiya; before Teḫip(?)-šarri son of Paliya; before Arip-parni son of Milkuya; before Šamaš-bārī, the scribe.

(35–36) (*seal impression*) Seal impression of Mikkiya; (*seal impression*) seal impression of Arip-parni; (*seal impression*) seal impression of Ipša-ḫalu.

COMMENTS

Collation of this document was undertaken using a pair of casts instead of the tablet itself. The original was returned to Baghdad by the Oriental Institute. Remarks made regarding the collation of JEN 726 (Maidman 1994, 192) apply, to some extent, here. Since the tablet seems to be in poor shape, since the scribe indulges in unique, even bizarre, writing practices, and since unusual personal names (and one geographical name) spelled unusually abound, this situation is especially to be regretted.

The tablet appears to have suffered some deterioration since it was copied. In other cases, however, signs are not visible probably owing to the defective nature of the casts rather than because of deterioration of the tablet. I note those latter instances by indicating that I could not see one or more signs.

The writer of this tablet wrote JEN 28 (most probably[21]), 33, 823, and 825. Like the present text, JEN 28 and 33 are tablets of real estate adoption, and appeal is made to those texts—especially JEN 33—in attempting to reconstruct the present contract.

This text seems actually to be mentioned in JEN 789:14, a phenomenon implicitly recognized by Lacheman through his close juxtaposition of these two texts in his publication plan. See further, below, JEN 789, Comments.

The citations of PNs from this text do not appear in *NPN*. This too is to be regretted since—and this is peculiar—names appearing here seem to occur nowhere else in the Nuzi texts: Šamaš-ilu (l. 5), Ibbi-ilu (l. 8), Ušeya (if correctly read; l. 26), and Nakata (l. 30).

NOTES

l. 1: *ú*. This sign is not entirely visible on the cast.

l. 2: [*ya*]. Cf. l. 9.

l. 3: *na*. This sign is not entirely visible on the cast.

l. 3: *ma-ru-ti*$_7$*-i-šu-nu*. This interpretation, as peculiar as it is, is preferable to Lacheman's *ma-ru-ti*$_7$ *i-<te-pu>-šu-nu*, with the verb repeated immediately afterwards. See also JEN 33:4 for another peculiar variation on *ma-ru-ti*.

l. 3: ⸢*pu-x*⸣*-šu*. I could not see these traces and sign. Lacheman reads the second trace: ⸢*uš*⸣.

l. 4: *ru*? GAL. Except for the final horizontal wedge of GAL, these signs are not visible on the cast. The former sign on the copy looks like RU. Lacheman once read RI, the expected sign.

---

21 Though not identified as the writer in the surviving text, his name appears in the witness list and as sealer (JEN 28:32, 35). More telling, perhaps, the tablet exhibits the same idiosyncrasies of vocabulary, orthography, and use of patronymics as appear in tablets known to have been written by this scribe.

l. 5: T[UR]. Lacheman reads G[AL]. However, Itḫ-apu son of Ḫašiya repeatedly acquired land in Ḫurāṣina-ṣeḫru. See, for example, JEN 785:3, 5; 786:3, 6.

l. 6: *A-ku*$_8$-⸢*ya*⸣!. This spelling of Akkuya has not, I believe, been attested before now.

l. 6: *wi*!?. The final wedge of this sign is now partially gone. The sign—and the copy—appear to reflect ŠI.

l. 7: [(?)]. Lacheman has [*i-na*].

l. 7: *Zi*?-*pu-ša*?/*zu*?. The first sign of this town name looks like a defective ZI. Cf. the defective PU in line 11. The last sign looks more like ŠA than ZU, but this interpretation is not certain. Lacheman and, later, Fincke (1993, 354) interpret the GN as "Zipuša," but, in the examples adduced by Fincke, nowhere is there a clear writing of this toponym.

l. 9: DUMU. I could not see this sign on the cast.

l. 10. Cf. JEN 33:8 for a similar form.

l. 12: *Mu*. I could not see this sign on the cast.

l. 13: ⸢*ta*⸣. This trace is not visible on the cast.

l. 13: [*ad-nu*]. Or the like. Cf. the spelling in JEN 33:11. Lacheman's [*din*] has the advantage of fitting the small gap more easily.

l. 15: *ta*. The sign does not appear as copied, but, rather, as  .

l. 15: ⸢*za*⸣-*a*[*k*]. These traces are not visible on the cast.

ll. 19–20. These lines define what it means to abrogate a contract.

l. 20: *il*!?-*ta-s*[*í*]. Lacheman reasonably reads *um-ta-*[ ] (though this yields no sense). Yet the first sign is unclear on the cast. The reading adopted is supported by the phrasing of line 19 and by JEN 28:20; 33:17, written by the same scribe.

l. 22: *ir*!-*wi*!-*ša*. Cf. JEN 28:24; 33:19.

l. 24: *y*⸢*a*⸣. This sign is hardly visible on the cast, but the reading is assured by the reappearance of this sealer as witness in line 29.

l. 25: ⸢DUMU *A*⸣?. The reading is adopted from Lacheman. However, ⸢DUMU⸣ *I*⸢*t*⸣ is an easier reading.

l. 25: DINGIR (= last sign). What appears on the cast is  .

l. 26: ⸢*Ú*⸣?-*še*. The second sign is not visible on the cast. The former trace appears as  .

l. 27: ⸢*Mi*⸣-*k*⸢*í*⸣-*ya*. For this reconstruction, cf. line 35.

l. 27: *Še-za-aḫ*. This appears to be a new spelling of Šien-zaḫ. See also above, JEN 786:24 with notes and the note to JEN 786:25.

l. 29: ⸢*iš*⸣. The rightmost vertical is not visible on the cast.

l. 30: *T*[*a*]-*a*. On the cast, the latter sign is not visible, and the former lacks the *Winkelhaken*s, so that the trace looks more like E than TA.

l. 32: *T[e?-ḫ]i?*. This reflects Lacheman's [*Te*]-*ḫi* and is the easiest, though not the only possible, reading of the traces.

l. 33: *Mi-il-ku*$_{8}$*-ú-a*. This spelling of Milkuya I believe appears for the first time here.

l. 36: *ri-pa?-ni*. Except for the first two wedges, these signs do not show up on the cast. One expects *pár*, not *pa*, here. Cf. l. 33. The two signs are similar and BAR may in fact have been written.

l. 36: ^{m} (second). This vertical is not visible on the cast.

JEN 788

OBVERSE

1 *ṭup-pí ma-ru-ti ša* ^{m}*Ak-ku-le-ni*
2 DUMU *It-ḫa-pu ù* ^{m}*Ḫi-il-pí-iš-šu-uḫ*
3 DUMU *Šu-ḫu-zi-ri-ru a-na ma-ru-ti*
4 *i-te-pu-uš* É.ḪÁ.MEŠ *ep-šú-tu*$_{4}$
5 *i+na* ŠÀ$^{-bi}$ URU *Te-em-te-na-aš*
6 *i-na e-le-et* É.ḪÁ.MEŠ *ša* ^{m}*Ma-at-te-šup*
7 ^{m}*Ak-ku-le-en+ni ki-i-•mu!* ḪA.LA-*šú*
8 *a!-na* ^{m}*Ḫi-il-pí-iš-[š]u-uḫ* SUM
9 2 ANŠE 6 BÁN ŠE.MEŠ ^{m}*Ḫi-il-pí-iš-šu-uḫ*
10 *ki-i-mu* NÍG.BA-*šú a-na* ^{m}*Ak-ku-le-ni* SUM
11 *šum-ma* É.ḪÁ.MEŠ *pa-qí-ra-na ir-ta-ši*
12 ^{m}*Ak-ku-le-ni ú-za-ak-ka*$_{4}$
13 *a-na* ^{m}*Ḫi-il-pí-iš-šu-uḫ i+na-an-din*
14 *ma-an!-nu ša* KI.BAL-*tu* 1 MA.NA KÙ.BABBAR
15 1 MA.NA KÙ.SIG$_{17}$ *ú-ma-al-la*

+———————————————————

16 IGI *Ma-at-te-šup* DUMU *Na-ni-ya*
17 IGI *Ḫu-i-te-šup* DUMU *Ta-a-ú-ki*
18 IGI *Wu-un-ni* DUMU *Ḫu-ti-pu-kùr*
19 IGI ⸢*T*⸣*a*-⸢*ú-š*⸣*e*-⸢*ya*⸣ ^{LÚ}*ṣa-ḫi-tù*
20 IGI *Ut-ḫáp-še* DUMU *A-ka*$_{4}$*-wa-til*
21 IGI *A-kap-še-eni* [D]UMU *A-ri-ka*$_{4}$*-ma-ri*
22 IGI *Ip-ša-ḫa-lu* DUMU *Šúk-ra-pu*
23 IGI *Še-ka*$_{4}$*-rù* DUMU *Ḫa-ši-ké-mar*

LOWER EDGE

24 IGI ^{d}XXX-ZAG^{-ti} ^{LÚ}•*ṣa-ḫi-tu*$_{4}$
25 IGI *Zi-il-tù-ri!*

REVERSE

26 DUMU ^{d}IM-*mu-šal-li*
27 IGI *Zi*-⸢*l*⸣*i-ya* DUMU *Pa-ak-ka*$_{4}$

28 IGI *Ad-d[á-š]e*$_{20}$*-ya* DUB.SAR$^{-rù}$

S.I. Po 34

29 ^{NA4}KIŠIB ^{m}*Ma-at-te-šup*

S.I. Po 61

30 ^{NA4}•KIŠIB ^{m}*Ḫi-il-pí-iš-šu-uḫ*

S.I. Po 176

31 ^{NA4}KIŠIB ^{md}XXX-ZAG^{-ti}

S.I. Po 116

32 ^{NA4}KIŠIB ^{m}*Zi-li-ya*

S.I. Po 116

33 ^{NA4}KIŠIB ^{m}*Ut-ḫáp-še*

LEFT EDGE

S.I.

34 ^{NA4}KIŠIB DUB.SAR$^{-rù}$

TRANSLATION

(1–4a) Tablet of adoption of Akkul-enni son of Itḫ-apu. He adopted Ḫilpiš-šuḫ son of Šuḫun-zirira.

(4b–8) Akkul-enni gave to Ḫilpiš-šuḫ as his inheritance share built up structures in the town of Temtena(š) itself, to the east (??) of the structures of Mat-tešup.

(9–10) Ḫilpiš-šuḫ gave to Akkul-enni as his gift 2.6 homers of barley.

(11–13) Should the structures have claimants, Akkul-enni shall clear (the structures and) give (them) to Ḫilpiš-šuḫ.

(14–15) He who abrogates (this contract) shall pay 1 mina of silver (and) 1 mina of gold.

(16–28) Before Mat-tešup son of Naniya; before Ḫui-tešup son of Tayuki; before Wunni son of Ḫutip-ukur; before Tauševa, the oil preparer; before Utḫap-še son of Akawatil; before Akap-šenni son of Arik-kamari; before Ipša-ḫalu son of Šukr-apu; before Šekaru son of Ḫašik-kewar; before Sin-imitti, the oil preparer; before Ṣill-dûri son of Adad-mušalli(m); before Ziliya son of Pakka; before Adaššeya, the scribe.

(29–34) (*seal impression*) Seal impression of Mat-tešup; (*seal impression*) seal impression of Ḫilpiš-šuḫ; (*seal impression*) seal impression of Sin-imitti; (*seal impression*) seal impression of Ziliya; (*seal impression*) seal impression of Utḫap-še; (*starburst incision; seal impression*) seal impression of the scribe.

Comments

This tablet has suffered almost no deterioration since it was copied or since it was first written.

The scribe of this text occasionally adds wedges to signs, seemingly as a flourish. See lines 7 (MU and possibly EN+NI), 8 (A), and 25 (RI).[22]

Notes

l. 1: *ru*. The copy is imprecise: a second *Winkelhaken* appears to the right of the first.

l. 4: *ep-šú-tu*$_4$. Cf. JEN 690:6 and Maidman 1994, 71–72, note to line 6.

l. 6: *e-le-et*. Cf. JEN 698:5 and Maidman 1994, 98, note to line 5.

l. 7: *en+ni*. This combination seems to be not so much a ligature as a superimposition of NI over EN. Alternately, once could read *en*!-<*ni*> or –*ni*!. The last would accord with the spellings of the PN in lines 1, 10, and 12.

l. 9: 6 BÁN. For this way of recording dry capacity, see above, note to JEN 786:12.

l. 14: *an*!. The sign appears as MAŠ, not AN as depicted.

l. 19: ^{LÚ}*ṣa-ḫi-tù*. For further on this occupation, see the dictionaries, and for further examples from Nuzi, see Mayer 1978, 177–178.

l. 28: *Ad-d*[*á-š*]*e*$_{20}$*-ya*. The restoration of this PN follows a suggestion of Lacheman, taken up, apparently, by Porada and—approximately—by *NPN*.[23]

l. 33: *še*. The sign is typical (as, for example, ŠE in line 23), not as depicted.

l. 34. The starburst shape above this line is incised. Similar designs appear elsewhere among the Nuzi tablets. I recall seeing one in the British Museum collection.

JEN 789

OBVERSE

1 [ṭup-pí] ⸢ma⸣-ru-ti ša
2 [^{m}Še-še-e]r-pá DUMU It-ḫa-[p]u
3 [ù ^{m}•H]u-•i-te DUMU Mu-š[e]-⸢y⸣a
4 [a-na m]a-ru-ti i-[pu]-⸢u⸣š
5 [um?-ma? ^{m}]⸢Še⸣-še-e[r-pá]-ma
6 [ ] ⸢x x⸣ [A].⸢ŠÀ⸣?.ḪI.M[EŠ]
7 ù ⸢É⸣.[ḪI.MEŠ (ù)] ma-ag-[ra-at-tu$_4$]^{MEŠ}-ya
8 GIŠ.KIRI$_6$.M[EŠ?]⸢ù⸣? ḪA.LA.[ME]Š?-ya
9 mar-ZI-⸢x⸣-[ME]Š!?-⸢ya⸣ š[a URU KÙ.SI]G$_{17}$-na-TUR
10 ù ša URU ⸢x⸣-[a-na] ⸢^{m}⸣Ḫ⸢u-i-te⸣ at-ta-din!
11 um-ma ^{m}Še-še-⸢er⸣-p[á-m]a [m]a ḫi

22 But note also line 14 (AN) where a stroke is missing.

23 *NPN*, p. 39a, *sub* ADAŠŠEỊA 3).

12 ṭup-pu ša Ša-al-[l]u?-ya it-ti A.ŠÀ.•ME[Š]⸢x⸣
13 ṭup-pu ša Šu-mu-•d[á-r]i it-ti A.ŠÀ.MEŠ
14 ṭup-pu ša Zu-ú-me [i]t-ti A.ŠÀ.MEŠ!
15 ṭup-pu ša A-ri-ka$_4$-m[a]-ri it-ti A.ŠÀ
16 ṭup-pu ša Šúk-ra-⸢pu i⸣t-ti A.ŠÀ.MEŠ
17 ṭup-pu ša Tu-•r[a]-⸢ri it⸣-ti A.ŠÀ.M[EŠ]
18 ṭ[up]-pá-tu$_4^{\text{MEŠ}}$ [an]-nu-tu$_4$ ⸢it⸣-[ti A.ŠÀ.MEŠ]
19 ⸢a-na ^{m}⸣Ḫu-i-⸢te⸣ at-ta-d[in]
20 i-lik-šu ⸢ša⸣ ^{m}Še-še-er-pá
21 a-na ^{m}Ḫu-i-⸢te⸣ na-ši
22 ù ^{m}Še-še-[e]r-pá la ⸢na⸣-[ši]

LOWER EDGE

23 šum-ma A.ŠÀ.[M]EŠ É.M[EŠ?]
24 pí-ir-qa [ir-•t]a-•ši
25 •ù ^{m} {m}Še-[še-er-•p]á ú-za-ka$_4$
26 a-na ^{m}[Ḫu-i-te] i-na-an-•din

REVERSE

27 i-⸢x⸣[ ] ⸢DUMU⸣? ÌR?-a-ḫi-šu-ma
28 ⸢m⸣[Še-še-e]r-pá ù ^{m}Ḫu-i-t[e]
29 [ ]⸢x x x⸣ la mi i+na UD$^{-m[i]}$
30 [GÌR.M]EŠ ša Še-še-er-pá iš-tu [A.ŠÀ.MEŠ]
31 ⸢ù⸣? iš-tu É.ḪI.⸢MEŠ$^{-ti}$⸣ uš-t[e-li ù]
32 ⸢GÌR⸣.MEŠ ša ^{m}Ḫu-i-te i⸢š⸣-[ta-k]a$_4$-[an]
33 ù ^{m}Ḫu-i-te 1 sí-a-na-[tu$_4$ (?)]
34 [1? +] 5 MA.NA an!-na-ku 1 BÁN ŠE ki-mu NÍ[G.BA-šu]
35 a-na ^{m}Še!-še-er-pá it-ta-[din]
36 ma-an-nu-um-me!-e i+na bi$_4$-ri-š[u-nu (ša)]
37 i-bala-ka$_4$-tu$_4$ 2 MA.NA KÙ.BABBAR 2 M[A.N]A KÙ.SIG$_{17}$
38 ú-ma-al-la DIŠ ù ^{m}Ḫu-i-⸢te⸣
39 2 É i+na ṣé-re-ti a-na ^{m}Še-š[e-e]r-pá SUM^{-din}
40 wa-ar-ka$_4$-sú ša 2 É an-[nu-t]u$_4$
41 ša ^{m}Ḫu-i-te-ma ṭup-pu an-nu-[ú?]
42 i+na EGIR^{-ki} šu-du-ti
43 i+na URU KÙ.⸢S⸣IG$_{17}$-na-TUR šá-ṭì-ir ⸢x⸣
44 IGI El-ḫi-ip-til-la D[UMU]-el-[t]e-e
45 IGI Ḫa-ši-ya DUMU ⸢X⸣-[ ]-⸢x⸣-ya
46 IGI Tup-ka$_4$-pu DU[MU] ⸢x⸣-še-en-ni
47 IGI •Um-pí-•y[a DUMU] Še-el-wi-ya
48 IGI Ki-pí-[til?-l]a? DUMU Šúk-ra-pu
49 [IG]I Ut-⸢ḫap⸣?-[ta?]-⸢e⸣? DUMU Ḫi-in-ti-ya
50 [IGI]-⸢x⸣-ya DUMU ⸢X⸣-zi-y⸢a⸣

51 [IGI]-˹*y*˺*a* ^{LÚ}˹*a-b*˺*u-ul-*[*t*]*a-an-*[*n*]*u* DUMU *Na-i-te-šup*
52 [IGI *I*]-˹*ri*˺-*ri* DUB.SAR$^{\text{-rù}}$
53 [IGI?] ^{LÚ}*ḫa-zi-an-*˹*nu*!? x˺
54 [LÚ.MEŠ *an-nu-t*]*ù*? A.ŠÀ.MEŠ *an-nu-tu*$_4$ [ ] ˹x x˺ *a-na ši-mi*
55 [ ] *na-din i* ˹*šu*˺? ˹x x˺ [^{m}]*Ḫu-i-te*
:*iq-ta-*˹*bi*˺?-•*ma*

UPPER EDGE

[S.I.?]
56 [NA$_4$] ˹*x*˺-*ki-ya*
57 [$^{\text{NA4}}$KIŠI]B ^{m}*Še-še-er-pá*
S.I.
58 [ ]-*ya*

LEFT EDGE

59 $^{+}$NA$_4$ $^{+\text{m}}$*Ki-pí-til-la* $^{+}$ S.I.
60 S.I. $^{\text{NA4}}$KIŠIB ^{f}/SAL [ ]-•AŠ?

Translation

(1–4) [Tablet] of adoption of Šešerpa son of Itḫ-apu. He adopted Ḫui-te son of Mušeya.

(5–10) [Thus?] Šešerpa: "I have given [to] Ḫui-te …, fields and structures [(and)] my threshing floors, orchard[s?] …? and(?) inheritance share, my …(?), my property(!) in (lit. "of") [the town of] Ḫurāṣina-ṣeḫru and in (lit. "of") the town of … ."

(11–19) Thus Šešerpa, further …: "I have given to Ḫui-te the tablet of Šalluya(?) together with the fields (described therein) …, the tablet of Šumu-dârī together with the fields (described therein), the tablet of Zume together with the fields (described therein), the tablet of Arik-kamari together with the field (described therein), the tablet of Šukr-apu together with the fields (described therein), the tablet of Turari together with the fields (described therein), (all) these tablets together with [the fields (described therein)].

(20–22) And Šešerpa's (erstwhile) *ilku* is for Ḫui-te to bear(?); and Šešerpa shall not bear it.

(23–26) Should the fields (and) structures have a claim, then Šešerpa shall clear (them) and give (them) to [Ḫui-te].

(27–35) … Šešerpa and Ḫui-te … on the day … that(?) Šešerpa lifts (his) feet (lit. "he lifts Šešerpa's feet") from [the fields] and from the structures [and] Ḫui-te sets his feet (lit. "he sets Ḫui-te's feet") (on them), then Ḫui-te will give (lit. "gave") to Šešerpa as [his] gift 1 blanket, …(?), 5 [+1?] minas of tin (and) .1 homer of barley.

(36–38a) Whoever between them abrogates (this contract) shall pay two minas of silver (and) 2 minas of gold.

(38b–41a) And he (i.e., Ḫui-te) gave to Šešerpa 2 structures in the suburbs; but the rear of these 2 structures belongs to Ḫui-te.

(41b–43) This tablet was written …(?) after the proclamation in the town of Ḫurāṣina-ṣeḫru.

(44–53) Before Elḫip-tilla son of …-el-teya; before Ḫašiya son of …-ya; before Tupk-apu son of Akku-šenni; before Umpiya [son of] Šelwiya; before Kipi-tilla son of Šukr-apu; before Utḫap-tae(?) son of Ḫintiya; [before] …-ya son of …-ziya; [before] …-ya the gatekeeper, son of Nai-Tešup; [before] Iriri, the scribe; [before?] …, the mayor.

(54–55) "And these(?) n men(?) gave(?) these fields … (in exchange) for (their) price," Ḫui-te said(?).

(56–60) [(*seal impression*)? seal impression of] …-kiya; seal impression of Šešerpa (*seal impression*); [(?)] …-ya; seal impression of Kipi-tilla (*seal impression*); (*seal impression*) seal impression of … .

COMMENTS

This tablet has suffered little deterioration since it was copied. It should be noted, though, that a join effected before the copy was made appears to involve pieces whose writing is in two sizes.[24] Nevertheless, the joined artifact is, in fact, one tablet. "Šešerpa" appears in both and a reasonable context emerges. Since the text is unusual and contains an important catalogue of tablets, special attention was paid to collation.

The alignment of lines in this text edition does not follow that adopted by the Oriental Institute, Lacheman, and derivative sources.[25] The current line 6 is skipped in preliminary treatments, resulting in a misalignment of parts of the subsequent lines. On the other hand, a phantom line 11 is inserted where none exists, so lines 12ff. maintain a correct line numbering until line 48 where there is a further misidentification of lines. The reader is urged to read the present transliteration and its attendant notes in tandem with the copy.

The structure of this document is unusual and involves ambiguities, quite apart from lack of clarity stemming from the damaged nature of the tablet. It is clearly and explicitly a tablet of real estate adoption (ll. 1–4). However, the description of the land ceded (ll. 5–10), the "inheritance share," does not appear in the expected third person but in the first (*-ya* [l. 7]; *attadin* [l. 10]), the direct discourse perhaps introduced by *umma* (l. 5; cf. l. 11). This is followed by a description of real estate tablets to be ceded by the same vendor together with the land described therein (ll. 11–19), again as a declaration in the first person (ll. 11, 19). It is unclear whether the second declaration, stressing the tablets, is an elaboration of the first or an additional element in the sale. Note that fields, structures, and a threshing floor, mentioned in the first part, are echoed in original tablets alluded to in the second part. (See below for the identification

24 The ends of lines 37–44 align more closely to the start of these lines than indicated in the copy.

25 See, for example, Richter 1995, 75, n. 35.

of those original tablets.) But as far as can be determined, the orchards of the first part find no counterpart in the second.[26]

The sections describing the ceded land are followed by the *ilku*-clause (ll. 20–22), not the expected "gift" (i.e., price) clause. The clear title clause then follows (ll. 23–26). Only then does there appear a "gift" clause (ll. 27–35), but in an unusual form.[27] In a very broken context, the tendering of payment seems to be delayed until some sort of cession of ownership rights take place.[28]

In a further departure from the norm, the penalty clause is now introduced (ll. 36–38a). And then a major departure (ll. 38b–41a): the buyer gives to the seller some real estate. Is this legally part of the original price or not? If not, does one link each of the two payments with each of what appear to be two clusters of real estate sold? The relationship(s) between real estate and payment for same (including real estate as part of the purchase price!) is unclear.

After this comes a statement regarding when and where the document was written (ll. 41b–43) and the witness list (ll. 44–53).

Before the expected seal impressions and legends (ll. 56–60), there appears a broken and intriguing section (ll. 54–55) seemingly identifying the witnesses as transferrers of the land and of the price for that land (but what of the delayed nature of the "gift"?), but ending with a puzzling note that "(so) Ḫui-te said." That we may be dealing here with an afterthought (obscured by the broken tablet), may follow from the insertion of the last word, *iqtabi*, as an appendage to line 55.[29]

Curious as the document already is, the contents include points of additional considerable interest. In particular, the function of the *ṭuppi mārūti* as a simple real estate sale contract is confirmed in two different ways. First, the appearance of the term *šīmu* as the *quid pro quo* for the real estate transferred (l. 54) reveals the true nature of *qīštu* (l. 34; acknowledged and publicized by the contracting parties themselves), not only in this text, but in all adoption tablets where "gifts" are tendered for land.[30] Second, the *ilku* is here said to be transferred,

---

26 The implications of this observation ought not be pressed too far: not all of the original tablets have been identified; and mention of specialized plots of land may be masked by the general "land / field," A.ŠÀ.

27 See below, note to ll. 30–32.

28 Might this have been more common than we suppose? Other common, but usually unstated, features of real estate adoption (transfer of the *ilku*, identification of the "gift" as price) are made explicit in this document. See below.

Although the remaining verb in the clause is in the perfect, future action seems to be indicated by *ina ūmi* (l. 29).

29 Indeed, if it is an appendage, then the broken tablet hides precisely where on line 54 we are to initiate the inserted thought unit.

30 The "gift" is most often mobilia. In the present text, structures *may* also be part of the "gift" (l. 39). To this extent, the boundary between real estate sale and exchange (i.e., *šupe''ultu*) becomes blurred. Possibly, this contract qualifies as an "adoption" with the price in mobilia and some realia (almost literally as an afterthought), rather than as a real estate exchange with a *quid pro quo* of land plus an Ú-*tu* payment of mobilia as inducement, because there can be no illusion that the real estate obtained (ll. 6–18) is at all equivalent to

together with the real estate, to the latest owner (ll. 20–22). As in the case of *šīmu*, here is a rare explicit statement of what was the norm in real estate transfers: the *ilku*-tax attached to the land and became the responsibility of whoever happened to own the land at the moment. See also above, JEN 782, Comments.

Another point of considerable interest is the catalogue of tablets appearing in lines 12–18. This is a rare explicit statement of what also must have been routine: written real estate contracts moved to new owners of the land described (as, in similar fashion, responsibility for the *ilku* moved).

According to this catalogue, Šešerpa son of Itḫ-apu is said to give to Ḫui-te son of Mušeya tablets (with the real estate represented by these tablets) of Šalluya(?), Šumu-dârī, Zume, Arik-kamari, Šukr-apu, and Turari (ll. 12–17). No surviving transaction links Šešerpa with any individual so named. However, the written contracts could have involved these persons and someone other than Šešerpa. The tablets could subsequently have come into Šešerpa's possession. In that case, Šešerpa's name would not, of course, have appeared on the relevant tablets. To ferret out such possible tablets, two steps may be taken. First, determine, if possible, any patterns linking real estate transfer from Šešerpa to Ḫui-te. Then, if such patterns emerge, determine if the same patterns may be discerned in contracts where the key PNs appear as principal parties. If that proves productive, it suggests that those tablets may have come into the possession of Šešerpa, then to pass on to Ḫui-te.[31]

As for the first step, there is, happily, clear evidence for real estate transfer from Šešerpa to Ḫui-te:

JEN 189 (room 4): antichretic loan; a structure in Ḫurāṣina-ṣeḫru.

JEN 300 (room 1): antichretic loan; land in Ḫurāṣina-ṣeḫru.

JEN 784 (room 1): adoption; a structure in Ḫurāṣina-ṣeḫru; document written in Ḫurāṣina-ṣeḫru. See also, above, JEN 784, Comments.

JEN 789 (room 1; the present text): adoption; real estate in Ḫurāṣina-ṣeḫru; document written in Ḫurāṣina-ṣeḫru.

JEN 822[32] (room ?): antichretic loan; land.

JEN 824 (room 1): antichretic loan; land in Ḫurāṣina-ṣeḫru; document written in Ḫurāṣina-ṣeḫru(?).[33]

---

that tendered (l. 39; and ll. 40–41 limits even that!). Yet one may not advance convincing solutions based on such limited evidence.

31 It is recognized that land could ultimately have been alienated by Šešerpa from more than one area or region, thus rendering any pattern worthless for purposes of analysis. This procedure is suggestive of what might have taken place, no more.

32 Ḫui-te's patronymic is here broken away.

33 Note also the following texts involving Šešerpa son of Itḫ-apu:

JEN 823 (room 4): He cedes to Taya son of Qîšteya land by means of an antichretic loan.
JEN 825 (room 1): He cedes to Taya son of Qîšteya land by means of an antichretic loan; Ḫui-te son of Mušeya is a witness.
JEN*u* 1158 (room?): He may cede property. The text is largely broken away.

The following pattern emerges. Šešerpa cedes real estate, usually land, in Ḫurāṣina-ṣeḫru. The documents were found usually in room 1, once in room 4, in a complex of buildings in the western suburbs of Nuzi (Lacheman 1958, vi).

Proceeding to the next step, can these characteristics be attached to transactions wherein a principal party—preferably the vendor—bears a name appearing among the six in ll. 12–17? They can.

Zume (l. 14). JEN 787 (room 1): land in Ḫurāṣina-ṣeḫru; ceded to Itḫ-apu son of Ḫašiya.

Arik-kamari (l. 15). JEN 89 (room 1): a threshing floor in Ḫurāṣina-ṣeḫru; ceded to Itḫ-apu son of Ḫašiya.

or

JEN 786 (room 1; the same individual who cedes in JEN 89): land in Ḫurāṣina-ṣeḫru; ceded to Itḫ-apu son of Ḫašiya.[34]

Šukr-apu (l. 16). JEN 47 (room 1): land in Ḫurāṣina-ṣeḫru; ceded to Itḫ-apu son of Ḫašiya.

Turari (l. 17). JEN 785 (room 1): land in Ḫurāṣina-ṣeḫru; ceded to Itḫ-apu son of Ḫašiya.[35]

Šumu-dârī (l. 13). No known links. But note that an individual bearing this name cedes land in Ḫurāṣina-ṣeḫru by antichretic loan *directly* to Ḫui-te son of Mušeya at least twice: JEN 292[36] (room 1) and JEN 833 (room 1). It is plausible that the same individual ceded land whose documentation reached Šešerpa.

Šalluya (if this is the correct PN; l. 12). No known links. But this rare name appears as the patronymic of a witness in JEN 786, one of whose principal parties is Arik-kamari. The same witness probably reappears in JEN 88, where one principal party is Mušeya son of Ḫašiya.[37]

In sum, of the six PNs appearing in JEN 789:12–17, four cede land, which could have gone to Šešerpa, in a common pattern and in a pattern by which Šešerpa son of Itḫ-apu himself cedes land to Ḫui-te son of Mušeya, while a fifth (Šumu-dârī) is likely to have done so, and the sixth (Šalluya?) could have.[38]

---

34 For the possible linkage between JEN 89 and 789, see already Zaccagnini 1984b, 714, n. 58. Only one tablet is mentioned in JEN 789:15. If JEN 89 or 786 is the referent, the nod should possibly go to JEN 89, which mentions a threshing floor. The threshing floor may be referred to in JEN 789:7, *if* lines 6–9 refer to the same real estate subsequently identified in lines 12–18.

35 The linkage of JEN 785 and 789 is noted by Zaccagnini 1984b, 714, n. 59.

36 JEN 491 may refer to the contract spelled out in JEN 292 (room 1). See already Zaccagnini 1984a, 83–84.

37 For the relevance of Mušeya son of Ḫašiya for the present discussion, see below, n. 42.

38 This is not to suggest that persons bearing these PNs could not or did not engage in real estate transactions where these patterns did *not* appear. The point of the exercise, however,

Thus, it is likely that we have located four of the six tablets mentioned in lines 12–17. This likelihood is reenforced by the emergence of yet another pattern. In each of the tablets identified as likely referents, JEN 787, 89 (or 786), 47, 785, the recipient of the real estate is the same person, one Itḫ-apu son of Ḫašiya.[39] Given that inheritance of land normally proceeds from father to son(s), and given that the land and its tablets succeeded to Šešerpa son of Itḫ-apu (on its way to Ḫui-te son of Mušeya), it is altogether plausible that Šešerpa's father, Itḫ-apu, is the son of Ḫašiya, the purchaser of the several items of real estate in Ḫurāṣina-ṣeḫru. Unfortunately, explicit proof of the three-link chain,[40] Šešerpa son of Itḫ-apu son of Ḫašiya is lacking.

Finally, the idea that the several tablets are the ones referred to in JEN 789:12–17 gains further strength from their common findspot, room 1. This room has been posited by Lacheman (1958, vi) as the archive of (amongst others) Ḫui-te son of Mušeya. This would make sense, of course, and would identify these tablets as "background" texts[41] to a subsequent acquisition (or acquisitions) of Ḫui-te.[42]

The fact that some of Šešerpa's presumed holdings are not named in JEN 789 (e.g., JEN 786 [or 89], 821) means that he did not give up all his property (and tablets) through this contract. The fact that all his documents appear to have been excavated from Ḫui-te's archive (rooms 1 and 4) means that, in the end, he may have ceded all (except for what is named in JEN 789:39). JEN 789 could be the culmination of the process.

NOTES

l. 3: [*ù*]. The size of the gap starting this line favors such a restoration.

l. 4: *i*-[*pu*]-⌜*u*⌝*š*. The Oriental Institute Nuzi files record PU as preserved. Lacheman reconstructs: *i*-[*te-pu*]-*uš*.

l. 5: [*um?-ma?*]. Lacheman restores *um-ma*, as does Zaccagnini.[43] Cf. line 11 in support of this restoration.

---

is to establish if such PNs made contracts where the pattern of Šešerpa's own real estate contracts resurface. This has now been established.

39 That JEN 785, 786, and 787 relate to JEN 789 shows that Lacheman, in ordering texts for publication, understood the significance of this complex of texts.

40 See Maidman 1976–77, 133 for this notion.

41 For this notion, see Maidman 1979, 5. See also above, JEN 782, Comments.

42 One may, at this point, muse that the Ḫašiya father of Itḫ-apu (plausibly) father of Šešerpa and of Ḫaniu (see JEN 825:2–3) may be none other than Ḫašiya father of Mušeya, who himself *may* be the Mušeya father of Ḫui-te. Thus, all these transactions may represent a shifting of economic power among branches of the same family, a phenomenon already well known in the Teḫip-tilla Family. This maximalist position regarding the linkage of PNs was already adopted by Lacheman (1958, vi). See also, above, note to JEN 785:30.

43 The restoration is implicit in his translation (1984b, 714). All references to Zaccagnini's readings in the notes to JEN 789 are, unless otherwise indicated, to Zaccagnini 1984b, 714.

l. 6: ḪI.M[EŠ]. Cf. the formation of the plural in line 31 and, above, JEN 784:19, 27.

l. 7: ˹É˺. The trace appears, not as depicted, but, rather, as .

l. 7: [ḪI.MEŠ]. See above, note to line 6.

l. 9: *mar*-ZI-˹x˺-[ ]. The context of this clause, an enumeration of different kinds of realia, suggests we see here some sort of spelling of *maršītu*. See *CAD* M/1, p. 295b for similar Nuzi contexts. In fact, the Oriental Institute Nuzi files records the second sign as ŠI. But this is wishful thinking, and Lacheman himself repeatedly (and correctly) read ZI. One must assume that the scribe meant here to render *maršītiya* or the like.

l. 9: [ME]Š!?. The trace is not part of a *Winkelhaken* as drawn, but, rather, the head of a vertical wedge.

l. 10: URU ˹x˺. Cf. HSS, XIII, 143:9 for a possible parallel. Lacheman may already have noted this possible connection.

ll. 11–12. At the very ends of these two lines a sign and sign fragments appear. But nothing in the context of these lines (or in any of those immediately following) seems missing.

l. 12: [*l*]*u*?. The Oriental Institute files read [*l*]*i*, an interpretation accepted by *NPN*, p. 123a *sub* ŠALLIḬA 4), and by Zaccagnini. My own reading is colored by JEN 786:26. See above, Comments.

l. 12: ˹x˺. This trace was also noted by Lacheman. The trace, appearing just below and to the left of [*m*]*a* (l. 11), does not have three remaining strokes but a single one, a small horizontal (i.e., AŠ). See also above, note to ll. 11–12.

l. 13: *d*[*á-r*]*i*. This reading already appears in the Oriental Institute files, Lacheman, and Zaccagnini. See also above, Comments, for the significance of this PN in this text.

ll. 20–22. For this formulation of the *ilku*-clause, see above, note to JEN 782:17–19.

l. 20. Note that the *ilku* is here defined by the erstwhile owner of the real estate, not by the real estate itself, as is usual. Cf., e.g., JEN 783:9.[44] That the *ilku* really does attach to the land and not to any particular owner is quickly demonstrated in the next two lines.

l. 21: *ši*. Collation confirms that the sign is clearly ŠI. The copy itself does not make this clear. Cf. also, above, note to JEN 785:19.

l. 22: ˹*na*˺-[*ši*]. The traces appear less elongated than depicted but contain the same elements. The Oriental Institute files record ŠI as preserved.

---

44 The reading ˹*ša*˺ in JEN 789:20 (rather than ˹*ma*˺) is established by comparison with JEN 784:17, written by the same scribe.

l. 23. The Oriental Institute files and Zaccagnini render this line, in effect: *šumma* A.ŠÀ [GIŠ.ŠAR] É.

l. 24: [*ir-t*]*a*. The Oriental Institute files record these signs as preserved.

l. 25: [*še-er-p*]*á*. The Oriental Institute files record these signs as preserved.

l. 25: *ka*$_4$. Lacheman adds: [*-ma*].

l. 26: *na* ᵐ. These signs are normal, not as depicted.

l. 27: *i*-⸢*x*⸣. The traces at the very start of this line appear, not as depicted, but, rather, as .

l. 27: ⸢DUMU⸣? ÌR?. Contrary to the copy, I see here: 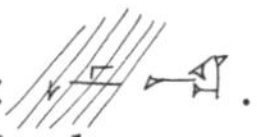. The PN (here as patronymic?) ÌR-*a-ḫi-šu* is not recognized here by Lacheman or by *NPN*. For ÌR?, Lacheman reads *ša*; the Oriental Institute Nuzi files have *na/la*.

ll. 28–29. The faint traces at the start of these lines shown in the copy are to be ignored; they are not present on the tablet.

l. 29: ⸢x⸣ *la mi*. The Oriental Institute files record: *al?-la-mi*.

ll. 30–32. These acts, whether symbolic or not, signify transfer of title to real property. See Zaccagnini 1984a, 88–89 for a discussion and survey of the four Nuzi examples available at that time. Those examples, JEN 59:10–11; 206:15–16; HSS, V, 58:9–10; XIII, 143:11–17, provide the basis for the restorations hazarded in these three lines of the present text.

l. 30: [A.ŠÀ.MEŠ]. Or the like. Zaccagnini assumes this reading as well.

l. 32: ⸢GÌR⸣. The sign appears, not as depicted, but, rather, as .

l. 34: *an*!. The sign appears, not as depicted, but, rather, as MAŠ.

l. 35: *Še*!. The sign appears, not as depicted, but, rather, as KUR.

l. 37: [N]A. The trace appears, not as depicted, but, rather, as .

l. 38: DIŠ. Correct as copied. Might this be an *ad hoc* indicator of a new, intrusive clause at this point in the contract?

ll. 40 (or 41)–43. The cramped writing of these lines indicates that the clause noting when and where the tablet was written was an afterthought (after the writing of the witness list).

l. 40: É. Not É.MEŠ, as in *CAD* A/2, p. 275b.

l. 41: [*ú*?]. Lacheman recorded, at this point: *-tu*$_4$.

l. 44: [ ]-*el*-[*t*]*e-e*. Lacheman restores: [*Še-ḫe*]-*el*-[*t*]*e-e*. The resulting individual is nowhere else attested.

l. 45: ⸢X⸣-[ ]-⸢x⸣-*ya*. The Oriental Institute Nuzi files record here [ ]-*pu?-ya*. Lacheman reads: [*Ku-uš-š*]*i-ya*. The resulting individual is nowhere else attested.

l. 46: [ ]-⸢x⸣-*še-en-ni*. The Oriental Institute Nuzi files restore [*A-k*]*u*-. This is attractive since the resulting individual reappears together with the next witness, Umpiya son of Šelwiya, in JEN 292. He is also a witness in JEN 825, a text (as is JEN 789) of Šešerpa son of Itḫ-apu.

l. 47: [DUMU]. The Oriental Institute Nuzi files record this sign as preserved.

l. 48: *Ki-pí-*[*til*?-*l*]*a*?. This restoration follows the Oriental Institute Nuzi files. The resulting individual is nowhere else attested, but the Kipi-tilla attested as a sealer below, line 59, may well be the witness in line 48.

l. 49: *Ut-*⸢*ḫap*⸣?-[*ta*?]-⸢*e*⸣?. The Oriental Institute Nuzi files restore: *Ut-ḫ*[*a-ap-ta*]-*e*. This identification is tentatively accepted in *NPN*, p. 168b *sub* UTḪAP-TAE 8). This individual is nowhere else attested.

l. 51: [ ]-⸢*y*⸣*a*. Porada identifies this gatekeeper as Akiya. See below, note to line 56.

l. 52. For this scribe, see above, JEN 784, Comments.

l. 53: *nu*!?. The Oriental Institute and Lacheman render this: *nu*. *na*! is also possible.

ll. 54–55. Except for A.ŠÀ.MEŠ *an-nu-*tu_4 (l. 54), *a-na ši-mi* (l. 54), and $^{[m]}$*Ḫu-i-te* (l. 55), everything in these lines is conjectural.[45] The Oriental Institute Nuzi files reconstruct the first surviving traces of line 55: *ta-din i-ba*?-*aš-ši*. Lacheman has: *ta-din i-na*.

l. 56: [NA_4]. Or the like.

l. 56: ⸢*x*⸣. Lacheman reads: *A*. In this connection, see above, note to line 51.

l. 59: $NA_4{}^{m}$. Both signs are complete and clear.

l. 60: ^{f}/SAL. The wedges appear, not as coped, but, rather, as  .

l. 60: AŠ?. Only the tail of this sign is preserved.

BIBLIOGRAPHY

Cassin, E., and J.-J. Glassner

1977 *Anthroponymie et Anthropologie de Nuzi, vol. 1: Les Anthroponymes.* Malibu: Undena Publications.

Fincke, Jeanette.

1993 *Die Orts- und Gewässernamen der Nuzi-Texte.* RGTC, 10. Wiesbaden: Dr. Ludwig Reichert Verlag.

Gelb, I.J., P.M. Purves, and A.A. MacRae.

1943 *Nuzi Personal Names.* OIP, 57. Chicago: University of Chicago Press.

Jordan, G.D.

1990 "Usury, Slavery and Land-Tenure: The Nuzi *tidennūtu* Transaction," *ZA* 80, 76–92.

---

45 But these three instances are themselves valuable gains. See, in part, above, Comments.

Lacheman, E.R.

1939 *Miscellaneous Texts.* JEN VI. New Haven: American Schools of Oriental Research.

1958 *Economic and Social Documents.* HSS 16. Cambridge, Mass.: Harvard U. Press.

Lacheman, E.R. and M.P. Maidman

1989 *Joint Expedition with the Iraq Museum at Nuzi VII: Miscellaneous Texts. SCCNH* 3. Winona Lake, Ind.: Eisenbrauns.

Maidman, M.P.

1976 "A Socio-economic Analysis of a Nuzi Family Archive," Ph. D. Dissertation, University of Pennsylvania.

1976–77 "The Teḫip-tilla Family of Nuzi: A Genealogical Reconstruction," *JCS* 28, 127–155; 29, 64.

1979 "A Nuzi Private Archive: Morphological Considerations," *Assur* 1, 179–86.

1994 *Two Hundred Nuzi Texts from the Oriental Institute of the University of Chicago, Part I. SCCNH* 6.

1998 "JEN 775–780: The Text Editions," *SCCNH* 9, 95–123.

Mayer, W.

1978 *Nuzistudien I: Die Archive des Palastes und die Prosopographie der Berufe.* AOAT 205/1. Kevelaer: Butzon & Bercker.

Porada, E.

1947 *Seal Impressions of Nuzi.* AASOR, 24. New Haven: American Schools of Oriental Research.

Richter, T.

1995 "Die Tenne in den Texten aus Nuzi," *SCCNH* 7, 69–79.

Von Soden, W.

1965–81 *Akkadisches Handwörterbuch.* Wiesbaden: Otto Harrassowitz.

Zaccagnini, C.

1984a "Land Tenure and Transfer of Land at Nuzi (XV-XIV Century B.C.)." In *Land Tenure and Social Transformation in the Middle East*, ed. by Tarif Khalidi, 79–94. [Beirut:] American University of Beirut.

1984b "Proprieta' fondiaria e dipendenza rurale nella Mesopotamia settentrionale (XV- XIV secola a.C.)," *Studi Storici* 3, 697–723.

Zum hurritischen Gilgameš-Epos: Ein neuer Zusammenschluß [1]

MITSUO NAKAMURA
Sanyo Gakuen University, Okayama

The author argues for an indirect join of two fragments of the Hurrian version of the Gilgameš epic from Ḫattuša (KBo 19.124 and KBo 33.10) on the basis of internal evidence and collation. He discusses the relative position of the fragments and the course of the narrative. According to his hypothetical reconstruction, the tablet contained the second half of the epic from Gilgameš's despair after Enkidu's death to Ullu's (= Utnapištim's) account of the flood.

1. *Zu den beiden Fragmenten des hurritischen Gilgameš-Epos KBo 19.124 und KBo 33.10.*

Unter den zahlreichen Tontafelfragmenten aus Boğazköy sind neben den Fragmenten des akkadischen und hethitischen Gilgameš-Epos bisher fünf Fragmente des hurritischen Gilgameš-Epos bekannt (1: KUB 8.61+KBo 8.144, 2: KUB 47.10, 3. KUB 8.60(+)[?]KUB 47.9, 4: KBo 19.124, 5: KBo 33.10)[2], worüber der Verfasser dieser Zeilen sich in seinem Beitrag zu A. Tsukimotos japanischer Übersetzung des Epos[3] und seinem in japanischer Sprache verfaßten Aufsatz[4] in BSNESJ 39/1 (1996) 61–63 geäußert hat. In diesem Beitrag werden die beiden letztgenannten Fragmente (4: KBo 19.124 und 5: KBo 33.10) erneut behandelt. Von KBo 19.124 ist nur die rechte Schulter erhalten. Sowohl auf der Vorderseite als auch auf der Rückseite sind jeweils elf Zeilen erhalten. Dieses Fragment unterscheidet sich insofern von dem Fragment 1 (=KUB 8.61+KBo 8.144) sowie

[1] Es handelt sich bei dem vorliegenden Beitrag um die deutsche Fassung des in japanischer Sprache in *Bulletin of the Society for Near Eastern Studies in Japan*(=*BSNESJ*) 41/1 (1998) 157–62 erschienenen Aufsatzes. Für die freundliche Aufnahme meines Aufsatzes in die *SCCNH* gilt mein aufrichtiger Dank Herrn Prof. Dr. G. Wilhelm.

[2] Vgl. zuletzt M. Salvini, „Die hurritischen Überlieferungen des Gilgameš-Epos und der Kešši-Erzählung", in: V. Haas (Hrdg.), *Hurriter und Hurritisch* (Konstanz 1988) 157–72 sowie G. del Monte, bei G. Pettinato, *La saga di Gilgamesh* (Milano 1992) 389.

[3] A. Tsukimoto, *Gilgameš-jojishi* (Tokyo: Iwanami Shoten, 1996).

[4] *BSNESJ* 39/1 (1996) 52–68.

Studies on the Civilization and Culture of Nuzi and the Hurrians - 10

von dem Fragment 3 (= KUB 8.60(+)$^{?}$KUB 47.9), als der Name Gilgameš auf der Vorderseite dieses Fragmentes genauso wie in der hethitischen Version des Epos als ^{d}GIŠ.GIM.MAŠ geschrieben wird. In Rs. 4' scheint der Ausdruck „von Susa, susäisch" (^{URU}*šu-šu-ḫé*[ ) vorzuliegen[5]. Demgegenüber ist von KBo 33.10 ein Teil des linken Randes erhalten; auf der Vorderseite sind zwölf Zeilen erhalten, und Wörter wie etwa „Land" sowie „Weg" scheinen vorzukommen. Auf der Rückseite kommt der Personenname Ullu in Z. 2' vor. Das war fast der einzige Anhaltspunkt für die Zuordnung dieses Fragmentes zum Gilgameš-Epos in meinen oben genannten früheren Arbeiten. Außerdem tritt die Göttin Ištar in ihrer hurritischen Form Šauška auf;[6] in meinen früheren Arbeiten ist auch auf den etwaigen Zusammenhang mit Ištars Schrei bei der Sintflut, die in ZZ. 116–17 der Taf. XI der Ninive-Version geschildert wird, hingewiesen worden[7].

2. *Zur Zuordnung der beiden Fragmente*

Nach der Kollation der beiden genannten Fragmente, die im Sommer 1996 vorgenommen worden ist[8], erscheinen sie nach Tonfarbe (schwarz) und Schrift sehr ähnlich. Es ist so gut wie sicher, daß die beiden Fragmente, ohne Anschluß, zu ein und derselben Tontafel gehören. In diesem Fall gibt KBo 33.10 den linken Rand der Tafel, während KBo 19.124 die rechte Schulter derselben Tafel liefert. Es ist nicht bestimmbar, wieviele Kolumnen sie hat. Obwohl der Herausgeber der Edition KBo 19 davon ausgeht, daß es sich bei KBo 19.124 um eine vierkolumnige Tafel handelt, kann man die Möglichkeit nicht ausschließen, daß es sich dabei doch um eine sechskolumnige Tafel handelt. Wenn man die Zusammengehörigkeit der beiden Fragmente voraussetzt, darf man den Inhalt des Textes folgendermaßen beschreiben. In Vs. Kol. i (KBo 33.10) finden sich Wörter wie „Land" sowie „Weg", die in Beziehung zu Reisen stehen, während in Kol. ii (bzw. iii) (KBo 19.124) der Name Gilgameš mindestens dreimal genannt wird und der Ausdruck für „großer Herr" vorkommt[9]. Außer Gilgameš kommt anscheinend in Z. 1 der Wettergott[10] vor. Ferner findet sich in Z. 6 das Wort für „Wort"[11]. Vermutlich werden in diesem Textteil Dialoge wiedergegeben. Auf der Rückseite kann man in Kol. iii (bzw. iv) außer dem

---

5 Verf. bei A. Tsukimoto, *Gilgameš-jojishi*, 279f.; Verf., *BSNESJ* 39/1 (1996) 63.

6 Zum Verständnis des Götternamens Šauška, s. I. Wegner, *SCCNH* 7 (1995) 117–20.

7 Verf. bei A. Tsukimoto, *Gilgameš-jojishi*, 280 ; Verf., *BSNESJ* 39/1 (1996) 63.

8 Mein aufrichtiger Dank für die Genehmigung meiner Arbeit im Museum für anatolische Zivilisationen/Ankara gilt der türkischen Regierung und für die freundliche Aufnahme und stete Hilfsbereitschaft dem Museumsdirektor Sayın Dr. Ilhan Temizsoy sowie den Kustodinnen Sayın Rukiye Akdoğan und Sayın Ismet Aykut.

9 Z. 3': da-la-$u̯u_{u}$-ši eb-r[i] (talāv=o=ži evri, Erg. Prof. G. Wilhelm); cf. G. Wilhelm, *Or*NS 61 (1992) 134; *GLH* 252; I. Wegner, *SCCNH* 7 (1995) 119; E. Neu, *Hethitica* 13 (1996) 68.

10 Cf. KBo 19, S. xiii.

11 Cf. te-$u̯e_{e}$-n[a, cf. *GLH* 268.

KBo 19.124(+)KBo 33.10

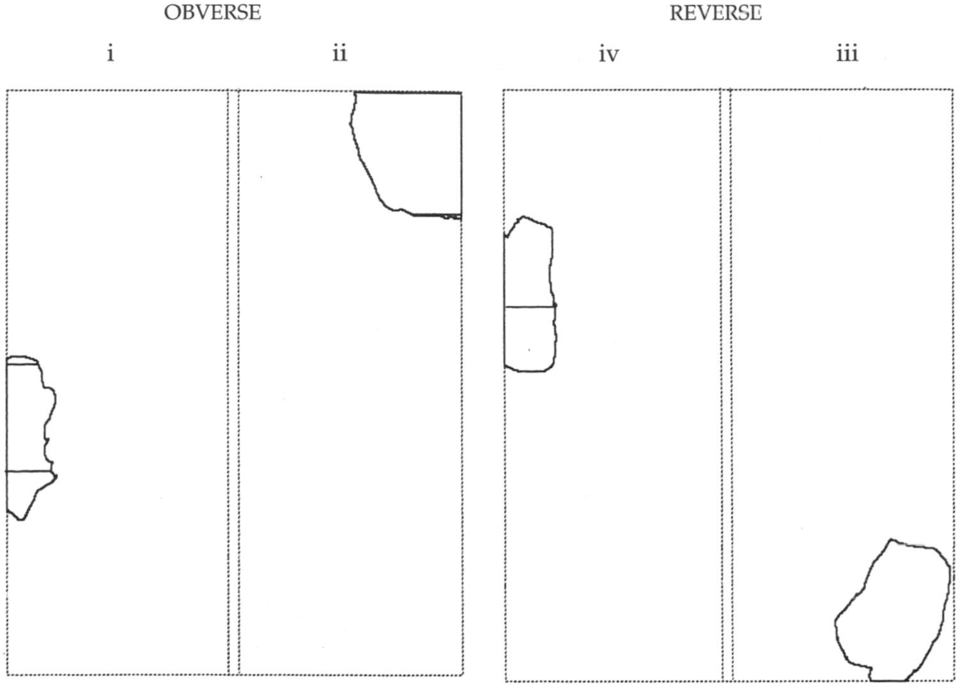

oben genannten Wort „susäisch, von Susa“ auch noch das Wort „dem Herzen“ (Z. 5')[12] sowie das Sumerogramm für „Berg“ (Z. 7') finden. Nach einer nicht kleinen Lücke tritt die Persönlichkeit Ullu, die angeblich dem Ut-napištim entsprechen soll, in der letzten Kolumne (iv bzw. vi) in Z. 2' auf. Wie oben schon gesagt, tritt auch die Göttin Šauška auf. Noch einige weitere Wörter sind hier zu lesen.

3. *Zur Verhältnis des Textes zu den bisher bekannten Gilgameš-Überlieferungen*

Wie verhält der neugewonnene Text sich zu den bisher bekannten Gilgameš-Überlieferungen? Folgende Entsprechungen werden nur hypothetisch vorgeschlagen:

Kol. i. Das verzweifelte Herumirren Gilgamešs nach dem Tode Enkidus, seines Freundes, und sein Aufbruch zur Suche nach dem Sinn des Lebens (Ninive-Version, Taf. IX [Kol. I]);

Kol. ii (iii): Gespräche Gilgamešs, der wohl das Gebirge Māšu erreicht hat, mit einem Skorpionmenschen (Ninive-Version, Taf. IX [Kol. ii]);

12 te-ša-a-u̯[a, cf. *GLH* 266.

Kol. iii (iv): Entweder Fortsetzung der Gespräche zwischen Gilgameš und dem Skorpionmenschen oder schon Gespräche mit der Schenkin über seine bisherige Reise(?);

Kol. iv(vi): Vielleicht Ullus Erzählung über die Sintflut.

Hier sind Szenen wie etwa die Reise ins Gebirge Māšu und die Begegnung mit den Skorpionmenschen, die in der hethitischen Version des Epos nicht erhalten(?) sind, angenommen. Es ist möglich, aber nicht als sicher zu betrachten, daß schon in Kol. i die Begegnung Gilgamešs mit der Schenkin erzählt wird. Was Kol. iii(iv) anbetrifft, erinnert diese Kolumne an solche Szenen wie das Herumwandern Gilgamešs und seine Jagden im Gebirge, seine Begegnung mit Löwen und Löwenjagd, die in einem der Fragmente der hethitischen Version des Epos (KUB 8.50(+)KBo 22.91), Kol. ii geschildert werden[13], was an einen derartigen Zusammenhang ernsthaft denken läßt.

Jedenfalls ist die Annahme einer Reise nach Osten aufgrund des Ausdrucks „von Susa, susäisch" wenig überraschend; eine Reise ins (von Uruk gesehen) in östlicher Richtung zu suchende Gebirge Māšu[14] wäre wahrscheinlicher als eine Reise in den im Zagros-Gebirge zu suchenden Zedernwald, wie Verf. sie in seiner früheren Arbeit vermutet hat.[15] Was Kol. iv (bzw. vi) anbetrifft, so ist es nicht endgültig zu entscheiden, ob die Persönlichkeit Ullu (als Entsprechung für Ut-napištim?) selbst bereits aufgetreten ist oder ob lediglich von ihm die Rede ist. Ob diese Partie schon zur Erzählung der Sintflut gehört, sei ebenfalls dahingestellt. Da der Inhalt des trotz des Zusammenschlusses immer noch schlecht erhaltenen Textes sprachlich noch immer nur schwer verständlich ist und da wir noch nicht wissen, wie die hurritische Version des Gilgameš-Epos als Ganzes aussah, ist die genaue Anordnung des Textes der Zukunft zu überlassen.

---

13 Verf. bei A. Tsukimoto, *Gilgameš-jojishi*, 259 und Anm. 18 (S. 11).

14 Der Anfang der Ninive-Version, Taf. I, Kol. i 36 ff. lautet: Der da fand die Eingänge in das Gebirge (= Gilgameš), / (37) Der dürstete nach den Zisternen am Rande des Steppenlandes. / (38) Der die See überfuhr, das weite, zum Sonnenaufgang hin liegende Meer. / (39) Der die Weltränder ins Auge faßte, überall das Leben suchend, der in seiner Stärke gelangte bis hin zum fernen Utnapištim. (Übersetzung nach W. von Soden, *Das Gilgamesch-Epos* [Stuttgart: Reclam, 1988] 16). „Zum Sonnenaufgang (= Osten) hin" *adi ṣīt šamši* heißt sicherlich „zum Gebirge Māšu, wo die Sonne aufgeht, hin" (vgl. Taf. IX, Kol. ii; A. Tsukimoto, *Gilgameš-jojishi*, 309).

15 Verf., *BSNESJ* 39/1 (1996) 63.

Eine Tontafel aus der Antikensammlung Bassermann–Jordan*

DORIS PRECHEL — FELIX BLOCHER
Ruprecht-Karls-Universität, Heidelberg

The authors edit and discuss a cuneiform tablet in a German private collection that belongs to the wider corpus of Nuzi tablets (i.e., including those from other places such as Arrapḫa and Kurruḫanni). It is a *Sammelurkunde* consisting of three loans of emmer given out by a certain Zike, (son of Allaituraḫḫe?). The place where the grain is to be returned is not mentioned. Neither the creditor, Zike, nor the groups of debtors can be traced prosopographically with certainty. Thus, the origin of this tablet remains open. Special attention is given to the seal impressions.

Weder die Umstände, unter denen die Tafel in den Privatbesitz der Familie Bassermann-Jordan gelangte, noch der Fundort des Stückes sind zu klären. Es handelt sich um eine Sammelurkunde mit verzinslichen Emmerdarlehen von Zike an jeweils drei Schuldnergemeinschaften verschiedener Größe. Wie sehr oft bei diesen Darlehen üblich, wird die Rückgabe des Getreides auf den Zeitpunkt nach der Ernte vereinbart.

Das Formular setzt sich mit Variationen aus folgenden Abschnitten zusammen (Owen 1970, 36ff., Wilhelm 1992, 12ff.):

(1) Nennung der Schuldner mit Angabe des Vaternamens
(2) Empfangsquittung mit Nennung des gesamten Darlehensgegenstandes
(3) Rückgabeklausel mit Bestimmung des Rückgabezeitpunktes
(4) Klausel gegenseitiger Bürgschaft

Aufmerksamkeit verdient allerdings die sonst nicht in dem Formular von Darlehensurkunden verwendete Anzeige, welcher Person die Schuldner unterstellt sind (s. Kommentar zu Z. 19).

Bei der Beschriftung der Tafel hat der Schreiber sichtlich Platzprobleme bekommen. In der unteren Hälfte der Vorderseite listet er zwei Personennamen

* Wir danken der Direktion des Historischen Landesmuseums der Pfalz, Speyer und Herrn Dr. Lothar Sperber für die Möglichkeit, den Text publizieren zu können. Doris Prechel ist für den philologischen, Felix Blocher für den archäologischen Teil verantwortlich.

Studies on the Civilization and Culture of Nuzi and the Hurrians - 10

samt Filiation auf, was dazu führt, daß ein erheblicher Teil der Rückseite mit in Anspruch genommen werden mußte. Es ist ihm wohl darauf angekommen, mit der neuen Tafelseite auch eine neue Darlehensbeurkundung zu verbinden. Interessanterweise setzen nach den ersten vier Zeilen Tilgungen über sechs bereits geschriebene Zeilen ein und zwar genau dort, wo ein Teil der Vorderseite ein Drittel der Rückseite beansprucht. Aus den erhaltenen Spuren wird zumindest deutlich, daß vor der Rasur nicht die Empfangsquittung für das Darlehen folgte, sondern weitere Personennamen notiert waren. Nach der Tilgung wird die Anzahl der Schuldner korrekt mit vier Personen summiert. Das folgende Formular ist gegenüber den vorangehenden verkürzt, obwohl die Rückseite erst zur Hälfte beschrieben ist. Durch diese Raumbeschränkungen sah sich der Schreiber veranlaßt, einige Variationen in den Schreibungen wie *kunīšu* / ZÍZ.AN.NA, *na-ad-nu* / SUM-*nu*, BURU$_{14}$(*-ri*) im Formular zu verwenden.

Maße: 12,9 x 7,3 cm (Abb. 1-5)

Vs.

1 ^{I}⸢*wa-aḫ*⸣*-ra-a-bi* DUMU *du-ra-ri*
2 ⸢^{I}⸣[ ]x DUMU *zi-li-ip-*LUGAL*-rù*
3 ^{I}[DU]MU *a-ri-ip-a-pu*
4 ^{I}[DUM]U *zi-qa-a-a*
5 ^{I}[x x x DUMU] *ki-pu-ú-uš*
6 ^{I}[ ]x DUMU *a-ri-ip-a-pu*
7 ^{I}*a-kip-*⸢*ša*⸣*-*⸢*lì*⸣ *ù* ^{I}*a-kip-til-la* DUMU *ka-a-a*
8 ^{I}*e-en-na-*⸢*pa*⸣*-li* DUMU *ḫe-er-ši-it-ta*
9 ^{I}*ḫa-ni-ku-*⸢*uz*⸣*-zi* DUMU *ḫu-ti-ia*
10 ^{I}*ku-uš-ši-ia* DUMU *ḫa-ni-ú*
11 ^{I}*tu-ú-ra* DUMU *ir-ti-ba-a-na*
12 12 LÚ.MEŠ *an-nu-tu*$_{4}$ *ù*
13 48 ANŠE ZÍZ.AN.NA.MEŠ *ša* ^{I}*zi-ge*
14 *a-na* MÁŠ*-ti il-qú-ú ù i+na* EGIR*-ki*
15 BURU$_{14}$*-ri it-t*[*i*] MÁŠ*-šu-nu*.MEŠ *a-na* 72 ANŠE ZÍZ.⸢AN.NA⸣
16 *ú-ta-ar-*[*r*]*u ù ku-ni-šu* SIG$_{5}$*-qú ka-ab-bá-r*[*u*]
17 LÚ *a-na* LÚ *m*[*a*]*-ḫi-iṣ pu-ti ša aš-bu*
18 *i+na* ŠÀ*-šu-nu* [*ku*]*-ni-šu* SA$_{5}$*-la ù šu-nu*
19 *i+na* ŠU ^{I}*a-w*[*i*]-DINGIR *na-ad-nu*

---

20 ^{I}*du-ra-ri* DUMU *ki-in-du-ia* ^{I}*mu-šu-ia* DUMU *an-zi*$^{?}$*-*[
21 ^{I}*el-ḫi-ip-til-la* DUMU EN*-ia* ^{I}*ḫa-ši-ip-te-šup* DUMU *tal-*⸢*li-ú*⸣
22 ^{I}*ip-šá-ḫa-lu* DUMU *te-ḫi-ip-*LUGAL ^{I}*i-ri-it-te* DUMU *šu-a-n*[*i*]*-*⸢*e*⸣
23 ^{I}*ta-i-qa* DUMU *mil-qa-a-pu* ^{I}*el-la-tu*$_{4}$ DUMU *al-ki-ia*
24 ^{I}*ur-ḫi-ia* DUMU *ar-ḫa-ma-an-na*
25 ^{I}*na-i-še-ri* DUMU *we-el-la-at-ku-i*

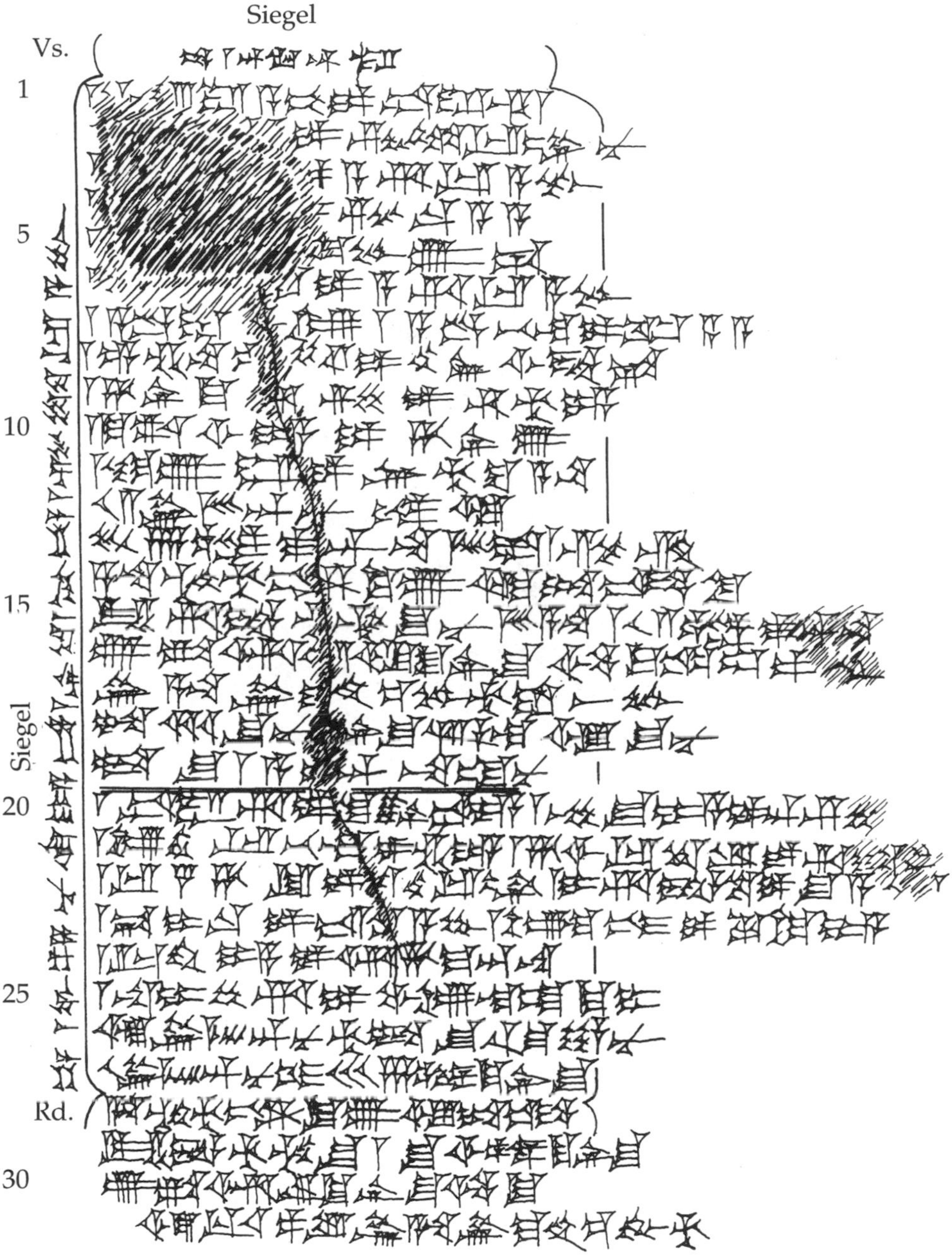

Abb. 1: Tontafel in der Antikensammlung Bassermann-Jordan (Kopie D. Prechel)

Rs.

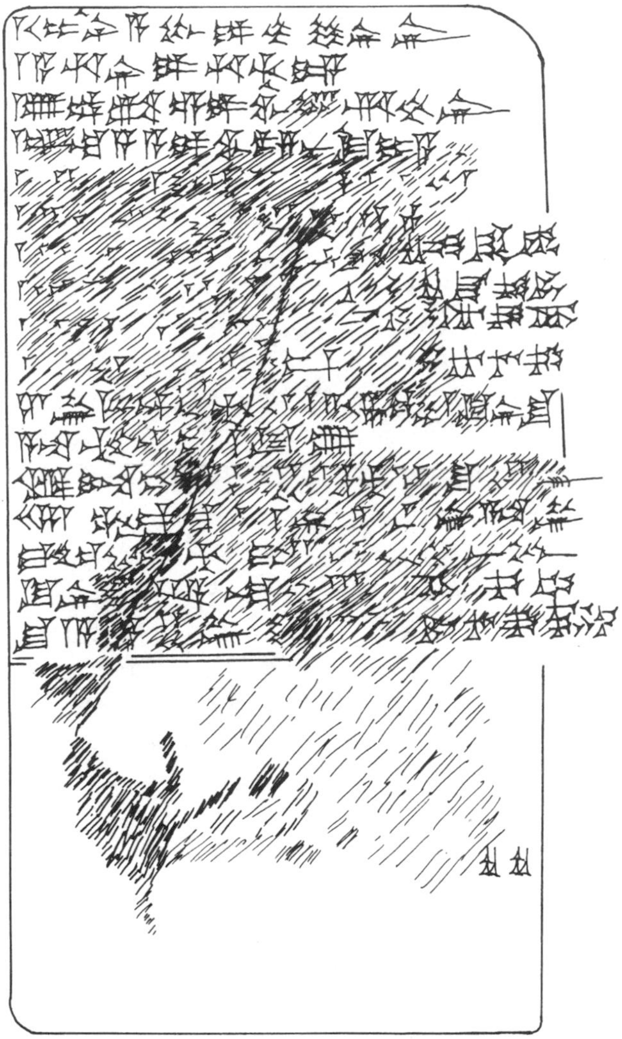

Abb. 2: Tontafel in der Antikensammlung Bassermann-Jordan (Kopie D. Prechel)

26 *ù* LÚ.MEŠ *an-nu-ti i+na* ŠU-*šú-ma* SUM-*nu*
27 10 LÚ.MEŠ *an-nu-tu*$_4$ 36 ANŠE *ku-ni-šu*

u. Rd.

28 *a-na* MÁŠ-*ti il-qú-ú ù i+na* EGIR
29 BURU$_{14}$ *it-ti* MÁŠ-*šu* 1 *šu-ši* ANŠE *ku-ni-šu*
30 *ú-ta-ar-ru ku-ni-šu* SIG$_5$-*qú*
31 *ù kab-bá-ru* LÚ *a-na* LÚ *ma-ḫi-iṣ pu-ti*

Rs.

32 ^{I}MI.NI$^{!}$-*a-bu* DUMU *še-in-ni*
33 ^{I}*a-ḫu-ni* DUMU *ḫu-ti-ia*
34 ^{I}*ú-nap-ta-e* DUMU *wa-*⸢*aḫ*⸣*-ri-še-ni*
35 ^{I}*ú-na*$^{!}$*-a-a* DUMU *wu-un-nu-ki-ia*
36 ^{I}x (Rasur)
37 ^{I}x (Rasur)
38 ^{I}x (Rasur)
39 ^{I}x (Rasur)
40 ^{I}x (Rasur)
41 ^{I}x (Rasur)
42 4 LÚ.MEŠ *an-nu-ti* ⸢*ù*⸣ 15 ⸢ANŠE⸣ *ku-ni-šu*
43 *a-na* MÁŠ-*t*⸢*i*⸣ ⸢*il*⸣-⸢*qú*⸣-*ú*
44 *ù i+na* ⸢EGIR⸣-[*k*]*i* [BU]RU$_{14}$ ⸢*it*⸣-*t*[*i*] M[ÁŠ]-*šu* x x
45 25 ⸢ANŠE⸣ [*ku-ni-š*]*u* ⸢*ú*⸣$^{?}$-⸢*ta*⸣$^{?}$-⸢*ru*$^{?}$⸣ (Rasur) ⸢LÚ⸣ *a-na* LÚ
46 *ma-ḫi-iṣ pu-ti* ⸢*ša*$^{?}$⸣ (Rasur) *aš-bu*
47 *ku-ni-š*[*u* S]A$_5$-*la*
48 ŠU ^{I}*a-*[*ki*]*p*$^{?}$-E[N$^{?}$] LÚ.D[UB.SAR]

---

o. Rd. Siegel

49 NA$_4$ $^{I\ d}$AK-DINGIR.RA

l. Rd. Siegel

50 NA$_4$ ^{I}*wu-un-nu-ki-ia* NA$_4$ ^{I}*ni-zu-uk* NA$_4$ ^{I}*zi-li-ip-a-pu*

ÜBERSETZUNG

Vs.

1 Waḫr-abi, Sohn des Turari,
2 [S2], Sohn des Zilib-šarri,
3 [S3, So]hn des Arib-abu,
4 [S4, Soh]n des Zikai̯a,
5 [S5, Sohn des] Kipuš,
6 [S6], Sohn des Arib-abu,
7 Akib-šali, Akib-tilla, Söhne des Kai̯a,

8 Enna-pali, Sohn des Ḫeršitta,
9 Ḫanikuzzi, Sohn des Ḫutii̯a,
10 Kuššii̯a, Sohn des Ḫaniu,
11 Tūra, Sohn des Irtib-ana.
12 Diese 12 Männer haben
13 48 Homer Emmer des Zike
14 für Zins genommen. Nach
15 der Ernte werden sie mit zugehörigem Zins 72 Homer Emmer
16 zurückgeben, und (zwar) hochwertigen, dicken Emmer.
17 Ein Mann ist für den anderen Bürge. Wer anwesend ist
18 von ihnen, wird Emmer in voller Höhe geben. Sie
19 sind in die Hand des Awīlu gegeben.

---

20 Turari, Sohn des Kindui̯a, Mušui̯a, Sohn des Anzi[ ],
21 Elḫib-tilla, Sohn des Bēlii̯a, Ḫašib-Tešup, Sohn des Talliu,
22 Ibša-ḫalu, Sohn des Teḫib-šarri, Iritte, Sohn des Šuani?,
23 Taiqa, Sohn des Milqāpu, Ellatu, Sohn des Alkii̯a,
24 Urḫii̯a, Sohn des Ari-ḫamanna,
25 Nai-šeri, Sohn der Wellatkui.
26 Diese Männer sind (also) in seine Hand gegeben.
27 Diese 10 Männer haben 36 Homer Emmer
u. Rd.
28 für Zins genommen. Nach
29 der Ernte werden sie mit dem Zins 60 Homer Emmer
30 zurückgeben, (und zwar) hochwertigen Emmer
31 und dicken. Ein Mann ist für den anderen Bürge.
Rs.
32 Ṣilli-abu, Sohn des Šenni,
33 Aḫuni, Sohn des Ḫutii̯a,
34 Unap-tae, Sohn des Waḫri-šeni,
35 Unai̯a, Sohn des Wunnukii̯a.
36-41 (Rasur)
42 Diese 4 Männer haben 16 Homer Emmer
43 für Zins genommen.
44 Nach der Ernte werden sie mit Zins
45 25 Homer [Emm]er zurückgeben. Ein Mann ist für den anderen
46 Bürge. Wer anwesend ist,
47 wird den Emmer in voller Höhe geben.
48 Hand des A⸢kib-bēli⸣, des Sch[reibers].

---

49 Siegel des ^{d}AK-DINGIR.RA
50 Siegel des Wunnukii̯a Siegel des Nizzuk Siegel des Zilib-abu

Abb. 3: Tontafel in der Antikensammlung Bassermann-Jordan: Vorderseite und rechter Rand

Abb. 4: Tontafel in der Antikensammlung Bassermann-Jordan: linker Rand und Rückseite

Abb. 5: Tontafel in der Antikensammlung Bassermann-Jordan:
oberer und unterer Rand

KOMMENTAR[1]

12: Zum „resumptiven u" nach Subjekt und vor direktem Objekt s. Wilhelm 1970, 60, vgl. Z. 42.

15: Die Zinssätze sind mit 50% im vorliegenden Fall und 66% in den beiden folgenden Beurkundungen unterschiedlich festgesetzt, entsprechen jedoch in ihrer Höhe den üblichen Forderungen, s. Owen 1970, 42.

16: Das präpositionale Objekt ist hinter das Verb gesetzt, zu diesem Interferenzphänomen des Ḫurro-Akkadischen von Nuzi s. Wilhelm 1970, 84f.; *kabbaru*, nach *AHw* s.v. „sehr dick" ist zur Spezifikation von Getreide auch belegt KAJ 66: 6, 8 *še-um šu-ub-ri damqu kab-ru*, nach David/Ebeling 1929: Nr. 55 „fettes, gutes, dickes Korn"; s. auch die *CAD* K sub *kabāru* gebuchten Belege, die sich auf das Gewicht der Getreideähren beziehen. vgl. Z. 30f.

17: *māḫiṣ pūti* „Bürge", s. Koschaker 1911, 216, 226ff., Petschow 1956, 81f. Anm. 242.

17f.: Die vollständige Wendung lautet *mannu*(*mmê*) *ina libbišunu ša ašbu* „Wer unter ihnen anwesend ist", zur Solidarhaftung s. Koschaker 1928, 121ff., Wilhelm 1992, 17; so auch Z. 46f., nicht jedoch auf Z. 31 folgend.

19: *ina* ŠU PN *nadnu*: festgestellt wird, in wessen Dienste sich die Angehörigen der Schuldnergemeinschaft befinden, wohl um die Personalexekution zu sichern. Gewöhnlich wird die Formel durch die Präposition *ana* eingeleitet, während *ina qāti* einen Vorgang aus dem Amtsbereich heraus beschreibt.

20: PN Kinduia̯ vielleicht Variante zu assimiliertem Kidduia̯, s. Müller 1998: Nr. 40:1, 7 und HSS XV 12:6. Der Beginn des Namens am Zeilenende ist mir unklar.

21: PN Talliu ist bislang nicht belegt, vgl. aber Talliia̯, *NPN* 145.

22: PN Iritte Sohn des Šuani nur noch HSS XV 25:51 belegt.

25: Wellatkui ist bisher nur als femininer PN gebucht, *NPN* 173 und Müller 1998: Nr. 21:14.

26: Vgl. Z. 19.

31: Aus Platzgründen scheint hier das vollständige Formular zur Solidarhaftung nicht geschrieben.

48: PN in der vorgeschlagenen Lesung bislang nicht belegt.

50: Zu gemeinsamen Aktivitäten des Nizzuk und Zilib-abu, s. Müller 1998, 72f. zu Nr. 20, 96 Nr. 30; C.J. Gadd, *RA* 23 (1926) 137 Nr. 68. Auch in der vorliegenden Urkunde scheint der Kassite Nizzuk für Zike, den Sohn der Allaituraḫḫe und des Šurki-tilla das Geschäft abzuwickeln.

---

[1] Ich danke Prof. Dr. G. Wilhelm, Würzburg, und Frau Dr. J. Fincke, Heidelberg, für eine kritische Durchsicht des Manuskriptes und wichtige Anmerkungen.

Von den genannten Personen sind bislang lediglich Urḫii̯a (JEN 342/ JENu 721), Kuššii̯a (HSS V 77:3; *NPN* 54), Iritte (HSS XV 25:51) und Taiqa (HSS XV 56:5) mit der vorliegenden Filiation belegt.

DIE SIEGELABROLLUNGEN

Die in der Antikensammlung Bassermann-Jordan aufbewahrte Tontafel trägt auf dem oberen und dem linken Rand Siegelabrollungen. Ob auch auf der unteren Hälfte der Rückseite Siegelabrollungen angebracht waren, läßt sich ohne Autopsie der Tafel, zu der ich leider keine Gelegenheit hatte, nicht entscheiden, es ist jedoch nicht wahrscheinlich. Sichtbar sind schwache Linien, die wohl eher von einem Gewebe als von einem Siegel herrühren dürften (Abb. 4). Auffällig ist außerdem eine sternförmige Ritzung (oder lediglich Beschädigung?). Auf eigene Umzeichnungen nach den Fotografien habe ich verzichtet.

Oberer Rand (Abb. 5)

Auf dem oberen Rand ist das bekannte Siegel des Schreibers ᵈAK-DINGIR.RA (Nabû-ila) abgerollt (Abb. 6). Das Siegel ist in seinem ganzen Umfang einmal abgerollt, der Tafelrand bot jedoch nur für dessen obere Hälfte Platz. Der untere Teil der Abrollung ist durch die Siegelbeischrift zerstört. Das Siegel ist von Stein 1993: Nr. 167 publiziert worden; zusätzliche Abrollungen davon sind jetzt von U. Löw in: Müller 1998: Taf. CIVff. Nrr. 2A, 26A, 43A, 52C, 53A, 135B vorgelegt worden.

Linker Rand (Abb. 4)

Abb. 6: Das Siegel des Schreibers ᵈAK-DINGIR.RA (Nabû-ila), Stein 1993: Nr. 167 (Umzeichnung D.L. Stein)

Die Siegelungen auf dem linken Rand bieten mehr Schwierigkeiten als diejenige des oberen Randes. Vom unteren Rand her beginnend, in der Leserichtung der Siegelbeischriften (Wunnukiia – Nizzuk – Zilib-abu, vgl. Abb. 1), sind folgende Einzelheiten zu sehen:

1. Spuren von Abrollungen, die nicht zu deuten sind;
2. zwei einander gegenüberstehende geflügelte Raubkatzen; aus dem Maul der rechten kommen (Feuer-)Strahlen; zwischen Flügel und Kopf der linken Raubkatze ein Kreis mit eingezeichnetem Punkt (Rest eines Flechtbandes), zwischen Kopf und Flügel der rechten ein Stern;
3. (umgekehrt abgerollt) Reste eines angewinkelten Armes mit einem Flügel darunter sowie zwei Arme, die eine Standarte halten;
4. zwei Zeilen einer Siegellegende mit Begrenzungslinien;
5. Kopf eines Cerviden in Vorderansicht, Tier in Seitenansicht (wohl hockender Affe);
6. Oberkörper und Reste von Köpfen zweier nach rechts (?) gerichteten menschlichen Gestalten;
7. zwischen den Köpfen von 6. (umgekehrt abgerollt) Rest eines Flügels wohl eines Mischwesens;
8. Rest einer Siegellegende mit Begrenzungslinie.

Abb. 7: Das Siegel des Kassiten Nizzuk, Müller 1998: Taf. CVI Nr. 23A (Umzeichnung U. Löw)

Die Zuordnung der Abrollungsspuren zu den Siegelbeischriften ist nur teilweise durchführbar. Zunächst ist festzuhalten, daß das Siegel des Schreibers Nabû-ila, dasselbe wie auf dem oberen Rand (Abb. 5–6), welches an mindestens einem, wenn nicht zwei Elementen klar zu erkennen ist (Nr. 3, 7?), keine eigene Beischrift aufweist.

Das Siegel des Wunnukiia (Nr. 1), wohl des Vaters des in Z. 35 genannten Schuldners Ulaia, läßt sich nicht beschreiben.

Nr. 2 ist das Siegel des Kassiten Nizzuk, Müller 1998: Taf. CVI Nr. 23A (Abb. 7), das mit seinen einander gegenüberstehenden Raubkatzen ein beliebtes

Motiv der Mittani-Glyptik aufweist; vgl. Stein 1993: Nr. 237. Allerdings ist fast immer ein Bäumchen, eine Standarte oder ähnliches zwischen den Tieren abgebildet, vgl. ebenda Fig. XIVf. (Gruppe 3).

Die Elemente Nr. 4, 5, 6 und 8 dürften zum Siegel des Zilib-abu gehören, Müller 1998: Taf. CVIII Nr. 30A (Abb. 8). Die Füllmotive Cervidenkopf und hockender Affe (Nr. 5) sind für Siegel der Mittani-Zeit ungewöhnlich; Vergleiche lassen sich dagegen im Corpus der kassitischen und pseudokassitischen Glyptik finden; vgl. Matthews 1992: Nr. 76, 94, 97; Matthews 1990: Nr. 80; wohin das Siegel zu gehören scheint. Was die Elemente Nr. 4 und 8 betrifft, so sind sie nicht sicher mit den von U. Löw kopierten Legendenresten auf dem Zilib-abu-Siegel (Abb. 8) in Übereinstimmung zu bringen. Sie gehören aber auch nicht zum Siegel Nabû-ilas (Abb. 5–6). Es besteht also die Möglichkeit, daß auch die Elemente Nr. 4 und 8 zu weiteren Siegeln, die ohne eigene Beischrift geblieben sind, gehören.

Zur Verteilung der Siegelabrollungen auf der Tafel

Zu erwarten wären Siegelungen vor allem auf der Freifläche der Rückseite (untere Hälfte), wo sie aber sehr wahrscheinlich fehlen. Siegelungen des oberen Randes sind gängig: Der obere Rand stellt die Anschlußfläche der unteren Hälfte der Rückseite dar. Für Siegelungen des linken Randes vgl. z. B. Müller 1998: Nr. 14, 15, 17, 18, 19, 22, 24, 27, 28, 39, 41, 54, 56, 76, 77, 152, 154, 157: Auf den linken Rand wird offensichtlich dann ausgewichen, wenn die untere Hälfte der Rückseite und der obere Rand voll sind mit Siegelabrollungen. Der rechte Rand steht hierfür meistens nicht zur Verfügung, weil er die Enden der überlangen Zeilen aufnehmen muß. Daß der linke Rand trotz der wohl freigebliebenen Rückseite gesiegelt ist, und daß das Siegel des Schreibers auch dort noch einmal abgerollt ist, könnte mit den Problemen zusammenhängen, die bei der Platzberechnung der Tafel aufgetreten sind (siehe dazu D. Prechel, oben).

Abb. 8: Das Siegel Zilib-abus, Müller 1998: Taf. CVIII Nr. 30A
(Umzeichnung U. Löw)

Bibliographie

David, Martin/Ebeling, Erich

1929 *Assyrische Rechtsurkunden*, Stuttgart: Enke

Koschaker, Paul

1911 *Babylonisch-assyrisches Bürgschaftsrecht*, Leipzig/Berlin: Teubner

1928 *Neue keilschriftliche Rechtsurkunden aus der El-Amarna-Zeit*. Leipzig: Hirzel

Matthews, Donald M.

1990 *Principles of Composition in Near Eastern Glyptic of the Later Second Millennium B.C.*, Freiburg/Schweiz: Universitätsverlag, Göttingen: Vandenhoeck & Ruprecht (Orbis Biblicus et Orientalis, Series Archaeologica 8)

1992 *The Kassite Glyptic of Nippur*, Freiburg/Schweiz: Universitätsverlag, Göttingen: Vandenhoeck & Ruprecht (Orbis Biblicus et Orientalis 116)

Müller, Gerfrid G.W.

1998 *Londoner Nuzi-Texte*, Wiesbaden: Harrassowitz (SANTAG 4)

Owen, David I.

1970 "The Loan Documents from Nuzu," Ann Arbor: University Microfilms

Petschow, Herbert

1956 *Neubabylonisches Pfandrecht*, Berlin: Akademie-Verlag

Stein, Diana L.

1993 *The Seal Impressions*, Wiesbaden: Harrassowitz (Das Archiv des Šilwa-Teššup 8–9)

Wilhelm, Gernot

1970 *Untersuchungen zum Ḫurro-Akkadischen von Nuzi*, Kevelaer: Butzon & Bercker (Alter Orient und Altes Testament 9)

1992 *Darlehensurkunden und verwandte Texte*, Wiesbaden: Harrassowitz (Das Archiv des Šilwa-Teššup 4)

Hurritologische Miszellen[1]

INGEBORG RÖSELER
Julius-Maximilians-Universität, Würzburg

The Allaiturahhe ritual from Boğazköy contains several quasi-bilingual passages that establish the meanings of five Hurrian words: *hežalli*, „colleague"; *eari*, „lion"; *zani* or *ani*, „fear"; *palali*, „horror"; and *tuinn-* „boil" (tr.). By the same token, three ghost words have been eliminated: **šalli-* ChS I/5, 2 Vs. 24'; **šumki* ChS I/5, 2 Rs. 89'; and **zi-né-e-a* ChS I/5, 23 II 16'. This study provides the evidence for these conclusions.

1. *hežalli* „Kollege"

Die Rituale der Beschwörerin Allaiturahhe aus Mukiš wurden von V. Haas und I. Wegner in Umschrift wiedergegeben[2] und zuletzt von V. Haas ausführlicher behandelt[3]. Die Beschwörungsworte gegen die „wütenden Augen" liegen in ChS I/5, 2 Vs. in hurritischer Sprache vor und haben eine hethitische Parallelstelle in ChS I/5, 15 III 2'ff. Die zu beschwörenden „wütenden Augen" sind die einzelner Gottheiten (hurr.: ChS I/5, 2 Vs. 12'–16'; heth.: ChS I/5, 15 III 2'–5') sowie diejenigen einzelner Menschen bzw. Gruppen von Menschen (hurr.:ChS I/5, 2 Vs. 17'–26'; heth.: ChS I/5, 15 III 18'–26'). Der hethitische Text zählt die „wütenden Augen des Landes, des Königs, der Königin, der Stadt, des Hauses, des Vaters, der Mutter, der Großen, des Bürgermeisters, des Herrn der Verwaltung, der Pagen, der Menge, des Hausgesindes" auf. Der hurritische Text ist leider so fragmentarisch, daß nicht für alle diese Wörter eine Entsprechung festgestellt werden kann. Eine der Personen, deren „wütende Augen" die

---

1 Der vorliegende Aufsatz wurde durch ein Seminar im Institut für Orientalische Philologie der Universität Würzburg im Wintersemester 1997/98 angeregt. Herrn Prof. G. Wilhelm danke ich für eine kritische Durchsicht des Manuskripts und manche Anregungen.

2 V. Haas und I. Wegner, *Die Rituale der Beschwörerinnen* ^{SAL}ŠU.GI (ChS I/5), Roma 1988.

3 V. Haas, „Die hurritisch-hethitischen Rituale der Beschwörerin Allaiturah(h)i und ihr literarhistorischer Hintergrund", in: V. Haas (Hrsg.), *Hurriter und Hurritisch* (Xenia 21), Konstanz: Universitätsverlag 1988, 117–43.

Studies on the Civilization and Culture of Nuzi and the Hurrians - 10

Beschwörerin „wegwischt", ist mit *ḫe/ižalli* bezeichnet (ChS I/5, 2 Vs. 24'): *ḫi-ša-al-li-ip-wi*$_i$*-na* KI.MIN.[4]

Die Form lautet in analytischer Umschrift *ḫe/ižalli=p=pe=na*, sie weist also dieselben Suffixe auf wie—nach einer weiteren Lücke in Zeile 25'—das Wort *purammi=p=pe=na*, d.h. das Possessivsuffix der 2. Pers. sg., das Genitivsuffix und das Pluralsuffix *-na*, welches Kongruenz zum im Absolutiv Plural stehenden Bezugswort herstellt (KI.MIN, d.h. „wütende Augen").

Ein Wort *ḫežalli-* ist in Mit IV 121 belegt[5]: *še-e-en-n[u-u]ḫ-ḫa ḫé-šal-lu-uḫ-ḫa-a-til-la-a-an ta-a-du-ka-a-ri-iš.*

> *šēnn(i)=o=ḫḫ(e)=a: šenni*, die häufig in PN bezeugte Form von *šena* „Bruder" mit individualisierendem Suffix *-ni*[6], ist in Ugarit auch lexikalisch bezeugt[7]. Es folgt der Derivationsvokal *-o-* vor dem Zugehörigkeitssuffix *-ḫḫe* und der Essivendung: „in brüderlicher Art und Weise";
>
> *ḫežall(i)=o=ḫḫ(e)=ā=dill(a)=ān*: Das zu besprechende Wort mit denselben Suffixen sowie zusätzlich dem enklitischen Pronomen der 1. Pers.pl. und dem Konnektiv: „und in ... Art und Weise wir";
>
> *tād=ugār=i=ž*: Wurzel *tād-* „lieben", erweitert um das Suffix der Reziprozität; die Suffixe *-i-* und *-ž* (Plural) zusammen mit dem enklitischen Pronomen der 1. Ps. Pl. am vorausgehenden Wort geben der Form die Bedeutung eines Voluntativs: „wir wollen einander lieben".

Diese Textstelle zeigt, daß es sich bei dem Begriff *ḫežalli* nicht um einen Bediensteten oder Untergebenen handeln kann, sondern nach der Sprache des Mittani-Briefes nur um einen Gleichgestellten. Die Nebeneinanderstellung der Begriffe *šēnn(i)=o=ḫḫ(e)=a* und *ḫežall(i)=o=ḫḫ(e)=a* könnte zunächst zu der Vermutung führen, daß hier der neue Verwandtschaftsgrad angesprochen ist, der Amenophis III. und Tušratta durch die Heirat des Pharao mit der Tochter des Mittani-Königs verbindet. In eine andere Richtung führt jedoch das neue

---

4 V. Haas und I. Wegner (s.o.) haben bei der Transkription der Stelle das Zeichen *ḫi* zum vorherigen Wort gezogen: *...l]i(-)⸢pu⸣?(-)ú-mu-uš-ši-ḫi ša-al-li-ip-wi*$_i$*-na* ..., merken aber an: „Oder: ⸢SAL⸣*ú-mu-uš-ši*"; so auch in der Letztbearbeitung von V. Haas, in V. Haas (Hrsg.), *Hurriter und Hurritisch*, 122. E. Laroche, *GLH*, 103, bucht die Stelle nach der Keilschriftedition (KBo XXIII 23,6) als *ḫi-ša-al-li-iw-wi*$_i$*-na.*

5 So bereits von E. Laroche, l.c., gebucht.

6 S. zuletzt G. Wilhelm, „Name, Namengebung. D. Bei den Hurritern", *RlA* 9/1.–2. Lfg. (1998) 124 f.

7 RS 21.62 Vo. 19' (*Ugaritica* 5, 239), s. J. Huehnergard, *Ugaritic Vocabulary in Syllabic Transcription* (HSS 32), Atlanta: Scholars Press, 1987, 34 f., No. 159.1; RS 94-2939 IV 10', s. B. André-Salvini und M. Salvini, „Un nouveau vocabulaire trilingue sumérien-akkadien-hourrite de Ras Shamra", *SCCNH* 9 (1998) 7. (Die dort S. 16 gebotene Analyse ist nicht zutreffend; es gibt kein Thema **šeni*, sondern nur den Konsonantstamm *šen*, den *a*-Stamm *šēna* und die Form mit dem individualisierenden Suffix *-ni šen=ni.*)

dreisprachige Exemplar von Sª aus Ugarit RS 94-2939[8], das in Kol. III 20 die folgenden Entsprechungen aufweist:

sum. TAB || akk. *tap-pu* || ḫurr. ⌜*ḫi/še*?*-ša*?*-al*?*-li*?⌝.

Die Editoren halten die Lesung *ḫi* zwar für wahrscheinlicher, favorisieren aber andererseits die Lesung *še*, da ein Wort *še-eš-ša-al-li* bzw. [*še-š*]*a-al-li-ni* in ChS I/1 9 IV 2 bzw. IV 4 belegt ist. Das akkadische Wort *tappû* in der Bedeutung „Genosse, Gefährte, Kompagnon, Kollege" (*AHw* 1321b) zielt auf die Gleichrangigkeit einer Beziehung ab, wie sie in der besprochenen Stelle des Mittani-Briefes gefordert wird. Bei der Lesung der Vokabularstelle sollte daher **še-ša-al-li* zugunsten von *ḫi-ša-al-li* aufgegeben werden. Mit der Entsprechung *tappû* || *he/ižalli* ergibt sich etwa die folgende Übersetzung von Mit IV 121: „Wir wollen einander in brüderlicher und kollegialer Weise lieben".

Das Wort findet sich auch in dem Fragment eines Geburtsrituals (ChS I/5, 102: 5') in unklarem Kontext: *ḫe-e-ša-al-l*[*a*]. In Nuzi ist Ḫišalla/e als männlicher Personenname in verschiedenen Schreibungen belegt[9]. Als Element in zusammengesetzten Namen liegt der Begriff nicht vor.

2. **šumgi*

Das *Corpus der hurritischen Sprachdenkmäler* bucht ein Wort ⌜*šu*⌝*-um-ki-i*[10] in einem Beschwörungsritual, das dem Allaiturahhe-Ritual zuzuordnen ist und von V. Haas als hurritische Vorlage für Teile der 5. und 6. Tafel der letzteren erkannt wurde. Auf die zitierten Zeichen folgen die hethitischen Wörter *ḫuppanniiaš uddār* „Worte des *ḫuppani*-Steins".

In der vorausgehenden Beschwörung, auf die der hethitische Vermerk Bezug nimmt (ChS I/5, 2 Rs. 84'–89'), begegnen mehrfach Verbalformen mit der Wurzel *pirž-*[11]: 85': *bi-ir-ša-am*, 86': *bi-ir-ša-ap*, 86': *bi-ir-šu-um*, 87': *bi*]*-ir-šu-um*,

---

8 S. Anm. 7.

9 *NPN* 60b. Der Name lautet überwiegend auf *-a* aus, seltener auf *-e/i*. In einem Fall scheint derselbe Namensträger einmal mit *-a* und einmal mit *-e/i* geschrieben zu sein: IGI *Ḫi-šal-la-a* DUMU *Pal-te-šup* (JEN 219:21) ᵐ*Ḫé-šal-le/i* DUMU *Pal-te-šup* (JEN 514:5). Die häufigen Schreibungen des Namens mit *ḫé* deuten darauf hin, daß ebenso wie im Mittani-Brief der erste Vokal als *e* anzusetzen ist.

10 V. Haas / I. Wegner, *Die Rituale der Beschwörerinnen* ˢᴬᴸŠU.GI. *Teil II: Das Glossar* (ChS I/5), Roma 1988, 57, letzte Zeile, bezogen auf die Textstelle ChS I/5, 2 Rs. 89', die als]*ši-bi-*⌜*ni*⌝ ⌜*šu*⌝*-um-ki-i* wiedergegeben wird. Ähnlich ( ]*-ši-bi-ni šu*(?)*-um-ki-i*) bereits V. Haas / H.J. Thiel, *Die Beschwörungsrituale der Allaituraḫ(ḫ)i und verwandte Texte* (AOAT 31), Kevelaer/ Neukirchen-Vluyn: Neukirchener Verlag, 1978, 212 Z. 71'.

11 In der korrespondierenden hethitischen Passsage ChS I/5, 19 I 56–62 begegnen dreimal Formen des Verbs *lā-* „lösen" (DU_8*-it* Z. 59, 61, [(*la-a*)]*-iš-ki-*⌜*ia-at*⌝ 62), das daher wohl mit *pirž-* gleichzusetzen ist. G. Wilhelm weist mich darauf hin, daß zu derselben Wurzel wahrscheinlich ein unbezeugtes Nomen **pirža* gehört, welches der Bezeichnung einer bei Zizza im mittleren Osttigrisland gelegenen *dimtu* („Turmbereich") Pirža=ḫḫe, Pirža=nni zugrundeliegt (s. dazu J. Fincke, *Die Orts- und Gewässernamen der Nuzi-Texte* [RGTC 10], Wiesbaden 1993, 224 ff.). Möglicherweise ist *pirž-* mit der Wurzel *fir-* „lösen" zu verbinden.

88': *bi-ir-š*]*u-um*. Mit einer solchen Verbalform enden auch die Beschwörungsworte, denn das auf *bi-* folgende Zeichen kann, wie die Schraffur in der Autographie zeigt, außer ⸢*ni*⸣ auch ⸢*ir*⸣ gelesen werden. Der Befund ist nur dadurch verunklart, daß die Verbalform nicht durch Spatien abgetrennt ist. Bei dem folgenden *ki-i* handelt es sich um das zum Folgenden zu ziehende hethitische Demonstrativpronomen, also „dies sind die Worte des *ḫuppani*-Steines". **šumki* erweist sich damit als „ghost-word".

3. *eari* „Löwe"

ChS I/5, 19, eine bis auf die IV. Kolumne durchgehend hethitischsprachige, großenteils erhaltene Tafel, die V. Haas zufolge als die 6. des Rituals der ^{MUNUS}ŠU.GI Allaituraḫḫe von Mukiš bestimmt werden kann[12], hat in längeren Passagen quasi-bilingue Entsprechungen in Ritualen mit hurritischen Beschwörungen. In einigen Fällen sind die Entsprechungen evident[13], in anderen sind derzeit nur Anklänge zu erkennen. Nach der synoptischen Textzusammenstellung von V. Haas[14] entsprechen sich ChS I/5, 19 III 34–48 (hethitisch) und ChS I/5, 23 II 3'–16' (hurritisch)[15]. In der Tat sind sowohl in dem beiden Versionen gemeinsamen hethitischen Passus ChS I/5, 19 III 40–41 // ChS I/5, 23 II 8'–9' als auch in der Abfolge von Götternamen (^{D}Ḫebat - ^{D}IŠTAR - ^{D}Ea ChS I/5, 19 III 44–46, 23 II 12', 14') und im Vokabular (DINGIR^{MEŠ}-*uš* - LUGAL^{MEŠ}-*i̯a-kán* ChS I/5, 19 III 34 f. // DINGIR^{MEŠ}-*na* - ⸢*e-ep*⸣-*re*-⸢*en*$_{6}$⸣-*na* 23 II 3' f., [(*ne-pí*)]⸢*ša-az*⸣- 19 III 42 // *ḫa-wu*$_{u}$*-ru-un-né-en*$_{6}$ 23 II 10') deutliche Parallelen erkennbar.

Ein Vergleich von ChS I/5, 19 III 46–48 (= KBo 12,85 III 5'–7') mit ChS I/5, 23 (= KBo 19,139) II 14'–16' eröffnet die Möglichkeit, die beiden Versionen noch enger zu verknüpfen und dabei ein weiteres hurritisches Lexem zu gewinnen.

(1)	ChS I/5, 19 III 46:	*na-at PA-NI* ⸢^{D}⸣É.A *ma-uš-ta*
	ChS I/5, 23 II 14':	^{D}É.A-*wa*$_{a}$ *ḫa*-⸢*šar*⸣-*ri a*-[*bi-d*]*a*$^{!?}$ *ku-du*[*r*]-*ri*
	Heth.:	„und es fiel vor Ea"
(2)	ChS I/5, 19 III 46–47:	⸢Ì⸣$^{?}$[.DÙG.GA$^{?}$] *za-nu-ut*
	ChS I/5, 23 II 14'–15':	⸢^{D}⸣É.A-*aš* ⸢*ḫa*⸣-*šar-ri du-ú-en-nu*-⸢*un*⸣[(*-ni/na*)?]
	Heth.:	„Ö[l(?)] kochte er"
(3)	ChS I/5, 19 III 47–48:	*nu* ⸢IGI-*an-da*⸣ *ŠA* ⸢UR.MAḪ⸣ *na-aḫ-š*[*a-ra-at-ta-an*] *ŠA* MUŠ-*ia* ⸢*ú-e-ri*⸣-*te-ma-an* ...
	ChS I/5, 23 II 15'–16':	⸢*za*⸣/⸢*a*⸣-*na-a-i e-a-ar-re-e-a* [*a*]*p*-⸢*še*⸣-*né-e-a pa-la-la-a*-⸢*e*$^{?}$⸣

---

12 Erstmals in V. Haas / H.J. Thiel, *Die Rituale der Allaituraḫ(ḫ)e*, 16, 181.

13 Cf. V. Haas, in: V. Haas (Hrsg.), *Hurriter und Hurritisch*, 120–24.

14 V. Haas / H.J. Thiel, *Die Beschwörungsrituale der Allaituraḫ(ḫ)i*, 129–53.

15 Cf. auch V. Haas, in: V. Haas (Hrsg.), *Hurriter und Hurritisch*, 128 f.

Heth.: „und gegenüber, das Furchterregende des Löwen und das Schreckeneinflößende der Schlange ..."[16]

Zu (1): Die Ergänzung der Postposition *ab(i)=i=da*, die den Dativ regiert, beruht auf der hethitischen Fassung; *ab(i)=i=da*, wenn richtig ergänzt, steht hier nicht direkt hinter dem Bezugswort, sondern ist vielmehr von ihm durch *ḫažarri* getrennt, wie dies auch in KBo 32 13 I 11 belegt ist: ^{D}IŠKUR-*up-pa pí-du-úw-wa*$_{a}$ *a-wi*$_{i}$*-ta* „sie drehte sich vor dem Wettergott"[17].

In der hethitischen Fassung ist das Subjekt nur durch das Pronomen *-at* repräsentiert. Der hurritische Text nennt hier wie auch in der folgenden Zeile sowie zweimal am Anfang der Beschwörung *ḫažarri*. Dieses Wort ist offenkundig der Schlüsselbegriff dieser Beschwörung. Trotz der Doppelschreibung muß es mit *ḫažari* „Öl" identifiziert werden, denn die vorherige hethitische Ritualanweisung spricht von der Salbung des Opfermandanten (*nu=za iškizzi* „er salbt sich" ChS I/5, 23 II 9'), und die ^{MUNUS}ŠU.GI spricht dazu die hier behandelte Beschwörung, die sich durch die einleitenden Worte *a-ú-u-ni an-ni* ⸢*ḫa*⸣*-a-šar-*[*ri* ..] „Siehe(?), dieses Öl ..." (Z. 10') und die stete weitere Bezugnahme auf Öl in mythologischem Zusammenhang als eine Kultmittelbeschwörung zu erkennen gibt. Dieses Öl—auch die hethitische Fassung ChS I/5, 19 III 42 spricht hier wahrscheinlich von Öl: VBoT 120 III 19 lies wohl *ku-*⸢*it* Ì.DÙG⸣.[GA][18]—stammt anscheinend „vom Himmel" [(*ne-pí*)]⸢*ša-az*⸣- 19 III 42 // *ḫa-wu*$_{u}$*-ru-un-né-en*$_{6}$ 23 II 10'.

Die Entsprechung von hurr. *kudurri* und heth. *maušta* erlaubt es, die hurritische Form von der aus der hurritisch-hethitischen Parabelsammlung KBo 32,14 bekannten Wurzel *kud-* abzuleiten, die sowohl als transitives Verb „fällen" wie auch als intransitives „fallen" verwendet wird[19]. Das Wort *kudurre* in ChS I/5, 23 II 5' (Schreibung: ⸢*ku*⸣*-dur-*⸢*e*⸣) ist in ChS I/5, 19 III 36–37 mit hethitisch ⸢*ku-it-kán ne-pí*⸣-[*ša-az*] *kat-*⸢*ta ú-it*⸣ wiedergegeben; hier entspricht hurr. *kud-* also heth. *katta uu̯a-* „herabkommen"[20].

---

16 Cf. *CHD* L-N, 344b: „opposite, [he ...-ed] the lion's fearsomeness and the snake's ability to terrify".

17 Cf. dazu I.M. Rowe: „The interpretation of Hurrian *pid=(u)u̯a* in the light of Hittite, Akkadian and Urartian data", *Aula Orientalis* 14 (1996) 283–84.

18 Zum hethitischen Wort für „Öl" s. H.A. Hoffner, Jr., „The Hittite word for 'Oil' and Its Derivatives", *HS* 107 (1994) 222–30.

19 G. Wilhelm, „Hurritische Lexikographie und Grammatik", *Or*NS 61 (1992) 131.

20 Die übrigen hethitischen Wiedergaben des hurritischen Textes in ChS I/5 Nr. 19 III 36–37 divergieren teilweise stark; als Entsprechungen können gelten: (1) Hurr. *en=na* „Götter" (DINGIR^{MEŠ}*-na* ChS I/5, 23 II 3') und heth. DINGIR^{MEŠ}*-uš* ChS I/5, 19 III 34 (zur Lesung s. G. Beckman, *BiOr* 48 [1991] 587); (2) hurr. *evren=na* „Könige" (⸢*e-ep*⸣*-re-*⸢*en*$_{6}$⸣*-na* ChS I/5, 23 II 4') und heth. LUGAL^{MEŠ}*-i̯a-kán* ChS I/5, 19 III 35; (3) hurr. *ōmīni* „Land, Bevölkerung" (*u-mi-ne* ChS I/5, 23 II 6') und ⸢DUMU.LÚ⸣.U$_{19}$.LU*-aš* „Mensch(enkind)" ChS I/5, 19 III 36 (VBoT 120 III 13; zur Lesung s. E. Neu, *Or* 60 [1991] 378); (4) hurr. *kunduri* (⸢*ku*⸣-[*u*]*n-*⸢*du*⸣*-u-ri* ChS I/5, 23 II 5') liegt anscheinend der heth. Übersetzung ⸢*ne-pí*⸣-[*ša-az*] „vom Himmel" (ChS I/5, 19 III 36) zugrunde; V. Haas und H.-J. Thiel, *Die Beschwörungsrituale der Allaituraḫ(ḫ)i*, 199

Die grammatikalische Deutung der Form *kudurri/e* ist schwierig. Es könnte sich um das patiensorientierte Partizip auf *-aure* handeln[21], wobei der Diphtong monophtongisiert ist. Eine solche Monophtongisierung von *-aure* ist vielleicht auch für das Wort *ḫuž=aure* „Gefangener“[22] anzunehmen, wenn das dreimal bezeugte, allerdings nicht kontextbestimmte Wort *ḫu-(u-)šu-ur-ra-(a)-ša*[23] (Nomen im Dat. pl.: =**n*(*a*)=*až*=*a*) hier angeschlossen werden darf (*ḫuž=aure* >? *ḫuž=ure*). Man könnte auch erwägen, ob hier ein bisher nicht beobachtetes Partizip des intransitiven Verbs vorliegt, welches in Parallelität zu dem Partizip des transitiven Verbs auf *-iri*[24] wie im Urartäischen mit einem Vokal *-o/u-* gebildet ist (urart. *uš-tu-(ú-)ri* „zu Felde gezogen seiend“ HchI 103 § 8 III, UKN 155 E 43 und *ka-ú-ri* „überquert habend“ UKN 158:7[25] sowie vom Zustandsverb *man- man=uri* „vorhanden seiend“, *passim*). Schwierig zu erklären ist auch die Doppelkonsonanz; vielleicht handelt es sich um ein graphisch-phonologisches Phänomen ohne morphologischen Hintergrund, wie es wohl auch bei *ḫa-šar-ri* in demselben Text Z. 11', 14' und 15' (s.o., Absolutiv: *ḫāžari*) der Fall ist.

---

bieten dafür die Übersetzung „Göttergemach“, was auf Gleichsetzung mit heth. ^{É}*kuntarra-* bzw. einem diesem wohl zugrundeliegenden hurr. *kundāri* beruht (s. dazu E. Laroche, *GLH* 154, und J. Tischler, *HEG* I, 635 mit Lit.).

Darüber hinaus schlägt G. Wilhelm folgende Entsprechungen vor: Hurr. ⸢*šu*⸣-[*u*(*ḫ-ḫ*)*u*]-⸢*un-ni*⸣ (ChS I/5, 23 II 6', erg. nach ChS I/5, 24:17') und heth. $^{\text{⸢MUNUS⸣}}$ÙMMEDA „Amme, Kinderwärterin“ (ChS I/5, 19 III 39), was zu *šuḫḫ-* „säugen“ passe, welches seinerseits aus *šuḫḫ=ar-* (*šu-uḫ*$_5$*-ḫa-ar*[- AdŠ 122:28, folgt auf den Namen einer Frau, die an anderer Stelle als *mušēniqtu* bezeichnet wird, s. G. Wilhelm, AdŠ 3 [1985] 85) und *šuḫḫ=ar=amb=aš=ḫe* „Ammenlohn, Ammenverköstigung“ (Essiv: Getreide *šu-uḫ*$_5$*-ḫa-ra-am-pa-áš-ḫa-a* AdŠ 109:19; *šu-ḫa-ra-am-pa-áš-ḫa* AdŠ 109:49, s. dazu K. Deller, *Or*NS 53 (1984) 107; anders, aber wegen des hier besprochenen Belegs aus Boğazköy irrig, G. Wilhelm, AdŠ 3 [1985] 85; zur Bildungsweise s. J. Fincke, *SCCNH* 7 [1995] 6–12 mit Deutung *teġ=amb=aš=ḫe* „Zahlung für das Aufziehen von Säuglingen“).—Die folgenden—durch Spatium abgetrennten!—fünf Zeichen ⸢*bi-ni-ia-aš-ši*⸣ (Duplikat ChS I/5, 24: 17' mit *wa*$_a$*-ni-i-e-an* abweichend) sei eine nominalisierte Verbalform wie *ašḫ=i=a=šše* „Opfermandant“, wörtl. „e., der opfert“, *am=om=i=a=šše* „Würdenträger“, wörtl. „e., der (etwas) beaufsichtigt“, *tād=i=a=šše* „Liebende“, wörtl. „e., die (jdn.) liebt“; sie entspreche heth. ⸢*ku-iš*⸣ ... ⸢*kar*⸣*-pa-an* [*ḫar-zi*] (ChS I/5, 19 III 39), woraus demnach—Korrektheit der ansonsten stark fehlerhaften Überlieferung unterstellt—eine Wurzel *p/fin-* oder *p/fen-* mit der Bedeutung „hochheben“ gewonnen werden könne; zu vergleichen sei (am Anfang einer Zeile!) *bi-na-a-nu-šu* (ChS I/5, 23 III 14) mit Dupl. *wi*$_i$*-na-nu*$^!$*-u*$^!$*-*⸢*šu*⸣$^{!?}$ (ChS I/5, 19 IV 7).—*ḫa-ni-ik-*[ ]*-an* sei als *kk*-Erweiterung von *ḫani* „Kind“ zu verstehen wie *aštakka* zu *ašti* „Frau“, *taḫḫakka* zu *taḫḫe* „Mann“, LUGAL-*ka* „König“ (Lesung auf Grund eines unv. Textes aus Emar nach frdl. Mitteilung von M. Salvini *evernakka*) und Ziel der in der nominalisierten Verbalform beschriebenen Handlung.

21 G. Wilhelm, „Gedanken zur Frühgeschichte der Hurriter und zum hurritisch-urartäischen Sprachvergleich“ in: V. Haas (Hrsg.), *Hurriter und Hurritisch*, 53–67.

22 Cf. G. Wilhelm, in: V. Haas (Hrsg.), *Hurriter und Hurritisch*, 57–62.

23 E. Laroche, *GLH*, 116.

24 Cf. G. Wilhelm, in: V. Haas (Hrsg.), *Hurriter und Hurritisch*, 55–57.

25 Cf. M. van Loon, „The Euphrates mentioned by Sarduri II of Urartu“, *Anatolian Studies Presented to Hans Gustav Güterbock*, Istanbul 1974, 187–94.

Die hurritische Fassung von Kolon (1) (ChS I/5, 23 II 14') ist demnach folgendermaßen zu übersetzen: „Vor Ea war das Öl herabgefallen(?)".

Zu (2): Der Satz besteht aus einem Ergativ (*Ea=ž*), einem Absolutiv (*ḫāžarri* „Öl") und der schwierig zu deutenden Form *tūennun*[ ], in der das Prädikat gesucht werden muß. In der hethitischen Fassung ist die Entsprechung dieses Satzes bis auf das Prädikat *zanut* „er kochte" ChS I/5, 19 III 47 abgebrochen.

Die Wurzel des hurritischen Verbs müßte *tu-*, *tue-* oder *tuenn-* lauten, wobei im letzteren Falle wohl bereits eine Wurzelerweiterung enthalten wäre.[26]

Die hurritische Fassung von Kolon (2) (ChS I/5, 23 II 14' f.) ist also zu übersetzen: „Ea kochte das Öl".

Zu (3): Falls zum Prädikat des vorausgehenden Satzes (*du-ú-en-nu-*⌜*un*⌝) noch—wie es wahrscheinlich ist—ein weiteres Zeichen gehört (eventuell *-nna* Pron. 3. Ps. Sg.?), verbleibt für den Anfang des ersten Wortes von Kolon (3) so wenig Raum, daß nach den Zeichenspuren nur ⌜*a*⌝- oder [*z*]*a-*, eventuell ⌜*e*⌝- in Frage kommen. Die Endung deutet auf einen Instrumental auf *-ai*.

Das folgende Wort, *e-a-ar-re-e-a*, enthält den assimilierten Relator, wofür besonders die Pleneschreibung des e-Vokals spricht, also: *ear*(*i*)=*re*=*a*. Dieselbe Endung weist das folgende Wort auf: [*a*]*p-še-né-e-a*[27]. Die Bedeutung des Wortes *apše* ist durch die neue Trilingue aus Ugarit[28] geklärt: Es ist mit sum. MUŠ und akk. *ṣīru* „Schlange" geglichen. Durch die Korrektur der Lesung und die neue Erkenntnis der Bedeutung von *apše* ergibt sich eine Übereinstimmung mit dem hethitischen Text ChS I/5, 19, der in III 48' ebenfalls das Wort für „Schlange" in der Schreibung MUŠ bietet.

Die Endung *-a*, die bei beiden Wörtern auf den Relator folgt, ist problematisch. Man könnte an einen Dativ mit jeweils ausgefallenem /*v*/ denken, doch sind hierzu bisher keine Parallelen beschrieben worden.

Das letzte Zeichen des folgenden Wortes *pa-la-la-a-*x[ ] ist nach der Kopie wahrscheinlich ⌜*e*⌝, da nur für ein Zeichen Raum vorhanden ist und

---

26 Zu einer Verbalwurzel *tu-* könnte die ergative pluralische Form *du-i-du*(*-um/-ma*) gestellt werden, die sich in ChS I/1, 11 Vs. 18–29 wiederholt neben dem Absolutiv *ḫažari* findet. Die Formen *tu-u-in-ni*(*-ib-bi*) in ChS I/1, 41 Vs. II 48 und 49 sind wohl nominal aufzufassen.

G. Wilhelm weist noch auf das Nomen *tue*, *tuve* in den Nuzi-Texten hin, das in Texten über Textilbearbeitung vorkommt (*du-e-na*.MEŠ HSS 13, 494 = AdŠ 507:15, 17, *du-e* HSS 15, 225 = AdŠ 508:1, 3, 5, 7, *du-e*[ ] HSS 15, 226 = AdŠ 509:6, [*d*]*u-ú-*[*w*]*e-né/ni* HSS 14, 250=566 = AdŠ 483:2 [alle koll.]; s. auch E. Laroche, *GLH*, 269). Es handelt sich um eine Substanz, die in Gewichtsmengen von 1–10 Sekeln ausgegeben wird und wohl zur Färbung von Wolle und Textilien dient. Eine semantische Brücke zu der hier diskutierten Verbalform könnte, so Wilhelm, der Vergleich mit akk. *bašālu* „kochen", *šubšulu* „färben" eröffnen.

27 ChS I/5, 23 II 16' bietet [*z*]*i*, doch zeigt die Kopie ein deutliches ⌜*še*⌝; auch ist der Abstand zwischen dem senkrechten Keil und dem folgenden Keilkomplex im Vergleich zu ZI drei Zeilen zuvor deutlich größer.

28 B. André-Salvini und M. Salvini, *SCCNH* 9 (1998) 7, 9 f.

demzufolge nach der Analogie von ⌜*za*⌝/⌜*a*⌝*-na-a-i* Z. 15' am ehesten ebenfalls die Instrumentalendung *-ae/i* anzusetzen ist. Für *palal(i)=ae* ergibt sich aus dem Vergleich mit der hethitischen Fassung ein Wort für „Schrecken" oder „Schreckeneinflößendes", und entsprechend läge in *zan(i)=ai* oder *an(i)=ai* dann ein Wort für „Furcht" oder „Furchteinflößendes" vor. Anders als in der hethitischen Fassung stehen die beiden Wortgruppen *za/an=ai ear=re=a* und [*a*]*pše=ne=a palal=ae*? in Chiasmus zueinander, was wohl als literarisches Stilmittel gedeutet werden kann. Die hethitische Übersetzung konstruiert UR.MAḪ „Löwe" und MUŠ „Schlange" als Genitive zu *naḫ-š*[*arattan*] „das Furchterregende" bzw. *weriteman* „das Schreckeneinflößende" (beide im Akkusativ) und weicht damit von der Konstruktion des hurritischen Textes ab.

Nach dieser Interpretation ergibt sich für das hurritische Wort *eari* die Bedeutung „Löwe". Die Wörter *apše* „Schlange" und *eari* stehen im Festritual zur Reinigung des Tempelgeräts, direkt nebeneinander: ChS I/9[29], 75 (KBo 35, 140), Z. 19': ⌜*e*⌝*-ri i-ia-a-ri ap-še š*[(*e-e-ri ša-a-ri*)]. Ein Zusammenhang zwischen den beiden Lexemen scheint auch in CHS I/5, 87 gegeben zu sein, wo in Vs. II 22' *ap-še-ne-we*$_e$ *ir-ḫa-a-ri* (*apše=ne=ve irḫari*) die „Schlange" im Genitiv Sg. zu einem Nomen im Absolutiv Sg. vorliegt und in Vs. II 25'–26' *e-ia-ar-re-we*$_e$*-na-ma kúl-we*$_e$*-na-a-ma* (*ear(i)=re=ve=na=ma kulve=nā=ma*); möglicherweise handelt es sich aber auch um zwei unabhängige Nomina, da an beide Worte das Konnektiv *-ma* suffigiert ist, wobei *ear(i)=ve-* dann als freischwebender Genitiv aufzufassen wäre. In dem mantischen Text ChS I/7, 40[30] (KBo 8, 146), Z. 3' findet sich dasselbe Wort in der Schreibung *e-ia-ar-re*[*-eš*$_{15}$?][31]. In Zeile 5' des Textes steht *pé-e-ta-ar-re-eš*$_{15}$ (*pidari* „Rind", Ergativ: *pidar(i)=re=ž*). Die Parallelität läßt vermuten, daß hier mit *ear(i)=re=ž* ebenfalls ein (mächtiges) Tier gemeint ist, was gut zu dem Ansatz „Löwe" paßt. Ein Zusammenhang mit hebr. *ʾarī* „Löwe" ist wahrscheinlich[32].

Weitere Belege bleiben wegen der Unverständlichkeit des Kontextes unsicher. So erscheint in ChS I/5, 132 (= KUB 32, 31) Z. 4' ein *e-a-ru-*WA, das dieselbe Endung aufweist wie in der folgenden Zeile *ḫa-še-ru-*WA (wohl zu *ḫažeri* „Dolch"). Noch unsicherer—und wohl kaum unter Heranziehung des hier diskutierten Lexems zu deuten—ist die Stelle aus einer Beschwörung aus Mari: [*k*]*u-um-di* ⌜*i*⌝*-ia-ru-*⌜*e*⌝ „Turm des/r ..." Mari hurr. 1:15, see F. Thureau-Dangin, „Tablettes hurrites provenant de Mâri", *RA* 36 (1939) 4.—In unverständlichem Kontext finden sich noch *i-ia-ra* (ChS I/1, 65 II 11' mit Parallelstelle 66:8'), *i-ia-ri* (ChS I/1, 43 I 21'), *i-ia-a-ri* (ChS I/1, 11 Vs. 17'), [ ]*ia-a-ri-ia* (KUB 27, 29 IV 2), *i-ia-a-ri a*[*p*?*-še*??] (KBo 33, 169 r. Kol. 13).

---

29 V. Haas, *Die hurritischen Ritualtermini in hethitischem Kontext* (ChS I/9), Roma 1998.

30 St. de Martino, *Die mantischen Texte* (ChS I/7), Roma 1998; der Text ist dort unter „Die Zeichen des Rindes" eingeordnet.

31 Die Doppelkonsonanz deutet auf einen assimilierten Relator *-ne* > *-re*, die Ergänzung zum Ergativ erfolgte aufgrund der Ergativendung von *pé-e-ta-ar-re-eš*$_{15}$ in Zeile 5' desselben Textes.

32 Frdl. Hinweis Jared Miller.

Öle und Fette in Nuzi

HELGA SCHNEIDER-LUDORFF
Johann Wolfgang Goethe-Universität Frankfurt/Main

Oil was one of the most important commodities in antiquity. Nuzi was situated in an area of sesame cultivation and the sesame seeds were processed for their oil. Sesame oil was stored in various kinds of containers and was used for many purposes. This article discusses the data from the Nuzi archives that relate to sesame production and use.

In den altorientalischen Kulturen gehörten Salböle neben Nahrung und Kleidung zum täglichen Bedarf der Menschen. Sie dienten gegen die Austrocknung der Haut, gegen Sandreiz und Insektenplagen. Öle wurden neben der Körperpflege außerdem noch genutzt bei der Zubereitung von Heilmitteln[1], zum Kochen, für Beleuchtungszwecke, zur Herstellung von Seifen, um nur einige Anwendungen zu nennen[2].

Daneben spielten die aromatischen Öle eine große Rolle bei den Kulthandlungen für die Götter, bei Bestattungszeremonien sowie bei anderen symbolischen Handlungen wie beispielsweise Grundsteinlegungen von Tempeln und Palästen[3].

Besonders aus dem alten Ägypten ist bekannt, daß dort eine besondere Vorliebe auch für duftende Salben, Schminken und Parfümwässer bestand[4]. So ist auch die Herstellung der wohlriechenden Salböle eine Erfindung des Vorderen Orients[5].

---

1 Dietlinde Goltz, *Studien zur altorientalischen und griechischen Heilkunde. Therapie—Arzneibereitung—Rezeptstruktur.* 1974.

2 Postgate über die Bedeutung des Öls zitiert Frankena, *Tākultu: de sacrale Maaltijd in het Assyrische Ritueel* (1954) 8: Col. x.29–34: „Yet it (the oil) was important enough to figure in a list of the essentials of a good life: 'corn, silver, oil, wool, salt for your meals and a wick (?) for your lamps'."

3 Die Gründungstafeln wurden nach den Bauinschriften mit Öl und Honig übergossen.

4 R.J. Forbes, *Studies in Ancient Technology*, Vol. III, 2. Siehe auch Emmerich Paszthory, „Laboratorien in ptolemäischen Tempelanlagen", *Antike Welt* 1988/2, S. 2–20.

5 Für die mittelassyrischen Rezepte zur Bereitung von wohlriechenden Salben s. E.

Studies on the Civilization and Culture of Nuzi and the Hurrians - 10

Fette und Öle sind Substanzen, die tierischen oder pflanzlichen Ursprungs sein können. Das Wort „Öl" selbst ist eine Sammelbezeichnung für wasserunlösliche, hydrophobe, bei Raumtemperatur flüssige organische Verbindungen, deren gemeinsames Merkmal nicht die chemische Zusammensetzung, sondern die ähnliche physikalische Konsistenz ist. Sowohl bei den pflanzlichen als auch den tierischen fetten Ölen handelt es sich um Glyceride gesättigter und ungesättigter Fettsäuren. Bei den ätherischen Ölen handelt es sich dagegen um flüchtige pflanzliche Riechstoffe von unterschiedlicher chemischer Zusammensetzung[6].

Der wichtigste pflanzliche Öllieferant in Nuzi war Sesam. Bereits um 2000 v.Chr. muß das Ost-Tigris-Gebiet ein wichtiges Anbaugebiet von Sesam gewesen sein[7]. Auf die Bedeutung des Sesamanbaus im Königreich Arrapḫa weist die in den Texten von Nuzi erwähnte Stadt ŠE.Ì.GIŠ-*we* bzw. *Šamšammue* hin[8]. Der Sesamanbau läßt sich außerdem in den Texten von Nuzi nachweisen; so ist durch HSS 14,72 die Ausgabe von Saatgut für Sesam (ŠE.Ì.GIŠ *ana* NUMUN) an eine Reihe von Persönlichkeiten, die teilweise auch in entfernteren Städten des Königreichs Arrapḫa lebten, belegt, darunter auch an die *ēntu* von Abenaš. Leider wird hier nicht angegeben, in welchem Monat die Ausgabe erfolgte[9].

Sesamum indicum L.,—in den Nuzi-Texten ŠE.Ì.GIŠ[10] geschrieben—wurde während der Sommermonate angebaut und bedurfte einer Bewässerung, obwohl er im Gegensatz zu anderen Ölpflanzen besser Trockenheit vertragen

---

Ebeling, *Or*NS 17 (1948) 129–45; 299–313; *Or*NS 18 (1949) 404–18; *Or*NS 19 (1950) 265–78. Erst durch ihre Kriegszüge lernten die Griechen die duftenden Salböle von den Persern kennen und schätzen. Daraus entwickelte sich sodann eine rege Handelstätigkeit. Siehe hierzu E. Paszthory, „Salben, Schminken und Parfüme im Altertum", *Antike Welt* Sondernummer 1990, S. 47.

6 M.P. Charles, „An Introduction to the Legumes and Oil Plants of Mesopotamia", *BSA* 2 (1985) 39–61.

7 So sind Importe von Sesam aus dem Gebiet von Karḫar bezeugt. Siehe hierzu H. Waetzoldt, „Ölpflanzen und Pflanzenöle", *BSA* 2 (1985) 80. Die Bedeutung des Sesamanbaus in dieser Gegend blieb auch bis in das 1. Jt. v.Chr. erhalten: bei Ausgrabungen im urartäischen Karmir Blur, das sich als ein bedeutendes Wirtschaftszentrum des Staates Urartu herausstellte, zeigte sich, daß bestimmte Bereiche der Zitadelle speziell der Produktion von Sesamöl gewidmet waren. Die große Menge der Ölkuchenrückstände lassen auf eine nicht unerhebliche Menge von verarbeitetem Sesam schließen (Bedigian, *BSA* 2 [1985] 168 ff.). Für die weite Verbreitung der Ölpflanze in Nordmesopotamien im 2. Jt. s. auch Postgate, *BSA* 2 (1985) 148.

8 A. Fadhil, *Studien zur Topographie und Prosopographie der Provinzstädte des Königreichs Arrapḫe*. BaF 6, 140–43. Fadhil ist allerdings noch davon ausgegangen, daß ŠE.Ì.GIŠ Leinsamen ist.

9 In der Provinz Lagaš ist die Ausgabe dieses Saatguts in der Regel im 2. Monat, nur einmal im 3. Monat bezeugt (H. Waetzoldt, *BSA* 2 [1985] 80).

10 Im Gegensatz zu dem sonst in Assyrien und Babylonien verwendeten *šamaššammu*. S. hierzu J.N. Postgate, „The 'Oil-Plant' in Assyria", *BSA* 2 (1985) 145.

konnte. Er war dagegen aber weniger tolerant gegen hohen Salzgehalt im Wasser[11]. Sesam konnte sowohl auf Feldern angebaut werden, auf denen gerade das Wintergetreide abgeerntet war, als auch auf Feldern, die im Winter brach gelegen hatten[12]. Im heutigen Iraq gibt es sowohl einen normalen Termin für die Aussaat (April, Ernte im September und Oktober) als auch einen frühen Termin (Mitte März, Ernte Mitte Juli)[13]. M. Stol konnte diese beiden Termine auch in altbabylonischen Texten nachweisen[14].

Gemessen wurde der Sesam in der Maßeinheit BÁN zu 8 *qa* (*ina* GIŠ.BÁN *ša* 8 *qa*)[15]. Das Sesamöl wurde aus den Samenkörnern des Sesam gewonnen. Für die Gewinnung war der LÚ *ṣāḫitu*[16] zuständig, der Ölpresser. In den Palasttexten von Nuzi sind zwei Männer dieser Berufsgruppe namentlich erwähnt: HSS 16,227 nennt den *ṣāḫitu* Eteš-šenni, in HSS 14,72 erhält ein Zikaia ŠE.Ì.GIŠ *ana ṣaḫāti*. *ṣaḫātu*[17] ist also der Prozeß der Ölgewinnung[18]. Altbabylonischen Texten zufolge benutzte der Ölpresser für seine Tätigkeit ein spezielles *kannu*-Gefäß *ša ṣaḫāti*, 1 NA_4 *erû* Ì.GIŠ[19] und 1 *esittu* Ì.GIŠ, „einen Mahlstein (für Sesam) und einen Stößel"[20].

Vor dem eigentlichen Preßvorgang mußten die Sesamkörner zerstoßen werden. So wurde in AASOR 16, 89 zwischen ŠE.Ì.GIŠ *la za-ku* und ŠE.Ì.GIŠ *za-ku*[21] unterschieden. Möglicherweise wurde nicht die gesamte Sesamernte auf

---

11 M.P. Charles, „An Introduction [...]", *BSA* 2 (1985) 48 f.

12 Ebd., S. 49. Das ermöglichte zugleich den Fruchtwechsel auf den Feldern von Getreide und Sesam.

13 Marten Stol, „Remarks on the Cultivation of Sesame and the Extraction of Its Oil", *BSA* 2 (1985) 119.

14 Ebd. Für die Aussaat und Ernte von Sesam siehe F.R. Kraus, „Sesam im Alten Mesopotamien", *JAOS* 88 (1968) 115–18; sowie Waetzoldt, *BSA* 2 (1985) 80 f.

15 Öl wird in HSS 13,488: 23–24 (=AdŠ 694) angegeben mit [...] 1 TAL Ì *ina* GIŠ.BÁN *ša* LÚ *ṣāḫiti*, was dann wohl auch dem BÁN zu 8 *qa* entsprechen dürfte. Siehe hierzu M.A. Powell, „Maße und Gewichte", *RlA* 7/3–4, 501.

16 LÚ.Ì.SUR. *CAD* Ṣ „preparer of sesame oil". S. auch Postgate, *BSA* 2 (1985) 146.

17 *CAD* Ṣ 60a f. *ṣaḫātum* „to extract oil"; „the verb seems to refer to the whole process of obtaining oil from sesame [...]". Das Pressen wurde ursprünglich auch durch Treten/Trampeln durch Mensch oder Tier ausgeführt, so wie auch das Korn durch Ochsen „gedroschen" wurde. S. hierzu Forbes, *Studies in Ancient Technology*, Vol. III, 131.

18 Postgate, *BSA* 2 (1985) 146.

19 Bzw. na_4.ur_5.še.giš.ì = *erû šamaššammi* (ḪAR-ra XVI 254).

20 Stol, Sesame. *BSA* 2 (1985) 122; Postgate, a.a.O., 147; Stol/Whiting, „A Rental of Tools Used in Processing Sesame", *BSA* 2 (1985) 179 f. Diese Geräte wurden auch bei der Herstellung von Heilmitteln zum Zerstoßen der Drogen benutzt (Goltz, a.a.O., 22: BAM 42 Vs. 5). Neben dem *kannu*-Gefäß ist auch ein dug.šagan! še.giš.ì bekannt.

21 *CAD* S *sīku* „powdered, crushed"? *AHw* 1013 a. Siehe hierzu Dietlinde Goltz, *Studien*, S. 33, *sâku* (auch *zâku*) „zerstoßen, stoßen". Der Vorgang des Zerkleinerns findet sich auch bei der Herstellung von Heilmitteln, wobei die verschiedenen Drogen vor der Weiterverarbeitung zerstoßen werden müssen.

einmal verarbeitet, sondern die Sesamkörner wurden als solche aufbewahrt[22], um bei Bedarf verarbeitet zu werden.

Aus anderen Quellen[23] gibt es Hinweise, daß die Sesamkörner vor dem Zerstoßen gewaschen und enthülst wurden. Das durch das Zerstoßen der Samen gewonnene „Mehl" wird sodann kalt gepreßt und anschließend gefiltert[24]. Das Produkt ist ein Öl von hoher Qualität. Der Rückstand aus diesem Prozeß, der sog. „Ölkuchen"[25], besteht aus zerstoßenen Hülsen[26] und Samenkörnern[27]. Dieser Ölkuchen ist noch stark ölhaltig und kann durch weiteres (heißes) Pressen weiter verarbeitet werden. Das dadurch gewonnene Öl weist allerdings einen hohen Verunreinigungsgrad auf und ist daher nur von minderer Qualität[28]. Es konnte allerdings durch einen weiteren Reinigungs—bzw. Filtervorgang verbessert werden[29].

Alternativ kann der Ölkuchen, da besonders reich an Proteinen, auch an das Vieh verfüttert werden, er ist aber auch ein wertvolles Nahrungsmittel für den Menschen[30]. Möglicherweise wurden aus diesen Rückständen auch besondere Opferspeisen für die Götter hergestellt[31].

---

22 Dafür, daß Sesam außer zur Ölgewinnung als Frucht selbst aufbewahrt wurde, siehe Postgate, *BSA* 2 (1985) 146, sowie auch Waetzoldt, *BSA* 2 (1985) 82.—Bei dem Prozeß des *ḫalāṣu*, der dem eigentlichen *ṣaḫātu* nach den von Postgate angeführten Beispielen vorangeht, könnte es sich entweder um das bereits beim Zerstoßen der Körner gewonnene „olio vergine" (entsprechend dem Ì.GIŠ.SAG [*rēštu*]?) handeln oder es beschreibt den Vorgang des „Kaltpressens" im Gegensatz zum „Heißpressen". Siehe hierzu M. Levey, *Chemistry and Chemical Technology in Ancient Mesopotamia*, S. 90; Waetzoldt, *BSA* 2 (1985) 84 ff. und zu *ḫalaṣu* auch D. Goltz, a.a.O., 38 f.

23 M. Stol, a.a.O., 120 f.; M.P. Charles, a.a.O., 51 f.; H. Waetzoldt, „Ölpflanzen und Pflanzenöle", *BSA* 2 (1985) 85; Dorothea Bedigian, „Is še-giš-ì Sesame or Flax?", *BSA* 2 (1985) 159–78.

24 D. Goltz, a.a.O., 39.

25 duḫ še.giš.ì = *kuspī*; cf. Stol, *BSA* 2 (1985) 122. Siehe auch Levey, a.a.O., 91.

26 Falls nicht vorher enthülst.

27 Aus Ägypten ist die Anwendung der Sackpresse bekannt. Abbildungen zeigen, wie das Sacktuch mittels zweier Stöcke, die am Rand befestigt wurden, entgegengesetzt gedreht wird, um dadurch einen höheren Preßdruck zu erreichen. S. hierzu R.J. Forbes, *Studies in Ancient Technology*, Vol III, 132.

28 Möglicherweise bestand die Methode auch darin, heißes Wasser zuzufügen, so daß das restliche Öl an der Oberfläche abgeschöpft werden konnte. Auf einen zweiten Pressvorgang weist vielleicht die Passage *ana šamni ša* 2 *ḫilaṣu* (Levey, a.a.O., 91).

29 Für Qualitätsbezeichnungen von Öl in der Ur-III-Zeit s. Waetzoldt, *BSA* 2 (1985) 85.

30 H. Waetzoldt, *BSA* 2 (1985) 82: „Gegessen wurden übrigens auch die Preßrückstände [...]".

31 Siehe die Angabe bei Postgate, a.a.O., 149, über die vier „Ziqqurräte", die—wohl mit weiteren Zutaten—von einem Ölpresser hergestellt werden sollen, wie sie auf mittelassyrischen Siegeln auf Opferaltären zu sehen sind.

Der Ölertrag betrug mehr als 20% der ursprünglichen Menge von Sesamkörnern[32]. Aufbewahrt wurden die Ölvorräte im Vorratshaus, dem É *nakamti*[33], in speziellen Ölbehältern.

Es gibt in den Nuzi-Texten verschiedene Bezeichnungen für Öl. Neben Ì ohne jeglichen Zusatz findet sich Ì.*ellu*[34]. Bei Ì.DÙG.GA scheint es sich nicht per se um Sesamöl zu handeln, da in HSS 15,167 Ì *ša* DÙG.GA *ša* ŠE.Ì.GIŠ (gutes Sesamöl) und Ì *ša* DÙG.GA *ša* ŠAḪ (gutes Schweineschmalz) unterschieden werden. Daneben wird es einmal als Ì DÙG.GA *tertennu* und einmal als Ì DÙG.GA *elli* näher spezifiziert. Zumindest Ì ohne Zusatz und Ì *ellu* wurden vermutlich alternativ, ohne Bedeutungsunterschied, verwendet. So finden sich beide Bezeichnungen sowohl bei den regelmäßigen Ölrationen für die Frauen und die Kinder des Königssohns Šilwa-teššup als auch bei den Angaben für die übrigen Verwendungen, wie z.B. für die Pferdepflege und für die Stoff- und Lederverarbeitung[35]. Auch die Königin erhielt Ì.MEŠ *ellu*[36]. Für die Kinder (*ana* TUR.TUR.MEŠ) wurde in HSS 15,247 5 *qa* Sesamöl aus gegeben, das hier explizit mit Ì.MEŠ ŠE.Ì.GIŠ.MEŠ bezeichnet wird.

Belege für Ì DÙG.GA dagegen finden sich nicht so oft. Bei den Einträgen HSS 14,248: 30: 1 DUG *bu-zu ša* 2 *qa* Ì DUG.GA *el!-li* und HSS 13,225: 23-24: 1 TAL Ì DÙG.GA *te-er-te-en-n*[*u*] 1 TAL Ì.[ ] *ù* 4 *qa* Ì DÙG.GA ist leider die Verwendung nicht bekannt.

In HSS 13,123 erhält eine Königstochter Ì.MEŠ DÙG.GA[37]. Auch die Götter erhielten meist Ì DÙG.GA, daneben aber auch Ì *ellu*; lediglich einige Gottheiten (AASOR 16,50) erhielten nur Ì *ellu*. Denkbar wäre, daß es sich bei dem Ì DÙG.GA um ein Öl handelte, das durch aromatische Beimischungen verfeinert war[38]. Gutes Öl wird auch in den Geschenklisten Tušrattas erwähnt[39].

---

32 Postgate, *BSA* 2 (1985) 149. Waetzoldt, *BSA* 2 (1985) 81.

33 HSS 13,198 = AdŠ III, Nr. 79 und HSS 16,422. In altassyrischer Zeit gab es ein É *ḫuburni*, nach dem möglicherweise das mass. bekannte BÁN-Maß für Öl benannt war (*ina* GIŠ.BÁN *ša* É *ḫiburni*: Postgate, *The Archive of Urad-Šerūa amd his Family*, Nr. 24:9). Für die Haltbarkeit der Öle waren sowohl dunkle Räume als auch große hohe Gefäße von Vorteil (Eckey, *Vegetable Fats and Oils*, S. 175). So wird denn auch von großen Tongefäßen mit einem Fassungsvermögen von 84 bis 174 Litern berichtet (H. Waetzoldt, *BSA* 2 [1985] 82).

34 [Ì] *ellum* according to the dictionaries specifically „sesame oil" (M. Stol, *BSA* 2 [1985] 122). Zu altbabylonischem *šamnum e-li-im/e-la-am* siehe ebd. Zu einer möglichen Übernahme aus dem indischen Raum s. D. Bedigian, a.a.O., 162 ff.

35 Ì ohne nähere Bezeichnung: AdŠ 3, Nr. 70–75; Nr. 78 und 79. HSS 15,291 aus dem Palast Raum N 120. Ì.MEŠ *ellu* : AdŠ 3, Nr. 76 und Nr. 79.

36 EN 9/3, 105 (identisch mit EN 9/3, 491 ?): 8 TAL Ì.MEŠ *ellu* im Monat *arkuzzi* für die Königin von Nuzi.

37 Möglicherweise in ihrer Eigenschaft als *ēntu*?

38 Emmerich Paszthory, a.a.O., S.9, „Die für kosmetische Zwecke benutzten Salböle wurden auch als 'gutes Öl' bezeichnet".

39 Krüge oder Näpfe *ša* Ì *ṭāba malû*. H.-P. Adler, *Das Akkadische des Königs Tušratta von Mitanni*, (AOAT 201) Kevelaer/Neukirchen-Vluyn 1976, S. 350.

Die Grundlage für die „guten" Salböle bildeten meist tierische Fette, denen aromatische Öle beigemischt wurden, wobei Extrakte aus Myrrhe immer einen existentiellen Bestandteil darstellten. Myrrhe war besonders kostbar, da sie von weither gebracht werden mußte[40]. Besonders für kultische Zwecke wurde das Öl mit Myrrhenextrakt und anderen wohlriechenden Zusätzen versehen. In HSS 13,119 ist die Ausgabe von Weihrauch für Öl bezeugt und in HSS 14,243 (=14,574) wird konstatiert, daß der Kaufmann Ikišeia noch 2 Talente und 15 Minen „Zedernöl" (GIŠ *erinu ša* Ì.MEŠ) zu liefern hatte[41]. Außer Ì.GIŠ *a-si-*[*i*?] und [Ì?].GIŠ *dabrāni* werden in HSS 14,247: 60 auch 6 TAL *zinzillu a-na* <*na*>?-*ru* aufgeführt.

Möglicherweise war die Herstellung der Parfümöle[42] im mesopotamischen Raum ähnlich der in Ägypten, wo stark duftende Blüten, Balsame und Harze in Ölen oder geschmolzenen Fetten ausgekocht und die Masse über eine Sackpresse ausgepreßt wurde. Eine andere Möglichkeit war, das sich nach tagelangem Kochen an der Oberfläche bildende Öl abzuschöpfen[43].

Die Produktion von Salben war ein ziemlich langwieriger Prozeß, der in den mittelassyrischen Texten zur Salbenbereitung sehr gut beschrieben wurde[44]. Es ist anzunehmen, daß es auch in Nuzi zumindest eine Salbenbereiterin gegeben hat, allerdings ist eine *muraqqītu* in den Texten nicht nachzuweisen[45]. Die hurritisch-hethitische Bilingue hat das hurritische Lexem für Öl (*hāšari*) geliefert und erklärt damit auch die Berufsbezeichnung *hašartennu*[46]. In HSS 13,109 wird die Palastsklavin Kušuḫ-elli einem Palastbeamten *ana ḫašartennu* übergeben, wobei es sich um das Amt der Salbenmischerin handeln könnte. Viele Handwerker und Handwerkerinnen werden aber oft in den Texten nicht mit ihrem Berufsstand genannt[47], so daß auch andere Frauen in diesem Bereich beschäftigt gewesen sein könnten[48].

---

40 Die Heimat dieses Strauches war Südarabien, von wo die Myrrhe sowie auch der Weihrauch nach Ägypten gelangte (siehe Paszthory, *Antike Welt* 1988/2, S. 18 f.). In den Gräbern ist die Lieferung der Waren aus Punt dargestellt (William J. Martin, *Tribut und Tributleistungen bei den Assyrern*, S. 10). Von Ägypten wurde sie dann weiter verhandelt. EA 22 III 29 nennt ein NA$_4$ *tāpāte ša murri* „eine Steinbüchse mit Myrrhe" (Adler, a.a.O., 322.)

41 Bei diesem „Zedernöl" handelt es sich um das duftende Wacholderbeeröl des Juniperus L. (Paszthory, *Salben, Schminken und Parfüme* [...], 24.). In Mari ist dagegen auch Zypressenöl (Ì.GIŠ ŠU.ÚR.MAN) belegt: ARM 22, 2 Nr. 269:1.

42 „Ätherische" Öle in unserem Sinne konnten zu der Zeit noch nicht hergestellt werden, es handelte sich vielmehr um in pflanzlichen Ölen gelöste Konzentrate (E. Paszthory, *Salben, Schminken, Parfüme*, a.a.O., S. 12).

43 Paszthory, a.a.O., S. 20, sowie *Antike Welt* 1988/2, S. 9.

44 Zu den Salbenrezepten der *muraqqîtu* der mittelassyrischen Zeit siehe E. Ebeling, Anm. 5.

45 W. Mayer, *UF* 8 (1976) 209 hat die MÍ *iškiḫuru* als Salbenmischerin vorgeschlagen nach dem hethit. *išk-* „salben". Dies läßt sich aber nicht auf das Hurritische übertragen. S. G. Wilhelm, „Notizen zum hurritischen Wörterbuch", *SMEA* 29 (1992) 245–47, bes. Fn. 12.

46 G. Wilhelm, a.a.O., S. 245 f.

47 So wird Kušuḫ-elli in HSS 14,621 ohne jede weitere Bezeichnung aufgeführt.

48 Eine Dame namens Wirzu erhält in HSS 13,119 Weihrauch, unter anderem auch für Öl.

Die zugefügten Drogenextrakte dienten gleichermaßen auch einer gewissen Konservierung[49]. Diese Konservierung war besonders bei tierischen Fetten nötig, die ja die Grundlage zur Herstellung der meisten Salböle bildeten[50]. Zu den tierischen Fetten gehörten das Butterfett (Ì.NUN[51], *ḫimētu*), das Fett von Schweinen (Ì.ŠAḪ, *lipû*) und das Fett von Schafen[52]. Auch beim Schweineschmalz/-fett gab es Unterschiede in der Qualität. Während es sich in HSS 15,258 um Ì *ša* ŠAḪ.MEŠ handelt, ist in HSS 15,167 auch von Ì *ša* DÙG.GA *ša* ŠAḪ.MEŠ die Rede. Schweineschmalz wurde verwendet sowohl bei der Lederverarbeitung[53], bei der Herstellung von Stoffen[54] als auch bei der Verarbeitung der ledernen Teile von Streitwagen[55]. Fette wurden im Gegensatz zu Öl gewogen, die Gewichtseinheit dafür war Talent und Mine[56].

Die Ölrationen für die Götter wurden, wie auch die der Palastangehörigen[57], jährlich ausgegeben; Empfänger waren die jeweiligen Priester[58]. Sesamöl ist dafür bekannt, daß es ein besonders haltbares Öl ist, das nicht so schnell ranzig wird und daher längere Zeit aufbewahrt werden kann[59].

So könnte es sich bei dieser Dame durchaus um eine in der Parfümeriebranche Beschäftigte handeln. In einem anderen Text (HSS 14,200) erhält dieselbe Dame *nirwe*, eine Substanz, für deren Deutung es bisher keinerlei Hinweis gibt.

49 Eckers, a.a.O., S. 174.

50 Paszthory, „Laboratorien in ptolemäischen Tempelanlagen", *Antike Welt* 1988/2, S. 8.

51 Lit. „fürstliches Öl". Wie verschiedene Texte zeigen, wurde diese Fettart in Gefäßen aufbewahrt, die auch für Öl und andere Flüssigkeiten gebraucht wurden, so daß es sich dabei auch um eine eher flüssige Substanz handelt (Stol, *BSA* 7 [1993] 103; er übersetzt dies daher mit „clarified butter").

52 In Mari z.B. ist auch Fischöl und Öl von Vögeln belegt. S. ARM Nr. 22.2, Nr. 269: 5–6. Siehe auch Pract. Vocab. of Aššur Nr. 135–40.

53 HSS 13,142 = AdŠ 72: 12–13; 15,257 = AdŠ 74: 13–14.

54 Z.B. HSS 16,630 = AdŠ 78 „Öl *ana* TÚG.MEŠ *eškarāti*"; HSS 13,198 = AdŠ 79: 11: 2 MA.NA *lipû ana* 2 TÚG *ša nuḫi*. Außer zum Walken von Stoffen (Öl *ana* TÚG.MEŠ *ašlakēna* [HSS 15,257=AdŠ 74:17–18] wurde Öl auch zur Appretur von Kleidern benutzt und auch, um Leinenstoffen einen besonders schönen Glanz zu verleihen (Pasthory, *Salben, Schminken, Parfüme*, a.a.O., 37.)

55 HSS 13,142 = AdŠ 72; 14,229 = AdŠ 689; 15,246 = AdŠ 690.

56 HSS 13,198:11 = AdŠ III Nr. 79 : 2 MA.NA *lipû*; bei HSS 14,243 = 14,576 2 GÚN 15 MA.NA GIŠ *erēnu ša* Ì.MEŠ dürfte es sich daher auch um eine festere Substanz handeln (Zedernharz?).

57 HSS 16,421 = AdŠ 75; HSS 16,423 = AdŠ 70, wo die Damen des Königssohns Šilwa-Teššup sowie seine Söhne und deren Familien ihre Salbölration für das Jahr (*ana* MU-*ti-šu*) erhalten. Auch erhielten die vom Palast abhängigen Arbeiter und Arbeiterinnen neben ihren regelmäßigen Rationen von Wolle und Gerste Ölzuteilungen (z.B. HSS 13,124 = AdŠ 76 *ana šattukki nīs* É-*ti*). In HSS 13,482 erhalten 13 *esrētu*-Frauen Öl.

58 Aus Mari-Texten ist zu entnehmen, daß das Öl u.a. vorgesehen war für das „Baden" bzw. Reinigen der Götterfiguren. S. hierzu G. Dossin, „Tablettes de Mari, 1. Le 'bain' des déesses", *RA* 69 (1975) 23–30.

59 Es ist gegen Oxidation durch das bei der Gewinnung aus dem Sesamolin entstehende Sesamöl recht widerstandsfähig und daher lagerfähig. Siehe M. Levey, a.a.O., S. 90; E.W. Eckers, *Vegetable Fats and Oils*, N.Y. 1954. S. 67. Es besteht daher auch keinerlei Zweifel mehr

Möglicherweise war die Ausgabe des Öls für die Götter in Nuzi mit dem *kenūni*-Fest verbunden (nach der Sesamernte), da es in AASOR 16,48 heißt, daß die Ölausgabe bestimmt ist vom Monat *kenūni* von Nuzi bis zum Monat *kenūni* von Nuzi (des nächsten Jahres). In diesem Monat wurde das *isinni kenūni*[60] gefeiert[61].

Für die Aufbewahrung der Öle dienten Krüge und Kannen. Von den in den Vorratshäusern aufbewahrten großen Krügen wurde das Öl wohl in kleinere Gefäße zum Gebrauch abgefüllt, die ein Fassungsvermögen von 2 bis 8 *qû* hatten. Das in Nuzi am häufigsten für Öl benutzte Gefäß war das *kukkupu*-Gefäß. *kukkupu*-Gefäße konnten sowohl ein Volumen von 4 *qû*[62] als auch von 2 *qû* haben (HSS 15,248 2–3: ⸢6⸣ DUG *kukkupu ša* 4 *qa* [n] DUG *kukkupu ša* 2 *qa*; HSS 15,249 5: 2 *kukkupu ša* 4 *qa a-dá-gu-ru*).

Neben Öl (HSS 15,291 6–7: *ù* DUG *kuk<ku>pu ṣalmu ša* Ì.MEŠ) dienten diese Gefäße jedoch auch zur Aufnahme von anderen Flüssigkeiten (in HSS 15,249 für Bier). *kukkupu*-Gefäße werden auch in den Amarna-Briefen erwähnt, die zusätzlich den ägyptischen bzw. manchmal auch mehrere ägyptische Namen dafür nennen[63]. Edel nimmt an, daß die ägyptischen Bezeichnungen je für ein bestimmtes Hohlmaß stehen, „die nicht durch ein akkadisches Äquivalent ohne komplizierte Umrechnungen ausgedrückt werden konnten"[64]. Auch aus Texten der mittelassyrischen Zeit ist das *kukkupu*-Gefäß bekannt[65].

Für den persönlichen Ölbedarf gab es kleinere *ḫuburnu*-Gefäße[66]. Diese Gefäße führten die Frauen auf ihren Reisen neben ihren Kleidern und sonstigen

---

daran, daß es sich bei *šamaššammu* um Sesamöl und nicht um Leinöl handelt, da Leinöl nur sehr begrenzt haltbar ist. (Siehe hierzu auch Waetzoldt, *BSA* 2 [1985] 84 ff.) Sesamöl war daher auch ein bedeutender Exportartikel (Paszthory, *Salben, Schminken, Parfüme* [...], S. 26).

60 Der Zeitpunkt dieses Festes dürfte somit nach der Sesamernte im September bzw. Oktober gelegen haben. Siehe hierzu auch Kraus, Sesam im Alten Mesopotamien, a.a.O., S. 118 f. Durch die jeweilige Angabe der Stadt nach dem Monats—bzw. Festnamen (Nuzi bzw. Arrapḫa) kann angenommen werden, daß diese Feste in beiden Städten zu unterschiedlichen Zeiten gefeiert wurden, vielleicht da sonst die Anwesenheit des Königs bei beiden Feierlichkeiten nicht gewährleistet gewesen wäre.

61 In Mari wurde Sesam im 7. Monat, ebenfalls dem Monat *kinūnum*, geerntet (Oktober) (Stol, *BSA* 2 [1985] 120). Zu Öl in Mari s. auch ARMT 21 (1983) 126–65.

62 Marvin A. Powell, „On the Absolute Value of the Assyrian *qa* and *emār*", *Iraq* 46 (1984) 57–61.

63 Einer der ägyptischen Name für *kukkupu* war *namša*, eine „Art Krug zum Wassergießen". (Edel, *Beiträge* [..], 102). Ein weiteres Gefäß, das auch mit ägypt. *namša* bezeichnet wurde, ist das *kabkabu* (EA 14 I 67).

64 Elmar Edel, „Weitere Beiträge zum Verständnis der Geschenklisten des Amarnabriefes Nr. 14", *Documentum Asiae Minoris Antiquae. Festschrift für Heinrich Otten zum 75. Geburtstag.* Wiesbaden 1988. S.99–114; hier: 109–11.

65 S. Amir Harrak, „La liste de vaisselle et de nourriture VAT 18046", *AoF* 17 (1990) 70–75. Hier: Z. 19: 3 *ku-ku-ba-tu.*

66 Sicher zu unterscheiden von den *ḫiburnu*/*ḫuburnu*-Vorratsgefäßen, die bereits aus altassyrischer Zeit bekannt sind und im É *ḫiburni* aufgestellt waren. Siehe hierzu auch

Utensilien mit sich[67]. In HSS 13,123 wird jeweils zusammen mit einem dünnen Gewand *mala ḫuburnu* Ì.MEŠ und Ì.MEŠ DÙG.GA (letzteres für eine Königstochter) ausgegeben[68].

Bei manchen Ölgefäßen, wie beispielsweise dem *tallu*, handelt es sich um Gefäße, die gleichzeitig als Hohlmaße dienten[69]. Die entsprechenden Hohlmaße für Flüssigkeiten waren ANŠE (= 10 TAL), TAL (= 8 *qû*)[70] und *qû*[71], während die nächstkleinere Einheit *kāsu*[72] war.

Ein *ušbu* findet sich einmal in einem Inventartext (HSS 15,130 41: 2 *ušbu ša* Ì.MEŠ), sowie in zwei der sog. „Ölrationentexte für die Götter"[73], wo die Zuteilungen von Öl in *ušbu* angegeben werden ([n] *ušbi* Ì.MEŠ), manchmal mit dem Zusatz GAL „groß"[74].

Ein *buzu*-Gefäß mit einem Volumen von 2 *qa*, das (auch) für Öl gebraucht wurde, wird lediglich in einem Text genannt: HSS 14,248 30: 1 DUG *bu-zu ša* 2 *qa* Ì DUG.GA *el!-li*.

Auch die Bezeichnung *tapte* für ein Ölgefäß ist in Nuzi singulär: HSS 5,23 6–7: 1 *ta-ap-te* [*š*]*a* Ì.MEŠ *ma-lu-ú ana* ᶠPN *nadnu*. Dagegen finden sich in der Amarna-Korrespondenz öfter *tapātu*-Gefäße mit gutem Öl[75], Myrrhe[76] sowie anderen kostbaren Inhalten[77]. Hierbei handelt es sich möglicherweise um einen

---

Salonen, *Die Hausgeräte der alten Mesopotamier*, S. 200 f., und für *ḫuburnu* als kleine Ölflasche S. 229 f. In mittelassyrischer Zeit gab es ein spezielles BÁN-Maß für Öl: BÁN *ša* É *ḫiburni* (s. hierzu Postgate, *The Archive of Urad-Šerūa and His Family*, Nr. 24: 9).

67 Z.B. HSS 16,395 7–9: *itti* TÚG.MEŠ-*šunu itti* TÚG *ḫaštiwušrišunu qadu ḫuburnišunu ù* Ì.MEŠ-*šunu*.

68 Bei *mala ḫuburni* handelt es sich vielleicht um ein Gefäß von nur der Hälfte des Volumens der sonstigen Gefäße. Von dem *ḫuburni*-Gefäß sind aber sonst keine Volumina angegeben. Zu *mala* s. Oppenheim, „Arraphäisch *māla* – 'Hälfte'", *AfO* 11 (1936) 237–39.

69 C. Zaccagnini, „The tallu Measure of Capacity at Nuzi", *Assur* 2/1 (1979) 29–34. Zu dem GIŠ.BÁN-Meßgefäß siehe auch Salonen, *Die Hausgeräte* [..], S. 297 ff.

70 Siehe auch Powell, Maße und Gewichte, *RlA* 7/3–4, S. 510. Die Entsprechung von 8 *qa* für ein TAL wird auch bestätigt durch HSS 13,142 = AdŠ 72, wo die Summierung von 2 TAL und 48 *qa* 8 TAL ergibt.

71 Marvin A. Powell, „On the Absolute Value of the Assyrian *qa* and *emār*", *Iraq* 46 (1984) 57–59.

72 Zu *kāsu* siehe G. Wilhelm, AdŠ II, 43: („Becher") ist hier zweifellos als Maßangabe zu betrachten. HSS 13,157: 1–2 [n] *qa ù* 1 *ka₄-sú* [Ì].MEŠ *ša* É.GAL-*lì*. Powell vermutet nach den neuassyrischen Texten (The Nimrud winelists), daß 10 *kāsu* 1 *qû* entsprechen. In den Nuzi-Texten gibt es dafür (bisher?) keine Bestätigung. Zaccagnini hält dies für unwahrscheinlich („it seems clear that the Nuzian *kāsu* does not correspond to 1/10 *qa*"; a.a.O., 34).

73 HSS 13,799 (Pl. VIII) = AASOR 16,49; HSS 13,2153+2154 (Pl.X) = AASOR 16,50.

74 S. auch D. Cross, *Movable Property in the Nuzi Documents*, (AOS 10) New Haven 1937, S. 15.

75 1 *tapātu* Ì *ṭāba malû* (EA 17,44).

76 1 NA₄ *tapātu ša murri* (EA 22 III 29).

77 1 NA₄ *tapātu ša iarutti* (EA 22 III 30).

der Salb- und Parfümbehälter, die entsprechend ihrem kostbaren Inhalt aus wertvollem Material und meist recht aufwendig gestaltet waren.

Besonders aus Ägypten sind Salbschalen aus Diorit, Alabaster und Glas bekannt, die zum Teil in verschiedenen Tierformen vorkamen[78].

Salblöffel, wie sie z.B. in Ägypten bereits aus der 2. Hälfte des 4. Jt. gefunden wurden[79], sind ebenfalls in den Inventarlisten von Nuzi aufgeführt: HSS 15,130 49: 8 GIŠ *itquru ša* Ì[80].

Bei den in HSS 13,198 = AdŠ 79: 13–15 genannten 4 *mišmunnu*, die für Streitwagen ausgegeben werden, könnte es sich um einen genormten Behälter handeln, der vielleicht speziell für Fette vorgesehen war[81]. Dafür spricht, daß in HSS 13,142 = AdŠ 72 für die Streitwagen zwei Minen *lipû* ausgegeben werden[82].

Postscriptum

Der Artikel „Dialogues between Ancient Near Eastern Texts and the Archaeological Record: Test Cases from Bronze Age Syria" von Marie-Henriette Gates (*BASOR* 270 [1988], 63–91) ist mir leider erst nach Fertigstellung meines Manuskripts bekannt geworden. Verf. behandelt darin u.a. die Aufbewahrung von Rohöl und die Weiterverarbeitung von Öl zu Salbölen und unternimmt den interessanten Versuch, die verschiedenen Arbeitsgänge Räumen des Palastes von Mari zuzuordnen, wo die in den Texten genannten Beamten (ARMT 21 und ARMT 23/AAM I) ihr Umfeld hatten (S. 75–83).

---

78 Kleine Salböltöpfe aus kostbarem Stein konnten mit Schnurösen versehen sein, so daß sie zum täglichen Gebrauch mitgeführt werden konnten. (Paszthory, *Salben, Schminken und Parfüme*, a.a.O., 23; in dem Heft sind auch weitere gute Abbildungen von Salb- und Parfümbehältern zu finden.) Solche kostbaren Salbölgefäße gehörten auch zur Mitgift der mitannischen Prinzessin Tadu-ḫepa. In den Listen finden sich mindestens 42 Exemplare aufgeführt. J.A. Knudtzon, *Die Amarna-Tafeln*. Neudruck 1964, S. 209–11.

79 Paszthory, *Salben, Schminken und Parfüme*, a.a.O., 13.

80 EA 14, II: 10 und 55 führt dagegen kostbare *nalbattu*-Schalen, teilweise aus Silber, auf.

81 S.G. Wilhelm, AdŠ 3, S.45, Fn. 13; K. Deller, *Or*NS 53 (1984) 103 sq. Bedeutungsansatz „Maßeinheit oder ein genormter Behälter für 'Fett'".

82 Handelt es sich dabei vielleicht um eine bei Fetten verwendete Untereinheit der Mine?

Kešše

GERNOT WILHELM
Julius-Maximilians-Universität, Würzburg

Keše, the hunter-hero of a lengthy cuneiform composition attested in the Hurrian and Hittite languages from Ḫattuša, is explained, on grammatical grounds, as a Hurrian nominalized form in *-šše*. The root is *ke-*, *kev/b-*, which corrresponds to Akkadian *šakānu*. The same root is also present in the profession term *kebli*, "hunter" (perhaps better "trapper"), which is attributed to *Kešše* in the Hurrian text.

Der Name des Jägers Keše, des Protagonisten einer weitgehend verlorengegangenen hurritischsprachigen, mehr als 14 Tafeln umfassenden Serie aus Ḫattuša, ist bisher ungedeutet geblieben. Die übliche Zitierform „Kešši" folgt den Fragmenten einer hethitischen Fassung des Stoffes, das kleine Fragment eines wohl ebenfalls zugehörigen akkadischen Textes aus Amarna bietet die Schreibung *Ki-iš-ši*. Anscheinend ist in der bisherigen Literatur[1] nicht einmal

[1] Erste Erwähnungen: E. Forrer, „Die Inschriften und Sprachen des Ḫatti-Reiches", *ZDMG* 76 [= N.F. 1] (1922) 188; H. Ehelolf, *Mythen und Rituale* (KUB 17), Berlin 1926, Vorwort, ad Nr. 1 mit Anm. 1; *idem*, „Zum hethitischen Lexikon", *Kleinasiatische Forschungen* I/1 (1927) 148 n. 2; J. Friedrich, „Die hethitischen Bruchstücke des Gilgameš-Epos", *ZA* 39 [= N.F. 5] (1930) 75–76, 81; Bearbeitung der hethitischen Fragmente: J. Friedrich, „Churritische Märchen und Sagen in hethitischer Sprache", *ZA* 49 (1950) 213–55; letzte Bearbeitung des akkadischen Fragments: Sh. Izre'el, *The Amarna Scholarly Tablets* (Cuneiform Monographs 9), Groningen: Styx, 1997, 17–19. Weitere Lit. (in Auswahl): Neuere Übersetzung: L. Jakob-Rost, *Das Lied von Ullikummi*, Leipzig: Insel-Verlag, 1977, 76–77; H.A. Hoffner, Jr., *Hittite Myths* (Writings from the Ancient World 2), Atlanta: Scholars Press, 1990, 67 f.; A. Ünal, „Das Märchen vom Jäger Keschschi, *CTH* 361", in: O. Kaiser (Hrsg.), *Texte aus der Umwelt des Alten Testaments* III/4, Gütersloh: Gütersloher Verlagshaus, 1994, 851–52; Erwähnungen in Lexika, Namen- und Wörterbüchern: E. von Schuler, „Kešši", in: H.W. Haussig (Hrsg.), *Wörterbuch der Mythologie*, I/1, Stuttgart: Ernst Klett Verlag, 1965, 181–82; A. Ünal, „Kešši", in: *RlA* 5 (1976–1980) 578; E. Laroche, *Les noms des hittites*, Paris: Librairie C. Klincksieck, 1966, 94 no. 588 (ohne Erwähnung im systematischen Teil); *idem*, *Glossaire de la langue hourrite*, Paris: Editions Klincksieck, 1980, 144; R.S. Hess, *Amarna Personal Names*, Winona Lake, Ind.: Eisenbrauns, 1993, 100; Aufsätze zum Text: M. Salvini, Sui testi mitologici in lingua hurrica", *SMEA* 18 (1977) 79; *idem*, „Die hurritischen Überlieferungen des Gilgameš-Epos und der Kešši-Erzählung", in: V. Haas (Hrg.), *Hurriter und Hurritisch* (Xenia 21),

Studies on the Civilization and Culture of Nuzi and the Hurrians - 10

die Frage der sprachlichen Zugehörigkeit dieses Namens diskutiert worden, sieht man von einem frühen und rasch aufgegebenen Versuch H. Ehelolfs ab, ihn mit der altbabylonischen Schreibung des Namens „Gilgameš" (GIŠ) in Verbindung zu bringen[2]. Der Name ist außerhalb des Mythos anscheinend nicht belegt, in den Corpora hurritischer Personennamen erscheint er nicht.

Eine Deutung eröffnet die Beobachtung der Schreibung und Konstruktion des Namens in Verbindung mit neueren Erkenntnissen zur hurritischen Grammatik und Lexik.

Die hurritischen Fragmente schreiben den Namen zumeist mit /e/ in der ersten Silbe und im Auslaut:

^{m}*Ke-e[š-*	KUB 47, 1 I 9
[^{m}*K]e-eš-še-ni-*⌜*i*⌝*-i[l*$_5$ (Ergativ)	KUB 47, 1 I 1''
^{m}*Ke-eš-š[e*	KUB 47, 1 I 10''
[^{m}*Ke-e]š-še-en*$_6$[3] (Absolutiv)	KUB 47, 1 II 3''
^{m}*Ke-eš-še-ni-w[a*$_a$ (Dativ)	KUB 47, 1 III 11'
^{m}*Ke-e[š*$_{15}$[4]*-*	KUB 47, 1 IV 3'
^{m}*Ke-eš-še-ni-we*$_e$*!-ni-i-we*$_e$*!-ni-i[l*$_5$[5]	KUB 47, 2 I 12
^{m}*Ke-eš-še-ni-i-il*$_5$ (Ergativ)	KUB 47, 2 IV 6', 10'
^{m}*Ke-eš-še-ni-iš-ša* (Ergativ)	KUB 47, 2 l.Rd. I 8
^{m}*Ke-eš-še* (in Kolophon)	KUB 47, 2 l.Rd. II 2
^{m}*Ke-eš-ši-ip-pa-an*	KUB 47, 3: 5', 6'
[^{m}*Ke]-eš-ši-in* (Absolutiv)	KUB 47, 3: 10'
[^{m}]*Ke-eš-še-e[n*$_6$ (Absolutiv)	KUB 47, 4 IV 2'
^{m}*Ke-eš-še-n[i-* (Ergativ)	KUB 47, 4 IV 3'
[^{m}*K]e-eš-še* (in Kolophon)	KUB 47, 4 l.Rd.
[^{m}*Ke-e]š*$_{15}$*-ši-il*$_5$ (Ergativ)	KUB 47, 7: 3'
^{m}*Ke-eš-še* (Absolutiv)	KBo 12, 79, 5'
^{m}*Ke-eš*$_{15}$*-ši[* (Absolutiv)	KBo 27, 218 6'

Konstanz: Universitätsverlag, 1988, 157–72; P. Xella, „Remarques comparatives sur le «roman de Kešši»", *RHA* 36 (1978) 215–24; E. Neu, „Kešše-Epos und Epos der Freilassung", *SMEA* 31 (1993) 111–20; Berücksichtigung in Monographien zur hurritischen Religion und Literatur: G. Wilhelm, *Grundzüge der Geschichte und Kultur der Hurriter*, Darmstadt: Wissenschaftliche Buchgesellschaft, 1982, 87 (= *idem*, *The Hurrians*, Warminster: Aris & Phillips, 1989, 62); M. Popko, *Huryci*, Warszawa: Państwowy Instytut Wydawniczy, 1992, 128–29.

2 S. Anm. 1.

3 Zur Lesung, cf. M. Giorgieri / G. Wilhelm, „Privative Opposition im Syllabar der hurritischen Texte aus Boğazköy", *SCCNH* 7 (1995) 52 f.

4 Zur Lesung, cf. M. Giorgieri / G. Wilhelm, *SCCNH* 7 (1995) 49 f.

5 Genitiv mit sonst nicht belegter doppelter Suffixaufnahme (Genitiv und Ergativ) oder Schreiberversehen? Cf. zur doppelten Suffixaufnahme, G. Wilhelm, „Suffixaufnahme in Hurrian and Urartean", in: F. Plank (ed.), *Double Case. Agreement by Suffixaufnahme*, New York / Oxford: Oxford University Press, 1995, 128–29, und I. Wegner, „Suffixaufnahme in Hurrian: Normal Cases and Special Cases", *ibid.*, 142–43.

Die Formen mit Kasusendung weisen—im Gegensatz zum Absolutiv—fast ausnahmslos den Relator *-ne-* auf. Dieses Verteilungsmuster ist auch sonst gut bezeugt[6], allerdings findet es sich bei Namen nur in bestimmten Fällen, nämlich wenn es sich um Appellativa handelt wie z.B. bei Kumarb / vi „der von Kumar", Šimīge, womit gleichermaßen der Sonnengott und der Himmelskörper bezeichnet wird, *Kiyaže* Name des Meergottes, aber auch „Meer"[7], oder Ea-šarri, bei dem das auch sonst bezeugte *šarri* „(Götter-)König" zweifellos als Appellativ verstanden wurde. Ansonsten tritt die Kasusendung unmittelbar an den Namen; aus der großen Zahl von Belegen seien hier nur einige aus dem Mittani-Brief genannt: ^{d}*Ša-uš-kaš* (Erg.) Mit. I 76, ^{d}*A-m*[*a*]*-a-nu-ú-e* (Gen.) Mit. II 77, ^{d}*Te-e-eš-šu-pa-aš* (Erg.) Mit. I 24, 76, II 65, IV 118, ^{d}*Te-e-eš-šu-u-ub-be* (Gen.) Mit. II 77, ^{m}*Ar-ta-ta-a-maš* (Erg.) Mit. III 52, ^{m}*Ge-li-i-aš* (Erg.) Mit. I 92, IV 26, IV 27, ^{m}*Ma-né-e-ta* (Dir.) Mit. I 53, II 19, ^{m}*Ma-né-e-ra-la-an* (Kom.) Mit. II 116, ^{m}*Du-uš-rat-ta-a-we* (Gen.) Mit. III 103. Texte anderer Provenienz folgen demselben Muster; es genügt hier, auf die Indizes des *Corpus der hurritischen Sprachdenkmäler* zu verweisen[8].

Dies bedeutet aber auch, daß jeder Name, der mit Relator konstruiert wird, daraufhin untersucht werden muß, ob womöglich ein Appellativ vorliegt. Im Falle des Namens Keššе fällt dies nicht schwer:

Die Berufsbezeichnung des Keššе, *kebli* „Jäger", ist von einer Wurzel gebildet, die als *ke-* (Ugarit: akk.-hurr. Bil., Quadrilingue; Mit.), *keb-* (Ugarit, sum.-hurr. Bil.) und wohl auch *kev-* (Nuzi) erscheint und akk. *šakānu* „setzen, stellen" entspricht[9]. Verf. hat im Zusammenhang der Isolierung eines Berufsbezeichnungen bildenden Suffixes *-li* diese Wurzel als Basis für die Berufsbezeichnung *kebli* bestimmt und eine Grundbedeutung „Fallensteller" vermutet[10]. Dieselbe Wurzel liegt, nominalisiert mit *-šše*, in dem Namen selbst vor. Er ist also ein Bezeichnungsname, der—da er im Anthroponomastikon anscheinend sonst nicht begegnet—speziell für den Protagonisten des „Jagdmythos"[11] geprägt wurde.

---

6 G. Wilhelm, „Zur Grammatik und zum Lexikon des Hurritischen", *ZA* 83 (1993) 107–9.

7 [...] *šarri=n(a)=až=e* ^{D}*Kiyaže=ne=vi=n(a)=až=e* [...] der (göttlichen) Könige des Meer(gott)es" KUB 27, 38 I 4'; zu *kiyaže* „Meer" (// A.AB.BA) s. N. Na'aman, *OA* 19 (1980) 109; M. Dietrich / W. Mayer, *UF* 28 (1996 [=1998]) 184–87 und vergleiche noch *ši-i-ra-a-ti-le ki-i-ia-ši* „ich will das Meer besingen(?)" KUB 45, 63 I 3 in einem Text, in dem laut Kolophon das „Meer" im Mittelpunkt steht (zu *šir=ad=i=l=e* cf. KBo 32, 11 I 1).

8 Auf Grund dieser Verteilung darf angenommen werden, daß der ebenfalls mit *-ne-* konstruierte Name des Herrschers von Ebla in der hurritisch-hethitischen Serie „Freilassung", Mēgi, ein Bezeichungsname ist. –Die Form **Ta-aš-mi-*^{D}LUGAL*-ma-ni-wi*$_{i}$, die der Index zu ChS I/5, S. 282, bietet, beruht auf den beiden Stellen [ ]*ni*(= [LUGA]L$^{?}$)*-ma-ni-wi*$_{i}$ KUB 45, 20 (= ChS I/5 Nr. 48) III 17 und [ ]x(= ⌜*ni*⌝$^{?}$)*-wi*$_{i}$ KUB 7, 58 (= ChS I/5 Nr. 47 III 5); die Parallelität der beiden Stellen ist ebenso unsicher wie die Ergänzung, so daß der hier festgestellte Sachverhalt als Hilfsargument gegen die Textherstellung berücksichtigt werden kann.

9 Zuletzt M. Giorgieri, „Die erste Beschwörung der 8. Tafel des Šalašu-Rituals", *SCCNH* 9 (1998) 78 n. 18 mit Lit.

10 G. Wilhelm, „Hurritische Berufsbezeichnungen auf *-li*", *SMEA* 29 (1988) 242 f.

11 P. Xella, *RHA* 36 (1978) 215–24.

turoni „Unterseite, Grundplatte, Basis" im Hurritischen von Qaṭna

GERNOT WILHELM
Julius-Maximilians-Universität, Würzburg

The term *tu-ru-ni*, that seems to be attested exclusively in the inventories from Qaṭna, is interpreted here as the metal base of ornaments and possibly of small figurines used as parts of necklaces. It is suggested that *tu-ru-ni* is to be derived from Hurrian *turi*, „below, low," and analyzed as *tur(i)=o=ni*, according to a well established pattern of Hurrian word-formation.

Die Qaṭna-Inventare[1] sind neben den mittanischen Geschenklisten aus Amarna die reichhaltigste schriftliche Quelle für das Formenrepertoire, das Material und die Terminologie spätbronzezeitlichen Schmucks. Die Inventare der Schätze des Ninegal-Tempels in Qaṭna verwenden zur Beschreibung der Geräte und Schmuckstücke der Gottheit neben zahlreichen akkadischen bekanntlich auch eine Reihe von hurritischen Termini.[2] Auch aus den in Amarna gefundenen

---

1 J. Bottéro, „Les inventaires de Qatna", *RA* 43 (1949) 1–40, 137–215. Zur Geschichte Qaṭnas s. H. Klengel, *Geschichte Syriens im 2. Jahrtausend v.u.Z.*, Berlin: Akademie-Verlag, 1969, 96–138.

2 Die meisten dieser hurritischen Termini sind bisher lexikalisch nicht genau gedeutet. Eine systematische Benutzung der heute verfügbaren hurritologischen Kenntnisse kann allerdings hier und da noch weiter führen. So ist das *ḫu-ru-up-pu* genannte goldene Gerät, das nach Inv. I 2–3 zu der dort beschriebenen Statuette der Göttin gehört (*ina qātī-šu* „in ihrer(!) Hand"), mit dem KBo 32, 13 I 30 genannten *ḫu-ú-ru-úw-we*$_{⌜e⌝}$- (*ḫūruffe*) zu identifizieren, bei dem es sich nach der hethitischen Übersetzung um ein *BIBRÛ*, also ein—oft tierförmiges—Trinkgefäß, handelt; s. E. Neu, „Neue Wege im Hurritischen", in: E. von Schuler (ed.), *XXIII. Deutscher Orientalistentag* (*ZDMG* Suppl. VII), Stuttgart: Franz Steiner Verlag, 1989, 297, *idem*, *Das Hurritische: Eine altorientalische Sprache in neuem Licht*, Mainz/Stuttgart: F. Steiner Verlag, 1988, 15. Eine ältere Deutung von E. Laroche apud J. Bottéro, *RA* 43 (1949) 138 f., Anm. 15, derzufolge *ḫuruppu* wahrscheinlich die Bedeutung „Schwert" habe und die Göttin also bewaffnet dargestellt sei, beruht auf KUB 27, 1 III 41 // 6 I 10, wo unter verschiedenen Kultobjekten—meist Waffen von Gottheiten—auch ^{D}U-*ub-(bi) ḫu-(u-)ru-ub-bi* „*ḫ*. des Teššob" genannt ist; in seinem *Glossaire de la langue hourrite*, p. 115, hat Laroche diese Deutung aufgegeben und unter Hinweis auf *CAD* Ḫ, 256 („a dish made of metal") durch die Bedeutung „un récipient" ersetzt. Auch I. Wegner, *Hurritische Opferlisten aus hethitischen Festbeschreibungen, Teil I: Texte für* Ištar-*Ša(w)uška* (ChS I/3–1), Roma: Bonsignori

Studies on the Civilization and Culture of Nuzi and the Hurrians - 10

Briefen des Akizzi von Qaṭna an Amenophis IV. (40er Jahre des 14. Jhs. v.Chr.) geht hervor, daß die hurritische Sprache dort Verwendung fand[3], wie auch der Name des Königs Akizzi dem Hurritischen zuzurechnen ist[4].

In der Beschreibung von Schmuckstücken begegnet mehrfach in vergleichbarem Kontext das Wort *tu-ru-ni,* das anscheinend außerhalb von Qaṭna nicht nachzuweisen ist. Es handelt sich um folgende Stellen (Belegstellen, an denen die Bezeichnung des mit *tu-ru-ni* verbundenen Objekts nicht erhalten ist, sind nicht berücksichtigt):

(1) 1 *qar-da-na-an* ZA.GÌN *i-na tu-ru-ni* KÙ.SIG$_{17}$ *n*[*a-di*] „ein *q*. aus Lapislazuli, in einem *t.* aus Gold lie[gt es]" Inv. I 44 (Bottéro, *RA* 43, 142; Kopie Expl. B: 191, Expl. D: 199).

(2) GÚ ŠÀ 1 ALAM ZA.GÌN *i-na tu-ru-ni* KÙ.SIG$_{17}$ ... 1 AŠ.ME ZA.GÌN *i-na tu-ru-ni* KÙ.SIG$_{17}$ *na-d*[*i*] (Var.: om.) „ein Halsschmuck, darin eine Figur aus Lapislazuli, in einem *t.* aus Gold <liegt sie> ... eine Sonnenscheibe aus Lapislazuli, in einem *t.* aus Gold liegt sie" Inv. I 45, 47 (Bottéro, *RA* 43, 142; Kopie Expl. B: 192, Expl. D: 200).

Editore, 1995, 49, übersetzt „*ḫurubbi*-(Gefäß)". Cf. noch den Essiv pl. *ḫu-u-ru-up-pa-ša* ChS I/ 1, 43 III 28′ sowie *ḫu-u-ru-ub-bi* ChS I/5, 145: 9′. *ḫ.* ist auch als Lehnwort im Hethitischen bezeugt und auch hier mit *BIBRÛ*-Gefäßen assoziiert (s. z.B. [D]U *ḫu-u-ru-up-pí-in BI-IB-RI*[ḪI.A]-*ja ḫu-u-ma-an-du-uš* KUB 46, 47 Vs. 13′). Das Wort selbst ist bereits in der Ur III-Zeit, später vereinzelt in Assyrien belegt (s. *AHw* 360b, *CAD* Ḫ, 256; die Erwähnung im Zusammenhang einer Eheschließung in § 42 des Assyrischen Rechtsbuches KAV 1 bezieht sich also nicht auf Hochzeitsgeschenke, sondern auf die bei der Hochzeitsfeier verwendeten Trinkbecher; cf. G. Cardascia, *Les lois assyriennes*, Paris: Les Editions du Cerf, 1969, 209, Anm. b mit Lit.). Seine Herkunft ist unklar; folgt man M.L. Khačikyan, *Churritskij i urartskij jazyki*, Jerevan: Izdatel'stvo AN Armjanskoj SSR, 1985, 47, Nr. 31, die das Wort mit hurr. *ḫurišḫe* zusammenstellt und von einer Wurzel *ḫûr-* ableitet, so müßte es sich um eine sehr frühe Entlehnung aus dem Hurritischen ins Akkadische handeln.

3 Die fremdsprachigen Glossen in EA 52 und 53 werden seit langem als hurritisch aufgefaßt, auch wenn eine lexikalische Deutung bisher nicht möglich war; cf. J. Friedrich, *Kleine Beiträge zur churritischen Grammatik* (MVAeG 42/2), Leipzig: J.C. Hinrichs Verlag, 1939, 53–58; A. Goetze, „An Unrecognized Ḫurrian Verbal Form", *RHA* 5/35 (1939) 103–8; J. Friedrich, „Zur Sprache von Qatna", *WZKM* 47 (1940) 202–14; E.A. Speiser, *Introduction to Hurrian* (AASOR 20), New Haven: ASOR, 1941, 195; E. Laroche, *Glossaire de la langue hourrite*, Paris: Editions Klincksieck, 1980, 133; W.L. Moran, *The Amarna Letters*, Baltimore/ London: Johns Hopkins University Press, 1992, 123–26.

Für das Lexem *kad-* in den oft diskutierten Formen *ka$_4$-ti-ḫi* EA 53:64 und *ka$_4$-ti-ḫu-le-eš* EA 53:65, für das auf Grund des Kontextes bereits von Goetze, l.c., 107, Anm. 22, eine Bedeutung wie akk. *maqātu* „fallen" angesetzt wurde, läßt sich nun ein Anschluß im Hurritischen der hurritisch-hethitischen Bilingue aus Ḫattuša finden, wo die Wurzel *kud-* „fallen" (intr.) bzw. „fällen" (tr.) bedeutet (Schreibungen: *ku-ú-du* „er soll fallen [gefällt sein]" KBo 32, 14 I 57, *ku-ut-te* „sie mögen es zu Fall bringen" [**kud=id=e*(*n*)] KBo 32, 14 I 11; ⸢*ku-ú-ta*⸣*-i-iš* „es möge fallen" KBo 32, 14 Rs. 40, jeweils mit einer Form von heth. *mau(š)-* übersetzt. Der Unterschied im Vokal ist vielleicht dialektal bedingt.

4 R.S. Hess, *Amarna Personal Names* (ASOR-Diss. 9), Winona Lake, Ind.: Eisenbrauns, 1993, 27 f. – Cf. noch den in Inv. I 44a erwähnten hurritischen Namen eines Königs oder einer anderen hochgestellten Persönlichkeit *E-wa-ri-šar-ri* // EN-LUGAL.

(3) GÚ ŠÀ 1 ALAM ZA.GÌN *ba-aš-lu/lu*$_4$ *i-na tu-ru-ni* (Var.: <*-ni*>) KÙ.SIG$_{17}$ „ein Halsschmuck, darin eine Figur aus künstlichem Lapislazuli (Fritte?), in einem *t.* aus Gold <liegt sie>" Inv. I 74 (Bottéro, *RA* 43, 144; Kopie Expl. B: 193, Expl. D: 200).

(4) GÚ ŠÀ ... 1 AŠ.ME AN.GUG.ME *i-na tu-ru-ni* KÙ.SIG$_{17}$ *n*[*a-di*] „ein Halsschmuck, darin ..., eine Sonnenscheibe aus ...-Stein, in einem *t.* aus Gold lie[gt sie]" Inv. I 92 (Bottéro, *RA* 43, 146; Kopie Expl. B: 193, Expl. D: 201).

(5) GÚ ŠÀ ... 1 *nim-ša-ḫu* ZA.GÌN *i-na tu-ru-ni* KÙ.SIG$_{17}$ *na-di* (Var.: om.) ... 1 AŠ.ME ZA.GÌN *i-na tu-ru-ni* KÙ.SIG$_{17}$ „ein Halsschmuck, darin ..., ein *n.* aus Lapislazuli, in einem *t.* aus Gold liegt es ..., eine Sonnenscheibe aus Lapislazuli, in einem *t.* aus Gold <liegt sie>" Inv. I 98, 101 (Bottéro, *RA* 43, 148; Kopie Expl. B: 194, Expl. D: 201).

(6) GÚ ŠÀ ... 1 AŠ.ME ZA.GÌN *i-na tu-ru-ni* KÙ.SIG$_{17}$ „ein Halsschmuck, darin ..., eine Sonnenscheibe aus Lapislazuli, in einem *t.* aus Gold <liegt sie>" Inv. I 103 (Bottéro, *RA* 43, 148; Kopie Expl. B: 194, Expl. D: 201).

(7) GÚ ŠÀ 1 IGI UDU BABBAR.DIL *tam-li* ZA.GÌN DU$_8$.ŠI+A *i-na tu-ru-ni* KÙ.SIG$_{17}$ „ein Halsschmuck, darin ein „Schafsauge" aus *p.*-Stein, die Einlage aus Lapislazuli (und) Bergkristall, in einem *t.* aus Gold <liegt es>" Inv. I 106 (Bottéro, *RA* 43, 148; Kopie Expl. B: 194, Expl. D: 202).

(8) GÚ ŠÀ ... 1 ^{na4}NUNUZ ZA.GÌN *i-na tu-ru-ni* KÙ.SIG$_{17}$ „ein Halsschmuck, darin ... eine eiförmige Perle aus Lapislazuli, in einem *t.* aus Gold <liegt sie>" Inv. I 129 (Bottéro, *RA* 43, 150; Kopie Expl. B: 195).

(9) GÚ ŠÀ ... 1 SAG.PIRIG DU$_8$.ŠI+A (Var.: GUG) *i-na tu-ru-ni* KÙ.SIG$_{17}$ *na-di* (Var.: om.) „ein Halsschmuck, darin ... ein Löwenkopf aus Bergkristall (Var.: Karneol), in einem *t.* aus Gold liegt er" Inv. I 148 (Bottéro, *RA* 43, 152; Kopie Expl. B: 196, Expl. D: 203).

(10) GÚ ŠÀ ... 1 AŠ.ME ZA.GÌN *i-na tu-ru-ni* KÙ.SIG$_{17}$ ... 1 AŠ.ME DU$_8$.ŠI+A *i-na tu-ru-ni* (Var.: *pí-i*) KÙ.SIG$_{17}$ „ein Halsschmuck, darin ... eine Sonnenscheibe aus Lapislazuli, in einem *t.* aus Gold <liegt sie>, ..., eine Sonnenscheibe aus Bergkristall, in einem *t.* (Var.: Mund/Öffnung) aus Gold <liegt sie>" Inv. I 154 f. (Bottéro, *RA* 43, 152; Kopie Expl. B: 196).

(11) GÚ ŠÀ ... 1 AŠ.ME AN.BAR (Var.: ZA.GÌN SIG$_5$) *i-na tu-ru-ni* KÙ.SIG$_{17}$ „ein Halsschmuck, darin ... eine Sonnenscheibe aus Eisen (Var.: gutem Lapislazuli), in einem *t.* aus Gold <liegt sie>" Inv. I 165 (Bottéro, *RA* 43, 154; Kopie Expl. B: 196, Expl. D: 203).

(12) GÚ ŠÀ ... 1 ALAM ZA.GÌN *i-na tu-ru-ni* KÙ.SIG$_{17}$ 1 *tal-lu*$_4$ (Var.: *ta-*) *i-na tu-ru-ni* KÙ.SIG$_{17}$ „ein Halsschmuck, darin ..., eine Figur aus Lapislazuli, in einem *t.* aus Gold <liegt sie>, ein Salbgefäß, in einem *t.* aus Gold <liegt es>" Inv. I 171 f. (Bottéro, *RA* 43, 154; Kopie Expl. B: 197, Expl. D: 204).

(13) GÚ ŠÀ ... 2 AŠ.ME AN.BAR *i-na tu-ru-ni* KÙ.SIG$_{17}$ *na-di* (Var.: om.) „ein Halsschmuck, darin ... zwei Sonnenscheiben aus Eisen, in einem *t.* aus Gold liegen sie(!)" Inv. I 177 (Bottéro, *RA* 43, 156; Kopie Expl. B: 197, Expl. D: 204).

(14) GÚ ŠÀ ... 1 AŠ.ME AN.GUG.ME *i-na tu-ru-ni* KÙ.SIG$_{17}$ *na-di* (Var.: om.) „ein Halsschmuck, darin ... eine Sonnenscheibe aus ...-Stein, in einem *t.* aus Gold liegen sie(!)" Inv. I 209 (Bottéro, *RA* 43, 158; Kopie, Expl. D: 205).

(15) GÚ [ŠÀ ...] 1 SAG AMAR ZA.GÌN *i-*[*na tu-ru*]*-ni* KÙ.SIG$_{17}$ *na-di* „ein Halsschmuck, [darin ...] ein Jungstierkopf aus Lapislazuli, i[n einem *t.*] aus Gold <liegt er>" Inv. I 236 (Bottéro, *RA* 43, 162).

(16) *ša* [*na*]*-piš-ti* [ŠÀ] ... 2? *ṣí-nu* ZA.GÌN (Expl. C: über KÙ.SIG$_{17}$) *i-na tu-ru-ni* KÙ.SIG$_{17}$ *na-di* (Var.: om.) 2 ^{na4}NUNUZ ZA.GÌN *i-na tu-ru-ni* KÙ.SIG$_{17}$ *na-di* (Var.: om.) 1 SAG L[Ú ...] *i-na tu-ru-ni* KÙ.SIG$_{17}$ *na-di* (Var.: om.) „ein Halsschmuck (*ša napišti* „der Kehle"), [darin ...] zwei(?) Palmetten aus Lapislazuli, in einem *t.* aus Gold liegen sie(!), zwei eiförmige Perlen aus Lapislazuli, in einem *t.* aus Gold liegen sie(!)" Inv. I 258, 259, 260 (Bottéro, *RA* 43, 164).

(17) ... 1 *ṣí-nu* ZA.GÌN [*i-na t*]*u-ru-ni* KÙ.SI[G$_{17}$] *na-di* „... eine Palmette aus Lapislazuli, in einem *t.* aus Gold liegt sie" Inv. I 298 (Bottéro, *RA* 43, 166).

(18) ... 3 *ṣí-nu* AN.BAR *i-*[*na t*]*u-ru-ni* KÙ.SIG$_{17}$ „... drei Palmetten aus Eisen, in einem *t.* aus Gold <liegen sie(!)>" Inv. I 310 (Bottéro, *RA* 43, 166).

(19) GÚ ŠÀ ... 1 ^{na4}NUNUZ ZA.GÌN *i-na tu-ru-ni* KÙ.SIG$_{17}$ „ein Halsschmuck, darin ... eine eiförmige Perle aus Lapislazuli, in einem *t.* aus Gold <liegt sie>" Inv. I 322 (Bottéro, *RA* 43, 168).

(20) GÚ ŠÀ ... 2 *ši-li-na* BABBAR.DIL *i-na tu-ru-ni* [KÙ.SIG$_{17}$] 1 *iz-zi-ḫu* BABBAR.DIL *i-na tu-ru-ni* KÙ.S[IG$_{17}$] „ein Halsschmuck, darin ... zwei *šili* aus *p.*-Stein, in einem *t.* [aus Gold] <liegen sie(!)>, ein *i.* aus *p.*-Stein, in einem *t.* aus Gold <liegen sie(!)>" Inv. I 350, 351 (Bottéro, *RA* 43, 170).

(21) GÚ ŠÀ ... 1 *ṣí-nu* ZA.GÌN SIG$_5$ *ḫi-mu-šu tam-li* ZA.GÌN *i-na tu-ru-ni* KÙ.SIG$_{17}$ „ein Halsschmuck, darin ... eine Palmette aus gutem Lapislazuli – ihr *ḫ.* (hat) eine Einlage aus Lapislazuli -, in einem *t.* aus Gold <liegt sie>" Inv. II 17 (Bottéro, *RA* 43, 174, Kopie Expl. A: 209).

(22) GÚ ŠÀ ... 2 *ṣí-nu* AN.GUG.ME *i-na tu-ru-ni* KÙ.SIG$_{17}$ (Var. add.(?): *n*[*a-di*]) 1 *ṣí-nu* ZA.GÌN *i-*[*na*] (Var.: *i-*<*na*>) *tu-ru-ni* KÙ.SIG$_{17}$ „ein Halsschmuck, darin... zwei Palmetten aus ...-Stein, in einem *t.* aus Gold liegen sie(!), eine Palmette aus Lapislazuli, in einem *t.* aus Gold <liegt sie>" Inv. II 23 (Bottéro, *RA* 43, 176, Kopie Expl. A: 209).

(23) GÚ ŠÀ ... 1 AŠ.ME ZA.GÌN *i-na tu-ru-ni* KÙ.SIG$_{17}$ „ein Halsschmuck, darin ... eine Sonnenscheibe aus Lapislazuli, in einem *t.* aus Gold <liegt sie>" Inv. II 25 (Bottéro, *RA* 43, 176, Kopie Expl. A: 210).

(24) GÚ ŠÀ ... 1 ^{na4}NUNUZ ZA.GÌN *i-na tu-r*[*u-n*]*i* KÙ.SIG$_{17}$ *na-di* „ein Halsschmuck, darin ... eine eiförmige Perle aus Lapislazuli, in einem *t.* aus Gold liegt sie" Inv. II 28 (Bottéro, *RA* 43, 176, Kopie Expl. A: 210).

(25) GÚ ŠÀ ... 2 *ṣí-nu* AN.GUG.ME *i-na tu-ru-ni* KÙ.SIG$_{17}$ „ein Halsschmuck, darin... zwei Palmetten aus ...-Stein, in einem *t.* aus Gold <liegen sie>" Inv. II 33 (Bottéro, *RA* 43, 176, Kopie Expl. A: 210).

(26) [^{na4}NUN]UZ ... 1 GUG *i-na tu-ru-*[*ni* KÙ.SIG$_{17}$] ⌜*na-du*⌝ „[eine] ... [eiförmige Per]le (und) ein Karneol, in einem *t.* [aus Gold] liegen sie" Inv. III, Fragment a, Rs. 22 (Bottéro, *RA* 43, 182, Kopie: 214).

(27) 1 GÚ ŠÀ 1 *b/pu-ku/qú* ZA.GÌN *i-na tu-ru-ni* KÙ.SIG$_{17}$ „ein Halsschmuck, darin ein b. aus Lapislazuli, in einem *t.* aus Gold <liegt es>" Inv. III, Fragment b, 20 (Bottéro, *RA* 43, 184, Kopie: 215).

Der *tu-ru-ni* genannte Schmuckteil ist demnach ausnahmslos aus Gold. Er erscheint fast ausschließlich nach *ina*, nur einmal (Inv. I 311) ist die Rede von 2 *tu-ru-ni* KÙ.SIG$_{17}$. Häufig folgt der Stativ *nadi* „liegt" (Nr. 1, 2, 4, 5, 9, 13, 14, 15, 16, 17, 22, 24), der sich auf das „*i-na tu-ru-ni*" liegende Schmuckobjekt bezieht; die Form steht meist auch dann—schematisch—im Singular, wenn das Bezugswort pluralisch ist (Ausnahme: Nr. 26). *nadi* fehlt öfter, wobei auch die verschiedenen Exemplare des Textes an derselben Stelle voneinander abweichen können, ist aber gewiß immer implizit gemeint.[5] Die betreffenden Schmuckelemente lassen sich folgendermaßen ordnen:

Bildliche Darstellung (ALAM; Relief oder Statuette): Nr. 1, 3, 12
„Schafsauge": Nr. 7
„Löwenkopf": Nr. 9
„Jungstierkopf": Nr. 15
„Sonnenscheibe" (AŠ.ME): Nr. 2, 4, 6, 10, 11, 13, 14
Palmette (*ṣīnu*): Nr. 16, 17, 18, 21, 22, 25
Eiförmige Perle (NUNUZ): Nr. 8, 16, 19, 24, 26
Karneol (GUG): Nr. 26
qardanan: Nr. 1
nimšāhu: Nr. 5
šili=na: Nr. 20
buk/qu: Nr. 27
„Salbgefäß" (*tallu*): Nr. 12

J. Bottéro deutete *tu-ru-ni* als eine Fassung („un 'cerclage' qui enferme l'objet par son contour"); er übersetzt *nadi* dementsprechend „enfoncé (dans)", „pris (dans)"[6]. Diese Deutung wurde von W. von Soden mit einer Andeutung von Unsicherheit übernommen[7]. *CAD* enthält sich bisher einer Übersetzung[8]. J.-M. Durand schließt sich in einer wichtigen Studie zum Schmuck in Mari der Deutung Bottéros an, vergleicht das in Mari bezeugte *kawārum*, das er als „cercle extérieur formant le rebord de l'objet" definiert und erwägt einen Zusammenhang mit akk. *dūrum* „Mauer"[9].

---

5 J. Bottéro, *RA* 43 (1949) 24.

6 J. Bottéro, *RA* 43 (1949) 24.

7 *AHw* 1373b: „*turun(n)u* (churr. Fw.?) eine Goldfassung?".

8 *CAD* N/II, 235b sub *nimšaḫu*, *CAD* Š/II, 444a sub *šilina*.

9 J.-M. Durand, „La culture matérielle à Mari (I): Le bijou *ḪUB-TIL-LÁ / 'GUR$_7$.ME'", *M.A.R.I.* 6 (1990) 125–58, zu *tu-ru-ni* p. 155 f.

Die Bedeutung „Fassung" ist plausibel und prinzipiell an den meisten Stellen wohl auch richtig. So fungiert *tu-ru-ni* bei den eiförmigen Perlen gewiß als Fassung; diese kann aber z.B. so beschaffen sein, wie bei jener mittelbronzezeitlichen Halskette aus dem Hypogäum Q 78 A in Ebla, in der die Perle in eine goldene Platte eingelassen ist[10], und bei den ovalen Anhängern in Form einer ornamentierten goldenen Scheibe mit eingelegtem Stein aus der mittelassyrischen Gruft 34 aus Assur[11]; oder wie die goldenen runden Scheiben aus dem Grab 135 in Mari, die jeweils mit einer Achatperle belegt sind[12], oder schließlich wie die Fassungen der vorderen „eiförmigen" Steine der Halskette aus dem Grab 236 in Mari, die in eine ihrer Form entsprechenden Fassung gebettet sind[13]. In keinem Falle handelt es sich hier nur um einen Metalldraht oder -streifen, der das Schmuckstück in der Außenkontur umgibt, sondern jeweils um eine Unterlage, in die das Schmuckstück eingebettet oder auf die es aufgebracht ist, wobei es dann von einem Draht oder Steg umrahmt werden kann.

Die in den Qaṭna-Inventaren aufgeführten „Sonnenscheiben" sind zumeist aus Gold; sind sie aus einem anderen Material wie Lapislazuli oder Bergkristall, so „liegen" sie in einem *tu-ru-ni* aus Gold. Solche „Sonnenscheiben" aus zwei Materialien—Stein und Gold—sind anscheinend bisher aus Ausgrabungen nicht bekannt[14], doch ist es auch hier gut möglich, daß die Steinscheiben auf eine—eventuell an den Rändern aufgebogene oder mit angelötetem Golddraht oder -streifen gerahmte—Goldplatte aufgebracht und nicht nur von einer ringartigen Fassung umgeben waren.

Schwieriger sind die in den Texten genannten Anhänger in Form bildlicher Darstellungen (ALAM) zu beurteilen. Im Falle von Reliefs könnte es sich um Fassungen mit einer Grundplatte handeln, wie wir sie für die Perlen oder die „Sonnenscheiben" erwogen haben. Grundsätzlich wäre dies auch bei einem der Vollplastik nahekommenden Hochrelief möglich, wie etwa bei einem Anhänger aus dem spätbronzezeitlichen Königsgrab von Kāmid el-Lōz: Hier ist die als Hochrelief beschriebene Figur eines zusammengekauerten Kalbes zusammen mit zwei tropfenförmigen Perlen aus Lapislazuli und einem Fritteplättchen auf eine Unterlage aus Goldblech aufgebracht, wobei die—eventuell aufgelötete—Figur von zwei gezwirnten Doppeldrähten umlegt ist

10 P. Matthiae, „Scavi a Tell Mardikh-Ebla, 1978: Rapporto sommario", *SEb* 1/9–12 (1979) 160 und Fig. 74; bessere Abbildungen: *idem*, „Die Fürstengräber des Palastes Q in Ebla", *Antike Welt* 13/1 (1982) 7 Abb. 11; *Land des Baal*, Mainz: Verlag Philipp von Zabern, 1982, 93.

11 W. Andrae, „Gruft 45 Ass. 14630 ...", in: A. Haller, *Die Gräber und Grüfte von Assur* (WVDOG 65), Berlin: Verlag Gebr. Mann, 1954, 144b, „10. Paar", Taf. 34 t, v; vgl. *Das Vorderasiatische Museum zu Berlin*, Mainz: Verlag Philipp von Zabern, 1992, 154 f.

12 B. Musche, *Vorderasiatischer Schmuck von den Anfängen bis zur Zeit der Achaemeniden* (HdO VII/1, 2, B, 7), Leiden etc.: E.J. Brill, 1992, 188, Nr. 2, Tf. LXV 2.

13 Musche, *Vorderasiatischer Schmuck*, 189, Nr. 4, Tf. LXV 4.

14 Vgl. Musche, *Vorderasiatischer Schmuck*, 189, Nr. 8, wo solche Scheiben aus Kāmid el-Lōz als „Scheibenanhänger mit Sternsymbol" bezeichnet werden. Für „Sonnenscheiben" aus Silber und Bronze s. *ibid.* 194 mit Tf. LXX, 1.1.

und die Perlen von Stegen gerahmt und mit einem keramischen Kleber befestigt sind[15].

Man könnte aber auch an kleine vollplastische Statuetten denken, wie sie als Anhänger in der Späten Bronzezeit—vor allem in Anatolien—tatsächlich bezeugt sind[16]. In diesem Falle ist weniger an eine „Fassung“ zu denken, die das Objekt umgibt, als vielmehr an eine Bodenplatte, wie sie die ausgegrabenen Objekte mehrfach zeigen. Eine solche Bodenplatte kann gesondert gearbeitet und eventuell aus einem anderen Material sein[17]. Auch bei dem Salbgefäß (Nr. 12) denkt man eher an den Fuß als an eine Fassung.

Die literarischen und archäologischen Kontexte lassen sich demnach problemlos mit einer Deutung harmonisieren, die *tu-ru-ni* mit dem wohlbekannten hurritischen Wort *turi* „unten“, „untere(s/r)“ verbindet. *tu-ru-ni* kann als die reguläre Ableitung mit dem Derivativvokal *-o-* und dem Suffix *-ni* analysiert werden, wie sie auch sonst bezeugt ist[18].

Als Grundbedeutung von *tur(i)=o=ni* ist demnach wohl „untere(s/r)“ anzusetzen, was substantiviert („Unterseite“) zu einem terminus technicus für „Grundplatte“, „Basis“ o.ä. geworden wäre.

---

15 Farbphoto: *Frühe Phöniker im Libanon*, Mainz: Verlag Philipp von Zabern, 1983, 2; zur Technik s. R. Echt / W.-R. Thiele, „Werkstoffkundliche Untersuchungen an Goldschmuck aus dem 'Schatzhaus'“, in: R. Hachmann (ed.), Kāmid el-Lōz 16. 'Schatzhaus'-Studien (Saarbrücker Beiträge zur Altertumskunde 59), Bonn: Dr. Rudolf Habelt GmbH, 1996, 294, 296.

16 Musche, *Vorderasiatischer Schmuck*, Tf. LXIX.

17 Musche, *Vorderasiatischer Schmuck*, 193, Nr. 3.2 mit Tf. LXIX.

18 Cf. *te(yi)=ō=n=ae* „in vielfacher Weise“ o.ä. (zu *teyi*(?) „viel“, mit adverbiell verwendetem Instrumental auf *-ae*), Mit. II 49, 55, 62, 64, 112, III 92, 109, IV 111, 113; *faǧr=o=n=ne=n* „in schöner Weise“ (*faǧr-* „schön sein“) Mit. I 81; *pic=o=n=ne=n* „in erfreulicher Weise“ (*pic-* „sich freuen“ Mit. I 79, *pic=ô=nē=n* Mit. III 4; wohl auch *pend=o=n*[*=ne=n*](?) „in rechter Weise“ Mit. II 87. Bei den früher als Optativen mißverstandenen (cf. F.W. Bush, *A Grammar of the Hurrian Language*, Dissertation Brandeis University 1964, 210, 215) Formen auf *-onnen* handelt es sich jeweils um den Instrumental auf *-ne/i* mit kurzem Allomorph *-n* in adverbieller Funktion nach Relator; s. M. Giorgieri in diesem Bande.

Part III

NUZI NOTES, 54–62

Nuzi Notes

54. A New Writing of the Arrapḫa Place Name URU.Turzanzi / Dūrzanzi

According to the tablets excavated at Yorġān Tepe (Nuzi), the place name Turzanzi, Durzanzi, or Dūr-zanzi was written URU *du-ur-za-an-zi* or URU *dur-za-an-zi*; see J. Fincke, RCTC 10 (1993) 312–13 *s.v.* Turzanzi, and G.G.W. Müller, *Studien zur Siedlungsgeschichte und Bevölkerung des mittleren Osttigrisgebietes* (HSAO 7), Heidelberg 1994, pp. 132–33, no. 2.186 *s.v.* Durzanzi.

Recently, some 163 more tablets and fragments from accidental finds at Kirkūk (Arrapḫe) and Yorġān Tepe were published by G.G.W. Müller in his *Londoner Nuzi-Texte* (SANTAG 4), Wiesbaden 1998. One of these texts provides a third spelling for this Arrapḫaen place name and reveals the interchange of the name element *zanzi* / *zamzi*:

SANTAG 4 no. 101 (BM 95277) obv. 3': [... L]Ú.MEŠ *ša* URU BÀD-*za-am-z*[*i*].

This place name was misread by G.G.W. Müller, SANTAG 4 no. 101, *s.v.* Zakku-zamti, and J. Fincke, RGTC 10 (1993) 116, *s.v.* Ilzam-x[...].

J. Fincke

55. EN 10/1, 38 Joined to HSS 13, 300.

The fragment published as EN 10/1, 38 (SMN 1608) turned out to fill the lacuna on the obverse (the copy of EN 10/1, 38 is wrongly labeled as reverse)[1] of HSS 13, 300 (SMN 300). The tablet is a memorandum of those individuals who did (reverse) or did not pay (obverse) their *iškaru*-tax to the palace. The *iškaru*-tax in this case is either part of the harvest of their fields (obv. ll. 9–11) or their work

1 The information this fragment to be AdŠ 527 given in the catalogue of EN 10/1 is not correct. AdŠ 527 is another fragment with the same SMN number.

Studies on the Civilization and Culture of Nuzi and the Hurrians - 10

as harvesters (rev. ll. 19–20), probable on fields of the palace. The individuals who did their duty already received their *iškaru*-delivery (upper edge ll. 20–21). For *iškaru*, see E. Cassin, *RA* 52 (1958) 24ff. and G. Dosch, HSAO 5, 1993, 39, n. 129. According to G. Dosch, all individuals named in this memorandum are chariot-drivers (*rākib narkabti*).

Room number: A 34; measurements: 83.3 x 61.5 x 27.3 mm; join (Jan. 7.) and transliteration (Sept.): 1997.

Obv. 1 <m>*Tup-ki-til-la* DUMU *Be-la-a+*[*a*]

2 ^{m}*Ki-in-tar* DUMU *Šúk-ri-i*[*a*]

3 ^{m}*Še-el-wu-*⸢*ḫu*⸣ DUMU *Ar-z*[*i-i*]*z-*⸢*za*⸣

4 ^{m}*Ki-ir-ru-*⸢*qa*⸣*-az-zi* DUMU *Ta-ú-ka*

5 ^{m}*Ú-a-ta* [D]UMU *A-kip*-LUGAL

6 ^{m}*Ma-an-n*[*i-i*]*m-ma-ḫi-ir-šu* DUMU *Pal-te-šup*

7 ^{m}*A-kip-t*[*a*]*-še-en-ni* DUMU *A-kap-dug-ge*

8 ^{m}*Ta-ḫi-r*[*i-i*]*a* DUMU *A-ri-ip-pa-ap-ni*

(one line uninscribed)

9 ⸢*an-nu-tu*$_4$⸣ [L]Ú.MEŠ *ša i+na* A.ŠÀ.MEŠ-*šu-nu* ḪA.LA.MEŠ-*šu-nu*

10 [*iš-ka*$_4$*-ri ša*] ⸢É⸣.GAL >*la*<

11 [*ša l*]*a i-ṣí-du*

Rev. 12 ⸢m⸣*Ḫu-ti-ia* DUMU *A-kip*-LUGAL

13 ^{m}*Šá-ḫi-ni* DUMU *Mu-uš-te-šup*

14 ^{m}*Ú-nap-te-šup* DUMU *Ar-ku*

15 ^{m}*Še-qar-til-la* DUMU *Tar-wa-za-aḫ*

16 DUMU.MEŠ *ša* ^{m}*Ni-iḫ-ri-ia* DUMU LUGAL

17 ^{m}*Ḫu-ti-ia* DUMU *Zi-li-ia*

18 ^{m}*Ak-ku-le-en-ni* DUMU *Še-en-na-a+a*

(seal impression)

19 ⸢*an*⸣*-nu-tu*$_4$ LÚ.MEŠ *i+na iš-ka*$_4$*-ri ša* É.⸢GAL⸣-*lì*

U. e. 20 ⸢*ša i-ṣí*⸣*-du ù iš-ka*$_4$*-ri-šu-nu*

21 [*il-q*]*ú-ú-šu-um-ma* [(__ __ __)]

J. Fincke

56. One Fragment from NTF P 181 Joined to HSS 15, 26

Although the tablet HSS 15, 26 (SMN 2122+2236) was returned to the Iraq Museum, a join can be made with help of a cast of the tablet at the Harvard Semitic Museum. The fragment from NTF P 181 joins lines 3–7 of HSS 15, 26, obverse.

The text lists a number of ŠEŠ.MEŠ, "brothers, companions" of different individuals who did not come or arrive (ll. 20, 21: *ša lā illikūni*). For this text, see G. Dosch, HSAO 5, 1993, 20f.

Room number: N 120; measurements: 77.5 x 110 x 26.8 mm; join and transliteration: Sept. 15. 1997.

Obv. 1 [n ŠEŠ.MEŠ *ša* Š]U ^{m}*Mar-ḫa-ar-ta-e*
2 [n ŠEŠ.MEŠ *ša* Š]U ^{m}*A-ru-pa-*⸢*a*⸣*-aḫ*
3 [n ŠEŠ.MEŠ *ša* Š]U ^{m}*Qa-wi-in-ni*
4 10+⸢1⸣ [ŠE]Š.MEŠ *ša* ⸢ŠU ^{m}*A-kip*⸣-[*š*]*e-en-ni*
5 10 ŠEŠ.MEŠ *ša* URU *Qu-ra-*[*a*]*r-te-šup*
6 20 ŠEŠ.MEŠ *ša* ŠU ^{m}*Ti-e-eš-*⸢*ur-ḫe*⸣
7 13 ŠEŠ.MEŠ *ša* ŠU ^{m}*Ša-ar-*⸢*te-šup*⸣
8 15 ŠEŠ.MEŠ *ša* ŠU ^{m}*Ku-ur-me-še-en-ni*
9 4 ŠEŠ.MEŠ *ša* ŠU ^{m}*I-ri-til-la*
10 4 ŠEŠ.MEŠ *ša* ŠU ^{m}*Na-an-te-šup*
11 10 ŠEŠ.MEŠ *ša* ŠU ^{m}*Tar-mi-ip-ta-še-en-ni*
12 13 ŠEŠ.MEŠ *ša* ŠU ^{m}*Du-li-pa-pu*
13 10 ŠEŠ.MEŠ *ša* ŠU ^{m}*Te-ḫi-ip-til-la*
14 6 ŠEŠ.MEŠ *ša* ŠU ^{m}*I-ri-ri-te-šup*
15 15 ŠEŠ.MEŠ *ša* ŠU ^{m}*Ge-el-te-šup*
16 12 ŠEŠ.MEŠ *ša* ŠU ^{m}*A-kip-ta-še-en-ni*
17 13 ŠEŠ.MEŠ *ša* ŠU ^{m}*Ur-ḫi-til-la*
Lo. e.
18 ⸢15⸣ ŠEŠ.MEŠ *ša* ŠU ^{m}*Tar-mi-til-la*

Rev. 19 ŠU.NÍGIN 2 ⸢*ma-ti* 1 (erasure)⸣ ŠEŠ.MEŠ <*ša*>

20 *la* ⸢DU-*ku*⸣.MEŠ-*ni* ⸢GÙB⸣
(rest of reverse not inscribed)
U. e. 21 [ŠEŠ.MEŠ *š*]*a la* DU-*ku*.M[EŠ]-*ni*

J. Fincke

57. HSS 19, 108 Joined to EN 9/1, 139

The fragment HSS 19, 108 (SMN 3766), which has not yet been identified in the collection of the HSM, fills the lacuna on obverse of EN 9/1, 139 (SMN 755). The tablet is a receipt of the dowry and bride price of the marriage between Zišaja, sister of Wunnukia, and daughter of Arn-urḫe, and Ar-teja, son of Ḫašip-aralla.

No room number; measurements of HSS 19, 108 (according to HSS 19) 41(frg.) x 31(frg.) x 8(frg.); measurements of EN 9/1, 139: 67.5 x 93.3 x 29 mm; join: Jan. 29, 1996.

Obv. 1 ^{m}*Wu-u*[*n-n*]*u-*⸢*ki-ia*⸣ D[UMU] ⸢*Ar*⸣-[*nu-ur-ḫe*]
2 NIN-[*sú* ^{f}*Z*]*i-i*$^{!}$*-ša-ia a-na aš-š*[*u-t*]*i a-na*
3 <m>*Ar-*[*te-i*]*a* DUMU *Ḫa-ši-ib-ba-ra-*[*a*]*l-la* SUM.MEŠ *ù* <m>*Ar-te-ia*
4 É.Ḫ[I.A.MEŠ *k*]*i-ma te-er*$^{!}$*-ḫa-t*[*i* S]UM.MEŠ
5 *ù* <m>*Wu-*[*un-n*]*u-ki-ia* NIN-*sú*.MEŠ ⸢É⸣.[ME]Š KÙ.BABBAR.MEŠ
6 *ki-ma mu-*⸢*lu-ú*⸣*-gi*$_{5}$*-šu id-dì-*⸢*na*⸣-[*šu*]
7 *ma-an-nu ša i+na bi-r*[*i-š*]*u-*⸢*nu*⸣ <*ina*> [EG]IR <UD-*mi*>
8 KI.BAL-*tù* 1 GUN KÙ.BABBAR 1 GUN KÙ.SIG$_{17}$
9 Ì.[L]Á.E.MEŠ

---

10 ^{m}*Ar-zi-iz-za* DUMU *Zi-ge*
11 ^{m}*La-qè-pu* DUMU *Pu-ḫi-ia*
12 ^{m}⸢*Ta*⸣*-e-na* DUMU *Ḫa-*⸢*ši*⸣*-ia*
13 [*an*]*-nu-*[*t*]*u* LÚ.MEŠ *ša ta-ap-pé-e* **ḫa-ṭá*$^{!}$(DU)-*a* ⸢*ša*$^{!?}$⸣*[2] ⸢É⸣.ḪI.A.MEŠ SUM-*nu*
14 ⸢m⸣*W*[*a-a*]*r-dú* DUMU *A-ḫu-ia*
15 [^{m}]*E-te-te* DUMU *Pu-i-ta-e*
16 [^{m}]*A-li-ib-bi-ia* DUMU *Ki-iz-zi-ḫar-be*
17 [^{m}]*Ta-ḫi-ri-iš-ti* DUMU *Ta-a+a-ti*
18 ^{m}AQ.QA-DINGIR.RA DUB.SAR DUMU ^{d}30-*na-ap-ši-ir*
(seal impression)
19 NA$_{4}$.KIŠIB *ša* ^{m}*A-li-ib-bi-ia*
Lo. e. 20 DUMU *Ki-iz-zi-ḫar-be*

---

2 *...* these signs could also be read: *ḫa-ṭù a-*⸢*šar*⸣$^{!?}$.

Rev. (seal impression)
21 NA$_4$.KIŠIB *ša* ^{m}*Ar-te-ia* DUMU
22 *Ḫa-ši-ib-ba-ra-al-la*
(seal impression)
23 NA$_4$.KIŠIB ˹*ša Wu-un*˺-*nu-ki-ia*
24 DUMU *Ar-*[*nu*]*-ur-ḫe*
(seal impression)
25 NA$_4$.KIŠIB ^{m}AQ.QA-DINGIR.RA DUB.SAR
26 DUMU ^{d}30-*na-ap-ši-ir*

J. Fincke

58. Two Fragments from NTF P 2 and 'Clay bullae' nos. 770 and 772 Joined to EN 9/2, 16

The joining fragments provide enough evidence to nearly completely reconstruct all phrases and lines of the tablet published as EN 9/2, 16 (SMN 2128), although the very top of the tablet is still missing. This *ṭuppi mārūti* states that Wantiš-šenni, son of Ninu-atal, adopted Tarmia, son of Ḫuja, and gave him a field west of the street going to Tarkulli. For the archive of Ḫuja, see M.A. Morrison, *SCCNH* 4 (1993) 21–46.

Room number: S 151; measurements: 79.4 x 100.6(frg.) x 35 mm. Join and transliteration: Sept. 16. 1997.

Obv. 1 [*ṭup-pí ma-ru-ti ša*]
2 [^{m}*Tar-mi-ia* DUMU *Ḫu-ú-ia*]
3 [*ù* ^{m}*Wa-a*]*n-*˹*ti*˺*-i*[*š-še-en-ni* DUMU *Ni-nu-a-tal*]
4 [*a-na m*]*a-ru-ti i*[*te-pu-uš*]
5 ˹4˺+[n$^{?}$] GIŠ.APIN A.ŠÀ *i+na šu-*˹*pa*˺*-*[*al* KASKAL(*-ni*)]
6 *ša* URU *Ta-ar-ku-ul-*˹*li i*˺+[*na*] *e-l*[*e-en*]
7 A.ŠÀ *ša* ^{m}*Zi-ge* DUMU *Na-qè-pu ki-ma*
8 ḪA.LA-*šu a-na* ^{m}*Tar-mi-ia* DUMU *Ḫu-ú-ia* [SUM]
9 *ù* ^{m}*Tar-mi-ia* 2 UDU 1 *en-zum* 5 MA.N[A KÙ.BABBAR.MEŠ]
10 1 BÁN 2 SÌLA ŠE *ki-ma* NÍG.BA-*šu a-na*
11 ^{m}*Wa-an-ti-iš-še-en-ni* DUMU *Ni-nu-a-tal* SU[M]
12 *šum-ma* A.ŠÀ GAL *la i+na-ak-ki-is šum-m*[*a* (A.ŠÀ)]
13 TUR *la ú-ra-ad-dá šum-ma* A.ŠÀ *ba-q*[*í-ra-na*]
14 *i-ra-aš-ši* ^{m}*Wa-an-ti-iš-še-en-n*[*i*(*-ma*)]
15 *ú-za-ak-ka$_4$-ma a-na* ^{m}*Tar-mi-i*[*a i+na-an-din*]
16 *il-ka$_4$-šu ša* A.ŠÀ ^{m}*Wa-an-ti-*[*iš-še-ni*]
17 *na-ši ù* ^{m}*Tar-mi-ia la na-š*[*i*]
18 *ma-an-nu-um-me-e i+na be-r*[*i-šu-nu*]

19 [š]*a* KI.BAL-*tu*$_4$ 1 MA.NA K[Ù.BABBAR/SIG$_{17}$ SA$_5$]
20 [EM]E-*šu ša* ^{m}*Wa-an-ti-i*[*š-še-en-ni*]
21 [*a+na pa*]-⸢*ni*⸣ LÚ.MEŠ *ši-bu-ti* [*ki-a-am*]
22 [*iq-ta-b*]*i* 2 UDU 1 *en-zum*
Lo. e. 23 [5 MA.NA K]Ù.⸢BABBAR⸣.MEŠ 1 BÁN 2 SÌLA ŠE
24 [*a-šar* ^{m}*Tar*]-*mi-ia el-te-qè-mi*
Rev. 25 [*ù* A.ŠÀ (-*ia*)] ⸢*a*⸣-*na* ^{m}*Tar-mi-ia at-ta-din*
26 ⸢*ù qa*⸣-*an-na-šu a-na pa-ni* LÚ.MEŠ *ši-b*[*u-ti*]
27 ^{m}*Tar-mi-ia im-ta-šar*

---

28 IGI *Zi-qa-du* DUMU *Ku-ri-iš-n*[*i*]
29 IGI *Ni-in-ki-ia* DUMU *Ša-an-*[
30 IGI *Ḫu-zi-ri* DUMU *Ša-at-*[
31 *an-nu-tù* LÚ.MEŠ *ša* A.ŠÀ *mu-*[*šel*$_4$*-mu-ú*]
32 IGI *Ki-in-zi-it-ti* DUMU _[_
33 IGI *Ku-ud-du* DUMU *Ge-l*[*i-*
34 IGI *Ú-náp-ta-e* DUM[U
35 ŠU *Du-ra-ar-te-š*[*up*
36 *an-nu-tù* LÚ.MEŠ *š*[*a* KÙ.BABBAR.MEŠ SUM-*nu*]
(seal impression) | (seal im[pression)]
37 NA$_4$ *Ku-ut-ti* | [
(seal impression) [
38 [NA$_4$ *Z*]*i-*[*qa-du*
(rest of reverse is broken off)
Le. e. 39' ⸢*ṭup*⸣-*pí i+na* EGIR-*ki šu-du-ti ina pa-ni*
40' [K]Á.GAL *Ti-iš-ša-e* ⸢*ša*$_{10}$⸣-*ṭe*$_4$-*er*

J. Fincke

59. SMN 2797 Joined to HSS 19, 30

The fragment SMN 2729 was published in transliteration by D.I. Owen, *SCCNH* 2 (1987) 352. The tablet HSS 19, 30 (SMN 2509 or 2709), which was returned to the Iraq Museum, Baghdad, was transliterated and discussed by K. Deller, *SCCNH* 1 = Fs. Lacheman (1981) 57ff.

This tablet, from the archive of Tarmia, son of Ḫuja, was previously interpreted as an adoption text (*ṭuppi mārūti*, cf. M. Morrison, *SCCNH* 4 [1993] 36) or as a tablet of share (*ṭuppi zitti*, cf. K. Deller, *op. cit*, 59; G. Dosch, HSAO 5, 1993, 11). The joining fragment SMN 2729 shows that the interpretation of Deller and Dosch is correct.

No room number; join: Dec. 3. 1997; transliteration according to *editio princeps*.

Obv. 1 [ṭ]up-pí ḪA.LA-ti ša [^{m}Te-ḫi-ip-til-la ù]
2 [š]a ^{m}Pa-i-til-la DU[MU.MEŠ Šúk-ri-ia]
3 ù ša Tar-mi-i[a DUMU Ḫu-(ú-)ia]
4 i-na be-ri-šu-nu _[_ 4 GIŠ.APIN A.ŠÀ]
5 i-na e-le-en [
6 [i+na il]-⸢ta-an A.ŠÀ⸣ [ša ^{m}
7 [i+na] sú-ta-an A.ŠÀ ša [
8 [ù] ⸢i⸣+na šu-pá-al a-tap-pí [an-zu-g]al-lì
9 ⸢ù⸣ [š]a-nu-ú aš-lu 3 GIŠ.API[N A.ŠÀ]
10 ⸢i⸣+[na] ⸢e⸣-le-e[n] A.ŠÀ ša ^{m}⸢A/Za⸣-[
11 ⸢i⸣+[na i]l-ta-[n]a-an A.ŠÀ ⸢ša⸣ ^{m}Ni-iḫ-ri-ia
12 ⸢i⸣-[na s]u-ta-⸢an⸣ A.ŠÀ ša ^{m}Tar-mi-ia
13 ⸢ù⸣ i+na šu-pa-al A.ŠÀ ša ^{m}[_]_-ni-ia
14 ⸢ŠU.NÍGIN⸣ 7 GIŠ.APIN A.ŠÀ an-nu-[ú]
15 i+na AN.ZA.GÀR ša ^{m}Ḫu-ia ^{m}Te$^{!}$(it)-ḫi-ip-til-la
16 [ù ^{m}]Ba-i-til-la ki-ma ḪA.LA-šu
17 [a-n]a ^{m}Tar-mi-ia it-ta-ad-nu-uš
18 ⸢ù⸣ ^{m}Tar-mi-ia 3 ANŠE 3 BÁN ŠE
19 ⸢ù⸣ [n] UDU ki-ma ḪA.LA-šu-nu a-na
20 [^{m}Te-ḫi-i]p-til-la ù ⸢a⸣-n[a] ⸢^{m}⸣[Ba-i-til-la]
21 [it-t]a-⸢din⸣-[
(rest of obverse is broken off)
(lower edge is missing)

Rev. (beginning is broken off)
1' [_]_ ⸢__⸣ [... KÙ.BABBAR(.MEŠ) ša pí-i]
2' [ṭ]up-pí an-ni-⸢i a⸣-š[ar ^{m}Tar-mi-ia]
3' ni-il-te-qè ap-la-[ku-mi um-ma]
4' ^{f}Wa-ar-ḫi-nu-zu-ma a-n[a-ku
5' a-na a-bu-ti la ep-ša-ku-m[i]
6' ma-an-nu i+na be-ri-šu-nu ib-bal-kat
7' 1 MA.NA KÙ.BABBAR 1 MA.NA KÙ.SIG$_{17}$ ú-ma-al-la ṭup-pí
8' an-ni-i i+na EGIR-ki šu-du-ti i+na URU
9' Nu-zi i+na ba-ab É.GAL-lì ina ITU.ḫu-tal-ši
10' šá-ṭì-ir IGI Ut-ḫap-ta-e DUMU Ki-ba-a+a
11' IGI Du-ra-ri DUMU Ta-i-še-en-ni
12' IGI Ka-a+a DUMU En-na-ma-ti
13' IGI Te-eš-ta-e DUMU E-ge-ge 4 LÚ.MEŠ an-nu-tu$_{4}$
14' ša KÙ.BABBAR na-dì-na-nu
15' IGI ^{d}30-KUR-ni DUB.SAR DUMU A-mur-LUGAL
16' IGI Zi-líp-a-pu DUMU Ge-el-ša-a-pu
17' IGI Še-ḫa-al-te-šup DUMU Ḫu-ur-bi-še-e[n-ni]
18' ⸢IGI A-kip⸣-[til-l]a DUMU Ik-ki-ia

19' (seal impression) NA$_4$ ^{m}*Te-eš-*[*ta-e*]
19' NA$_4$ ^{m}*Ut-ḫap-ta-e*
(seal impression)
20' [N]A$_4$ ^{m}*Zi-líp-a-pu* NA$_4$ ^{m}*Še-*[*ḫa-al-te-šup*]
(seal impression)
21' [N]A$_4$ ^{m}*A-kip-til-la* NA$_4$ ^{m}_[_
Le. e. (seal impression) (seal impression)$^?$
22' NA$_4$ ^{m}*A-kip-*[*t*]*il-la* NA$_4$ DUB.SAR

J. Fincke

60. 'Clay bulla' no. 573 Joined to EN 9/2, 362

Fragment no. 573 from the clay bullae collection fills the upper right part of EN 9/2, 362 (SMN 2335). Kinni, son of Ḫaniu, borrows 5 ANŠE grain from Puḫišenni, son of Mušapu. For the archive of the family Mušapu, see M.A. Morrison, *SCCNH* 4 (1993) 66–94.

Room number: S 129; measurements: 54.7 x 49.7 x 21.2 mm; join and transliteration Sept. 4. 1997.

Obv. 1 5 ANŠE ŠE.MEŠ *ša*
2 ^{m}*Pu-ḫi-še-*⸢*en*⸣*-ni* DUMU *Mu-ša-pu*
3 *a+na* UR$_5$.RA ^{m}*K*[*i*]-⸢*in*⸣*-ni*
4 DUMU *Ḫa-ni-ù* ⸢*il-qè*⸣
5 *i+na* EGIR BURU$_{14}$ ŠE.MEŠ SAG.DU MÁŠ-*šu*
6 ^{m}*Ki-in-ni a+na* ^{m}*Pu-ḫi-še-en-ni* GUR

---

7 IGI *Ḫa-ni-e* DUMU *Šúk-ri-ia*
8 IGI *Še-qa-rù* DUMU *Ḫa-ši-pa-pu*
9 IGI *A-ri-il-lu*
Lo. e. 10 DUMU *Ša-qa-ra-ak-*⸢*ti*⸣
Rev. 11 IGI *El-ḫi-ip-til-la* DUB.SAR
(one line not inscribed)
12 NA$_4$ ^{m}*Ki-in-ni*
(seal impression)
13 NA$_4$ ^{m}*Ḫa-ni-e*
(seal impression)
14 NA$_4$ ^{m}*A-ri-il-lu*
U. e. (seal impression)
Le. e. (seal impression)
15 NA$_4$ ^{m}DUB.SAR-*rù*

J. Fincke

61. Notes to Cumulative Catalogue, *SCCNH* 5 (1995) 147–48: Texts Found in Square S

The archives excavated in square S, corresponding to groups 17, 18A, and 19, have been studied recently by M. Morrison in *SCCNH* 4. Below are a few additions and corrections to the list of texts found in square S, compiled in the "Cumulative Room List to Excavations at Nuzi 9," *SCCNH* 5, pp. 147–48.

Delete Rm 130 EN 9/3 501 = SMN 2343. This tablet comes from S 130, cf. *SCCNH* 5, p. 133.

Delete Rm 151 EN 9/3 523 = SMN 2524. This tablet comes from S 151, cf. *SCCNH* 5, p. 135.

Delete S 019 EN 9/3 385 = SMN 3056; the tablet comes in fact from C 19, has been pointed out by J. Fincke, *SCCNH* 8, p. 353.

S 110: add EN 9/1 351 = SMN 2160, cf. *SCCNH* 2, pp. 371 and 383,
EN 9/2 354 = SMN 2158,
EN 9/2 363 = SMN 2108,
EN 9/2 450 = SMN 2127,

according to *SCCNH* 4, pp. 11 and 145–47 (but in *SCCNH* 4, p. 150, the same texts are said to come from S 112).

The assignment of these four tablets to room S 110 is correct in the catalogue, *SCCNH* 5, pp. 121–22 and 129, but the first was left out in the room list and the last three were assigned to S 112. Tablets EN 9/2 322, coming from the same room, EN 9/1 351, EN 9/2 363, and EN 9/2 450 were previously thought to come from N 120 in the palace; cf. W. Mayer, *Nuzi-Studien I, Die Archive des Palastes und die Prosopographie der Berufe* (AOAT 205/1; Neukirchen-Vluyn 1978), p. 51, nos. 227–30.

S 112: delete EN 9/2 354 = SMN 2158,
EN 9/2 363 = SMN 2108,
EN 9/2 450 = SMN 2127.

S 113: delete EN 9/1 156 = SMN 2013.
add EN 9/2 298 = SMN 2011, according to *SCCNH* 4, pp. 11, 142 (p. 150 overlooked) and *SCCNH* 5, p. 117.

S 124: delete EN 9/1 419 = SMN 2309.
instead of EN 9/2 530 (which does not exist), read EN 9/3 526.
instead of EN 9/2 531 (which does not exist), read EN 9/3 527.

S 130: add EN 9/3 501 = SMN 2343.

S 131: delete EN 9/2 298 = SMN 2011, which comes from S 113 (same mistake: *SCCNH* 4, p. 151).

S 132: delete EN 9/1 102 = SMN 2380.
add EN 9/1 350 = SMN 2392, cf. *SCCHN* 2, pp. 371, 383 and *SCCHN* 5, p. 121.

delete EN 9/1 371 = SMN 2358.
add EN 9/3 514 = EN 9/2 371, cf. M.P. Maidman, *SCCNH* 8, p. 368.

S 133: add EN 9/2 529 = SMN 3620, cf. *SCCNH* 4, pp. 18, 148, 151 and *SCCNH* 5, p. 135.

S 151: delete EN 9/1 29 = SMN 2133.
EN 9/1 153 = SMN 2493.
EN 9/1 444 = SMN 2525.
EN 9/1 461 = SMN 2525 has been found in S 151.
EN 9/1 444 = SMN 3588; its room number is unknown according to *SCCNH* 2, pp. 376, 382 and *SCCNH* 5, pp. 129 and 144.
add EN 9/3 523 = SMN 2524.

B. LION

62. Additions and Corrections to *SCCNH* 9 (1998) 3–40.

Nous proposons des lectures nouvelles pour certains mots de la tablette RS 94-2939 publiée dans *SCCNH* 9 (1998) 3–40. Elle correspond au début du vocabulaire S^a. Dans sons état originel la tablette devait comporter toutes les entrées du vocabulaire trilingue S^a.

RS 94-2939
COL. I

1	[A]	⸢*mu-ú*	ši-e⸣	"eau"
2	[A]	*a-bu*	⸢at⸣-ta-ni	"père"
3	[ŠUR]	*zu-un-nu*	i-še-na	"pluie(s), ruissellements, écoulements"
4	[ŠUK]	*za-ḫa*	ku-ru-ma-ti	"ration (de nourriture)"(?)
5	[ḪAR]	*ḫa-*SU*-ú*	tu-ur-še-na	"les poumons"
6	[ḪAR]	⸢*ka-bi-tù*⸣	ur-mi	"foie"
7	[ḪAR]	⸢*še*⸣*-me-ru*	ḫa-ap-te	"bracelet"
8	[ḪAR]	*e-ru*	ḫi-še	"pierre de meule"
9	[U]Ḫ	*kál-ma-*⸢*tu*⸣	ap-ḫé	"vermine, pou"
10	[UḪ]	⸢*pur?*⸣*-ḫu-šu*	ta-me	"puce"
11	⸢MUŠEN⸣	*iṣ-ṣú-ru*	i-ra-te	"oiseau"
12	⸢ḪU?/RI?⸣	TA-AŠ-BU	ḫa-al-li	"?"
13	⸢RI⸣	*tal-lu*	⸢aš?-di?-we?-el-te?⸣	"traverse, diagonale"
14	BI	[ ] x	[x]-⸢an?-ni⸣	
15	BI [		]x[	
16	N[I			
17	B[U			
18	Š[UD?			

19 T[UKUL

20 L[U

(la reste de la colonne est perdu)

ligne 4 – La position de ce mot au début de la liste S^a, permettrait de penser qu'il s'agit d'une inversion faite par le scribe entre la colonne akkadienne et la colonne hourrite. Mais, d'autre part, kurumati pourrait être un emprunt hourrite à l'akkadien *kurummatu*, comme c'est le cas, par exemple, pour SUKKAL = *šuk-kál-lu* = ⸢šuk-kál-li⸣ (col. III 21). Toutefois zaḫa ne correspond ni à un mot akkadien ni à un mot hourrite connus.

ligne 5 – A lire *ḫašû*. Cela explique le pluriel hourrite turše=na, qui est un hapax.

ligne 8 – La colonne akkadienne devrait comporter *e-ru-ú* (*erû*).

ligne 10 – Graphie alternative de *perš/sa'u, puršu'u* "puce" (*AHw* 855b); voir aussi D. Arnaud, *EMAR* VI/4, p. 12 = No. 537, 71: *pí-ir-ša-'-u / pí-ir-še-'-ú*.

ligne 12 – La place de ce mot dans la liste semble exclure notre première lecture KU_7 pour le sumérien, en faveur de ḪU ou RI, ce qui remet en cause l'interprétation de la colonne akkadienne comme *dá-aš-pu* "doux."

COL. II

5	KAM	*⸢mé⸣-re-él-tu*	ša-ri-iš-še!	"désir" (de šar- "désirer")
23	[KA	*ap*]-*⸢pu⸣*	wu-uḫ-ḫi	"nez"
27	[DU	*iz-zu?-zu*]	⸢um?-ma?⸣-[	"se tenir debout"
		(Huehnergard [cf. note 3], n. 53.2, et p. 65, *izzuzu*, "to stand")		

COL. III

12	⸢TU⸣	*sú-um-⸢ma-tu⸣* :?	[ ]	"colombe"

COL. V

1'	⸢BAL⸣	[*pí-la-ak*]-*⸢ku⸣*	t[e-a-ri]	"fuseau"

B. ANDRÉ-SALVINI and M. SALVINI

Part IV

LEXICAL INDEX

Lexical Index

D. I. OWEN – G. WILHELM

Akkadian

[a]-bar-ti 182
a-bu-ul-li 69
abullu 69
abullu ša šupūli 73[41]
a-dá-gu-ru 408
aḫāti 321
aḫatūti 324
ālik ilki 96
ana 220[12], 321, 406
ana aḫatūti 324
ana mārūti epēšu 71
an-du-ra-ra 318
an-du-ra-ri(-im) 315, 321, 323
andurārum 290, 313–321, 323–327
annaku 310
annû 310
annûti 310
arad ekalli 95
ardu 95, 96
arki 320
a-si-[i] 406
aššābu 96
ašbu 388
ašlakēna 407[54]
atappu 309

ba-a-ru 269
bāqirānu rašû 71
ba-aq-ri(-im) 315
baqrim 316
ba-aš-lu/lu₄ 417
bēlu 297[9]
birqu rašû 71
bīt ḫiburni 405[33], 409[66]
bīt ḫurizati 71, 72
bīt ḫurši 135
bīt nakamti 405
bīt rimki 135
bu-k/qu 419
buk/qu 419
būru šupūli 73[41]
bu-zu 405
buzu 409

dabābum 74
dabrani 406
da-da-a-ia 166[167]
damqu 388
da-núm 176
dan-nu 208[30]
dârum 74
dikmēnu 298
dimātu 85, 87
dimtu 85, 309, 395[11]
dimtu ša išparāti 85
dūrum 420

edû 320[29]
ekalli 69, 71, 72, 95
ekallu 135
e-la-am 405[34]
e-li-im 405[34]
el-li 405
elli 405
ellu(m) 405, 405[34], 405[36]
e-nu 269

Studies on the Civilization and Culture of Nuzi and the Hurrians - 10

Egyptian

Elamite

Hebrew

Hittite

HURRIAN

KASSITE

LUWIAN

PERSIAN

SUMERIAN, SUMEROGRAMS

Ugaritic

Urartian

Studies on the
Civilization and Culture of
NUZI AND THE HURRIANS

***

Volume 1.	*In Honor of Ernest R. Lacheman on His Seventy-fifth Birthday, April 29, 1981*. Edited by M.A. Morrison and D.I. Owen. Winona Lake: Eisenbrauns, 1982. Pp. xxi + 496. ISBN 0-931464-08-0.
Volume 2.	*General Studies and Excavations at Nuzi 9/1*. Edited by D.I. Owen and M.A. Morrison. Winona Lake: Eisenbrauns, 1987. Pp. ix + 723 + 1 foldout. ISBN 0-931464-37-4.
Volume 3.	*Joint Expedition with the Iraq Museum at Nuzi VII: Miscellaneous Texts*. By E.R. Lacheman and M.P. Maidman Edited by D.I. Owen and M.A. Morrison. Winona Lake: Eisenbrauns, 1989. Pp. xii + 307. ISBN 0-931464-45-5.
Volume 4.	*The Eastern Archives of Nuzi and Excavations at Nuzi 9/2*. Edited by D.I. Owen and M.A. Morrison. Winona Lake: Eisenbrauns, 1993. Pp. xii + 420. ISBN 0-931464-64-1.
Volume 5.	*General Studies and Excavations at Nuzi 9/3*. Edited by D.I. Owen. Winona Lake: Eisenbrauns, 1995 . Pp. ix + 357. ISBN 0-931464-67-6.
Volume 6.	*Two Hundred Nuzi Texts from the Oriental Institute of the University of Chicago*, Part 1. By M.P. Maidman. Edited by D.I. Owen. Bethesda: CDL Press, 1994. Pp. xvi + 440. ISBN 1-883053-05-6.
Volume 7.	*Edith Porada Memorial Volume*. Edited by D.I. Owen and G. Wilhelm. Bethesda: CDL Press, 1995. Pp. x + 159. ISBN 1-883053-07-2.
Volume 8.	*Richard F.S. Starr Memorial Volume*. Edited by D.I. Owen and G. Wilhelm. Bethesda: CDL Press, 1996. Pp. 484. ISBN 1-883053-10-2.
Volume 9.	*General Studies and Excavations at Nuzi 10/2*. Edited by D.I. Owen and G. Wilhelm. Bethesda: CDL Press, 1997. Pp. viii+396. ISBN 1-883053-26-9.
Volume 10.	*Nuzi at Seventy-Five*. Edited by D.I. Owen and G. Wilhelm. Bethesda: CDL Press, 1999. Pp. xi+451. ISBN 1-883053-50-1.